THE COMPLETE ILLUSTRATED ENCYCLOPEDIA OF

BIRDS
OF THE WORLD

THE COMPLETE ILLUSTRATED ENCYCLOPEDIA OF
BIRDS
OF THE WORLD

A DETAILED VISUAL REFERENCE GUIDE TO 1600 BIRDS AND THEIR HABITATS, SHOWN IN MORE THAN 1800 PICTURES

DAVID ALDERTON

WITH ILLUSTRATIONS BY PETER BARRETT

LORENZ BOOKS

This edition is published by Lorenz Books, an imprint of Anness Publishing Ltd,
108 Great Russell Street, London WC1B 3NA; info@anness.com

www.lorenzbooks.com; www.annesspublishing.com; twitter: @Anness_Books

If you like the images in this book and would like to investigate using them
for publishing, promotions or advertising, please visit our website
www.practicalpictures.com for more information.

© Anness Publishing Ltd 2017

A CIP catalogue record for this book is available from the British Library.

Publisher: Joanna Lorenz
Editorial Director: Helen Sudell
Project Editors: Debra Mayhew and Catherine Stuart
Text Editors: Jen Green, Molly Perham, Ian Woodward and Dawn Titmus
Book and Jacket Design: Nigel Partridge
Chief Illustrator: Peter Barrett

PICTURE ACKNOWLEDGEMENTS
David Alderton: 15, 16, 17B, 18, 19; Ardea: 2, 21TR, 25TM, 25TR, 205, 385, 449BR, 450R, 451, 455, 456, 457BR, 458BL,
459, 460B, 461B, 462T, 463T, 465, 466, 467M, 469B, 470, 471T, 471M, 472, 473T, 473M, 474T, 486BL, 488TL, 488B, 490,
492T, 494T, 496M, 498T; Dennis Avon: 12, 20B, 21B, 22; Oxford Scientific: 8, 25TL, 447, 449TL, 449TR, 449ML, 449MR,
449BL, 452T, 453TL, 453ML, 454, 457BL, 460T, 461TL, 461TR, 462BL, 462BR, 464, 467T, 467B, 469T, 471B, 473B, 474B,
475, 477, 481, 482, 484T, 486T, 486BR, 488TR, 492B, 494B, 496T, 496B, 498B; Papilio: 10, 478 (Bryan Knox), 444 (John Farmer).

The Publishers would like to thank the following illustrators for contributing their artwork to this book:
Peter Barrett, Anna Childs, Studio Galante, Martin Knowelden, Janos Marffy, Andrew Robinson, Tim Thackeray.
Anthony Duke supplied the distribution maps for pages 24–443 and 476.

Illustrations appearing on pages 1–7 are as follows: p1, forest weaver (*Ploceus bicolor*); p2, gila woodpecker
(*Melanerpes uropygialis*); p3, northern saw-whet owls (*Aegolius acadicus*), p4, red-faced mousebird (*Urocolius indicus*);
p5 (clockwise from top-left), robin (European robin, *Erithacus rubecula*); saddle-billed woodstork (saddle bill,
Ephippiorhynchus senegalensis); pygmy kingfisher (*Chloroceryle aenea*); l'iwi (*Vestiaria coccinea*);
white-tailed ptarmigan (*Lagopus leucurus*); eastern screech owl (*Otus asio*); mallard ducklings (*Anas platyrhynchos*);
giant coot (*Fulica gigantea*); crested auklets (*Aethia cristatella*); sooty shearwater (*Puffinus griseus*); p6 (clockwise from top-left),
puffin (*Fratercula arctica*); brambling (*Fringilla montifringilla*); peach-faced lovebird (rosy-faced lovebird, *Agapornis roseicollis*);
orange-breasted waxbill (golden-breasted waxbill, *Amandava subflava*); yellow-billed hornbill (*Tockus flavirostris*);
kingfisher (common kingfisher; *Alcedo atthis*); stone curlew (thick knee, *Burhinus oedicnemus*); p7 (clockwise from top-left),
wandering albatross (snowy albatross, *Diomeda exulans*); yellow warblers (*Dendroica petechia*);
African red-eyed bulbul (*Picnonotus nigricans*); king penguins (*Aptenodytes patagonicus*);
coppersmith barbet (crimson-breasted barbet, *Megalaima haemacephala*); Gouldian finch (*Chloebia gouldiae*);
giant pittas (great blue pitta, *Pitta caerulea*); watercocks (kora, *Gallicrex cinerea*);
collared kingfisher (mangrove kingfisher, *Halcyon chloris*).

PUBLISHER'S NOTE
Although the information in this book is believed to be accurate and true at the time of going to press,
neither the authors nor the publisher can accept any legal responsibility or liability
for any errors or omissions that may have been made.

CONTENTS

BIRDS OF GREAT BRITAIN, EUROPE AND AFRICA 204

INTRODUCTION

Birds have been a source of fascination and inspiration to people since the dawn of history. Birds' mastery of the skies not only inspired humans to invent flying machines but also helped to facilitate the development of modern aircraft, as designers working within this industry used the aerodynamic features of birds to revolutionize the workings of modern planes. This has greatly enhanced our ability to travel between different continents – just as many migratory birds do.

Birds have also influenced our cultures in a spiritual way, as reflected, for example, by the phoenix featured in the mythologies of ancient civilizations. To this day, the connection between birds and religious or cultural events remains strong throughout the world. The European robin (*Erithacus rubecula*) is often linked with Christmas on that continent, while the return of the American robin (*Turdus migratorius*), which is in fact unrelated to its European namesake, to North American backyards is eagerly awaited as a sign of spring. In Japan, a folded paper crane has become a symbol of peace, due to its connection with the true story of Sadako Sasaki in World War II. These birds are often launched in their thousands at international festivals, an example being the 2002 soccer World Cup.

Below: Birds can live and feed in a wide range of habitats. This puffin (Fratercula arctica) *is returning from a successful fishing trip at sea.*

Above: Being large in size may make birds more conspicuous, like the Australian cassowary (Casuarius casuarius), *but it can mean they are less vulnerable to predators too.*

It may seem surprising, but new species of birds are still being discovered even today, especially in remote areas of the world. A recent expedition to the Foja Mountains in western New Guinea, one of the last true wilderness areas of rainforest on the planet, reported finding what is thought to be a completely new species of honeyeater (Meliphagidae). It also solved a mystery dating back over a century, as to whether Berlepsch's six-wired bird of paradise *(Parotia berlepschi)*, first described in the 19th century and named after German ornithologist Hans von Berlepsch, survived, and also gave new insights into the distribution and behaviour

Left: An apparently new addition to the bird life of New Guinea, this particular honeyeater was discovered for the first time in 2005. It is the first hitherto unknown species of bird to be found on this island for more than 60 years. The expedition to the somewhat impenetrable region of tropical forest in the Foja Mountains found many other new species there, including unusual flora, frogs, butterflies and a tree kangaroo.

Left: Berlepsch's six-wired bird of paradise (Parotia berlepschi), named for its curious crest of wires above the eyes, was first reported in 1897. The "sighting" was not of a live bird in the wild, however, but of a museum specimen belonging to the private collection of Hans von Berlepsch. Its rediscovery in the Foja Mountains has helped to pinpoint its habitat.

of the golden-fronted bowerbird (*Amblyornis flavifrons*). It is quite likely that other new species still await discovery in this highly inaccessible forested region, the heart of which is entirely unpopulated by people.

In recent years, there have been some remarkable rediscoveries of species which were previously thought to have become extinct. Generally, a species is assumed to have died out if no sightings are recorded over a period of 50 years. Yet the continued survival of the New Zealand storm petrel (*Fregetta maoriana*) was recently confirmed after an absence of 150 years. A group of between 10 and 20 of these petrels was spotted by birdwatchers in the Hauraki Gulf region, although they are thought to be seasonal visitors rather than permanent residents. Conservationists are now trying to locate the whereabouts of their breeding grounds, to assess the health of this small population.

There are now about 9,000 bird species present on Earth, which dwarfs the number of mammals. Their colonization of much of the planet is partly due to their mobility – a number of species can fly or swim extraordinary distances – and their ability to inhabit, reproduce and nest in some of the most desolate areas of the world, from arid desserts and remote islands to the freezing wasteland of Antarctica. But the success of this class of the animal kingdom is also due to another important characteristic: its adaptable feeding habits. Birds eat an enormous variety of foods, from microscopic plankton in the oceans to the carcasses of large mammals, as well as numerous invertebrates and all types of vegetation.

Despite these qualities, human activities have made an increasingly harmful impact on avian populations around the world, and have mounted such a challenge to the lifestyle of some species that their very existence hangs in the balance. On a more positive note, the predicament of critically endangered birds has prompted decisive action from conservationists, and

technology is being applied as never before to make sure that rarities such as the Californian condor (*Gymnogyps californianus*) do not become extinct.

Birdwatching has also benefited from technological advances, such as the Internet, which enables details of new sightings to be relayed instantly to enthusiasts. Undoubtedly, webcam opportunities to observe bird sites, even on the other side of the world, will increase in the years ahead. One of the reasons why bird-watching has become such a popular pastime is that it can be carried out anywhere. No specialized equipment is necessarily required, although binoculars, sketchpads and similar items can add greatly to your enjoyment and understanding of avian life.

This book is a celebration of birds that sets out to reveal the diversity that exists in both their form and lifestyles, and to paint a vivid picture of the contrasting environments they inhabit. Even if you do not have the opportunity to visit far-flung places such as tropical rain-forests and frozen tundra, you can still marvel at the diversity of avian life, as portrayed in these pages.

Below: A male golden-fronted bowerbird (Amblyornis flavifrons). This species was also first identified in the 1890s, from three specimens purchased by the famous naturalist Lord Rothschild. Virtually nothing has been recorded about it since then. Following a series of frustrating attempts to document the wildlife at the heart of the remote tropical forest in the Foja mountains, where these birds were thought to live, scientists finally succeeded in photographing a cock bird for the first time during their month-long expedition in 2005. In seeking to attract a mate, the bird had constructed a huge display bower made of twigs, decorated with blue berries.

DISCOVERING BIRDS

Birds have been observed and documented by humankind since the two began

their co-existence on the Earth. Among the earliest records are the stone

paintings, or pteroglyphs, of northern Africa which show ostriches (*Struthio*

camelus) being hunted by dogs, while ancient mythologies often depicted

supernatural beings of part-human, part-avian form. Birds continue to feature in

the folklore and art of many cultures around the world, while, more prosaically,

they have also been hunted or kept as a source of food for many centuries.

Tragically, these hunting pressures, coupled with environmental hazards such as

pollution and habitat clearance, have resulted in many species becoming scarce

or even extinct. Increasing efforts are being made to safeguard the world's

remaining endangered populations, using a variety of methods from intensive

captive-breeding schemes to habitat preservation. It is even possible for the

casual observer to monitor the progress of various species via webcams which

now offer a window on even the most isolated habitats of the world.

Left: Although wide ranging throughout much of the world, the osprey (Pandion haliaetus) remains an endangered
species in parts of Europe, due to long-running pressures such as persecution and use of the banned substance DDT.
Above from left: Goliath heron (Ardea goliath), black-crowned night heron (Nycticorax nycticorax),
blue and yellow macaw (Ara ararauna).

BIRDS AND MYTH

The unique qualities of birds – their feathers, flight, speed and agility – were coveted and eulogized by early civilizations, who sought to arm their gods and rulers with similar powers. To this day, heraldic symbols continue to associate birds with noble characteristics such as bravery, fortune and fertility.

Many ancient cultures associated birds with kings, deities and the creation of great cities. Some even held that birds were the spiritual ancestors of the human race. The Algonquin tribes of America, for example, referred to the supernatural thunderbirds as Our Grandfathers. These mighty creatures could unleash a storm with just the blink of an eye, or a flap of the wing.

Legend of the fire bird

One of the most enduring of all bird myths is the legend of the fire bird rising from the ashes. It has become symbolic of birth and renewal. The Egyptians were the first to speak of this mythical bird, which they called "Benu", but it also appears in Greek and Roman mythology as "Phoenix", and bears some similarity to Garuda, the golden-bodied bird of Hindu culture which acted as Vishnu's mount.

Benu was the sacred bird of Heliopolis, a great city on the Nile

Below: The green and gold plumage of the yellow wagtail, a migratory bird found in Europe and north-west Africa, inspired depictions of sun deities in Ancient Egypt.

delta that was at the centre of sun worship. There are conflicting accounts of Benu's birth, with some stories depicting a fiery creation amid the burning branches of the sacred Persea tree, and others describing its first appearance on the city's *benben* – a tall stone monument, pointed at the apex, which may indeed have acted as a prototype for the first pyramid. This standing stone is believed to have been the first point in the city to be hit by the rays of the rising sun, and the benu-bird is often connected with regeneration, rebirth and fertility.

The Greek writers Herodotus and Pliny described Benu's self-sacrifice on a nest of sticks engulfed by the fires of the rising sun. From the ashes, a new bird arose, young and strong. Yet, while Egyptian mythology does point to Benu's ascension at sunrise, it is likely that this story of death and eternal life has become entwined with the Phoenix of Greco-Roman legend.

Egyptian iconography depicts the benu-bird in the form of a heron, with two prominent feathers protruding from its crest. Its plumage is often

greenish-gold, which some suggest was inspired by the feathers of the yellow wagtail (*Motacilla flava*), a bird which was itself believed to be a manifestation of the sun god, Atum.

In Greek mythology, the Phoenix is likened more to the appearance of a peacock (*Pavo cristatus*), while other accounts describe an eagle-like bird rising from the ashes. Often depicted as a feminine bird, it was, however, believed that the Phoenix could not reproduce, but must die before another such creature could be created.

Winged messengers

It is perhaps fitting that creatures with the power of flight should come to symbolize a winged ascension – a closer connection with gods and the afterlife. The Egyptian god Horus, with whom kings of Egypt were often associated, was represented as a falcon, and his name translates as "He Who Is Above", reflecting his status as a god of the sky. But the ability of birds to soar above the earth, and travel great distances, also led ancient civilizations to put their faith in them as portents. According to Aztec legend, the pioneers of this great mesoamerican civilization chose the site for their capital city, Tenochtitlán, after the god Huitzilopochtli instructed them to build where they saw an eagle with its serpentine prey, perched atop a cactus. The national flag of Mexico continues to depict this legend. As well as effectively mythologizing and deifying the city's origins, legends such as these were used by rulers to encourage the population to trust in their wisdom.

The secret of long life

Other avian characteristics have been seized upon by myth-makers and story-tellers. Cranes (Gruidae) have become symbolic of long life in Japan, China and Asia, as legend holds that they

Above: Cranes symbolize long life and fidelity in Japanese culture, due to the fact that pairs often mate for life. Motifs of these birds may adorn kimonos and wedding cakes at nuptials.

may live for many thousands of years. In China, eggs were traditionally used in potions by medics and witch doctors who promised to bestow long life.

Birds and heraldry

The papal states of the Holy Roman Empire regularly depicted birds in heraldic design. An eagle is often featured on the standard of their armies, indicating courage, strength and imperial ambition, and black eagles are viewed as particularly brave.

During the Middle Ages, Pelicans (Pelecanidae) were often linked with self-sacrifice, due to the bird's habit of pecking at its own breast during preening. Representations of heraldic birds such as these were often far from lifelike, but they became quite popular, particularly in British designs, despite the fact that the more oft-used subjects such as pelicans were not necessarily native to the British Isles.

Many other birds, real and fanciful, are depicted in medieval heraldry, and not all are of a recognizable form. The identity of the martlet – associated with various European coats of arms – remains something of a mystery. Crusaders claim to have seen the bird in the Holy Land, and it has been suggested that it could be based on a type of martin, which it resembles in silhouette. It is depicted without legs, as medieval writers believed that the bird could not set foot on land. The martlet was often given as a heraldic charge to younger sons of nobility, as a reminder to "trust to the wings of virtue and merit, and not to their legs, having no land of their own to put their feet on." In France, the martlet often

resembles a duckling, although some sources suggest it was derived from the image of a blackbird (*Turdus merula*). In Germany, the symbol more closely resembles a lark (Alaudidae).

A significant change occurred in European heraldry in 1550 when a non-European species, the turkey (*Meleagris gallopavo*), was included on the coat of arms of one William Strickland. A cabin boy who sailed with John Cabot's crew to the New World, Strickland was reputedly the first to introduce these birds to Europe from their North American home.

Left: The ambitious Roman fiefdom of Sabbioneta in the Po Valley honoured its independence from Mantua by depicting a victorious two-headed black eagle on its coat of arms.

DOCUMENTING BIRDS

As world trade thrived during the 1600s, the drive to find new resources prompted daring expeditions across the oceans in search of undiscovered lands. These early explorers marvelled at the new birds they found, and some species were brought home, where they aroused much fascination.

Eyewitness accounts of new creatures in foreign lands have never failed to capture public imagination. However, they did not always reflect anatomical accuracy, particularly if descriptions originated from a brief, awestruck sighting or a perilous encounter. The legend of Sinbad's rescue by a Roc may have come from the stories of sailors who spotted the mighty elephant bird (*Aepyornis maximus*) on Madagascar. At 3.5m (10ft) high, and weighing perhaps as much as 454kg (1,000lb), this now extinct species would have dwarfed a modern ostrich (*Struthio camelus*), with eggs the equivalent in volume of up to seven ostrich eggs.

Exotic finds

The prospect of carrying home a live elephant bird was less than feasible, but other species proved more easily captured by explorers. In 1493,

Below: Eyewitness accounts of birds in new territories were often prone to exaggeration and fantasy. It is thought that the legend of the roc (below), an enormous bird capable of carrying three elephants while in flight, was born out of sightings of the elephant bird on Madagascar. Although a match for its mythical counterpart in size and strength, the elephant bird – a member of the Ratitae group – did not possess the power of flight.

Christopher Columbus paraded a pair of Cuban Amazon parrots (*Amazona leucocephala*) in the streets of Barcelona, as part of the celebrations to mark his safe return. These exotic birds were prized for their powers of mimicry and their colourful plumage, and unsurprisingly, owning a New World parrot became a significant status symbol for the wealthy and well-connected in Renaissance Europe.

A flightless pigeon of the Indian Ocean, already hunted to extinction by 1690, caused perhaps the greatest stir of all. Several living dodos (*Raphus cucullatus*) were brought to Europe, where their ungainly appearance made them a highly popular exhibit among fashionable society there. Yet, despite enduring interest in the dodo, there is not a complete surviving specimen of this bird in any museum in the world today. Nor should contemporary portraits be entirely trusted. Public enthusiasm for the grotesque may have encouraged artists to exaggerate the dodo's already striking features, while the rather bulky, ungainly appearance we have come to associate with the bird may have resulted from enforced domesticity and poor diet. Many ornithologists now believe that the endemic species was quite athletic in its natural habitat.

Advent of ornithology

By the dawn of the nineteenth century, naturalists had made considerable progress with their study of plant and animal species around the world, and often accompanied prominent seamen on their voyages. The Andes had been documented by the German naturalist Alexander von Humboldt (1769–1859)

Left: From the scant evidence that remains, it appears that the dodo's most striking feature was its large and hooked bill. Its wings were reduced to little more than stumps hanging on each side of its plump body, and it also appears to have had a short tail. By contrast, the bird's legs were thick and strong, which not only aided the distribution of its considerable body weight, but may also have helped it to move fast through the thick woodland of Mauritius.

and his French compatriot Aimé Bonpland (1773–1858), and countless other geologists, botanists and ornithologists brought home accounts, or actual samples, of their discoveries. As knowledge of the many kinds of birds in existence grew, the need to find a logical means of grouping them prompted a Swedish botanist, Carl Linnaeus (1707–78), to devise a universal system of

Below: Trying to remove new birds from their natural habitat was not always easy, particularly if the naturalist knew little of their behavioural traits. Although toucans (Ramphastidae) are normally shy and nervous, they can be aggressive if threatened. When the naturalist Henry Bates tried to capture one in the Amazon, he was subsequently attacked by the rest of the flock.

classification, so practical in its application that it is still used today.

Earlier attempts at grouping living creatures had actually appeared in the work of the Greek philosopher, Aristotle, almost 2,500 years ago. Yet whereas Aristotle indicated distinctions based on lifestyle, the anatomical differences which form the basis of today's categorization did not gain significance until Sir Francis Willughby (1635–72), an English ornithologist, had his work *Ornithologia* published posthumously in 1676. Willughby saw the need for what was essentially an identification key that would enable readers to find an unknown bird by means of special tables, devised purely for this purpose. By organizing species according to this hierarchical – or taxonomic – structure, Willughby's work marked a new era in scientific ornithology in Europe.

Willughby's work concentrated solely on birds, but it was Linnaeus who extended this classificatory scheme to cover all living organisms, in a branch of science now known as systemics. His approach is outlined in the classic work, *Systema Naturae*, which was first published in 1735, and subsequently refined and updated in a series of new editions.

Theory of evolution

As differences between species, and subspecies, of birds and other animals became more widely recognized among naturalists, subsequent research by Charles Darwin (1809–82), Alfred Wallace (1823–1913) and Henry Bates (1825–92) paved the way for a revolution in biological science – the theory of evolution by natural selection. Birds were in fact a focal point of Darwin's studies. The various finches native to the Galapagos islands in the American Pacific, recorded by Darwin during his expedition on board the *Beagle* in the 1830s, vitally supported his theory that animals of identical parentage could undergo specific mutations in order to survive in a specific habitat. Darwin's hallmark work, *The Origin of Species*, was finally published in 1859, and,

Above: There are many forms of avian art besides painting. These quails (Phasianidae), which adorn the Emperor's Imperial Palace in China, have been fashioned from wood. They are still often depicted on oriental porcelain.

although an instant bestseller, divided creationists and revisionists in its implications for the roots of humanity.

Ornithological art and books

The anatomical distinctions between birds have been documented by a long line of eminent artists. There is little doubt that their work reflects a natural desire to capture the beauty and brilliance of their subjects, yet the growing popularity of avian painting during the early eighteenth century also made it a potentially lucrative profession. One of the first artists to capitalize on the growing appreciation of birds in art was English-born Mark Catesby (1682?–1749) who, prompted by wealthy patrons, visited North America and ultimately published *A Natural History of Carolina* in the 1730s. This work incorporated colourful portraits of native birds surrounded by evidence of their habitat. Another Englishman, Eleazer Albin, completed *A Natural History of British Birds* during the same decade, and subsequently portrayed various foreign birds gaining popularity in his homeland, including the African grey parrot (*Psittacus erithacus*).

Audubon and Gould

It was to be the illegitimate son of a seafaring Frenchman, born on the Caribbean island of Haiti, who transformed ornithological painting.

The name of John James Audubon (1785–1851) is now inextricably linked with his mammoth project, *The Birds of America*. A collection of 435 colourful life-size plates, first published in eight parts from 1839–44, it set the standard for modern-day avian artists, and individual plates now fetch huge sums at auctions.

British-born entrepreneur John Gould (1804–81) also acted on the desire for fine ornithological books displayed by wealthy collectors. Despite his lowly origins and lack of artistic talent, Gould was a shrewd businessman, and his wife Elizabeth proved an able lithographer. Travelling with a zoologist, the Goulds roamed through Asia, Australia and the East Indies, and oversaw the production of a series of limited-edition monographs of birds. Gould's most ambitious project was *The Birds of Australia*, published in seven volumes between 1840 and 1848, which was illustrated by 600 magnificent hand-coloured plates. The content and accuracy of the work – which documented many hitherto unknown species – brought acclaim for Gould from within the scientific community, as well as from his fellow avian artists.

DOMESTICATION OF BIRDS

Many introduced species, as well as native birds, have been domesticated by humans throughout the world, and the fact that some birds are bred specifically for food, companionship or a variety of other purposes has led to distinct evolutionary changes in those species.

The Chinese were among the first of the early civilizations to domesticate birds. Cormorants (*Phalacrocorax*) were trained to fish with loops around their necks, a technique that prevented the birds from swallowing their catch. The fish was then collected when the cormorant resurfaced. This traditional method is still used in some Chinese communities today, just as it has been for thousands of years.

Birds of prey were also valued for their hunting skills, and pitted against a number of targets ranging from pigeons to rabbits, their kill providing food. Raptors are, on occasion, still used in combination with hounds in parts of North Africa, to harry their target and make it easier for the dog to catch its quarry.

Rearing birds for food

As farming became more settled and widespread in Europe during the early Middle Ages, birds were increasingly

Below: Ornamental dovecotes became fashionable again during the early twentieth century. These essentially decorative constructions were home to much smaller colonies than their monastic predecessors.

Above: Waterfowl continue to be valued throughout the world for their meat and eggs, their downy feathers, and as pets.

reared for food. Many monasteries had a dovecote, which became home to perhaps hundreds of pairs of doves (Columbiformes). The young hatchling doves, called squabs, were highly valued as a source of food, but lay farmers living close to the monasteries were often furious about the way in which the adult birds plundered their fields. The practice of rearing doves on monastic land came to an end with the dissolution of the monasteries in mainland Europe during the 1500s, but small-scale ornamental dovecotes were revived during the early 20th century, thanks to the influence of garden designers such as Gertrude Jekyll (1843–1932).

Chickens have become the most widely kept of all farm birds, and remain a vital component of the poultry-rearing industry throughout the world. It is believed that domestic chickens are descended from red junglefowl (*Gallus gallus*), which roamed the Indus Valley of India as long ago as 2500BC. Some of the common mutations associated with particular breeds of poultry today,

including silkies, which are particularly prized for their egg-laying capacity, were first recorded many centuries ago. Indeed, domestic chickens were present in British society by around AD10.

Waterfowl, namely ducks and geese (Anatidae), were domesticated later than chickens, and evidence suggests that the pioneers of this culture were, again, the ancient Chinese. Today's domestic duck breeds are mainly descended from mallards (*Anas platyrhynchos*), and, quite apart from the distinctive differences in size and colour that have resulted, domestic ducks are also not able to fly well. They are kept as a source of both eggs and meat, and growth rates in domestic strains are such that they may be sold at just eight weeks old.

There is also considerable interest in keeping rare and exotic breeds of waterfowl on artificial lakes, a trend which began among the European nobility. Hardy and easy to maintain, these birds' attractive plumage meant

Above: Affluent Romans prized rose-ringed parakeets as pets, and kept these birds in ornamental cages. Domestic staff or slaves were tasked with tending to the needs of the bird, and encouraging it to speak.

that they rapidly became very popular on landed estates. The escapees from these collections help to explain how free-flying waterfowl, such as Carolina wood ducks (*Aix sponsa*), came to be present in Europe, far from their American homeland.

Exotic birds as pets

Interest in birds as companions seems to date back to the campaigns of Alexander the Great (4th century BC), when soldiers returned home with the parakeets which now bear his name. What fascinated their owners was the way in which these Alexandrine parakeets (*Psittacula eupatria*) could mimic human speech, with a repertoire extending to several languages. Interest in talking birds also apparently existed in Roman society, where rose-ringed parakeets (*Psittacula krameri*) were kept in elaborate cages crafted from tortoiseshell or precious metals, and

chattering magpies (*Pica pica*) were placed outside barbers' shops in a bid to draw in customers.

As journeys to the New World increased the profile of parrots among European society, the crowned heads of Europe also fell under the spell of these birds. Henry VIII (1491–1547) kept a rather talented African grey parrot (*Psittacus erithacus*) at his palace at Hampton Court, London, in the early 1500s. The bird apparently summoned the boatman across the Thames river, and then demanded that the man be paid for his trip!

It was John Gould's brother-in-law, Charles Coxen, who raised the first budgerigars (*Melopsittacus undulatus*) in Europe in 1840, although a single live specimen had been exhibited nine years earlier at the Linnean Society Museum in London. Gould himself created a detailed profile of these parakeets in *Birds of Australia*. The popularity of budgies was such that, by the end of the century, they were being bred in huge numbers in aviaries in France – a single establishment might be home to more than 100,000 birds. As domestication of budgerigars continued, the many garish colour morphs we now associate with them began to develop. Today, we see shades of blue and yellow in their bright plumage, which diverge considerably from the native light green coloration of these birds.

Domestic birds in industry

While affluent Victorian society was drawn to the budgerigar, it was a small finch, native to Madeira and the Canary Islands, that became popular among the labouring classes. The canary (*Serinus canaria*) was first brought to mainland Europe during the 1400s, and was originally bred for its song. Over time, "type breeds" with distinctive physical attributes began to emerge.

Canaries served a special purpose in twentieth century industralized culture. When taken underground into coal mines, the songbirds displayed signs of breathing distress if they came into contact with heightened levels of the explosive gas methane, before the miners themselves were affected. As time went on, treatment of canaries showed greater consideration. During the latter years of their employment, some cages were equipped with small cylinders of oxygen, so that the birds could be revived if they ingested too much methane. Canaries were eventually replaced with handheld gas detectors displaying digital readings, and the mining industry lost a most faithful friend. They remain popular pets, however, and if well cared for may live for up to 10 years.

Below: Growing awareness of the nutritional needs of parrots has meant that more are being successfully hand-reared in Europe and North America than at any time in the past.

THREATS TO HABITAT

Birds face a growing number of hazards in the world today, many of which are linked in some way to human activity. Although widescale habitat destruction has grabbed the headlines in recent decades, other perils include pollution, pesticides and the impact of climate change.

In view of the serious environmental threats now facing avian species around the world, it is hard to imagine that some birds were once culled in tens of thousands simply for use as fashion accessories. The feathers of hummingbirds (Trochilidae) were once used to adorn the hats and clothes of the wealthy classes in late nineteenth-century Europe and America, and the colourful plumes of the scarlet ibis (*Eudocimus ruber*) were similarly prized for ornamentation.

Environmental hazards

While activities such as these have, thankfully, been curtailed, other less deliberate incidents have also taken their toll on bird populations. The wrecking of the crude oil tanker, the *Torrey Canyon*, in 1967, which went down off the south-west coast of England, was one of the first environmental disasters of its kind. Thousands of seabirds nesting on the beaches there died in the polluted waters. Eighteen years later the *Exxon Valdez*, which sank off the Alaskan coast, resulted in the deaths of huge

Above: Plume-hunters almost drove wading birds such as this scarlet ibis to extinction in US states such as Florida. The governor of the latter finally passed a law in 1910, banning this practice in the region.

numbers of birds, including the common diver (*Gavia immer*), the harlequin duck (*Histrionicus histrionicus*), various cormorants

(*Phalacrocorax*) and the pigeon guillemot (*Cepphus columba*). In addition, the polluting of nearby sounds severely disrupted the breeding patterns of other birds such as bald eagles (*Haliaeetus leucocephalus*). Although methods of dealing with oil spillages at sea have improved, the risk of another incident remains a depressingly inevitable prospect.

Overfishing can also have devastating effects, particularly on the breeding colonies of seabirds which depend on fish in order to sustain themselves and their young. Global shortages are forcing fishermen to bolster their stocks by targeting catch that was previously of little value commercially, but which nevertheless represents an important part of seabirds' diets. Allied to this problem is the way in which the fish are caught. In longline fishing, baited hooks – sometimes up to 80 miles (129km) long – are towed behind vessels, often

Below: Human activities such as overfishing and pollution can seriously affect the breeding patterns and very existence of seabirds that reside near these waters.

Above: Vultures are often unpopular in human habitations, due to their grisly reputation as carrion-eaters. Yet they remain a vital part of the ecosystem, helping to clear up waste and thus lessening the spread of harmful bacteria.

perilously close to birds foraging on the surface of the water. The impact on colonies of various albatross species (Diomedeidae), for instance, has been colossal, with the resulting decline in numbers causing great concern among environmental groups. These losses are particularly critical for a group of birds that are slow to attain maturity and reproduce. Longline fishing is currently under review, with hopes to minimize its risks to seabirds.

On land, pesticides and herbicides sprayed on to agricultural land can decimate bird populations, by reducing the quantities of plant matter and animal prey available for them to eat. The release of harmful industrial chemicals into the air, soil or water represents further hazards. Some unpopular species of birds, such as vultures (*Cathartes*), may even be deliberately poisoned with bait. India's vulture population has fallen at an alarming rate in recent years, with one region reporting a ninety per cent drop in the number of white-rumped vultures (*Gyps bengalensis*) over less than a decade, partly due to pest control.

Ironically, the decline has prompted a corresponding increase in the number of rabid feral dogs in the region, as – no longer facing competition from the vultures – these new pests are free to prowl the streets to pick the mounting numbers of carcasses of deceased livestock and other carrion.

Climate change and habitat loss

In the very near future, global warming, resulting at least partly from increased emissions of carbon dioxide and other industrial gases, is likely to affect many birds and their habitats. If specific types of vegetation, insect prey or small vertebrates are decimated as a result of the changing climate, and the dietary needs of the predatory birds cannot adapt in time, every link in the corresponding food chain may subsequently disappear.

Rising global temperatures will also unleash other hazards. The melting of the polar ice caps, for example, will swell water levels throughout the world, gradually swamping traditional shoreline nesting areas, and low-lying wetlands favoured by wading birds.

Mention of habitat clearance often conjures up images of massive rainforest destruction, and certainly this can devastate woodland birds with specialized feeding and nesting habits. Yet small-scale, localized felling of trees can be just as damaging if it goes

unchecked. Many birds depend on tree holes as nesting sites, and are less likely to breed if these havens are not available. On a more positive note, increasing recognition of this problem has encouraged new conservation measures whereby artificial nestboxes are affixed to younger trees, or poles, to replace the older trees that have been felled.

The fact that habitat destruction is as much a consequence of agricultural development as of urban expansion may come as something of a surprise, yet the clearance of land for cereal production or livestock pasture may severely reduce feeding opportunities for birds in this type of terrain. In the absence of their natural foods, avian populations may resort to foraging on the crops, which will in turn prompt compensatory action by the farmers. In parts of Africa, populations of red-billed queleas (*Quelea quelea*) have grown increasingly reliant on supplies of wheat, sorghum and barley, feeding on ripened grain and flattening young plants. Increasingly, the queleas are being targeted with pesticides, and this has caused outrage among bird protection groups who point out that the extension of arable land is in fact responsible for the change in the diet of these supposed "pests".

Below: Mature trees provide essential nesting sites for many woodland species.

ENDANGERED SPECIES AND CONSERVATION

Some of the world's most distinctive birds have evolved in relative isolation, on islands such as New Zealand, once home to the moas (Dinorsis), Hawaii, Madagascar and Mauritius. Many of the indigenous species of these regions are already extinct, with conservationists in a race against time to save others.

Humankind has been responsible for introducing numerous bird species into new environments, far from their natural range, as can be seen from histories of trade, game hunting and domestication. Such measures have not been without consequence. The European starling (*Sturnus vulgaris*), introduced to the United States during the 1890s, is now also found across much of Australia, and its aggressive nature means that it can drive out other birds sharing its habitat. Feral pigeons (*Columba livia*) have also become something of a hazard in cities throughout the world. Their droppings contaminate buildings, and the birds themselves may peck at the mortar, weakening the structure.

In the same way, the introduction of domestic animals by the first voyagers to the New World into habitats that had, in some cases, never been subject to artiodactyls (mammals with cloven hooves), wreaked havoc on some of the local bird populations. Grazing animals, particularly goats, released on

Below: The waldrapp, or bald, ibis (Geronticus eremita) of north Africa is now the subject of intense conservation efforts to build on its dwindling numbers.

to islands by passing ships to provide meat for subsequent visits, often overgrazed the sparse native vegetation, drastically reducing the food supply of native plant-eating birds. Feral rodents such as rats and mice, stowaways on colonial ships, represented another hazard, especially for ground-nesting birds, their eggs and offspring.

Feral cats have been responsible for wiping out many island species, a famous example being the Stephen Island wren (*Traversia lyalli*), off the coast of mainland New Zealand. The last example of this species was caught and killed by the lighthouse keeper's cat, even before it had been officially documented by scientists. Today, our knowledge of this species is largely a product of posthumous study and a certain amount of guesswork.

Control programmes are now in place to counter the continuing impact of this uneasy co-existence between birds and feral mammals, and a boost in the numbers of some rare species, including the flightless cormorant (*Phalacrocorax harrisi*), a flightless shore bird, suggests some success.

Above and right: Providing artificial nesting sites for birds can help to encourage breeding of many species, including the peregrine falcon (Falco peregrinus), even in urban areas. In addition, the use of avian images on stamps, such as this Irish portrait of a peregrine, has become a popular way of raising public awareness about local bird life.

Captive breeding programmes

Preserving habitat is undoubtedly the best and most cost-effective way of ensuring that birds not only survive in their environment, but also co-exist in relative harmony with other creatures sharing their home. A worldwide network of national parks and reserves helps to protect at least some natural habitats, although enforcement of anti-hunting and anti-poaching laws, even here, can be difficult to accomplish.

Conservationists may, subsequently, be compelled to take interventionist measures to safeguard the future of a particularly threatened species. Captive breeding is a viable option, and this has revived threatened populations such as the California condor

(*Gymnogyps californianus*), a species of vulture that teetered on the brink of extinction in the USA during the 1980s. Every surviving condor in the country was captured, and nurtured in captivity, before numbers were judged sufficiently improved to prompt the first tentative releases into the wild. The echo parakeet (*Psittacula eques*) of Mauritius has also been subject to an intensive captive breeding programme. Numbers of these psittacines dropped to as few as 12 individuals at one perilous point in the species' history, before concerted conservation efforts pushed the global population to just above 100. This parakeet remains a severely threatened species.

Rearing young birds

In some cases, artificial insemination has been used to fertilize the eggs of endangered birds directly, and these may then be transferred to incubators to be hatched. This method can potentially double the number of chicks reared at any one time, as removing the eggs often stimulates the hen to lay again more quickly than usual. Hand-rearing chicks on formulated diets helps to ensure the survival of the hatchlings in the absence of their parents. When hand-reared chicks are eventually released into the wild, it is vital that they bond with their own kind and retain a

Below: Golden eagles have been translocated to new and suitable breeding grounds, to boost global numbers of these birds.

natural fear of people, so glove puppets shaped like parent birds are often used to feed the chicks.

Reintroduction programmes

Breeding endangered birds in captivity is relatively easy compared with the difficulties of reintroducing a species to its former habitat, as such schemes are extremely costly. Staff are needed to care for the aviary stock, rear the chicks and monitor habitat through detailed studies. These assess the dangers the birds will face after their reintroduction into the wild, and help to pinpoint suitable release sites. The birds may then be fed with carrion while acclimatizing to the habitat, are often fitted with PVC wing tags and monitored with the aid of radio.

Translocation

In some cases, hatchlings are removed from their native environment and reared in a new location that has been judged suitable for their habitation. Populations of golden eagles (*Aquila chrysaetos*) in the south-west of Scotland have, in recent years, proved slow to reproduce, and a co-operative scheme between Scottish Natural Heritage and the government of the Irish Republic has been launched to re-introduce these birds into parts of Eire, where they have been extinct since 1910. Eaglets are removed from their nests at approximately six weeks of age, at which point they can feed themselves and regulate their body

Above: Glove puppets resembling the parent bird's head are often used when hand-rearing chicks, to encourage the birds to bond with their own kind when they are released.

temperature, and taken to designated sites in Ireland where they are housed in specially-designed avian cages. There follows a further six-week period of hand rearing, during which time the conditions of the originally nesting site are replicated as closely as possible, before intricate preparations for their release are made.

Ecotourism

Working with local people and gaining their support is often essential to the long-term success of conservation programmes. This "hearts and minds" approach has been used successfully on some of the Caribbean islands, such as St Vincent, which is home to various Amazon parrots (*Amazona*). Clearance of the island's native forests, a growing human population, hunting and the illegal pet trade were all pressures threatening the survival of these colourful psittacines.

Publicity about the birds' plight, including illustrations on currency and postage stamps, helped to raise local awareness about the island's natural heritage. Education programmes in schools taught young islanders about the plight of the birds, thus ensuring that conservation efforts would continue among future generations. As ecotourism within the region increased as a result of international attention, bringing in much-needed hard currency, the Amazons' economic and cultural value was re-affirmed in the eyes of the islanders, improving their survival prospects on St Vincent.

CLASSIFICATION OF BIRDS

New species of birds are still being discovered and, following detailed observation, can be fitted into the framework of Carl Linnaeus's classificatory system. The Linnean system continues to influence the way in which we group and name birds, although DNA testing has called for the revision of some existing classifications.

The Linnean system operates via a series of ranks. Starting from a very general base, the ranks become increasingly specific, splitting into smaller groups until, finally, individual types of birds can be identified.

How the system works

Birds, as animals, belong to the kingdom Animalia, and, having backbones, they are members of the phylum Chordata, which includes all vertebrates. The class Aves is the first division at which birds are separated from other vertebrates such as mammals, and they alone comprise this major grouping. Common characteristics between members of a group call for further subdivisions, down to the level of subspecies. The rose-ringed parakeet (*Psittacula krameri*), for example, is classified as follows:
Order: Psittaciformes
Family: Psittaculidae
Genus: *Psittacula*
Species: *Psittacula krameri*
Subspecies: *Psittacula krameri krameri*, *Psittacula krameri pavirostris* etc.

Below: The so-called nominate subspecies of the timneh parrot, known scientifically as Psittacus timneh timneh.

Above: The African race of (Psittacula krameri krameri), *the green coloration is of a more yellowish shade, while the bill is darker.*

If you are unsure where you are in the ranking, the way in which the names are written gives a clear indication. The names of orders end in "-formes", while family names terminate with "-idae". At and below genus level, all names are italicized, with the genus comprising one or more species. The scientific name of a species always consists of two descriptions, with the genus names being written first. Species are the fundamental level in the taxonomic tree, and enable particular types of birds to be named individually. Members of a particular species generally identify with each other and do not normally interbreed with other species. However, if interbreeding does occur, the resulting offspring are known as hybrids.

At the most specific level of the taxonomic tree are subspecies: closely related forms of the same species that are nevertheless distinct enough to be identified separately. These are often defined on the basis of their size or by differences in coloration. In the case of the African grey parrot given above, the nominate form, which is the first form to have been recognized, is *Psittacula krameri krameri*, as indicated by a repetition of the "trivial" name *krameri*. The krameri subspecies is slightly smaller in size, and has more yellowish coloration a darker bill.

In order to be recognized as a species, an example of the bird, known as the "type specimen", has to be held in a museum collection, enabling a detailed description to be written up as part of the identification process.

What's in a name?

Even the choice of scientific names is not random. Often derived from Latin, they can give an insight into a bird's appearance or distribution. The name *flavinucha*, for example, indicates yellow plumage around the neck; the description *peruviana* in the case of the parrot-billed seedeater (*Sporophila peruviana*) indicates the bird's distribution in South America. In a few instances, the species' description features a person's name, for example *Erythrura gouldiae* – the Gouldian finch – which John Gould named after his wife Elizabeth, because of its beauty.

HOW THE DIRECTORY WORKS

Despite a good acquaintance with birds and their habitats, identifying species can be tricky, particularly if you have a relatively brief sighting. This illustrated directory been designed to simplify the task of identification as much as possible, by allowing the reader to clarify sightings with information on size, shape, colour, behaviour and location.

The directory is divided into three large geographical regions, which are split into the particular types of habitat – oceanic, shore, estuarine, freshwater, woodland, open country and urban – in which birds are most likely to be seen. This system is not infallible, as some birds are highly adaptable and may range widely through different environments, so it is well worth checking the corresponding habitat

types of the other geographical regions if you cannot find the bird you are looking for. It is not possible to include every species in the world here, but the representative sample means that you should at least be able to identify the type of bird you saw, and distinguish it from others in the same group.

Browsing through these pages also affords an opportunity to learn more about the varying lifestyles and habits

of the world's birds, ranging from the hornbills living in the west African rainforests to the owls and waterfowl inhabiting the Arctic Circle. The directory is followed by sections on bird behaviour and avian habitats, and there is an extensive index of species, which will enable the reader to locate a description of a particular bird by looking up either its common name or its scientific denomination.

Associated descriptions break down the key characteristics of a species, from unique dietary preferences to breeding behaviour and average life span

Common name

Alternative common name (as may be known in native country or elsewhere within its range)

Classificatory name, consisting of genus and species denominations. If followed by an (E), the species is endangered

---

Black kite (*Milvus migrans*): 60cm (24in)
Present on much of mainland Europe to Asia and Australia. Also occurs in North Africa and overwinters south of the Sahara. Mainly brown but darker on the wings. The underparts are decidedly rufous. Barring on the tail. Some grey markings on the head. Sexes are alike.

Common black-shouldered kite (*Elanus caeruleus*): 30cm (12in)
Present in North Africa and widely distributed south of the Sahara. Grey head, extending down the back over the wings. Whitish sides to the face and white underparts. Prominent black area on each wing extending from the shoulders. Sexes are alike.

Montagu's harrier (*Circus pygargus*): 50cm (20in)
Found in Europe and North Africa, east to Asia. Overwinters in central and eastern Africa south of the Sahara. Predominantly grey, with barring on the lower underparts. Narrow white rump. Hens are larger, with brown plumage replacing the grey. In the dark morph, males are blackish and hens are a dark chocolate-brown.

Black harrier (*Circus maurus*): 52½cm (21in)
Restricted to southern Africa, including parts of Namibia and South Africa. Cock is brownish-black, with white feathering on the rump, grey flight feathers and grey bands on the tail, which also has a white tip. Black bill, yellow cere, and yellowish legs and feet. Sexes are alike. Young birds have rufous-brown edging on the wings, and buff underparts also streaked with brown.

Sparrowhawk
Eurasian sparrowhawk *Accipiter nisus*

These hawks favour preying on groundfeeding birds, and males generally take smaller quarry than females, reflecting the difference in their respective sizes. Even females rarely take birds much larger than pigeons, although they will prey on thrushes. Pairs nest later in the year than many songbirds, so there are plenty of nestlings to prey on and feed to their own chicks. Sparrowhawks have short wings and are very agile in flight, able to manoeuvre easily in wooded areas. They approach quietly with the aim of catching their target unawares, seizing their prey using their powerful feet.

Identification: Grey head, back and wings, with darker barring on the grey tail. The underparts are also barred. Bare yellow legs and feet, with long toes. Cock birds are smaller than hens and have pale rufous areas on the lower sides of the face, extending to the chest, while the barring on their underparts is browner.

Left: Young male sparrowhawks fledge several days before their heavier siblings.

Intricate colour artworks create a lifelike profile of a species, with careful attention to shape, posture and colour

Maps indicate the full range of a species, with specific information on breeding and wintering locations given under 'distribution', directly below

Distribution: Resident in most of Europe (except the far north of Scandinavia), North Africa and the Canary Islands. Migratory birds overwinter around the Red Sea. Extends east to Asia.
Size: 28cm (11in).
Habitat: Light woodland.
Nest: Made of sticks.
Eggs: 4–6, pale blue with reddish-brown markings.
Food: Mainly birds.

The maximum size of a species is given in metric and imperial measurements. Where there are marked differences in the sizes of the male and female, or if the female is the larger of the two, this is also indicated

Preferred habitat

Information on nesting, eggs and food builds a picture of the species' lifestyle

Special features or particular habits of a species may also be illustrated where this will be of interest

Related species box, indicating close relatives or birds sharing similar characteristics to those illustrated on the page

Detailed identification guide to the bird's appearance will enable the keen observer to distinguish between a cock bird and a hen, to pinpoint seasonal changes in colour (known as eclipse plumage), or to identify a species during flight or from its call

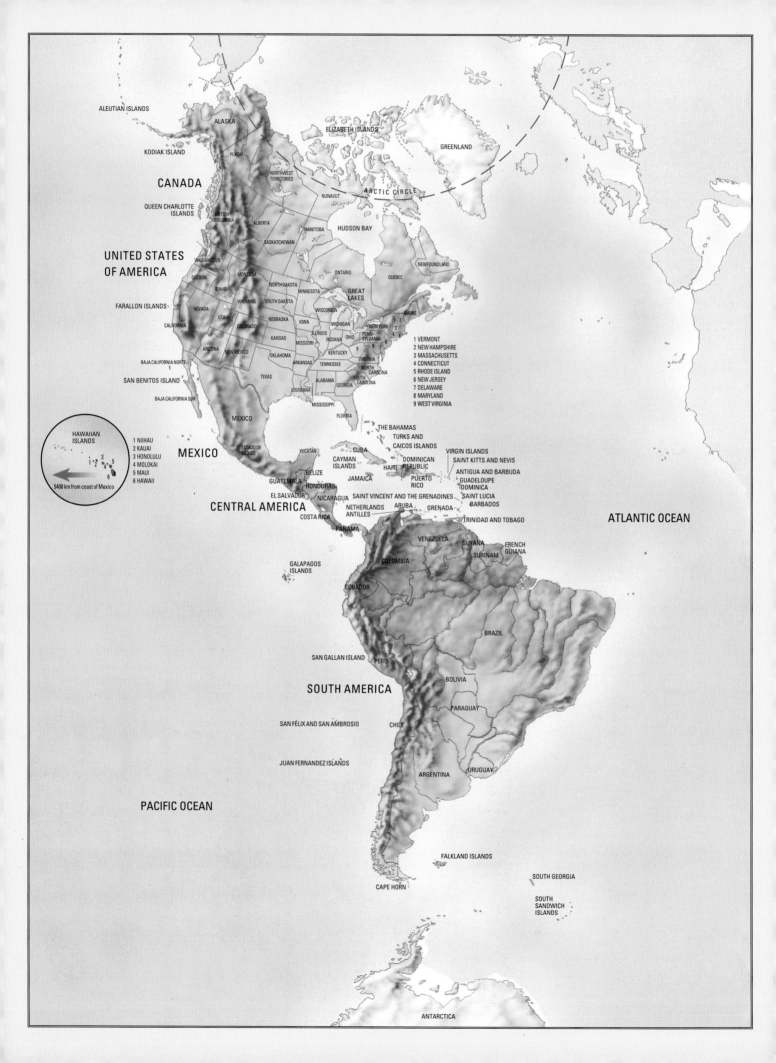

BIRDS OF AMERICA

There is a significant divide between the avifauna of the South American continent, and those families represented in North America, with the Central American isthmus serving as a crossover zone. This is partly a reflection of the feeding habits of the birds, with many fruit-eating species of the Amazonian region, for example, being restricted to this rainforest area, where they are guaranteed a constant supply of food throughout the year. Some of the most unusual birds in the world, including toucans with their bizarre and often colourful bills, are found in this region and nowhere else. Hummingbirds, which include the smallest bird in the world, do range across both continents, and through the Caribbean, although they reach their greatest diversity on the southern continent. The localized distribution of some birds in parts of South America, combined with the often inaccessible terrain, means that new species are still found there quite regularly.

Above from left: Roadrunner (Geococcyx californianus), *Virginian cardinal* (Cardinalis cardinalis), *toco toucan* (Ramphastos toco).

OCEAN WANDERERS

These birds often have a wide distribution, roaming far out from the shore over the oceans. They will only return to land in order to nest, frequently choosing remote islands for this purpose, so they are unlikely to be seen by the casual observer. However, they may be attracted to passing ships, particularly trawlers, in search of offerings of food.

Laysan albatross

Phoebastria immutabilis

The Laysan is the most common albatross of the northern Pacific region. According to reports of sightings, especially from the larger islands, these birds now appear to be venturing closer to the shoreline of the Hawaiian islands. Unlike many albatrosses, the Laysan rarely follows ships, and comes to land only during the breeding season. It is thought that pairs remain together for life, and albatrosses rank among the longest-lived of all birds, having a life expectancy often exceeding half a century. These birds face few natural enemies, but, sadly, a number are dying prematurely after seizing baited hooks intended for fish left on long lines by fishing boats. Albatrosses usually feed by scooping up prey from the surface of the ocean while in flight.

Identification: Relatively small. Predominantly white with a sooty-brown back, upperwings, and tail, and dark feathering around the eyes. In flight, the largish, pinkish feet extend beyond the tail. Yellow curved bill has a black tip. Sexes are alike.

Distribution: Extends from the northern Pacific Ocean to the western coast of North America. Especially common on Midway and Laysan Islands, Hawaii.
Size: 91cm (36in).
Habitat: Open ocean.
Nest: Area of ground.
Eggs: 1, white, may be blotched.
Food: Fish and other aquatic creatures.

Short-tailed albatross

Phoebastria albatrus (E)

Distribution: Occurs off the west coast of North America, up to the Gulf of Alaska. Has been sighted very rarely as far south as Hawaii.
Size: 94cm (37in).
Habitat: Open ocean.
Nest: Earth mound incorporating plant matter.
Eggs: 1, white.
Food: Mainly fish and squid.

Short-tailed albatrosses breed mainly on Torishima Island, which is part of the Izu group lying off the south-east of Japan. They return every second year, with the nesting season starting in October. However, Torishima has an active volcano at its core, which has led to a dramatic decline in their numbers, as repeated eruptions have decimated the breeding population. In addition to this, they were also once hunted for their plumage. These long-lived ocean wanderers were thought to have become extinct during the 1940s, but some of them had survived, and now about 70 chicks are reared annually on Torishima, where they are protected. Another breeding population is established on Minami-kojima, in the nearby South Ryukyu Islands, where the albatrosses use cliffs for nesting. Out at sea, birds may scavenge scraps thrown overboard from trawlers, and hunt squid at night.

Identification: Mainly white, with black patches extending from tips of wings and on tip of tail. Yellowish-orange on the head. Pinkish bill with pale blue tip. Sexes are alike. Young have dark-brown plumage.

White-tailed tropicbird

Phaethon lepturus

These tropicbirds vary in appearance over their wide range, with some having more evident black markings on their primaries than others. The most distinctive race (*P. l. fulvus*) is found in the vicinity of Christmas Island in the Indian Ocean, with its plumage having a golden suffusion. White-tailed tropicbirds tend to be more commonly seen in coastal areas than other species, being relatively common in the Caribbean. They catch flying fish above the water, but will frequently dive down into the ocean as well, to obtain other fish and invertebrates such as small squid. Breeding takes place on remote islands, and in some localities, pairs nest throughout the year. Both young and adults can range over wide areas.

Above: The tropicbird nests in a shallow scrape on the ground.

Identification: Black markings on the wing tips, V-shaped black markings running from the lower back on each side of the body and through each eye, and a narrow dark stripe down the centre of the base of the tail. Rest of plumage is white, with pinkish bill. Legs and feet greyish. Sexes are alike. Young birds display barred markings.

Distribution: Found in American waters off the coast of Florida and in parts of the Caribbean, as well as off the central-eastern coast of South America. Largely circumglobal through the world's oceans, mainly south of the Equator, but absent from the eastern Pacific.
Size: 82cm (32in).
Habitat: Largely open ocean, but sometimes in more coastal areas.
Nest: Scrape on the ground, often under a rock.
Eggs: 1, pinkish with darker markings.
Food: Fish and some invertebrates.

Buller's albatross (*Thalassarche bulleri*): 81cm (32in)
Ranges from western South America across the southern Pacific to south-east Australia. White crown, grey sides to the face. Back of the wings and leading edge as well as the tips beneath edged grey, remainder of underparts white. Bill pale yellow top and bottom, brown on the sides. Sexes are alike. Young birds have brown bills and heads.

Black-footed albatross (*Phoebastria nigripes*): 91cm (36in)
Found in the northern Pacific Ocean, extending from western North America to the Asiatic coast. Lives on the open ocean. Predominantly brownish grey with a white face and undertail coverts, although occasionally paler. Feet are black. Sexes are alike.

Waved albatross (*Phoebastria irrorata*): 93cm (37in)
Occurs off the north-west coast of South America, west to the Galapagos Islands. Easily recognized by the combination of a whitish head and neck with a yellow suffusion, plus brown plumage elsewhere on the body. May be observed feeding at night, when squid are nearer the surface of the water. Sexes are alike.

Northern fulmar

Fulmarus glacialis

Northern fulmars are versatile in their feeding habits. They often track the path of trawlers, and may congregate in large groups in the wake of boats, seeking food. These seabirds scoop up fish during the day and find squid at night, when these invertebrates rise up from the depths. If necessary, they will dive into the sea to catch food. They are also adept scavengers, feeding on the remains of whales and other marine mammals washed onto beaches. They nest communally, usually on sheer cliff faces, where they can colonize inaccessible ledges. In some parts of their range they may build their nests on buildings inland, but they generally favour islands and other remote sites rather than the mainland. Northern fulmars are thought to have a life expectancy of about 34 years. Fulmar chicks may not breed for more than a decade after fledging.

Distribution: Occurs right around the Northern Hemisphere, being present both on the Atlantic and Pacific coasts of North America, extending right up to the far north.
Size: 50cm (20in).
Habitat: Open ocean.
Nest: Bare cliff ledge.
Eggs: 1, white.
Food: Fish, squid and sometimes carrion.

Identification: Varies in colour throughout its range, with light and dark morphs. The light form has a whitish head and underparts with grey above; dark morphs are greyish brown overall. Sexes are alike, but males are larger.

PETRELS

Many of the seabirds found in American waters have a wide distribution, which can be pan-global, often extending around the southern oceans and sometimes even further afield. Petrels are well adapted to spending virtually their entire lives over these waters, even to the extent of being able to scoop up their food directly from the surface of the ocean and sleeping on the wing as they glide.

Hawaiian petrel

Pterodroma sandwichensis (E)

Split from the Galapagos petrel (*Pterodroma phaeopygia*), it does not have a clear identification, since various petrels display a similar dark rump. The Hawaiian petrel appears to be quite rare compared to other species and is thought to be declining in numbers. It spends its time at sea, coming on to land to breed. The largest colony is found around the Haleakala Crater on Maui. These petrels nest in burrows underground, remaining there during the day and emerging to search for food at night. Outside the breeding period, Hawaiian petrels are most likely to be sighted to the south-east of the Hawaiian islands.

Identification: Black upperparts, with white plumage just above the bill and extending right across the underparts. The undersides of the wings are also mainly white, with a black area evident on each of the leading edges when seen from below. There is usually a white, V-shaped marking present at the base of the uppertail coverts, above the tail. Sexes are alike.

Distribution: Pacific Ocean, Hawaiian Islands.
Size: 43cm (17in).
Habitat: Open ocean.
Nest: Sited in underground burrows.
Eggs: 1, white.
Food: Fish and other aquatic creatures.

Mottled petrel

Pterodroma inexpectata

Distribution: Very wide-ranging, occurring in the Pacific Ocean from the Gulf of Alaska southward down the west coast of North America, and has been recorded off the southern tip of South America.
Size: 35cm (14in).
Habitat: Lives at sea, only comes on land to nest.
Nest: Rocky crevices or underground, in colonies on remote islands and outcrops.
Eggs: 1, white.
Food: Fish, squid, and crustaceans.

These petrels spend most of their lives flying across the oceans. They range over a very wide area along the Antarctic coastline, with their distribution extending as far south as the pack ice. In the north, they occur throughout the central Pacific area but are rarely sighted close to land. Mottled petrels migrate south across the Equator before the nesting period, which begins in October. Only at this stage do they come to land, nesting colonially on small rocky outcrops and remote islands. The incubation period is lengthy, lasting approximately 50 days. After hatching, nestlings may spend up to three and a half months in the nest. By the time the petrels are ready to head north again, the dark days of the southern winter are descending. Mottled petrels have disappeared from some parts of their former breeding range, notably New Zealand and nearby islands, where the introduction of land predators such as cats has greatly reduced their success rate.

Identification: Upperparts are dark. A black stripe on the underside of each wing joins to form a characteristic M-shape when viewed from below. The sides of the head are greyish, with a black stripe through the eyes. The underparts are white, apart from a distinctive grey patch running across the centre of the body. Sexes are similar in appearance.

Kermadec petrel (*Pterodroma neglecta*): 38cm (15in)
Ranges right across the southern Pacific, from the western coast of South America to Australia's east coast, and extending north up to Central America. Both light and dark morphs are recognized. Very pale grey suffusion on the head is a distinguishing feature of the light morph, while consistently blackish coloration over the entire body is a feature of the dark morph, although there are variants between these two extremes as well. Sexes are alike.

Soft-plumaged petrel (*Pterodroma mollis*): 37cm (14¹/₂in)
Distribution extends widely through the southern oceans from close to New Zealand around the world to south-eastern South America. Generally only exists in a light phase, although the breadth of the dark throat collar varies in width and definition. Basic coloration otherwise similar to other related petrels, with dark upperparts and mainly white underparts.

Great-winged petrel (*Pterodroma macroptera*): 40cm (16in)
Distribution extends from east of New Zealand through the southern oceans, coming close to the southern coast of South America. Distinguishable from other petrels in this region by its consistently dark brown coloration. Sexes are similar, but hens are smaller. The nearest breeding grounds to South America are on islands off the south-west coast of Africa. Nesting occurs during the southern winter.

Herald petrel

Pterodroma heraldica

The coloration of these petrels is quite variable, since intermediate forms exist between the light and dark colour morphs. Darker birds tend to be more common in eastern parts of both the Atlantic and Pacific ranges. The variation in colour can make these petrels hard to identify, particularly in areas where similar species are found. Herald petrels may be seen in the company of wedge-tailed shearwaters, which occur in similar colour morphs. They seek out inaccessible breeding sites. They do not migrate over large distances, though young birds may travel further after fledging.

Distribution: One population occurs in the central Pacific, extending westward as far as north-eastern Australia, while another is found in the Atlantic, off the eastern coast of South America. A third is isolated around Mauritius in the Indian Ocean.
Size: 39cm (15in).
Habitat: Open ocean.
Nest: Cliffs and underground burrows.
Eggs: 1, white.
Food: Squid; and probably other fish.

Identification: The Atlantic race or Trindade petrel (*P. arminjoniana*) is greyish-brown on its back and wings, with a similar band across the throat and around the eyes. The remaining underparts are white, with dark spotting on the flanks. The dark morph has darker underparts. Sexes are alike.

Stejneger's petrel

Pterodroma longirostris

As with many petrels, relatively little is known about the habits of this oceanic wanderer. There is little to constrain its range through the Pacific Ocean, so it is not surprising that there have been a number of reported sightings of Stejneger's petrels far away from where it is most commonly observed. Stejneger himself first recorded the petrel in Japan in 1893. The breeding period starts in November. Pairs return from further north to Alejandro Selkirk Island, part of the Juan Fernandez group off the west coast of South America. They nest inland in areas of tree fern forest, in underground burrows, usually alongside the Juan Fernandez petrel. The young possess darker plumage than the adults. They leave the nest by the following March, and then disperse over the Pacific, often not returning for several years.

Identification: Dark greyish-black lines create an M-shaped pattern over the wings when viewed from behind, with the centre point of the letter being located on the lower back. The head is blackish, as is the tip of the tail, and the remaining upperparts are whitish. Pale white under-wing area, with a very faint bar running across the underside. Sexes are alike.

Distribution: Typically encountered from Japan down to the western-central coast of South America. Occasionally sighted outside this range in localities including coastal parts of California.
Size: 31cm (12in).
Habitat: Open ocean.
Nest: Burrows.
Eggs: 1, white.
Food: Probably fish and other marine creatures.

DEEP-SEA HUNTERS

Keen eyesight, possibly assisted by a sense of smell, aids these seabirds in finding sources of food in the oceans. Marine invertebrates feature prominently in their diet, and they will often congregate in areas where krill are to be found, along with other predatory creatures such as whales. They tend to seek out inconspicuous places to nest, such as underground burrows or the crevices in a rocky cliff face.

Black-capped petrel

Pterodroma hasitata

Occurring further north than many petrels, this species ranges out into the Atlantic and has even crossed to the UK on very rare occasions. Its main breeding grounds are on Haiti, where it nests high up in the mountainous areas, seeking the safety of cliffs. Plants help to conceal the presence of its burrows. Nevertheless, black-capped petrels are still hunted there, and their numbers have fallen in recent years. It is even feared that the completely black melanistic race known as *P. h. caribbea*, which used to frequent the island of Jamaica, is now extinct. It is thought that mongooses brought to the islands in the 1870s to control the rat population started raiding the nests of these petrels, causing a rapid decline in their numbers. An unusual feature of the young of the surviving race is that they have yellow rather than grey down, reflecting the fact that their plumage overall is not as dark as that of many other petrels.

Identification: This species has white plumage on the back of the neck and black on the head. The wings are dark, the rump and uppertail coverts white. A narrow black streak extends down the sides of the neck. The body is white, with black stripes near the leading edge of the wings, and black wing tips. Sexes are alike.

Distribution: North Carolina and both coasts of Florida southward via the Caribbean islands of Cuba and Hispaniola as far as the island of Guadeloupe, and reaching the coast of north-eastern Brazil, but not Central America.
Size: 40cm (16in).
Habitat: Open ocean.
Nest: Rocky areas and underground burrows.
Eggs: 1, white.
Food: Fish, squid and perhaps jellyfish.

Audubon's shearwater

Puffinus lherminieri

Distribution: From north of Florida through the Caribbean region to the coast of northern South America. Another population is present in the southern Pacific Ocean, off the north-west coast of South America.
Size: 33cm (13in).
Habitat: Out over the sea.
Nest: Rocky hollows. Sometimes underground.
Eggs: 1, white.
Food: Fish, krill, and squid.

Audubon's shearwater has a discontinuous distribution through the world's oceans. There is a distinct, separate Pacific population off the coasts of Asia and Australia, and another in the Indian Ocean. Breeding periods vary accordingly in different parts of its range. Small, remote islands, many of which are uninhabited by people, are favoured for breeding. These shearwaters usually stay close to the shore when nesting, breeding colonially yet preferring an inconspicuous site, which may sometimes be underground rather than on a bare cliff face. The young, who may not fledge until they are nearly 11 weeks old, disperse to the sea. They are slow to mature, and unlikely to breed until they have reached approximately eight years old. Individuals from the Caribbean population have occasionally been recorded as far north as north-eastern Canada.

Identification: Brownish back and wings, with brown coloration extending to the sides of the head. The throat area and underparts are white, with brown edging visible on the extended underside of the wings. This species has a dark bill, pinkish legs and brown undertail coverts. Sexes are alike, and younger birds often closely resemble the adults.

Black storm petrel (*Oceanodroma melania*):
23cm (9in)
Extends along the California coastline and offshore islands. This is the most common and largest of the black-coloured petrels, with a pale wing bar and a relatively slow flight pattern. Calls at night from underground burrows. Sexes are alike.

Black-bellied storm petrel (*Fregetta tropica*):
20cm (8in)
Occurs virtually throughout the oceans of the southern hemisphere up to the equator, including right around South America south of the equator, breeding on remote islands close to Antarctica. From beneath, a well-defined central black stripe bisects the white breast feathering, down to the black lower belly and undertail coverts. There are also whitish areas on the underside of the wings. Sexes are alike.

Least storm petrel (*Oceanodroma microsoma*):
15cm (6in)
Relatively narrow range in the Pacific, sighted not far from the western coast of Baja California, breeding on small islands and rocky outcrops in the Golfo de California. This is the smallest storm petrel, dark in overall coloration, with paler edging apparent across the wing coverts. Forked tail feathers help with recognition. Sexes are alike.

Hornby's storm petrel (*Oceanodroma hornbyi*):
23cm (9in)
Occurs offshore in an area extending down the western coast of South America from the equator as far as Chile. Distinguished by its dark cap, lighter throat and hindcollar. Greyish on the upperparts, with slightly darker flight feathers. Underparts white. Bill black, as are the legs and feet. Sexes are alike. Young birds resemble adults.

Wedge-rumped storm petrel

Galapagos storm petrel *Oceanodroma tethys*

These storm petrels often roam extensively through their range. However, on the Galapagos Islands there is a permanent population throughout the year, not just during the breeding period, which usually commences in May. There, however, they are vulnerable to short-eared owls (*Asio flammeus*), which regularly prey on them. Their other main breeding area is on the Piscadores and San Gallan Islands, off the coast of Peru. Part of the reason for their wandering is that they are able to track the Humboldt Current, which helps to provide them with a ready source of food. (Note that this can be disrupted during years when weather patterns and sea currents are affected by the El Niño phenomenon.) Wedge-rumped storm petrels catch their food in a variety of ways, including while swimming on the ocean surface and by diving underwater.

Identification: Distinguishable by the extensive area of white plumage on the rump and uppertail coverts, which separates this species from other storm petrels. The upper surfaces of the wings are dark, with light areas across the wing coverts, and a white central area on the underside of each wing. The head is dark. Sexes are alike.

Distribution: Extends through the eastern Pacific region, from California southward to Peru, including the Galapagos Islands.
Size: 20cm (8in).
Habitat: Out over the ocean.
Nest: Crevices in rocks or under plants.
Eggs: 1, white.
Food: Fish, krill, and squid.

Fork-tailed storm petrel

Grey storm petrel *Oceanodroma furcata*

The bluish coloration of the fork-tailed petrel sets it apart from all other related species. These birds are most likely to be seen over open sea, swooping down to break the surface of the water occasionally with their legs. They feed both on the wing and on the ocean surface. Like other storm petrels, they come ashore to breed, often on islands, seeking the security of underground burrows at this time. Breeding colonies can be savaged by introduced mammals, notably cats and rats. The nostrils of fork-tailed petrels are located in a tube above the bill, and serve to excrete excess salt from the body, ingested as a result of the bird's environment and diet.

Identification: Distinctive bluish-grey plumage is lighter on the throat and the undertail coverts. The tail is forked and the wings are a duskier shade of blue. Both the bill and the legs are black. The plumage around the eyes is mainly blackish. Sexes are alike.

Distribution: The west coast of North America and south to California. Also found on the Aleutians and nearby islands.
Size: 23cm (9in).
Habitat: Open ocean.
Nest: Underground burrow.
Eggs: 1, white.
Food: Fish, invertebrates and plankton.

SOME LONG-DISTANCE TRAVELLERS

It is remarkable just how far some seabirds will fly to and from their nesting grounds each year.
They may effectively traverse the globe on an annual basis, as in the case of those that nest in the far
north and return to the Antarctic region by the start of the northern winter. These extensive journeys are
made all the more remarkable for entailing little or no rest on land.

Wilson's storm petrel

Oceanites oceanicus

Identification: Dark brownish, with a prominent white rump and square tail. Paler buff barring on wing coverts. Short wings and long yellow legs conspicuous in flight. Sexes are alike.

Breeding Wilson's storm petrels may excavate their own nesting burrows, which typically extend about 38cm (15in) below ground, although on cliff faces and other rocky areas these seabirds seek out sanctuary in a suitable crevice. The nesting period typically begins in November. However, unpredictable snowstorms can sometimes obscure the entrances to nesting burrows, forcing the birds to abandon them. Incubation lasts about six weeks, with the chick fledging about 7½ weeks later. Both adult birds assist in its care. These storm petrels feed in a number of ways, sometimes swooping down to take krill from the water surface, and at others flying very close to the surface, just staying airborne. It is believed that Wilson's storm petrels rely partly on a keen sense of smell to find food, especially carrion, which may form part of their diet. They may also follow ships, particularly fishing vessels, in search of scraps.

Distribution: Has one of the most extensive ranges of any seabird, being found along the entire eastern seaboard of North America and the northern Caribbean, around South America, down to Antarctica, and across both Atlantic and Pacific oceans.
Size: 19cm (7½in).
Habitat: Open ocean.
Nest: Rocky crevice or underground burrow.
Eggs: 1, white.
Food: Krill and fish.

Long-tailed skua

Long-tailed jaeger *Stercorarius longicaudus*

The long tail feathers of this skua account for as much as 23cm (9in) of its overall length, and it is actually still the smallest member of this group of seabirds. Long-tailed skuas breed in the Arctic region of North America, spending the winter at sea. Only on rare occasions are they observed on freshwater lakes. Skuas can be considered the pirates of the skies, menacing gulls and terns and harrying them to drop fish or other quarry, which they quickly swoop down on and seize before the prey disappears into the water. The long-tailed skua is especially agile in flight, as is reflected by its long, pointed wings, while its hooked bill is a formidable weapon. On occasion, long-tailed skuas have been known to resort to attacking other nesting seabirds, taking both their eggs and the chicks.

Identification: Characteristic long, narrow tail feathers. Underparts are whitish, with a greyer tone on the flanks and around the vent. Head is blackish and the wings are dark. Sexes are alike.

Distribution: Occurs throughout the far north of North America and Greenland during the summer breeding period. Then flies south to overwinter around the coasts of South America and western South Africa, extending down into sub-Antarctic areas.
Size: 58cm (23in).
Habitat: Mainly open ocean.
Nest: Depression on the ground.
Eggs: 1–2, olive with dark spots.
Food: Fish and other small aquatic and land creatures.

Arctic skua

Parasitic jaeger *Stercorarius parasiticus*

The diet of these skuas alters dramatically though the year. They are known as parasitic skuas due to their habit of stealing fish from other seabirds, preferring this method of feeding more than any related species. Yet they are also effective hunters, catching lemmings in their northern breeding grounds, and also feeding on insects and even berries during the brief Arctic summer. Their nests, in turn, are commonly raided by Arctic foxes (*Alopex lagopus*). Once the surviving chicks have migrated southward, beginning their journey in August, they may remain in the southern hemisphere for their first year rather than return back north. Unlike many seabirds, parasitic skuas often migrate over land, possibly because they will stay close to coasts on arrival, rather than ranging widely over the ocean.

Identification: Sleek, gull-like appearance with long, narrow tail extensions averaging nearly 9cm (3¹/₂in) in the summer. Dark crown, with brownish-grey wings and tail, with white underparts at this stage too. The dark colour morph displays no white plumage, while youngsters have a barred appearance. Sexes are alike. Young birds have blue legs.

Distribution: Overwinters south of the equator, including Atlantic and Pacific coasts of South America from Peru to Brazil. Migrates to breed in the north, including the USA and Greenland.
Size: 44cm (17in)
Habitat: Open ocean.
Nest: Scrape on the ground.
Eggs: 1–2, olive with dark spots.
Food: Fish and rodents.

Southern giant petrel (*Macronectes giganteus*): 99cm (39in)
Circumpolar in the Antarctic and up both sides of South America, to Chile in the west and Argentina in the east. Brownish overall, although darker on the lower underparts toward the vent. Paler greyish-brown head and neck. Bill is yellowish. White morph displays odd speckled brownish feathering on otherwise white plumage. Hens are smaller.

Fairy prion (*Pachyptila turtur*): 28cm (11in)
Found in three separate areas in the southern oceans, one extending eastward from the extreme south-east of South America. Grey crown, wings and back, with white underparts and a dark tail tip. Blackish patterning across the wings. Sexes are alike.

Blue petrel (*Halobaena caerulea*): 32cm (12¹/₂in)
Another circumpolar species of the southern oceans. Ranges from the Atlantic to the Pacific coast of South America, with young birds seen off the Peruvian coast. Bluish-grey wings with a black M-shaped marking over the rump to the tail. Tail has a distinctive black subterminal band, with broad white tips to the feathers. The top of the head, including the eyes, is black, with white plumage below, extending to the underparts. Sexes are alike.

Black petrel (*Procellaria parkinsoni*): 46cm (18in)
Ranges from the west coast of Central America down to north-western South America, typically far offshore, and across the Pacific to New Zealand. Relatively large, with black plumage. Bill yellowish-orange, darker at tip. Sexes are alike.

Pomarine skua

Pomarine jaeger *Stercorarius pomarinus*

Pomarine skuas are exceedingly effective predators of lemmings, and are even able to dig these small rodents out of their underground burrows using their strong bills. There is a direct link between the number of lemmings and the breeding success of these skuas: when lemmings are plentiful, it is not uncommon for young pomarine skuas to breed before they have acquired full adult plumage. However, during the periods following a collapse in the lemming population, food becomes scarce, forcing these skuas to turn their attentions to other prey, which can include anything from carrion to the eggs of other birds. They will also kill and eat smaller seabirds. Pairs lay in the far north, directly on the ground, without constructing a nest of any kind. After leaving the tundra region in September, pomarine skuas will feed mainly on fish, which they prefer to steal from other seabirds, rather than catch themselves.

Distribution: Breeds in the Arctic along the northern coastline of North America, and migrates south in the winter to both the Pacific and Atlantic coasts of Central America, occurring widely throughout the Caribbean. Also present on Hawaii. A separate population is found on the south-eastern coast of South America.
Size: 50cm (20in).
Habitat: Open ocean.
Nest: Scrape on the ground.
Eggs: 2, olive with dark spots.
Food: Fish and lemmings.

Identification: Mainly black head; back of neck is pale yellowish. Back, wings and vent area dark grey. White underparts, with grey barring on chest and flanks. Bill pinkish with dark tip. Juvenile has white wing bars.

PREDATORS AND PIRATES

Seabirds are adaptable by nature, as shown by the way they will occasionally scavenge, following trawlers for unwanted parts of a catch that fishermen may throw back overboard. Some birds are even more resourceful, and aggressive, in obtaining their food, notably pirates such as skuas, which will harry other seabirds in order to steal their catch.

South polar skua

Stercorarius maccormicki

South polar skuas are long-distance migrants, flying from their breeding grounds in the Antarctic up to the edge of the Arctic. The time of year obviously affects the likelihood of observing them. During the northern summer they can be seen on the Grand Bank of Newfoundland in relatively large numbers. They leave the north in August, after moulting for the journey, and begin arriving at their breeding grounds in October. South polar skuas are highly territorial when breeding, with nest locality affecting breeding success. If both eggs hatch, the younger, weaker individual may be killed by its sibling. Many skuas seen in the northern hemisphere are young birds, not ready to breed until over six years old. In the Antarctic, the two colour morphs are often observed in different locations: the dark morph more commonly on the Antarctic peninsula; the light morph in the Ross Sea.

Identification: Two distinctive colour morphs recognized. Dark morphs are dark brown overall, with wings slightly darker than the body. In pale morphs the head and underparts are significantly paler than the brown wings. Males are darker overall and smaller in size.

Distribution: Occurs in the eastern Pacific, off the coast of North America in an area extending from Baja California to Alaska, and also on the Atlantic seaboard, extending right up to Greenland. Breeds in the Antarctic, in the Ross Sea area and on the Antarctic peninsula.
Size: 55cm (22in).
Habitat: Open ocean.
Nest: Scrape on the ground.
Eggs: 1–2, olive with dark spots.
Food: Mainly fish.

Great skua

Northern skua *Stercorarius skua*

Distribution: Occurs in the vicinity of Newfoundland, Canada, and also through the outer Caribbean region down to the area off northern Brazil.
Size: 58cm (23in).
Habitat: Open ocean.
Nest: Scrape lined with grass.
Eggs: 1–2, olive green with dark spots.
Food: Mainly fish

These skuas are transatlantic migrants, breeding in the far north of Europe, with some individuals overwintering along parts of the eastern American seaboard. Most of these birds are thought to be of Icelandic origin, rather than from further east in Europe. Great skuas prefer to nest in fairly remote locations on level ground, often in proximity to other seabird colonies. They are very resourceful in obtaining food, since not only will they catch fish themselves, but they will also torment other birds, such as puffins (*Fratercula arctica*), into dropping their catches. They will feed on carrion too, as well as edible items thrown overboard from boats. Sand eels are often very significant in their diet during the breeding period. Great skuas migrate southward at the end of the summer, returning north to their traditional nesting grounds again in March. Occasionally, individuals may be found inland as the result of severe storms, young birds especially.

Identification: Large and predominantly brown, with a powerful black bill. The sides and top of the head are entirely dark in colour, but there is lighter streaking down the neck onto the chest, broadening over the wings. Short tail and blackish webbed feet. Sexes are alike.

Pink-footed shearwater

Ardenna creatopus

Pink-footed shearwaters overwinter off the shores of eastern North America, where they are sometimes sighted as far north as the Gulf of Alaska. They head south to their breeding grounds, on the Juan Fernandez islands, located off the coast of central Chile, arriving there by November. Their nesting sites are often located far away from the shore, as these birds will instinctively seek out areas where vegetation provides good cover for their burrows. Single eggs are laid underground. The young will have left their nests by the following April, when the shearwaters head north again, leaving the southern winter behind. They may sometimes disperse far outside their natural range, however, having been recorded on the other side of the Pacific, off the coasts of New Zealand and eastern Australia. When feeding, pink-footed shearwaters grab their prey at the surface of the water, but they are also adept at diving beneath the waves.

Identification: Predominantly greyish-brown, with paler underparts displaying a variable amount of mottled brown coloration, especially on the sides of the body. Paler plumage also under the wings. Flesh-pink bill with a dark tip, and similarly coloured feet. Sexes and young birds are alike.

Distribution: Eastern Pacific, particularly off the coast of the Americas, although absent from the far north and extreme south. Also on Hawaii.
Size: 48cm (19in).
Habitat: Open ocean.
Nest: Underground burrows.
Eggs: 1, white.
Food: Fish and squid.

Manx shearwater (*Puffinus puffinus*): 35cm (14in)
Widely distributed through the North Atlantic, seen in the vicinity of Canada and breeding on Newfoundland. Overwinters down the eastern coast of South America. Sooty black upperparts, white beneath including the undertail coverts. Sexes are alike.

Black-vented shearwater (*Puffinus opisthomelas*): 38cm (15in)
Very limited distribution off the coast of Baja California, breeding on islands in this area. Upperparts are dark, as are the undersurfaces of the primaries. The whitish underparts are suffused with brown, with dark plumage around the vent. Sexes are alike.

Great shearwater (*Ardenna gravis*): 51cm (20in)
Present throughout the Atlantic Ocean, breeding on the Falkland Islands during the southern summer. Relatively large in size, with dark upperparts and a white band on the uppertail coverts. Underparts below the eyes are also whitish, with variable darker mottling on the belly, and dark edges to undersides of wings. Sexes are alike.

Chilean skua (*Stercorarius chilensis*): 58cm (23in)
Overwinters north to Peru, although more common from Chilean coast to southern Argentina. May reach the Falkland Islands. Light cinnamon underparts and sides of the face, darker brown with cinnamon edging on the neck and wings. Crown is dark blackish-brown. Bill pale blue, darker at the tip. Legs and feet greyish. Sexes are alike. Cinnamon coloration most pronounced in young birds.

Sooty shearwater

Ardenna grisea

The largest populations of sooty shearwaters are found in the northern Pacific, rather than the Atlantic. Their location varies according to the season, however, with their American breeding grounds located at the very tip of South America, including the Falkland Islands. They nest in large colonies, with the breeding season commencing in October. Subsequently they will head north, remaining relatively close to the western coast of the continent while crossing the equator, although some will overwinter in southern waters. Sooty shearwaters are often observed feeding in the company of unrelated species, including penguins in the far south. They usually obtain their food underwater, rather than trawling for it at the surface while in flight. The difficulty of mastering this skill probably helps to explain why young birds will follow ships, especially trawlers, in the hope that edible items will be thrown overboard that they can scavenge.

Distribution: Occurs right around the entire coast of the Americas, except the Caribbean and the far north, ranging out across the Pacific and Atlantic oceans.
Size: 50cm (20in).
Habitat: Open ocean.
Nest: Underground burrows.
Eggs: 1, white.
Food: Fish and marine invertebrates.

Identification: Dark sooty black, reflecting its common name, with paler areas evident under the wings. Black bill and yellowish feet. Young birds resemble the adults. Sexes are alike.

AUKLETS

The six members of this group of seabirds occurring around the shores of America are much more at home on the sea surface than in the air. They often struggle to take off, paddling to raise their body up before they can use their wings to get clear of the water. Once in the air, a group will often fly behind each other in a straight line, rather than opting for a V-shaped formation.

Crested auklet

Aethia cristatella

Crested auklets spend much of the winter period at sea, before returning to their breeding islands in the spring after the snow has melted. Huge numbers, sometimes as many as 100,000 birds, may congregate at these colonies. Dominant individuals with the tallest crests are favoured breeding partners, though members of an existing pair will return to breed together every year. Unusually, while males are responsible for brooding the young, it is the females who provide the majority of food for the chicks, frequently travelling distances of 50km (31 miles) or more from the nest site, carrying the food back in their throat pouches. Egg-laying occurs at roughly the same time in a colony, which means that most of the young will fledge together within a short period. This brings survival advantages by increasing the percentage of young that are likely to escape waiting predators. Once at sea, crested auklets remain in large groups.

Identification: Dark grey underparts, blacker head, back and wings, with a white stripe behind the eyes. A forward-pointing, semicircular crest of feathers on the head. Breeding adults develop orange plates on the face. Sexes are alike. Young have a tuft of feathers instead of a crest.

Distribution: Extreme northern Pacific, extending between Alaska across to Asia, through the Gulf of Alaska, especially near Kodiak Island.
Size: 20cm (8in).
Habitat: Ocean and shore.
Nest: Rocky crevices and crags.
Eggs: 1, white.
Food: Mainly crustaceans, plus fish.

Parakeet auklet

Aethia psittacula

Distribution: Occurs in northern Pacific Ocean, extending between north-eastern Asia and the far north-west of North America, and southward down as far as California.
Size: 25cm (10in).
Habitat: Ocean and shore.
Nest: Underground holes.
Eggs: 1, white.
Food: Crustaceans and fish.

These auklets breed along the western coast of North America, as well as in the Aleutians and other islands. Large colonies may be formed in areas where nesting sites are available. Breeding underground offers a degree of security from larger predators, but the eggs and young chicks are still vulnerable to attack by voles. It takes approximately five weeks for the chicks to reach fledging size, at which stage they will emerge from the nest under cover of darkness and head directly to the sea. The young are unlikely to breed until they are three years old. Parakeet auklets have been known to dive as deep as 30m (100ft) in search of food, and they are capable of remaining underwater for at least a minute. They spend much of their winter at sea, typically heading south, away from the Gulf of Alaska, and are commonly seen in the vicinity of Washington and California.

Identification: Dark upperparts, with white underparts and an intervening mottled grey area. A thin white streak extends back from the eye on each side of the head. Bill reddish outside the breeding season, brighter in breeding adults. Sexes are alike. Young birds are duller, with light blue rather than white eyes.

Cassin's auklet

Ptychoramphus aleuticus

These auklets do not venture across the Pacific, preferring to stay around the shore of north-western North America. They remain close to their breeding grounds, even during the winter, although the nesting period varies significantly depending on the latitude. It can begin as early as March in southern California, but not until July in Alaska. Cassin's auklets may excavate their own nesting burrows, which can be 1m (3ft) in length, but elsewhere, in rocky areas, they seek out suitable retreats among the rocks. Nesting communally, however, often draws the attention of predatory species such as gulls, resulting in the loss of both eggs and chicks. Unique among members of the alcid family, the Farallon Islands population of Cassin's auklets regularly nests twice during the same season, with females laying both in April and July.

Identification: Rather stumpy, plump body shape, with a short, straight and rather broad bill with a pale spot at its base. Predominantly greyish, with small white, crescent-shaped markings above and below the eyes. The underparts are whitish. Sexes are alike. Young birds have dark eyes and black bills.

Distribution: Through the Aleutian Islands to the coast of Alaska and south to Baja California, including offshore islands through this region.
Size: 23cm (9in).
Habitat: Ocean and shore.
Nest: Underground burrow or crevice.
Eggs: 1, white.
Food: Crustaceans and fish.

Least auklet (*Aethia pusilla*): 16cm (6¼in)
This auklet is found off western Alaska, wintering in the Aleutian Islands, and has sometimes been recorded as far south as California. White plumes extend back from each eye, with bristly feathers on the forehead and lores (between the bill and the eyes). There is a white area under the chin, and the underparts vary from lightly mottled to blackish, depending on each individual. With winter plumage, the upperparts are black with a white wing bar, and the underparts completely white. Sexes are alike.

Whiskered auklet (*Aethia pygmaea*): 20cm (8in)
The whiskered auklet ranges through the Aleutian Islands off the south-west coast of Alaska. Three relatively long, white plumes are present on each side of the face, and the auklet has a raised, forward-curling black crest of feathers in the centre of the forehead. Undertail coverts are white, and the bill is bright red. Out of breeding condition, both plumes and crest are less evident, and the bill appears darker. Males and females are alike. Young birds lack the crest.

Rhinoceros auklet

Cerorhinca monocerata

Rhinoceros auklets congregate in areas where they can come ashore and excavate their nests in relative safety. They breed communally, with nesting densities of approximately seven birds per square metre (square yard) having been recorded on Forrester Island, Alaska. Rhinoceros auklets dig long underground tunnels, using their bills and feet to excavate these burrows during the night. It will typically take a pair about 14 nights to construct an average tunnel about 213cm (7ft) long. The hen lays a single egg in a chamber at the end.

Distribution: Western coast of North America, extending to the Aleutian Islands across the Bering Sea.
Size: 38cm (15in).
Habitat: Coastal areas.
Nest: Underground chamber, may be lined with vegetation.
Eggs: 1, white spotted.
Food: Fish, such as anchovies, sand launce, and herrings.

Identification: Dark brown upperparts. Underparts from the chin down to the chest and flanks are whitish, with a brownish-grey tone especially evident on the breast. White streaks evident on the face, creating a mustached effect, plus white crests extending from the eyes back to the nape of the neck that are less distinctive outside the breeding season. Orangish bill with characteristic horn-like swelling at the base of the upper bill, which largely disappears during the winter. Sexes are alike.

PUFFINS AND AUKS

Although seabirds generally have a reputation for being quite dull in terms of coloration, members of this group often undergo a striking transformation in appearance at the onset of the breeding period. In flight or at a distance, puffins can generally be distinguished from other alcids since they tend to fly relatively high above the water, rather than skimming low over the waves.

Puffin

Atlantic puffin *Fratercula arctica*

These auks have unmistakable bills, said to resemble those of parrots. Young puffins have much narrower and less brightly coloured bills than the adults. Puffins come ashore to nest in colonies on cliffs and in coastal areas where they can breed largely hidden from predators. Sand eels figure prominently in their diet at this time, and adult birds often fly quite long distances to obtain food. When underwater, puffins use their wings like flippers, which enables them to swim faster. Adult birds fly back to their young with eels arranged in a row, hanging down each side of their bills. They can carry as many as ten fish at a time in this way.

Identification: Distinctive whitish sides to the face, with black extending back over the crown. Black neck, back and wings; underparts white, with a grey area on the flanks. Broad, flattened bill has a red area running down its length and across the tip, and a greyish base with a yellow area intervening. During the winter, the bill is less brightly coloured, and the sides of the face turn greyish. Sexes are alike.

Above: The appearance of the puffin's bill varies depending on the bird's age and the time of year.

Right: Puffins excavate nesting tunnels underground or use existing holes.

Distribution: Extends from the far north of eastern Canada south, occasionally as far down as Long Island.
Size: 32cm (13in).
Habitat: Ocean and coastal areas.
Nest: Underground burrows.
Eggs: 1, white.
Food: Fish.

Tufted puffin

Fratercula cirrhata

After nesting at high densities, both on the coast of North America and on islands including the Aleutians, tufted puffins disperse widely through their extensive range. These puffins prefer to nest in burrows, which they dig in grassy areas. The single egg is laid at the end of the burrow on the bare soil, or sometimes on a bed of feathers. Puffins react badly to human disturbance when nesting, a likely reason why the small southerly breeding population in California has declined over the past century. Further north, in the breeding grounds on the Alaskan peninsula, predators such as Arctic foxes take their toll, while gulls are a hazard on the Aleutians. Young puffins leave the nest after dark and head out to sea.

Identification: Breeding plumage is mostly blackish, with prominent white areas on the face and long, straw-coloured tufts of feathers that extend over the back. The large bill is red, with a prominent horn-coloured area at its upper base. Entire body is greyish black in winter, the bill being red with a brownish base (those of young birds are completely brown).

Distribution: Ranges right up into the polar region and throughout the northern Pacific, occurring as far south as the Farallon Islands off central California.
Size: 41cm (16in).
Habitat: Ocean and shore.
Nest: Burrows, sometimes rocky crevices.
Eggs: 1, white, often spotted.
Food: Fish and squid form the bulk of the diet.

Marbled murrelet (*Brachyramphus marmoratus*): 25cm (10in)
Extends from south-east Alaska across the Pacific to the coast of Asia via the Aleutian Islands, and south down North America's west coast to California. Dark brown coloration, especially on the sides of the head and over the back, with whitish mottling on the breast and underparts, but no white area there. In winter, black extends around the eyes, with a white collar evident on the back of the neck. Sexes are alike.

Kittlitz's murrelet (*Brachyramphus brevirostris*): 23cm (9in)
From the western coast of Alaska to Asia via the Bering Sea. Present also through the Aleutian Islands and in North America, on rare occasions as far south as California. Greyish-brown on the throat, breast and flanks, with only the centre of the belly being white. Brown flight feathers and a brown area on the wing coverts. In winter, a black stripe extends over the top of the head. Wings and back predominantly greyish. Sides of the face and underparts are white, with slight mottling on the breast. Sexes are alike.

Craveri's murrelet (*Synthliboramphus craveri*): 20cm (8in)
Occurs on the western side of North America, in the Golfo de California and Baja California north as far as the San Benito Islands. This species has black upperparts, with white crescents directly above and below the eyes, and white underparts, with a blackish collar curving slightly onto the breast. Underwing area is grey. Narrow black bill. Sexes are alike.

Horned puffin

Fratercula corniculata

Horned puffins are most frequently observed in northern parts of North America. However, they do venture south outside their traditional wintering grounds, and can occasionally be seen on the shorelines of Oregon and California. Records reveal they may even reach the western Hawaiian islands. The determining factor that affects their range, especially at this time of year, is the availability of fish. Within a colony, egg-laying is a synchronized process usually occurring over the course of a week, which means that the chicks will subsequently hatch together. There may be a few later young, usually resulting from pairs who lost their initial egg soon after it was laid. (This in turn has the effect of triggering the hen to lay again.) Horned puffins will not stray far from their breeding grounds when obtaining food for their young, who are reared mainly on sand eels caught under-water by the adults.

Identification: White underparts and black on the upper body, with a huge bill and grey coloration on the sides of the face, distinguish this species. During the breeding period, the sides of the face become white and the bill, with its horn-coloured base, is much brighter. Sexes are alike. Young birds have dark and much narrower bills.

Distribution: Ranges right up into the polar region and throughout the northern Pacific, occurring as far south as the Queen Charlotte Islands, British Columbia.
Size: 41cm (16in).
Habitat: Ocean and shore
Nest: Rocky crevices and burrows.
Eggs: 1, white with dark spots.
Food: Mainly fish and squid.

Guadalupe murrelet

Synthliboramphus hypoleucus

These auks occur in the same area as their close relatives, Craveri's (*S. craveri*) and Scripps's (*S. scrippsi*), but can be distinguished from the latter by their paler underwing coloration. Chicks typically hatch after a period of nearly five weeks, and, within a couple of days, will head into the sea with their parents. The family unit swims to feeding grounds away from the shore, where the chicks will be fed by their parents for the first time. There are just four major breeding colonies. Murrelets are vulnerable to the effects of deer mice (*Peromyscus maniculatus*), which not only disturb sitting birds but may also eat their eggs. There are also fears that overfishing within their range, and possible oil spillages, could also endanger them.

Identification: Black plumage extends from head and beneath the eyes down the neck. May display slight greyish edging to the black plumage over the back and wings. Underparts are white, with some greyish-black on the flanks. Whitish under the wings. Black bill narrow and pointed; legs and large feet are blackish. Hens typically larger in size. Young birds display dark barring on the flanks.

Distribution: Western coast of North America, breeding on islands off southern California and Baja California. Winters as far north as southern British Columbia.
Size: 25cm (10in).
Habitat: Ocean and shore.
Nest: Burrows.
Eggs: 2, brownish-green with darker spots.
Food: Fish and squid.

SOCIAL SEABIRDS

Although seabirds generally feed on fish, their bills can differ significantly in shape, as revealed by a comparison between the pointed bill of the guillemots, the relatively stumpy bill of the murrelets and the distinctive stocky, sheathed bill of the greater sheathbill. These differences can be very helpful when trying to identify birds such as these from their silhouettes.

Ancient murrelet

Grey-headed murrelet *Synthliboramphus antiquus*

The unusual name of these members of the auk family comes from the white streaks in the plumage of breeding adults, which suggest an old appearance. Though occurring right across the Pacific to the eastern coast of Asia, the ancient murrelet can sometimes be found on inland waters in North America, and may even extend as far south as northern Baja California. It is possible to distinguish between these and other murrelets thanks to their flight pattern, since they keep their head in a more upright position rather than extending it horizontally. Ancient murrelets prefer to nest in burrows that they excavate themselves. Weaning takes place rapidly, with the adult pair simply abandoning their young, forcing them to emerge. The family group then fly off, usually at night, and will travel a long distance, typically up to 50km (30 miles), within a day of leaving the nesting grounds.

Identification: White underparts and sides of the neck, with grey on the back and wings. Black bib and head, which is variably streaked with white. Black barring on the sides of the body too, usually concealed by the wings. Sexes are alike, and the throat region of young birds is mainly white.

Distribution: Represented through the Aleutian chain and southern Alaska southward along the North American coast to northern California.
Size: 27cm (11in).
Habitat: Ocean and shore.
Nest: Burrows and crevices.
Eggs: 2, brownish green with darker spots.
Food: Crustaceans and fish.

Snowy sheathbill

Greater sheathbill, Pale-faced sheathbill *Chionis albus*

These rather strange seabirds are often encountered amongst penguin colonies, on the look-out for opportunities to obtain food, seizing either young chicks or eggs, and sometimes stealing items such as squid caught by the penguins. They will also wander amongst groups of mammals such as seals, scavenging on the afterbirth or suckling milk alongside seal pups. When foraging for themselves, they often feed on marine algae, as well as invertebrates. Snowy sheathbills breed in the Antarctic summer, arriving here from October onwards, and then head north, overwintering from Tierra del Fuego up to Uruguay and around the coasts of the Falkland Islands. During these journeys, they may even rest on drifting icebergs. They also hitch rides on passing ships, and as a result turned up unexpectedly in England following the Falklands War.

Identification: Upright stance, with dense white plumage covering the body. Pale pinkish, wattled area of skin on the cheeks, encircling the eyes, with the stout bill being brownish at its tip, with an evident sheath. Legs and feet greyish. Hens are smaller in overall size. Young birds may still show greyish down after fledging and have little evident wattling.

Distribution: Breeds on Antarctica and islands forming the Scotia Arc, including South Georgia. Present also in south-eastern parts of South America.
Size: 40cm (16in).
Habitat: Coastline, and on icebergs.
Nest: Made of any available debris.
Eggs: 1–4, greyish white.
Food: Omnivorous.

Pigeon guillemot

Cepphus columba

These guillemots are most conspicuous during the early summer when they come ashore to breed, with pairs returning to the same site throughout their lives. Southerly populations are likely to be seen around six weeks before egg-laying commences in April, returning about a month later further north. The adults are determined hunters, submerging to catch fish and other prey for up to 2^1/$_2$ minutes. They comb the seabed for fish, invertebrates, crabs, other crustaceans, and molluscs. Chicks are normally fed on fish such as sand eels. The young are independent once they leave the nest at just over five weeks old, although this period may be longer if food is scarce. They are unlikely to breed until at least three years old.

Identification: Relatively long neck and pointed bill. Adult breeding birds are black with a white area on the wings, and have a mottled back, whitish neck and white underparts in the winter. The area around the eyes remains dark, as does the bill. Sexes are alike. Young birds display more pronounced greyer mottling on the neck than the adults.

Distribution: Northern Pacific region, on both the east coast of Asia and the western coast of North America, reaching as far south as southern California.
Size: 37cm (14^1/$_2$in).
Habitat: Ocean and shore.
Nest: Rock crevices, burrows.
Eggs: 2, whitish with dark spots.
Food: Fish and marine invertebrates.

South Georgia diving petrel (*Pelecanoides georgicus*): 20cm (8in)
Circumpolar distribution through the southern oceans, being named after the breeding colony on South Georgia. Other nesting grounds are off the south of New Zealand and to the south-east of Africa. Predominantly blackish upperparts and white beneath, with a dusky area each side of the neck. White edging on the feathers above the shoulders. Very similar to other diving petrels, distinguishable by shape of the nostrils. Bill, legs and feet black. Sexes are alike. Young birds resemble adults.

Magellanic diving petrel (*Pelecanoides magellani*): 20cm (8in)
Restricted to the southern region of South America, extending from southern Chile around Tierra del Fuego to southern Argentina, on small islands lying offshore or in fjords. Most easily identified of the diving petrels, thanks to the extensive white edging to the black plumage of the upperparts, with the underside of the body being white. Sexes are alike. Young birds have reduced white edging on their upperparts, but have a partial white collar.

Bulwer's petrel (*Bulweria bulweri*): 28cm (11in)
Extends across the Atlantic, from the coast of South America to the northern half of Africa. Also ranges through the Pacific region, east of Madagascar. May range outside these areas on occasion, sometimes being observed as far north as the British Isles. Dark brownish coloration overall, with a paler bar evident on the upper coverts when the wings are held open. Tail appears quite narrow, but is actually wedge-shaped. Bill, legs and feet dark. Sexes are alike.

Common murre

Guillemot *Uria aalge*

The upright resting stance of the common murre and its ability to hop, combined with its black and white coloration and fish-eating habits, have led to these birds being described as the penguins of the north. However, unlike penguins they can fly. This enables them to reach their rocky and inhospitable nesting sites, where large numbers pack on to ledges. The sheer density of numbers there offers protection against raiding gulls since there is little space for the predators to land, and they will be met with a fearsome barrier of sharp, pointed bills if they swoop down. As many as twenty breeding pairs can crowd every 1 square metre (11 square feet). Depleted fish stocks and pollution have had an adverse effect on numbers.

Identification: Black head, neck and upperparts, apart from a white area at the edge of the wing coverts. Slight mottling on the flanks, otherwise underparts completely white. Outside the breeding season the entire throat and sides of the neck are white. Sexes are alike. Dark plumage extends up the sides of the neck in young birds.

Distribution: Northern waters right across the Atlantic and Pacific oceans, from Alaska to California in the west down to the Gulf of Maine on the east coast.
Size: 43cm (17in)
Habitat: Ocean and shore.
Nest: Cliff ledges and crevices.
Eggs: 1, bluish green, dark spots.
Food: Fish and marine invertebrates.

PELICANS AND BOOBIES

These large birds, which belong to the same family, both hunt fish, but whereas pelicans are well-equipped to trawl for fish by virtue of their pouches, boobies are more opportunistic, relying sometimes on their size to harry and dispossess other birds of their catches. Both groups possess webbed feet, which are ideally suited to swimming in watery habitats.

American white pelican

Rough-billed pelican *Pelecanus erythrorhynchos*

These pelicans are found mainly on stretches of fresh water, sometimes hunting in groups for fish and other creatures such as crayfish. They are also seen in saltwater habitats but do not venture far from coasts. Occasionally, they may fly long distances to obtain food if the waters that they inhabit have a low fish population. On migration, American white pelicans fly over land rather than the ocean, although populations in the southern part of their range will remain in the same region throughout the year. These birds breed communally, usually on quite inaccessible islands. Their chicks associate together in groups, known as pods, before they are fully fledged.

Identification: Predominantly white plumage with contrasting black primary flight feathers. The large yellow bill develops a distinctive raised area on the ridge toward the tip from late winter through the breeding season. Sexes are alike, but the female is smaller.

Distribution: Western and central areas of North America, extending as far south as Guatemala and Costa Rica during the winter.
Size: 178cm (70in)
Habitat: Both freshwater and saltwater areas, not ranging far out to sea.
Nest: On the ground.
Eggs: 2–3, whitish with darker markings.
Food: Fish and other aquatic creatures.

Left: The pelican's pouch is used to trawl for food.

Brown pelican

Pelecanus occidentalis

Distribution: Ranges down the Pacific coast of America, from California to Chile, and on the Galapagos Islands. Another population is centred on the Caribbean.
Size: 152cm (60in).
Habitat: Ocean and shore, but not venturing inland.
Nest: On the ground or in trees.
Eggs: 2–3, white.
Food: Mainly fish.

Brown pelicans trawl for fish at the surface, but also dive to depths of 10m (30ft), where small fish are numerous, returning to the surface to swallow their catch. They also fly in formation close to the surface and spot fish below with their good eyesight. Brown pelicans frequent ports in search of fish leftovers, but retreat to islands and other remote locations to breed. They usually nest on the ground, but build more substantial platform nests in mangrove swamps, with chicks taking longer to fledge there.

Identification: Golden-yellow area on head, greyish-brown body and white neck, with the white becoming browner in the breeding season. The top of the head becomes speckled when adults are rearing young. Sexes are alike. Young birds have brown heads and are duller overall.

Blue-faced booby

Masked booby *Sula dactylatra*

The blue-faced species is the largest of the boobies, and preys upon correspondingly larger fish, swallowing those of up to 41cm (16in) without difficulty. Although these birds often dive quite deeply in search of fish, they may also catch flying fish at the surface. They sometimes lose their catch to frigatebirds that harry them as they fly back to land. Blue-faced boobies live in colonies, and prefer to nest on cliff faces. On remote islands in the absence of major predators, however, pairs may breed on the ground. While the hen is likely to lay two eggs, only one chick is normally reared, and the weaker chick loses out to its stronger sibling in the competition for food. Blue-faced boobies are long-lived, and young birds may not breed until their third year. These birds frequent tropical oceans on both sides of America. Sadly, their numbers are declining in some areas due to increased development disturbing their habitat. A large colony can still be found around the Galapagos Islands, off the western coast of South America.

Identification: Predominantly white but with black on the wings and a distinctive black tail. Has dark feathering on the face around the eyes, with a bluish tinge extending on to the yellowish bill. In hens, the bill is significantly duller.

Distribution: Range is pan-global around the equator. This species occurs both on the Atlantic and Pacific coasts of America, and also in the Caribbean.
Size: 91cm (36in)
Habitat: Tropical oceans.
Nest: Constructed from accumulated droppings.
Eggs: 2, pale blue.
Food: Fish form the main element of diet.

Peruvian booby (*Sula variegata*): 76cm (30in)
Ranges along the western coast of South America, in the vicinity of the Humboldt Current. Breeds from northern Peru south to central Chile, sometimes being observed as far north as south-west Ecuador. White head and neck, with blackish bill and black area around the eyes. Brown wings with white edging over the feathers, and similar mottling behind the legs and on the rump. Dark feet. Sexes are alike.

Red-footed booby (*Sula sula*): 77cm (31in)
Occurs both in the Caribbean and south-west Atlantic, off the coast of Brazil. Also in the Pacific, with a distribution including the whole coast of Central America. Occurs in a variety of colour morphs. Black-tailed white morph with black flight feathers is found on the Galapagos Islands. Brown morph also recognized. May also have a distinctive white tail in some cases. Sexes are alike.

Blue-footed booby (*Sula nebouxii*): 84cm (33in)
Eastern Pacific, extending from the Golfo de California south to Peru, and to the Galapagos Islands. Black area around the eyes and similar bill. Brown and white markings from top of head to base of neck. Throat and underparts whitish. Wings brown; plumage on back is edged with white. Distinctive blue feet. Sexes are alike.

Brown booby

Sula leucogaster

The noise of these boobies in a colony is deafening, but out over the sea they hunt quietly, often not far from the coast. They are very agile both above and below the water surface, able to catch flying fish as they break above the waves, as well as pursuing their prey underwater, using their wings like paddles. Brown boobies are rarely seen on the surface of the ocean, however. Females especially will also rob other seabirds of their catches as they head back to shore. Pairs usually nest on the ground, favouring offshore islands, nesting almost throughout the year in some parts of their range, although usually only one chick survives through to fledging. The young spend several months with their parents after fledging, before leaving the colony. This gives them a chance to learn basic fishing techniques that will be essential to survival.

Distribution: Virtually circumtropical. Populations present off the coast of Central America and in the Caribbean, as well as eastern-central South America.
Size: 81cm (32in)
Habitat: Ocean and shore.
Nest: Loose pile of twigs.
Eggs: 2, pale chalky blue.
Food: Flying fish and squid.

Identification: Adults generally have dark brownish head, upperparts and wings, with pale yellowish bill and feet. The remainder of the body is white, including much of the underwing area. Sexes are alike. Young birds are entirely brown at first, and have duller coloration around the face.

CORMORANTS

Cormorants are generally dark, which can make it hard to distinguish between different species from a distance. These seabirds are often sighted on harbour poles and buoys, with their wings outstretched. This is essential behaviour, allowing their plumage to dry off, since it is not as water-repellent as that of other seabirds. When in flight, cormorants flap their wings often, and they will dive down to catch fish.

Neotropic cormorant

Phalacrocorax brasilianus

Distribution: Southern USA, east to Cuba and the Bahamas, also Central and South America to Cape Horn.
Size: 73cm (29in).
Habitat: Coastal areas and inland.
Nest: On ground, or in bushes.
Eggs: 1–7, whitish-blue.
Food: Fish, other aquatic creatures.

A widely distributed species likely to be found in a variety of aquatic habitats. These cormorants will even move into temporarily flooded areas, and are a relatively common sight in the Andean lakes. In coastal districts they seek out sheltered bays and coves, rather than venturing far out in open sea. Social by nature, neotropic cormorants will fish in groups, collaborating together. When breeding they form large aggregations, often in the company of other birds such as herons, and their nest site is directly influenced by their habitat. If trees or bushes are available they will nest off the ground, where they will be safer from predators, but on remote islands they can breed at ground level with little fear of persecution. Pairs often hatch more chicks than they can successfully rear, with the older, dominant individuals winning in the competition for food with their younger siblings.

Identification: Blackish plumage, more mottled over the wings. Dull yellow throat-patch edged with white, which becomes pinker in the breeding season. Long, hooked bill and characteristic long tail. Sexes are alike. Young birds are much browner.

Double-crested cormorant

Phalacrocorax auritus

These cormorants are found mainly in coastal waters, sometimes using unorthodox sites such as wrecked ships as perches. They also venture to inland areas, where they are found on suitable stretches of water. They can form large flocks, often hunting together for fish, which form the main ingredient of their diet. In the past, double-crested cormorant numbers have plummeted in some parts of their range due to DDT entering the food chain. This pesticide has had a harmful effect on eggshell thickness, and, as a result, has significantly reduced the number of chicks that hatch. The ban on DDT has seen their numbers rise again. These cormorants have also benefited from the increasing number of freshwater reservoirs in various parts of their range, providing them with additional areas of habitat.

Identification: Adults are entirely black. Immatures show a whitish hue to their underparts. A double crest of feathers is evident on the back of the head during the breeding period, with a variable amount of white coloration. Has bare yellowish-orange skin around the face, with a powerful hooked bill. Females are smaller in size. Several different races are recognized through their range, differing in the extent of the white feathering forming the crest as well as in the depth of coloration.

Distribution: Much of the USA, south to parts of Central America in the winter. Also in parts of the Caribbean, from Florida to Cuba.
Size: 91cm (36in).
Habitat: Areas of fresh water and sea water.
Nest: Built of sticks and often seaweed.
Eggs: 3–4, pale blue.
Food: Fish and other aquatic creatures.

Imperial shag (*Leucocarbo atriceps*):
76cm (30in)
Southern South America, from Chile to Argentina and Uruguay, and the Falkland Islands. Loose black crest with black plumage extending from above the upper bill over the head, back and wings to the tail. White on the sides of the head down over the underparts,with white patches on wings. Blue skin encircling the eyes. Sexes are alike.

Great cormorant (*Phalacrocorax carbo*):
102cm (40in)
Great cormorants breed from Newfoundland and around the Gulf of St. Lawrence southward as far as Maine. May move further south for the winter, sometimes as far as Florida. Different races occur elsewhere in the world. Nominate North American race is blackish overall, with purplish hue on the wings and white patches in the throat region and near the top of the legs when in breeding condition. Bluish skin around the eyes, and horn-coloured bill with a darker tip. Sexes are alike.

Red-faced cormorant (*Phalacrocorax urile*):
89cm (35in)
This species occurs on southern coasts of Alaska extending via the Aleutian Islands to Asia. Blackish overall, with white plumage at the top of the legs. Slight crest on the top of the head and another behind. Red areas of bare skin encircle the eyes. Relatively pale bill. Crests and white areas are breeding characteristics. Hens are smaller in size.

Pelagic cormorant

Phalacrocorax pelagicus

Occasionally sighted as far south as Hawaii, the pelagic cormorant is smaller than related species from the American Pacific region. Their size enables them to colonize small rocky shelves on the faces of cliffs, which can be adopted for breeding purposes without conflicting with their larger relatives. Flying into a site such as this is one thing, but, with insufficient room to turn around, the birds may have to take off again by throwing themselves backward off the ledge. Pelagic cormorants usually nest in small groups, and in some locations individual pairs may even breed on their own. The nest is constructed of seaweed or similar material, held together by their droppings. It is unusual for more than four chicks to be reared successfully through to fledging, even in locations where fish are plentiful. Pairs will return in future years, renovating the nest site as necessary. On occasions, these cormorants may also be sighted inshore.

Distribution: Northern Pacific region, from Asia to North America southward from Alaska, including the Aleutian Islands, as far as north-western Mexico.
Size: 76cm (30in)
Habitat: Sea and seashore.
Nest: Cliff ledges and caves.
Eggs: 2-7, whitish blue.
Food: Mainly fish.

Identification: Glossy greenish black. During the breeding period gains white areas on the flanks, and tufts of longer feathers on the nape and crown, with the skin around the eyes also becoming redder. Sexes are alike. Young birds are brown in colour.

Brandt's cormorant

Phalacrocorax penicillatus

The social behaviour of these cormorants is fascinating to observe, as they sometimes join together in their hundreds to head out over the sea in search of fish. When a shoal is discovered the cormorants dive down, collectively harrying the fish and working together to maximize their catch. These birds also breed colonially, and, although males return to the same nest site each year, they may choose a new partner. The nest is sited on the ground on a larger area than the cliff nests of pelagic cormorants. Breeding success is influenced greatly by the availability of a plentiful supply of food, and in years when the El Niño effect alters the pattern of ocean currents off the coast, and thus the distribution of anchovies and other fish, success may plummet accordingly. This generally has no lasting effect on the cormorant population, however, because they are long-lived birds with a potential life expectancy of more than a decade.

Distribution: Restricted to the western coast of North America, from southern British Columbia down to Baja California in Mexico.
Size: 89cm (35in).
Habitat: Ocean and shore.
Nest: Gently sloping cliffs.
Eggs: 3–6, whitish blue.
Food: Mainly fish.

Identification: Relatively large. Buff feathers across throat, pouch bright blue at outset of breeding. Plumage generally blackish, apart from a few white feathers on the head at this time. Sexes are alike. Young are brown.

PENGUINS AND GEESE

Bright plumage is not a feature generally associated with seabirds, in which more subdued hues of black, brown and white predominate. There are exceptions, however, most noticeably in the case of geese that have spread to the marine environment from the freshwater haunts more usually occupied by waterfowl. These birds have adapted their diets accordingly, often feeding on seaweed.

Galapagos penguin

Spheniscus mendiculus

These penguins have colonized the volcanic outcrops of the Galapagos Islands, seeking out fish such as sardines, which feature prominently in their diet in coastal waters.

Galapagos penguins usually fish together in pairs but sometimes hunt in larger groups too. When there is a change in the pattern of the ocean currents owing to El Niño, and fish then become scarce, penguin numbers may plummet. This decline occurred most dramatically in the early 1980s, when just a few hundred Galapagos penguins survived. Their numbers have since undergone a good recovery, aided by the fact that they can breed throughout the year.

Above: Penguins may not be able to fly, but their wings make powerful flippers underwater.

Distribution: Confined to the Galapagos Islands.
Size: 53cm (21in)
Habitat: Coastal regions.
Nest: In caves or crevices.
Eggs: 2, whitish.
Food: Fish.

Identification: A relatively small penguin, especially when compared with related species. A very thin white stripe extends from the eye around the throat, and the sides of the face are dark. White area under the lower bill and over much of the underparts, apart from an uneven, mainly black circle of feathers. Bill is pinkish at the base. Sexes are alike, and patterning is less clearly defined in young birds.

Southern rockhopper penguin

Eudyptes crysocome

Distribution: Occurs on the south-eastern side of South America. Other populations found off Australia's south coast and between Africa and Australia.
Size: 62cm (24¹/₂in)
Habitat: Ocean and close to the shoreline.
Nest: Made of grass and other available materials.
Eggs: 2, bluish white.
Food: Mainly krill. Some fish.

These penguins are so called because of the way they hop across land instead of walking. They live communally in rookeries, using their sharp bills to ward off gulls and other predatory birds that may land in their midst. Despite its relatively small size, the rockhopper is the most aggressive of all penguins. It is also one of the most adaptable, and is found even in temperate areas. These penguins feed underwater, using their wings like flippers to steer themselves. If danger threatens, they swim toward the shore and leap out of the water on to the land with considerable force.

Identification: White underparts. Black head, flippers and tail although the ear coverts appear slightly paler. The bill is red, as are the irises. A line of golden plumage forms a crest toward the rear on each side of the head. Hens are smaller and have less stout bills.

Above: These ungainly hopping penguins are elegant swimmers.

Humboldt penguin (*Spheniscus humboldti*): 70cm (28in)
Occurs in the vicinity of the Humbolt Current along the shores of Chile and Peru. Distinctive pink fleshy edges at the base of the bill. Otherwise black and white, with a prominent white area on the throat. Sexes are alike.

Magellanic penguin (*Spheniscus magellanicus*): 76cm (30in)
This species occurs around the southern part of South America, from central Chile via Cape Horn north to central Argentina. Also present on the Falkland Islands. Similar to the Humbolt penguin, but can be distinguished by the much wider white stripe extending around the side of the head, and the pink coloration not extending below the level of the upper bill. This species is also slightly larger. Sexes are alike.

Chubut steamer duck (*Tachyeres leucocephalus*): 74cm (29in)
These Chubut steamer ducks are restricted to the coastal region of Chubut in Argentina, South America. The drake has a greyish head with white patches on the sides of the face and down the neck when in breeding condition. White is also evident on the wings, and the remainder of the plumage is greyish with black edging to the feathers. A narrow black band extends around the bill, which is yellowish. Ducks have a darker head, and reddish-brown, rather than whitish, plumage. The bill is also darker. Young birds have brown rather than grey markings on the head.

Emperor goose

Beach goose *Anser canagicus*

The numbers of emperor geese found in North America are larger than those occurring in Asia. In the summer, they are commonly encountered in the Arctic tundra here, often close to coastal lagoons. They nest in secluded localities, but only a relatively small percentage of the overall population appears to breed each year. Much larger numbers of non-breeding birds congregate at their traditional moulting grounds, which, in the case of the Alaskan population, are located in the vicinity of St Lawrence Island. These geese then move southwards to the Aleutian Islands for the duration of the winter. On occasions, however, emperor geese have also been recorded well away from their normal wintering range, in localities which include California and even Hawaii. During this period, emperor geese forage almost entirely along the coastline, grazing not just on seaweed but also nibbling invertebrates such as barnacles off the rocks at low tide, whereas in the summer, they feed largely on herbage.

Identification: White plumage on the head, extending down the back of the neck, with a black throat. Remainder of the plumage purplish, with the individual feathers especially on the back having a black band adjacent to a white area on the edge. Tail white. Bill predominantly reddish, with the legs and feet pinkish. Sexes are alike. Young birds have greyish markings on the white of the head, and a dark bill.

Distribution: The Aleutian islands, extending from south-western Alaska across the Bering Strait to north-eastern Siberia.
Size: 89cm (35in).
Habitat: Coastal areas.
Nest: Scrape in the ground, lined with feathers.
Eggs: 1–8, whitish.
Food: Seaweed, grass and other vegetation.

Kelp goose

Chloephaga hybrida

The distinctive white plumage of the male kelp goose may be more suggestive of swans, but these geese have a stocky body shape. They live on the coast, foraging in beds of kelp at low tide, and then retreat to rocky areas of the coast when the tide comes in. Kelp geese can swim well, but tend to do so when the tide is going out, starting to feed at this stage by dipping their heads under the water. They are also occasionally seen inland. A strong bond is formed between pairs, with the breeding period beginning in October. The nest is built close to water, sometimes near fresh water, with the incubation period lasting 30 days. Kelp geese are largely sedentary, but after breeding they may move further north, up both coasts of South America.

Identification: Males are pure white in colour. Hens have a black head, neck, back and wings, with the feathers on the underparts being edged with white, with the lower abdomen being entirely white. Bill yellowish in hen, dark grey in cock; legs and feet yellowish. Young males are similar to adult hens in colour, but their legs are greenish-yellow.

Distribution: South South America, extending as far north as southern Chile, and east to the Falkland Islands.
Size: 65cm (26in)
Habitat: Mainly seen in coastal areas.
Nest: Made of grass, lined with feathers.
Eggs: 3–7, creamy white.
Food: Seaweed, grasses, other vegetation and berries.

GULLS

Gulls are linked in many people's minds with the seaside, but some species have proved very adept at adjusting to living closely alongside humans, and generally profiting from this association. A number of different gulls have now spread to various inland locations as a result. Shades of white and grey generally predominate in the plumage of these birds, making them quite easy to recognize.

Heermann's gull

Larus heermanni

Distribution: Occurs along much of the Pacific coastline of North America, being recorded from Vancouver Island down as far south as Panama.
Size: 53cm (21in).
Habitat: Ocean and shore.
Nest: Scrape on the ground.
Eggs: 2–3, buff-coloured.
Food: Fish and various invertebrates form the bulk of the diet.

Like most of its kind, Heermann's gull is very adaptable, ever ready to obtain food opportunistically. These gulls may harry pelicans, persuading them to disgorge their catches, or dart in among feeding sea lions to grab food. They often follow fishing boats too, swooping on waste thrown overboard, and will scavenge on the shoreline for edible items. When Heermann's gulls obtain their own food they usually do so inland, seizing lizards and invertebrates, although they are able to catch fish in the ocean also. While most migrants head south for the winter, these gulls will often move further north. Some prefer to head to warmer climates further south of their breeding grounds, which are centred on Isla Raza and other neighbouring islands in the Golfo de California, as well as the San Benito Islands, lying off western Baja California.

Identification: Dark grey back and wings, with the body being lighter in colour and the tail edged with white. Head whitish, becoming streaked in winter. Bill bright red with a dark tip. Sexes are alike. Young birds are dark brownish black, lightening over successive moults and gaining a buff tail tip in their second year.

Brown-hooded gull

Pink-breasted gull *Chroicocephalus maculipennis*

These South American gulls can be encountered in a wide range of localities, especially in winter when they disperse further afield from their breeding grounds. They tend to nest inland, often near marshy ground and lakes. Their diet varies through their range, with brown-hooded gulls being opportunistic in their feeding habits. They will congregate in ploughed fields, seeking grubs and worms here, but equally, they also catch fish, or scavenge in harbours and other localities for carrion. The breeding season begins in October, by which stage they will have moulted to acquire their distinctive dark head feathering. Pairs may nest communally, often at quite high densities, sometimes even constructing floating nests in calm freshwater areas. Their nests may suffer predation by other birds, although members of a breeding colony will join together to mob and drive off would-be intruders.

Identification: Brown hood on the head, darker towards the rear when in breeding condition, otherwise white, like the neck. Back and wings grey. White, crescent-shaped markings behind the eyes. Underparts whitish, usually with an evident pinkish suffusion. Outer primary feathers also white, with the tips of the other feathers here being black. Bill dark at its base, reddish towards the tip. Legs and feet orangish red. Sexes are alike. Young birds have brownish mottled upperparts, and a narrow black tail bar, with brownish legs.

Distribution: Southern parts of South America, occurring on both the Pacific and Atlantic coasts, extending from northern Chile right around to central region of Brazil. Also present on the Falkland Islands.
Size: 36cm (14in).
Habitat: Coastal areas, breeding inland.
Nest: Made of vegetation.
Eggs: 2–4, buff olive and blotched.
Food: Invertebrates and fish.

Andean gull (*Chroicocephalus serranus*): 48cm (19in)
Western South America, through the Andean region, occurring on lakes here, and to the coast, especially in winter. Ranges from northern Ecuador to southern Chile. Glossy black feathering on the head when in breeding condition, with white eyelids. Neck and underparts white, as is the tail. Underparts may show a pinkish suffusion. Back and wings grey, with the longer flight feathers being white with black tips. Bill blackish, legs and feet dark grey. Sexes are alike.

Little gull (*Hydrocoloeus minutus*): 28cm (11in)
This species is now breeding in Ontario and Wisconsin, though its main area of distribution extends from central Europe to Siberia. Breeding population overwinters on the Great Lakes and the coastal area from New Brunswick south to New Jersey. Pale grey back and wings, with a black head, the black extending right down to the neck. Red legs and feet. In winter, has a dark spot toward the rear of the head, which is otherwise whitish apart from a mottled area on the crown. Sexes are alike.

Black-tailed gull (*Larus crassirostris*): 18½in (47cm)
Seen as a vagrant on western parts of North America, from Alaska southwards to California although main area of distribution is in eastern Asia. Greyish wings with black tips on the ends. Underside of the wings and body are white. Tail has a broad black band and narrower white tip. Head becomes brownish in winter. Bill is yellow, with a dark tip. Legs and feet yellow. Young are brownish overall, paler on the wings with white area on the vent.

Thayer's gull

Larus thayeri

Similar in appearance to the herring gull (*L. argentatus*), with which it overlaps in some parts of its range, Thayer's gull is nevertheless slightly smaller in size, and generally displays less intensive black coloration on its flight feathers above, with these feathers being white beneath. In some parts of its range, however, notably in the vicinity of Hudson Bay, it interbreeds with the Iceland gull (*L. glaucoides*), adding to the confusion over the identity of these gulls. Pairs normally nest in small colonies on cliff ledges, often with larger species breeding above them. Occasionally, pairs may be forced to nest on the ground in some areas, and their chicks instinctively react differently to danger, trying to run off if approached, whereas those in nests on cliff faces remain still if disturbed. Thayer's gull overwinters along the Pacific coast, with young birds tending to head further south than adults, although occasionally, they have also been recorded in north-eastern parts of the USA at this stage.

Distribution: Breeding grounds lie in the far north of Canada, extending to western Greenland, overwintering along the Pacific Ocean from British Columbia southwards to Baja California.
Size: 63.5cm (25in).
Habitat: Coastal areas.
Nest: Cup-shaped, made of seaweed and grass.
Eggs: 2–3, tan with brown spotting.
Food: Marine invertebrates, fish, offal.

Identification:
Predominantly white in colour, with grey back and wings. Flight feathers are slate-black, with white markings. Bill yellow, with a prominent red spot at its tip. Legs deep pink. Sexes are alike. Young birds are whitish, with brownish mottling on their bodies.

Great black-backed gull

Larus marinus

These large gulls can be extremely disruptive when close to nesting seabird colonies. Not only will they harry returning birds for their catches of fish, but they also take eggs and chicks on occasion too. In winter, great black-backed gulls move inland to scavenge on rubbish tips, although they are generally wary of people and are unlikely to be seen in urban areas. These gulls have now become relatively common on the eastern Great Lakes, and may be moving progressively westward in this part of North America, where there are large stretches of accessible water. When breeding, pairs can be quite solitary, especially near human habitation, but they are more likely to nest in colonies on uninhabited islands.

Identification: Has a white head and underparts with black on the back and wings. A large gull with a white-spotted black tail and a large area of white apparent at the wing tips in flight. Bill yellow with a red tip to the lower bill. Has pale pinkish legs. Sexes are alike.

Distribution: Extends down the northern Atlantic coastline, expanding its range progressively to Florida but still uncommon along the Gulf coast. This species occurs inland too.
Size: 74cm (29in).
Habitat: Coastal areas.
Nest: Pile of vegetation.
Eggs: 2–3, brownish with dark markings.
Food: Fish and carrion.

ISLAND GULLS

The adaptable nature of gulls is further revealed by the way in which they occur not just around the coastline, from the north right down to the south of America, but out to many of the world's more remote islands too, including Hawaii, the Galapagos Islands and the Falklands. Young gulls are usually easy to spot by their darker plumage.

California gull

Larus californicus

California gulls are particularly adaptable, as is reflected in the wide range of habitats they frequent. They will eat an equally diverse range of food, including grain and various types of invertebrates, and will scavenge at garbage dumps for anything edible. These gulls will also take eggs and hunt ducklings and other young birds, and may even cannibalize the carcasses of their own dead. They seem to have an insight into where food may be readily available, often appearing to plague strawberry farms for fruit when the crop is ripening. Famously, flocks of California gulls rescued the early Mormon settlers around the Great Salt Lake from imminent starvation by devouring a plague of locusts that was threatening to destroy their crops, an event marked by a statue in Salt Lake City. California gulls breed in colonies on islands in large inland lakes.

Identification: White underparts and head, with the back of the head being mottled in the winter. Wings grey, with the flight feathers appearing black and white with the wing closed. The bill is yellow with a red tip. Legs and feet are also yellow. Sexes are alike. Young birds have brown mottling, a dark bill and pink legs.

Distribution: Central north-western North America, in the prairie regions, overwintering on the coast from Oregon south via California to Baja California.
Size: 58cm (23in).
Habitat: Coastal areas and inland.
Nest: Twigs and other vegetation.
Eggs: 2–3, buff olive with blotches.
Food: Omnivorous.

Ring-billed gull

Larus delawarensis

Identification: Named for the black ring circling yellow bill close to its tip. Typical gull patterning, with white head showing mottling in winter. Wings greyish, white markings on black wing tips. Legs yellow. Sexes are alike. Young show light mottling.

Winter sees a return to the coastline for these gulls. Most move to the more southerly parts of their range, although some wander north as far as Alaska. Over recent years they have become relatively common in Florida, where they were first recorded in 1930. They have also extended their distribution from California in 1940 up to British Columbia by 1974. Even more remarkably, since the 1970s they have been crossing the Atlantic in large numbers, so that they are no longer considered rare vagrants in the U.K. Ring-billed gulls are adaptable feeders. In the prairies they congregate in flocks to pick up grubs from the soil as the land is ploughed. They catch fish underwater when hunting at sea.

Distribution: Range extends north to the prairie region of Canada, and east to the Great Lakes. Also extends down the Atlantic seaboard, past Florida and around the Caribbean to Central America.
Size: 53cm (21in)
Habitat: Coastal areas and inland.
Nest: Made of vegetation.
Eggs: 3, buff-coloured and blotched.
Food: Omnivorous.

Glaucous-winged gull

Larus glaucescens

Glaucous-winged gulls breed in large colonies on islands and remote areas of coastline, returning during the spring and early summer to nest. Pairs are strongly territorial, driving away would-be rivals. However, violent squabbling between adjacent pairs can result in nearly half the chicks being killed, especially while they are young. When feeding, glaucous-winged gulls will hunt and scavenge for any edible animal matter, even learning to crack shellfish by dropping them on to rocks. In areas close to human habitation they have become scavengers, flying surprisingly long distances of over 64km (40 miles) to seek food on rubbish dumps. As their range gradually expands, in some areas glaucous-winged gulls are increasingly hybridizing with related species, such as western gulls (*L. occidentalis*) in Washington state.

Identification: Pale grey wings and flight feathers with white edging, help to distinguish this gull. Head and underparts are white, the bill is yellow with a red spot, and the feet are pink. Sexes are alike. Young birds are predominantly fawn-brown with a dark bill.

Distribution: Extends right across the Pacific, from the coast of eastern Asia via the Aleutian Islands down the western coast of North America to Baja California.
Size: 69cm (27in)
Habitat: Ocean and shore.
Nest: Made of vegetation.
Eggs: 2–3, pale olive brown with speckles.
Food: Omnivorous.

Dolphin gull (*Leucophaeus scoresbii*): 46cm (18in)
Southern Chile around Tierra del Fuego to southern Argentina and the Falklands. Light dolphin-grey head and underparts. Dark grey on head when not breeding. Wings slate-grey with white tips, flight feathers black with white markings. Red bill, legs and feet. Sexes are alike.

Olrog's gull (*Larus atlanticus*): 56cm (22in)
Ranges from Puerto Deseado in Argentina north to south-eastern Uruguay; breeds solely in Argentina. White head and underparts, black wings. Black tail band, white band at bottom of tail feathers. Bill has yellowish base, blackish and red tip. Legs and feet yellow. Sexes are alike.

Lava gull (*Leucophaeus fuliginosus*): 55cm (22in)
Restricted to the Galapagos Islands. Very distinctive sooty-black head with remainder of the body being greyish, lighter on the lower underparts. Whitish tail coverts and eyelids. Bill black, slightly swollen along its length. Legs and feet dark. Sexes are alike. Young birds are sooty-brown in colour.

Grey-headed gull (*Chroicocephalus cirrocephalus*): 43cm (17in)
Found on both coasts of South America, ranging along the coastlines of Peru and Ecuador on the west. On the Atlantic coast from Argentina to central Brazil, ranging inland to Santa Fe. Characterized by grey head, with dark edge over back of head. Wings greyish, flight feathers black. Neck and underparts are white. Reddish bill, legs and feet. Sexes are alike.

Belcher's gull

Band-tailed gull *Larus belcheri*

Belcher's gulls track the Humboldt Current, although much of their food is gathered along the shoreline rather than out over the sea. They will readily take eggs and young from colonies of other seabirds too. They generally associate in small groups, typically comprising fewer than 100 pairs. The largest colony is to be found on San Gallan Island, off central Peru, where thousands of these gulls may be present. Their eggs are laid on the ground, sometimes directly on to the sand above the high-water mark, or concealed among rocks on the shoreline. In the past, Belcher's gulls were subjected to heavy persecution at their breeding sites, since their droppings, known as guano, were sold in huge quantities as a fertilizer. Today their numbers can be adversely affected by the El Niño effect, which typically occurs every five years, altering the sea currents and thus the availability of fish in this region.

Identification: Dark wings and a black band across the base of the tail are evident in flight. This gull has a dark head in winter. Bill tip is red, with a black bar behind. Eyes have a yellow orbital ring. Sexes are alike. Young birds have mottled brown wings and a dark head, with a black-tipped, dull yellow bill.

Distribution: Coastal area of South America, from northern Ecuador southward as far as central Chile, typically breeding between northern Peru and northern Chile.
Size: 52cm (20½in)
Habitat: Ocean and shore.
Nest: Hollow on the ground.
Eggs: 1–3, dark olive brown with speckles.
Food: Fish, shellfish and carrion.

LARGER SEABIRDS

Larger seabirds tend to be quite opportunistic in their feeding habits. Although they are able to catch fish very effectively, as shown by the gannet, some of these birds are often seen scavenging on the coastline or soaring around seabird colonies, seeking other opportunities to obtain food. This is a reflection of their aerial agility and strength. They tend to be long-lived as well.

Ross's gull

Rhodostethia rosea

Breeding in the Arctic region, this northern gull appears to be extending its range, with reports of sightings from much further south in North America. Increasing numbers of vagrants are also being spotted in European localities, including parts of the British Isles. Pairs nest in loose colonies on the bare tundra during the brief summer period, using whatever vegetation is available to construct their nest. The task of incubation is shared by both parents and lasts for just over three weeks. Young gulls hatch covered in thick down to give them some protection against hypothermia, and they are able to fly by three weeks old. Prior to this, they will leave their nests and congregate together in groups. The gulls leave their nesting grounds by late July. It is thought that the majority overwinter on the unfrozen waters surrounding the Arctic, and they have also been observed on drifting ice floes.

Identification: Has a very distinctive black band running around the throat and up around the back of the head in summer plumage, with the head being white. Back and wings grey, with the underparts being white with a pinkish suffusion. During the winter, the collar is replaced by an ear spot in front of the eye. Relatively long, pointed tail. Sexes are alike. Bill black, legs and feet red. Young birds display evident black areas on the wings, and have pinkish legs and feet.

Distribution: Far north of North America and Northern Siberia. Also recorded as breeding on Greenland, but precise range not well-documented.
Size: 35.5cm (14in).
Habitat: The Arctic, nesting on the tundra.
Nest: Cup of vegetation on the ground.
Eggs: 2–3, olive green with brown spots.
Food: Invertebrates, including crustaceans.

Black-legged kittiwake

Rissa tridactyla

Identification: Head usually whitish with a black marking on the back. Back and wings greyish. Flight feathers black, white spots on tips. Bill yellow, legs black. Sexes are alike. Young birds have a black bill, and black band across the neck, wings and on tail tip.

The largest breeding colonies of black-legged kittiwakes in the Arctic comprise literally hundreds of thousands of birds. They seek out high, steep-sided cliffs, with so many birds packing on to these ledges that both adults may encounter difficulty in landing at the same time. These sites are defended from takeover most of the year, not just during the nesting period. The nest is made using scraps of vegetation, especially seaweed, combined with feathers and bound together with mud. The narrow, shelf-like nature of the site may make it difficult for aerial predators to attack the kittiwakes, but in some parts of their range, such as Newfoundland, it also reduces breeding success. Away from the nest, these birds remain largely on the wing, swooping down to gather food from the ocean surface.

Distribution: Circumpolar, extending from the far north of Alaska southward as far as Mexico. Occurs down to the northeastern USA in the north Atlantic. Also on Greenland. The commonest gull in the Arctic region.
Size: 40cm (16in).
Habitat: Ocean and shore.
Nest: Cliff ledge.
Eggs: 2, buff olive and blotched.
Food: Fish and marine invertebrates.

Iceland gull (*Larus glaucoides*): 64cm (25in) Iceland gulls occur in the north Atlantic, being present in Iceland, Greenland and north-east Canada. They overwinter south from Labrador down to Virginia and inland to the Great Lakes. This species has a relatively pale grey area on the back and wings, with the head and underparts being white. The bill is yellowish, with a red spot on the lower mandible. The legs and feet are pink. Sexes are alike.

Red-legged kittiwake (*Rissa brevirostris*): 38cm (15in) Red-legged kittiwakes are found in the northern Pacific, occurring off the south-west coast of Alaska and through the Aleutian Islands. Their head and underparts are white. The wings are relatively dark grey, with white edging on the longer feathers. The flight feathers are black with white markings. These birds have a white tail and yellowish bill. Their reddish legs and feet help to distinguish them from other species.

Gannet

Northern gannet *Morus bassanus*

This species is the largest of all gannets and can weigh up to 3.6kg (8lb). It is the only member of this group found around the North Atlantic. These gannets are powerful in the air. Their keen eyesight allows them to detect shoals of fish such as herring and mackerel in the ocean below. When feeding, gannets dive down into a shoal, often from a considerable height, seizing fish from under the water. Their streamlined shape also enables them to swim. Breeding occurs in the spring when the birds form large colonies in which there is often a lot of squabbling. The young mature slowly, and are unlikely to breed until they are at least four years of age.

Distribution: Occurs on both sides of the Atlantic, along the eastern seaboard of North America and across the Atlantic to northern Europe. South through the Atlantic to the western coast of Africa. Also in the Mediterranean.
Size: 88–100cm (35–9in).
Habitat: Ocean.
Nest: Cliff top, from seaweed and other marine debris.
Eggs: 1, whitish.
Food: Fish.

Identification: Mainly white, apart from pale creamy yellow plumage on the head extending down the neck, and black flight feathers. Tail feathers are white, and the feet are dark grey. Sexes are alike. Young birds are dark brown in colour.

Man o'war bird

Magnificent frigatebird *Fregata magnificens*

Distribution: Throughout the eastern Pacific Ocean, Gulf of Mexico and tropical parts of the Atlantic Ocean.
Size: 101cm (40in).
Habitat: Oceanic coastlines.
Nest: Platform of sticks.
Eggs: 1, white.
Food: Fish and invertebrates, including jellyfish. Also preys on baby turtles and seabird chicks.

These birds can glide for long periods, relying on their huge 229cm (7¹/₂ft) wingspan to help keep them airborne on the air currents. The male's throat pouch, prominent at close quarters, is far less visible when in the air. Pairs nest on the coast in areas where there are other smaller, fish-eating seabirds that can be harried for their catches, so that the frigatebirds do not have to obtain their own food. If necessary, however, they often catch flying fish, as well as other creatures found near the surface, including baby turtles. It is believed that although cock birds may breed annually if the opportunity is there, most hens nest only every second year.

Identification: Jet black, with a bare, bright red throat patch that can be inflated for display purposes. Hens are similar, but can be easily distinguished by white feathering on the breast. In immature birds, the plumage on the head is also white.

TERNS

Terns as a group can usually be distinguished quite easily, even from gulls, by their relatively elongated shape. Their long, pointed wings are an indication of their aerial ability, and some terns regularly fly longer distances than other migrants. Not surprisingly, their flight appears to be almost effortless. When breeding, terns generally nest in colonies.

Black skimmer

Rynchops niger

Distribution: Southern North America, from California in the west and North Carolina on the Atlantic coast south through Central and South America as far as Chile and northern parts of Brazil.
Size: 46cm (18in).
Habitat: Coastal areas and rivers.
Nest: Depression in the sand.
Eggs: 2–6, bluish with dark spots.
Food: Mainly fish.

As their name suggests, these narrow-bodied birds with long wings have a distinctive way of feeding, skimming over the surface of the water with their mouth open and lower bill beneath the water level. Contact with a fish will result in the skimmer snapping its bill shut, with its head briefly disappearing under its body before it moves forward and takes off. The catch is consumed either in flight or once it has landed. This fairly specialized method of fishing is most suited to the shallows, so when hunting inshore in rivers these birds favour areas near sandbars, becoming most active in tidal rivers at low water. Black skimmers breed colonially, with up to 1,000 pairs nesting on beaches in remote localities. The North American population overwinters in Central America. Those breeding in South America also head south, while pairs nesting along rivers in eastern Brazil move to coasts.

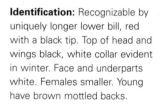

Identification: Recognizable by uniquely longer lower bill, red with a black tip. Top of head and wings black, white collar evident in winter. Face and underparts white. Females smaller. Young have brown mottled backs.

Chilean tern

Peruvian tern *Sternula lorata*

Identification: White forehead and chin, with a black stripe extending back on each side of the head from the base of the bill. This joins up with the more extensive black area which runs from the crown and rear part of the head down the back of the neck. Chest and underparts are light grey; back and wings are a slightly darker shade. Bill yellow with a black tip. Legs and feet greyish. Young birds have buff underparts.

The Peruvian population of these terns is thought not to exceed 10,000 individuals in total, and numbers are likely to be adversely affected during so-called El Niño years, when food is harder to find, causing their breeding success to fall significantly. They normally nest in small groups, sometimes in desert areas inland. Pairs often choose a location near a landmark, such as a rock, which may help them to orientate themselves when travelling back with food. Unfortunately, nesting inland increases the risk of predators such as grey foxes (*Duscicyon culpaeus*) disrupting breeding attempts, as these terns breed on the open ground and rely on camouflage to escape danger. Chicks hatch covered in greyish down, with black markings on the head and neck, and fledge by the end of January, but both they and adult terns can fall victim to peregrine falcons (*Falco peregrinus*) swooping over the breeding grounds in search of prey.

Distribution: Occurs along the western coast of South America, ranging from the central part of Ecuador southwards as far as northern Chile.
Size: 24cm (9¹/₂in).
Habitat: Generally sandy areas of coastline.
Nest: Scrape on the ground.
Eggs: 1–2, brownish with darker markings.
Food: Mainly fish, some krill.

Snowy-crowned tern (*Sterna trudeaui*): 35cm (13½in)
Southern South America, extending down the Chilean coast, and also from southern Brazil to Uruguay in the east, and inland to Bolivia. White head, with a black stripe extending from just in front of the eyes to the sides of the neck. Stripe greyer when birds are not in breeding condition. Underparts light grey, wings slightly darker. Bill yellow, with a black band near the tip and red legs.

Elegant tern (*Thalasseus elegans*): 43cm (17in)
Ranges down the Pacific coast of America, from British Columbia to northern Chile, outside the breeding season. Breeding range restricted to the vicinity of California. Narrow black area above the bill extends back to encompass the eyes, with feathers at the back of the neck forming hair-like projections. Back and wings light grey, with the remainder of the body being white. Bill reddish, paler at the tip, with the legs and feet black, although, strangely, about 1 in 10 of a typical population have orange legs and feet. Sexes are alike. Forehead and crown white when not in breeding condition. Young birds have mottled upperparts and yellow bills.

South American tern (*Sterna hirundinacea*): 43cm (17in)
Coastal areas from Ecuador around the southern tip of the continent to Tierra del Fuego. Also on the Falkland Islands. Breeding range extends from southern Peru to central Brazil. Black cap on the head, reaching down to the eyes, narrowing over the neck, with the remainder of the face being white. Body grey, with flight feathers darker. Tail white. Bill, legs and feet red. Forehead white when not breeding. Young birds have white crowns, showing variable darker mottling, with black bills and dull yellow feet.

Amazon tern

Yellow-billed tern *Sternula superciliaris*

Unlike most other related species, the Amazon tern is frequently seen far inland, in the vicinity of rivers and lakes where breeding takes place, often on sandbars exposed during the relatively short dry season. Should the rainfall pattern prove unreliable, however, nests are likely to be lost if the river levels rise too fast, even before the eggs have hatched. These terns usually breed in small colonies, although their nests are often widely-spaced, which may help to guard against flooding. Younger individuals are likely to be observed in coastal areas, where they are often joined by adults outside the breeding season. Pairs have been observed nesting during July in Peru, but may not breed in Uruguay until December. Small fish, which are caught by diving down into the shallows, are a significant item in the diet of these terns, but frequently, they also hunt invertebrates of various types, sometimes even catching these in flight.

Distribution: Much of eastern South America, east of the Andes, from Eastern Colombia around to central parts of Argentina and Uruguay.
Size: 23cm (9in).
Habitat: Ranges extensively inland, breeding here.
Nest: Scrape on the ground.
Eggs: 2–3, brownish with darker markings.
Food: Fish and invertebrates.

Identification: A black stripe passes through each eye from the base of the bill, joining with a prominent area of black plumage running from the crown down the back of the neck. Remainder of plumage on the head is white, with the underparts also being white. Grey back and wings, with dark, blackish outer flight feathers, while the remainder of the underside of the open wing is white. Bill, legs and feet yellow. Sexes are alike. Young birds have greyish upperparts.

Spectacled tern

Grey-backed tern *Onychoprion lunatus*

Highly oceanic by nature, spectacled terns breed on islands through their range, with their nesting period being variable. Where they occur alongside sooty terns (*O. fuscata*), they will begin to nest up to two months before their near relatives. When the gap between nesting periods is shorter, competition for nest sites results in territorial conflicts between adult birds. The nest sites themselves may be on cliffs or concealed in amongst rocks. Spectacled terns can be sighted over a wide area outside the breeding season, and are potentially long-lived, with a life expectancy of over 15 years.

Identification: White forehead, with black crown and neck. Pale streaking on the forecrown when out of breeding condition. A black stripe extends from each side of the bill through the eyes, with the sides of the face, chest and underparts being white. Back and wings grey, with the flight feathers being a slightly darker shade of grey. Bill black, legs and feet dark grey. Sexes are alike. Young birds have dusky edging to the breast and buff markings on the upperparts.

Distribution: Through the Pacific from the Hawaiian Islands down to Fiji and Easter Island. Ranges west through Micronesia.
Size: 38cm (15in).
Habitat: Islands and open ocean.
Nest: Usually on the ground.
Eggs: 1, brownish with darker markings.
Food: Mainly fish and squid.

SANDPIPERS

This group of waders tend to have a fairly compact body shape, and are not especially brightly coloured. They have thin, narrow bills that are used for probing, although they also provide a very efficient means of grabbing the invertebrates that feature in their diets. The way in which they feed and move on the ground can aid identification.

Spotted sandpiper

Actitis macularius

Distribution: Northern Alaska through most of Canada and the USA. Moves south in the winter, heading down into South America.
Size: 20cm (8in).
Habitat: Shores and waterways.
Nest: Scrape in the ground.
Eggs: 4, greenish buff with brown spots.
Food: Invertebrates and fish.

In spotted sandpipers, some aspects of the traditional breeding roles of male and female are reversed. It is the female that returns first to the breeding grounds in the far north and establishes the breeding territory, driving off would-be rivals. During the breeding season she is likely to mate with a number of males, producing several clutches of eggs in succession. These are incubated and hatched by the male on his own, although occasionally the bond is strong enough for the female to stay and assist him. Spotted sandpipers start to leave the breeding grounds in June, heading south. Although some birds may only travel as far as British Columbia, the majority fly much closer to the equator, overwintering in the Caribbean and as far south as northern parts of Chile and Argentina. They are also not uncommon on the Galapagos Islands at this time.

Identification: Dark upperparts with darker brown speckling, white stripe above each eye and a long red bill with a dark tip. Underparts are white with dark spotting, with streaking on the sides of the face. Outside the breeding period the underparts are white, with speckling also absent from the wings, and the bill is yellowish brown. Sexes are alike. Young birds resemble adults not in breeding plumage.

Dunlin

Red-breasted sandpiper *Calidris alpina*

Identification: The Alaskan (*C. a. pacifica*) and Canadian (*C. a. hudsonia*) races are the largest. Coloration is quite variable. Generally greyish head and wings in winter, with streaking on the breast. Underparts white. In summer, underparts display black streaking, with brownish and black on wings. Centre of abdomen black, flanks white. Sexes are alike.

Dunlin favour muddy estuaries rather than sandy coasts, and outside the breeding season may be seen in large flocks numbering hundreds of birds. They feed by probing repeatedly in one area, then dart off and begin probing again nearby, a distinctive feeding method that enables them to be identified from a distance. Flocks invariably head north early in the year to nest, but if the winter is more prolonged than normal the pools and marshland where they feed will still be frozen over. This forces the dunlin to return south for a further period, before they venture north once again to begin breeding. They construct a simple nest using grass and other vegetation, which helps to conceal their eggs from would-be predators. Both members of the pair are involved in caring for the brood.

Distribution: Circumpolar, breeding along the coast of Alaska and through northern Canada around to the western shore of Hudson Bay. Winters south down the Pacific coast of North America, and along much of the Atlantic coast too.
Size: 20cm (8in).
Habitat: Frequents tundra and beaches.
Nest: Cup on the ground.
Eggs: 4, greenish brown with dark spotting.
Food: Invertebrates are the main constituent of diet.

Baird's sandpiper

Calidris bairdii

The female Baird's sandpiper lays her eggs on a scape in dry ground on the tundra, with both members of the pair incubating the clutch. Once the breeding season ends in July, these sandpipers begin to head south, with the females setting out first, followed by their partners and finally the young birds, who are unlikely to be seen in Argentina before the end of August. Here the sandpipers can be encountered in a wide range of habitats, with some found in the vicinity of lakes in the high Andes. They start to head north again during March, passing back over Central America and the prairies of North America, where they are likely to be observed during late April and early May. Baird's sandpiper is less social by nature than some of its kind and does not form large groups when feeding. These birds often prefer to seek their food along the shoreline, rather than actually wading.

Identification: Mottled appearance over the back and wings, with more of a striped pattern on the sides of the face and upper chest during the breeding period. Underparts are white, and the narrow bill is blackish. Upperparts more uniform in colour, with light edging to the brownish plumage. Sides of the face whitish with a brownish breast band. Legs and feet are dark. Sexes are alike. Young birds have an evident scaly patterning on their wings and streaky buff feathering on the chest.

Distribution: Summer breeding range is circumpolar. Overwintering grounds are mainly in the southern half of South America, including the Falkland Islands.
Size: 19cm (7¹/₂in).
Habitat: Breeds on tundra.
Nest: Scrape in the ground.
Eggs: 4, olive with dark markings.
Food: Invertebrates.

Sanderling (*Calidris alba*): 20cm (8in)
Breeds in the far north of Canada and Greenland, overwintering along the Atlantic coast of the USA down through the Caribbean. Also present from southern Alaska right down the Pacific coast. Reddish coloration and black speckling on the breast. The underparts are white, while the back and wings are grey with black and buff markings. In winter plumage, reddish markings are less evident, but a broad wing bar with black edging is seen in flight. Sexes are alike.

Red-necked stint (*Calidris ruficollis*): 15cm (6in)
Migrates regularly from eastern Asia across the Bering Sea to western Alaska and its offshore islands. Variable depth of reddish coloration on the head and upper chest, with the underparts being white. In paler individuals throat area may be whitish. Wings are chestnut and black, with white edging to the plumage. Bill and legs are blackish. Sexes are alike.

Purple sandpiper (*Calidris maritima*): 23cm (9in)
This species breeds on the southern coast of Greenland, plus Queen Elizabeth and neighbouring islands off Canada's northern coast. Streaked patterning is evident on the head, with a dark crescent-shaped marking seen behind the eyes. The back is mottled, with the wings being mainly brownish. Underparts becoming whiter, with striations down the flanks. The bill and legs are yellowish in colour, and the bill has a dark tip. Dark, greyish-brown head in winter plumage. Sexes are alike.

Stilt sandpiper

Calidris himantopus

The long legs of stilt sandpipers help distinguish them from similar species. Wading through water, they will submerge their heads as they search for food such as aquatic snails. They are observed feeding with dowitchers. Males lay claim to breeding territories on the tundra, flying conspicuously and calling loudly to attract females. The pair both incubate the eggs, the cock bird typically sitting through the day and his partner at night. In due course, they leave their young for the southerly wintering grounds. From mid-July the females head south, followed by their partners. Fledglings spend a further month before departing. Most fly straight down across North America, but some take a more easterly route down the Atlantic coast.

Distribution: Northern Alaska and Canada eastwards as far as Hudson's Bay. Moves south to southern California, Florida, and parts of South America for the winter.
Size: 22cm (8¹/₂in).
Habitat: Tundra and coastal areas.
Nest: Hidden in grass.
Eggs: 4, buff with brown markings.
Food: Mainly invertebrates.

Identification: Breeding adults have chestnut patch on each side of the head, conspicuous behind the eyes. White underparts heavily barred, top of the head is darker. Black and white markings on back and wings. In winter, much greyer overall, with underparts much whiter. Long, narrow bill is still blackish. Sexes are alike. Young lack chestnut patches.

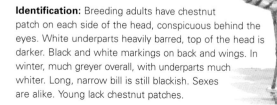

WADERS

Like their smaller counterparts, these birds may travel long distances to and from their breeding grounds, which are typically in the Arctic region. The nature of the climate here means the nesting period is necessarily short, and cover in this treeless part of the world is limited. In this environment, barred plumage of any type is helpful in providing camouflage.

Wilson's phalarope

Phalaropus tricolor

This is the largest species of phalarope. It moves inland when overwintering in South America, and is found around lakes and ponds rather than at sea like its relatives. A distinctive feature of Wilson's phalarope is the way its legs change colour during the year, being dull yellow in non-breeding birds before darkening to black at the start of the nesting period. Hens are more colourful, and will compete with each other to attract mates. Having laid her eggs, the hen leaves her partner to hatch them and rear their chicks alone. Wilson's phalarope has a very slender bill, which enables it to hunt invertebrates very effectively. Unlike other phalaropes this species does not have webbed feet, and so swims less frequently, but it does possess an unusual habit of stirring up the water by spinning around, and then looking for invertebrate food items that have been disturbed.

Identification: Breeding females have a broad reddish area down the side of the neck, with similar spots of coloration on the grey wings. Orange feathering on the throat. Underparts white with yellowish edging. Cock birds are duller in colour, with brownish wings. In winter plumage, both sexes have grey upperparts and white underparts. Young birds have brownish, mottled wings and white underparts.

Distribution: Generally breeds in an area from southern Yukon and Minnesota south to California and Kansas. Occasionally in the Great Lakes region, and also Massachusetts. Migrates south to the tropics for the winter, but some individuals may remain in California and Texas.
Size: 24cm (9½in).
Habitat: Coastal bays and lakes.
Nest: Scrape on the ground.
Eggs: 4, buff with brown spotting.
Food: Invertebrates.

Eskimo curlew

Numenius borealis (E)

Identification: Pale stripe above eye, with dark stripe running through it. Underparts buff with blackish markings. Long, narrow slightly down-curving bill and grey legs and feet. Hens similar but may be slightly bigger. Young birds have more buff coloration on underparts.

The total world population of these curlews is thought to be comprised of fewer than 50 individuals, yet in the early 1800s, they were regarded as being numerous. Shooting on their northern migratory route appears to have led to a decline in their numbers, and habitat changes may have subsequently prevented a recovery in their numbers. They arrive at their northern nesting grounds in May, seeking out areas where crowberries are common, although little is known about their breeding habits. Eskimo curlews then start to head south from late July onwards, travelling a distance of some 5,000km (3,125 miles) at this stage, heading down over the Atlantic, having crossed the coast over Labrador or Newfoundland. Their route back up north in the following spring takes a more westerly course over land, heading back over Texas. Sadly, conservation measures as yet seem to have had little impact on increasing their numbers, leaving this species on the edge of extinction.

Distribution: Breeds in the central coastal area of northern Canada, overwintering right down in parts of Argentina and Uruguay in South America.
Size: 34cm (13in).
Habitat: Tundra and pampas grassland.
Nest: Hollow, lined with leaves.
Eggs: 3–4, bluish green with brown spots.
Food: Invertebrates and berries.

Long-billed curlew

Numenius americanus

The distinctive song of these birds helps to explain their name, and announces their return to the northern breeding grounds each spring. Over the past century, however, their numbers have declined significantly. They nest in grassland areas, but are most likely to be seen feeding in groups on mudflats when the tide is low. They use their long bill to probe in the mud for worms and similar edible items. They are shy by nature, and will not generally tolerate a close approach. Long-billed curlews move south from May onwards, travelling relatively short distances in flocks to their wintering grounds, which include parts of Central America. They are opportunistic feeders, particularly when migrating. Their diet may include marine invertebrates caught on beaches and grasshoppers on the prairies, as well as berries and even seeds on occasion.

Identification: Brownish overall, with barring running across the feathers of the back and wings. Underparts slightly paler, less cinnamon in coloration, with striations becoming less apparent on the abdomen. Long, slightly down-curving bill, with grey legs and feet. Sexes are alike. Young birds are similar but have shorter, straighter bills.

Distribution: Breeding range extends from southern Canada down to northern California, running through parts of Utah, New Mexico, and Texas. Overwinters in southern USA southward.
Size: 58cm (23in).
Habitat: Salt marshes and prairies.
Nest: Grass-lined scrape.
Eggs: 4, olive with darker spotting.
Food: Mainly invertebrates, occasionally berries, seeds.

Bristle-thighed curlew (*Numenius tahitiensis*): 46cm (18in)
This species of curlew breeds only in Alaska, wintering in parts of Asia, including some Pacific islands. Very similar to the whimbrel, with mottled plumage and a dark streak behind the eyes, but distinguished by buff coloration on the rump and tail. Flanks display stiff feathers. Black, down-curving bill and grey legs. Sexes alike.

Rock sandpiper (*Calidris ptilocnemis*): 23cm (8.5in)
This sandpiper breeds in western Alaska and the Aleutians and winters on the western coast of North America. Also present in eastern Siberia. Appearance varies according to race. Upperparts are brownish with paler buff-white edging to the wings and streaking on the breast. Lower underparts are whitish, bill is dark and the legs are yellowish-grey. Often greyer in winter plumage. Sexes are alike. Young birds distinguished by their brighter buff patterning.

Magellanic plover (*Pluvianellus socialis*): 20cm (8in)
This species occurs on the south-eastern side of South America, in coastal parts of Argentina. Pale grey upperparts, with a darker eye stripe, white throat and a broad grey band across the chest. Remainder of the underparts are white. A darker grey central stripe is evident on the tail. Bill blackish, legs pinkish. Sexes are alike. Young birds have mottled grey upperparts and white streaking on the breast.

Surfbird

Calidris virgata

When nesting, surfbirds can be found inland on the Arctic tundra, where they feed largely on flies and other insects. The chicks grow rapidly, leaving the nest before they are a month old. In this open country, camouflage may not be sufficient to conceal their nest site from predators, so surfbirds are highly aggressive if threatened. They will fly directly at any perceived threat, even striking out at people passing close to their nest, flapping around their heads while calling loudly. Once the breeding season ends, surfbirds move further south to the coast, ranging close to where waves are breaking over rocks. This has led to them being called surfbirds. They use their strong bills to hammer invertebrates such as limpets and barnacles off the rocks. Flocks of surfbirds, numbering up to 100 individuals, may congregate in areas along the shoreline.

Distribution: Central and southern parts of Alaska, and central Yukon when breeding. Overwinters on Pacific coast, from Alaska to the southern tip of South America.
Size: 25cm (10in).
Habitat: Tundra and coast.
Nest: Hollow on the ground, lined with some vegetation.
Eggs: 3–4, buff with reddish-brown spotting.
Food: Invertebrates and even fish eggs.

Identification: White with rows of clustered, dark arrow-shaped markings. Wings have broad, buff orange band. Flight feathers black. Bill blackish, but with a lighter area at the base of the lower bill. Legs and feet pinkish. Sexes are alike. Young birds have a brownish breast.

OTHER NORTHERN WADERS

In the inhospitable region of the far north there is a restricted choice of food, but the presence of mosquito larvae, breeding in the shallow pools that develop here as the water is trapped by the deep-frozen permafrost beneath, guarantees a valuable source of protein for nesting birds, which they can use as a rearing food for their young.

Willet

Tringa semipalmata

The loud calls of the willet help to betray its presence, particularly as when alarmed it calls more frequently. Its unusual name is derived from its contact call, which sounds like "pee ... wee ... willet." Occurring in small flocks, willets keep in touch with each other by calling, especially if disturbed on their feeding grounds. They are found in a range of habitats, from mud flats to salt marshes, sometimes venturing into water to grab prey. Small crabs often feature prominently in their diet. Willets breed over a relatively wide area. The Caribbean population does not stray far, but those breeding further north head toward warmer climates in July. The young birds later follow their parents.

Identification: Breeding adults have a vibrant mottled appearance, with a white central area to the abdomen, and greyish wings with black flight feathers. Birds from the east have more evident barring than those from the west, as well as being slightly smaller too. The bill is long and straight. In winter plumage, grey overall becoming lighter on the underparts. Sexes are alike, with brownish tone to the back and wings.

Distribution: Breeding range extends from central Canada to north-eastern parts of California and Nevada. A second breeding population extends south from Nova Scotia down along the Gulf coast.
Size: 38cm (15in).
Habitat: Muddy shores and coastal marshes.
Nest: Grassy scrape.
Eggs: 3–4, buff with darker spots.
Food: Invertebrates and seeds.

Greater yellowlegs

Tringa melanoleuca

The muskeg area of Canada, characterized by its marshy ponds and relatively few trees, is the greater yellowlegs' breeding habitat. They move further south for the winter, where they are found on muddy coasts and sometimes further inland, in areas of both brackish and fresh water. These sandpipers will wade into deep water, up to the top of their legs, and have developed diverse feeding techniques. They chase after small fish, bending to seize them with their long bill, and pick up invertebrates on the shoreline. These waders undertake a relatively long migration, with some birds leaving as early as July, stragglers as late as November. They return from South America in March, reaching the breeding grounds again in April. Some young birds may remain behind, not heading north until ready to breed the following year.

Identification: Legs can vary in colour from yellow through to orange. Black lines on the neck are more distinctive in breeding plumage, with brown areas apparent on the wings. Centre of the abdomen is white. The contrast in coloration is less distinctive in birds in winter plumage, with the brown and black areas in the wings becoming grey. Sexes are alike. In young birds, more brownish colouring is seen over the wings.

Distribution: Breeds in south-west Alaska, and across Canada to Newfoundland. Overwinters in coastal and southern USA, from Washington southward and Virginia in the east, and through South America.
Size: 36cm (14in).
Habitat: Wet meadows and marshes.
Nest: Scrape on the ground.
Eggs: 4, dark spotted buff or greyish.
Food: Small fish and invertebrates.

Wandering tattler

Tringa incana

As its name suggests, the wandering tattler travels over a very wide area and can be found in a diverse range of habitats, depending on the time of year. Pairs breed alongside flowing streams in Alaska, nesting on the ground on gravel, sometimes constructing a nest for their eggs. They remain there between late May and August, before heading south to their wintering grounds, which include Hawaii. It is not common to see wandering tattlers feeding in large groups, but they will roost communally, and are not unduly shy. They sometimes seek to avoid danger by freezing rather than taking flight, although they are very agile on the wing and able to fly with little obvious effort.

Away from their breeding grounds, these waders are often found in rocky areas, rather than the mudflats favoured by the related Siberian or grey-tailed tattler (*T. brevipes*).

Identification: Dark grey upperparts, with the head and breast being heavily streaked and barred with grey markings. Pointed black bill, with yellow legs and feet. Outside the breeding season the markings on the underparts are replaced by consistent grey coloration on the breast and along the flanks, with a white central area on the underparts. Sexes are alike. Young birds similar but distinguishable by white spots on their upperparts.

Distribution: Breeds in south-central Alaska and northern British Columbia. Overwinters on Pacific islands and along the Pacific coast from central California south as far as Ecuador.
Size: 28cm (11in).
Habitat: Coastal areas and mountain streams.
Nest: Made of twigs and leaves.
Eggs: 4, greenish and spotted.
Food: Invertebrates.

White-rumped sandpiper (*Calidris fuscicollis*): 18cm (7in)
Breeds in northern America, overwinters from central Brazil down to the tip of South America. Black speckling over the top of the head, white chin. Ashy-brown head in non-breeding birds. Dark arrow-like patterning in rows on the chest, underparts white. Prominent black markings on the mottled wings. Bill, legs and feet black. Hens larger. Young birds have streaked breasts.

Black turnstone (*Arenaria melanocephala*): 24cm (9in)
Breeds around the Alaskan coast, moving further south to Baja California in winter. Mainly black upperparts with some white markings, including conspicuous spot above bill. Underparts white. In winter head, back, and breast are brown.

Hudsonian godwit (*Limosa haemastica*): 38cm (15in)
Far north of North America, wintering in south-eastern South America. Greyish head and neck, with chestnut featuring on underparts. Speckled white plumage on the wings, with distinctive black underwing feathering. Long bill, reddish at the base. Hen is larger, with whiter underparts.

Buff-breasted sandpiper (*Calidris subruficollis*): 20cm (8in)
Northern coast of Alaska eastward to the Queen Elizabeth Islands when breeding, migrates to South America for winter. Buff coloration on sides of face and underparts, becoming white. Large eyes, narrow black bill, yellow legs. Blackish-brown feathering edged with white on the back. Sexes are alike.

Ruddy turnstone

Arenaria interpres

Pairs of ruddy turnstones return to their Arctic breeding grounds during May, using their distinctive facial patterning and fanning their black and white tails for display. They will subsequently travel widely to their overwintering grounds, which lie in coastal areas and even on Pacific islands such as Hawaii. As their name suggests, ruddy turnstones have a distinctive way of seeking food. They utilize their strong neck and bill to flip over small rocks, shells, and seaweed on the beach, which may be hiding small crabs and other invertebrates. In sandy areas these sandpipers will dig too. They also scavenge on the remains of invertebrates caught by oystercatchers for example, and will even eat carrion. Ruddy turnstones are relatively tame birds and often seek to run away from danger, only taking flight as a last resort.

Identification: Distinctive ruddy coloration on wings in breeding plumage, broken by black. Black markings around the eye down on to the chest, with remaining underparts white. Bill black, legs reddish. Hens not as brightly coloured. In winter, brown and blackish streaks appear on head and back, with black wing patch and bib unaltered. Young birds have browner heads.

Distribution: Northwestern Alaska and Canadian Arctic, including Queen Elizabeth Islands. Found all along the coastline from Oregon to Connecticut in the USA, and all around South America.
Size: 24cm (9½in).
Habitat: Coastal tundra.
Nest: Scrape on the ground.
Eggs: 4, greyish-green with darker markings.
Food: Invertebrates.

PLOVERS AND DOWITCHERS

Many shorebirds occur over a wide area, but on occasion they may additionally be sighted in areas well outside their natural range. The young birds especially can become disorientated and end up in the wrong location, sometimes after being blown off course by gales and storms, which may force them to travel further inland than normal.

American golden plover

Lesser golden plover *Pluvialis dominica*

Distribution: Breeds in far north of North America, overwinters in South America.
Size: 28cm (11in).
Habitat: In summer tundra, in winter mudflats and marshes.
Nest: Scrape in ground.
Eggs: 3–4, buff with black and brown markings.
Food: Invertebrates and berries.

These long-distance migrants may fly almost twice the length of the American continents to and from their breeding grounds, travelling as far as 32,000km (20,000 miles) annually. Incredibly, they may undertake the southward journey without resting and can reach speeds of as much as 112kph (70mph) in flight. They then head back north over a different route up through South America and the Gulf of Mexico to Texas, usually pausing here on this leg, before continuing northwards to Canada, arriving from late May onwards. Heavily hunted for food in the late 1800s, the American golden plover is now less numerous than it was in the past, but the population appears stable. It often overwinters in flocks, frequently in estuarine areas rather than on the coast, and may be observed inland at this stage too, in open pasture, using its stout bill to seek worms and other invertebrates.

Identification: White forehead, extending as a stripe above each eye, narrowing out down the sides of the neck. Area beneath is black, as is the throat and underparts when in breeding plumage. Crown, back and wings are mottled, with buff, black and white evident here. Bill, legs and feet black. Hens have more extensive white on the flanks. Young birds have heavily marked grey underparts.

Wilson's plover

Thick-billed plover *Charadrius wilsonia*

Wilson's plovers, also known as thick-billed plovers, are widely distributed in North America. They frequent sandy coasts and mud flats, where they use their relatively large bill to feed on crabs and other invertebrates. They tend to avoid hunting directly on the shoreline, preferring the upper areas of the beach instead. Wilson's plovers nest on sandy beaches, sometimes close to coastal lagoons, but they do not usually venture far inland. In winter the northern population heads south as far as Brazil, leaving just a remnant overwintering population in southern Florida. On the Pacific coast, many of the Wilson's plovers that spend the summer there retreat as far south as central Peru for the duration of the winter. The young birds moult rapidly, and are indiscernible from the adults within months of fledging. It is not uncommon to see Wilson's plovers in the company of similar species.

Identification: In breeding plumage males have a black area on the centre of the crown and a broad black chest bar, with brown areas on the head and extending down over the wings. The underparts are white. Hens lack the male's black areas, which are replaced by brown feathering; this also applies to cock birds outside the breeding period. Young birds have scaly areas on the head, chest, back and wings.

Distribution: Breeding range from southern New Jersey south to Texas and Florida. Winters mainly in Florida, along the Gulf coast and in northern South America
Size: 20cm (8in).
Habitat: Sandy beaches and mud flats.
Nest: Scrape in sand.
Eggs: 3–4, buff with dark markings.
Food: Invertebrates.

Short-billed dowitcher

Limnodromus griseus

Breeds in northern areas, typically the marshy and sparsely wooded muskegs of Canada. The short-billed dowitcher is one of the first shorebirds that nest in this region to head back south again, with females leaving in late June. The young will follow slightly behind the adults, seeking out their coastal wintering grounds. These dowitchers can be encountered on both Atlantic and Pacific coasts, as well as through the Caribbean region, though some travel down to South America. The three distinctive races all follow separate routes as they leave the Arctic. Short-billed dowitchers form large flocks in their wintering grounds. They feed by probing with their bills for edible items underwater, often submerging their heads while doing so. On the return journey, southerly populations start to pass through the USA from March onwards.

Identification: Crown of breeding birds dark, with pale orange area on underparts broken by blackish speckling. Wings are black and grey with pale edging, although races differ. Sexes are similar. Silvery-grey winter plumage, becoming paler on the underparts. Young birds resemble breeding adults, but underparts are much whiter.

Distribution: Breeding range from southern Alaska across central Canada to Hudson Bay and northern Quebec. Overwinters on coasts south from California in the west and Virginia in the east as far as tip of South America.
Size: 28cm (11in).
Habitat: Tundra and tidal marshes.
Nest: Scrape on the ground.
Eggs: 4–5, white.
Food: Invertebrates.

Grey plover (*Pluvialis squatarola*): 30cm (12in)
Breeds from northern Alaska eastward to the vicinity of Hudson's Bay. Migrates south to the Pacific coast of North America and via Florida through the Caribbean. Prominent black area on face and belly, with white patches on the sides of the body. Mottled black and white plumage over the wings and white undertail coverts. Hens are similar, but black on the underparts has white barring. In winter upperparts are silvery-grey, with similar streaking on white underparts.

Rufous-chested plover (*Charadrius modestus*): 22cm (8¹/₂in)
Southern South America, overwintering in south-eastern Brazil, northern Chile and the Falkland Islands. Bright white stripe extends round the forehead over the eyes, grey below. Brown top to the head. Breast is rufous, with a black band on the lower chest. The underparts are white. Back and wings dark brown. Bill, legs and feet blackish. Hens duller. Out of breeding plumage, rufous and grey areas are brown, with young birds similar, but with buff edging on the breast.

Long-billed dowitcher (*Limnodromus scolopaceus*): 30cm (12in)
Breeds on the north Alaskan coast and offshore islands, migrating south to the Pacific coast and across the southern USA into Central America. Only the hen has a longer bill than the short-billed dowitcher. In breeding plumage all of the underparts are orangish, with a white stripe above the eyes. In winter, these birds become silvery-grey with whiter underparts.

American oystercatcher

Haematopus palliatus

This wader's large size and noisy nature make it quite conspicuous. The powerful bill is an adaptable tool, used to force mussel shells apart, hammer limpets off groynes, prey on crabs and even catch worms in the sand. Individuals will defend favoured feeding sites such as mussel beds from others of their kind. They are not likely to be observed in large groups, and tend to be quite sedentary. It takes young birds two years to gain their full adult coloration.

Identification: Black head, white underparts, brown back and wings. White wing bar. Large reddish-orange bill, reddish eye ring, legs and feet pink. Sexes are alike. Young birds have brown head with speckled wings.

Distribution: Breeding range from Baja California in the west to Massachusetts in the east. Winters along the Gulf coast from North Carolina, and into South America.
Size: 47cm (18¹/₂in).
Habitat: Tidal mud flats.
Nest: Scrape on the ground.
Eggs: 2–4, light buff with blackish-brown markings.
Food: Various invertebrates.

LARGER WADERS

Colourful in some cases and highly adapted to their environment, larger waders use their bills as sensory devices, probing for aquatic prey concealed in mud or under loose stones underwater. Their long legs facilitate feeding in beyond the shallows, while their height allows them to spot potential prey, such as a shoal of fish, from some distance away.

Scarlet ibis

Eudocimus ruber

The beautiful appearance of these ibis is derived in part from their diet, which helps to provide the pigment that gives them their characteristic coloration. They live in groups and comb the mud flats for crabs and other food with their stout but pointed bills. The scarlet ibis prefers to nest on islands, building a loose nest of sticks off the ground, often in mangrove swamps above the waterline. This can bring dangers, however, from crocodiles that lie in wait, hoping to seize chicks that have just left the nest and fall into the water.

Identification: Brilliant scarlet plumage, besides blackish ends to four longest primary flight feathers. Bill black in breeding birds, reddish rest of year. Sexes are alike. Young birds duller, with brown and white areas.

Distribution: Concentrated in northern South America, from parts of Colombia and Ecuador through Venezuela (including Guyana to French Guiana) along the coast of Brazil to the Amazon Delta. Has recently reappeared around São Paulo at Santos Bay, Brazil.
Size: 69cm (27in).
Habitat: Mangroves, mud flats and estuaries.
Nest: Sticks.
Eggs: 2, pale blue or greenish with brown blotches.
Food: Crustaceans, small fish and amphibians.

American white ibis

Eudocimus albus

These ibis use their long bill to probe underwater, seeking out the crabs that figure prominently in their diet, although they will also prey on other creatures, including fish and amphibians. White ibis are usually seen in groups, roosting and breeding in colonies which may number many thousands of birds, and which are frequently centred in mangrove areas. The eggs take three weeks to hatch, with the new chicks initially having a covering of black down. The young will leave the nest five weeks after hatching. Although populations are largely sedentary, these ibis may fly some distance to find food. When flying in groups they adopt a typical V-shaped formation. Numbers have declined in some areas, but there are still colonies of up to 40,000 ibis in parts of south-eastern USA.

Identification: Snow-white plumage and red legs. Reddish bill with a darker tip and bare reddish facial skin, which becomes darker as birds come into breeding condition. Blackish tips to the primary feathers are revealed in flight. Sexes are alike. Young birds have brown streaking on the head and neck, brownish wings and white underparts. Bill and legs paler than in adults.

Distribution: From North Carolina in the east, west to Baja California, and down through the Caribbean and Central America to Colombia and north-west Venezuela. Extends to western Ecuador and north-western Peru.
Size: 64cm (25in).
Habitat: Mangrove and wetland areas.
Nest: Platform of sticks.
Eggs: 2–3, bluish green with dark blotches.
Food: Crustaceans, small vertebrates.

Little egret (*Egretta garzetta*): 65cm (26in)
One of the Old World species that occasionally crops up on the east coast of North America during the summer, recorded from Newfoundland down to the mid-Atlantic states. White plumage with a blue-grey area at the base of the bill. Long white nuptial plumes at breeding time. Legs are blackish, but with highly distinctive yellowish toes. Sexes are alike.

Glossy ibis (*Plegadis falcinellus*): 65cm (26in)
Eastern coast of the USA, down through Florida and along the Gulf coast. Has been recorded as far west as Colorado. Dark brown overall, but some white streaking on head. Wings and rump green, legs and bill dark. Green and brownish plumage on head replaced by streaking in winter. Sexes are alike.

Western cattle egret (*Bubulcus ibis*): 56cm (22in)
Established in America after arriving from Africa. Moved north to Florida by the 1950s, reaching California by the 1960s. Pale buff coloration on head and throat extends on to breast, also on back and rump. Remaining plumage white. May have traces of white plumage around yellow bill.

Western reef heron (*Egretta gularis*): 65cm (25¹/₂in)
Occurs on Puerto Rico, Barbados and St Lucia. Dark phase birds are grey with darker band on wings and browner underparts. White at base of bill, down to throat. Legs dark, with yellowish-green feet. White phase birds are pure white with two long plumes on hindneck. Sexes are alike. Young birds are brown and white.

Tricoloured heron

Egretta tricolor

Although most commonly found in coastal areas, tricoloured herons may occasionally be seen inland as well, with breeding records from both Kansas and North Dakota. They frequent both mud flats and mangrove swamps, the latter providing them with trees where they can construct their nests in relative safety. They prefer to nest there rather than on the ground. Although rather solitary when seeking food, these herons will breed in relatively large colonies, sometimes alongside related species, with as many as 1,500 nests being recorded in the same area. Tricoloured herons display some seasonal movements, with the USA populations usually heading south to northern parts of South America to overwinter, swelling the local population. In recent years the species has also ranged further north up the US Atlantic coast.

Distribution: From southern and eastern parts of the USA through the Caribbean and along the northern coast of South America. Also present on the western coast, through Ecuador down to northern Peru.
Size: 66cm (26in).
Habitat: Salt marshes and mangrove swamps.
Nest: Platform of sticks.
Eggs: 3–4, greenish-blue.
Food: Fish and other aquatic creatures.

Identification: Bluish head, back and wings, with white underparts and a brownish area over the back. Sexes are alike. Young birds have a chestnut hind neck, with the chestnut extending on to the wing coverts.

Reddish egret

Egretta rufescens

Only young reddish egrets are likely to venture inland, and even they are a rare sight. These egrets are most commonly sighted around the shoreline. They are solitary hunters, catching food in a variety of ways. This includes scratching in the water with a foot to stir up creatures lurking on the bottom, and opening the wings to create a shadow on the water, which may draw fish within reach. They may even chase larger quarry through the shallows. Reddish egrets prefer to nest on islands or in mangroves, which provide some protection from predators. The colour morphs can be distinguished on hatching, since the white birds have corresponding white down. This form is only likely to be seen in the Bahamas, however. The overall range of reddish egrets has declined during the past century, initially as the result of hunting, as plumage was used to decorate hats.

Identification: Shaggy reddish-chestnut plumage on head and neck extends to upper chest, with greyish-black plumage over rest of body, and cobalt-blue legs. Pure white form has same bill and leg colours. Plumage less shaggy and bill dark when not breeding. Sexes are alike. Young birds greyish, with cinnamon on head.

Distribution: Extreme south of the USA, around the Gulf coast on the eastern side, and eastern Mexico as well as parts of the Caribbean. Also occurs in South America in the most northerly parts of Colombia and Venezuela.
Size: 81cm (32in).
Habitat: Shallow salt pans.
Nest: Made of sticks.
Eggs: 2–7, greenish blue.
Food: Mainly fish.

WATERFOWL AND RAILS

While members of both these groups are typically more widespread in freshwater zones, there are certain species which have adapted to living in proximity to tidal areas. In the case of rails, the regular fall-off in water level in this type of environment provides increased feeding opportunities. Like waterfowl, they can feed both in water and on land.

Mottled duck

Anas fulvigula

Distribution: From just north of Florida on Atlantic coast around the Gulf of Mexico down to south Mexico. Now introduced to South Carolina.
Size: 56cm (22in).
Habitat: Coastal waters.
Nest: Made of grass.
Eggs: 4–18, greyish-green.
Food: Aquatic vegetation and invertebrates.

Closely related to the well-known mallard (*Anas platyrhynchos*), these dabbling ducks are usually encountered in relatively shallow waters, where they dip their heads down under the surface to obtain water plants and invertebrates. During the summer they are more likely to be found on stretches of fresh water, but will usually be seen in salt marshes through the winter period. Flocks start to pair off early in the year, beginning in January. They breed on the ground, choosing a secluded site under vegetation for their nest and lining it with feathers. The incubation period takes approximately four weeks, with the young ducklings having dark brown upperparts at first, and much lighter underparts. They will be sexually mature at one year old. Mottled ducks can be distinguished from mallards by their darker overall plumage, with females having no white area in their tails.

Identification: Drake has a yellow bill with a dark tip. Predominantly brownish plumage, with paler, unstreaked sides to the face and on the throat. Mottled underparts, with more evident scalloping to the feathers on the flanks, and over the back and wings. Blue wing speculum. Yellowish-orange legs and feet. Sexes are similar, although females can be instantly recognized by the greener coloration of their bills.

Fuegian steamer duck

Tachyeres pteneres

The short flight feathers on the wings confirm the inability of this species to fly. They have acquired the name of "steamer" because of the way they paddle furiously with their powerful legs to escape danger, rather like a paddle steamer moving along the coast. These ducks are largely marine, seeking food such as crustaceans in beds of kelp close to the shore, generally at high tide, although they can sometimes be observed several miles out to sea. They rarely venture inland in search of fresh water, but drink regularly from streams running down to the shore.

Fuegian steamer ducks are relatively solitary by nature, and highly territorial during the breeding period, which begins in September. The nests themselves are very well-concealed in coastal vegetation, being located just a short distance from the sea, allowing the sitting bird to escape if danger threatens. Calm bays and coves are especially favoured as nesting sites, with the incubation period lasting about 30 days.

Identification: Drakes have a greyish head, with darker edging to the plumage on the body, with a prominent white area on the underparts. There is also a white wing bar. Tail feathers are short. Prominent orangish bill, with a dark tip. Stocky legs and feet. Ducks smaller, with a purplish suffusion on the sides of the head. Young birds duller, with a narrow and pale eye-ring.

Distribution: Southern South America, extending from Tierra del Fuego north to central Chile, and to southern Argentina.
Size: 84cm (33in).
Habitat: Coastal region, especially in bays.
Nest: Built in vegetation, lined with feathers.
Eggs: 5–8, creamy-white.
Food: Mainly marine invertebrates, as well as small fish.

Clapper rail

Rallus crepitans

The population of clapper rails has declined in some areas, notably on the west coast, as a result of the introduction of red foxes (*Vulpes vulpes*), which hunt these birds to the extent that the brightly coloured *R. obsoletus levipes* is now regarded as endangered. There are approximately 8 different subspecies of this rail recognized through their New World distribution, differing not just in coloration but also in size. Clapper rails were given their name because of the sound of their distinctive calls. They use their long bills to probe for food, hunting by sight in most cases, although they can catch fish by diving underwater. The best time to spot these secretive birds is when the tide is low, but they rarely emerge from cover for long and will dart back at the slightest hint of danger. Pairs are very territorial when nesting.

Identification: Greyish sides to the face, with a speckled brown back. The throat is white with variable brown and white barring on the flanks and white undertail coverts. The chest area can be cinnamon, although duller in some cases, depending on the species concerned. Long, dark-coloured straight bill. Hens are significantly smaller in size.

Distribution: Occurs mainly in coastal areas, extending through Mexico and parts of the Caribbean region southward to northern Peru and southern Brazil in South America.
Size: 41cm (16in).
Habitat: Salt marshes.
Nest: Cup-shaped.
Eggs: 3–14, creamy-white with dark blotches.
Food: Small invertebrates and seeds.

West Indian whistling duck (mangrove duck, *Dendrocygna arborea*): 56cm (22in)
Occurs widely through the Caribbean, from the Bahamas south via Cuba, the Cayman Islands and Jamaica east to Puerto Rico, Antigua, and Barbuda. Also on the Virgin Islands. Dark crown, neck and wings. Yellowish-brown markings on the sides of the face; and white upper throat is mottled with black lower down. Prominent black and white markings on the flanks. Brown on chest, becoming mottled and paler on lower underparts. Sexes are alike. Young birds duller.

Flying steamer duck (*Tachyeres patachonicus*): 71cm (28in)
Southern South America, on both sides of Cape Horn, from Chile to northern Argentina, and also on the Falklands. Plain grey head, with black edging to the grey feathering on the body. White wing speculum. Grey back and white underparts. Drakes have yellowish-orange bills with a black tip, whereas hens have a darker bluish shade on the bill. Yellow legs.

Barrow's goldeneye (*Bucephala islandica*): 53cm (21in)
Western North America, from the Aleutian Islands and southern Alaska down the Pacific coast to California. Also occurs on northeastern Canada and Greenland. Metallic green head, black over the back with white underparts, and a prominent white area on each side of the black bill, with golden eyes. Hens, in contrast, have brown head and greyish underparts, with a dull yellow tip to the bill. Drakes out of colour resemble hens, apart from their dark bill and black and white wing markings.

Little wood rail

Aramides mangle

Since it was first described back in 1825, very little has been documented about the habits of this species, which is the smallest of the wood rails. In some parts of its range, however, it does appear to be quite numerous. The best time to see little wood rails is at low tide, when the falling water level draws the birds out from the relative sanctuary of the mangroves to search for food on the mud banks. It is thought that little wood rails feed chiefly on invertebrates. They also venture further inland on occasions, being recorded from forests near the mangroves. Little wood rails are shy by nature, and if disturbed will fly up and perch in branches, where they will be relatively safe from danger. It is likely that they will nest off the ground too, but no information is recorded about their breeding habits, nor their eggs. Even the appearance of the young birds remains unrecorded, though it is probable they are simply not as brightly coloured as the adults.

Distribution: Restricted to South America, where it can be found in the eastern coastal areas of Brazil.
Size: 32cm (11in).
Habitat: Coastal swamps and mangroves.
Nest: Unknown.
Eggs: Unknown.
Food: Probably invertebrates.

Identification: Bluish-grey plumage on the head, extending down the back, with the chin and throat being whitish. Olive-green coloration extends down to the upper back, while the lower back and rump is sepia. Tail and surrounding region are black, with the underparts being tawny-red. Lower flanks and abdomen are olive. The sharp, pointed bill is yellowish-green. Legs and feet are red. Sexes alike.

LOCALIZED SPECIES

Coastal areas, including mangroves, are home not just to various types of water birds but also to members of groups such as sparrows, whose relatives are typically found further inland. These species have adapted well to this type of habitat, and yet in a number of respects their lifestyles are not entirely dissimilar to those of their more widely distributed relatives.

Mangrove cuckoo

Coccyzus minor

Hard to spot in the mangroves and forested areas where they occur, these cuckoos effectively conceal their presence by perching near the centre of a tree, rather than on the outer branches. Their slim shape enables them to slip through vegetation without creating a disturbance or drawing attention to themselves. Mangrove cuckoos fly straight and fast, slipping out of sight rapidly. They are more likely to reveal their location by their song, which can be heard during the nesting period. Unlike many cuckoos, the mangrove rears its own chicks. The nest is built in trees or bushes, where it is well concealed, sometimes at a relatively low height. As with other related species, the young will grow quickly, and are reared mainly on invertebrates.

Identification: The Florida race (*C. m. maynardi*) has a greyish-white throat with yellow underparts. In other cases, however, this part of the body is entirely yellowish buff. The head is greyish, with a black band behind each eye and browner wings and tail. Underside is black and white. It has a powerful, down-curving bill. Sexes are alike. Young birds have paler faces, and the contrast on the tail is less marked.

Distribution: Occurs in southern Florida and throughout the Caribbean. Also occurs on mainland parts of Central America, from Mexico extending south along the west coast of South America.
Size: 30cm (12in).
Habitat: Mangrove swamps.
Nest: Bowl of twigs.
Eggs: 2, white.
Food: Invertebrates, some berries.

Fish crow

Corvus ossifragus

It can be difficult to distinguish this species from the American crow, especially from a distance, although fish crows are a little smaller, with longer tails. The situation is made more complex by the fact that these two corvids sometimes feed together. However, the calls of the two species offer a means of distinction, with fish crows uttering short, low-pitched "car" notes and higher-pitched, two-tone "ca-hah" calls, whereas adult American crows utter a more strident "caw." Fish crows hunt along the seashore, and will even wade into the water in search of food. They are sufficiently agile to catch small fish by plucking them from the water with their claws while hovering overhead. Fish crows may form small colonies when breeding in the spring, but each pair occupies its own tree, with the nest of twigs being built in a convenient fork. The young fledge with blue eyes, although these soon darken to the brown of adult birds.

Identification: Jet black, but can be distinguished from the similar American crow (*C. brachyrhynchos*) by its slightly smaller size, and perhaps most noticeably by its longer tail. The head and bill are also smaller, while in flight it has a more jerky flight pattern. Sexes are alike. Young have a more dusky head and underparts.

Distribution: Occurs in eastern parts of the USA, from New England down to Florida and along the Gulf coast to the vicinity of Galveston, Texas. May be sighted further inland during the summer, in the Mississippi valleys as far as southern Illinois.
Size: 39cm (15¹/₂in).
Habitat: Salty marshes and rivers.
Nest: Bowl of twigs.
Eggs: 4–5, bluish green with dark blotches.
Food: Omnivorous.

Black-whiskered vireo

Vireo altiloquus

Distribution: Centred on the Caribbean, sometimes recorded on the Caribbean coast. Also ranges north to Florida.
Size: 16cm (6¹/₄in).
Habitat: Mangrove swamps.
Nest: Cup of grass.
Eggs: 2–3, white with brown spots.
Food: Invertebrates and berries.

These small insect-eaters are relatively inconspicuous, especially when obscured in vegetation, but they have a surprisingly loud song, which betrays their presence, reported to sound like the words "Whip Tom Kelly." In the Caribbean, these vireos have developed various local song dialects. Their characteristic stripe is not that apparent unless the bird is seen at close quarters. Typically occurring in mangroves, as in the vicinity of Miami on the mainland, black-whiskered vireos construct a small nest in a tree fork. While in some parts of their range, as in the Lesser Antilles, they are present throughout the year, populations from elsewhere migrate southward to northern South America in September, after the end of the breeding season, and return early the following year.

Identification: A characteristic black stripe extends down each side of the face from the base of the bill. The crown is grey, and there is also a broad grey stripe running through the eyes, which have bright orange-red pupils, with a whitish stripe above. The wings and back are olive green, and the underparts are a whitish shade, with yellow suffusion on the flanks. Sexes are alike.

Saltmarsh sparrow (*Ammodramus caudacutus*): 13cm (5in)
Found on the eastern coasts of the USA. Dark crown, with orange area on the sides of the face, encircling the grey patches behind each eye. Underparts streaked on the chest and flanks, centre of abdomen white. Some chestnut coloration on the wings, with three rows of distinctive white markings down the back. The bill is relatively long and flat.

Boat-tailed grackle (*Quiscalus major*): cock 42cm (6¹/₂in); hen 37cm (14¹/₂in)
Ranges down the Atlantic coast through Florida to coastal areas of Louisiana and Texas. Mature cock birds have iridescent bluish-black coloration, with a long, keel-shaped tail. Eye colour varies from brown to yellow. Hens significantly smaller and tawny brown, with wings and tail darker.

Tricoloured blackbird (*Agelaius tricolor*): 23cm (9in)
Occurs on south-western coast of the USA extending inland, nesting in marshes. Breeding cock is predominantly black, with a bold red wing patch and white stripe behind. Hens sooty brown overall, with speckled lines running over the breast and a light stripe above the eye. Greyish-buff edging on the upperparts seen in both sexes following the late summer moult.

Grey kingbird (*Tyrannus dominicensis*): 23cm (9in)
Found in the Florida Keys, occasionally north up the Atlantic seaboard, and along the Gulf coast to Texas. Often seen in mangroves. Darker grey head and back, with broad black streak through the eyes. Red patch on crown is hard to spot. Underparts whitish with a yellowish suffusion extending to undertail coverts. Forked tail, strong black bill. Sexes are alike.

Seaside sparrow

Ammodramus maritimus

Distribution: From New England down to Florida on the eastern side of the USA, and along the Gulf coast as far as Texas.
Size: 15cm (6in).
Habitat: Tidal marshes.
Nest: Woven grass.
Eggs: 4–5, white with brown blotches.
Food: Invertebrates and seeds.

These unusual finches live in the grasslands of tidal salt marshes, having adapted to this habitat, with local races also having arisen. (These included the sadly extinct Cape sable sparrow [*A. m. mirabilis*], which had particularly strong green coloration, and the dusky seaside sparrow [*A. m. nigrescens*], one of the latest additions to the annals of extinct North American birds, the last known example dying in June 1987. The contrast in the plumage of *A. m. nigrescens*, between its dark upperparts and darkly streaked white underparts, was particularly marked.) The habitat has influenced the diet of seaside sparrows, since they feed more on small creatures such as crabs and snails in the tidal area than on seeds. They are inconspicuous, often spending time near the ground foraging, but can also be seen singing in prominent sites.

Identification: Differs quite widely in coloration, depending on the individual race. The common nominate race (*A. m. maritimus*) has greyish-olive upperparts with brown marking on the wings, and a small yellowish area above each eye. Throat is whitish grey, with a darker stripe extending from the corner of the bill. Underparts are greyish, with darker streaked patterning. Sexes are alike. Young birds are browner.

DIVERS AND GREBES

Most wetland birds that breed in the far north during the summer cannot stay there throughout the year because the winter conditions are too harsh. While some head to warmer climates further south, others may seek sanctuary along the coast, where the ocean is unlikely to freeze even in winter. This shift usually brings a dramatic change in both the bird's lifestyle and diet.

Red-throated diver

Red-throated loon *Gavia stellata*

Distribution: Throughout far north of North America and in parts of Greenland when breeding. Overwinters further south, from the Aleutians down to California in the west and on the Atlantic seaboard down to Florida.
Size: 64cm (25in).
Habitat: Pools, open country.
Nest: Pile of vegetation.
Eggs: 1–3, olive brown with dark spots.
Food: Mainly fish.

Red-throated divers pair up for life and stay together throughout the year. In May they return to their northern nesting grounds, revisiting the same location each year. Their nest, usually located among vegetation and surrounded by water, is simply a loose pile of plant matter. This is added to during the incubation period, potentially developing into a large mound. Both parents share incubation duties, although the female normally sits for longer than the male. Young red-throated divers can take to the water almost immediately after hatching, but usually remain at the nest for the first few days. Even once the chicks have entered the water they may still occasionally be carried on their parents' backs. Survival rates can be low, but if they make it through the critical early months of life, these divers may live for up to 23 years.

Identification: Distinctive red throat patch present in adults of both sexes during the breeding period. The head is grey, and the back of the neck is streaked black and white. Upperparts are brown, underparts white. During winter it has a pale grey crown, with speckling extending down the back of the neck and white spotting on the back, while remaining underparts are white. Yellowish-grey bill. Young birds can be identified by their greyish-brown heads.

Horned grebe

Podiceps auritus

Horned grebes return to their freshwater breeding grounds in spring, after overwintering in bays and other sheltered locations along the coast. The nest consists of a mass of floating aquatic plants, although it is sometimes built on rocks. The young, which hatch covered in striped down, can take to the water almost immediately, but prefer to be carried on their parents' backs. Horned grebes obtain much of their food by diving rather than feeding at the surface. Their natural underwater agility enables them to catch fish with ease. Diet varies according to season and location. At sea during winter they eat mostly fish, while brine shrimps are important when passing the Great Salt Lakes on migration. Diet is more varied on the breeding grounds.

Identification: Distinctive golden horns created by raised feathers on each side toward rear of head. A red-brown area extends from bill to eyes, with others on the neck and flanks. Remainder of head black, as are wings. Much duller plumage in winter, when black on top of head extends down back of the neck to the wings. Throat and area below eyes remain white. Iris is reddish, bill black. Sexes are alike.

Distribution: Breeds in much of Alaska and south-east across Canada to the shores of the Great Lakes. Overwinters through the Aleutians and down the west coast of Canada to mainland USA, and down the eastern seaboard to Florida and Texas on the Gulf coast.
Size: 34cm (13½in).
Habitat: Marshland, ponds and lakes.
Nest: Pile of vegetation.
Eggs: 1–7, bluish white.
Food: Fish and invertebrates.

Western grebe

Aechmophorus occidentalis

Identification: Black head, encompassing the eyes when breeding, with a narrow white stripe running to the bill. Black plumage extends down back of neck over back and wings, with some mottling on flanks. Iris reddish, bill black in centre, with yellowish sides. Area around eyes mottled in winter. Sexes are alike.

Western grebes hunt fish by diving, becoming most active when the sun is high in the sky, illuminating the water and improving visibility. Their habitat alters significantly through the year, as they range between the coast and their freshwater breeding haunts in the north. Western grebes begin nesting during May, often forming large groups comprised of thousands of birds. It is not uncommon for hens to lay in nests other than their own, which can result in some nests containing ten or more eggs. Once the chicks have fledged, typically about ten weeks after hatching, the grebes head south to their wintering grounds, migrating over land during the hours of darkness. The habits of the Mexican population are rather different, as they have a more extended nesting season, with egg-laying continuing until October. Mexican birds are also more sedentary by nature, and significantly smaller in size than their northern cousins.

Distribution: Breeds in south-central and south-western parts of Canada, and in western and central parts of the USA. Overwinters down the Pacific coast to Baja California, with a separate Mexican population. Also present on the Gulf coast in winter.
Size: 64cm (25in).
Habitat: Lakes and reservoirs, overwinters on coasts.
Nest: Pile of vegetation.
Eggs: 3–4, bluish white with buff markings.
Food: Fish form the bulk of the diet.

Junin flightless grebe (*Podiceps taczanowskii*): 38cm (15in) (E)
Occurs naturally only on Lake Junin, central Peru, but introduced to other nearby lakes, to help its conservation. Greyish head, with a black area extending down the neck (only in breeding plumage) from the hindcrown over the back. White throat and underparts. Bill, legs and feet greyish. Prominent red iris. Sexes are alike. Young resemble adults outside the breeding period.

Least grebe (*Tachybaptus dominicus*): 25cm (10in)
Southern Texas and Baja California to northern Argentina and southern Brazil, also Caribbean. Greyish head and neck, darker crown, browner on chest, with dark flanks. Chin and throat are white, and flanks pale, outside the breeding season. Iris is yellowish. Sexes are alike. Young resemble non-breeding adults, except for stripes on sides of the head.

White-tufted grebe (*Rollandia rolland*): 36cm (14in)
Found in central Peru and south-eastern Brazil down to tip of South America; also Falklands. Has a unique black and white tuft of feathers on head, with black crown, neck, chest, and wings. Red-brown barring on flanks and red-brown underparts. Browner overall when not breeding, with a white throat and underparts. Sexes are alike. Young birds similar to adults out of breeding colour, but with black striping across the cheeks.

Sungrebe

Heliornis fulica

The sungrebe is the smallest member of the finfoot family. Shy by nature, its habits have proved hard to determine, partly because it prefers wooded areas with dense vegetation by waterways. Sungrebes usually feed on the water, but may also venture onto land. They feed on insects such as dragonflies and their larvae, also hunting crayfish and amphibians. When breeding, males choose a nest site overhanging the water, typically only 1m (3ft) from the surface. The incubation period is short, lasting just ten days. The male sungrebe then carries the helpless chicks in a special pocket created by a skin fold under each wing, and can even fly with them in there. This method of care is completely unique.

Identification: Black and white stripes on top of head, running through eyes. White throat and underparts, yellowish hue on upper breast. Back and wings are brownish. Legs and especially feet banded gray and yellow. White tail tip. Breeding hens have chestnut area on sides of the head and red upper bill, plus scarlet eyelids.

Distribution: Extends from south-eastern Mexico through Central America down to Peru in the west, and across much of northern South America east of the Andes down as far as northern Argentina.
Size: 33cm (13in).
Habitat: Streams, rivers and lakes.
Nest: Platform of twigs.
Eggs: 2–3, buff with darker markings.
Food: Mainly aquatic invertebrates.

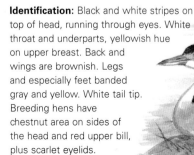

FLAMINGOS AND OTHER LARGER WATERBIRDS

A number of relatively large birds, including flamingos and cranes, have evolved to live in wetland areas, where their height can be an advantage in finding food and wading through the water. Unfortunately, some have become so specialized in their habits that changes in their environment, such as pollution of waterways or clearing of land, could have serious consequences.

American flamingo

Phoenicopterus ruber

The distinctive coloration of these birds comes from their diet of algae or small creatures that have eaten the microscopic plants. They feed in a unique fashion by walking along with their head submerged, their long neck allowing them to filter relatively large quantities of water by sweeping their unusually shaped bill from side to side. As a result of their highly specific feeding requirements, American flamingos are vulnerable to habitat loss or pollution of the shallow coastal lagoons that they inhabit. Young are reared on nests of mud raised above the water level, and are covered in a whitish-grey down at first. At a month old, they moult into a brownish down. Their bills are short and straight at this stage. American flamingos are known to live for more than 30 years in the wild.

Identification: Bright, almost reddish plumage on the neck, with a paler pink body. Bill also has a pink hue behind the black tip. Outstretched wings in flight show black areas. Sexes are alike.

Distribution: The Caribbean Islands, Mexico, the north coast of South America and the Galapagos Islands. Other subspecies found in parts of southern Europe, Africa, and Madagascar, extending through the Red Sea into Asia.
Size: 145cm (57in) tall.
Habitat: Shallow saline lagoons.
Nest: Mud.
Eggs: 1, white.
Food: Small molluscs, crustaceans and plant matter.

Chilean flamingo

Phoenicopterus chilensis

Distribution: Ranges from highlands of Peru to Tierra del Fuego at the tip of the continent.
Size: Up to 105cm (41in) tall. Hens shorter and smaller.
Habitat: Highland salt lakes.
Nest: Mud.
Eggs: 1, white.
Food: Algae and invertebrates.

This is the most widely distributed South American flamingo, with a range extending more than 4,000km (2,500 miles). In the altiplano region of the Andes, they are usually observed at altitudes of 3,500–4,500m (11,500–15,000ft), but in parts of Argentina, east of the Andes, they occur at lower levels. In suitable areas, Chilean flamingos will congregate in large numbers, and as many as 100,000 have been counted on Lake Poopo in Bolivia. Lake Titicaca, found on the Bolivian border with Peru, is home to even greater numbers. Their calls are similar to the honking notes of geese.

Identification: Pinkish with crimson coloration over the back. Black area on the tip of the bill, extending back beyond the bend, with the remainder being whitish. No yellow coloration is evident here. Characteristic reddish knee joints and feet. Sexes are alike.

Sandhill crane

Antigone canadensis

Young sandhill cranes take around 2¹/₂ years to acquire full adult coloration. However, adults may smear themselves with iron-rich mud when preening, which gives their plumage a reddish-brown colour, not dissimilar to that of immature birds. Sandhill cranes migrate long distances to the Caribbean from their tundra breeding grounds, but are often difficult to spot as they fly at a high altitude. Southern populations tend to be more sedentary, although they may move in search of food. During late summer and early autumn they are more likely to be sighted in agricultural areas, feeding on spilt corn and taking invertebrates such as earthworms.

Identification: Mostly grey, with whitish colour on sides of face and throat. Vibrant red area on crown and lores; bill, legs, and feet grey. Sexes are alike. Young birds have tawny neck and head, and brownish mottling on the body.

Distribution: Breeds along the Arctic coast of North America, and at Great Lakes. Winters in southern USA and Mexico. Also found in Florida and the Caribbean.
Size: 122cm (48in).
Habitat: Wetland areas.
Nest: Mound of vegetation.
Eggs: 2, buff with brown markings.
Food: Omnivorous.

James's flamingo
(*Phoenicoparrus jamesi*):
92cm (36in)
Confined to a small part of the Andes, the Puna has the smallest range of any flamingo. Pinkish suffusion to the head and body, with a whitish neck and a reddish-pink streak along the breast and back when breeding. Flight feathers are black. Bare red skin around the eyes; yellowish bill with a black tip. Pink legs and feet, with no hind toe on either foot. Young have fawn-coloured feathering with black streaking across upperparts.

Southern screamer (*Chauna torquata*):
95cm (37in)
South America, extending southward from Bolivia and southern Brazil down to northern Argentina. Mostly grey, darker over back and wings, with a short crest at the back of the head. Bare red skin around the eyes; bill is greyish. Narrow white band around the neck, with a broader black band beneath. In flight, a white area can be seen on the wings. Sexes are alike. Young birds are duller in colour with shorter spurs on the feet.

Northern screamer (*Chauna chavaria*):
91cm (36in)
North-west Colombia and neighbouring north-western Venezuela. Predominantly dark, slate grey with whitish striations on the breast. Top of the head is paler grey, with a backward-pointing crest and a large white area extending from the top of the head down under the bill. Neck almost entirely black. Sexes are alike. Young birds duller in coloration.

Whooping crane

Grus americana (E)

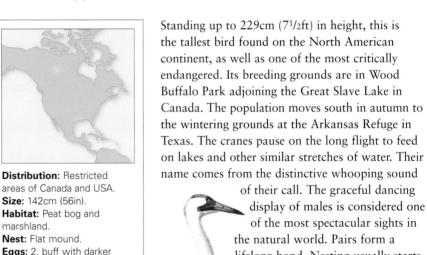

Distribution: Restricted areas of Canada and USA.
Size: 142cm (56in).
Habitat: Peat bog and marshland.
Nest: Flat mound.
Eggs: 2, buff with darker blotches.
Food: Omnivorous.

Standing up to 229cm (7¹/₂ft) in height, this is the tallest bird found on the North American continent, as well as one of the most critically endangered. Its breeding grounds are in Wood Buffalo Park adjoining the Great Slave Lake in Canada. The population moves south in autumn to the wintering grounds at the Arkansas Refuge in Texas. The cranes pause on the long flight to feed on lakes and other similar stretches of water. Their name comes from the distinctive whooping sound of their call. The graceful dancing display of males is considered one of the most spectacular sights in the natural world. Pairs form a lifelong bond. Nesting usually starts in May.

Identification: Red face and white plumage, black primaries. Sexes are alike. Young birds have a rusty hue, particularly on head and neck.

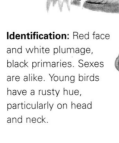

LONG-LEGGED WADING BIRDS

These birds are all well equipped to forage in wetland areas, their long legs enabling them to wade easily through the shallows while also giving them a good field of vision to detect possible prey. A powerful bill and rapid reflexes make them formidable hunters of small aquatic creatures. They may also be encountered in open areas close to stretches of water.

Wood stork

Wood ibis *Mycteria americana*

Although usually it is most likely to be encountered in freshwater areas, the wood stork may be seen in mangrove swamps where food is abundant. These birds are opportunistic predators, and are equipped with a powerful bill to seize creatures ranging from fish to young turtles and alligators. These large birds breed colonially, often on nesting sites surrounded by water. Up to 50 pairs or more may be found in the same area where conditions are favourable. Pairs accomplish nest-building quite quickly, in about three days, and the hen lays the eggs on a nest lining of leaves. These storks are long-lived, and their young are therefore slow to mature, often not breeding until they are five years old.

Identification: Bare, dark and unfeathered head is offset against the white plumage. The black feathering is confined to the wings and tail. Long bill, powerful at its base. White plumage in young birds tends to appear slightly soiled.

Distribution: Southern parts of the USA south as far as north-west Argentina.
Size: 119cm (47in).
Habitat: Marshland and lakes.
Nest: Made of sticks.
Eggs: 2–5, creamy white.
Food: Fish, amphibians and crustaceans.

White-faced ibis

Plegadis chihi

Studies have revealed the long distances that these ibises may travel, even in the southern part of their range where they do not undergo any apparent seasonal migrations. Not surprisingly, they may occasionally be encountered well outside their normal range, occurring as far south as Tierra del Fuego and even on Hawaii on rare occasions, though they fly over the ocean less than related species. White-faced ibises feed in large flocks, sometimes comprised of thousands of individuals. They eat a range of invertebrates, some of which may be gathered in water, while others such as earthworms are found by probing in mud. Unfortunately, in some areas pesticide residues have had an adverse affect on their numbers, since they interfere with the hatching of their eggs. The nest site is usually well concealed in vegetation. These ibises often nest together in large colonies, sometimes in the company of other birds, including gulls.

Identification: Distinguishable in breeding plumage by the white line that encircles the bare red skin on each side of the face. The remainder of the plumage is chestnut and green, with bronzy tones apparent over the wings. The legs and feet are reddish, while the horn-coloured bill is long and down-curving. In winter, the appearance is much duller, with brown and black streaking extending over the head and neck, no greenish cap on the crown, and paler red skin. Sexes are alike. Young birds are much less brightly coloured, being predominantly brownish on the head, with speckled feathering.

Distribution: Occurs in the north-west USA and central California, extending down the coasts of Mexico. Also found in southern-central parts of South America, from Paraguay, southern parts of Bolivia, and Brazil southward to northern parts of Chile and Argentina. Also occurs in Uruguay.
Size: 58cm (23in).
Habitat: Shallow areas of fresh water.
Nest: Cup-shaped, made of reeds.
Eggs: 3–5, pale green.
Food: Mainly invertebrates.

Great egret

Ardea alba

Identification: Tall and snow-white, with plumes over the back and on the chest of breeding birds. Skin in front of eyes blue, bill yellowish with bluish hue on top. Legs and feet are black. Sexes are alike. Birds lack both plumes and blue coloration in winter.

By the early 1900s, the great white egret had become a very rare species in the USA. These birds were heavily hunted for their plumes, which were used to decorate women's hats. Numbers have now recovered and their range has expanded up the Atlantic coast. These birds move south to the Caribbean for winter, while further west, populations are found from California down through Central America. Great white egrets are adaptable, and are found on farmland and even in pasture some distance from water. Here they feed on rodents and other small mammals, insects, and reptiles such as snakes. Breeding occurs in colonies sometimes consisting of several hundred pairs. Nests may be sited either on the ground or high in trees, usually over water, which offers protection from predators.

Distribution: Breeds south of the Great Lakes in the eastern USA, and along the Atlantic coast. Winters in southwest USA, through much of Central America and the Caribbean down across most of South America, as far as central Argentina.
Size: 99cm (39in).
Habitat: Marshland, flooded areas.
Nest: Stick-type nest.
Eggs: 3–5, pale blue.
Food: Fish and small invertebrates.

Green ibis (*Mesembrinibis cayennensis*): 58cm (23in)
Eastern Costa Rica and Panama across much of South America east of the Andes. Very dark overall with greenish suffusion on wings and loose greenish plumage at back of head. Young lack the gloss on their plumage. Sexes are alike.

Bare-faced ibis (*Phimosus infuscatus*): 54cm (21in)
Two separate populations: one across northern South America from eastern Ecuador eastward; the other south of the Amazon in Brazil, Bolivia, Paraguay, Argentina, and Uruguay. Blackish overall, with a bare area of reddish skin on face. Bill is yellowish, legs reddish. Sexes are alike.

Buff-necked ibis (*Theristicus caudatus*): 76cm (30in)
Colombia, Venezuela, and French Guiana south to northern Argentina and Uruguay. Buff neck, darker on the crown. Mainly grey wings, with a characteristic white area. Buff on the chest, with black underparts. Sexes are alike.

Agami heron (chestnut-bellied heron, *Agamia agami*): 71cm (28in)
Southeastern Mexico to Ecuador and Amazon region in Brazil. Very colourful: dark mauve head with white stripe down throat. Lower neck and back silvery-blue, with plumes of this colour on crown. Metallic green wings, rufous underparts. Long, narrow, straight bill. Sexes are alike. Young birds browner, with a white stripe.

Limpkin

Aramus guarauna

This large bird, about the size of a goose, can be recognized by its long, pointed bill. It is not easily observed, being shy by nature and mostly active at night, when its wailing call echoes across the marshes. This disconcerting noise, which can sound like a person crying out, has led to the limpkin being called the crying bird. The impression of distress is reinforced by the fact that the birds have a limping gait which suggests they are in pain. Limpkins use their pointed bill to feed on aquatic apple snails, and are able to pull the molluscs from their shells without crushing them. They also prey on other invertebrates and amphibians. Pairs usually nest in secluded sites on the ground, but occasionally choose a low bush and use sticks to make a nest platform.

Identification: Tall, brownish with prominent white streaking on the head and neck, extending down over the upper wings. Strong, powerful, darkish horn-coloured bill, with a blackish tip. Greyish-green legs and feet, with long toes. Sexes are alike. Young birds paler overall in coloration.

Distribution: Northern breeding range is centred on Florida, occasionally seen in neighbouring parts of southern USA. Also parts of Central America and South America east of the Andes.
Size: 66cm (26in).
Habitat: Wetlands, swamps.
Nest: Pile of vegetation.
Eggs: 5–8, buff with dark markings.
Food: Aquatic invertebrates and amphibians.

BITTERNS AND OTHER WATERBIRDS

Although some waterbirds, such as bitterns, feed in a similar fashion to waders, their larger size allows them to wander into deeper water, giving greater opportunities to feed and enabling them to take larger prey such as fish. Certain waterbirds, such as the anhinga, will actually disappear under the water in search of food, rather than hunting from above.

American bittern

Botaurus lentiginosus

These shy birds adopt a characteristic frozen pose when alarmed, with their head pointing vertically upward, in the hope of avoiding detection. This disguise is very effective in the reed beds that they frequent, especially as they move their head slightly to resemble a reed waving in the wind. Their presence is clearly audible during the nesting period, however, thanks to their booming calls, which can be heard over 0.8km (¹/₂ mile) away. American bitterns are solitary hunters, becoming active at dusk. These waders rely simply on standing quietly and seizing unsuspecting prey that comes within reach, though with their long neck and slim shape they can also chase prey through the water. Apart from fish, American bitterns will feed on a host of other creatures, including amphibians and reptiles, as well as invertebrates such as water snails and crayfish.

Identification: White streak extending above the eye. Throat is also white, with dark edging apparent, and striped throat markings too. The back and wings are mottled, and the flight feathers are dark. Underparts slightly paler around the vent. Bill is yellowish, as are the legs and feet. Sexes are alike. Young birds lack the black markings on the throat.

Distribution: Breeds central Canada eastward along the southern shore of Hudson Bay to the Atlantic seaboard. Overwinters south of the breeding range and along the Pacific coast, notably throughout Central America and the Caribbean.
Size: 71cm (28in).
Habitat: Marshland and shallow water.
Nest: Platform made of marsh plants.
Eggs: 2–6, buff.
Food: Mainly fish.

Sunbittern

Eurypyga helias

The sunbittern has no close relatives and resembles a rail in some respects. It has a relatively long tail, and there is no webbing apparent between its toes. This bird has a fiery, brilliant coloration on the flight feathers and uses these to stunning effect during its mating display. Relatively little is known about the habits of these rather shy birds, which are most likely to be encountered on their own, or sometimes as pairs in damp areas of tropical forest. These bitterns use their bills to probe for food in wet areas, but rarely enter the water itself, and they do not fly far.

Identification: Black head with prominent white stripes above and below the eyes, and another white area on the throat. Neck and upperparts are brownish, broken with variable markings ranging from chestnut through grey to black. Orange areas on the wings are most apparent in flight. Dark markings also on the brownish breast, which becomes paler, almost whitish, on the underparts. Bill is straight and yellowish on the lower part. Legs are orangish yellow. Sexes are alike.

Distribution: From southern Mexico south to western Ecuador and east to northern parts of Brazil. Occasionally seen in Chile.
Size: 48cm (19in).
Habitat: Near streams in wooded areas.
Nest: Globular in shape, made of vegetation and mud.
Eggs: 2, buff with dark spots at the larger end.
Food: Invertebrates.

Pinnated bittern (*Botaurus pinnatus*): 76cm (30in)
Eastern Mexico south across northern South America to Ecuador and the north of Argentina. Pale brown and black striations across neck, with further black markings over the back. Buff area behind the eyes, with a narrow white stripe here and white plumage under the throat. Brown and white underparts. Hens smaller, with brown rather than black tail feathers. Young birds reddish.

Least bittern (*Ixobrychus exilis*): 36cm (14in)
Breeds from southern Canada near the Great Lakes, southward across eastern USA. Also Pacific coast down to Baja California, Caribbean and through Central America to northern and eastern parts of South America. Cock bird has a black stripe over head, less prominent in hen. Sides of face and neck yellowish brown, back blackish with a white stripe on each side. White stripes on underparts too. Large buff areas on wings.

Stripe-backed bittern (*Ixobrychus involucris*): 33cm (13in)
Occurs in four separate areas of South America. Distinctive dark stripes on the head and down the wings and back. Sides of the head greyish, with a whitish throat. Rest of body light brown, with whitish stripes on underparts. Bill, legs, and feet yellowish. Sexes are alike.

Anhinga

Snakebird *Anhinga anhinga*

The shape of the anhinga's body in the water has led to these darters being known as snakebirds. They swim with their body submerged, the long, narrow neck above the water giving the impression of a snake. Since their feathering is not waterproof, anhingas favour stretches of water with trees close by so they can roost and dry their plumage. They are most often seen perching with wings held out to dry, or flying high in circles over a favoured tree. Anhingas feed mainly on fish, the rough edges on the sides of the bill making it easier to grasp their quarry. They catch fish by stabbing them and tossing them into the air, then catching and swallowing them head-first. Amphibians and reptiles, even baby alligators, may also be taken.

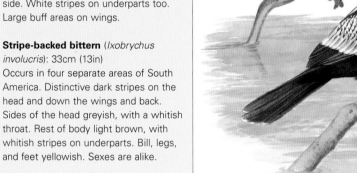

Distribution: Breeds from North Carolina to Florida and west to Texas, up along the Mississippi to southern Missouri and Kentucky. Range contracts southward in winter, from South Carolina along the Gulf coast. Also Central America south to northern Argentina and the Caribbean.
Size: 89cm (35in).
Habitat: Ponds and swamps.
Nest: Sticks, with leaf lining.
Eggs: 3–5, chalky blue.
Food: Mainly fish.

Identification: Cock bird has predominantly black plumage with a green iridescence. White and silvery-white spotted markings are evident on the wings. During the breeding period the bare facial skin becomes brighter in colour, and long, fine plumes can be seen on the back of the neck. Hens have brownish heads.

Roseate spoonbill

Platalea ajaja

The distinctively enlarged and flattened tips on the spoonbill's beak are very sensitive. They act like a pair of hands, allowing these birds both to detect and grab crabs and similar creatures underwater without difficulty. Roseate spoonbills sometimes immerse their entire head when feeding, although they are more likely to be observed sweeping the head from side to side, rather like the American flamingo and other tall waders. These birds are often seen in small flocks on marshes and similar wetlands near the coast. They nest off the ground, building loose piles of sticks.

Identification: Predominantly pink in colour, variable in hue, with a more prominent scarlet patch on the shoulders. Has the characteristic spoon-shaped bill and bare greenish skin on the face. Sexes are alike. Young birds are much paler, with whiter areas on head, neck, and breast.

Distribution: From southern USA into northern and eastern parts of South America as far south as Argentina. Also occurs in the Caribbean.
Size: 81cm (32in).
Habitat: Wetland areas, typically coastal areas including mangrove swamps.
Nest: Made of sticks.
Eggs: 3, white, brown spots.
Food: Small fish, amphibians and other aquatic creatures.

HERONS

Colourful in some cases and highly adapted to their environments, herons are well equipped for their predatory lifestyle, with powerful, sharp bills and long necks enabling them to lunge at prey which would otherwise be out of reach. In spite of their size, however, herons are not always easy to observe, being shy by nature and blending in well with their surroundings.

Boat-billed heron

Cochlearius cochlearius

Unique among herons, the characteristic broad bill of this species is thought to have evolved to enable it to scoop up food whether in water or on land. Boat-billed herons rarely feed during the day, seeking their prey as dusk falls. They do not actively pursue their quarry, relying instead on stealth, and will sometimes catch small mammals as well as aquatic creatures. Their breeding season varies through their wide range, influenced by the rains that make it easier to obtain food for the nestlings. Pairs nest on their own or in small groups, occasionally associating with other herons. They may return to the same nest each year, adding new material to it, or even adopt an abandoned nest of another bird. Boat-billed herons prefer wooded areas of habitat close to water, and can be seen in mangroves as well as freshwater areas.

Identification: Black area runs across the top of the head and down the centre of the back. Wings are greyish, with rufous underparts. Sides of the face and breast vary in colour depending on race, from white through to reddish grey, with a similar area of colour just above the bill. Hens have smaller crest plumes. Young birds are duller, with rufous back and wings.

Distribution: Extends south from both the Caribbean and Pacific coasts of Mexico, through parts of Central America and via Panama to South America. Here the species ranges east to French Guiana and over a broad area in the centre, as far south as north-east Argentina.
Size: 50cm (20in).
Habitat: Lakes and marshes.
Nest: Platform of sticks.
Eggs: 2–4, pale blue.
Food: Invertebrates and small vertebrates.

Whistling heron

Syrigma sibilatrix

Distribution: Two distinct populations in South America: one in eastern Colombia and Venezuela; the other further south, extending from Bolivia as far as south-east Brazil and north-east Argentina.
Size: 61cm (24in).
Habitat: Mainly wet grassland.
Nest: Platform of sticks.
Eggs: 3–4, pale blue with speckles.
Food: Invertebrates, also amphibians and reptiles.

Unlike most members of the heron family, the Ardeidae, the whistling heron is often encountered in areas of wet grassland rather than standing in water, although it may be observed in flooded fields and similar locations. The slender but stout bill enables it to capture both invertebrate and vertebrate prey, the latter including frogs and reptiles. In suitable areas where food can be found in abundance, these herons may congregate in groups of more than 100 birds, although they are more likely to be observed individually or in pairs. Their name is derived from their whistling calls, which have been likened to the sound of a flute.

Identification: Rigid black plumes at the rear of the head. The face is mainly black, with a white area under the chin and a large area of blue skin encircling the eyes. The neck and breast are a buff colour, becoming paler on the underparts. The back is greyish with black edging to the brownish feathers on each wing. The legs are fairly dark. The reddish bill becomes dark at the tip. Sexes are alike. Young birds have streaking on the neck.

Bare-throated tiger heron

Tigrisoma mexicanum

Distribution: Range extends from coastal and western parts of Mexico down through Central America and as far south as north-western Colombia in South America.
Size: 81cm (32in).
Habitat: Both streams and rivers.
Nest: Platform of sticks.
Eggs: 1–3, pale blue.
Food: Mainly fish.

Tiger herons are so-called because of their evident striped patterning, and this is the only species characterized by a lack of throat plumage. It is found further north than its two relatives, and also has a more limited area of distribution. Bare-throated tiger herons are often found not just in marshland and wooded swamps but also in coastal areas, where they hunt in mangroves. They are generally solitary when seeking food, and prefer to feed at dusk, often being content simply for unsuspecting prey to wander within reach of their sharp bills. In addition to fish, these herons also take amphibians and larger invertebrates, including crustaceans. The breeding period varies through their range, being delayed further north. The nest is usually constructed in a tree overhanging water, which affords the birds greater security from predators at this vulnerable time. The site may be up to 15m (48ft) off the ground.

Identification: Black area extending over the top of the head, grey sides to the neck, with horizontal black striations running around the neck down to the sides of the body. Wings marked with black and brown lines. White area on the chest extends to the flanks, underparts are pale rufous. Bare area around eyes, and also lower bill, yellowish-green. Bare skin on the throat yellowish, especially in breeding birds. Legs and feet greyish. Sexes alike. Young birds have brownish barring and spotting, with darker wings than adults.

Zigzag heron (*Zebrilus undulatus*): 33cm (13in)
Precise distribution is unclear, but range probably extends from parts of eastern Colombia and Venezuela across to French Guiana and northern Brazil; also eastern Peru and north-east Bolivia. Dark, heavily mottled body in various shades of brown, with darker barring over the back and wings. Sexes are alike. Young birds have a more rufous coloration overall.

Black-crowned night heron (*Nycticorax nycticorax*): 65cm (26in)
Global range, including from southern Canada southward as far as northern Chile and Argentina in South America. Also present in the Caribbean. Breeds in central parts of North America, moving southward and to the coast during the winter. Predominantly black top to the head, with a thin white streak above the bill extending above the eyes. White areas on sides of the face, with the underparts greyish. The wings are black, with a white area on the back.

Rufescent tiger heron (*Tigrisoma lineatum*): 76cm (30in)
South-east Mexico through Central America down to Ecuador and over much of northern South America, from Amazonia to the Brazilian coast and southward as far as north-east Argentina. Head and neck rufous, with grey back and wings. Black-edged white stripe extending down both sides of the chest from the base of the bill to the flanks. Underparts also reddish brown. Sexes are alike. Young birds are a paler cinnamon-buff, with black barring on their bodies disappearing lastly from the neck region.

Little blue heron

Egretta caerulea

These herons are a common sight through much of their range. They prefer to feed on invertebrates rather than fish, hunting crayfish in the water, and crickets on drier ground. These birds sometimes follow behind ploughs to hunt worms brought to the surface. Breeding starts in April in the north, earlier in Florida and the Caribbean. Pairs often breed in mixed groups with larger herons. Young birds are occasionally seen well beyond their normal range, even as far as Greenland and Paraguay.

Distribution: Southern parts of the USA; breeds in various locations from southern California east to New England. Moves south in winter from New Jersey down to Florida, along the Gulf coast, and down through Central America to southern Peru and southern Brazil.
Size: 61cm (24in).
Habitat: Ponds, lakes, marshes.
Nest: Platform of sticks.
Eggs: 3–5, pale blue-green.
Food: Invertebrates.

Identification: Slate-blue, with dark purple feathers on head and neck. In breeding birds, these areas are reddish purple, with plumes on the chest and a head crest. Legs and feet change from dull green to black. Sexes alike. Young birds white, with black tips to flight feathers.

CRAKES

The rail family, Rallidae, to which crakes belong, includes coots and gallinules as well as rails. These birds may be observed in the open, but if frightened will usually dart back into cover along the edges of the water. They can all be recognized by their relatively narrow body shape, which enables them to slip easily and quietly through reeds and similar vegetation.

Moorhen

Common moorhen *Gallinula chloropus*

Identification: Slate-grey head, back and underparts. Greyish-black wings. A prominent white line runs down the sides of the body. The area under the tail is white and has a black central stripe. Greenish-yellow legs have a small red area at the top. The bill is red apart from a yellow tip. Sexes are alike.

Although usually found in areas of fresh water, moorhens are occasionally seen in brackish areas, with infrequent sightings in eastern parts of the USA, such as Connecticut. Their long toes enable them to walk over aquatic vegetation, and they also feed when swimming or browsing on land. Their diet varies according to the season, although seeds of various types make up the bulk of their food. Moorhens are less wary than most rails or crakes, swimming in open water. If danger threatens, they will either dive or swim underwater. They are adept divers, staying submerged by grasping onto underwater vegetation with their bills. In public parks, moorhens can become quite tame, darting in to obtain food provided for ducks. During the breeding season, pairs of moorhens set up and defend territories and perform complex courtship rituals.

Distribution: South from the Great Lakes to much of the eastern USA. Also Florida, the Gulf Coast and California, right through Central America. Common in much of South America except the north-east and far south.
Size: 30cm (12in).
Habitat: Ponds and other areas of water edged by dense vegetation.
Nest: Domed structure hidden in reeds.
Eggs: 4–7, buff to light green with dark markings.
Food: Omnivorous.

Grey-necked wood rail

Cayenne wood rail *Aramides cajaneus*

These rails may expand their range during the wet season, moving into areas of tropical forest that have become flooded. Like many rails, they are shy, unobtrusive birds, preferring to escape danger by slipping away through undergrowth rather than by flying and revealing their presence. They are highly adaptable feeders, using their powerful bills to kill snakes and snails and to smash open palm nuts to feed on the edible kernel. They are even known to dig in cattle dung, to feed on insects there. Grey-necked wood rails form lifelong pairs. Their nest, constructed using a range of materials, is well-hidden, usually situated off the ground but remaining close to water. The chicks hatch after about three weeks, and leave the nest a day or two later. They grow rapidly, becoming indistinguishable from adults by the age of seven weeks old.

Identification: Appearance varies throughout its wide range. Characterized by the grey coloration of the neck, sometimes with a red cap on the crown. Wings are pale brown, with orange-chestnut underparts, and the rear of the body is dark blackish brown. Legs and feet are red. Bill is yellow, being greener at the tip.

Distribution: Occurs over much of South America, extending south from southern Mexico via the Yucatan Peninsula to eastern Ecuador and Peru, and across Brazil to northern parts of Argentina and Uruguay.
Size: 42cm (17in).
Habitat: Forested areas with water.
Nest: Bowl of vegetation.
Eggs: 3–7, creamy buff with brownish markings.
Food: Invertebrates, frogs, fruits, seeds and nuts.

Giant wood rail (*Aramides ypecaha*):
45cm (18in)
Eastern and south-eastern Brazil, Bolivia, Paraguay, north-eastern Argentina and Uruguay. Bluish-grey sides to the face extend over the breast, with a white area under the bill. Back of the head and neck chestnut, as are most of the underparts. Mantle, back and wings are greenish brown. Rump and the corresponding undertail coverts are black. Area at the top of the legs is grey. Stout, pointed bill is yellowish green, with legs and feet red, as is the iris. Hens similar, but smaller. Young birds duller overall, with brownish-black plumage.

Brown wood rail (*Aramides wolfi*): 36cm (14in)
North-west Colombia south to western parts of Ecuador, and probably the far north-west of Peru. Ash-grey head and nape, with white throat. Upper back and underparts are rufous-chestnut, with the rest of the back and wings olive brown. Rump and tail are black. A small yellowish patch is apparent on the centre of the forehead, above the greenish-yellow bill. The legs are reddish. Sexes are alike.

Blackish rail (*Pardirallus nigricans*): 32cm (13in)
Widely separated distribution across South America, with several areas of population in the north-west, from south-western Colombia down through Ecuador and Peru. Also in Bolivia, Paraguay, and over much of eastern Brazil, south to north-eastern Argentina. Dark in colour, with a bluish-slate head and underparts, except for a white area on the throat. Back and wings brownish, with the lower belly, undertail and uppertail coverts, and tail all black. Bill greenish yellow. Legs and feet red, as is the iris. Sexes are alike. Young birds have browner plumage.

American purple gallinule

Porphyrio martinica; previously Porphyrula martinica

These gallinules are very agile, athletic birds, able to walk across lily pads, climb trees, swim, and even dive underwater. They are also powerful in flight, with much of the North American population migrating across the Gulf of Mexico each year. Occasionally they are sighted far outside their usual range, in locations as far apart as Greenland and the Falkland Islands. Elsewhere, except at the far south of their range, these gallinules do not migrate. The breeding season begins in May in the USA, but not until December in Argentina. Pairs may also breed regularly through the year, as in Costa Rica. Both parents help to incubate and rear the young. Chicks start to seek out food for themselves at three weeks old, but cannot fly for a further two weeks or more after this.

Identification: Bluish shield on the top of the head. Head also has a purplish area, becoming bluer on the underparts and much greener on the back and wings. White undertail coverts. Prominent bill is reddish, with a yellow tip. Legs and feet are also yellow. Sexes are alike. Young birds are predominantly brownish, with greenish suffusion on the wings and lighter underparts.

Distribution: Breeds in the eastern USA, almost to the Great Lakes. Winters further south, along the Gulf coast and south through Central America as far as Argentina. Also in the Caribbean.
Size: 33cm (13in).
Habitat: Marshes and swamps.
Nest: Built on floating vegetation.
Eggs: 3–10, buff with red markings.
Food: Mainly plant matter.

Azure gallinule

Little gallinule *Porphyrio flavirostris*

The smallest member of its genus, the azure gallinule has a discontinuous distribution through South America. It tends to favour areas of deep water where there is much vegetation growing over the surface. In spite of its long legs, it can swim if necessary, as well as sometimes flying up and perching to escape danger. Azure gallinules also use their long legs to climb up and trample down seeding grasses, which allows them to extract the seeds. They are more likely to be seen in forested areas rather than savanna, and are known to undertake seasonal movements.

Identification: Azure plumage on the wings. The sides of the head down to the breast are a bluish grey, and the rest of the underparts are white. A band of brown extends from the centre of the head down over the back and part of the wings. The bill and shield are a greenish yellow colour. Sexes are alike.

Distribution: From Colombia eastward to French Guiana and south through Peru to Bolivia, southern Brazil and into northern Argentina.
Size: 25cm (10in).
Habitat: Marshland with good cover.
Nest: Open cup of vegetation.
Eggs: 4–5, creamy with reddish-brown spots.
Food: Grass seeds and invertebrates.

OTHER RAILS AND RELATED SPECIES

Although shy by nature, members of this group are sometimes sighted in cultivated areas. Their large toes help to prevent them from sinking into marshy ground, and leave an unmistakable impression in mud at the water's edge. Some species of rail display a distinctive flattened, unfeathered area, known as the frontal shield, above the bill.

Giant coot

Fulica gigantea

Occurring in the puna zone of the Andes at altitudes as high as 6,500m (21,320ft), these coots are reputedly not able to fly when adult, although young birds will fly quite readily, often moving down to lakes at lower altitudes for a time. They then return to their traditional haunts for breeding, and have specific nesting requirements. Giant coots construct huge platforms of water weed, often 3m (10ft) or more in length, in the shallows for nesting. The hen lays her eggs in a relatively small, raised cup area, and the same nest site is used and maintained over a number of years. The rim of the nest helps to conceal the chicks once they hatch and also protects them from cold winds.

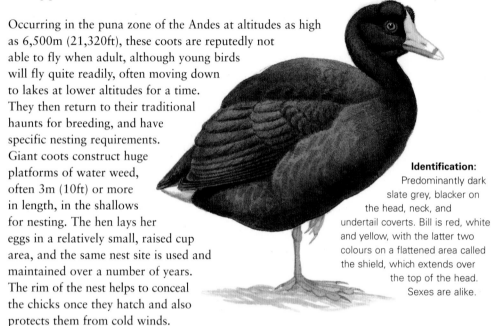

Identification: Predominantly dark slate grey, blacker on the head, neck, and undertail coverts. Bill is red, white and yellow, with the latter two colours on a flattened area called the shield, which extends over the top of the head. Sexes are alike.

Distribution: Central Peru to Bolivia, Chile and north-west Argentina.
Size: 59cm (23in).
Habitat: Shallow lakes and smaller areas of water.
Nest: Large platform built on dense patches of water weed.
Eggs: 3–7, creamy grey with reddish-brown spots.
Food: Aquatic vegetation.

American coot

Fulica americana

Although there are no striking plumage differences between cock and hen, they can be distinguished by a marked difference in their calls. Unlike some related species, American coots have proved to be highly adaptable, to the extent that their numbers appear to have increased overall in recent years. They rapidly colonize new areas of suitable habitat, although populations can be adversely affected by cold springtime weather, which makes food hard to find. American coots often migrate south in large numbers to avoid the worst of the winter.

Identification: Predominantly slate grey, more blackish on the head. White undertail coverts. Bill is whitish, with red near the tip, enlarging into a broad shield with red at the top. Sexes are alike, although hens are often significantly smaller. Young birds are predominantly brown, with duller bills.

Distribution: From Alaska southward across much of North America through Central America and the Caribbean into parts of Colombia in South America.
Size: 43cm (17in).
Habitat: Permanent areas of wetland.
Nest: Floating heap of dead aquatic vegetation.
Eggs: 3–12, buff with dense, fine blackish spotting.
Food: Diet consists of aquatic vegetation.

King rail

Rallus elegans

Distribution: From southern Canada through eastern USA to parts of Mexico. Also present on Cuba and the neighbouring Isle of Youth.
Size: 48cm (19in).
Habitat: Freshwater and brackish marshes.
Nest: Cup-shaped.
Eggs: 10–12, creamy buff with purplish-brown spots.
Food: Both plant and animal matter.

Like many of the rails occurring in North America, king rails move south in winter to areas where the temperature is unlikely to drop significantly below freezing, as this would turn their feeding grounds to ice. Aquatic invertebrates feature prominently in their diet, but they are actually omnivorous, eating grass seeds and even fruit, such as blackberries, on occasion. They also prey on frogs and small water snakes. Sadly, in some parts of their range the numbers of king rail have fallen dramatically because of use of pesticides on agricultural land. Many are killed each year by passing traffic. They can also fall victim to a wide range of predators that may include alligators, raccoons and great horned owls.

Identification: Rusty brown, with darker scalloped patterning over the back and wings. Grey on the ear coverts behind the eyes. Cinnamon underparts with vertical black and white barring on the flanks. Long bill, brown at the tip and orangish further back. Sexes are similar but hens are smaller in size.

Yellow rail (*Coturnicops noveboracensis*): 17cm (7in)
Marshland in central and south-eastern parts of Canada to north-eastern USA, wintering further south in Louisiana and Texas. Brown on top of the head, with a buff stripe above the eyes, and a brown stripe running across the eye. Sexes are alike, but males may be slightly larger.

Dot-winged crake (*Porzana spiloptera*): 15cm (6in)
Occurs in northern Argentina and southern Uruguay. Blackish head and chest, with white edging to the plumage on the lower underparts. Back brown with black streaks and some white. Red iris. Dark bill and legs. Sexes are alike. Young birds have whitish faces.

Sora (Carolina rail, *Porzana carolina*): 25cm (10in)
Freshwater marshland from south-eastern Alaska across much of the USA, also in brackish marshes when migrating. Black area at base of bill extends to forehead, white spot behind eyes, with greyish sides to face, and barring on flanks. Upperparts show dark streaks. Sexes are alike.

Galapagos crake (*Laterallus spilonota*): 15cm (6in)
Endemic to the Galapagos Islands. Dark, mainly chocolate-brown coloration, with a blackish head. Dark grey neck and breast, belly dark chocolate with white spots. White barring on undertail coverts. White spotting on wings and back when breeding. Bill blackish, legs and feet dark. Iris is orange. Hens may have paler throat coloration. Young have no white spots on their underparts.

Ruddy crake

Laterallus ruber

Much still remains to be discovered about the ruddy crake. It may only be present in Costa Rica for part of the year. It is shy by nature, blending in with the vegetation, but may be recognized by its calls, which are uttered with increasing frequency in the breeding season. The most obvious of these is a loud trilling call, which falls off in frequency. These crakes hide for much of the time, but will emerge into the open by day in search of food. If frightened, they run to cover or fly off with their long legs hanging down. They probably feed mainly on invertebrates, with some seeds. Ruddy crakes appear to nest in reed beds, constructing a woven nest lined with thin stems of grass, and

a narrow entrance at one side.

Distribution: Occurs in eastern Mexico, also down the west coast and possibly right across the southern part of Mexico too, ranging to parts of Honduras and Nicaragua in Central America, as far south as Costa Rica.
Size: 15cm (6in).
Habitat: Marshland and ditches.
Nest: Ball of grass and other plants.
Eggs: 3–6, cream with dark reddish markings.
Food: Unknown.

Identification: Cock has blackish area over top of the head, with bluish ear coverts. Throat whitish, underparts reddish. Back and wings brownish, darker on the flight feathers. Hen similar, but darker area to uppertail coverts is reddish. Legs and feet pinkish, iris orange, bill black. Young resemble adults but pale on belly.

WATERFOWL

This group of birds has diversified to occupy a wide range of habitats, and has adopted a correspondingly broad range of lifestyles, ranging from grazing in wetland areas through to hunting for fish. Breeding habits vary significantly too, with some members of the group choosing to breed on the ground, while others prefer the relative safety afforded by tree hollows.

Carolina wood duck

American wood duck *Aix sponsa*

Distribution: Occurs widely over much of North America and south to Mexico, being present in western, central and south-eastern parts of the continent, as well as on western Cuba.
Size: 51cm (20in).
Habitat: Wooded stretches of fresh water.
Nest: In tree holes.
Eggs: 5–9, buff.
Food: Mainly vegetable matter, from acorns to aquatic plants.

Although these ducks have been seen as far north as Alaska, they move south to warmer climates for the winter months. In some areas their numbers have benefited from the provision of artificial nesting boxes, so that today they rank among the most common waterfowl in the United States. Carolina wood ducks are likely to be seen dabbling for food in open stretches of water, dipping their heads under the surface, but they also come ashore to nibble at vegetation. Although vagrants sometimes appear in the Caribbean, Carolina wood ducks observed in other parts of the world will be descendants of escapees from waterfowl collections.

Identification: Crest with glossy green and purple tones in breeding plumage. The lower neck and breast are chestnut with white speckling, while the abdomen is buff with barring on the flanks. Cock in eclipse plumage resembles the hen, but with a more brightly coloured bill. The hen is duller in overall coloration, with dark brown underparts.

Muscovy duck

Cairina moschata

These dull-coloured waterfowl are far removed in appearance from their more brightly coloured domesticated counterparts. They prefer freshwater areas but sometimes move into saltwater lagoons during the dry season. Muscovies live in groups and are arboreal by nature, with powerful claws that help them to climb trees and roost easily on branches. They generally prefer to nest off the ground, but in areas where they are not commonly hunted, hens may lay eggs on the ground in spots that are well camouflaged by surrounding vegetation. The young develop the white wing patches at one year of age.

Identification: Mainly black but with white patches on the wings and glossy greenish suffusion on the surrounding plumage. Has a prominent, dull reddish-purple bill knob. Hens are smaller and lack the knob on the bill. Young birds can be distinguished by their lack of white plumage.

Distribution: From Mexico south to parts of Argentina and Uruguay.
Size: 84cm (33in).
Habitat: Forested lakes and marshes.
Nest: Usually in a tree hollow.
Eggs: 8–15, white with greenish suffusion.
Food: Omnivorous.

Hooded merganser

Lophodytes cucullatus

These ducks occur only in small groups of often less than a dozen individuals. They can be difficult to observe, either when resting by the water or even when swimming and darting under the surface in search of food. In the far north, hooded mergansers fly south when their freshwater habitat starts to freeze at the onset of winter, often moving to coastal estuaries. They breed off the ground and sometimes nest as high as 25m (80ft) up in suitable trees. These waterfowl can fly well, displaying great manoeuvrability at low levels.

Identification: Drakes have a white fan, edged with black, at the rear of the head. The face is black. The chest is white with black-and-white striping behind. The flanks are chestnut and the back is black. Ducks are mainly brown with a bushy crest. Cocks in eclipse plumage resemble hens but have yellowish rather than brown irises, and darker bills.

Distribution: Two distinct populations, one ranging south from Alaska on the western side of North America. The other extends widely over the east of the continent.
Size: 50cm (20in).
Habitat: Lakes and slow-flowing areas of water near woodland.
Nest: In tree hollows.
Eggs: 6–12, white.
Food: Mainly fish.

Northern pintail (*Anas acuta*): 62cm (24in)
Throughout North America and the Caribbean. Moves south in winter, when rarely seen north of the Great Lakes. Long, narrow black tail. Head blackish, with white stripes on breast. Grey flanks. Wings greyish with prominent stripes. Hens brown, with darker patterning and a long, pointed tail with white edge to wings in flight.

Ruddy duck (*Oxyura jamaicensis*): 43cm (17in)
Much of North America and down the west side of South America. Broad bill and upright tail feathers. Chestnut-brown coloration (brown in eclipse), with black and usually white on head. Some regional variations. Hens mainly brown.

White-winged scoter (*Melanitta deglandi*): 60cm (24in)
Breeds in Alaska and west and central Canada. Overwinters along west coast of North America as far south as California and on the Atlantic coast from Newfoundland to the Carolinas, and even Florida and Texas. Drakes blackish, with white secondaries and a white area behind the eyes. Ducks brown with white patches on sides of head. Young similar to hens but paler brown.

Black scoter (*Melanitta americana*): 53cm (21in)
Breeds in western Alaska, and also Labrador and Newfoundland. Overwinters on the Pacific from Alaska to California, and from Newfoundland down to the Carolinas in the east, sometimes south to the Gulf coast; also on the Great Lakes. Drake blackish with mainly yellow bill. Ducks dark brown with paler sides to head and neck. Young similar but with white bellies.

Common merganser

Goosander *Mergus merganser*

Like many waterfowl found in the far north, the common merganser occurs at similar latitudes in Europe and Asia. Diving rather than dabbling ducks, they are called sawbills because of the small sharp projections running down the sides of their bills, which help them to grab fish more easily. Seen in wooded areas close to water, pairs will nest in a hollow tree or even a nest box, lining it with down to insulate the eggs and prevent them rolling around. Outside the breeding period, common mergansers form large flocks numbering thousands of birds on lakes and similar stretches of fresh water. They may, however, prefer to fish in nearby rivers, returning to the lake at dusk. Common mergansers tend to remain in their nesting location until the water starts to freeze over, whereupon they head south. They pair up mainly over winter, returning north to breed the following spring.

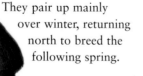

Distribution: Ranges right across North America, from Alaska to Newfoundland, moving southward to overwinter in southern parts of the USA and Mexico.
Size: 64cm (25in).
Habitat: Lakes and rivers.
Nest: Uses a tree hole.
Eggs: 6–17, ivory or pale buff.
Food: Predominantly fish.

Identification: Narrow body shape. Drake has dark green head and neck, with green on the primary flight feathers evident in flight. Underparts white, back is greyish. Ducks have chestnut-brown head and white area under throat. Bill and legs red. Drakes in eclipse plumage have white areas at front of wings.

DUCKS

Waterfowl are generally conspicuous birds on water, but their appearance and distribution can differ markedly through the year. Drakes often resemble hens outside the breeding season, when their plumage becomes much plainer. Some species are migratory, heading to warmer climates to escape freezing conditions, although others may fly to coastal areas, seeking out estuaries and sheltered bays.

American wigeon

Anas americana

These wigeon are sometimes seen well outside their normal range, with reports of sightings in locations as far apart as Hawaii, the Komandorskie islands off Siberia, and Europe. Almost every year a few vagrant American wigeon are recorded by birdwatchers in the British Isles. The ability of these ducks to cross the Atlantic Ocean is all the more surprising because they are essentially vegetarian in their feeding habits, browsing on plants in and out of the water. A number of American wigeon also migrate south each year to South America, and are observed here in larger numbers outside the breeding season.

Identification: In breeding condition, a prominent white stripe extends back over the top of the head, with a broad dark green area incorporating the eyes, and speckling beneath. The remainder of the plumage is brownish with a white belly and broader white area on the lower body close to the tail. Ducks have completely speckled heads and lack the drake's white forewing, which is retained in the eclipse plumage. The duck has paler chestnut coloration than the drake in eclipse plumage.

Distribution: Much of North America, including the far north. Often moves southward in winter.
Size: 56cm (22in).
Habitat: Freshwater marshland.
Nest: In a hollow often hidden in grass, lined with down feathers.
Eggs: 6–12, creamy white.
Food: Aquatic vegetation, small aquatic invertebrates.

Hawaiian duck

Koloa *Anas wyvilliana*

Considered a smaller relative of the mallard, Hawaiian ducks have declined over recent years. This is due to a combination of hunting pressures, drainage schemes and predation by introduced species such as cats and mongooses. However, it has proved possible to breed these waterfowl successfully in captivity, and this has provided the nucleus of stock for release schemes in areas where they formerly occurred. Already there are indications that they may be re-establishing themselves on Oahu. Hawaiian ducks are shy. Where they do occur in the company of mallards, the populations tend not to mix, although hybridization is a possibility, confirming their close relationship. Hawaiian ducks usually breed between March and June, choosing a well-hidden site for their nest. Although often feeding by dabbling in the water, these ducks may sometimes feed on land, especially in agricultural areas.

Identification: Some variation in appearance. Drakes have a dark greenish top to their heads, with a fine brown speckled area on the cheeks and neck. Chestnut markings with black scalloping on the chest, and brownish underparts. Darker over the back and wings. Drakes have an olive-green bill. Ducks similar, but of a lighter shade overall, with a dull orange or sometimes greyish bill.

Distribution: Restricted to the Hawaiian Islands, mainly on Kauai but reintroduced to both Oahu and Hawaii. Formerly also on Maui, Molokai and Niihau.
Size: 49cm (19in).
Habitat: Freshwater areas.
Nest: Scrape on the ground.
Eggs: 7–16, greyish green.
Food: Plant matter and invertebrates.

Rosy-billed pochard (*Netta peposaca*): 56cm (22in)
Southern South America, from Tierra del Fuego northwards, ranging to southern Brazil, Paraguay and central Chile. Also recorded on the Falkland islands. Drakes display glossy black plumage with a white undertail area and greyish flanks. Bill reddish, with a black tip and darkest at its base. Hens are mainly brown, darker over the back, with a whitish area on the face. Bill greyish in this case, with a black tip, yellowish legs and feet. Young birds like hens, but with less white on the underparts.

Black-headed duck (*Heteronetta atricapilla*): 40cm (15¾in)
Central South America, from Chile to Argentina, south to Buenos Aires. Drake has blackish head, brownish upperparts, and sometimes a white area on the throat. Lighter overall, with a slight rufous suffusion on the breast becoming greyer on the lower underparts. Bill grey, with a reddish area at the base. Ducks have paler heads and less rufous underparts, with no red spot on the bill. Legs and feet grey. Young have more rufous upperparts than ducks, being yellower below.

Gadwall (*Anas strepera*): 50cm (20in)
Ranges extensively through North America, up as far as southern Canada. Winters further south, down to Mexico, and also on Caribbean islands. Drake is finely speckled on the breast, browner on flanks, with a dark crown and black bill. A black area runs through the eyes, with a white area on the wings. In eclipse plumage, the flanks and wings are speckled and the bill is yellowish. Ducks are mottled with rufous edging on the feathers, especially on the wings.

Blue-winged teal

Anas discors

Blue-winged teal return to their northern breeding grounds in May, nesting on their own rather than in colonies and choosing sites concealed in vegetation. The eggs take nearly four weeks to hatch, with the young being unable to fly for a further five weeks or so. They feed by dabbling, up-ending themselves rather than diving for food. They feed on aquatic snails, crustaceans, and virtually any plant matter. Blue-winged teal are long-distance travellers. Their regular migratory routes take them over land to South America rather than across the Gulf of Mexico. Strong and fast in flight, they are sometimes found well outside their usual range, including on Hawaii and the Galapagos Islands. Blue-winged teal also regularly cross the Atlantic to reach the UK and sites as far south as north-west parts of Africa.

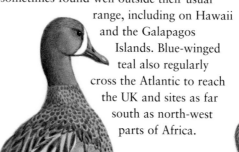

Distribution: Breeds in south Alaska, Newfoundland, and central USA. Winters along Pacific and Atlantic coasts. Also present in Caribbean and Central America, extending to northern part of South America, even as far as Chile.
Size: 41cm (16in).
Habitat: Marshes and shallow lakes.
Nest: Down-lined scrape.
Eggs: 6–15, greyish green to buff.
Food: Plants, invertebrates.

Identification: Blue upperwing coverts with a green speculum. Drake has a white area around base of bill, and a greyish head with darker crown. Underparts red-brown with black speckles. White areas on sides, black rump. Male in eclipse similar to female. Duck brownish, with whitish area at base of bill. Young have spotted underparts.

Shoveler

Northern shoveler *Anas clypeata*

The broad bills of these waterfowl enable them to feed more easily in shallow water. They typically swim with their bill open, trailing it through the water to catch invertebrates, although they also forage both by upending and by catching insects on reeds. Shovelers choose wet ground, often some distance from open water, as a nesting site, where the female retreats from the attention of other drakes. Like the young of other waterfowl, young shovelers take to the water soon after hatching.

Identification: Dark metallic-green head and orange eye. White chest and chestnut-brown flanks and belly, and a black area around the tail. Both back and wings are black and white. The remainder of the body is predominantly white. Broad blue wing stripe, which enables drakes to be recognized even in eclipse plumage, when they resemble hens. Very broad black bill. Hens are predominantly brownish, but with darker blotching. The bill has yellowish edges. A paler area of plumage can be seen on the sides of the tail feathers.

Distribution: Breeds in western North America, moving south to winter in warmer parts such as Texas and Central America. Smaller populations on east coast.
Size: 52cm (20in).
Habitat: Shallow coastal and freshwater areas.
Nest: Down-lined scrape.
Eggs: 8–12, green to buff white.
Food: Plants, invertebrates.

OTHER COMMON DUCKS

Ducks are a diverse group of waterfowl, but can be distinguished by their relatively small size compared with swans and geese. They inhabit stretches of open water, though typically become more secretive when nesting. Drakes usually moult into more colourful plumage before the onset of the breeding season. For the rest of the year they have duller "eclipse" plumage more closely resembling the hens.

Mallard

Anas platyrhynchos

Distribution: Occurs throughout much of North America, though is more scarce in the far north of Canada. Also in Mexico.
Size: 60cm (24in).
Habitat: Open areas of water.
Nest: Scrape lined with down feathers.
Eggs: 7–16, buff to greyish green.
Food: Plant matter and some invertebrates.

These ducks are a common sight, even on stretches of water in towns and cities, such as rivers and canals. They may congregate in quite large flocks, especially outside the breeding season, but they are most evident in the spring, when groups of unpaired males chase potential mates. The nest is often constructed close to water and is frequently hidden under vegetation, especially in urban areas. These birds feed both on water, up-ending themselves or dabbling at the surface, and on land.

Identification: Metallic-green head with a white ring around the neck. Chest is brownish with grey underparts, and blackish area surrounds the vent. Bluish speculum in the wing, most evident in flight, bordered by black and white stripes. Hen is brownish buff overall with darker patterning, and displays same wing markings as drake. Hen's bill is orange, whereas that of male in eclipse plumage is yellow, with a rufous tinge to the breast.

Redhead

Aythya americana

In April, redheads return to their northern breeding grounds in the prairie marshes, constructing a nest from dead vegetation concealed in among reedbeds. Although these waterfowl tend to nest singly, rather than in groups, it is not unusual for ducks to lay in the nests of other redheads. As a result, the number of eggs in a nest can vary significantly. Females may even deposit their eggs in the nests of other waterfowl. After breeding, large numbers of redheads often congregate over the winter period, when they can be seen in coastal districts as well as inland. They have even been recorded overwintering as far west as the Hawaiian islands in the Pacific Ocean. Redheads usually feed by diving, rather than dabbling at the surface, and although they feed mainly on plant matter they will also prey on crustaceans in coastal areas.

Identification: Drake has a chestnut-red head, with a black chest and smoky-grey back and sides. Black feathering also around the base of the tail. Bill is very pale blue with a dark tip. Ducks are brownish overall, darker on the crown, with a slaty bill and a narrow whitish area around the black tip. Out of colour, the drakes resemble the ducks.

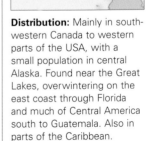

Distribution: Mainly in south-western Canada to western parts of the USA, with a small population in central Alaska. Found near the Great Lakes, overwintering on the east coast through Florida and much of Central America south to Guatemala. Also in parts of the Caribbean.
Size: 48cm (19in).
Habitat: Ponds, lakes, and marshes.
Nest: Made of vegetation.
Eggs: 6–9, greenish grey.
Food: Mainly plant matter.

Bufflehead

Bucephala albeola

The bufflehead's breeding grounds spread through the forested areas of northern North America, where they are likely to be seen close to water. These waterfowl will dive in search of invertebrate prey, feeding mainly on insects during the summer and switching to snails and crustaceans in winter. They also take plant matter. Breeding starts in April, with a pair often colonizing a hole made by a common flicker or other woodpecker. When not nesting, these ducks spend most of their time on the water. They are less social than many other diving ducks, rarely forming large aggregations even outside the nesting period. It appears that their range in the eastern part of North America, in the vicinity of the Great Lakes, is expanding, but these and other tree-nesting waterfowl are obviously adversely affected by deforestation.

Identification: When in colour, drakes have an unmistakable large, fluffy white area on the head, extending back behind the eyes. The front of the face and neck are glossy black. Back and wings are dark, contrasting with the white underparts. The duck's head is brownish grey, with a smaller patch of white plumage below the eyes. Wings are darker, and flanks appear greyish rather than white. Males out of colour indistinguishable from females.

Distribution: Ranges from Alaska eastward through Canada, reaching the Great Lakes and Hudson Bay. Overwinters further south, from the Aleutians down the southern coast of Alaska south to Mexico. Also ranging over much of southern USA as well as down the north-eastern seaboard to Florida.
Size: 34cm (13$\frac{1}{2}$in).
Habitat: Ponds and small lakes.
Nest: Hollow trees.
Eggs: 5–12, pale green.
Food: Invertebrates, some fish.

Common pochard (*Aythya ferina*): 49cm (19in) Primarily Eurasian, but also the Aleutian and Pribilof islands, and from southern Alaska down to southern California. Similar in appearance to the redhead (see left), with a chestnut-brown head and neck, black chest, a broad grey band encircling the wings and body, and black feathering on the hindquarters. Hens have a brownish head and chest, greyer over rest of the body. Bill has distinctive black band extending down over the nostrils, not seen in redheads.

Canvasback (*Aythya valisineria*): 53cm (21in) Drake has a rufous head and black chest, with a silvery area on the back and wings, and black plumage on the rear. In eclipse plumage, chest area becomes blackish brown, with silvery-brown coloration in place of the silver. Bill has a distinctive prominent silvery band across it. Ducks also display this feature, being recognizable by the pale stripe through the eye. Head and chest brownish overall. Young birds are a more even shade of brown.

Ring-necked duck (*Aythya collaris*): 46cm (18in) Drakes in breeding plumage have a blackish head, chest, back and wings, with silvery flanks and a distinctive white ring on the underside of the body at the base of the neck. Ducks are much browner, with a band of white plumage at the base of the bill and a similar eye-stripe. Their underparts are mainly brownish. Young birds are similar to hens, but with a less apparent white eye-stripe. They also lack the white bill stripe seen in adults, behind the black tip.

Torrent duck

Merganetta armata

Torrent ducks are associated with the Andes but may also be found at lower altitudes, even close to sea level in some areas. The appearance of these waterfowl varies throughout their extensive range, with six different races being recognized. However, some of these may be naturally occurring colour morphs. Torrent ducks favour fast-flowing rivers, where they probe for food around boulders. They will also dive in search of prey, including small fish. Their nests are generally well-concealed, often on cliff ledges or in rocky crevices.

Identification: Drake has a black stripe extending down the centre of the head and neck, with another stripe through the eye. Body colour varies with race, with chests being black or speckled. Hens have chestnut throats and underparts. The rest of the head is greyish, with a similar band around the bill. Young birds are greyish, with streaking on the back and barring on the flanks.

Distribution: Extends down the western side of South America, from Venezuela through most of the Andean region via Bolivia and Chile to Argentina.
Size: 46cm (18in).
Habitat: Fast-flowing rivers.
Nest: Dry plant matter.
Eggs: 3–4, pale green.
Food: Aquatic invertebrates.

SWANS AND GEESE

These large, unmistakable birds regularly fly long distances to and from their breeding grounds. They rank among the longest-lived of all waterfowl, with a potential life expectancy of more than two decades. Young birds are unlikely to breed until they are three or four years old. When observing them, remember that both geese and swans can be aggressive, especially when breeding.

Coscoroba swan

Coscoroba coscoroba

The status of this swan is a cause for debate among zoologists, with some suggesting that it represents a link between the true swans (of the genus *Cygnus*) and geese. Others regard this species as a relative of the whistling ducks. Coscoroba swans feed by dabbling in the shallows, although they will also seek food on land by grazing. Pairs tend to be solitary by nature. They build a typical swan-like nest consisting of a pile of vegetation, often concealed in a reed bed or on an island. The centre of the mound is lined with soft downy feathers, serving as a receptacle for the eggs. The nesting period varies throughout their range. Once the young birds hatch they will swim after their parents, but, unlike other swans, these waterfowl do not appear to carry their cygnets on their backs. Subsequently these South American swans may be seen in flocks, numbering as many as a hundred individuals.

Identification: Predominantly whitish overall, but with distinctive black tips to the primary feathers that are even apparent when the wings are closed. Bill, legs and feet pinkish. A brown rather than reddish iris distinguishes the hen. Young birds have brownish feathering on the head.

Distribution: Southern part of South America, extending north from Tierra del Fuego to central parts of Chile and northern Argentina. This species overwinters further north in Brazil.
Size: 115cm (45in).
Habitat: Lakes and lagoons.
Nest: Mound of vegetation.
Eggs: 4–7, pale green.
Food: Plant matter and invertebrates.

Tundra swan

Whistling swan *Cygnus columbianus*

Tundra swans arrive on their breeding grounds during May. They choose an elevated nest site, and are very territorial at this stage. The majority of pairs breed in western Alaska, and adopt set flight paths to and from their northern range. In the vicinity of Niagara Falls, the swans can easily be swept over the falls to their death if they misjudge the current in the river, since their weight renders them unable to take off directly from the water's surface without paddling along first to gain momentum. The swans leave the tundra in October, roughly splitting into two groups and flying south to their wintering grounds on either side of the USA. Here they may sometimes invade areas of farmland to feed on crops, especially winter cereals. Despite their alternative name of the whistling swan, these waterfowl honk, not whistle.

Identification: Large, white with blackish legs and a mainly black bill. Small yellow area below each eye. This feature is larger in the Eurasian form, Berwick's swan, seen occasionally on the west coast. Males often larger. Young have grey-pink bills.

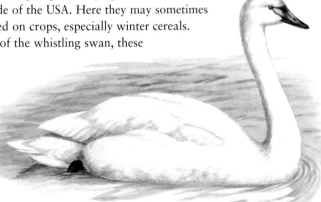

Distribution: Breeds across the extreme northern coast of North America, moving south to coastal locations in western and eastern parts of the USA for the winter.
Size: 132cm (52in).
Habitat: Tundra, ponds, and lakes.
Nest: Mound of vegetation.
Eggs: 2–6, pale green.
Food: Mainly vegetation.

Ross's goose (*Anser rossii*): 66cm (26in)
Breeds in the far north of central Canada, near the Perry River, wintering in south-west USA and along the Mexican border. Occurs in both snow (white) and blue phases, like its relative, the snow goose, retaining the white plumage on the head in its blue phase. Sexes are alike, but males are often larger.

Greater white-fronted goose (*Anser albifrons*): 85cm (33½in)
Circumpolar, including Alaska, north-west Canada and south-west Greenland, overwintering in western USA, including the Gulf of Mexico. White band at base of bill (lacking in young birds), with brown head. White edging to body plumage; white undertail area. Pinkish bill, legs and feet. Sexes are alike.

Trumpeter swan (*Cygnus buccinator*): 180cm (71in)
Breeding grounds are in Alaska and neighbouring Canada, wintering grounds extends south into the USA from British Columbia. Resident also in some areas of the north-western USA. White in colour overall, distinguishable by its black bill, with a narrow band of black extending up to each eye. Legs and feet dark grey. Pens smaller than cobs, with young birds having some greyish plumage.

Black-necked swan (*Cygnus melancoryphus*): 124cm (49in)
Southern South America, overwintering as far north as south-eastern Brazil. Also present on the Falkland Islands. Unmistakable appearance, with a black neck and head, apart from a narrow white line passing through the eyes. Remainder of the body white. Grey bill, yellowish at the tip and with red swellings at its base. Legs and feet pink. Hens smaller. Young birds lack the red area on the bill.

Canada goose

Branta canadensis

A number of different races of Canada goose are recognized, which all differ from one another a little in terms of plumage and size. This species has proved to be highly adaptable. Its numbers have grown considerably in Europe, especially in farming areas, where these geese descend in flocks to feed on crops during the winter once other food has become more scarce. When migrating, flocks fly in a clear V-shaped formation. In common with many waterfowl, Canada geese are not able to fly when moulting, but they take readily to the water at this time and can dive to escape danger if necessary. These handsome black-necked geese prefer to graze on land, returning to the relative safety of the water during the hours of darkness.

Identification: Distinctive black head and neck. A small area of white plumage runs in a broad stripe from behind the eyes to under the throat. A whitish area of feathering at the base of the neck merges into brown on the chest. The wings are dark brown, and there is white on the abdomen. The legs and feet are blackish. Sexes are alike.

Distribution: Breeds across North America from Alaska to Labrador, south to California and south of Great Lakes. The smallest race occurs in western Alaska, while geese from the Canadian prairies are almost four times as heavy. Overwinters near west and east coasts of the USA, south to the Caribbean.
Size: 55–110cm (22–43in).
Habitat: Usually near water.
Nest: Vegetation on the ground.
Eggs: 4–7, whitish.
Food: Vegetarian.

Snow goose

Anser caerulescens

Although most common in the far north, migratory snow geese also visit the southerly coasts of the USA, and can even be seen in northern Mexico. These geese are especially attracted to farmland, where grazing opportunities are plentiful, and this appears to be helping them to extend their range. As with all waterfowl, however, there is always the possibility that sightings of snow geese indicate an escape from domestic waterfowl collections, rather than actual wild individuals. The calls of snow geese have been likened to the barking of a dog.

Above: Blue geese are less common than white-phase geese.

Identification: Blue-phase birds (above) are dark and blackish, with white heads and white borders to some wing feathers. Young birds of this colour phase have dark heads. White-phase birds (left) are mostly white, with dark primary wing feathers. Young have greyish markings on their heads. Sexes are alike.

Distribution: Breeds in the high Arctic, migrating to the Klamath marshes and south to California, while some remain at Puget Sound. Others overwinter on the east coast, and along the Gulf coast to Mexico.
Size: 84cm (33in).
Habitat: Tundra and coasts.
Nest: Depression lined with vegetation.
Eggs: 4–10, whitish.
Food: Vegetarian.

SHY WADERS

There are a number of long-legged yet small birds that inhabit freshwater locations. They are rather shy by nature, and tend to be found in the shallows, although some species are capable of not only swimming but also diving, and are able to escape would-be predators and obtain food in this way. Although their feet are not webbed like those of waterfowl, their toes are frequently elongated.

Northern jacana

Jacana spinosa

The long toes of this jacana help to distribute its weight over a wide area as it walks, enabling it to move over dense aquatic vegetation on the surface of pools and shallow lakes. This species feeds almost entirely on invertebrates, using its slender bill to probe in surface vegetation and among the roots of water plants. Small fish and water-lily seeds are sometimes eaten too. Breeding habits are unusual, since it is the female who maintains a larger territory, encompassing that of several males. The nest, constructed by the male, is often partially submerged, and the hen will mate with, and lay in the nests of, all males sharing her territory. In turn, each male is responsible for hatching the eggs, and rears the chicks until they are three months old.

Identification: Head and neck are black, merging into dark rufous body and wings. Flight feathers yellow, evident in flight. Frontal shield bright yellow, with bluish area above bill. Grey legs, and very long toes. Prominent spurs at the bend of the wings. Hens larger. Young birds have white underparts, with a white stripe running from each eye down the neck, and adjacent plumage is black. Back and wings brown.

Distribution: May breed as far north as southern Texas, but usually ranges from Mexico south through Central America to western parts of Panama. Also occurs in the Caribbean region, on Cuba, the Isle of Pines, Hispaniola, and Jamaica.
Size: 24cm (9¹/₂in).
Habitat: Marshes and ponds.
Nest: Made on floating vegetation.
Eggs: 4, pale buff with black markings.
Food: Invertebrates.

American avocet

Recurvirostra americana

These avocets head north to their breeding grounds in April, nesting around shallow lakes and similar expanses of water, sometimes in large numbers. Females sometimes lay in nests other than their own. Both sexes share the incubation and rearing, with the young fledging at around four weeks of age. American avocets leave their nesting grounds from August, often heading to coasts. They are less common on the eastern seaboard, but appear to be increasing there again after being hunted and almost exterminated in the 1800s. These birds have a distinctive method of feeding in water, sweeping their head from side to side in search of worms, crustaceans, and other prey. On land they catch grasshoppers in a more conventional way, grabbing them with their bill, and sometimes eat seeds too.

Identification: Slender and long-legged, with a narrow, greyish bill slightly upturned at its tip, especially in females, and longer in males. Black areas on the wings separated by a broad white band, with the underparts being white. The head and neck are of a rusty shade when breeding, becoming greyish-white in winter. Young birds have a slight cinnamon wash on their neck.

Distribution: Breeds from south-eastern parts of British Columbia across to south-western Ontario, down to Baja California and central Texas. Also occurs in the eastern USA and central Mexico. Winters in the vicinity of Florida, Texas and the Caribbean, as well as California. Also ranges south to Guatemala.
Size: 46cm (18in).
Habitat: Marshes and ponds.
Nest: Grass-lined scrape.
Eggs: 4, olive-buff with darker spots.
Food: Invertebrates.

Black-necked stilt

Himantopus mexicanus

This species is sometimes regarded as a subspecies of the black-winged stilt (*H. himantopus*), which has a much wider distribution especially in southern latitudes. Other subspecies occur on the Hawaiian islands and southern parts of South America. The black-necked stilt can be distinguished from other mainland forms, which have a white top to the head, by its black top. These stilts breed in colonies and defend their nests aggressively, harrying would-be predators by dive-bombing and calling loudly. Later birds in northern parts migrate southward for winter, but nearer the equator they remain all year around. They seek invertebrates in water by probing and swinging their bill from side to side. Black-necked stilts also take fish, and on land are known to catch butterflies and other insects.

Identification: Slender, with a straight, narrow bill. Distinctive red legs and feet. Upperparts of the cock are predominantly black, with a white area at the base of the bill and above each eye. Black feathering extends out at the base of the neck. Hens are blackish brown, while young birds have brown rather than black upperparts.

Distribution: Widely distributed through western and central parts of the USA, and via Central America to parts of Ecuador and Peru in western South America, extending as far as north-eastern Brazil. Also occurs in the Caribbean.
Size: 41cm (16in).
Habitat: Marshland.
Nest: Grass-lined scrape.
Eggs: 3–4, buff with darker markings.
Food: Mainly invertebrates.

Pied plover (*Hoploxypterus cayanus*): 22¹/₂cm (9in)
Occurs in Northern South America, east of the Andes from the Caribbean south to Argentina. Broad black stripe on the sides of the face, extending down the neck and encircling the lower breast. Black cap on the head; remainder of throat, breast and head is white. Broad black stripes run across the wings, with the upperparts being greyish. Underparts are white. Legs and feet red. Sexes are alike. Young birds are brownish where adults have black markings.

Wattled jacana (*Jacana jacana*): 25cm (10in)
From western Panama through Colombia and Venezuela, across much of South America east of the Andes to northern Argentina and Uruguay. Separate population exists in Ecuador and Peru. Distinctive red frontal shield above and on the sides of the yellowish bill. Head and chest are a glossy bluish black; wings are chestnut red with yellow evident in the flight feathers. Legs and long toes are grey. Regional variations exist, with the northern race blackish, with no chestnut markings on the back and wings. Hens larger, with bluish edging to the upper part of the comb. Young have a smaller frontal shield.

Andean avocet (*Recurvirostra andina*): 48cm (19in)
Found throughout western South America, from central Peru and western Bolivia to northern Chile; also north-west Argentina. Found high in the Andes. White head and body, blackish wings and narrow, up-curved black bill. White feathering on breast is often stained. Orange-red iris. Greyish feet and legs. Sexes are alike.

Marbled godwit

Limosa fedoa

The call of these birds, most commonly uttered when they are nesting, explains why they are known as godwits. They eat a variety of foods, depending on habitat, feeding largely on insects when breeding. Marbled godwits nest in small colonies close to pools, and may start to lay as early as May. Both parents share the three-week incubation, with the young fledging after a further three weeks. Soon after the birds head south, mostly overwintering on coasts, especially in North America. Occasionally they may head much further south, with records of this species as far south as northern Chile. One of the best sites to see flocks returning north is at Cheyenne Bottoms in Kansas, where they traditionally break their journey. Marbled godwits can be long-lived, with a life expectancy in excess of 25 years.

Identification: Long, slightly upturned bill, orangish-pink at its base and dark at the tip. Tawny-brown overall, with relatively heavy black mottling on the upperparts and lighter barring beneath, especially during the winter months. Cinnamon plumage under the wings evident in flight. Sexes are alike. Young birds resemble adults in winter plumage.

Distribution: Breeds in North America from Saskatchewan to Minnesota, also in southern Alaska and south of Hudson Bay. Moves south for winter to California, and from Virginia along Gulf coast to Panama and South America.
Size: 46cm (18in).
Habitat: Grassy areas, shallow waters.
Nest: Grass-lined scrape.
Eggs: 4, olive-buff with darker markings.
Food: Mainly invertebrates.

KINGFISHERS

There are only seven species of kingfisher in America. Although fish feature prominently in the diets of these birds, they may also hunt invertebrates in flight. Their dependence on stretches of open water means that they leave the freezing latitudes of the far north for the winter, and may sometimes move to coasts during unexpected cold spells elsewhere.

Ringed kingfisher

Megaceryle torquata

Ringed kingfishers are rather solitary by nature, and hence not especially conspicuous. They are very patient when fishing, and can spend up to two hours on a favoured branch waiting for a fish. The bird then dives down to seize the fish, returning to the perch to stun it before swallowing it head-first. Ringed kingfishers tend to be sedentary, but in southern areas they move north from Tierra del Fuego to winter. Pairs usually nest in riverbanks. The tunnel leading to the nest chamber is up to 2.7m (8.8ft) long, while the chamber itself is small. The young remain there until five weeks old, and can fly from the time of fledging.

Identification: Male has pale grey head, with a white spot in front of the eye and a narrow white line beneath. A broad white collar encircles the neck. Back and wings are grey, with grey and white upper tail feathers. Underparts rufous, with white undertail coverts. Hens have a grey area on the breast with a narrow white band below, and rufous underparts. Young birds similar to females, but grey of the breast has a rufous suffusion.

Distribution: Ranges as far north as the Rio Grande and south Sinaloa down through Central America. Also present on Guadaloupe. Occurs through much of South America apart from the Andean region.
Size: 40cm (16in).
Habitat: Lakes and rivers.
Nest: In a burrow.
Eggs: 3–6, white.
Food: Mainly small fish.

Belted kingfisher

Megaceryle alcyon

The loud, rattling call of these kingfishers, uttered in flight, betrays their presence. Their preference for fish means they will move south in the winter, to areas of water that will not freeze over. They are generally found on tranquil stretches of water, where they can observe fish easily, but on occasions they have been spotted feeding up to 1 km (0.6miles) offshore. They may also visit garden ponds. Various invertebrates from butterflies to crayfish feature in the diet of belted kingfishers. Their large size means they can also prey on water shrews and the young chicks of other birds. If faced with a shortage of food in winter, they will even resort to feeding on berries. The area beneath their regular roosting spot is littered with regurgitated pellets containing the indigestible remains of their prey. As in the case of owls, this evidence enables zoologists to pinpoint the feeding preferences of these and other kingfishers.

Identification: Cock birds are mainly grey on the head, back and wings, except for a white collar, white underparts below a grey breast-band, and a white spot by each eye. Hens have a rufous breast-band with grey markings. and are rufous on the flanks too. Young have a second tawny breast-band.

Distribution: Ranges from the Aleutian Islands into south-west Alaska and down through southern Canada to the Gulf coast and Mexico. May be seen in other parts of Central America, the Caribbean and along the north-eastern coasts of South America in winter.
Size: 37cm (14¹/₂in).
Habitat: Ponds, lakes and rivers.
Nest: In a burrow.
Eggs: 5–8, white.
Food: Mainly fish.

Amazon kingfisher

Chloroceryle amazona

As their name suggests, Amazonian kingfishers are more common in South America than further north, preferring lowland areas of habitat. Their calls are quite harsh, but they do have a song that is occasionally uttered when perched, with the bird's wings held open and

its bill raised vertically. A pair will excavate the nest tunnel in a vertical bank, extending back up to 1.6m (5¼ft) and broadening into a chamber about 25cm (10in) wide and 45cm (18in) long. The narrow dimensions of the nest mean that adult birds are forced to back out along the tunnel, rather than being able to emerge again head-first. Both members of the pair share the incubation, which lasts about 22 days, and subsequently care for the young, which leave the nest site when just over a month old.

Identification: Dark green head and back, with some prominent green streaks on the flanks. A white collar extends around the neck, beneath the black bill. A rufous area is present on the breast of cock birds, with the underparts being white in hens.

Distribution: From the Yucatan Peninsula in Central America southward to Ecuador and across central and eastern South America as far as central Argentina.
Size: 30cm (12in).
Habitat: Wooded areas near water.
Nest: In a burrow.
Eggs: 3–4, white.
Food: Fish and prawns.

Green kingfisher (*Chloroceryle americana*): 22cm (9in)
May be seen as far north as Arizona and New Mexico, and more frequently in Texas, down through Central America across much of north-eastern South America to Argentina, as well as the north-western coastal area, reaching northern Chile. Cock birds have a green head, back and wings, with two lines of white barring extending across the wings. The throat is white, with a collar extending from the throat around the neck. Rufous chest and white underparts, apart from prominent black spotting on the flanks and across the lower chest. Hens are similar, but with a very pale rufous chest band and a speckled greenish band.

Green-and-rufous kingfisher (*Chloroceryle inda*): 24cm (9½in)
The green-and-rufous kingfisher ranges from south-eastern Nicaragua, Costa Rica, and Panama southward through northern South America east of the Amazon, and south as far as Santa Catarina in Brazil. Also present down the western coast of South America through Ecuador and Peru. Head, back and wings dark green, with pale white spots on the wings. Underparts are rufous. A small rufous stripe extends back to the eye on each side of the head from the base of the dark bill. Hens can be easily recognized by the green speckling on a white band across the upper breast.

American pygmy kingfisher

Chloroceryle aenea

Quiet by nature and blending in well with their forest background, these small kingfishers are often difficult to observe. They are not uncommon, however, and are most likely to be found near streams and other areas of water. American pygmy kingfishers hunt in a similar way to their larger relatives, perching on a convenient branch overlooking a calm stretch of water and waiting for small fish, tadpoles or other aquatic creatures to come to the surface. These kingfishers catch insects in flight too. They are solitary except when breeding. The nest may be excavated a short distance into a riverbank, or sometimes in an arboreal termite mound, where the termites help to protect the birds from predators.

Distribution: Extends southward from the Sierra Madre del Sur and Puebla in Mexico down through Central America and eastward across South America as far as Rio de Janeiro.
Size: 13cm (5in).
Habitat: Forest pools and rivers.
Nest: In a burrow.
Eggs: 3–5, white.
Food: Fish and invertebrates.

Identification: Cock has a bright green head, back and wings, with a rufous collar. The chest and flanks are rufous, with the centre of the underparts being white, as are the undertail coverts. A rufous area extends from the bill above the eye. Hens can be distinguished by their green breast band. Young birds have pale speckling on the wings and very pale rufous upperparts.

OTHER FRESHWATER PREDATORS

As with other species, there are a number of predatory birds which have adapted to lakes, rivers and other freshwater habitats, while their relatives are more commonly encountered in other localities. Examples here include several fish-eating species, ranging from a freshwater tern to various birds of prey, with their lifestyles varying accordingly.

Large-billed tern

Phaetusa simplex

These unusual terns are typically found on freshwater lakes and rivers, where they breed on sand bars. They sometimes nest in large colonies of up to 100 pairs. Large-billed terns lay directly on to the sand but change their breeding sites annually, possibly to avoid predation. Nevertheless, nesting on the ground still has its dangers, with a variety of predators, including boa constrictors, seeking out their nests. Outside the breeding period they may be found in other habitats, often moving to coasts. Large-billed terns mostly feed by diving into the water, but may also swoop down and trawl at the surface using their large bill. Along with aquatic prey they also catch flying insects, and on farmland may seek out invertebrates exposed by the plough.

Identification: Black cap on the head, with black also on the primary flight feathers and adjacent areas. Back and leading edges of the wings are grey, the rest is white. Forehead paler when not breeding. Large bill and feet are yellow. Sexes are alike.

Distribution: Mainly eastern half of South America, with a small population in western Ecuador, down to Argentina and Uruguay. May range further north in spring, being recorded in Ohio, Illinois, and New Jersey in the USA, and also from Bermuda as well as Cuba.
Size: 37cm (14^1/$_2$in).
Habitat: Freshwater areas.
Nest: On sand bars.
Eggs: 2–3, brownish with darker markings.
Food: Fish and invertebrates.

Common black hawk

Buteogallus anthracinus

Common black hawks are summer visitors to North America, migrating south in the autumn, although they appear to be sedentary further south. Occupying large territories means these birds of prey are not especially evident. A study in Mexico along the River Bavispe revealed that individual pairs typically occupy a territory of some 3km (1.8 miles) long, although in other areas they may occur at higher densities. They are not very conspicuous, often perching quietly in trees, and briefly swooping down to seize their quarry. Fish figure prominently in their diet, although a wide range of other prey, from crabs to iguanas, may also be eaten. Breeding pairs in North America start laying in May, while nesting takes place earlier closer to the equator. The incubation period lasts nearly six weeks, with fledging occurring after a further six weeks.

Identification: Predominantly blackish, with a white tip to the tail and a broader white band across the tail. Some relatively inconspicuous white flecking on the thighs and also at the base of the primary flight feathers, evident in flight. Cere area incorporating the nostrils is yellow, as are the legs. Sexes are alike. Juveniles have streaked underparts, with a series of bands across the tail. Yellow on the face less prominent.

Distribution: Ranges from southern Utah, Arizona, New Mexico, and Texas down through western and eastern Central America to Colombia, Venezuela, and Guyana. Present on various Caribbean islands as well. Generally migrates south from the USA for winter.
Size: 53cm (21in).
Habitat: Wooded areas near rivers.
Nest: Made of sticks.
Eggs: 1–3, white and spotted.
Food: Amphibians, crabs, and fish.

Western osprey

Pandion haliaetus

The natural range of the osprey extends to all inhabited continents, making it one of the most widely distributed of all birds. Ospreys have adapted to feeding on stretches of fresh water as well as on estuaries and even the open ocean, swooping to grab fish from just below the surface using their powerful talons. They are capable of carrying fish typically weighing up to 300g (11oz) without difficulty, although there are reports of birds being dragged underwater and subsequently drowning while grappling with extremely heavy prey. They live in coastal colonies and often return to the same nesting grounds year after year. Their call is a high, rapidly repeated and rather plaintive whistle.

Left: Osprey feed only on fish, pouncing on those just below the surface.

Identification: Brown stripes running across the eyes down over the back and wings. Eyes are yellow. Top of the head and underparts are white, with brown striations across the breast, which are most marked in hens. Tall, upright stance, powerful grey legs and talons. Hens are significantly heavier than cocks.

Distribution: Ranges across North America, from British Columbia to eastern coasts north of the Great Lakes. Breeding grounds are also extensive, stretching from Florida to Labrador. Winters from South Carolina to north and eastern South America.
Size: 58cm (23in).
Habitat: Close to stretches of water.
Nest: Platform of sticks in a tree, high off the ground.
Eggs: 3, white with darker markings.
Food: Fish exclusively.

Rough-legged buzzard (*Buteo lagopus*): 56cm (22in)
Breeds across the far north of North America, wintering in the north-east and across much of the USA, except for the south-east. Heavily streaked brown and white plumage, with a brown area on the wings. Tail is banded in males, solid brown in females, edged with narrow black barring on lower side; feathers have white tips. Young birds have buff-coloured thighs. A dark morph also exists.

Slate-coloured hawk (*Buteogallus schistaceus*): 43cm (17in)
Amazonia region, from southern Colombia and Venezuela eastward to French Guiana and northern Brazil. Also south via Ecuador and Peru to Bolivia. Slaty grey overall, with a red area encircling the eyes and over the cere. Legs also red. Tail black with a white band across it, and a narrow white tip. Hens slightly larger. Young birds have narrow white barring on underparts and undersides of wings.

Barred owl (*Strix varia*): 53cm (21in)
North-western USA up to southern Alaska, across Canada and down across eastern USA. Dark circle outlining the face, with a line running to the top of the yellow bill. Thick brown barring across the upper breast, with streaking over rest of underparts. Back and wings have brown and white patterning. Whitish feathers on the feet, with the exposed tips of the toes being yellowish. Sexes are alike.

Crane hawk

Geranospiza caerulescens

Despite their extensive distribution relatively little is known about crane hawks, so-called because of their long legs and upright posture. These birds of prey are found in a variety of habitats, usually near water. They are adaptable hunters, catching quarry in flight as well as dropping down to seize prey on the ground. Their legs are double-jointed, allowing one foot to be used rather like a hand while the hawk anchors itself with the other; this is useful for reaching into tree holes or vegetation to grab small creatures. The breeding period extends through much of the year, apparently influenced by location, occurring in Venezuela during the rainy season. The nest site is located high up and lined with fresh vegetation. Egg-laying is preceded by aerial courtship displays.

Identification: Varies with race. Greyish to black overall. Long, broad tail has two prominent white bands. Dark bill, with red skin encircling the eyes, and pinkish-red legs. Sexes alike, but females larger. Young display white streaking on head, and brownish suffusion, with barring and buff on underparts.

Distribution: An isolated population in north-western Mexico, with the main range extending south through the rest of Central America and across much of northern South America to the north of Argentina and Uruguay.
Size: 51cm (20in).
Habitat: Often close to water.
Nest: Platform of sticks.
Eggs: 2, white and spotted.
Food: Larger invertebrates and vertebrates.

COTINGAS

The cotingas include some of the most colourful of all tropical birds, although their name comes from an Amazonian native American word meaning "washed white," which is used locally to describe the white bellbird. Their diet consists mainly of fruits and berries, and this group of birds is important in the dispersal of plants, as undigested seeds from their food are passed onto the ground.

Scarlet cock-of-the-rock

Andean cock-of-the-rock *Rupicola peruviana*

With their spectacular bright red plumage, males frequently congregate together at traditional display sites called leks, often deep in the forest. Here they seek to entice hens to mate with them. Their display calls have been likened to the squealing of pigs, although these cotingas are not noisy by nature. Their brilliant plumage blends into the dark background in the forest, making them hard to observe. The hen constructs her nest using damp mud.

Distribution: Colombia and Venezuela to parts of Ecuador, Peru, and Bolivia.
Size: 32cm (12¹/₂in).
Habitat: Humid, rocky areas of forest, often in ravines close to water.
Nest: Cup made of mud, located in a secluded rocky outcrop or cave.
Eggs: 2, buff with darker spotting.
Food: Mainly berries and other fruit.

Identification: Brilliant red dominates in the plumage, with crest feathers extending down over the bill, contrasting with black on the back and wings. Hens are significantly duller in colour, and are generally reddish brown with a smaller crest.

Fiery-throated fruiteater

Pipreola chlorolepidota

This is the smallest of the Andean fruiteaters. It is found at a lower altitude than related species, typically less than 1,000m (3,280ft) above sea level, in the foothills of the Andes. These members of the cotinga clan are most likely to be observed singly or in pairs. They may breed throughout the year, building a moss nest lined with small roots, usually close to the ground and often disguised in a creeper. The fiery-throated fruiteater is unusual in that it does venture up into the canopy of the forest, although it is also commonly seen in the lower levels, often seeking food in the company of other birds.

Identification: The underparts are dark green, with a yellowish-orange throat area; remainder of the plumage is also green. Bill is reddish. Hens closely resemble female scarlet-breasted fruiteater (*P. frontalis*), being predominantly green, with yellow barring extending from the throat over the entire underparts.

Distribution: Eastern areas of Ecuador and Peru.
Size: 11cm (4in).
Habitat: Humid tropical forest.
Nest: Cup-shaped.
Eggs: Probably 2, creamy and spotted.
Food: Mainly berries and other fruit, also invertebrates.

Orange cock-of-the-rock (Guianan cock-of-the-rock, *Rupicola rupicola*): 32cm (12¹/₂in)
Found in French Guiana west to Colombia, also in northern Brazil. Unmistakable shade of brilliant orange. The hen is mainly olive brown with an orange suffusion on the rump.

Pompadour cotinga (*Xipholena punicea*): 20cm (8in)
Extends from Colombia eastward to French Guiana and south to north-west Brazil. Wine-red plumage with white areas on the wings. Hens are grey, with white edging to some wing feathers. The eyes are whitish.

Plum-throated cotinga (*Cotinga maynana*): 19cm (7¹/₂in)
Ranges from south-eastern Colombia to northern Bolivia and Amazonian Brazil. Turquoise with a small plum-coloured throat patch. Hens are brown with pale edges to the feathers. They have cinnamon plumage on the lower abdomen.

Barred fruiteater (*Pipreola arcuata*): 22cm (8¹/₂in)
Found in the Andean region of western South America at altitudes of 3,200m (10,500ft) in cloud forest. Blackish head, with barring confined to the chest and underparts, which are green in hens.

Red-crested cotinga (*Ampelion rubrocristatus*): 23cm (9in)
Found in the Andean region of Colombia and western Venezuela south to northern Bolivia. Greyish brown, with a blacker tone on the head, back and wings. Reddish crest at the back of the head is often kept flat. Undertail coverts are streaked with white. White areas on the underside of the tail. Bill is white with a black tip. Iris is red. Sexes are alike.

Long-wattled umbrellabird

Cephalopterus penduliger

As the name suggests, the male of this species has a bizarre black-feathered wattle extending down from his chest that measures approximately 30cm (12in) long. It is inflated as part of his display, but shortened during flight and held close to the chest. The flight pattern of umbrellabirds is not dissimilar to that of woodpeckers, low and strong over the trees. Quiet by nature, solitary and rarely observed, males are most likely to be seen displaying on bare branches, when their booming calls are uttered. These calls are heard with increasing frequency during the nesting season, although it appears that the hen alone is responsible for rearing the offspring.

Identification:
Predominantly black in colour. Very long wattle, which is greatly reduced in females. Both have relatively small crests. Brown eyes help to distinguish these cotingas from related umbrellabirds.

Distribution: Western Colombia and north-western Ecuador.
Size: 51cm (20in) cock; 46cm (18in) hen.
Habitat: Lowland tropical forest.
Nest: Platform of twigs.
Eggs: 1, khaki-coloured.
Food: Mainly palm fruits and insects.

Purple-breasted cotinga

Cotinga cotinga

One of the most striking features of these cotingas is their small yet broad bills, which allow them to pluck and swallow quite large fruits whole. They belong to the group often known as the blue cotingas, so-called because of the predominant colour of the cock bird. Individuals are most likely to be seen perching on dead treetops, although they fly with a strange rattling noise, which is thought to be caused by the modified shape of their flight feathers. Little is known about their breeding habits, but it is believed that hens incubate and rear their chicks on their own.

Identification:
Silhouette is like that of a dove. Distinctive reddish-purple feathering from the throat down to the middle of the belly; the remainder of the body is violet blue, apart from the black wings and tail. Small yet broad bill. Hens are dark brown, with white edging to the feathers, creating a scaly appearance over the whole body.

Distribution: Eastern Colombia to the Guianas and Brazil.
Size: 19cm (7¹/₂in).
Habitat: Lowland tropical forest.
Nest: Small, flimsy and cup-shaped.
Eggs: Probably 1–2, bluish with rusty-brown markings.
Food: Primarily fruit.

JACAMARS, MOTMOTS AND PUFFBIRDS

These birds are unique to America. Jacamars are mainly found in South rather than Central America, and are characterized by their relatively slim body shape, long narrow tail, and slender bill. Motmots are easily recognized by the enlarged rackets on their surprisingly flexible tail. Like puffbirds, they feed on invertebrates and even small vertebrates.

Paradise jacamar

Galbula dea

Distribution: Northern South America to parts of Brazil, Peru and Bolivia.
Size: 30cm (12in).
Habitat: Occurs in forest and more open country.
Nest: May excavate into the mounds of arboreal termites or a suitable bank.
Eggs: 2–4, glossy white.
Food: Invertebrates.

The jacamars form a group closely related to woodpeckers, and are members of the avian order *Piciformes* (which includes woodpeckers and trogons). Like trogons, they have a zygodactyl perching grip, with two toes directed forward over the perch and two behind. In common with related species, the paradise jacamar has a long, thin bill. It hunts insects on the wing, using its bill to grab prey in flight. These are not especially shy birds, and are most likely to be seen either in pairs or small parties in forest clearings or sometimes when swooping out across water. Their call note is a distinctive "pip" sound that is repeated frequently. These jacamars, unlike other species, often remain in the tree canopy, where they are difficult to observe thanks in part to their coloration. Paradise jacamars will often accompany groups of other birds, seizing any invertebrates that are disturbed as a result of the other birds' movements.

Identification:
Distinctive dark body and a long tail that tapers along its length. White feathering under the throat and dark, glossy, green wings. Bill is long and black. Sexes are alike. The colour of the crown may be either pale grey or dark brown, depending on race.

Rufous-tailed jacamar

Galbula ruficauda

Distribution: Ranges from the south-eastern part of Mexico along the Atlantic seaboard down through Honduras into South America, extending to Ecuador in the west and down as far as Argentina on the eastern side.
Size: 22·5cm (9in).
Habitat: Evergreen forests.
Nest: In a burrow.
Eggs: 2–4, glossy white.
Food: Mainly flying insects.

Identification: Metallic green head, chest, and wings with glossy, iridescent upperparts and rufous-brown underparts. The bill is long and narrow, tapering to a point. Throat area in cock birds is white, and a pale cinnamon or buff colour in hens.

Like other jacamars, this wide-ranging Central and South American species perches for relatively long periods during the day, remaining alert to feeding opportunities. When an insect ventures within range it will dart off in pursuit with a swooping flight pattern. Having seized its quarry, it will return to beat the invertebrate fiercely against its perch. Dragonflies and butterflies rank amongst its favourite prey. Rufous-tailed jacamars inhabit evergreen forests including second growth forests, where they frequent forest clearings. They have very loud calls, which have been likened to human screams, and it is usually these that betray their presence in the forest, especially since they favour perches that are relatively exposed. Pairs will nest in burrows, with the nest often located at a relatively low height in a bank. The tunnel can be up to 45cm (18in) in length. Both members of the pair share incubation duties. The cock bird sits mainly during the day, with the hen taking over at dusk. The young birds, which have duller plumage, remain in the nest until they fledge at about three weeks old.

Amazonian motmot

Momotus momota

Amazonian motmots frequent lower branches in the canopy, sometimes venturing into more open areas of countryside, especially in the vicinity of rivers. They have a very distinctive way of moving their tail feathers from side to side, rather like the pendulum of a clock, usually when excited, and will also perch with their tail held at an angle. These motmots hawk insects on the wing and hunt small vertebrates such as lizards, as well as eating fruit and berries on occasion. They also follow columns of army ants moving across the forest floor, swooping down not on the ants but on other small creatures attempting to escape from these aggressive insects. The call of the Amazonian motmot is rather like that of an owl, often consisting of a double hooting, frequently uttered just before sunrise. A hole in a bank, often near water, is used for breeding, with the tunnel extending back some distance and broadening to form a nesting chamber at the end.

Identification: Quite variable, depending on the race. Black stripe, edged with blue, extends back a short distance down the side of the neck through the eyes. The crown may be blue (as in the north-east Mexican Blue-capped motmot *M. coeruliceps*) or can be black at the centre with a blue surrounding area. Upperparts may be green or olive green, sometimes with a chestnut collar. Underparts are olive green. The tail is long, green at the base and blue toward the tip, with two evident rackets. Sexes are alike.

Distribution: Range includes much of Central and South America, extending from Mexico down to north-western Peru and eastward to Paraguay, north-west Argentina and south-eastern Brazil. Also occurs on Trinidad and Tobago.
Size: 41cm (16in).
Habitat: Mainly forested areas.
Nest: In a burrow.
Eggs: 2–5, white.
Food: Invertebrates form the bulk of the diet.

White-eared jacamar (*Galbalcyrhynchus leucotis*): 20cm (8in)
Northern part of the Upper Amazonian region. Recognizable by its large, pinkish bill and white areas of plumage behind the eyes. Reddish chestnut overall with dark wings. Sexes are alike.

White-necked puffbird (*Notharchus hyperrhynchus*): 25cm (10in)
The five recognized subspecies of these puffbirds have a fairly extensive range through South America, from sightings in Mexico and Guatemala south as far as northern parts of Argentina. White on the forehead, chest and abdomen. Black elsewhere, in a band across the chest, around the eyes and on the wings. Barred on sides of body. Sexes are alike.

Spotted puffbird (*Bucco tamatia*): 18cm (7in)
Northern South America, including Colombia and Venezuela, south through Ecuador to Peru and east into Brazil. Cinnamon plumage across the throat, black-and-white barring beneath, with a black bar on the lower cheeks. Sexes are alike.

Rufous-capped motmot (*Baryphthengus ruficapillus*): 40cm (16in)
Ranges from eastern Honduras down to parts of Brazil and northern Argentina. Head and underparts are rufous, apart from an area of black feathering extending back from the bill. There may also be a small black spot on the belly. Back and wings are green, as is the tail and the area around the vent. Isolated south-eastern population lacks rackets on the tail and has olive underparts.

White-whiskered puffbird

Malacoptila panamensis

It is easy to miss these dark-coloured birds in the forest gloom. Puffbirds avoid the canopy, preferring to spend much of their time perching quietly at lower levels, flying only short distances. They hunt close to the ground, catching insects and small vertebrates in their stocky, hooked bills. Puffbirds are typically seen either on their own or in pairs. They nest in an underground tunnel, usually excavated on slightly sloping ground, which extends down to a depth of 60cm (2ft), and the eggs are laid in a chamber on a bed of leaves. Unusually, the male white-whiskered puffbird is largely responsible for incubating the eggs and brooding the chicks once they hatch, while the female is responsible for obtaining food. The entrance to the tunnel is carefully concealed with leaves and twigs, and the puffbirds fly directly up to the branches overhead as they leave the nest.

Identification: Cinnamon-brown streaking, with white spots over the back and wings. Paler brown underparts, with prominent white bushy lores and moustache. The iris is a deep reddish shade. Hens are paler and greyer overall, again with a white area surrounding the bill. Young birds are recognizable by the scaling on their upperparts, and they possess a smaller moustache.

Distribution: Ranges from south-eastern Mexico down through Central America to Ecuador.
Size: 20cm (8in).
Habitat: Evergreen forest.
Nest: In burrows.
Eggs: 2–3, white.
Food: Mainly invertebrates.

QUETZALS, TROGONS AND MANAKINS

Quetzals have a special mythical significance in ancient Central and South American culture and feature prominently in Mayan legend and symbolism. Trogons as a group have a much wider distribution, with relatives in Africa. They have a similar body shape to quetzals, with a broad, square-ending tail. Manakins form another colourful group of fruit-eating forest birds.

Crested quetzal

Pharomachrus antisianus

Distribution: Colombia and western Venezuela to Brazil in the east and southwards as far as Bolivia.
Size: 33cm (13in).
Habitat: Humid forest. Typically occurs in cloud forest in the Andean region up to an altitude of about 3,000m (9,840ft).
Nest: In tree holes or termite nests.
Eggs: 2, light blue.
Food: Berries, other fruit, and also invertebrates.

Quetzals have a distinctive, upright stance when perching, and they rest so quietly that they are easily overlooked. They are most likely to be seen close to the fruiting trees on which they feed. These quetzals have an undulating flight pattern, and their calls are a loud sequence of rolling notes. The plumage of crested quetzals, like that of related species, is brightly coloured but fades quite rapidly after death, so museum specimens rarely display the vibrancy of living birds. Another unusual feature is their very thin skin.

Identification: Distinguished from other quetzals by the white undersides to the tail feathers; hens have barred feathering. The hen can also be distinguished from the cock by her brown rather than green head, and a reduced area of red on the underparts. Young birds resemble the female.

Golden-winged manakin

Masius chrysopterus

These small birds are most likely to be spotted flying through the understorey in forests, sometimes heading up into the canopy in search of fruit. Golden-winged manakins normally seek out berries, which they can pluck on the wing, as well as invertebrates, which figure more prominently in their diet during the breeding period when there are chicks in the nest. Little is known of the habits of golden-winged manakins, but they appear to be relatively solitary by nature. The males use their bright wing coloration for display purposes.

Identification: This species has a distinctive golden-yellow edging to the wings and a yellow crest on the forehead, with this colour extending onto the throat and back over the head, where it becomes orangish. The remainder of the plumage is glossy black. The hen is greenish, but with prominent yellow feathering in the vicinity of the chin and belly.

Distribution: Occurs in the Andean region of South America, notably in Colombia, Venezuela, Ecuador and Peru.
Size: 11cm (4in).
Habitat: Cloud forest and woodland.
Nest: Suspended cup-shape, made of moss and rootlets.
Eggs: 2, cream with brown spots.
Food: Berries and some invertebrates.

Green-backed trogon

Amazonian white-tailed trogon *Trogon viridis*

Like other trogons, the green-backed may be sedentary for long periods, but is sufficiently agile to feed on fruit in flight, as well as to catch invertebrates on the wing. These trogons will also swoop on small vertebrate prey, such as lizards. The bill is short, but has a wide gape to facilitate swallowing. Their perching grip is unusual too, with two toes being directed in front of and behind the perch, rather than the more usual 3:1 perching configuration. In common with other trogons, they do not build a nest, with hens simply laying their eggs in a suitable chamber. They have even been known to use a termite nest, where the presence of termites deters would-be predators. Here the nesting chamber is a hollow, constructed at the end of a tunnel that usually leads in an upwardly diagonal direction.

Identification: Glossy violet feathering from the head to the chest. Yellow underparts and a dark green back, with a distinctive, mainly white underside to the tail. Blue eye rings. Bill is bluish white. The hen is duller in appearance, slate in colour with orangish-yellow underparts and a dusky upper bill.

Distribution: Costa Rica and Panama south to Colombia, Ecuador, Peru, and Brazil. Also on Trinidad.
Size: 28cm (11in).
Habitat: Humid forest.
Nest: Usually in a tree hole.
Eggs: 2, light blue.
Food: Berries, other fruit, and some invertebrates.

Pavonine quetzal (*Pharomachrus pavoninus*): 33cm (13in)
The only quetzal found east of the Andes, ranging south to northern Bolivia. Distinctive red bill and red lower underparts, otherwise the plumage is metallic emerald green. Hen is less colourful, with a black underside to the tail.

Black-throated trogon (*Trogon rufus*): 25cm (10in)
Ranges from south-eastern Honduras down to Paraguay and north-eastern Argentina. Distinctive green-and-yellow coloration, separated on the chest by a thin white band. The hen is distinguished from the cock by her brown and yellow feathering.

Eastern striped manakin (*Machaeropterus regulus*): 9cm (3¹/₂in)
Colombia and Venezuela south to Peru, Bolivia, and Brazil, occurring in the Andes up to 1,500m (4,900ft) . Brilliant red cap, with reddish streaking on the undersides. The hen is a dull shade of green overall, with paler, yellowish underparts and a white underside to the tail feathers. There are also darker streaks on the sides of the body, with a rufous hue on the flanks.

Guianan trogon (*Trogon violaceus*):22cm (9in)
Eastern Mexico, Central America down into Ecuador and Brazil. Entire head and throat of cock is purplish blue, with a white border separating this area from the bright yellow underparts. The back is a dark metallic shade of green, while the underside of the tail is white with black horizontal banding. Bill is horn-coloured and has a darker base. Hens have white feathering encircling each eye.

Elegant trogon

Trogon elegans

Elegant trogons frequent fruiting trees in the forest, being most commonly sighted individually or in pairs. Despite the bright coloration of the cock bird in particular, they blend in well with the background and are not easily observed. Elegant trogons are not especially active by nature. Their calls consist of chattering and hooting sounds. They may use their bill to excavate a nesting chamber, boring into rotten wood if no natural hole is available. Trogons may also dig into a wasps' nest or arboreal termite nest without disturbing the occupants, benefiting from the protection they offer.

Distribution: Occasionally observed in southern Arizona, more typically in Mexico and southward to northern parts of Costa Rica.
Size: 30cm (12in).
Habitat: Forested areas.
Nest: In hollows.
Eggs: 2–3, whitish.
Food: Fruit and invertebrates.

Identification: Cock has a dark green chest, head, and back, with greyish wings. Blackish area above the bill broadens to form circles on the sides of the face. A white band across the lower chest separates this area from the bright red underparts. The tail is yellowish brown on upper surface, white with fine horizontal black barring beneath, with a dark tip. Hens are brownish, with a white area behind the eyes. There is a faint white band across the chest, with red on the lower underparts. Upper surface of the tail is reddish brown, with pronounced barring beneath and a narrow dark tip.

BARBETS, BELLBIRDS AND FRUITCROWS

These birds are typical inhabitants of tropical forests. While fruitcrows and bellbirds are confined to America, barbets are well represented in parts of Asia and Africa. Like other fruit-eating species, they all have an important role in helping to spread the seeds of the plants on which they feed. A number of these species are found at high altitudes in the Andes, and may have a limited area of distribution.

Toucan barbet

Semnornis ramphastinus

Distribution: Western parts of Colombia and Ecuador. Typically between 1,000 and 2,400m (3,280 and 7,870ft).
Size: 20cm (8in).
Habitat: Humid mountain forests.
Nest: Tree hollow.
Eggs: 2, white.
Food: Berries, other fruit, and invertebrates.

The coloration of these barbets is not dissimilar to that of mountain toucans, which is how they got their name. Their bills, in contrast, are both stocky and powerful, enabling them to bore into wood to create or enlarge a nest in a tree hollow. Their tails are flexible, and can be carried either down or raised into a more vertical position. The toucan barbet's range is relatively restricted, and they tend not to be common, with just odd birds or pairs being sighted rather than groups. Like many barbets, they can call loudly, with members of a pair taking part in a duet of loud honking notes with each other. Calling of this type is most common during the nesting season.

Identification: Prominent bluish-grey areas on the sides of the face and chest. Orangish-red underparts, becoming more yellowish toward the vent, with an olive-brown back and yellowish rump. Wings and tail are bluish grey. Bill is tipped with black. Sexes are alike.

Five-coloured barbet

Capito quinticolor

These barbets are not perhaps as colourful as their name might suggest. They have a localized distribution on the western (Pacific) side of the Andes and they are not especially easy to observe, often occurring just as individuals hopping through the vegetation, or in pairs. They sometimes associate with other birds, possibly hoping to snatch invertebrates that may be disturbed as the flock moves from tree to tree. Five-coloured barbets do not range up into mountains, but are found in lowlands, at altitudes of 100m (330ft) or below.

Identification: Distinctive yellow V-shape at the top of the mainly black wings. The chest is predominantly white. Underparts are yellowish orange, with black spotting on the flanks and olive thighs. Hens have streaked upperparts and spotted underparts, and lack the crimson crown and nape seen in cocks.

Distribution: Restricted to western parts of Colombia, extending from Quibdó, Tadó and Chocó southward along the Pacific coast as far down as western Nariño.
Size: 18cm (7in).
Habitat: Forested areas of the coastal lowlands.
Nest: Cavity in a tree.
Eggs: 3, white.
Food: Berries, other fruit and invertebrates.

Prong-billed barbet (*Semnornis frantzii*):
18cm (7in)
Western Panama and Costa Rica. Olive-green upperparts with buff coloration on the upper breast. Crown is a dull, golden-brown shade, with a raised crest of glossy black feathers at the back of the head. Lower bill is divided, with the tip of the upper bill lying in the notch created where the two halves join. Hens lack black feathering.

Red-headed barbet (*Eubucco bourcierii*):
14cm (5½in)
Colombia, western Venezuela, Ecuador and the far north of Peru. Cock birds have a bright red head and upper breast, merging into the orange of the upper abdomen and becoming yellow on the lower underparts. A narrow whitish collar encircles the back of the neck, separating the red here from the green wings. Hens easily distinguished by the black plumage on the forehead, blue on the sides of the face and yellow-to-green shading over the back. The throat is grey, while all of the underparts are yellow. Lower underparts are whitish, with green streaking.

Scarlet-crowned barbet (*Capito aurovirens*):
16cm (6½in)
Occurs in southern Colombia, Ecuador, western Brazil, and the northern half of Peru. Cock bird has a bright red crown and nape, with brown on the sides of the face, extending over the back and wings. There is a white area under the chin. The upper breast is yellowish red and the lower underparts olive brown. Legs and feet are grey. Lower bill greyish with a black tip; upper bill is mostly black. Eyes have a vivid orange iris. Hens have whitish crown and nape, and a yellow breast.

Bare-throated bellbird

Procnias nudicollis

Bellbirds are named because of the sounds of the cock bird's call, which ranks as one of the loudest and most distinctive in the avian world. The hens, in contrast, remain quiet. When calling, the cock bird chooses a tall branch in the tree canopy, often in quite a conspicuous position, and subsequently drops down to another favoured branch lower in the canopy. It is here that mating may take place. The cock often uses these two perches to carry out a jumping display, dropping down on to the lower branch to land in a crouched position with his tail feathers spread. Studies on this species have revealed that bare-throated bellbirds move seasonally, descending to lower altitudes outside the breeding season.

Distribution: Southern Brazil, north-eastern Argentina, and Paraguay.
Size: 24cm (9½in).
Habitat: Montane forest.
Nest: Light and bowl-shaped, often in a tree fork.
Eggs: 1, light tan with brown mottling.
Food: Almost exclusively frugivorous, feeding on berries and other fruit.

Identification: Snowy-white feathering, with blackish bill and feet, plus a bare bluish-green area under the throat, extending just around the eyes. Contrasting dark irises, bill, and legs. The cock bird's calls are made by the syrinx, located in the throat. Hens are strikingly different, with a dark head, green wings, and yellow-streaked underparts, which become yellower on the lower abdomen. Young birds develop their bare throats by the time they are one year old.

Purple-throated fruitcrow

Querula purpurata

Like bellbirds, these are cotingas, not corvids as their common name might suggest. Purple-throated fruitcrows are not active birds by nature, which means they can be easily overlooked in forested areas. They are most conspicuous either when in flight or feeding, especially when they dart out quickly to seize berries or feed in the company of other frugivorous birds such as trogons. These fruitcrows live in groups of three or four individuals, and although only the female incubates, all members of the group provide food for the young bird. When displaying, males inflate their purple gorget of feathers, which then resembles a shield.

Left: The fruitcrow's nest may be at least 22m (70ft) off the ground.

Distribution: Costa Rica and Panama south to Amazonian region of Brazil and northern Bolivia.
Size: 28cm (11in).
Habitat: Tropical forest.
Nest: Cup-shaped, relatively high off the ground.
Eggs: 1, blackish.
Food: Berries, other fruits and invertebrates.

Identification: Predominantly black, with a distinctive area of purplish plumage under the throat. Hens are entirely black in colour, as are young birds of both sexes. Tail is quite short and wings are rounded.

TOUCANS, ARACARIS AND TOUCANETS

Members of the toucan clan are virtually unmistakable, although not all of them have large, brightly coloured bills. Active and restless by nature, they often congregate in large numbers in fruiting trees, hopping from branch to branch. When roosting and breeding in tree holes where their bill could be an encumbrance, they pull their tail feathers up vertically and tuck their bill over their back.

Crimson-rumped toucanet

Aulacorhynchus haematopygus

The term "toucanet" is applied to smaller members of this family, with green predominating in the plumage of all eleven *Aulacorhynchus* species. These toucanets are active and quite noisy birds, hopping from branch to branch in search of food. Eating is a two-stage process. Fruit is plucked and then skillfully tossed up into the air and swallowed whole. Pits are regurgitated later. Larger items can be held against the perch with the foot, allowing chunks to be torn off and then eaten in a similar way. The zygodactyl arrangement of these birds' toes, with two toes directed forward and two behind the perch, helps them to hold their food securely.

Identification: Predominantly green, darker on the wings with distinctive red plumage over the rump. Dark, reddish-brown bill, with white at the base and prominent dull reddish skin encircling the eyes. Sexes are alike.

Distribution: Colombia, Venezuela, and Ecuador.
Size: 41cm (16in).
Habitat: Humid forest and secondary woodland.
Nest: Tree hollow.
Eggs: 3–4, white.
Food: Fruit, small vertebrates and invertebrates. May also steal eggs and chicks.

Toco toucan

Ramphastos toco

Distribution: Guyana, Surinam and Guiana, south to Brazil, Paraguay, Bolivia and northern Argentina.
Size: 53cm (21in).
Habitat: Unusual in ranging from forest to savanna. On rare occasions, large flocks have moved into towns where ripening fruit is plentiful nearby.
Nest: Hollow in tree, sometimes previously occupied by woodpeckers.
Eggs: 2, white.
Food: Berries, other fruit, and invertebrates. Also raids nests of other birds.

Just why toucans have such large, brightly coloured bills is something of a mystery. These lightweight, honeycombed structures contain a long, fringed tongue. Its function is unknown, but it probably helps the toucans to swallow food. It is thought that the bill may enable these birds to pluck fruits that would otherwise be out of their reach at the end of thin branches. The bright colours set against their subdued plumage may also be a useful defensive aid, and certainly, the serrated edges of the bill can inflict a painful wound. Toco toucans are less social by nature than other members of the family, although they may congregate in large groups in areas where food is plentiful. They have a call that has been likened to the sound of deep snoring.

Identification: Largest of the toucans. Glossy black plumage with prominent white bib on the throat and red around the vent. Bare area of bright blue skin around the eyes, with small area of surrounding yellow feathering. Large, broad bill displays shades of yellow and yellowish-orange coloration, black at the base, with a prominent black tip to the upper bill. Sexes are alike.

Lettered aracari

Pteroglossus inscriptus

These aracaris get their name from the traces on their upper bill, which look like lettering. Aracaris are social by nature, and are most likely to be observed in groups. It is thought that in some cases, the young of the previous year may remain with their parents and assist in the rearing of the following year's young. The chicks hatch with heel pads that help them to keep their balance, although their bills at this time are relatively small. These pads fall off once the young birds have left the nest. Aracaris and other toucans rely on an adequate number of tree holes for breeding purposes because, unlike woodpeckers, their bills are not strong enough to allow them to bore effectively into trees.

Identification: The lack of banding across the yellow feathering of the chest is distinctive. Upperparts are greenish. Traces similar to letters on the upper bill, whereas lower bill is mainly black. Sexes are alike.

Distribution: Eastern Colombia to central and southern Brazil, and into northern Bolivia.
Size: 37cm (14¹/₂in).
Habitat: Forested areas and more open woodland.
Nest: Tree holes.
Eggs: 2–3, white.
Food: Berries, other fruit, invertebrates and small vertebrates.

White-throated toucan (*Ramphastos tucanus*): 61cm (24in)
Occurs in Venezuela, Guyana and French Guiana into parts of Brazil and eastern Bolivia. Dark reddish sides to the bill, yellow on top, with a white chest and red band beneath. Has mainly black plumage elsewhere, although the vent area is red. Sexes are alike.

Sulphur-breasted toucan (Keel-billed toucan, *Ramphastos sulfuratus*): 48cm (19in)
Found in Central America, from southern Mexico to northern Colombia and Venezuela. Bill is pea-green with orange stripe on upper part. Brilliant yellow plumage on the chest, predominantly black elsewhere. Sexes are alike.

Golden-collared toucanet (*Selenidera reinwardtii*): 33cm (13in)
Found in southern parts of Colombia, extending to parts of Ecuador, Peru and Brazil. Bill is a deep shade of red with a black tip. Plumage is mainly black and green, with a yellow collar and ear flashes. Hen has rufous coloration, not black.

Spot-billed toucanet (*Selenidera maculirostris*): 33cm (13in)
Confined to Brazil. Predominantly ivory bill with black markings. Mainly black head and chest, whereas the hen has reddish-brown plumage. Lower underparts are yellowish.

Many-banded aracari (*Pteroglossus pluricinctus*): 43cm (17in)
From Colombia and Venezuela south to northern Peru and Brazil. Black apart from ivory area down the sides of the upper bill. Two black bands run across the underparts, which are pale yellow with reddish markings. Upperparts are dark. Blue skin around the eyes. Rump is red. Sexes are alike.

Plate-billed mountain toucan

Andigena laminirostris

The four species of mountain toucan are all found at relatively high altitudes, and can be distinguished from the *Ramphastos* genus by their smaller bill. The plate-billed mountain toucan is so-called because of the presence of raised yellowish patches on each side of the beak. The function of these is unclear. Blue features prominently in the coloration of all mountain toucans, and the plumage is soft and quite loose. The wings of these toucans have the typical rounded shape associated with other members of the family, which means that they do not fly especially powerfully.

Identification: Characteristic yellow plate on each side of the upper bill, with black elsewhere and dull reddish base. Dark, sky-blue plumage on the underparts, with black cap on the head extending down the neck. Wings are olive brown. Sexes alike.

Distribution: Colombia and western parts of Ecuador.
Size: 51cm (20in).
Habitat: Humid and wet mountain forests.
Nest: Tree hollow.
Eggs: 2–3, white.
Food: Berries, other fruit, invertebrates and small vertebrates.

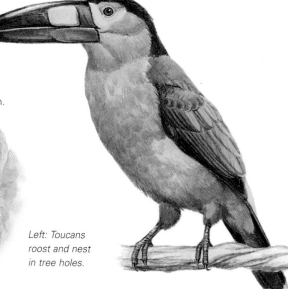

Left: Toucans roost and nest in tree holes.

CRACIDS, TINAMOUS AND GROUND BIRDS

There are a number of relatively large birds represented in America. The curassows, guans and chachalacas together form the family Cracidae. They tend to be more arboreal than the tinamous, which form a separate group. Antpittas and trumpeters are primarily ground-dwelling birds from this region, and they live and feed mainly on the forest floor.

Great tinamou

Tinamus major

Approximately 40 different species of tinamou occur from Mexico to the tip of South America. Like others of its kind, the great tinamou is difficult to observe, in spite of its size. These birds rarely fly unless there is danger close by, and they move quite quietly through the forest, where their coloration helps them to merge into the background. Their call consists of whistling notes, sometimes heard after dark. The nest is always well concealed in thick, inaccessible vegetation. The cock bird is believed to be largely responsible for incubating the eggs. The eggs themselves can vary quite widely in colour, even being violet in some cases. The chicks are able to move readily within a day of hatching. Their flight feathers grow rapidly, so that the young birds can fly when they are little bigger than a robin.

Identification: Large, plump appearance. Greyish-brown underparts, with a more olive hue across the back. White areas on throat, with chestnut feathering on the crown in many cases. Sexes are alike but hens may be larger. Young birds are darker in colour than adults.

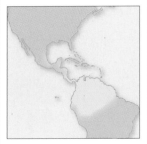

Distribution: From Mexico south to parts of Ecuador, Peru and Brazil, with approximately a dozen different subspecies being found throughout the area up to about 1,000m (3,280ft).
Size: 46cm (18in).
Habitat: Generally lowland areas in humid forests.
Nest: Leaf-lined scraping on the ground, often disguised in buttress roots.
Eggs: 6–7, glossy turquoise ranging to violet.
Food: Berries, seeds and invertebrates.

Andean guan

Penelope montagnii

These large birds are primarily arboreal by nature, living in groups of three to six individuals outside the breeding season. They tend to be encountered at higher altitudes than other guans, certainly in Colombia where they have been observed up to 3,500m (11,500ft). They sometimes leave the cover of dense forest in search of fruit, venturing into isolated trees where such food is plentiful. They usually forage in the branches, however, rather than on the ground. Andean guans have a loud honking call, which is heard more frequently during the breeding period. These birds have been heavily hunted, like related species, are shy, and avoid areas near human settlements.

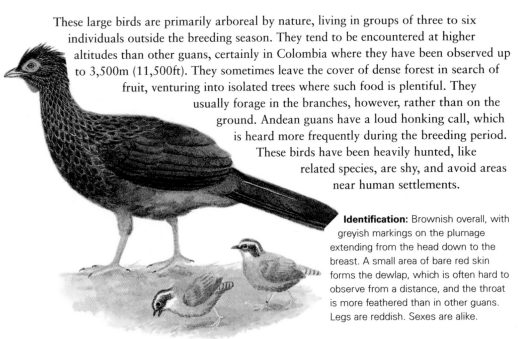

Identification: Brownish overall, with greyish markings on the plumage extending from the head down to the breast. A small area of bare red skin forms the dewlap, which is often hard to observe from a distance, and the throat is more feathered than in other guans. Legs are reddish. Sexes are alike.

Distribution: In the Andean region of Colombia, north-west Venezuela, Ecuador, Peru, and Bolivia. This species may extend as far south as north-western parts of Argentina, although this is doubtful.
Size: 61cm (24in).
Habitat: Forested areas at relatively high altitudes.
Nest: Platform of leaves and twigs.
Eggs: 1–3, white.
Food: Berries, other fruit and seeds.

Grey-winged trumpeter

Common trumpeter *Psophia crepitans*

Distribution: North-western South America eastward through to French Guiana.
Size: 61cm (24in).
Habitat: Rainforest.
Nest: Leaf-lined tree cavity.
Eggs: 6, white.
Food: Fruits, plant matter and invertebrates.

Trumpeters are a common sight around native American settlements, and are easily tamed if obtained young. They make useful watchdogs, uttering loud grunts as warning calls. They are also valued for their snake-killing abilities, and these reptiles may feature as part of their natural diet. The plumage on the head and neck is short and has a velvety texture. Their overall appearance resembles that of miniature rheas, although trumpeters retain four toes on each foot. Their legs are powerful, allowing them not just to run but also swim effectively. Trumpeters spend most of their time on the ground, although they prefer to roost in trees when not active after dark.

Identification: Plumage predominantly black, with purplish feathering at the base of the neck. The plumage on the head is very short and has a plush texture. Grey coloration is apparent on the wings. Upright stance. Sexes are alike.

Great curassow

Crax rubra

Distribution: Mexico southward to Colombia and Ecuador.
Size: 91cm (36in).
Habitat: Lowland forest.
Nest: Platform off the ground.
Eggs: 2, rough-shelled, white.
Food: Plant matter.

The curassows tend to be more terrestrial than other cracids, although they invariably roost off the ground. Pairs also nest off the ground, sometimes at heights of up to 30m (100ft) in a suitable tree. Great curassows are most likely to be encountered individually or in pairs, rather than in larger groups. Cocks of this species have a deep, booming call and also utter high-pitched whistling notes. Their range has contracted in some areas, such as along the Pacific coast of Colombia, because of the combined effect of overhunting and deforestation. In areas where great curassows are not persecuted, these large birds are quite conspicuous.

Identification: Mainly black, with a white abdomen and undertail coverts. Striking yellow knob on the upper bill, which is absent in hens and immatures. Hens are mainly chestnut, but with black-and-white barring on the head and neck. Those from Central America may be darker and display more barring.

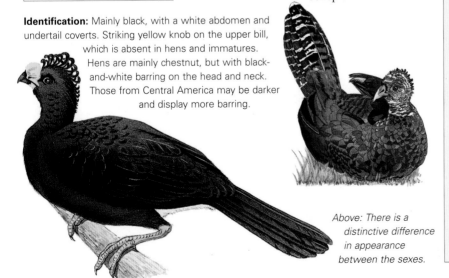

Above: There is a distinctive difference in appearance between the sexes.

Plain chachalaca (*Ortalis vetula*):
64cm (25in)
Southern Texas in the USA south to Mexico and Nicaragua, as well as the Honduran island of Utila. Predominantly brownish, with bare, blue skin on the face and a flesh-coloured throat. Relatively noisy and quite adaptable by nature, in the face of primary deforestation. Sexes are alike.

Band-tailed guan (*Penelope argyrotis*):
66cm (26in)
Found in parts of Venezuela and Colombia. Large red dewlap under the throat and frosty white plumage on the sides of the head. Has a distinctive pale tail band not seen in other guans, and also has a stocky appearance compared with related guans. Predominantly brown with white streaking on the breast and mantle. Sexes are alike.

Wattled curassow (*Crax globulosa*):
89cm (35in)
South-eastern Colombia south to northern Bolivia and the western upper Amazonian region of Brazil. Predominantly black with a curly crest. Two distinctive red wattles at the base of the lower mandible, with a similar knob on the top of the bill at its base. These swellings are sometimes yellowish. Sometimes a marbled plumage patterning is evident over the wings. Hens have no wattles or knob, and have a white rather than chestnut belly and undertail coverts.

Giant antpitta (*Grallaria gigantea*):
27cm (10½in)
Occurs in parts of Colombia and Ecuador, and lives on the forest floor. Reddish brown with black barring on the underparts. Olive-brown upperparts and greyish suffusion on the head. Sexes are alike.

WOODLAND GAME BIRDS

A variety of game birds are found in the woodlands of North America, extending southward. The most significant is undoubtedly the wild turkey, the original ancestor of all modern domestic strains worldwide. Grouse also occur in this region. All are shy and wary by nature, relying on cover to elude detection, and seeking their food at ground level. A number migrate.

American woodcock

Scolopax minor

The mottled appearance of the American woodcock provides exceptional camouflage when on the ground in forests, where these birds blend in with the leaf litter. They tend to rely on camouflage to escape danger, but if flushed will take off with a noisy flapping of their wings, flying not in a straight line but swerving from side to side. The courtship display of these woodcocks is spectacular, with males taking off and flying almost vertically before circling and plunging down again. The nest is sited in a secluded spot, and even the eggs blend in with the leaves, which are used to line the nest scrape. American woodcocks have relatively large eyes, which help them see well in the gloom of the forest. The position of the eyes high on the head also gives them excellent vision, so it is difficult for predators to creep up on them. The long bill is used to extract worms from muddy ground and catch insects.

Distribution: Ranges from Newfoundland and southern Manitoba in Canada down through eastern parts of the USA as far as Texas, Florida and the Gulf coast. Overwinters in these southerly areas.
Size: 28cm (11in).
Habitat: Wet woodland.
Nest: On the ground.
Eggs: 4, buff with brown spots.
Food: Invertebrates including earthworms and insects of various kinds.

Identification: Pale buff sides to the face, a barred crown, and grey above the bill and around the throat. A grey stripe extends down the edge of the wings, with a broader grey area across the wings. The rest of the back is mottled. Pale rufous-brown underparts, with the undersides of flight feathers grey, and a black band across a very short tail. Long, tapering bill. Sexes are alike.

Wilson's snipe

Gallinago delicata

Not easy to observe, Wilson's snipe tends to feed either at sunrise or toward dusk, probing the ground with jerky movements of its stocky bill. It remains out of sight for most of the day. If surprised in the open these birds will sometimes freeze in the hope of avoiding detection, relying on their cryptic plumage to provide camouflage. More commonly they take off in a zigzag fashion, flying quite low and fast before plunging back down into suitable cover. Cocks perch and call loudly on their display grounds in the far north. When plummeting down as part of their display flight, the movement of air through their tail feathers creates a distinctive hooting sound, which has been likened to the call of the boreal owl. They migrate south in the fall, flying in flocks under cover of darkness. Subsequently they split up and forage separately, which helps to conceal their presence.

Identification: Pale buff stripe runs down the centre of the crown, with pale stripes above and below the eyes. Dark mottled plumage on chest and wings. Blackish stripes on sides of the body, with white underparts. Wings have white stripes, tail is rufous. Long, pointed bill. Sexes alike.

Distribution: Breeds right across northern Alaska and Canada, southward to New Jersey in the east and California in the west. Wintering grounds extend up to British Columbia, to western and south-eastern USA, and all along the Gulf coast.
Size: 28cm (11in).
Habitat: Lightly wooded areas, and fields offering plenty of concealment.
Nest: Hidden in grass.
Eggs: 4, olive-brown with black spots.
Food: Mainly invertebrates.

Wild turkey

Meleagris gallopavo

These large members of the fowl family are difficult to spot in their natural woodland habitat because the barring on their plumage breaks up their outline very effectively to create good camouflage. Shafts of sunlight filtering through the trees highlight the natural iridescence in the plumage, with shades of green appearing on the feathering from some angles. The wild turkey is unmistakable, especially when the male erects his tail feathers into a fan-shape as part of his courtship display. The colour of his bare skin intensifies during the breeding season, and he often utters a loud gobbling call. Males, called stags, frequently live in the company of several females. It is only these wild turkeys that have rusty brown tips to their tail feathers, those of domestic turkeys being white.

Identification: Bare head, which is predominantly bluish. Has a prominent red beard extending down the throat, which is absent in hens. The body is bronzy brown in colour, with black barring on the wings and tail.

Distribution: Southern USA south into Mexico. It has a very patchy distribution that has given rise to numerous localized subspecies, especially in western parts of the range.
Size: 120cm (48in) cock; 91cm (36in) hen. Birds from the north are larger than those found further south.
Habitat: Wooded areas, including swampland.
Nest: Scrape on the ground.
Eggs: 8–15, buff with dark brown spots.
Food: Berries, seeds, and nuts, also invertebrates.

Spruce grouse (*Falcipennis canadensis*): 41cm (16in)
From Alaska south to northern parts of the neighbouring USA. Prominent red area above the eye. Forehead down to the throat and upper breast are black with a white border. White barring on the flanks. Greyish upperparts. Hens are much duller, lacking the red and black areas, and are significantly smaller in size.

Ruffed grouse (*Bonasa umbellus*): 46cm (18in)
Alaska and north-west Canada to central USA. Distinguishable by the slight crest and ruff of black or reddish-brown feathering on the neck. There are two colour phases; the reddish brown rather than grey phase predominates in south-west British Columbia. Hens have a shorter ruff and an incomplete tail band.

Dusky grouse (*Dendragapus obscurus*): 50cm (20in)
Western North America, from south-east Alaska down to San Francisco Bay. Also further inland in the Sierra Nevada and Rocky Mountains. Cock has sooty-grey plumage from the back of the neck to the yellow-orange comb on the head. Mottled brown markings with an inflatable neck sac apparent on the sides of the head, and surrounding plumage is white with brown edging. Brown plumage on the legs extends to the toes. Broad fan-shaped tail with whitish plumage around the vent. Hens much plainer, with mottled brown plumage edged with white. Flight feathers brown, spotted with white. Broad brown subterminal band across the tail feathers.

Ocellated turkey

Meleagris ocellata

Ocellated turkeys are shy, and despite their relatively large size are not easy to spot in the wild. However, the species has been domesticated in some parts, where birds are seen near settlements. They naturally live in groups, comprised of a single stag and several hens, and may emerge from wooded areas into clearings in search of food on the ground. If disturbed, they often run off rather than fly, as they are fairly clumsy in the air. When displaying, the stag inflates his wattle, which otherwise hangs down over his bill, and utters a call that has been likened to a motor being started. The nest is hidden in vegetation. The young grow rapidly but develop slowly, only gaining adult plumage at around three years old.

Distribution: Restricted to specific areas of Central America, such as the Yucatan Peninsula in Mexico, Belize and Guatemala.
Size: 102cm (40in) cock; 84cm (33in) hen.
Habitat: Largely deciduous woodland.
Nest: Scrape on the ground.
Eggs: 8–15, buff with brown markings.
Food: Seeds, berries and invertebrates.

Identification: Male has greenish-blue neck, underparts and back, merging with brown. Prominent copper wing patch. Whitish flight feathers. Broad tail with blue and coppery patches like ocelli. Pale blue skin on the head has warty areas. Female much smaller, with a pinkish bill. Young birds have greyish-brown feathers.

SPECIALIST FOREST-DWELLERS

Some of the smaller birds found in woodland environments tend to have the most specialized habits, as shown by the various birds featured here. Unfortunately, observing nocturnal species like the oilbird in the field, especially when they fly long distances, is difficult, but the widespread use of low-cost infra-red viewing equipment now gives a better insight into their behaviour than ever before.

Oilbird

Steatornis caripensis

Distribution: Western Panama through Colombia to Ecuador and Peru, and east to French Guiana.
Size: 48cm (19in).
Habitat: Caves and cliffs.
Nest: Made from regurgitated seed.
Eggs: 2–4, white with brown blotches.
Food: Fruit.

The oilbird is the only fruit-eating bird in the world that feeds at night. It spends its days roosting in the black interiors of caves. Oilbirds have large eyes that glow red when a light is shone at them. Like bats, they rely on a navigation system known as echolocation to avoid collisions with objects when flying around in darkness. The system involves the bird uttering a constant series of high-pitched calls while in flight, and listening to the echoes that bounce back, to avoid flying into objects. Oilbirds fly up to 25km (16 miles) from their roosting caves in search of fruit each night. A keen sense of smell may help the birds to find ripe fruit, which they swallow whole and digest the next day.

Identification: Prominent hooked bill and very long wings. Rufous-brown upperparts with white spots edged with black running across the wings. Similar but smaller white-spotted patterning on the head and underparts, which are otherwise cinnamon-white. Long, tapering tail barred with black. Cock is greyer than the hen.

Great potoo

Nyctibius grandis

The potoo family, the Nyctibiidae, contains about seven species of nocturnal birds, all living in Central and South America, and in the West Indies. The group is named after the wailing cry of some species. All potoos feed mainly on insects. During the daytime, the large eyes of the great potoo are dark, but they take on an eerie orange glow at night when these birds become active. They hunt large flying insects on the wing, swooping down to catch them. During the day great potoos rest motionless on a tall branch in a hunched-up position. Their cryptic coloration provides good camouflage, helping to conceal their presence from enemies. They generally call only on moonlit nights, when their vocalizations comprise a series of guttural notes followed by louder, harsh, grating sounds. When breeding, the hen does not build a nest but simply lays her single egg in a suitable hollow in a tree where it cannot roll away.

Distribution: Panama south to Peru and southern Brazil.
Size: 51cm (20in).
Habitat: Gallery forest, especially at the edges.
Nest: Knotholes or similar hollows in trees.
Eggs: 1, white with darker markings.
Food: Mainly insects.

Identification: Large birds with variable coloration. Typically greyish-white to brown upperparts, and white underparts that are finely barred. Black spots on the breast. Tail feathers are barred with black borders. Sexes are alike.

Lyre-tailed nightjar (*Uropsalis lyra*): 76cm (30in) cock; 25cm (10in) hen
In highland areas of Colombia and Venezuela to Ecuador and Peru. Very distinctive ribbon-like tail, up to three times as long as the body. Brownish black with rufous barring and spots. Hens have shorter tails that lack the white tips.

Squirrel cuckoo (*Piaya cayana*): 43cm (17in)
Ranges from north-western Mexico south to Bolivia, Paraguay, Argentina and Uruguay, with 18 different races being recognized. Chestnut-brown head and wings, with greyish lower underparts. Long tail with pale tips to the feathers. Bare skin around the eyes is red in birds found east of the Andes Mountains; greenish yellow elsewhere. Sexes are alike.

Scaly-throated leaftosser (*Sclerurus guatemalensis*): 18cm (7in)
Extends from south-eastern parts of Mexico down the Atlantic side of Central America to the western coast of Colombia and western Ecuador in South America. Predominantly dark brownish overall, with relatively inconspicuous paler markings on the throat. Long, straight, dark bill. Dark legs and tail. Sexes are alike.

Long-billed gnatwren (*Ramphocaenus melanurus*): 12cm (5in)
Extends from south-eastern parts of Mexico down through South America as far south as north-eastern Peru in the west, and south-eastern Brazil. Long narrow bill, with white throat offset against cinnamon plumage on the face and underparts. The vent area is also whitish. Upperparts greyish, with a relatively long, narrow tail, marked black and white.

Ovenbird

Seiurus aurocapilla

These unusual warblers spend most of their time on the ground searching for insect prey, walking rather than hopping like most birds. Ovenbirds prefer mature areas of woodland, where there is relatively little undergrowth. Their presence may be revealed by their song, which sounds like the word "teacher" repeated constantly. Their precise song pattern varies with region, with several dialects being identified. The ovenbird gets its name from the appearance of its nest, a domed structure that has been likened to a Dutch oven. The nest is located on the ground and made from a pile of leaves and other vegetation. The entrance hole is to the side, and the interior is lined with grass. Some males have more than one mate, while on occasions several males have been observed feeding a brood of chicks.

Identification: Rufous stripe edged with black extending back from the bill and up the crown. Upperparts are olive brown, throat is white with a dark stripe running down the sides from the lower corner of the bill. Dark streaking on the underparts, including the flanks. Narrow ring of white feathers encircles each eye. Bill darker on the upper surface, paler below, and the legs and feet are pinkish. Sexes are alike.

Distribution: Breeds in North America from western and central parts of Canada to the east coast and south to South Carolina and northern Gulf states. Moves southward for the winter, around the Caribbean including much of Central America down to northern parts of South America.
Size: 14cm (5¹/₂in).
Habitat: Mature woodland.
Nest: Dome of vegetation.
Eggs: 4–5, white with brown spots.
Food: Invertebrates.

Tawny-throated leaftosser

Sclerurus mexicanus

Relatively little is known about the habits of this group of forest birds, which were previously more commonly known as leafscrapers. Their current name is a more accurate reflection of their lifestyle, however, as they use their long bill to grab and flip over leaves on the forest floor in search of invertebrate prey lurking underneath. Leaftossers spend most of their time at ground level, normally flying a short distance if disturbed, calling loudly, before settling onto a low branch, bobbing up and down there at first. Tawny-throated leaftossers are most likely to be found in dense vegetation, where they are usually observed on their own. Pairs of these birds will breed in banks, digging out their nesting tunnel, which terminates in a larger chamber at the end, where the female lays her eggs.

Identification: Brown head and wings. Relatively short brown tail feathers with elongated tips. Throat and chest are chestnut in colour, as is the rump. Sexes are alike.

Distribution: Various populations occur from eastern parts of Mexico down through Central America and over a wide area of South America, from Colombia to French Guiana and the eastern coast of Brazil, south into Ecuador and Peru, and down to Bolivia.
Size: 16cm (6¹/₂in).
Habitat: Humid forest.
Nest: A burrow.
Eggs: 2, white.
Food: Invertebrates.

MACAWS

The macaws include the largest and most spectacular members of the entire parrot family. All 17 species are characterized by their long tails and the prominent, largely unfeathered areas of skin on their faces. Their distribution ranges from Central America through to the southern parts of South America.

Blue-and-gold macaw

Blue-and-yellow macaw *Ara ararauna*

Distribution: Eastern Panama and Colombia south through Amazonia to south-eastern Brazil, Bolivia, and Paraguay.
Size: 75–83cm (30–33in).
Habitat: Forested areas near water.
Nest: Tall hollow tree.
Eggs: 2, white.
Food: Nuts, fruits and seeds.

Wooded areas are the normal habitat of these colourful macaws, which usually feed in the treetops. Their presence there is revealed by their loud, raucous calls, which are also uttered when the birds are in flight. Although normally observed in pairs or small family groups, blue-and-gold macaws do form larger flocks, consisting of up to 25 individuals on occasion. They are most likely to be observed during the morning and again at dusk, as they fly back and forth between their roosting and feeding sites. One of the main factors restricting the distribution of these macaws is the availability of suitable palms as nesting sites. They are quite adaptable in their feeding habits, eating a wide variety of plant matter and even sometimes seeking nectar from flowers.

Identification: Predominantly blue upperparts, with contrasting golden-yellow underparts. Greenish area on the forehead above the bill. Bare, unfeathered white skin on the sides of the face, with small tracts of black feathers there and a black band beneath the throat. Sexes are alike. The rare Bolivian blue-throated macaw (*A. glaucogularis*) is similar in its overall coloration, but can be distinguished by its prominent blue cheek patches.

Red-and-green macaw

Green-winged macaw *Ara chloroptera*

As in related species, these large macaws display isolated feather tracts across the bare areas of skin on each side of their face. Rather like fingerprints, this feature is sufficiently distinctive to enable individuals to be identified at close quarters. Young birds display odd maroon rather than crimson feathers there, and also have dark eyes. Adult pairs remain together throughout the year, although they may not breed annually. They can live for more than 50 years. Red-and-green macaws usually feed in the canopy, and are sometimes seen there in the company of blue-and-gold macaws. These parrots are able to use their feet like hands to grasp their food. Pairs frequently engage in mutual preening when resting in trees during the hottest part of the day.

Identification: Rich crimson feathering predominates, with both bluish and distinctive green feathering evident on the lower part of the wings. Sexes are alike.

Distribution: Eastern Panama in Central America south across the Amazon Basin to Bolivia, Brazil, and northern Argentina. Now very rare in Panama and also at the southern tip of its range in Argentina, where there never appears to have been an established population.
Size: 73–95cm (29–37in).
Habitat: Forested areas.
Nest: Large hollow trees, sometimes on cliff faces.
Eggs: 2, white.
Food: Fruits, seeds and nuts.

Spix's macaw (Little blue macaw, *Cyanopsitta spixii*, E): 56cm (22in)
The last known survivor of this species in the wild disappeared toward the end of 2000, so the future of the species now depends on captive breeding of approximately 60 individuals surviving in collections around the world. These small macaws have only ever been sighted iin northern Bahia, north-eastern Brazil. Bluish plumage with a dark, greyish area of bare skin on the face. Sexes are alike.

Great green macaw (Buffon's macaw, *Ara ambiguus*, E): 77–85cm (30–33in)
There are several widely separated populations throughout its wide range, which extends from eastern Honduras to western parts of Colombia. Mainly green plumage with a prominent area of red plumage above the bill. Whitish facial skin. Blue flight feathers and a long reddish tail with a blue tip. Sexes are alike.

Blue-winged macaw (Illiger's macaw, *Primolius maracana*, E): 39cm (15in)
Deforestation has led to the disappearance of these small macaws from Argentina. They occur in wooded parts of Brazil, south of the Amazon, and to the south in Paraguay. Mainly green, with white skin around the eyes and a red forehead and rump. Some red on the belly. Sexes are alike.

Red-bellied macaw (*Orthopsittaca manilata*): 46cm (18in)
Northern South America, including Trinidad, south to Bolivia, Peru, and north-east Brazil. Mainly green, with a bluer head and flight feathers. Bare yellowish area of skin surrounding the eyes. Reddish belly. Sexes are alike.

Red-and-gold macaw

Scarlet macaw *Ara macao*
(E: Central America)

There are two different populations, with birds of Central American origin being recognizable by the blue tips to the prominent yellow feathers on the wings. Red-and-gold macaws are sometimes encountered in certain areas with other related multicoloured macaws, such as red and green macaws, although they do not appear to hybridize in the wild. Such mixed groups are most commonly observed congregating to feed on the soil of mineral-rich cliffs in parts of Peru. The mud that the parrots consume here is believed to neutralize plant toxins that they absorb as part of their diet. It appears that, certainly within some parts of their distribution, these macaws move seasonally in search of more plentiful feeding opportunities. They eat a considerable variety of foods, feeding in trees, rather than on or near the ground, which enables them to range widely across Central and South America.

Identification: The plumage of these large macaws is scarlet-red rather than crimson, which helps to distinguish them from the red-and-green macaw. Bright yellow plumage on the wings provides a further simple means of recognition. Sexes are alike.

Distribution: Southern Mexico to Panama; widely distributed across the Amazonian region to Bolivia.
Size: 80–96cm (31–38in).
Habitat: Forested areas and savanna.
Nest: Hollow chamber in a tall tree.
Eggs: 2, white.
Food: Fruits, seeds and nuts.

Hyacinthine macaw

Hyacinth macaw *Anodorhynchus hyacinthinus* (E)

These vividly coloured macaws are the biggest parrots in the world. They fly with slow wingbeats and are usually seen in pairs or small family groups. Young hyacinthine macaws are unlikely to breed until they are seven years or even older, but these are potentially long-lived birds, with a life expectancy that can be measured in decades. They face relatively few predators, although in spite of their size and very powerful bills, they can fall victim to harpy eagles. In some areas hyacinthine macaws can be seen flying after dark, when the moon is shining. They are often noisy by nature, uttering a wide range of calls.

Identification: Predominantly a distinctive, deep shade of glossy blue, with prominent areas of bare yellow skin encircling the eyes and also present on the sides of the lower bill. Sexes are alike.

Distribution: North-eastern Brazil, extending south and westward to parts of Bolivia and Paraguay.
Size: 90–100cm (35–39in).
Habitat: Areas where Mauritia and other palms are growing.
Nest: Either a hollow tree or among rocks on inaccessible cliff faces.
Eggs: 2, white.
Food: Palm nuts, fruits and even water snails.

CONURES

Conures are a group of parakeets whose distribution is confined to parts of Central and South America. Their unusual name comes from the old generic name Conurus. *They are quite social birds by nature and are often seen in noisy flocks, congregating in large numbers where food is plentiful, and even invading agricultural regions on occasion.*

Queen of Bavaria conure

Golden conure Golden parakeet *Guaruba guarouba* (E)

Ranking among the most colourful of all conures, this species is most commonly seen in small groups. It occurs in regions where the forest is not subject to seasonal flooding, and so is absent from areas immediately adjacent to the Amazon River. Females sometimes share the same nest hole, with chicks of widely different ages being reared inside. The nesting chamber can be surprising deep, extending down for at least 2m (6¹/₂ft). Deforestation is having an adverse effect on the numbers of these beautiful parrots, since they are dependent on older, more mature trees for nesting sites. Small flocks will sometimes descend to feed in fields, taking crops such as ripening maize, but they more commonly eat a variety of rainforest fruits and flowers.

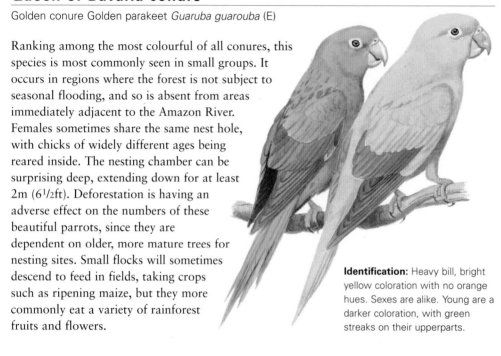

Identification: Heavy bill, bright yellow coloration with no orange hues. Sexes are alike. Young are a darker coloration, with green streaks on their upperparts.

Distribution: Centred on the Amazonia region of Brazil, south of the Amazon, and may range further afield.
Size: 36cm (14in).
Habitat: Rainforest extending to the edge of cultivated areas.
Nest: Cavity within a tree, up to 30m (100ft) above the ground.
Eggs: 2–4, white.
Food: Fruit and seeds, occasionally making raids on maize fields.

Sun conure

Sun parakeet *Aratinga solstitalis*

The fiery coloration of these conures explains their common name. They are very social by nature, but in spite of their bright plumage, they can be hard to spot when roosting quietly on branches. When in flight, however, their sharp, harsh calls are often heard, drawing attention to the flock as it passes overhead. The coloration of sun conures often differs slightly between individuals, with some being of a brighter shade than others. The pattern of coloration is quite variable too, so it is often possible to distinguish between individuals in a flock. Large numbers of these conures may feed together on trees, and they have also been observed eating the fruits of cacti on the ground. It is possible that they move through their range according to the season, splitting up into smaller groups for much of the year.

Identification: The orange hues on the yellow plumage, black bill and smaller size distinguish this conure from Queen of Bavaria conure. Sexes are alike. Young are much duller, being largely green.

Distribution: Occurs in north-eastern parts of South America, being found mainly in parts of Guyana, Surinam and northern areas of Brazil. May also occur in French Guiana to the east.
Size: 30cm (12in).
Habitat: Palm groves, savanna, and dry forest.
Nest: In hollows in palms or other trees.
Eggs: 3–4, white.
Food: Berries, other fruits, seeds and similar items. Sometimes cacti fruits.

Blue-crowned conure (Blue-crowned parakeet, *Thectocercus acuticaudatus*): 36cm (14in)
Occurs in separate populations in north-east, east and central-southern parts of South America. Green with dull bluish coloration on the crown. Sexes are alike.

Nanday conure (Nanday parakeet, *Aratinga nenday*): 30cm (12in)
The range of this conure extends from south-eastern Bolivia via parts of Brazil and Paraguay to Argentina. The entire head, including the bill, is black in colour, with a variable band of reddish feathers bordering the black. There is a pale blue wash in the vicinity of the throat, and red plumage at the top of the legs. The flight feathers are dark blue, with the underside of the tail being dark. The remainder of the body is green, slightly lighter on the rump and underparts. Sexes are alike. Blue wash less evident in young birds.

Dusky-headed conure (Dusky-headed parakeet, *Aratinga weddellii*): 28cm (11in)
The dusky-headed conure ranges from south-eastern parts of Colombia southward to eastern Bolivia. Dark, scaly-grey coloration is seen on the head, with the bill being black. The pale-coloured iris is surrounded by white peri-orbital skin. The flight feathers are dark.

Green conure (Green parakeet, *Psittacara holochlorus*): 32cm (12¹/₂in)
Extends from the far south of Texas in the USA south through Central America, occurring in eastern and southern Mexico south to northern Nicaragua. Predominantly green with a prominent white eye ring of bare skin and a pale bill. May be traces of yellow on the edge of the wings. The southern species, known as the red-throated conure or parakeet (*P. rubritorquis*), is easily distinguishable by its reddish throat.

Scarlet-fronted conure

Wagler's conure Scarlet-fronted parakeet *Psittacara wagleri*

Most conures of the genus *Psittacara* are predominantly green in colour, with the brighter coloration on their heads serving to distinguish the individual species. Scarlet-fronted conures are noisy by nature, and their call notes resemble the braying of a donkey. They often congregate in large flocks consisting of as many as 300 individuals. Cliffs are favoured both as roosting and breeding sites, and are an important factor in determining the precise distribution of these conures within their range. Flocks of scarlet-fronted conures sometimes descend into agricultural areas, where they are capable of causing serious damage to cultivated crops.

Identification: Red plumage may extend over the top of the head to just behind the eyes, depending on the race. Scattered red feathering may also be present on the throat. Thighs are red. Sexes are alike. Young birds have greatly reduced area of red on the head.

Distribution: Discontinuous distribution down the western side of South America in the Andes Mountains, from Venezuela to Peru.
Size: 36cm (14in).
Habitat: Most often in forested areas with cliffs nearby.
Nest: Often located on cliff faces.
Eggs: 3–4, white.
Food: A variety of wild and cultivated seeds and fruits, including maize crops.

El Oro conure

El Oro parakeet *Pyrrhura orcesi*

The *Pyrrhura* conures are sometimes known as the scaly-breasted conures because of the characteristic barring across their chest. Most of the species have restricted areas of distribution, and the El Oro conure was not discovered until 1980. It is believed to have a very restricted range, which may be no more than 100km (60 miles) long and 10km (6 miles) wide. There has been relatively little deforestation in this area, and the population appears to be quite stable where the forest is undisturbed. These conures are most likely to be observed feeding in the forest canopy, or flying overhead calling. They are typically seen in groups numbering from four to 12 individuals.

Identification: Red on the crown and bend of the wing. Chest barring is relatively indistinct in this particular species. Pale bill. Sexes are alike. Young birds display less red.

Distribution: Apparently centred on El Oro province, Ecuador.
Size: 22cm (9in).
Habitat: Cloud forest between 600 and 1,300m (2,000–4,300ft)
Nest: Probably tree hollows.
Eggs: Not recorded.
Food: Fruits and seeds.

CONURES AND PARROTS

In America, parrots are generally restricted to Central and South America, where they range widely, although they used to occur regularly in North America too. The northern continent was home to the now extinct Carolina parakeet, a species thought to have vanished around 1920. It should be noted that not all members of this family lay their eggs in hollow trees.

Thick-billed parrot

Rhynchopsitta pachyrhyncha (E)

Distribution: Restricted largely to western and central parts of Mexico. Range formerly extended north into New Mexico and Arizona.
Size: 38cm (15in).
Habitat: Coniferous (pine) forests.
Nest: In a tree hole.
Eggs: 2–4, white.
Food: Pine seeds and other vegetable matter.

Thick-billed parrots formerly ranged northward from Mexico to New Mexico and Arizona, and particularly to the Chiricahua Mountains in the USA. However, they have been severely affected by the clearance of pine forests, since pine cones provide a major source of food and the trees afford them nesting sites. Their breeding cycle is also closely tied to the ripening of the cones, which provide a plentiful supply of soft food for rearing the young. Their calls are very loud and raucous, and are audible at distances of up to 3km (2 miles). This can make it difficult to locate their precise whereabouts within a particular area. Attempts have recently been made to reintroduce these endangered parrots to Arizona, using individuals which had been illegally brought into the USA as well as captive-bred birds, but this has not proved entirely successful.

Identification: Large, stocky build. Mainly green, with a scarlet area on the forehead extending behind the eyes, which are encircled by white peri-orbital skin. Scarlet also on shoulders, leading edges of wings and legs. Heavy black bill, with grey legs and feet. Sexes are alike. Young birds are much greener, but with a red-brown band over the bill, and grey skin encircling the eyes.

Monk parakeet

Quaker parakeet *Myiopsitta monachus*

Identification: Grey on forehead, crown, and down to underparts, which may show barring. Rest of underparts yellowish green, with darker upperparts and bluish-purple flight feathers. Sexes are alike. Young birds greener on the forehead.

The breeding habits of the monk parakeet are very different to other parrots. This has helped this species to spread beyond its native range. Rather than nesting in tree holes, these conures construct their own roosts out of sticks. Pairs often nest communally in these structures, which are added to over time, and may eventually become so large they collapse. Some nests accommodate 20 or more pairs, and weigh over 200kg (40lb). The entrance hole is directed downward, so that the birds fly in from below, making it harder for predators to gain access. A number of other species, including caracaras and storks, may take advantage of these substantial tree platforms to build their own nests on top.

Distribution: Extends from the central region of Bolivia, parts of Paraguay, and southern Brazil southward to central parts of Argentina. Also introduced to various locations including Puerto Rico in the Caribbean, and parts of the USA.
Size: 30cm (12in).
Habitat: Dry, wooded areas.
Nest: Usually built of sticks.
Eggs: 4–6, white.
Food: Seeds, vegetable matter.

Patagonian conure

Burrowing parrot *Cyanoliseus patagonus*

Occasionally found in large flocks of up to a thousand birds, these conures can inflict serious damage in agricultural areas, especially when grain is ripening. In open country they are seen in groups perching on telephone lines, calling loudly, especially when alarmed. Patagonian conures nest communally in holes in either sandstone or limestone cliffs. Their breeding season varies through their range, with birds returning to nest sites in Argentina in September, as the peak laying period there is November and December. Most of these birds leave again by April, moving north for the southern winter. The distinctive Chilean race (*C. p. bloxami*) is bigger and has more extensive whitish areas on the sides of the breast, which often create a collar.

Identification: Mainly olive brown on the head and upperparts, with blue flight feathers. White skin encircles the eye. Underparts are rich yellow, with a reddish central area. Bill is black, legs pinkish. Sexes are alike. Newly fledged young have mainly white bills, with a blackish central stripe.

Distribution: South-eastern South America, centred on Argentina but also present in Uruguay. A small, distinctive, residual population also occurs in central Chile.
Size: 45cm (18in).
Habitat: Wooded areas and more open country.
Nest: In burrows.
Eggs: 2–4, white.
Food: Seeds and nuts.

Austral conure (Austral parakeet, *Enicognathus ferrugineus*): 33cm (13in)
Chile and Argentina down to Tierra del Fuego. Mainly green, with darker upperparts. A reddish area evident on the belly, with a smaller area above the bill. Body plumage is barred with dark edging. The tail is a dull reddish shade, with the bill dark on its upper surface. Sexes are alike. Young birds less brightly coloured overall.

Maroon-fronted parrot (*Rhynchopsitta terrisi*): 45cm (18in)
Restricted to the Sierra Madre Oriental, north-eastern Mexico. Similar to the thick-billed parrot, with a mainly green body. Red feathering on the leading edges of the wings, shoulders, and at the top of the legs. Dark maroon patch on the forehead. Sexes are alike. Young birds have a brownish rather than black bill.

Golden-plumed conure (Golden-plumed parakeet, *Leptosittaca branickii*, E): 35cm (14in)
Andean region in forested areas. Recognizable by elongated, tufted band of yellow plumage under the eyes; rest of the plumage is green. Orangish suffusion on the breast. Sexes are alike.

Yellow-eared parrot (*Ognorhynchus icterotis*, E): 42cm (16½in)
North Andean region of Ecuador and Colombia. Bright yellow plumage on the forehead extends to the lower bill and past the eyes. Yellowish suffusion on the underparts, while undersides of the tail feathers are rufous. Remainder of the body green. Dark, heavy bill, with narrow whitish area of skin encircling the eyes. Sexes are alike.

Slender-billed conure

Slender-billed parakeet *Enicognathus leptorhynchus*

The elongated upper bill of these conures is used to dig for edible roots. It is also used to split open the tough-cased nuts of the monkey-puzzle tree. Slender-billed conures live in flocks with a well-defined structure. When the flock is feeding, one bird perches nearby and alerts its companions by calling loudly if danger threatens. Large numbers gather at their roosting grounds, calling as dusk falls. Slender-billed conures nest communally, with several pairs occupying hollows in the same tree. Occasionally they lay on cliff faces and are even known to build nests of sticks in bamboo or trees. This species was thought to have declined as a result of the deadly Newcastle disease, which can spread from flocks of chickens, but numbers now appear stable.

Distribution: Occurs on the western side of Chile extending from Mocha Island, off Bio Bio, northward to Santiago.
Size: 42cm (16½in).
Habitat: Wooded areas.
Nest: In a tree hole.
Eggs: 5–6, white.
Food: Seeds and roots.

Identification: A vivid red area extends back from the forehead through the eyes, and a red patch is present on the belly between the legs. Apart from the dull reddish tail feathers, remainder of the body is green with darker barring, which is often most noticeable on the head. Has a long, pointed upper mandible that extends well below the lower bill. Sexes alike. Young birds have less red coloration and a shorter upper mandible.

AMAZONS AND OTHER PARROTS

Amazon parrots are widely distributed in America from the extreme south of the USA to Mexico south through Central America and the Caribbean to South America. They are sometimes described as green parrots because this colour predominates in the plumage of many species. Pionus parrots are smaller in size, while the bizarre hawk-head is the only member of its group.

Imperial Amazon

Dominican Amazon *Amazona imperialis* (E)

The largest of all 27 species of Amazons, these parrots are also unusually coloured because most Amazons are predominantly green. It is sometimes seen in the company of the red-necked Amazon, and both are most likely to be seen in the vicinity of Dominica's highest mountain, Morne Diablotin. Hurricanes and agricultural development pose serious threats to the survival of these Amazons. Imperial Amazons have a wide range of call notes, which are often loud. Their alarm call has been likened to the sound of a trumpet. Pairs nest in hollow trees, but research suggests that they may breed only every two years or so, rather than annually, and then produce only a single chick.

Distribution: The Caribbean island of Dominica in the Lesser Antilles.
Size: 45cm (18in).
Habitat: Mountainous forest.
Nest: Tree cavities.
Eggs: 2, white.
Food: Fruits, nuts, seeds and palm shoots.

Identification: Green back. Purple neck and underparts. They can be confused with birds of prey, owing to their large size and flight pattern (wingbeats followed by gliding). Sexes are alike. Young have green on the cheeks.

Black-billed Amazon

Amazona agilis

Distribution: Central and eastern parts of Jamaica.
Size: 25cm (10in).
Habitat: Wet limestone forests and agricultural areas.
Nest: Tree cavities at least 18m (59ft) off the ground.
Eggs: 2, white.
Food: Fruits, seeds and nuts.

Two distinctive species of Amazon parrot inhabit the Caribbean island of Jamaica and sometimes associate together in mixed flocks. As its name suggests, the black-billed type can be easily distinguished from the yellow-billed (*A. collaria*) by its beak coloration. Breeding occurs between March and May. These Amazons are shy birds by nature, and rarely tolerate a close approach. Their green plumage helps to conceal them in forests, making them very hard to spot, especially because they will remain silent if disturbed. Sadly, deforestation in various parts of the island is thought to be having an adverse effect on their numbers.

Identification: Mainly dark green with a bluish hue on the top of the head, black ear coverts and black edging to the feathers on the back of the head. Black bill. Sexes are alike, although hens may have some green feathers on the edge of the wings. Young birds lack any trace of red feathering on the wing edges, and this area is entirely green.

Mealy Amazon (*Amazona farinosa*): 38cm (15in)
Range extends from Central America, home of the distinctive blue-crowned race (*A. f. guatemalae*) across much of northern South America to Brazil. A large, green Amazon with a particularly raucous call. Sexes are alike.

Red-necked Amazon (*Amazona arausiaca*, E): 40cm (16in)
Restricted to the Caribbean island of Dominica. Distinguished from the imperial Amazon by its predominantly green coloration and distinctive red area of plumage across the throat, often extending to the upper breast. Sexes are alike.

Tucuman Amazon (Alder parrot, *Amazona tucumana*): 30cm (12in)
Occurs in the eastern Andean region of Bolivia and Argentina. Predominantly green overall, with black scalloping on the plumage, especially on the back. Red forehead and a red area on the upperwing. White peri-orbital skin and horn-coloured bill. Sexes are alike. Young birds have a much reduced red area on the head, and none on the wing.

Dusky pionus (*Pionus fuscus*): 24cm (9¹/₂in)
Occurs in lowland forests from the Colombian–Venezuelan border east to north-eastern Brazil. Unusual pinkish, purple and bluish-brown tones in its plumage. Sexes are alike.

Hawk-headed parrot

Red-fan parrot *Deroptyus accipitrinus*

Completely unique among parrots, the hawk-headed type displays a stunning ruff of blue-edged, claret-red feathers at the back of its neck, which it can raise like a fan as part of its display. These parrots may be seen in small groups outside the breeding season. They feed largely in the treetops rather than descending to the ground, and raise their young either in natural tree hollows or in old woodpecker nests. Hawk-heads are noisy parrots, possessing a wide array of call notes. They often call loudly and fan the ruff of feathers around their neck if alarmed.

Distribution: Northern South America, to the east of the Andes Mountains.
Size: 31cm (12in).
Habitat: Lowland rainforest.
Nest: Tree hollows, sometimes occupying old woodpecker nests.
Eggs: 2–3, white.
Food: Fruit, seeds, nuts and leaves.

Identification: These parrots fly quite slowly, with their tail feathers spread slightly apart. They may be confused with small hawks, thanks to the rounded tips of the wings and tail. Green back, wings and tail. Sexes are alike. Young have some green feathering on the crown.

Blue-headed pionus

Blue-headed parrot *Pionus menstruus*

The most widely distributed of the eight members of the *Pionus* genus, and one of the commonest New World parrots, the blue-headed is often seen either singly or in pairs, rather than in flocks. They do congregate in larger numbers in certain mineral-rich areas, consuming the soil in the company of other parrots. The mineral-rich soil is thought to neutralize toxins absorbed from their food, which is usually gathered in the forest canopy, although they occasionally raid maize fields. Blue-headed pionus are sometimes observed flying quite high and fast in a loose formation, when they become more conspicuous than many parrots. They often call loudly when in flight.

Identification: Rich dark blue head with black ear coverts. Otherwise green plumage overall. Bill has reddish markings on the sides. Sexes are alike. Young birds have mainly green heads.

Distribution: Two separate populations: from southern Costa Rica to northern South America; also present over a wide area of central South America east of the Andes.
Size: 28cm (11in).
Habitat: Lowland tropical forest, into agricultural areas.
Nest: Tree cavities, or nest sites created by other birds.
Eggs: 2–4, white.
Food: Seeds, fruit and nuts, and sometimes maize.

SMALLER PARROTS AND PARAKEETS

The parrots of South America display a great range in size, from large macaws down to the small parrotlets that are often not much larger than the width of a human hand. Small species are often the hardest to spot, especially in a rainforest setting, because their coloration as well as their size helps to conceal their presence in this habitat.

Vulturine parrot

Pyrilia vulturina

One of the most unusual of all parrots in terms of appearance, the vulturine parrot is so called because of its essentially unfeathered head, which is covered with fine, bristle-like plumage. It has been suggested that this characteristic has developed to stop the feathering becoming matted by fruit juices when these parrots feed. Young birds, distinguishable by their fully feathered heads, are believed to congregate in flocks on their own until they pair off for breeding. The call of the vulturine parrot is also very different from that of other parrots, and has a watery tone. These parrots are found in areas of lowland forest, where their presence is easily overlooked since they are quiet by nature.

Identification: Bald, blackish face with adjacent yellow area of plumage around the neck. Sexes are alike. Young birds have fully feathered greenish heads but less yellow on the neck. Like that of the adults, the base of the bill (cere) is unfeathered and very prominent.

Distribution: South of the Amazon River in north-eastern Brazil, extending in the east to the coastal zone of Brazil.
Size: 23cm (9in).
Habitat: Lowland tropical rainforest.
Nest: Unrecorded, probably in tree hollows.
Eggs: Unrecorded.
Food: Berries, other fruit and seeds gathered in the forest canopy.

White-bellied caique

White-bellied parrot Green-thighed parrot *Pionites leucogaster*

Most likely to be seen in small flocks, white-bellied caiques are quite bold by nature, and often tolerate a relatively close approach before flying off rapidly. Their wings make an unusual whirring sound as they become airborne, and are quite small relative to the birds' size. If disturbed, white-bellied caiques call out loudly. Their other call notes are more varied, and some have been likened to the sounds of tapirs. They sometimes associate in groups with blue-headed pionus, and can often be observed close to waterways, being less common in drier parts of their range in the south. Three distinct races of the white-bellied caique are recognized through the range of this species. They can be identified by subtle differences in colour, such as the tail feathers and thighs being yellow rather than green.

Identification: White underparts and a yellow head distinguish this caique from other parrots in the region, notably the black-headed caique, which borders its northerly range. Sexes are alike. Young birds have a brown crown and nape.

Distribution: Occurs in parts of central South America, south of the Amazon from Brazil to south-eastern Peru and northern Bolivia. Has also been reported in the eastern part of Ecuador, but its occurrence there is still to be verified.
Size: 23cm (9in).
Habitat: Lowland rainforest.
Nest: Usually high up in a tree cavity.
Eggs: 2–4, white.
Food: Berries, other fruit, seeds and nuts.

Red-winged parrotlet

Blue-fronted parrotlet *Touit dilectissima*

Distribution: Panama south into north-western South America where the species' precise range is still unclear. Extends south to near the Peruvian border.
Size: 15cm (6in).
Habitat: Wet forests, sometimes ranging up into cloud-forest areas.
Nest: Chamber located in arboreal termites' nests.
Eggs: Probably about 5, white.
Food: Berries, other fruit, blossoms and seeds.

The parrotlets can all be recognized by their small size and rather dumpy body shape, with short, squat tails. The red-winged type, like related parrotlets, is quiet and easily overlooked in the forest canopy. Although three separate populations of these inconspicuous parrotlets have been identified, it is possible that these are not actually isolated, although this species is considered to be scarce in Central America. Red-winged parrotlets feed and roost in small groups, eating seeds as well as whole fruit. They fly low over the trees, when their high-pitched calls are most likely to be heard. Their yellow underwing coverts are also conspicuous in flight.

Identification: Mainly green, with blue feathering on the front of the head. Pronounced areas of red feathering on the sides of the wings, reduced in hens. Young birds resemble hens, but their heads are predominantly green.

Spot-winged parrotlet (*Touit stictopterus*): 18cm (7in)
Scattered distribution in the eastern Andes, from Colombia to Peru, in mature, subtropical forests. Mainly green with blackish-brown area on the wings. Sexes are similar except that cocks have white, spot-like edging to some of the wing feathers.

Rusty-faced parrot (*Hapalopsittaca amazonina*): 23cm (9in)
Occurs at relatively high altitudes in the Andean cloud forests of Colombia and Venezuela. Mainly green, with yellow streaking on the sides of the heads, lacking in young birds. Sexes are alike.

Short-tailed parrot (*Graydidascalus brachyurus*): 23cm (9in)
Widely distributed along the Amazon and its tributaries, from Peru, Ecuador and Colombia in the west to French Guiana and Brazil. Predominantly green parrots with a plump appearance. Very noisy by nature. Often seen in large numbers on river islands. Sexes are alike.

Blue-bellied parrot (Purple-bellied parrot, *Triclaria malachitacea*): 28cm (11in)
Mainly south-eastern Brazil. Green overall, with a distinctive purplish patch extending from lower breast. Relatively broad, long tail. Horn-coloured bill. Hens lack the purplish colouring, though young birds may show traces of this patch.

Cobalt-winged parakeet

Blue-winged parakeet *Brotogeris cyanoptera*

Distribution: Western area of the Amazon Basin, from Venezuela to Bolivia.
Size: 18cm (7in).
Habitat: Forests and open areas where trees are available nearby for roosting.
Nest: Probably tree holes but may use arboreal termite mounds.
Eggs: 5, white.
Food: Fruit and seeds.

Identification: Predominantly green, with cobalt-blue flight feathers and an orange spot under the chin. Sexes are alike. Young birds have greyer bills.

The eight species of the *Brotogeris* group are represented in both Central and South America. They are quite dumpy birds, all of similar size, with relatively narrow tail feathers. Green usually predominates in their plumage. They tend to be noisy, social birds by nature. Cobalt-winged parakeets are fast on the wing. Although they are sometimes seen flying across open areas and clearings, they tend to spend more time in the forest canopy than other members of the group, where their size and coloration make them relatively hard to observe. They are most likely to be encountered in lowland forests, sometimes in areas where seasonal flooding occurs.

WOODPECKERS

These birds are highly adapted to living in woodlands, and are able to hop up vertical trunks supported by their rigid, prong-like tail feathers and their powerful feet and claws. The largest member of the family, the ivory-billed woodpecker (Campephilus principalis), which measures 50cm (20in), is now believed to be extinct in southeastern USA, with a tiny population surviving on Cuba.

Cream-coloured woodpecker

Celeus flavus

Distribution: Colombia and French Guiana south to Bolivia and Brazil.
Size: 28cm (11in).
Habitat: Wooded areas near water, ranging from mangrove to rainforest.
Nest: Tree hollow.
Eggs: 3, white.
Food: Invertebrates and possibly some vegetable matter.

In spite of their name, some of these woodpeckers are of a more yellowish shade than others, while buffish and cinnamon-white individuals are also known. Cream-coloured woodpeckers have a very distinctive call that sounds somewhat like a laugh. There is usually a close bond between members of a pair. These woodpeckers are likely to be encountered in a wide range of habitats, from mangrove swamps to savanna. They can also be found in agricultural areas, particularly coffee plantations, where they help to control insect pests.

Identification: Predominantly cream, although coloration can be quite variable, with an obvious crest. Crimson patches on the sides of the face. Wing coverts are brownish. Tail is black. Odd brown feathers may be apparent on the underparts. Hens lack the crimson plumage on the sides of the head.

Crimson-bellied woodpecker

Campephilus haematogaster

These large woodpeckers are not easy to spot, especially since they are more likely to be observed as individuals rather than as pairs or in larger groups. They are most commonly seen in the understorey, frequently quite low down on bigger trees in dense forest. They eat a variety of invertebrates, including the larvae of wood-boring beetles up to 15cm (6in) long, which they pull out from the bark using their strong, chisel-shaped bills. Crimson-bellied woodpeckers make a double rap when drumming, like related species, and have an alarm call that resembles a loud squeal. They tend to frequent relatively wet areas of montane habitat. The plumage of these woodpeckers typically appears less brightly coloured when it is worn, and the white barring on the undersides of the flight feathers can be seen only in flight.

Identification: Prominent area of red on the head. Two black stripes beneath, bordered by two yellowish-white stripes. The lower one is more extensive in hens, whose black feathering extends to the lower neck. Wings are black, rump is crimson. Underparts are crimson and black, and are blacker in the case of hens.

Distribution: Western Panama south to parts of Ecuador. Occurs in two apparently separate populations, with the nominate race ranging from eastern parts of Colombia south to Peru.
Size: 33cm (13in).
Habitat: Tropical forest.
Nest: Tree hollow.
Eggs: 2, white.
Food: Invertebrates.

Magellanic woodpecker (*Campephilus magellanicus*): 38cm (15in)
Found in southern parts of South America. The cock has a bright red head and crest, with a black body and white evident on the rump. The hen, in contrast, is almost completely black, apart from a greatly reduced area of red plumage around the base of the bill, which is otherwise greyish black. Young birds are similar to hens, but browner.

Guadeloupe woodpecker (*Melanerpes herminieri*): 29cm (11½in)
Restricted to the island of Guadeloupe in the southern Caribbean, though sometimes seen on Antigua. Predominantly black apart from slight reddish suffusion on the underparts, which is most apparent during the nesting period. Hens are similar, but with significantly shorter bills. Young birds duller overall.

Golden-naped woodpecker (*Melanerpes chrysauchen*): 19cm (7½in)
Costa Rica to Panama and northern Colombia. Distinctive golden-yellow nape and red crown, with black plumage extending from the sides of the head to the back, where there is a broad white stripe. Hens are less colourful overall. Often drums on wood with its bill.

Powerful woodpecker (*Campephilus pollens*): 37cm (14½in)
Andean region, from Colombia to Peru. Scarlet crest with white stripes extending from each side of the face over the wings, to create a V-shape. White back and rump. Underparts barred. Hens lack the scarlet on the head, and have darker underparts.

Black-backed woodpecker

Picoides arcticus

Ranging over a huge area, these woodpeckers are most likely to be seen where there are numerous dead pine trees, especially if the surrounding area is flooded. They often occur in groups, breeding together in close proximity where conditions are favourable. In some years, flocks may move further south than usual, occasionally crossing into the states of Nebraska, New Jersey, and Ohio in the USA. This type of movement, known as an irruption, is usually the result of a shortage of food.

Distribution: Canada and northern USA, from Alaska east to Newfoundland in the north and south to New York State and California.
Size: 24cm (9½in).
Habitat: Coniferous forest.
Nest: Tree hollow.
Eggs: 2–6, white.
Food: Mainly invertebrates, but also some vegetable matter, such as nuts.

Identification: Yellowish plumage on the head and crown, with two white stripes on each side of the face separated by an irregular, broad, black band. Wings and back are blackish, with some whitish feathering. The flanks of some birds are blacker than others, depending on the subspecies. The short inner hind toe, equivalent to the thumb, is missing, helping these birds to climb vertically. Hens are smaller with no yellow on the crown. Young birds are generally browner in colour, but with more white plumage on the wings. Markings on the underparts are not as clear as those of adults.

Red-headed woodpecker

Melanerpes erythrocephalus

These woodpeckers eat a wide range of plant and animal foods, and their diet is influenced by the season. They are unusual in that they hunt not only by clambering over the bark of trees, but also by hawking insects in flight. They will even swoop down onto the ground and hop along there seeking prey. Red-headed woodpeckers also raid the nests of other birds, seizing both eggs and chicks, as well as catching mice. In northern parts of their range, these woodpeckers often migrate southward during the colder months of the year, seeking plentiful supplies of acorns and beech nuts when other foods are in short supply. They also lay down stores of food, concealing larger insects in cavities or hiding them under the bark, and returning to eat them later.

Distribution: Canada and the USA, from Manitoba and southern Ontario in the north southward to Florida.
Size: 24cm (9½in).
Habitat: Open woodland.
Nest: Tree hollow.
Eggs: 4–10, white.
Food: Plant and animal matter.

Identification: Scarlet plumage covering the head, bordered by a narrow band of black feathering. White underparts, bluish-black coloration on the back, part of the wings, and the tail. Sexes are alike. Young birds are much browner overall, including the head.

OTHER TREE-CREEPING BIRDS

Members of this group of birds are to be found in woodland areas throughout America. Those living in the far north, where the climate can be harsh and invertebrates are often in short supply, lay down food stores to help them survive the winter period. A number of unique and localized species are also to be found on islands in the Caribbean.

Acorn woodpecker

Melanerpes formicivorus

These lively woodpeckers are typically found in oak forests, living in groups of up to 15 individuals. The colony creates special food stores, sometimes described as granaries, where they store acorns for use when food is in short supply. It can take years to build up these stores, which can involve the construction of as many as 50,000 holes in trees throughout the birds' territory. Such is their dependence on this food source that the size of the acorn crop has a direct effect on the number of woodpeckers living in the area. Food storage of this type is far more common in North American populations, since those occurring nearer the equator have a much wider range of foods available throughout the year. The nesting period also varies according to latitude, beginning in March in North America. Family groups will defend the nest site and also provide food for the chicks, which may include small lizards and similar creatures.

Identification: This species has a black area encircling the front of the face, with a white band behind which encircles the eyes. Black and white streaking is evident on the breast, with the remainder of the underparts being white. The scarlet area on the nape of the cock bird is missing in the hen. Young birds have browner upperparts, with an orange crown.

Distribution: Western North America, ranging from southern Oregon eastward to New Mexico and Texas, and south via Central America to Colombia.
Size: 22.5cm (9in).
Habitat: Oak woodland.
Nest: Tree hollow.
Eggs: 4–6, white.
Food: Mainly acorns, with some ants.

White-striped woodcreeper

Lepidocolaptes leucogaster

As their name suggests, woodcreepers are able to climb up the bark of trees like woodpeckers, although they belong to an unrelated family. Here they hunt invertebrates, using their long, slender bills to probe into the bark. White-striped woodcreepers comb the tree in a very methodical fashion, working their way up the trunk and then flying down to the bottom of a nearby tree to work up again. Their strong feet and sharp claws enable them to climb and maintain their grip on the tree. Like woodpeckers, their tail feathers have stiffened shafts that terminate in points which dig into the bark and help to support their weight. Though they do not associate in flocks, it is not uncommon for white-striped woodcreepers to forage in the company of other related species. This can make it difficult to determine the identity of these birds in the field, especially since they may only be seen from behind.

Identification: Whitish sides to the face and throat, with a blackish stripe above the eyes. Top of the head is dark brown mottled with white, while the chest is white with black scalloping to individual feathers. Lower underparts have whitish stripes. Upper back is tawny-brown. Flight feathers, rump and relatively long tail are all rufous. Narrow, slightly down-curved bill, with a dark upper surface and paler below. Greyish feet display claws. Sexes are alike.

Distribution: Occurs in central America, where this species is restricted to the mountainous region of western Mexico.
Size: 22.5cm (9in).
Habitat: Coniferous and oak woodlands.
Nest: Tree hollow.
Eggs: 2–3, white.
Food: Feeds exclusively on invertebrates.

Red-breasted nuthatch

Sitta canadensis

Lively and active by nature, red-breasted nuthatches are well-adapted to an arboreal lifestyle. Their small size and compact shape enable them to climb up and down tree trunks with ease, their strong toes and claws providing sufficient anchorage for them to descend head-first. Their tail feathers lack the stiff points at the tips that characterize woodpeckers, and their bills are not strong enough to bore into the trunk. However, these nuthatches are adept at pulling insects out from under the bark, and they will move along narrow branches to pluck invertebrates off leaves. The seeds of conifers help to sustain them through winter, when invertebrates are scarce. These birds have an unusual method of deterring predators from the nest hole, by smearing it with pine oil. This helps to obscure the scent of the nuthatches, whose plumage becomes heavily stained as they pass in and out of the nest.

Identification: Black cap across the top of the head, with a black line running through the eyes, separated by an intervening white stripe. White on the cheeks too. Back, wings and tail bluish-grey, with rust-coloured underparts. Short, narrow blackish bill, paler below, with black legs and feet. Hens have duller plumage on the head and paler underparts. Young birds are similar to hens.

Distribution: Breeding range extends right across Canada from south-eastern Alaska to Newfoundland. Winters across much of the USA, sometimes as far south as northern Florida, the Gulf coast and Mexico.
Size: 11.5cm (4¹/₂in).
Habitat: Coniferous and oak woodlands.
Nest: Tree hollows.
Eggs: 4–8, white with reddish-brown speckling.
Food: Invertebrates and pine nuts.

Fernandina's flicker (*Colaptes fernandinae*): 35cm (14in)
Very limited range, restricted to the Caribbean island of Cuba. Yellowish-tan overall, broken by black markings which are particularly evident on the upperparts, while the underparts tend to be lighter. Brownish sides to the face; eyes display a dark iris. Narrow, pointed black bill. Legs and feet are also blackish. Hens lack the distinctive moustache-like stripe seen in cocks.

White woodpecker (*Melanerpes candidus*): 24cm (9¹/₂in)
South America, from Surinam and French Guiana south via Brazil to parts of Bolivia, Paraguay, Argentina and Uruguay. Also extends westward to Peru. Mainly white, with a narrow dark stripe running from behind the eye, on each side of the head, down to the wings. Wings and tail are black. There is a bright yellow patch on the hind neck, and also in the centre of the belly. Hens show little striping on the head and no yellow on the hindneck. Young birds have blackish-brown upperparts and white areas are tinged with buff.

Puerto Rican woodpecker (*Melanerpes portoricensis*): 25cm (10in)
Occurs on the Caribbean island of Puerto Rico, and on nearby Vieques, where it is more scarce. Black head and upperparts, with prominent white lores and white encircling the eyes. Lower back and rump are white, with white edging sometimes seen on adjacent areas of the wings. Underparts are reddish with buff on the flanks. Hens and young birds are similar to cocks but with less red on their underparts.

Red-breasted sapsucker

Yellow-breasted sapsucker *Sphyrapicus ruber*

True to their name, red-breasted sapsuckers feed mainly on the sap of trees, which they drill into trunks to obtain. When the young hatch, however, the adults forage more widely to feed their hungry brood, seeking insects, especially ants on the ground. A pair will often start several nest holes, and may end up using one that has been partially created already, or one used in a previous year. Both parents share the task of incubation, which lasts just under two weeks, with the young remaining in the nest a further four weeks. During this time the male usually keeps the nest clean. As fall arrives they create new sap wells, to which they regularly return over winter. Sometimes these wells trap ants, which add to their diet. They rarely eat fruit.

Distribution: Western North America, breeding as far north as south-east Alaska, down to California and Nevada. Overwinters south as far as Baja California.
Size: 22.5 cm (9in).
Habitat: Mainly coniferous forest.
Nest: Tree hollow.
Eggs: 3–7, white.
Food: Sap and insects.

Identification: Red head, with white area above the bill, which may extend around sides of the head. Back and wings have white wing bars. Underparts yellowish, with darker speckling. Bill is narrow and black. Sexes are alike. Young have brown heads with little red, but white over the bill.

PIGEONS, DOVES AND CUCKOOS

Flying in a woodland environment obviously presents problems, not just because of the confined space but also because it draws attention to a bird's presence, which could place it in danger. It is much better to quietly slip away from a possible predator. This is exactly what many otherwise conspicuous, and often highly terrestrial, birds such as pigeons and cuckoos do.

Key West quail-dove

Geotrygon chrysia

Distribution: Occurs in the Caribbean on the Bahamas, in Hispaniola, and in Cuba. Also occurs locally on Puerto Rico.
Size: 30cm (12in).
Habitat: Forest and more open wooded terrain.
Nest: Loose platform.
Eggs: 1–2, buff.
Food: Seeds, fruit and invertebrates.

These quail-doves spend most of their time on or near the ground, often frequenting densely wooded countryside, where their dark coloration makes them difficult to observe. Their calls may betray their presence, consisting of a series of low-pitched cooing notes uttered in rapid succession. They use their bills to forage among the leaf litter, eating a varied diet that includes snails and caterpillars. If disturbed, Key West quail-doves will seek to walk away quietly, rather than try to fly and so betray their presence. They typically live alone, sometimes in pairs. Cocks begin to call in search of mates in January. The nesting period lasts from February to August, with pairs possibly nesting more than once. The birds sometimes conceal the nest, which is made with twigs and leaves, and sited up to 1m (3ft) off the ground in a bushy shrub or vine.

Identification: Metallic greenish area on the head, extending down the back of the neck. Prominent white banding under each eye, with reddish-brown upperparts. Underparts are pinkish-grey, becoming greyer on the abdomen. Legs and feet are reddish, and the bill is pink with a dark tip. Hens are generally duller. Young birds have brownish feathering on the underparts, and no iridescence.

Blue ground dove

Claravis pretiosa

The marked difference in colour between the male and the female blue ground dove is an extreme example of sexual dimorphism within this group. Their appearance in some parts of their range, notably in Central America, is seasonal, being driven by the availability of food. These doves do not occur at high altitudes, being found mostly in the foothills of the Andes, and are most likely to be seen on the forest floor. They are quiet by nature and do not associate in flocks, so are easily overlooked. The breeding season varies with location, starting in March in Panama but usually not until September in Bolivia. The cock bird displays by bowing with his tail raised and wings quivering. The nest is a fragile structure up to 6m (18ft) off the ground. The young often leave at just two weeks of age, before they can even fly properly.

Identification: Cock birds are very easily distinguished by their overall greyish-blue coloration, and are a darker shade of blue on the head, wings and upperparts. Variable patterning of black spotting and large black blotches on the wings, with flight feathers also black. Hens are brownish, with brown rather than black wing markings. Young birds resemble hens, but have blackish wing spots.

Distribution: Ranges from south-eastern parts of Mexico down through Central America to Peru in western South America, and as far as Argentina on the eastern side of the continent.
Size: 23cm (9in).
Habitat: Scrub and woodland.
Nest: Platform of twigs.
Eggs: 2, white.
Food: Seeds, fruits and invertebrates.

Pheasant cuckoo

Dromococcyx phasianellus

Distribution: Range extends from southern Mexico down through Central America as far as northern parts of Bolivia, Paraguay, and north-eastern Argentina.
Size: 35cm (14in).
Habitat: Rainforest.
Nest: Parasitic.
Eggs: White or buff, with reddish speckling.
Food: Omnivorous.

These large cuckoos are so called because they have a lifestyle similar to that of pheasants, spending much of their time on the ground. They inhabit woodland areas and plantations where there is dense cover, and will run through the undergrowth to elude pursuit. Their presence is most likely to be betrayed by their song, which sounds like a loud whistle. They often choose a prominent branch some distance off the ground to sing from, and this is where they are most likely to be observed. Like many members of their family, pheasant cuckoos do not build a nest and rear their own chicks. Instead, females lay single eggs in the nests of other birds, usually favouring domed nests that may be hanging freely. The host species varies throughout their range, but the yellow-olive flycatcher (flatbill) (*Tolmomyias sulphurescens cinereiceps*), found in Mexico, is typical.

Identification:
Thin head with a narrow rusty crest and a pale stripe running back from the eyes. Thinner dark stripe below from the base of the bill. Chest is pale buff with darker speckling, the remainder of the underparts are white. Back and wings brown, with lighter edging on the feathers. The tail is long and broad, narrowing down its length, with paler tips to the underside of the feathers. Long, pointed bill and dark feet. Sexes are alike. Young birds easily identifiable by their plain buff throat and chest.

Crested quail-dove (*Geotrygon versicolor*): 30cm (12in)
Restricted to Jamaica. Unusual short greyish crest, with buffy patches below the eyes extending backward. Bluish-grey neck and underparts, with a rufous area around the vent. Back and wings mainly purplish maroon. Flight feathers chestnut, rump and tail blackish. Hens have browner and paler underparts. Young birds display reddish-brown edging on the feathers.

Scaly-naped pigeon (*Patagioenas squamosa*): 40cm (16in)
Widely distributed through the Caribbean, but not on Jamaica, and has not been recorded from Aruba since 1973. Reddish-purple feathering extends over the head and neck to the breast. Rest of the body is slaty grey. Metallic coppery-red shade on the sides of the neck. Orbital skin is orangish, the bill has a red base and yellow tip. Legs and feet red. Sexes are alike. Young birds are less brightly coloured overall, with rusty tones on the head and wings.

Chilean pigeon (Chilean bandtail, *Patagioenas araucana*): 35cm (14in)
Ranges through forested areas, notably the beech forests of central and southern parts of Chile into western Argentina. Vinous-pink head, back and underparts, except for a narrow white stripe across the neck, with metallic green below. Tops of the wings are reddish purple, the rest of the wings and rump grey. Tail also grey with a broad black band. Hens duller, with less reddish purple on the wings. Young birds paler and greyer, with bluish-grey rump and tail.

Black-billed cuckoo

Coccyzus erythrophthalmus

Black-billed cuckoos are typically found below 1,100m (3,300ft). They are not easy to spot, being mainly solitary birds that prefer to hide in dense vegetation. Their calls are not very distinctive, resembling those of doves. Pairs sometimes nest quite close to the ground in a bush that gives good cover, or higher up in a tree fork. The diet of black-billed cuckoos varies with location, since they are opportunistic feeders. They may steal both eggs and chicks from the nests of smaller birds, as well as eating fruit and catching prey ranging from insects to lizards. In North America, these cuckoos are highly valued in farming areas due to the number of pests, especially tent caterpillars, they eat, which lessens damage to crops.

Distribution: From Alberta and Montana to the eastern coast of North America, south as far as South Carolina, Arkansas and Texas. Migrates to western South America as far south as northern Peru, but also recorded from Paraguay.
Size: 28cm (11in).
Habitat: Various types of woodland.
Nest: Platform of sticks.
Eggs: 2–4, pale bluish green.
Food: Omnivorous feeding habits.

Identification: Bronze-brown colour on the upperparts, with underparts white. Long, narrow tail feathers that are black with white tips. Orbital skin encircling the eyes is red. The bill is black.

TANAGERS

The tanager group is comprised of approximately 240 different species, with representatives found throughout America. The largest of the tanagers, up to 28cm (11in) long, is the magpie tanager (Cissopis leverianus), so called because of its black and white plumage. Tanagers occur at a wide range of altitudes, from sea level up into the Andean region. Some North American species are migratory.

Paradise tanager

Tangara chilensis

These tanagers are rather shy by nature, and their coloration makes them hard to recognize against a dark woodland background. They are lively, restless birds with alert, curious natures. They occur in loose flocks, typically made up of 10–15 individuals, and are sometimes seen in the company of related species. Paradise tanagers usually seek out food in the upper part of the canopy, hopping along the branches there and grabbing spiders and other invertebrates as well as seeking berries and fruit.

Left: A paradise tanager on its nest. The Yuracares Native American tribe calls these birds "yeri yeri" because of the sound of their calls.

Identification: Essentially green on the sides of the face, violet-blue throat with vibrant sky-blue underparts. Rump red, with the back of the head and wings black. Sexes are alike. There is some subspecific variation, and the rump colour is paler in immature birds.

Distribution: Colombia east to French Guiana and Brazil. Also present in Peru and Ecuador. Although their scientific name suggests otherwise, these tanagers are not found as far south as Chile, reaching only as far as northern Bolivia.
Size: 13cm (5in).
Habitat: Lowland areas of woodland and forest.
Nest: Cup-shaped, made of vegetation.
Eggs: 2, whitish with purple-red speckling.
Food: Fruit and invertebrates.

Beryl-spangled tanager

Tangara nigroviridis

Social by nature, beryl-spangled tanagers are usually observed either in pairs or small flocks comprised of up to 15 individuals. They move fast, rarely resting for any time on a perch. These tanagers remain relatively close to the ground when foraging. They adopt a distinctive posture with their head down when seeking spiders and similar creatures, peering under branches and leaves. Their necks are surprisingly flexible, allowing these tanagers to pluck invertebrates from relatively inaccessible sites. There is some variation between races in their bluish-green plumage.

Identification: Black plumage around the bill, extending in a band around the eyes and over the back, is separated by bluish-green plumage, which is also present on the crown. Violet hues apparent over the wings. The rump is greenish blue; the underparts are blackish with pronounced blue spangling. Sexes are alike.

Distribution: Colombia and Venezuela south to parts of Ecuador, Peru, and Bolivia.
Size: 13cm (5in).
Habitat: Relatively open areas of forest.
Nest: Cup-shaped, made of vegetation.
Eggs: 2, creamy white to pale green, with darker speckling.
Food: Berries, other fruit, and invertebrates.

Blue-winged mountain tanager

Anisognathus somptuosus

These relatively large tanagers are the most common member of their genus in Colombia. They tend to be encountered throughout their range at lower levels than other related species, usually frequenting altitudes of 1,400–2,600m (4,600–8,500ft). They are most likely to be observed toward the tree-tops, in groups comprised of up to ten individuals. Blue-winged mountain tanagers are quiet by nature; their trilling calls are unlikely to betray their presence from any distance away. Their gape enables them to swallow some berries whole, while on other occasions they pull the skin off first.

Identification: Yellow stripe running over the crown, bordering black areas of plumage on the head. Underparts a matching shade of rich yellow. Back olive yellow, with blue shoulder patches apparent on the wings. Colour of tail and rump varies, depending on subspecies. Sexes are alike.

Distribution: Colombia and Venezuela south into Bolivia.
Size: 19cm (7¹/₂in).
Habitat: Forested areas in the Andean region.
Nest: Cup-shaped, made of vegetation.
Eggs: 2, greenish white, speckled.
Food: Berries, other fruit and invertebrates.

Green-and-gold tanager (*Tangara schrankii*): 12cm (4¹/₂in) Colombia and Venezuela to Ecuador, Peru, Bolivia and Brazil. Green plumage on the sides of the body and tail. The crown, underparts and rump are golden yellow. The forehead and area surrounding the eyes are black. Hens and young birds have a green rump and black spotting on the crown.

Bay-headed tanager (*Tangara gyrola*): 12cm (4¹/₂in) Costa Rica via Panama to Colombia, French Guiana, Brazil, Ecuador, Peru and Bolivia. Quite variable in coloration through its wide range, but generally brown plumage on the head. Wings greenish, while underparts may vary from green to blue.

Crested ant tanager (*Habia cristata*, E): 19cm (7¹/₂in) Confined to the western Andes of Colombia. Long, narrow, scarlet crest feathers, with scarlet throat. Upperparts reddish, with brown wings, underparts greyish. Young birds predominantly brown and have no crest. Feeds mainly on various insects, swooping down to snatch army ants on the march.

Grass-green tanager (*Chlorornis riefferii*): 20cm (8in) Distribution extends through the Andean region, from Colombia via Peru to Bolivia. Brilliant grass-green coloration offset against chestnut-brown plumage on the sides of the face, and in the vent region. Bill and legs are red in adults. Bills of immatures are brown.

Purple honeycreeper

Cyanerpes caeruleus

Honeycreepers often move extensively through their range, with their local distribution being affected by the whereabouts of flowering trees. Their narrow, curving bills enable these birds to probe flowers to obtain nectar, but their bill shape also allows them to feed on seed pods and to seize small invertebrates. Purple honeycreepers are sufficiently agile to catch insects in flight, although they cannot hover in front of flowers as hummingbirds do. They will, however, dive down to seize spiders that try to escape off branches by dropping down on gossamer threads.

Identification: A rich shade of purple, with a black bib under the throat and black on the wings. Legs are yellow. Hens are green, with yellowish striations on the underparts. Sky-blue patches extending back from the corners of the bill and on the top of the head.

Distribution: Panama southeast via Colombia as far as French Guiana, and south to Ecuador, Peru, Bolivia and Brazil.
Size: 10cm (4in).
Habitat: Flowering trees.
Nest: Cup-shaped nest made of vegetation.
Eggs: 2, white with reddish-chocolate blotches.
Food: Nectar, berries, other fruit and invertebrates.

NEW WORLD BLACKBIRDS

The description "New World blackbirds" reflects not only the fact that these birds are restricted to America, but also that the colour black predominates in their plumage. These birds, often known as icterids, use their bills like knitting needles when constructing their intricate nests, weaving strands of plant matter together to create a remarkably stout, suspended structure.

Crested oropendola

Psarocolius decumanus

During the breeding season, the remarkable call of the male crested oropendola is heard frequently. It has been likened to the noise made by a finger repeatedly plucking the teeth of a plastic comb. These oropendolas live in colonies comprised of several cock birds, one of whom is dominant, and as many as 30 hens. The crest is used as part of the male's display, which consists of elaborate posturing as well as distinctive singing. Ordinary call notes are much shorter and harsher in tone, and are uttered by both sexes. When foraging for food, crested oropendolas frequently associate with jays (*Cyanocorax* species).

Identification: Mainly black, with striking blue eyes and a slight crest. Large, relatively straight, pointed white bill, which is characteristic. Chestnut-brown rump, with yellow in the tail feathers and brown undertail coverts. Hens are similar but duller, and lack a crest.

Distribution: Western Panama south via Colombia to northern Argentina and south-east Brazil.
Size: 43cm (17in) cock; hen typically 33cm (13in).
Habitat: Typically lowland wooded areas.
Nest: Suspended nest built off tree branches.
Eggs: 1–2, pale green or greyish.
Food: Mainly invertebrates.

Left: The entrance to the nest of the crested oropendola is at the top, and isolated trees are favoured for nesting.

Venezuelan troupial

Icterus icterus

These attractive icterids (blackbirds) are the national bird of Venezuela. They also occur naturally on the Netherlands Antilles and have been introduced to other islands in the Caribbean, notably Bonaire. It can be difficult to distinguish young birds from the adults on the basis of their plumage, but the bare area of skin surrounding the eyes is a duller shade of blue with a greyish hue in immature specimens (as pictured). They feed mainly on fruit, but also catch insects and may steal other birds' eggs. Unlike other icterids, troupials do not contruct their own nests. Instead, they take over those built by other birds, particularly rufous-fronted thornbirds (*Phacellodomus rufifrons*) and sometimes great kiskadees (*Pitangus sulphuratus*). The troupials then modify the nests by adding a new lining to meet their needs.

Identification: Black head and bill, with black on the back and on the wings, where there is also white plumage. The plumage itself is quite rough in texture here. The remainder of the body is orangish yellow in colour, with a black tail. Bluish area of skin surrounds the eyes. Sexes are alike.

Distribution: Northern South America from Colombia and Venezuela to the Caribbean.
Size: 23cm (9in).
Habitat: Relatively dry woodland.
Nest: Covered (roofed) nest.
Eggs: 3, white or pale pink with dark blotches.
Food: Mainly frugivorous, but also eats invertebrates, and may rob other nests for eggs.

Orange oriole (*Icterus auratus*): 19cm (7in)
Restricted to the Yucatan peninsula in Central America, but some birds may overwinter in north-east Belize. Mainly orange, becoming yellowish on rump and underparts. Narrow black lores, with black plumage extending along sides of the bill onto chest. Tail and wings black, with a small white wing bar and white edging to the flight feathers. Straight, pointed bill blackish-grey, with grey legs and feet. Hens and young are yellowish rather than orange, with an olive tone on the back and a less obvious wing patch.

Montezuma oropendola (*Psarocolius montezuma*): 48cm (19in)
Eastern Mexico to central Panama. Large, pointed pale yellow bill, extends back above the pale bluish eyes. Chestnut on the head, becoming blacker on the abdomen and chestnut again on the rump and lower underparts. Back and wings are blackish, upper tail feathers the same colour, with yellow below. Slight trailing crest of hair-like plumes at the back of the head. Legs and feet grey. Hens are smaller. Young birds duller, with entirely blackish underparts.

Black-cowled oriole (*Icterus prosthemelas*): 20cm (8in)
South-east Mexico to western Panama, also Caribbean. Cock has a black head, chest and back, with blackish wings and tail, and a yellow area at top of the wings. Rest of body yellow, except for small brownish area on the chest. Bill mostly black. Hens have less black on the head, with olive-green from the crown down over the wings. Young birds have a slight suffusion of black on the throat, and are more lemon in colour.

Baltimore oriole

Icterus galbula

These orioles and particularly their young vary in appearance, which makes them hard to identify. To add to the confusion, this species used to be considered the same as the Bullock's oriole found in the west, because of observations of interbreeding. From 1973-1995 they were classified as a single species known as the northern oriole. The orange eyebrows and cheeks of the cock distinguish the western form from the eastern. The increasing forestation of the Great Plains enabled these birds to meet and hybridize, to create what is in some respects a new species. Large flocks of these orioles migrate south in September, and return again in April.

Distribution: British Columbia in Canada eastward to Nova Scotia and across virtually all of the USA, except Florida and parts of the Gulf coast. Overwinters in Central America down to northern South America.
Size: 22cm (8¼in).
Habitat: Deciduous woodland.
Nest: Pendulous woven structure.
Eggs: 4–6, greyish with darker markings.
Food: Invertebrates and fruit.

Identification: Breeding adult male has a black head, with black extending over the back and wings. Narrow white bar above the flight feathers, which are edged with white. Rest of the body orange, vivid on the chest but paler on underparts. Rump orange, with black upper tail feathers, orange below. Narrow, pointed greyish bill, blacker on the upper surface. Hens have brown instead of black on the head and upperparts. Young have olive brown head and upperparts, and dull underparts with variable orange.

Southern mountain cacique

Cacicus chrysonotus

Typically found at altitudes between 1,500 and 3,300m (4,500–9,900ft), mountain caciques are most common in the southern part of their range, particularly in Bolivia, where they may be found at even higher altitudes. These caciques are noisy by nature, drawing attention to themselves with whistles and dueting as members of a group keep in contact with each other. Flocks are small, however, and typically comprise no more than half a dozen birds. They also forage in the company of other birds such as mountain tanagers, often venturing to higher branches than their companions to obtain food. Although members of a flock roost together, mountain caciques breed in pairs rather than groups. They construct a typical woven nest, hanging down from a branch where it will be relatively inaccessible to potential predators such as snakes.

Distribution: Occurs in the Andean region of South America, ranging from Venezuela through Colombia, eastern Ecuador, Peru, and down into Bolivia.
Size: 26cm (10¼in).
Habitat: Humid montane forest.
Nest: Pendulous woven structure.
Eggs: Apparently unrecorded.
Food: Berries and invertebrates.

Identification: Mainly black with a yellow lower back and rump. Often has yellow on the wings, depending on race. The Northern mountain cacique (*C. leucoramphus*) has a white collar largely hidden by white feathering on the nape, and orange on rump. Pale blue iris. Sexes are alike, but hens significantly smaller. Young birds are duller black, with a weaker, horn-coloured rather than mainly bluish-grey bill.

WOODLAND INSECT-CATCHERS

Insects caught on the wing feature in the diet of these birds, although hummingbirds also seek out forest flowers, which provide them with energy-rich sugar and protein-laden pollen. Hummingbirds do not occur outside America and often inhabit quite restricted areas, especially in the rainforest. In some cases the shape of the bill has evolved to enable the birds to feed on a particular type of flower.

White-tipped sicklebill

Eutoxeres aquila

The highly distinctive, downward-curving bill of these hummingbirds enables them to draw nectar from *Heliconia* flowers. They will frequently grasp on to blossoms with their sharp claws as they probe the flowers with their beak. Their relatively subdued coloration and small size means that white-tipped sicklebills are hard to observe in woodland, especially as they are solitary by nature. They are also shy in contrast to many hummingbirds, but become quite common near their main food plant. They also hunt for small invertebrates on bark. The nest of these hummingbirds hangs down, often suspended from a palm frond, with a "tail" made of plant fibres beneath.

Identification: Characteristic sickle-shaped bill, with lower part being yellow. Glossy deep-green upperparts, and heavy black-and-white streaking on the underparts. The bronzy-green tail feathers have broad white tips. Sexes are alike, but hens have slightly shorter wings compared to cocks.

Distribution: Costa Rica south to north-west Peru in the Andean region.
Size: 11.5cm (4¹/₂in).
Habitat: Lower areas of forest and woodland.
Nest: Cup-shaped, made of plant fibres.
Eggs: 2, white.
Food: Nectar, pollen and small invertebrates.

Long-tailed hermit

Phaethornis superciliosus

Distribution: Mexico south to northern Bolivia and the Amazonian region of Brazil, although distribution is not continuous through this area.
Size: 13cm (5in).
Habitat: Lower levels in forest and woodland.
Nest: Cone-shaped, made of plant fibres.
Eggs: 2, white.
Food: Nectar, pollen and small invertebrates.

The body of these hummingbirds is tiny compared with the length of their bill, which accounts for about a third of their body length, and their long tail feathers. As is usual behaviour with hummingbirds, males are highly territorial, and each establishes a small area, singing there for long periods and driving away potential rivals. The repetitive call note may be repeated up to 100 times each minute in an attempt to attract any female in the vicinity. After mating, the hen will build the nest and incubate and rear the chicks on her own. She keeps her head up when incubating, but the nest is usually concealed beneath a palm frond or similar leafy vegetation.

Left: The hen of the long-tailed hermit always incubates the eggs facing the vegetation that conceals the nest.

Identification: Dull shade of brown with bronzy-green suffusion over the back. Buff edging to the rump. Greyish-buff underparts, becoming buff on the belly, with distinctive white tips to the central tail feathers. Sexes are alike.

Tree swallow

White-bellied swallow *Tachycineta bicolor*

These swallows may be seen in huge flocks migrating to and from their breeding grounds. Nesting starts in early May in the far north of their range, with males laying claim to suitable tree holes. Nest sites are sometimes fought over, with rivals occasionally being killed in such encounters. (The incidence of these disputes is reduced in some areas thanks to the presence of alternative sites in the guise of nestboxes.) Females may also battle to obtain a mate, sometimes even driving out a sitting resident. The hen is responsible for collecting the material for the nest, which is usually made up of dry grass and pine needles, with the eggs being laid on top of a bed of feathers. Studies have revealed that during the nearly three-week period in which they remain in the nest, the nestlings are fed about every three minutes. Success is therefore dependent on the summer, and in bad weather, when invertebrates are scarce, fewer than one chick in four will survive through to fledging.

Identification: Predominantly metallic bluish-green head, extending down over the back, shoulder area and rump, while the wings and tail are blackish. Develops a less bluish hue after the breeding season. The remainder of the body is white. Sexes are alike. Young birds have brown upperparts to their bodies and often display a greyish band over the chest.

Distribution: North-central Alaska to Newfoundland south of Hudson's Bay, south to northern Louisiana and Mississippi. Winters from southern California east to the south of Virginia and down through Central America to Panama. Also in the Caribbean.
Size: 12.5cm (5in).
Habitat: Breeds in wooded terrain.
Nest: Tree cavity.
Eggs: 3–8, white.
Food: Invertebrates, some berries.

Gorgeted woodstar (*Chaetocercus heliodor*): 6.5cm (2½in)
Mountainous areas of eastern Panama south to Venezuela and north-west Ecuador. The gorgeted type is the smallest of the woodstars. Stunning pinkish gorget under the throat, lacking in hens, with white feathering on the chest. Remainder of the plumage is mainly green. The underparts of hens are cinnamon.

Geoffroy's wedgebill (Wedge-billed hummingbird, *Schistes geoffroyi*): 8.5cm (3½in)
Mountainous areas from Venezuela to Bolivia. Bronzy-green upperparts. White stripe extends downward from each eye, with a blackish area beneath. Short bill with a sharp point. Gorget is brilliant green with purple plumage. White band across upper chest. Hen has a duller gorget or even a white throat, depending on subspecies.

Purple-crowned fairy hummingbird (*Heliothryx barroti*): 11cm (4in)
South-eastern Mexico south to western Ecuador. Distinctive, shiny violet-purple plumage on the front of the crown, with a black stripe through the eyes. Glossy green upperparts and pure white underparts. Long tapering tail. Hen is slightly larger, with a green crown.

Hoary puffleg (*Haplophaedia lugens*): 8.5cm (3½in)
Uplands of south-west Colombia and the neighbouring area of northern Ecuador. Green upperparts with a coppery hue on head and rump. Greyish-black underparts. Sexes are alike.

Northern royal flycatcher

Onychorhynchus mexicanus

Northern royal flycatchers rarely reveal their distinctive crowned crest, except when displaying. They do not range high into the forest canopy, and are usually seen foraging at lower levels in the company of other birds, keeping a watchful eye for invertebrates. They often hunt near forest streams, where mosquitoes and other flying insects are likely to be found. They may also be seen either singly or in pairs, hawking on the wing or darting off from a branch to catch their quarry. These birds may betray their presence by their calls, made up of a series of whistling notes. Their nests are remarkable. Built from a mass of vegetation, they hang down from a branch and measure over 1m (36in) long, affording good protection from predators. The nest chamber is located within the side of the structure.

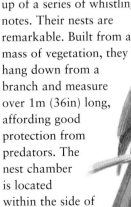

Distribution: Extends from south-eastern parts of Mexico down to north-western Peru and Bolivia, and via Venezuela to French Guiana, reaching down as far as south-eastern Brazil.
Size: 18cm (7in).
Habitat: Forest, often near streams.
Nest: Hanging oval structure.
Eggs: 2, reddish brown with darker markings.
Food: Invertebrates.

Identification: Brown head and wings, with greyer sides of the head. White throat with greyer breast. Underparts yellowish. Tail cinnamon with dark tip. Folded crest on head forms a half-circle when erect, and is red with blue edges and markings. Hens have orange in the crest. Young display dusky scalloping on chest and upperparts.

NORTHERN VISITORS

Woodland areas are rich in invertebrate life, so it is not surprising that a variety of birds seek their food there. Some have a highly specialized style of feeding, while others are opportunistic, which has helped them to spread over a wide area. Insectivorous species occurring particularly in northern areas of North America are forced to head south in the fall, in order to maintain their food supply.

Black-and-white warbler

Mniotilta varia

Distribution: From Canada (southern Mackenzie through central Manitoba to Newfoundland) to much of southern USA east of the Rockies. Overwinters along the Gulf coast and down through Central America into northern South America.
Size: 13cm (5in).
Habitat: Woodland.
Nest: Cup-shaped.
Eggs: 4–5, white with purple spots.
Food: Invertebrates.

With its bold patterning and a call that has been likened to a noisy wheelbarrow, the black and white warbler is relatively conspicuous. These birds arrive back in their breeding grounds during April, although they may head north before then, sometimes being spotted in more open country as well as in backyards and parks. These warblers are often better known by their traditional name of black and white creepers, due to their habit of foraging on tree trunks, probing for insects in the bark. They are surprisingly agile, being able to move both up and down the trunk. In their breeding territories, black and white warblers prefer stretches of deciduous woodland where good cover is available, since they breed on the ground. Here the pair will construct a well-disguised nest, usually close to a tree. They start to head south again from July onward. Like other wood warblers, these birds often forage as part of mixed species flocks, especially over winter.

Identification: In breeding plumage males have black feathering on the cheeks and in the vicinity of the throat, with the lower throat area becoming white over the winter. A prominent white stripe is evident above the eyes, with black and white streaking on the flanks. The lower underparts are white. Hens recognizable by their whitish cheeks, with a slight buff suffusion on the flanks. This is more apparent in young birds.

Worm-eating warbler

Helmitheros vermivorum

These warblers are difficult to observe since they frequent areas of dense undergrowth, their small size and coloration helping them to blend into their environment. Although their distribution is centred on the eastern USA they have on rare occasions been recorded in more westerly areas, even in California. Worm-eating warblers seek their food close to the ground, often on their own, although they can sometimes be found in the company of other warblers. This species is so called not because they favour earthworms but rather because they seek out caterpillars of various moths, which at this stage in their life-cycle resemble worms. Pairs return to their breeding grounds during April, and the males sing as they establish their breeding territories, often perching on a high branch, although even here they can be hard to observe. The nest is built on the ground, and is comprised mainly of dry leaves, with moss and feathers used to create a softer lining.

Identification: A black stripe extends up the sides of the crown down over the neck, with another black stripe passing through the eyes. Rest of upperparts are buff-coloured. Back and wings brownish olive. Narrow light-coloured bill with pink legs and feet. Sexes are alike.

Distribution: Breeds in the eastern USA, from south-east Iowa to New York and eastern parts of North Carolina, down as far as the central Gulf coast. Overwinters from south-eastern parts of Mexico down into South America.
Size: 14cm (5½in).
Habitat: Dry woodland.
Nest: Cup-shaped.
Eggs: 4–5, white with brown spots.
Food: Invertebrates.

Ruby-crowned kinglet

Regulus calendula

These small warblers breed in the taiga forest stretching across the far north of North America. They often search for food by hovering around the branches, darting down to seize insects such as caterpillars, and are able to balance right out at the tips of branches thanks to their small size. It is not always easy to recognize the distinctive ruby-red crown of the cock bird, since this feathering may be obscured. Ruby-crowned kinglets are very active birds, constantly on the move, and frequently flick their wings, as if something has startled them and they are about to take off. Their nest is woven with great skill and located close to the end of a branch of a spruce tree or similar conifer, where they will be relatively safe from predators. After the breeding season these small birds travel southward, arriving at their wintering grounds in September. Although sometimes sighted among mixed flocks there, they are not especially social over the winter period.

Identification: Olive-brown upperparts with a paler, whitish area encircling the eyes. Throat area pale grey, becoming yellowish on the underparts. Wings dark, with prominent white band at the top and across the wings of the cock bird. Ruby-red patch of feathering on the top of the crown. Hens lack this colour, and have more dusky stripes across the wings. Young birds are more brownish on their upperparts.

Distribution: Alaska across Canada south of Hudson's Bay to Newfoundland, south to the Great Lakes and New England. Overwinters from southern USA south through Central America as far as Guatemala.
Size: 11cm (4¼in).
Habitat: Forests and woodland.
Nest: Woven from plant matter.
Eggs: 5–10, creamy with fine darker speckling.
Food: Invertebrates.

Eye-ringed flatbill (*Rhynchocyclus brevirostris*): 17cm (6½in)
Southern parts of Mexico down through Central America to Ecuador. Greyish area surrounding the eyes, with a blackish border behind and a paler, greyish-whitish throat. White circle around each eye. Rest of upperparts olive green, with blackish areas on the wings and tail. Underparts lemon, with olive markings on upper abdomen. Narrow, pointed bill, blackish above and paler below. Grey legs and feet. Sexes are alike.

Stub-tailed spadebill (*Platyrinchus cancrominus*): 9cm (3½in)
South-east Mexico down to north-western Costa Rica. Rufous-brown crown, back and wings. A fawn stripe passes through the eyes and down behind the cheeks. A dark streak runs from the lores below the eyes. Throat whitish, with the underparts pale brownish. Centre of the belly and undertail coverts whitish lemon. Distinctive short, wide tail. Broad, pointed bill, dark above. Pinkish legs and feet. Male has a yellow patch on the crown, absent in the hen. Young birds have a less distinctive facial pattern.

Yellow-eyed junco (*Junco phaeonotus*): 16cm (6¼in)
South-eastern Arizona and south-western New Mexico south to Guatemala. Greyish head, with black lores highlighting the bright yellow eyes. Back and wings reddish brown, with pale grey underparts. Mottled bluish area at the shoulders, with reddish edging to the black flight feathers. Central tail feathers are dark. Sexes are alike. Young birds have dusky rather than yellow eyes.

Dark-eyed junco

Junco hyemalis

Although these finches display variable coloration through their wide range, the fact that they breed together freely and produce fertile offspring means that they rank as one species, not four. They are widely seen, mainly in woodlands but also in other habitats when migrating. Dark-eyed juncos are mainly terrestrial in their habits, living in loose flocks that may forage widely. They are prolific when nesting, with incubation lasting just 12 days and the young fledging after a similar period. The nest is well-disguised and sited close to the ground, so that if the young are disturbed they can escape a predator by running away on their surprisingly large feet. Hens produce up to three rounds of chicks over the summer. The young feed largely on invertebrates.

Identification: Variable appearance. Eastern North American birds are mainly slaty grey, with brownish-grey hens. In the west the Oregon junco (*J. h. thurberi*) has a black head and orange-red flanks and back, with paler brown hens. Other variants include the pink-sided type (*J. h. mearnsi*) of the central Rockies, and the white-winged type (*J. h. aikeni*), grey with white wing bars and white underparts. There are several grey-headed forms. Dark eyes in all cases. Sexes alike. Young birds have streaked patterning.

Distribution: Occurs over most of North America, breeding from Canada to Newfoundland, extending south to Mexico and Georgia in the east. Winters along the Gulf coast and into northern Mexico.
Size: 16cm (6¼in).
Habitat: Woodland.
Nest: Cup of vegetation.
Eggs: 3–6, pale green to blue, with brown spots.
Food: Seeds, berries, invertebrates.

HAWAIIAN FOREST DWELLERS

In appearance and lifestyle, native birds occurring on the Hawaiian Islands are among the most unusual to be found anywhere in the world, having developed in complete isolation from mainland species until relatively recently. However, a number of these species have, sadly, become extinct over recent years, largely as a direct result of human interference in their environment.

I'iwi

Drepanis coccinea

Distribution: Confined to the Hawaiian Islands; this species has become extinct on Lanai, and so now occurs only on Hawaii itself, Kaua'i, Maui, O'ahu and Molokai.
Size: 15cm (6in).
Habitat: Woodland.
Nest: Cup-shaped, made of vegetation.
Eggs: 1–3, white with brown markings.
Food: Nectar and invertebrates.

As with many of Hawaii's birds, the common name of this honeycreeper is derived from its native name. It is most likely to be spotted around flowering plants, both native and introduced. In spite of their vivid coloration i'iwis are not easy to observe; like other red forest birds, they blend very effectively with the background. Even if only briefly glimpsed, however, their downward-curving bill sets them apart from other Hawaiian birds of similar colour and size. I'iwis' calls are surprisingly varied, ranging from whistles to gurgles, their most distinctive vocalizations being likened to the sound of a rusty hinge creaking open. They are also talented mimics, replicating the calls of other species such as the Hawaii elepaio (*Chasiempis sandwichensis*). I'iwis are most commonly found above 600m (2,000ft), being less common on O'ahu and Molokai.

Identification: Brilliant red coloration over much of the body. Wings and tail are black, with a small area of white plumage at the top of the wings. Legs and bill, which is narrow and down-curved, are also red. Young birds much duller in coloration, being yellowish-green with dark barring over their body. The plumage on the back is darker than on the underparts. Wings are black, with paler edging on some of the feathers, with the tail also black. Bills of young birds are less brightly coloured than those of adults, lightening toward the tip.

'Akohekohe

Crested honeycreeper *Palmeria dolei* (E)

Identification: Highly distinctive loose, bushy crest extends up between the eyes, with buff above each eye and blue beneath on the cheeks. Remainder of the head is dark, with a reddish nape. Bluish markings on the throat, with blue and brownish patterning on the underparts. Wings similarly coloured on the top, with a blue band running across and blue edging to the flight feathers. Fan-shaped tail is black with a white tip, undercoverts greyish. Sexes are alike. Young birds have a much shorter crest and are much duller.

Another honeycreeper that is not always easy to spot. Its rather dark overall coloration and relatively small size help to conceal its presence in the treetops where it feeds. However, the 'akohekohe has a very lively nature and is highly vocal, uttering a series of buzzing and whistling sounds, some not unlike a person whistling. Unfortunately this species has seriously declined in numbers. It has already vanished from Molokai, although it is not uncommon on the eastern side of East Maui, where it inhabits the upland forest areas, frequenting ohia-lehua trees in particular. Here it can sometimes be seen in flight, although sightings are made difficult by the frequent misty weather that obscures visibility in this area. From a distance, the 'akohekohe may be confused with the smaller apapane (*Himatione sanguinea*).

Distribution: Hawaiian Islands; now believed to be extinct on Molokai, but still survives on Maui.
Size: 18cm (7in).
Habitat: Flowering trees.
Nest: Cup-shaped, made of vegetation.
Eggs: 2, white with brown markings.
Food: Nectar and invertebrates.

Maui nukupu'u

Hemignathus affinis (E)

The Maui nukupu'u occurs in thick ohia forest, using its strong legs to clamber up the bark of trees. Its slender bill is used to probe for invertebrates among the moss and crevices in the bark, and it may often be seen hanging upside down looking under leaves as well. Once three species existed. The O'ahu nukupu'u (*H. lucidus*) is already extinct and the Kaua'i species (*H. hanapepe*), with its distinctive white undertail coverts, was restricted to the Alakai swamp, however there have been no recent sightings. On Maui most sightings are likely to be on Haleakala's upper slopes. Much of the confusion surrounding its distribution there arose from its close likeness to the akiapola'au (*H. wilsoni*), which occurs on Hawaiian islands too. A very detailed comparison will reveal that the akiapola'au's straight rather than slightly curved lower mandible sets it apart.

Distribution: Now restricted to Maui.
Size: 14cm (5^1/$_2$in).
Habitat: Forest.
Nest: Apparently unrecorded.
Eggs: Believed to be 2, white with brown markings.
Food: Mainly invertebrates.

Identification: Cock bird has a yellow head and underparts, with paler undertail coverts. The plumage on the back of the head is relatively long. Back and wings are dark olive-green. Small black area of plumage around the eyes, with the legs black too. Narrow bill is dark, with the upper part being curved and much longer than the short lower part. Hens easily distinguished by their dull olive-green plumage. Young birds resemble hens.

Ou (*Psittirostra psittacea*, E): 17cm (6^1/$_2$in)
Hawaiian Islands, being found only in small numbers in the Alakai swamp on Kaua'i, and on Hawaii itself, between the Volcanoes National Park and Hamakua. Male is predominantly green with a yellow head. Bill is salmon pink and hooked at its tip. Legs are pink. Hens can be distinguished by their green heads.

Palila (*Loxioides bailleui*, E): 19cm (7^1/$_2$in)
Occurs only on the island of Hawaii, notably near Mauna Kea. Cock bird has a yellowish head and breast, with a narrow black area around the eyes. Rest of underparts are white. Back and rump slaty blue, with dark yellowish green on the wings. Bill and legs black. Hens duller, with grey merging with the yellow on the hindneck.

Maui parrotbill (*Pseudonestor xanthophrys*, E): 14cm (5^1/$_2$in)
Restricted to Maui, on the eastern side of Haleakala. The massive, dark-coloured and downward-curving upper bill of this species resembles that of a parrot. It has a bright yellow stripe above each eye. A dark olive stripe through the eyes separates the duller yellow cheeks and underparts. Dark olive-green area extends from the top of the bill over the wings. Hens less brightly coloured, with smaller bills.

'Akikiki (Kaua'i creeper, *Oreomystis bairdi*): 11cm (4^1/$_2$in)
Occurs only on Hawaii itself. Dark grey above, with greyish-whitish underparts and darker grey flanks. Short tail feathers and short, pointed, slightly down-curving pink bill. Young birds have white areas of plumage encircling their eyes.

Bishop's oo

Moho bishopi (E)

This relatively large nectar-feeder has very distinctive, flute-like tones in its song. The bishop's oo is exceedingly difficult to spot, however, as it inhabits dense areas of rainforest and prefers the upper level of the canopy. It is regarded now as being extinct, having vanished from both of the islands where it was sighted at the start of the 20th century. The bishop's oo did have an unconfirmed sighting on Maui in 1981 so it is possible that it still survives there today, notably on the north-eastern slope of Haleakala, but sadly there have been no sightings of the Molokai population since 1904. Like other honeyeaters, bishop's oos have tiny swellings on their tongue, called papillae, which act as brushes, helping them to collect flower pollen. Not surprisingly, honeyeaters are important pollinators of forest trees.

Distribution: Restricted to the Hawaiian Islands, being recorded only from Molokai and Maui.
Size: 30cm (12in).
Habitat: Dense forest.
Nest: Cup-shaped.
Eggs: 2, pinkish with dark spotting.
Food: Mainly nectar.

Identification: Predominantly blackish, with faint yellow streaking on the body and more prominent yellow areas behind the eyes and at the bend of the wing. Yellow undertail coverts. Long tail feathers, tapering to a point. Slightly down-curving bill, also tapering to a point, and black legs. Sexes are alike.

THE WOODLAND CHORUS

It is not always easy to identify birds with certainty, especially in the case of immatures coming into their adult plumage, a process that can involve several moults. There can also be regional variations in the appearance of some birds, particularly those that are widely distributed. Furthermore, distinctive colour forms can crop up among normally-coloured individuals. These are described as colour morphs.

Mexican jay

Grey-breasted jay *Aphelocoma wollweberi*

Identification: Predominantly bluish grey overall, differing in the depth of colour through its range. Bluish-grey plumage on the head and neck, extending over the wings, with the tail also bluish. Greyish-white underparts, becoming white around the vent and on the undertail coverts. Northern birds are paler than their southerly relatives. Sexes are alike. Young birds duller, typically displaying a yellowish area at the base of the bill.

Seven different races of the Mexican jay have been identified, though it is not always easy to distinguish them in the field, especially since juvenile coloration is a key factor. The length of time taken for the bills of young birds to change colour varies greatly, sometimes taking up to two years. Differences in vocalizations and lifestyle have also been identified. The race *A. w. couchii*, found in southern Texas and south across the border, has a harsher call and has adopted a more territorial lifestyle than the Arizona race (*A. w. arizonae*), which lives in flocks of up to 20 birds. These flocks are usually made up of an adult pair and their young from previous years that are not yet breeding, and so are able to help the parents rear the new brood.

Distribution: Ranges from Texas, Arizona, and New Mexico in south-western USA, down through much of Mexico.
Size: 33cm (13in).
Habitat: Arid woodland.
Nest: Cup-shaped platform of sticks.
Eggs: 4–7, blue to greenish blue.
Food: Omnivorous.

Clark's nutcracker

Nucifraga columbiana

These members of the corvid family are relatively conspicuous, often approaching campsites in search of food. Clark's nutcrackers have a varied diet, hunting small vertebrates and preying on the eggs and chicks of other birds, as well as searching rotting wood for invertebrates such as beetles. Pine nuts are also significant in their diet. They use their narrow, curved bill to prise out the seeds, sometimes wedging the pine cone in a rock crevice, which acts like a vice. Clark's nutcrackers are territorial by nature. In late summer a pair will begin to create stores of nuts and seeds. Although some of this food is consumed over winter, most of it is used to rear the chicks the following spring. If the pine crop fails, the birds are forced to abandon their territories and head elsewhere in search of food. This happens once every 15 years on average.

Identification: White crown and area around the eyes, with a white patch also evident on each wing and on the undertail coverts. Underside of the tail is also white. Wings and tail otherwise black, with the remainder of the body grey. Powerful, pointed black bill, with black legs and feet. Sexes are alike. Young birds duller, with a more brownish tone to their grey plumage.

Distribution: Western North America, from south-western Canada and western USA south to northern parts of Mexico. Sometimes irrupts into other areas from central Alaska to Texas, but uncommon in the Midwest.
Size: 30cm (12in).
Habitat: Typically montane coniferous forests.
Nest: Made of twigs and sticks.
Eggs: 2–6, green with dark brown markings.
Food: Omnivorous.

Unicoloured jay (*Aphelocoma unicolor*): 35.5cm (14in)
Parts of Mexico south to northern El Salvador and western Honduras, being found in cloud forest. Blue overall, with a darker blue area on sides of the head, extending below and behind the eyes. Some races are a more purplish-blue shade. Bill, legs and feet blackish. Sexes are alike. Young birds duller, with yellowish bills.

Pinyon jay (*Gymnorhinus cyanocephalus*): 28cm (11in)
Western USA south to northern Baja California. Dull blue, with whitish streaking around throat. Relatively narrow, pointed black bill. Sexes are alike. Young birds are greyer in colour.

Brown jay (*Psilorhinus morio*): 44cm (17in)
South-eastern Texas via Mexico and much of Central America to north-west Panama. Greyish-brown head, chest and upperparts, with greyish-white underparts. Bill, legs and feet are black. Southern individuals have white tips on inner tail feathers. Sexes alike. Young have yellowish bills.

Northern waterthrush (*Parkesia noveboracensis*): 15cm (6in)
Breeds from Alaska right across Canada except the far north, also northern USA. Winters in Mexico, Ecuador and Peru. Brown upperparts, with a fawn streak from the upper bill behind each eye. Spotted throat. Underparts lemon yellow, with darker streaking toward the vent. Undertail coverts white. Bill dark, legs and feet pinkish, bobbing as it walks. Sexes are alike.

Varied thrush

Ixoreus naevius

This migratory member of the thrush family is sometimes placed within the genus *Zoothera*. It is inconspicuous, often hard to observe in the dark woods and areas near water it frequents. Varied thrushes are not shy birds, however, and have a powerful song with buzzing tones which is most often uttered in the rain. They sing most at the start of the breeding period in March, from upper branches in the forest. Varied thrushes normally feed close to the ground, foraging for invertebrates as well as eating berries. They normally nest around 4.5m (15ft) off the ground. The bulky nest often includes moss. After the breeding period the thrushes leave Alaska, with many overwintering in British Columbia, while others head further south, where they may be seen in open woodland.

Identification: Bluish-grey upperparts, with a broad black stripe on the sides of the head and a prominent black band across the chest. Bright orange areas above the eyes and on the throat, upper chest, and lower underparts, the latter being mottled with grey. Orange bars also on the wings. Hens browner, with duller orange and an indistinct breastband. Young birds much duller, with brownish mottling on the throat and chest.

Distribution: Occurs in western North America, ranging from Alaska southward as far as northern parts of California.
Size: 25cm (10in).
Habitat: Coniferous forest.
Nest: Bulky and cup-shaped.
Eggs: 3–5, pale blue with dark spots.
Food: Invertebrates, some berries.

American redstart

Setophaga ruticilla

Belonging to the wood warbler rather than the thrush family, American redstarts are naturally very lively and active, almost constantly on the move seeking food, fanning open their tails and lowering their wings. Invertebrates may be hawked in flight or grabbed off bark. In parts of Latin America, where they overwinter, they are known locally as "candelita," since their jaunty nature and the coloration of cock birds combine to resemble the movements of a candle flame. Male American redstarts will sing loudly even before they gain adult plumage, which is not attained until they are over a year old. The song is most evident in spring at the start of the breeding season. The nest is built at a variable height in a suitable bush or tree, up to 23m (75ft) above the ground, and the hen incubates alone, with the eggs hatching after approximately 12 days. The young birds are reared almost entirely on invertebrates, and fledge about three weeks later.

Identification: Cock birds are very colourful, with orange patches on the wings and tail contrasting with the white plumage on the underparts and black elsewhere. Hens are a dull shade of olive brown, with yellow rather than orange markings. Young birds resemble hens.

Distribution: South-eastern Alaska to Newfoundland, south to California in the west and South Carolina in the east. Overwinters in extreme south of the USA and via Mexico to northern South America.
Size: 15cm (6in).
Habitat: Deciduous woodland.
Nest: Cup-shaped.
Eggs: 3–5, white to bluish, with brownish spots.
Food: Invertebrates and berries.

OWLS

Owls rank among the most distinctive of all birds, thanks partly to their facial shape. Representatives of this group are very widespread in America, ranging from the coniferous forests of the far north, through the Amazon rainforest and right down to Tierra del Fuego at the southern tip of South America. Although the majority are nocturnal by nature, some will actively hunt during the daytime.

Northern saw-whet owl

Aegolius acadicus

Despite their distinctive calls, which resemble the sound of a saw being sharpened, northern saw-whet owls are hard to observe due to their small size and nocturnal nature. They are also able to fly very quietly to escape detection. This is strictly a woodland species, not found in northern coniferous areas. In southern areas it can be seen in more open, drier deciduous forest. During the day the owls rest on a branch close to a tree trunk, where their colour and size make them hard to locate. They eat a variety of prey, especially rodents but also birds, invertebrates and frogs. Pairs only come together for breeding, with the male seeking a mate by singing close to his nest hole. The young remain in the nest for a month.

Identification: Brown and white area on the face above the eyes, with white spotted area on the nape. Brown markings on the sides of the face. Underparts are white with rufous-brown markings. Wings and tail brownish with white spotting. Bill is black, irides yellow. Young birds have white eyebrows and lores, while the rest of the face is brown. Their underparts are tawny brown in colour.

Distribution: Range extends across North America from British Columbia to Newfoundland, and south as far as Mexico. The race *A. a. brooksi* occurs on the Queen Charlotte Islands and *A. a. acadicus* in the full range down to northern Mexico.
Size: 19cm (7¹/₂in).
Habitat: Mainly coniferous forest.
Nest: Tree hole.
Eggs: 3–7, white.
Food: Mainly small vertebrates.

Northern hawk-owl

Surnia ulula

These owls, occurring in the far north where day length varies significantly through the year, can be encountered at any time. Northern hawk-owls are solitary by nature outside the breeding season. In late spring the male calls to attract a mate. The pair may choose from a variety of nesting sites, making use of a hole created by a woodpecker, taking over an abandoned stick nest, or simply choosing a site on top of a tree whose crown has snapped off, creating a depression. They make no attempt at nest-building themselves. The eggs are laid at two-day intervals, with the hen sitting alone and the male bringing food for her. Lemmings usually predominate in their diet, but in years when the lemming population plummets other prey, even small fish, may be caught. Breeding success is directly related to the availability of food. The young fledge at four weeks old, but it will be a further two weeks before they can fly, and they remain dependent on their parents for food for a further month.

Identification: Prominent white eyebrows and white cheeks, with whitish spotting on the dark head and wings. Broad black bars on each side of the neck. More brownish on the underparts and tail, with the underparts barred too. Eyes and bill pale yellow. Sexes are alike.

Distribution: Range is circumpolar, right across North America in the boreal region from southern Alaska east to Labrador. Also present in Newfoundland.
Size: 40cm (16in).
Habitat: Coniferous forest.
Nest: Tree holes.
Eggs: 5–13, white.
Food: Mainly small mammals.

Elf owl

Micrathene whitneyi

Five different races of this small, short-tailed owl are recognized. It is the only member of its genus, and lacks ear tufts. Elf owls are nocturnal, often roosting during the day in holes created by woodpeckers, although they may also be spotted on a branch. At night they hunt from a perch, and may be drawn to the light of a campfire, swooping down unexpectedly to catch moths. Their presence may also be betrayed by their high-pitched calls, some of which sound like whistles. Pairs sometimes choose nest holes in saguaro cacti, with the female building no nest, simply laying directly on the floor of the hollow. With the exception of the isolated population in Baja California, elf owls undertake seasonal movements on the mainland, leaving the USA and overwintering in central Mexico. In spring they return north again to establish breeding territories.

Identification: Plumage varies, with brown and grey morphs identified. Upperparts brown with white spotting on the head, back and wings, creating a line across the wings. The tail is barred. Face is rufous-brown, with more prominent narrow black markings. Underparts are brownish above, becoming whiter below with fine black barring. Eyes pale yellow, with a greyish-horn bill. Head and crown greyish in young birds.

Distribution: Extends from south-western California to central Mexico. Separate populations exist in Baja California and on Socorro Island.
Size: 14cm (5½in).
Habitat: Arid wooded areas.
Nest: Hollows in trees or cacti.
Eggs: 2–5, white.
Food: Mainly invertebrates.

Unspotted saw-whet owl (*Aegolius ridgwayi*): 19cm (7½in)
Southern parts of Mexico down to Costa Rica, Guatemala and Panama. Whitish eyebrows and lores, paler brown face. Rufous-brown upper chest, sides of the head and upperparts, with buff underparts. Short tail. Eyes yellow, bill black. Sexes are alike. Young birds may have faint streaking on the breast.

Buff-fronted owl (*Aegolius harrisii*): 20cm (8in)
Venezuela down via Ecuador to north-west Argentina, with an apparently separate population in eastern Brazil and adjacent parts of Argentina and Paraguay. Cream-coloured facial discs, with brown edging and eyebrows. Rest of the head mainly brown, with a wide yellowish-buff band around the neck and a similar line running down the wings; spotted patterning here and on the tail. Rest of upperparts brownish, with buff underparts. Sexes are alike.

Boreal owl (Tengmalm's owl, *Aegolius funereus*): 29cm (11½in)
Circumpolar, including northern North America, ranging as far south as Oregon and New Mexico in the USA. Blackish surround to the mainly white face, with white spotting on the forehead and a paler area on the back of the head. Dark throat patch. Underparts are a combination of rufous and white markings, with brown on the wings and tail, broken by white spots of variable size. Barring on the tail also. Eyes are yellow, bill pale horn-coloured. Sexes are alike, but the female is larger. Young birds are similar to adults after fledging, but may be darker.

Crested owl

Lophostrix cristata

Crested owls are most likely to be seen in areas relatively close to water, at altitudes up to 1,500m (4,500ft). Their pronounced ear tufts may assist them in detecting and homing in on invertebrate prey. Small vertebrates such as rodents also feature in their diet. Pairs will roost together on a suitable branch during the daytime, often in riverine areas, relying on their plumage to conceal their presence. If disturbed they will try to hide more effectively, by stretching themselves to appear slimmer, with their ear tufts held erect. Their breeding season appears to be linked to climate, since it occurs during drier months of the year, although little is documented about their reproductive habits. The subspecies *L. c. stricklandi*, seen here, is distinguished by its unusual yellow, rather than brown, eyes.

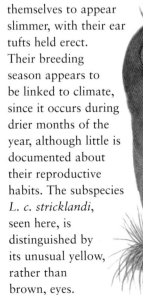

Distribution: Southern Mexico down through Central America and into northern South America, although its precise range there is unclear. Has been recorded as far south as parts of Peru, Bolivia and Brazil.
Size: 43cm (17in).
Habitat: Rainforest areas.
Nest: Tree holes.
Eggs: Not recorded.
Food: Mainly invertebrates.

Identification: White eyebrows extend to create tufts which can be raised. In the brown morph, the head and upper breast is chocolate-brown, the back and wings are paler with white spotting, and the eyes are dark. Red morph displays more even rufous colour; grey morphs have brownish-grey plumage. Young tend to be whiter.

OWLS WITH VARIABLE PLUMAGE

Variation in appearance is a feature of many owls, occurring as they do in different colour morphs. Such variants typically range from a reddish tone through to grey. Unlike true subspecies, these morphs occur alongside each other in the same area, even in the same nest. This diversity may have evolved to provide additional camouflage to the cryptic patterning that already characterizes these birds.

Stygian owl

Asio stygius

Stygian owls are found in highland areas, up to altitudes of 3,000m (9,000ft) or more where trees are present. They stay hidden during the daytime, roosting on a branch that allows them to get close to the trunk of a tree, keeping their ear tufts lowered unless they become frightened. They emerge to hunt under cover of darkness, flying in a distinctive manner that distinguishes them from other owls: by flapping their wings in a slow, deliberate fashion and gliding. Stygian owls are very agile in flight, however, and are able to catch bats on the wing. More typically they catch other prey, which can include birds taken from a perch. Their distinctive call is most likely to be heard at the start of the breeding season, with those of females being higher in pitch. While some pairs may nest on the ground, others often adopt tree nests abandoned by other birds.

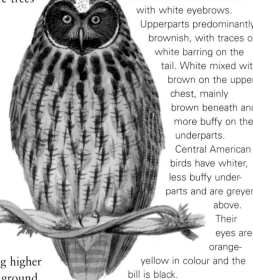

Identification: Prominent ear tufts. Brownish facial area with white eyebrows. Upperparts predominantly brownish, with traces of white barring on the tail. White mixed with brown on the upper chest, mainly brown beneath and more buffy on the underparts. Central American birds have whiter, less buffy underparts and are greyer above. Their eyes are orange-yellow in colour and the bill is black.

Distribution: Range extends from parts of Mexico through Central America to Nicaragua and Belize. Separate population in north-western South America, another extending south to northern Argentina and southeastern Brazil. Also on Cuba, Hispaniola, and smaller neighbouring islands.
Size: 46cm (18in)
Habitat: Montane forest.
Nest: Variable.
Eggs: 2, white.
Food: Mainly vertebrates.

Mottled owl

Strix virgata

Mottled owls vary not only in coloration but also in size, with the largest individuals originating from the vicinity of the Lower Amazon in Brazil. They are sedentary throughout their wide area of distribution, and also nocturnal in their habits, roosting quietly on branches in secluded places during the day. The breeding season also varies according to location, often starting as early as February in northern parts of their range, but restricted to September through to November in Argentina, at the southern end of their distribution. Males are very territorial when nesting, singing from the outset to attract a mate. Mottled owls are opportunistic hunters, preferring to catch their quarry from a perch rather than on the wing. They take a wide variety of prey, with rodents featuring prominently in their diet, although reptiles and amphibians may also be caught, along with various other invertebrates.

Identification: Rounded head with no ear tufts. Coloration variable, depending on race and colour morph, with some birds significantly darker than others. Generally, the head is brown, and the chest is lighter with short vertical markings, compared with the abdomen which is buff with white and brown markings. Tail heavily barred. Eyes dark brown, with a pale yellow bill.

Distribution: Exends from both coasts of Mexico down through Central America to northern parts of South America, ranging to Ecuador in the west and down to north-east Argentina and south-eastern Brazil on the Atlantic coast.
Size: 35cm (14in).
Habitat: Lowland forest.
Nest: Tree hole.
Eggs: 2, white.
Food: Small vertebrates and invertebrates.

Rufous-banded owl (*Strix albitarsis*):
35cm (14in)
Western South America, from Colombia and Venezuela south to Ecuador, north-west Peru, and Bolivia. Chestnut-brown facial disk, with prominent white lores and tawny and black barring on back of the head. Wings brownish, with grey and white flight feathers. Underparts are paler with white markings. Orange-yellow eyes and yellow bill. Sexes are alike but hens usually larger. Young birds have a blackish mask.

Black-banded owl (*Strix huhula*):
36cm (14½in)
Occurs over a wide area east of the Andes, south to northern Argentina and south-east Brazil. Blackish facial area, with fine white markings, and slight barring on the head. Barring more evident over the rest of the body, even on the feathering on the legs. Birds from the south are blacker than northern individuals, which have a brownish tinge to their plumage.

Mountain pygmy owl (*Glaucidium gnoma*):
16cm (6in)
South-western USA southward, probably to the far north-west of South America. Depth of coloration varies through its range. Whitish eyebrows, with light brown plumage speckled with white spots over the head. Darker collar, and brownish wings showing fine barring and speckling. Central area of the chest down to abdomen white, with dark brown flecking on the flanks. Eyes yellow, bill pale yellow. Sexes are alike, but hens may be bigger. Young birds display even grey coloration on the crown.

Great grey owl

Strix nebulosa

These owls move quite extensively through their large range, with North American individuals even having been sighted in the vicinity of New York on occasion. Much of this movement is triggered by the availability of food, especially voles, which these owls hunt almost exclusively during the breeding season. Pairs will often take over the abandoned nests of other birds of prey such as buzzards, although they sometimes nest on the ground. The number of eggs in the clutch is directly related to the availability of food, with breeding results therefore being closely correlated with fluctuations in vole populations.

Distribution: Circumpolar, from northern Canada and Alaska south to California, Idaho and Wyoming. A separate population extends across the far north of Europe and Asia.
Size: 69cm (27in).
Habitat: Coniferous forest.
Nest: Often a platform of sticks.
Eggs: 3–6, white.
Food: Small vertebrates, especially voles.

Identification: Plumage coloration consists mainly of grey streaking and barring on a white background. The dark markings on the so-called facial disk that surrounds the eyes form concentric rings. Yellowish bill, with a blackish patch beneath. Tail is relatively long. Hens are larger in size.

Great horned owl

Bubo virginianus

These owls are not found in areas of dense forest such as the Amazon. They prefer instead to hunt in semi-open terrain, where their keen eyesight enables them to swoop down on small mammals that form the basis of their diet. They are opportunistic hunters, however, and will take a much wider range of prey, from insects and amphibians to other birds, including smaller owls. Males are quite vocal, and sing loudly to attract a mate. Pairs split up at the end of the breeding season, but may reunite again later. They breed in a wide range of locations; an unpleasant stench may give away the location of the nest site because the male may stockpile food there for the offspring.

Identification: Variable through the species' wide range. Northerly populations generally have more brown in their plumage and on the facial disc. Populations further south have a more buff tone to the feathering. Bill is greyish black. Iris is yellow. Hens are larger than cocks.

Right: The name of these owls comes from the appearance of their so-called ear tufts.

Distribution: Alaska and Canada south over virtually the entire USA and Central America. South America from Colombia and Ecuador through Peru to Bolivia and east to Guyana; also south to Brazil and central Argentina.
Size: 56cm (22in).
Habitat: Lightly wooded areas.
Nest: Abandoned nest or on the ground.
Eggs: 2–6, white.
Food: Small vertebrates.

LARGER HUNTERS OF THE FOREST

A number of large diurnal birds of prey have adapted to life in woodlands, becoming skilled hunters in this terrain, where visibility is limited. They often range over a very wide area, and take a diverse range of prey.

Harpy eagle

Harpia harpyja

The immense power and strength of these eagles makes them fearsome predators, able to catch creatures ranging from birds such as large macaws to monkeys, sloths and even pigs. Reptiles such as iguanas and large snakes may also fall victim to these eagles. They are believed to use not just keen eyesight but also acute hearing to detect potential quarry in the forest canopy. However, they often prefer to hunt in clearings, or at areas where animals congregate, such as water sources. In the early morning, it is sometimes possible to see these magnificent eagles perched rather than flying overhead.

Identification: The female harpy eagle is much larger than the male, potentially weighing twice at much as her partner, up to 9kg (20lb). The head is greyish with a prominent, divided black crest. Upper chest is blackish, and underparts are white, aside from black-and-white barring on the tail feathers. There is fainter barring on the thighs. Wings are blackish. Young take at least five years to acquire full adult plumage. Their head and underparts are entirely white at first, changing gradually over successive moults.

Distribution: South Mexico through Central America, to Colombia and northern South America, ranging as far south as north-eastern Argentina, via eastern Bolivia and Brazil.
Size: Female 105cm (41in).
Habitat: Lowland tropical forest. They rarely soar over the forest, preferring instead to fly close to the canopy.
Nest: Platform of sticks.
Eggs: 2, whitish.
Food: Vertebrates.

Black-and-chestnut eagle

Spizaetus isidori

These eagles are most likely to be seen at altitudes of around 2,000m (6,600ft) but they have been observed from sea level up to 3,500m (11,500ft). Relatively little is known about their habits, and they are hard to observe since they hunt mainly in the canopy, preying on quite large creatures, including monkeys, which they seize in their powerful talons. Large trees are chosen to support the weight of their nest, which can be up to 2m (6½ft) in diameter. The cock bird is responsible for feeding the single chick, and appears to concentrate on hunting squirrels for it. The young eagle spends about four months in the nest, after which time its plumage darkens over successive moults until it assumes its adult coloration at four years old.

Identification: Head, including crest feathers, back, wings and top of the thighs are black. Lower chest and underparts are chestnut streaked with black. Tail is greyish with a black band at its tip. Iris is orange-yellow. Feet are yellow. The female can be up to 20cm (8in) larger than the male.

Distribution: North-east Colombia and adjacent Venezuela south through Ecuador and Peru to Bolivia. Possibly no longer occurs in Argentina.
Size: Female 80cm (31½in).
Habitat: Forested areas.
Nest: Platform of sticks.
Eggs: 1, whitish with brownish spots.
Food: Other vertebrates.

Crested eagle

Morphnus guianensis

These eagles vary considerably in appearance, with pronounced differences between the light morph and the grey morph, which has a much greyer head and chest, combined with black and white barring on the underparts. Crested eagles are solitary by nature outside the breeding season. They can sometimes be spotted on a branch high up in an exposed tree, watching for prey, although with large territories to cover, sightings can be infrequent. These are birds of the lowland forest, typically seen up to 1,600m (4,800ft). They are formidable predators, taking mammals the size of woolly monkeys, as well as larger forest birds, notably guans (Cracidae). Pairs typically nest around April close to the equator; elsewhere their breeding period is unknown. They build a massive nest, with a cup-shaped depression at the centre for the eggs.

Identification: Light and dark colour morphs. In light morph males, head is pale greyish-brown with a black crest at the rear, and a bare greyish area extending from the bill around the eyes. Underparts whitish with signs of brownish banding. Blackish wings, with the rump being edged with white, while the tail has alternating black and greyish bands. Hens are similar but abdomen usually free of barring. Young birds paler, with buff areas on the underparts.

Distribution: South-eastern Mexico down to Panama and across South America east of the Andes, ranging down through eastern Bolivia, Paraguay and Brazil. Very occasionally sighted in northern Argentina.
Size: 89cm (35in).
Habitat: Lowland tropical forest.
Nest: Large stick nest.
Eggs: 1–2, creamy white.
Food: Mainly mammals and birds.

Chaco eagle (Crowned solitary eagle, *Buteogallus coronatus*): 85cm (33^1/$_2$in) Eastern Bolivia, western Paraguay, southern Brazil and Argentina, also possibly Uruguay. Mainly dark grey, with a crest at the back of the head. Flight feathers and tail are darker. Tail has a broad white band and white tip. Bill mainly yellow with a dark tip. Legs and feet also yellow. Hens slightly larger. Young birds have brownish upperparts, with whitish streaking beneath.

Ornate hawk-eagle (*Spizaetus ornatus*): 67cm (26in) South-east Mexico to Bolivia, Paraguay and north Argentina. Dark brown crest at back of the head. Sides of face and neck rufous. Throat and underparts white, brown spots and barring on lower chest and abdomen. Undertail coverts white. Barred tail with black and white markings. Wings brownish with white edging. Irides orange. Yellow bill has dark tip, feet yellow. Hens larger. Young have whiter underparts.

Black hawk-eagle (*Spizaetus tyrannus*): 71cm (28in) Central Mexico down across much of northern South America to southern Brazil and north-east Argentina. Mainly black, with crest at back of the head having white at base of feathers. Lower abdomen and undertail coverts have white barring. Long, broad tail is banded black and grey. Irides yellow, bill black, feet yellow. Hens are larger. Young have more extensive white areas on the head and are browner overall.

Black-and-white hawk-eagle

Spizaetus melanoleucus

Sightings of this eagle are relatively unusual. Although distributed over a very wide area, it does not occur anywhere at high density. Large territories are essential to provide adequate hunting. Black and white hawk eagles take a wide variety of prey, from birds to opossums and probably small monkeys, also reptiles and amphibians. They hunt from high vantage points in the canopy, sometimes from fairly exposed branches. They prefer to hunt in clearings or on the edge of the forest, diving down from heights of 200m (650ft) or more, and may be heard whistling in flight. Little is known about their breeding habits, except that pairs construct a bulky platform of sticks located 40m (120ft) or more off the ground.

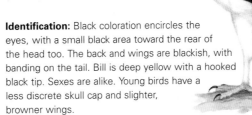

Identification: Black coloration encircles the eyes, with a small black area toward the rear of the head too. The back and wings are blackish, with banding on the tail. Bill is deep yellow with a hooked black tip. Sexes are alike. Young birds have a less discrete skull cap and slighter, browner wings.

Distribution: South Mexico through much of Central America. Isolated South American populations in Colombia, Venezuela and Peru but mostly found further east from Brazil to Bolivia and Paraguay, and in Argentina.
Size: 20cm (61in).
Habitat: Rainforest areas.
Nest: Stick nest.
Eggs: 1, white with dark brown blotches.
Food: Wide variety of prey.

OTHER HUNTERS OF THE FOREST

In addition to the larger birds of prey found in woodlands, a number of other predatory species are also encountered in this environment. They include the unusual caracaras, which are highly social by nature and feed largely on insect larvae. Other birds are more adaptable feeders, but studying these species is not always easy due to the relative inaccessibility of their habitats.

Red-throated caracara

Ibycter americanus; previously *Daptrius americanus*

Distribution: Ranges from southern Mexico through Central America to Ecuador, central Peru, and parts of northern and eastern Brazil, as far as southern Brazil.
Size: 61cm (24in)
Habitat: Rainforest.
Nest: Made of sticks.
Eggs: 2–3, whitish to buff, spotted with brown.
Food: Mainly invertebrates and some fruit.

Unusually among birds of prey, red-throated caracaras are highly social, living in established groups of up to ten individuals that all share and defend a territory. They break open small nests of wasps and bees to obtain the grubs, and remarkably escape being stung, even on their bare facial skin. It is believed that the caracaras have a natural insect-repellent on their plumage, since these normally aggressive insects do not even attempt to sting them. Occasionally, they also eat palm fruits and may even take turtle eggs. Red-throated caracaras breed infrequently, perhaps just once every five years, which may be a reflection of a stable and relatively long-lived population. Pairs may lay at a considerable height off the ground, with group members guarding the nest and gathering food for the chicks.

Identification: Mainly black on upperparts, back, wings and tail. Abdomen and undertail coverts white. Bare area of pinkish-red skin around eyes and on throat. Bill dark grey, legs and feet pink. Sexes are alike. Young have more yellowish areas of exposed skin.

Collared forest falcon

Micrastur semitorquatus

Identification: Three colour morphs. Black crown, with partial stripes extending down the sides of the face. Underparts and neck collar white or tawny, depending on the morph, with black back and wings. Long tail with white barring and a white tip. In dark morphs, head and underparts entirely black, except for slight white barring on the flanks. Bill black, with an area of greyish skin encircling the eyes. Legs and feet yellowish in all cases. Females larger. Upperparts of young birds more brown in colour.

It is thought that collared forest falcons deliberately deceive their prey, calling close to the ground to lure other birds within reach. They are effective hunters, able to dispatch much larger species such as ocellated turkeys, guans, currassows and other predatory birds, such as mottled owls. These falcons also appear to have very acute hearing. They nest in hollows in mature trees, with the larger female defending the site against other pairs. Incubation lasts over six weeks, with chicks spending a similar interval in the nest, where they are fed increasingly by the male. They are unlikely to start hunting alone until at least six weeks after fledging. Breeding pairs usually return to the same nest every year.

Distribution: Ranges from north-central parts of Mexico through Central America to parts of Colombia, Ecuador, and Peru. Extends over much of northern South America, as far south as Bolivia, Paraguay and northern Argentina.
Size: 56cm (22in).
Habitat: Lowland rainforest.
Nest: Tree cavities.
Eggs: 2, buff to brown, with darker brown markings.
Food: Mainly vertebrates.

Bat falcon

Falco rufigularis

In spite of its name, the bat falcon is not dependent on bats for its food, since it is an adept hunter of other flying creatures, including birds and invertebrates. Occasionally, these falcons catch rodents or lizards on the ground. They can also vary their hunting strategy, watching patiently from a perch or swooping down low over the forest canopy in the hope of disturbing prey. Pairs nest in tree holes that may previously have been occupied by birds such as parrots. They become noisy and territorial at this stage, driving away other birds of prey that enter the area. The male mainly hunts alone to feed the brood.

Identification: Dark slaty-grey head, with yellow cere and skin encircling each eye. Partial white collar extends up sides of the neck, edged with a chestnut band across chest. Greyish-black wings and tail, which is barred with white and has a white tip. Thighs and undertail coverts rufous. Lower underparts blackish with white barring. Bill black, legs and feet yellowish. Hens are larger. Young have black upperparts, with a buff-coloured throat.

Distribution: Extends from northern Mexico down through Central America west of the Andes to Ecuador, and eastward down as far as southern Brazil and northern Argentina.
Size: 29cm (11^1/$_2$in).
Habitat: Forested areas.
Nest: Tree holes.
Eggs: 2–9, creamy to reddish, with dark blotches.
Food: Flying creatures.

Sharp-shinned hawk (*Accipiter striatus*): 34cm (13in)
Much of North America from Alaska and Canada south to the USA as far as Panama, with birds moving south in winter. Also on various Caribbean islands. Slate-blue upperparts and barred tail with variable white-and-chestnut areas on the underparts. Females are larger.

Northern goshawk (*Accipiter gentilis*): 68cm (26^1/$_2$in)
North America to Mexico. A separate population is present through northern Europe and Asia. Variable depth of coloration. Wings are greyish. Underparts white with greyish barring extending up around the neck. Darker area of plumage on the head and behind the eyes. Hens are larger.

Plumbeous forest falcon (*Micrastur plumbeus*): 37cm (14^1/$_2$in)
South-west Colombia and northern Ecuador. Small, with dark greyish head and back. Barred underparts, with a characteristic single white band midway down the white-tipped tail feathers.

Hawaiian hawk (*Buteo solitarius*): 46cm (18in)
Restricted to the Hawaiian Islands. Endemic to Hawaii, has spread to Oahu and Maui. Brown overall, with pale rufous underparts. Females are much larger, the size difference being greater than in any other *Buteo* species. Young birds have tawny mottled plumage on the head and breast. In the pale morph, head and underparts are pale pinkish buff, with white undertail coverts. Wings are brownish with light markings, and the tail is grey with light banding. Young pale morph birds are golden-buff.

Ridgway's hawk

Buteo ridgwayi

These hawks can be seen in a variety of different habitats, having adjusted to some degree to forest clearance, but they are still very dependent on wooded areas for hunting and nesting. The nest is large, about 50cm (20in) in diameter. It is built mostly by the male, with the hen adding material to disguise its presence. Breeding pairs fly high above the canopy to perform a conspicuous aerial courtship. The eggs take about a month to hatch, and the chicks then remain on the nest until they fledge at around three months. They are reared largely on food provided by the male. Ridgway's hawk faces an uncertain future in its native habit unless sufficient areas can be protected from deforestation. It remains most widespread in the Los Haites region of Hispaniola. Although part of the island has been set aside as a national park, policing of these boundaries remains a difficult task.

Distribution: Restricted to the Caribbean region, where it occurs on the island of Hispaniola and neighbouring islets.
Size: 40cm (16in).
Habitat: Prefers undisturbed forest.
Nest: Platform of vegetation.
Eggs: 2–3, whitish with reddish blotches.
Food: Mainly vertebrates.

Identification: Greyish head, rufous underparts barred with white on chest and abdomen. Undertail coverts white. Back and wings brown, rufous-brown on the shoulders. Flight feathers dark, tail feathers dark with narrow white lines. Dull yellow bill has dark tip. Legs and feet yellow. Females duller brown above, with reddish-pink on underparts. Young are grey-brown with no rufous feathers.

GIANTS AND ODDITIES

Grassland areas are home to a surprisingly wide range of birds, including the flightless rheas, although the number of large species in South America is now significantly smaller than it was in the past. Fossil evidence has revealed how gigantic, fearsome avian carnivores roamed these plains as the age of the dinosaurs drew to a close, some 65 million years ago.

Greater rhea

Common rhea *Rhea americana*

The size of rheas prevents them from flying, but they are well equipped to defend themselves from most predators, and are able to run at speeds in excess of 60km/h (37mph) Their wings are larger than those of other flightless birds, with a claw on each so they can inflict serious injury at close quarters. Social by nature, rheas live in loose groups. When breeding, a number of hens are attracted to the male's nest and are persuaded to lay their eggs there. The eggs are golden yellow at first, changing to a whitish tone. The cock incubates the eggs and cares for the young chicks, which all hatch within a day or so of each other and start following him.

Identification: Tall and long-necked with greyish-brown plumage. Feathering only extends down the thighs, leaving the lower leg bare. Feet have three toes. Hens are lighter in colour and slightly smaller. Pure white albino individuals are surprisingly common, especially in the Argentinian race.

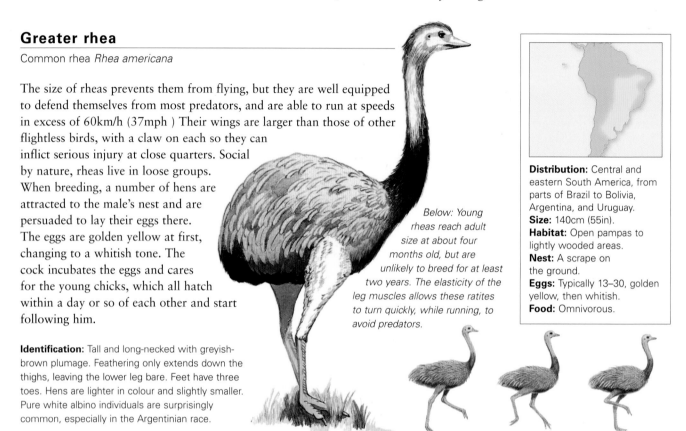

Below: Young rheas reach adult size at about four months old, but are unlikely to breed for at least two years. The elasticity of the leg muscles allows these ratites to turn quickly, while running, to avoid predators.

Distribution: Central and eastern South America, from parts of Brazil to Bolivia, Argentina, and Uruguay.
Size: 140cm (55in).
Habitat: Open pampas to lightly wooded areas.
Nest: A scrape on the ground.
Eggs: Typically 13–30, golden yellow, then whitish.
Food: Omnivorous.

Jabiru

Jabiru mycteria

The largest flying bird in America, the jabiru has a massive bill up to 33cm (13in) long. It uses this weapon to seize and kill its prey, which include fish, small mammals, other birds and their eggs. Jabirus are sometimes observed in groups. They are not shy, even seeking food in cultivated areas. Jabirus build a relatively large platform nest. Both the pair incubate the eggs, with chicks leaving the nest some four months after the eggs were laid. These large storks hop to aid take-off, but once airborne they fly with ease. In flight the neck is held out in a straight line, with legs trailing under the body. They are often seen circling at great heights.

Identification: Bare blackish skin on the head and neck, with a broad red band at its base. The nape of the neck is covered in downy white plumage, and all of the underparts are white. The legs and bill are black. Sexes are alike. Young birds have greyish upperparts and a duller red band, often with brownish feathering among the white.

Distribution: Ranges from south-eastern Mexico down through Central America, extending as far south as northern Argentina and Uruguay in South America.
Size: 132cm (52in)
Habitat: Marshy savannas.
Nest: Platform of sticks.
Eggs: 2–4, whitish.
Food: Mainly small vertebrates.

Hawaiian goose

Nene *Branta sandvicensis*

Hawaiian geese are unique, partly as a result of their environment. They display relatively little webbing between their toes, reflecting the fact that they live in a dry environment, foraging for food on larva screes. Another unusual feature is that they mate on land, rather than in water. They live in flocks from June to September, with pairs subsequently nesting on their own. In the late 1700s Hawaiian geese were very numerous, with an estimated population of around 25,000, but hunting and introduced animals from cats to mongooses, which killed the geese and ate their eggs, reduced the population to near-extinction. By the early 1950s only 30 individuals remained. However, a captive-breeding programme coupled with control of the predators has caused numbers of these geese to rise significantly again.

Distribution: Native range is restricted to the Hawaiian Islands, occurring on Hawaii itself and Maui. Captive-bred flocks occur in other areas, including Britain.
Size: 66cm (26in).
Habitat: Bare volcanic slopes.
Nest: Made of vegetation.
Eggs: 3–6, whitish green.
Food: Plant matter including vegetation and berries.

Identification: Black plumage on the head, with a buff-brown area at the back. Neck is mostly white but streaked with blackish markings, with a black band encircling the base. Underparts are whitish grey, and the area from the legs to the undertail coverts is white. Back and wings are greyish, with black and white edging to the feathers. Rump is white, with black tail feathers. Sexes are alike.

Greater roadrunner

Geococcyx californianus

These unusual members of the cuckoo clan are built for speed. Their common name derives from their habit of frequenting roads that attract lizards and other reptiles to bask on the heat of the tarmac early in the day to raise their body temperature. Greater roadrunners can run at speeds up to 37km/h (23mph), and although they can fly, they rarely take to the air. They have a distinct zygodactyl foot structure, with two toes directed forward and two behind, which may assist their balance, compared with the more usual 3:1 perching configuration. Their calls resemble the cooing of doves, and they also communicate by bill-chattering.

Distribution: South-western parts of the USA, across from California into Mexico.
Size: 61cm (24in).
Habitat: Open country, including desert areas.
Nest: Low platform of sticks.
Eggs: 4–10, white.
Food: Insects, lizards and small snakes.

Identification: Loose, ragged, dark crest spotted with white. Streaked upper chest becoming white on the underparts. Back and wings brown with buff and whitish edging to the feathers. Powerful, sharp-tipped bill. Grey rump and long tail. Strong legs. Sexes are alike.

Antillean nighthawk (*Chordeiles gundlachii*): 25cm (10in)
Breeds in the Caribbean, including on Jamaica, Hispaniola, Cuba, the Bahamas and the Cayman Islands, subsequently migrating to South America. Mottled tawny underparts with blackish mottled upperparts, white wing bars, and a lighter mottled stripe along the sides of the wings. Brown area below the eyes, white throat. Tiny, pointed black bill. Hens lack the white tail band of cocks.

Puna plover (*Charadrius alticola*): 17cm (7in)
Central Peru southward to north-eastern Chile, western Bolivia, and as far as north-western Argentina. White area above the bill, down onto sides of face and across underparts. Faint barring on the breast. Black stripe on the forehead, with buff-brown plumage on rest of the head. A blackish bar passes through the eyes down onto sides of the chest. Back and wings brownish. White evident on sides of the rump. Bill black. Hens have a rufous tinge on the nape. Young birds have no black markings on the head.

Rufous-bellied seedsnipe (*Attagis gayi*): 30cm (12in)
Isolated areas of Ecuador and central Peru through the Andean region down into Chile and to north-western Argentina. Heavily mottled rufous-brown overall, with black, white and brown areas on the individual feathers. Underparts are of a more pure chestnut shade. The southern population is paler overall compared with birds occurring further north. Sexes are alike.

QUAILS AND OTHER SMALL GROUND BIRDS

It is no coincidence that many of these birds have mottled upperparts, since they face danger from above, in the guise of avian predators swooping overhead. This characteristic patterning serves to break up their outline, making them hard to spot among the vegetation. They move largely on foot, which also helps to conceal their presence, and often fly only if they detect danger nearby.

Common bobwhite

Northern bobwhite *Colinus virginianus*

Taxonomists have recognized at least 22 different races of these quail, and colour variation is quite marked in some cases. Differences in size are also apparent, with individuals found in southern parts of their range being smaller than those occurring in northern regions. Common bobwhites live in groups, typically numbering around a dozen birds or so. They will invade agricultural areas to forage for food, especially when crops are ripening. These birds generally prefer to seek cover on the ground, where their cryptic coloration helps to conceal them from predators, but they will fly if threatened. Populations of these quails have also been introduced well outside their normal range, not only in other parts of the USA, including the north-west and on Hawaii, but also further afield in New Zealand.

Identification: There is considerable variation through the birds' wide range. Most races have a black stripe running from the bill through the eyes, with a white stripe above and a broader white area on the throat. Chestnut underparts, usually speckled with white. Wings are brownish. Hens are duller, having buff rather than white patches on the head.

Distribution: North-eastern USA southward through Mexico into western Guatemala.
Size: 25cm (10in).
Habitat: Woodland and farmland.
Nest: Scrape on the ground lined with vegetation.
Eggs: 10–15, dull white, often with blotches.
Food: Seeds and invertebrates.

California quail

Callipepla californica

California quail are highly adaptable through their range, and this characteristic has enabled breeding populations of these popular game birds to be established in locations as far apart as Hawaii, Chile and King Island, Australia. Nesting on the ground makes California quail vulnerable to predators, and although the young are able to move freely as soon as they have hatched, relatively few are likely to survive long enough to breed themselves the following year. Overgrazing by farm animals can adversely affect their numbers, presumably because this reduces the food that is available to the birds. However these quail also forage in crop-growing areas, and sometimes associate in groups of up to a thousand individuals where food is plentiful.

Identification: Prominent, raised black crest that slopes forward over the bill. Top of the head is chestnut, with a white band beneath and another bordering the black area of the face. Chest is greyish, flanks are speckled. Hens lack the black and white areas, with greyish faces and smaller crests.

Distribution: Native to western North America, ranging from British Columbia in Canada southward to the warmer climates of California and Mexico.
Size: 27cm (11in).
Habitat: Semi-desert to woodland.
Nest: Grass-lined scraping on the ground.
Eggs: About 15, creamy white with brownish patches.
Food: Seeds, vegetation and invertebrates.

Montezuma quail

Cyrtonyx montezumae

Like others of their kind, these quails are shy by nature and not easily observed unless flushed from their hiding places. They venture into woodland areas and can also be found in grassland, typically associating in small groups (described as coveys) comprised of about eight individuals, although groups of up to 25 may be observed. Montezuma quails have a varied diet, and when food is in short supply can survive on underground bulbs and tubers dug up with their powerful legs and sharp claws. As well as invertebrates, which figure prominently in their diet while breeding, they also seek out seeds and fruits. Pairs construct a domed nest up to 10cm (4in) tall, lined with leaves and grass. Both members of the pair are thought to share incubation duties. The young are able to walk on their own almost immediately after hatching, which occurs about 3¹/₂ weeks after egg-laying.

Identification: Males have black stripes above and below the eyes, with a black patch beneath each eye and under the throat, surrounded by white feathering. Upperparts are brownish with black mottling, possibly with a small crest on the back of the head. Depending on race, underparts may be black and white across the chest and down the flanks, with a central rufous area, or predominantly chestnut with light grey feathering broken by white spots on the flanks. Hens are less boldly marked, with no black and white markings on the face, and light rufous underparts.

Distribution: Ranges from parts of Texas, New Mexico and Arizona in the USA southward into Mexico.
Size: 22cm (9in).
Habitat: Brush and grassland.
Nest: Made of grass.
Eggs: 6–14, white, usually with darker markings.
Food: Vegetable matter and invertebrates.

Crested bobwhite (*Colinus cristatus*): 22cm (9in)
Panama to Colombia, Venezuela, French Guiana and northern Brazil. Appearance varies. Distinct crest, usually with a white stripe near the eyes. White speckling with thin, black borders on chestnut- or buff-coloured underparts. Hens duller with a shorter crest, and no eye stripe.

Scaled quail (*Callipepla squamata*): 29cm (11¹/₂in)
Southern USA south into Mexico. Blue-scaled plumage on the breast and neck down to the browner underparts. White-edged crest on the head. Wings brownish. Hens have a smaller crest, with brown streaking on the head and throat.

Lesser prairie chicken (*Tympanuchus pallidicinctus*): 41cm (16in)
Restricted to Colorado, Kansas, Oklahoma, Texas and New Mexico. Barred brownish and white plumage. Tail has dark banding near the tip. Buffish-yellow plumage above the eyes, with inflatable orange-red air sacs on sides of head. Sexes are similar, but hens lack dark tail banding.

Sharp-tailed grouse (*Tympanuchus phasianellus*): 48cm (19in)
Northern North America from Alaska across much of Canada, south into the USA, where its distribution has shrunk recently. Distinguishable from other barred members of the grouse family by pointed tail feathers. Has pinkish inflatable air sacs on head. Underparts speckled. Cocks significantly larger than hens.

Banded quail

Philortyx fasciatus

Hard to spot in their grassland habitat, these quails are perhaps more likely to be heard, uttering distinctive ringing notes to keep in touch with each other. They are social by nature, typically occurring in groups called coveys, comprised of up to a dozen individuals and sometimes more. They remain largely hidden during the day, tending to forage for food either at first light or towards dusk. At this stage, they may venture into fields in search of cultivated crops such as beans, sunflower and sesame. If disturbed, the members of the covey will usually fly off in different directions, reuniting once the danger has passed. Little is known about their breeding habits, although the hen sits alone, with the incubation period lasting about three weeks. The young are able to move on hatching, and will then start to moult at about two months of age. They attain adult plumage after a similar interval.

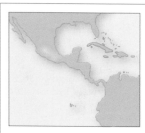

Distribution: Restricted to western-central Mexico, extending from southern Jalisco and Colima as far as central Guerrero and Puebla.
Size: 20cm (8in).
Habitat: Arid grassland areas.
Nest: Scrape with a partial grass dome above.
Eggs: 3–7, white.
Food: Seeds, some invertebrates.

Identification: Backwards-pointing brownish-black crest. Head brown with narrow buff stripe above eye and a broader blackish area behind. Throat white; upper breast brown with black edging. Wings dark centres with lighter buff edging. Hens have shorter crests. Young birds similar, but lack pure white throat.

GAME BIRDS

This group of birds also rely on their appearance to blend in with the background. The distribution of grouse extends to the frozen wastelands of the tundra zone in the far north. They are adapted to living on the ground there, moulting their plumage to match the seasons. They also have feathering that extends right down over the toes to restrict heat loss and guard against frostbite.

Greater prairie chicken

Tympanuchus cupido

The greater prairie chicken's range has declined significantly in recent years. The nominate race, called the heath hen, once had an extensive range in eastern parts of the USA, but is now presumed extinct. The smaller and darker form, Attwater's prairie chicken (*T. c. attwateri*), is now extinct in south-west Louisiana and struggling to survive in Texas. This is the result of hunting and also clearance of prairie habitat. Breeding males display communally at a lek, inflating their neck sacs and uttering a far-carrying, booming call. The nest is concealed by vegetation. Egg-laying occurs from early April.

Identification: Cock has yellowish-orange areas on head. Adjacent golden air sacs are inflated as part of the display, when the dark neck feathers are also raised. The body is barred with shades of brown. Paler underparts. Short tail is blackish in cock, barred in the hen. Sides of female's head and throat are speckled, with underparts having dark markings on a white background.

Distribution: Occurs mainly to the south and west of the Great Lakes, as far south as Oklahoma, with a separate population found in the coastal area of Texas.
Size: 47cm (18½in).
Habitat: Prairies and associated agricultural areas.
Nest: Scrape lined with feathers.
Eggs: 5–17, olive with brown blotching.
Food: Seeds and invertebrates.

Willow ptarmigan

Willow grouse, red grouse *Lagopus lagopus*

Identification: In summer plumage, cock has brownish head and upperparts, white wings and underparts, and black tail feathers. Hens can be distinguished by the speckled appearance of their underparts. During the winter, both sexes become white overall.

Living in a very inhospitable part of the world, where the earth is permanently frozen even in the summer, these grouse rely on meagre plant growth to sustain themselves. Willow (*Salix*) is vital as a food source over winter, when the ground is blanketed with snow, while in summer, berries and even invertebrates are sought. Breeding occurs during May and June, with the eggs being laid in a scrape on the ground. Both pairs share the task of incubation, with the young hatching after about three weeks. At this stage they are especially vulnerable to predators such as the Arctic fox, and studies suggest their lifespan is unlikely to exceed two years. Their transformation into white plumage helps them to merge with the background in winter. Sometimes, if conditions get very harsh, these grouse will move much further south, having been recorded in southern Ontario and northern Minnesota.

Distribution: Range is circumpolar, extending from the Aleutian Islands, Alaska, and north-west British Columbia right across northern Canada, including Arctic islands such as Victoria, down as far as Newfoundland on the east coast.
Size: 43cm (17in).
Habitat: Arctic tundra.
Nest: Scrape on the ground.
Eggs: 2–15, yellowish with brown blotches.
Food: Willow buds and twigs.

Sage grouse

Centrocercus urophasianus

The distribution of these grouse is tied to their primary food source, the sagebush (*Artemisia*), especially during winter when they feed almost exclusively on this plant. They even nest under cover of sagebushes. Breeding begins in April, with males displaying on their communal display grounds (leks), inflating their air sacs. The nest is well-concealed, with a lining of sagebush leaves and grass. Incubation lasts about a month. The young are able to move independently once hatched, and are reared on invertebrates.

Identification: Cock blackish around the bill, with an orange patch above each eye and greenish display sacs. V-shape created by blackish patches broken by a whitish area on the sides of the head and upper chest, with a whitish area on the lower breast and black on the abdomen. Upperparts heavily mottled, with white speckling on the flanks. Undertail coverts black with white edging. Long, tapering tail. Mottling extends down the legs. The bill is black. Hens are smaller, lacking white on the head or breast, this area being brownish instead. Young birds resemble hens, but paler.

Distribution: Central Washington, parts of Alberta, Saskatchewan, and the Dakotas to eastern California through Nevada, Utah, and western Colorado. Formerly southern British Columbia and northern parts of Oklahoma and New Mexico.
Size: 76cm (31in).
Habitat: Areas of sagebrush.
Nest: Scrape in the ground.
Eggs: 7–15, olive-buff with a few dark spots.
Food: Mainly sagebrush.

Gunnison grouse (*Centrocercus minimus*): 56cm (22in)
South-eastern Utah and south-central Colorado. Cock has orange on top of the head, with a long, downward-curving black crest at the back of the head. Prominent white breast with blackish central area, marked with brown on the lower chest. Rest of underparts dark. Wings mottled brown. Tail barred with white, with narrowing feathers. Hens are significantly smaller.

Chukar partridge (*Alectoris chukar*): 35cm (14in)
Southern British Columbia to Baja California and east to Colorado. Originally introduced as a game bird from Europe. Grey crown with a black stripe through each eye running down across the chest. Underparts greyish blue, becoming fawn, with black and white barring on flanks. Brownish on the back. Cream area on the sides of the face and chest. Bill is mainly red. Hens lack the tarsal swelling of cocks, with less colourful head patterning. Young birds mainly brownish in colour.

Grey partridge (Hungarian partridge, *Perdix perdix*): 32cm (12¹⁄₂in)
Ranges across prairies of northern USA and southern Canada. Introduced from Europe. Orangish-brown face, with a stripe extending further back. Crown, neck and much of underparts greyish, with dark edging on the plumage. Flanks barred with brown. Wings also brown with black speckling.

White-tailed ptarmigan

Lagopus leucura

The white-tailed is the only species of ptarmigan ranging south into the USA from Canada. It usually occurs at higher altitudes, although it descends in October to escape the worst winter weather. During summer, white-tailed ptarmigans are found close to the tree-line, where pairs establish breeding territories. The nest is concealed on the ground, and lined with feathers. Eggs are laid any time from late May until July. Hens incubate alone, with the young able to follow their parent after hatching. The population divides in winter, with males forming flocks on their own. When food is hard to find because of snow, ptarmigans feed on the buds of willow, birch and alder. Their fully feathered legs and feet afford protection from the cold.

Identification: In winter, both sexes are completely white, with males retaining a narrow red comb above the eyes. In summer, males have evident red comb with mottling on the head and upper breast, extending over the back and part of the wings, with white underparts. Hens slightly smaller and more mottled, with prominent black markings over the back, and lacking the comb. Slight variations depending on race. Young birds display barring all over the wings.

Distribution: Western North America, from Alaska through Canada into the USA in the Rocky Mountains, as far south as New Mexico. Now re-established in the High Sierras of California.
Size: 34cm (13in).
Habitat: Tundra and mountainous areas.
Nest: Scrape on the ground.
Eggs: 5–9, cinnamon-brown with dark spots.
Food: Vegetation.

HUMMINGBIRDS AND INSECT-HUNTERS

The feeding opportunities that exist in relatively open areas of country enable birds more commonly found in the woodland, such as hummingbirds, to live successfully in this habitat. As well as flowers, which provide high-energy nectar and protein-rich pollen, there is an abundance of small invertebrates. Other birds that catch insects in flight, such as flycatchers, can also be encountered here.

Beautiful hummingbird

Beautiful sheartail *Calothorax pulcher*

Hummingbirds as a group are restricted to the New World, with a number of species occurring in relatively open countryside, where they seek out flowers. The beautiful hummingbird feeds at a range of levels, from quite close to the ground right up into flowering trees. Like many species it has a very restricted range, which helps its identification. The speed at which beautiful hummingbirds fly and dart around makes them difficult to observe closely, especially on the wing, while their small size means they can be easily overlooked when perching. Furthermore, the brilliant colours of the male's gorget have an iridescent quality which, depending on the light, can actually make them even less conspicuous. There is no mistaking the male's display flight, however, as he soars upward to a height of perhaps 10m (30ft) before dropping back down right beside his mate. She builds the nest, and subsequently cares for their chicks on her own.

Identification: Cock has golden-green upperparts, with a black tail and wings. Underparts whitish, greener on the flanks. Area of deep rose-pink feathering with violet markings forms a gorget on the throat. Long, narrow, down-curved black bill. Hens lack the bright throat, with a buff tinge to the underparts and a pale grey streak extending from below the eyes. Tail feathers mainly black with a brown base and white tip. Young birds similar to hens.

Distribution: Occurs only in Central America, where its range is restricted to south-western parts of Mexico.
Size: 9cm (3$\frac{1}{2}$in).
Habitat: Scrubland.
Nest: Small, cup-shaped.
Eggs: 2, whitish.
Food: Nectar and invertebrates.

Giant hummingbird

Patagona gigas

Identification: Bronzy to cinnamon upperparts, sometimes with a greyish tone depending on the subspecies, and long, narrow wings. Forked tail paler at the base. Relatively thick, straight bill measuring approximately 3·5cm (1$\frac{1}{2}$in). Hens can be distinguished by the spotting on their underparts. Young birds are much greyer overall, with faint scaling on the upperparts.

As its name suggests, the giant hummingbird is the largest of over 300 species. It occurs in relatively inhospitable terrain through the Andean region, typically being found in valleys, ranging as high as 4,500m (14,800ft) in parts of Peru. Its size imposes constraints on its aerial manoeuverability compared with smaller relatives, and it has a flight pattern that more closely resembles that of a swallow. Giant hummingbirds can hover when feeding, spreading their tail feathers, but often prefer to perch on the puya or cacti flowers. They can be aggressive toward other hummingbirds, chasing them away while calling loudly. The female constructs her nest in the safety of a branching cactus, although cliff faces are also used. Giant hummingbirds appear to be extending their range northward into Colombia, having established themselves in neighbouring Ecuador.

Distribution: May range from the eastern Andes of Colombia southward via Ecuador, Peru and Bolivia to central parts of Chile and Argentina.
Size: 20cm (8in).
Habitat: Arid upland areas.
Nest: Small, cup-shaped.
Eggs: 2, whitish.
Food: Nectar and invertebrates.

Cassin's kingbird (*Tyrannus vociferans*): 23cm (9in)
Ranges from south-western USA through western Mexico as far south as Guatemala. Greyish plumage on the head and upper breast, extending down the back. Prominent white area under the throat, reaching to the base of the lower bill. Lower underparts are yellowish. Wings and tail feathers are brownish, with whitish edging to the flight feathers. Pointed bill, legs and feet are all blackish. Sexes are alike.

Mexican sheartail (*Doricha eliza*; previously *Calothorax eliza*): 10cm (4in)
Restricted to Veracruz in Mexico and the north Yucatan Peninsula. Iridescent green top to the head extends over the back, with greenish suffusion on the flanks. Throat is a metallic reddish purple, edged with a whitish area from the eyes on to the chest and central underparts. Wings and tail feathers blackish, as is the long, narrow, slightly down-curved bill. In flight the tail feathers may be held in a V-shape, revealing orange edging. Hens are slightly smaller, with completely white underparts.

Dusky hummingbird (*Cynanthus sordidus*): 9cm (3¹⁄₂in)
Restricted to south-western Mexico. A white stripe extends behind the eyes. Upperparts dull golden green, tail feathers greyish green. The wings are dusky grey, underparts greyish with a green suffusion on the flanks. Long, narrow bill is mainly red. Hens have paler underparts.

Rock wren

Salpinctes obsoletus

Ten subspecies of this wren have been identified, although one of these, the San Benedicto rock wren (*S. o. exsul*), from the island of that name on Mexico's west coast, was wiped out by a volcanic explosion in 1952. Rock wrens are lively and easy to observe since they are naturally quite tame and conspicuous, moving from boulder to boulder in search of invertebrates, although, if danger threatens, they slip away. Their relatively loud song is especially evident during the breeding period. These wrens seek out small crevices in rocks as nest sites, creating a snug lining. They frequently build the nest on a bed of small stones that they collect themselves, for reasons that are unclear, though it may have something to do with nest sanitation. They will gather a wide variety of material to incorporate into the nest site, ranging from rabbit bones to small pieces of rusty metal.

Identification: Dark greyish-brown upperparts with black streaky markings. Chestnut-brown rump, underparts whitish grey with fine dark streaking on the breast. Narrow, pointed greyish bill. Sexes alike. Young birds duller. Extent of black barring differs between races.

Distribution: Western North America. Breeding range extends to British Columbia; wanders widely outside the breeding period. Separate populations in parts of Mexico, Guatemala, Honduras, Nicaragua and north-western Costa Rica.
Size: 14cm (5¹⁄₂in).
Habitat: Rocky areas.
Nest: Made of vegetation.
Eggs: 4–10, white with reddish-brown speckling.
Food: Invertebrates.

Fork-tailed flycatcher

Tyrannus savana

Flycatchers belong to the same genus as kingbirds, *Tyrannus*. The very long, streaming tail plumes of this species are especially conspicuous in flight. The plumes of the young birds are less than half the length of those of the adults. Fork-tailed flycatchers inhabit open savanna country, often preferring areas where there are isolated bushes rather than trees. Here they frequently perch quite close to the ground, ever-alert to feeding opportunities. Their diet consists of invertebrates. Fork-tailed flycatchers can be quite social by nature, and have occasionally been recorded in groups of more than 50 individuals, with this flocking behaviour being most common outside the summer months. Although it has been suggested that these flycatchers undertake regular migrations, it now appears that they tend to be more nomadic in their habits, simply wandering from one area to another. They construct their nest from plant fibres of various types.

Identification: Black head, with white throat and underparts. The neck and back are grey, and the flight feathers are black with whitish edging. Distinctive, elongated forked tail feathers, which are longer in cock birds than in hens. Young birds recognizable by their much shorter forked tails and the dusky area on the crown.

Distribution: Ranges from southern parts of Mexico through much of Central and South America. Reaches Argentina at the most southerly point of its range.
Size: 13in (33cm).
Habitat: Savanna.
Nest: Cup-shaped, fashioned from plant fibres.
Eggs: 2–5, whitish with darker markings.
Food: Invertebrates.

PIGEONS AND DOVES

The characteristic dumpy appearance of pigeons and doves, along with their relatively subdued coloration, means that they can be quite easily identified. There is actually no strict zoological distinction between these two groups, although the term "pigeon" is usually applied to larger species, particularly members of the Columba *genus.*

Mourning dove

Carolina dove *Zenaida macroura*

These doves are so-called because of the plaintive, mournful sound of their calls. They have benefited from the provision of bird tables, particularly in the northern part of their range, and often visit gardens for the food being offered. Their powerful wings and sleek shape help these doves to fly long distances on migration, and northerly populations overwinter in Central America. In southern USA, such as Florida, mourning doves are resident throughout the year. They prefer to look for food on the ground if not feeding on a bird table, and groups often wander across fields in search of seeds and other edible items. Mourning doves are now overwintering further north than they did in the past, partly as a result of more feeding opportunities from bird tables.

Identification: There is some variation in appearance through these doves' wide range, with cocks displaying pinkish buff coloration on the face, extending down to the underparts, with a dark streak just above the neck. The upper surfaces of wings and tail are brown, with several large dark spots evident on the wings. Hens are duller in coloration, being browner overall.

Distribution: Extensive range across much of North America, from southern Canada southward across the USA through Central America to Costa Rica and Panama, but distribution is affected by the season. Also occurs on the Greater Antilles in the Caribbean.
Size: 34cm (13in).
Habitat: Lightly wooded areas.
Nest: Loose pile of twigs.
Eggs: 2, white.
Food: Seeds and some invertebrates.

Black-winged ground dove

Metriopelia melanoptera

The male black-winged ground dove has a very distinctive, rather attractive chirruping call, unlike the more usual cooing calls associated with this group of birds. His call is heard more frequently during the breeding season, as he fans his tail and flicks his wings, making the white areas of plumage on these areas more visible. These doves are often sighted in association with the smaller bare-faced ground dove (*M. ceciliae*), and frequently occur in the vicinity of puya shrubs, which provide both roosting and breeding sites. Pairs may also nest in buildings, however, and sometimes even on the ground among rocky outcrops that provide them with some protection from possible predators. The nest itself is a relatively loose structure, and is usually sited quite close to the ground.

Identification: Compact body shape. Predominantly brown, apart from the black flight feathers and tail, with a white area at the shoulder that is usually hidden. There is a slight pinkish tinge on the head, and bare orangish-red skin around the eyes. Hens are duller in colour and a slightly paler shade of brown. This colour tends to increase in depth during the breeding period.

Distribution: Western side of South America, from Colombia and Ecuador through Peru, Chile and Argentina to Tierra del Fuego at the southern tip of the continent.
Size: 23cm (9in).
Habitat: Upland arid areas.
Nest: Platform of twigs.
Eggs: 2, white.
Food: Seeds of grasses and other plants.

Buckley's ground dove (Ecuadorian ground dove, *Columbina buckleyi*): 18cm (7in)
North-western Ecuador to north-western Peru. Greyish-brown upperparts and more pinkish underparts, with greyish coloration most marked on the head. Black underwing coverts. Hen is browner, with less contrast in her plumage.

Eared dove (golden-necked dove, *Zenaida auriculata*): 28cm (11in)
Occurs over most of South America, aside from the Amazon region and Andean uplands. Very common, especially in north-eastern Brazil, where migratory flocks, thought to be comprised of a million birds, can occasionally be observed. Some variation in colour through the range. Two black lines behind and below the eyes, with a prominent green iridescent area behind the eyes. Wings are brownish with variable dark wing spots. Underparts are pinkish. Hens are duller in appearance.

Spot-winged pigeon (American spotted pigeon, *Patagioenas maculosa*): 33cm (13in)
Two separate populations. One ranges from south-west Peru into western Bolivia and Argentina, distinguishable by the white edging to the grey feathers on the wings. The other, with more pronounced white areas creating the impression of spots, extends southward into south-western Brazil, Paraguay and Uruguay. Head and underparts have a pinkish-grey tone. Hens greyer overall.

Scaled dove (*Columbina squammata*): 22cm (8 1/2in)
South America, with the more northerly population extending from northern Colombia to French Guinea; the other ranges from central-eastern Brazil down to northern Argentina. Greyish-brown upperparts, with black scaly edging to individual feathers over the entire body. Greyish-white forehead, a pinker tone on face and breast, becoming whitish on underparts. Hens are a duller pink. Young birds duller overall.

Gold-billed ground dove

Croaking ground dove *Columbina cruziana*

These small doves are a relatively common sight in gardens and parks, and have adapted well to changes in habitat throughout their range. They may sometimes be seen in large numbers where food is abundant, seeking seeds and other plant matter on the ground. The distinctive croaking calls uttered by cock birds are more likely to be heard during the breeding period. In common with many other pigeons and doves, the hen lays on a relatively flimsy nest. The young doves may leave the nest at just ten days old, before they are able to fly effectively, and hide in nearby vegetation.

Above: Both members of the pair incubate the eggs.

Identification: Predominantly brownish with pinker underparts and greyish head. Bluish-grey wing coverts display variably positioned reddish-brown spots across them and a magenta stripe across the top. The bill is yellow at the base, while the tip is black. Hens are similar, but are a much more even shade of brown overall. The tail is relatively short.

Distribution: Coastal region from Ecuador through Peru to northern Chile.
Size: 15cm (6in).
Habitat: Open woodland and scrub.
Nest: Loose platform of twigs.
Eggs: 2, white.
Food: Seeds of grasses and other plants.

Bare-faced ground dove

Bare-eyed ground dove *Metriopelia ceciliae*

These doves may range at altitudes up to 4,500m (15,000ft). When breeding, they will, unusually, seek out holes in cliffs or even the protection offered by buildings, rather than nesting in a tree or shrub. In the vicinity of human habitation, they often nest on houses, and forage for food in surrounding gardens. Elsewhere, they may fly quite long distances from their roosting sites in search of food. These doves are very quiet by nature, and are unlikely to betray their presence by their calls. They are also very adept at running along the ground to escape from danger.

Identification: Bright area of bare, yellowish-orange skin encircles the eyes. Back and wings are brownish with much paler, buff-coloured mottling at the centres of individual feathers. Chest is pinkish brown with brownish underparts. Hens are usually slightly duller in coloration.

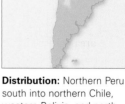

Distribution: Northern Peru south into northern Chile, western Bolivia, and north-west Argentina.
Size: 16cm (6in).
Habitat: Dry, upland country.
Nest: Loose platform.
Eggs: 2, white.
Food: Seeds of grasses and other plants.

SPARROWS AND FINCHES

Adaptable feeders, these relatively small birds can be encountered in a wide range of habitats, even in areas that are relatively inhospitable such as in the high Andean region or on the tundra of the frozen north. Occasionally they can be found well outside their normal distributions. Most are relatively conspicuous, certainly outside the nesting period, when they are likely to be sighted in small flocks.

Andean siskin

Spinus spinescens

Distribution: Occurs in the Andean region of northern South America, ranging from Venezuela and Colombia southward to northern Ecuador.
Size: 10cm (4in).
Habitat: Scrub and relatively open countryside.
Nest: Made of plant fibres of various kinds.
Eggs: 2, pale bluish white with darker markings.
Food: Seeds and also invertebrates.

These siskins have a high-pitched and attractive song, often uttered in flight. As their name asserts, they are native to the Andean region, where they are most likely to be observed at altitudes of between 1,500 to 4,100m (5,000 and 13,500ft). Here they favour scrubland and fairly open terrain. Andean siskins are sometimes hard to spot as they perch in taller trees. They are easier to observe when they venture on to the ground in search of food. These siskins may be encountered in small flocks, and sometimes forage in company with other finches, seeking *Espletia* seeds, a particular favourite. Their diet also includes insects, which provide protein. It is not uncommon among the Ecuadorian population for some birds resembling mature cocks actually to be hens. Their main area of distribution lies in the northern part of their range, and here they are quite common. It appears that these siskins are extending their range south-westward as well, with the first documented sighting of the species from northern Ecuador being made in 1982.

Identification: Has a black area extending from the bill to the top of the head. Plumage is greenish yellow elsewhere and of a brighter hue on the underparts. Wings are black with distinct yellow markings across the flight feathers. Hens are duller in coloration, lacking the black cap, and with less yellow on the wings.

Saffron finch

Sicalis flaveola

Distribution: Much of South America, from Colombia to Argentina; also on Trinidad.
Size: 14cm (5½in).
Habitat: Lightly wooded areas.
Nest: Tree cavities.
Eggs: 4, pale blue with brownish spots.
Food: Seeds and invertebrates.

Although there are other finches with predominantly yellow plumage, the saffron finch is the most brightly coloured member of the entire group, and also has one of the widest distributions. It has been introduced to various localities outside its natural range across much of South America, and is consequently seen in parts of Panama and Jamaica as well. These attractive finches can frequently be observed on the ground, foraging for food in the form of seeds and invertebrates, often in small groups or individual pairs. They are usually quite tame by nature, especially when encountered in parks and other urban areas.

Identification: Bright yellow underparts, becoming more orange at the front of the crown. Olive-brown wings and tail. Short, pointed bill. Hens have brown, streaked upperparts with whitish underparts. Young birds are also streaked, with young cocks developing a yellowish neck collar and matching chest when they first moult into adult plumage.

Grasshopper sparrow

Ammodramus savannarum

Known as grasshopper sparrows because of the way they hop over the ground in search of food, these small, rather plain-coloured birds are not always easy to spot in their grassland habitat. Males are most likely to betray their presence by their song, especially at the start of the breeding season. This is the time when they are most likely to be seen in the open, trilling on a fence post or a similar exposed perch. The nesting season varies through their range, typically occurring between May and August in the Caribbean. On some islands, such as Cuba, they overwinter in large numbers, yet elsewhere (Jamaica for example) they are present throughout the year. Unfortunately, grasshopper sparrows are very susceptible to habitat disturbance, and this has led to their decline in some areas, with even overgrazing reducing their numbers.

Identification: Some races have distinctive yellow plumage at the front of each eye stripe, and a white stripe on the crown. Pronounced black streaking with chestnut edging on the crown, becoming browner on the wings. Underparts are pale brown, becoming whitish close to the vent. Sexes are alike. Young birds have streaking on the breast.

Distribution: Breeding range extends north across British Columbia, Manitoba, and New Hampshire. Winters in southern USA through Panama to western Colombia and north-western Ecuador. Also through the Greater Antilles in the Caribbean.
Size: 13cm (5in).
Habitat: Grasslands.
Nest: Domed structure.
Eggs: 3, white with dark markings.
Food: Invertebrates and some seeds.

Hooded siskin (*Spinus magellanicus*):
14cm (5¹/₂in)
Central-southern South America, in Bolivia, Peru, Paraguay, Argentina and Uruguay. Also a northern Andean population, from Colombia to Peru, and another in south-east Venezuela, Guyana, and north-west Brazil. Black head and yellowish chest and upper abdomen, becoming whiter below, with a green back. Hens are duller, with a greyish head and greenish underparts.

Common redpoll (*Acanthis flammea*):
14cm (5¹/₂in)
Breeds across northern North America, from Alaska to British Columbia and east to Newfoundland. Winters through southern Canada into the USA from California via Oklahoma to the Carolinas. Crimson red cap and black lores, with streaked upperparts. Pinkish chest fading to white on the streaked abdomen. White wing bars, yellowish bill. Hens lack the pink throat. Young birds lack the red cap.

Pine siskin (*Spinus pinus*):
13cm (5in)
Breeds from southern Alaska across Canada south of Hudson's Bay to Newfoundland, and in the USA south to California and in the vicinity of the Great Lakes. Occurs widely through the USA in winter, extending south to parts of Florida, Texas and New Mexico. Dark streaky patterning over the entire body, with solid black areas and variable patches of yellow on the wings. Variable yellow patches at the base of the tail feathers too. Narrow, pointed bill which is darker above. Sexes are alike.

Hoary redpoll

Arctic redpoll *Acanthis hornemanni*

Similar in appearance to the common redpoll (*A. flammea*), this species can easily be distinguished by its plain rump and undertail coverts. Although both redpolls occur together in some parts of their range, they do not interbreed. The distribution of the hoary redpoll extends further north, and in the treeless tundra they are forced to breed on the ground, creating a warm, cup-shaped nest lined with feathers that may be concealed among rocks or under a shrub. The chicks are reared largely on a diet of insects, which are readily available in the Arctic through the summer months, while for the remainder of the year these finches subsist primarily on seed. They are often observed in pairs or family groups, although occasionally they may be spotted in larger flocks of up to 100 individuals. Occurring so far north, it is perhaps not surprising that this redpoll has a circumpolar distribution, being also found throughout the far north of Europe and Asia.

Distribution: Breeds along the Arctic coast of North America. In winter, found over much of Canada and northern parts of the USA
Size: 14cm (5¹/₂in).
Habitat: Tundra and open country.
Nest: Cup of vegetation.
Eggs: 5–6, pale blue with light brown spots.
Food: Seeds and invertebrates.

Identification: Red patch on the crown. Pale frosty grey streaked upperparts and a prominent white wing bar, with wings otherwise appearing black. A black area surrounds the base of the stocky bill. Breeding males have pinkish chests. Hens similar but with some streaking present on the flanks.

FARMLAND BIRDS

Areas of open country have increased significantly in the recent past, with vast amounts of land being cleared for the cultivation of crops, especially in the eastern USA. Natural habitats have also made way for towns and cities, while highways have cut across country. However, many birds have adapted well to these changes, and thrive in this altered environment.

Painted bunting

Passerina ciris

The cock painted bunting is popularly regarded as the most colourful of all North America's songbirds. Unfortunately, however, these relatively shy birds are not easily seen, often remaining concealed in vegetation, where their presence is more likely to be revealed by the cock's song. They have a warbling call as well as a short, harsh, warning note that is uttered at any hint of danger. The nest, too, is well hidden, and is constructed from a variety of vegetation. A pair may rear two broods in succession, and insects feature more prominently in their diet at this time. The hen builds the nest on her own and collects a variety of plant matter for this purpose, ranging from strips of bark and dead leaves to grass stems and rootlets. She chooses a well-concealed nest site, often in the fork of a tree.

Identification: Males are very colourful and unmistakable, with bluish-violet plumage on the head and a rose-red throat and underparts. The wings and back are green, with darker tail and flight feathers. Hens are drab in comparison, with green upperparts, becoming more yellowish on the underside of the body, and no bars on the wings, unlike many other finches.

Distribution: Widely distributed across the southern USA and Mexico, with populations moving south in the winter as far as Panama. Also present on Cuba.
Size: 14cm (5½in).
Habitat: Lightly wooded areas and brush.
Nest: Woven nest.
Eggs: 3–5, pale blue with darker spots.
Food: Mainly seeds, some invertebrates.

Dickcissel

Spiza americana

These finches take their unusual name from the sound of their song, which at times is repeated almost continuously from a suitable perch. Dickcissels are frequently seen in agricultural areas, often in hay fields where they can forage easily on the seeds that form the basis of their diet. When breeding, they choose a nest site close to the ground, and at ground level may hide the nest among clover or alfalfa. These finches undertake seasonal movements. On migration they sometimes form huge flocks consisting of thousands of individuals, with the birds flying in tight formation. Many spend the winter period (from October to April) in the Venezuelan llanos, although they may also congregate in agricultural areas at this time, mostly in rice fields. Dickcissels can occasionally be observed in various parts of the Caribbean, heading to and from their North American breeding grounds.

Identification: This species has a grey head with a yellow stripe above each eye leading back from the short, conical bill. A whitish area is present on the throat, with black beneath. Chest is yellowish, with white lower underparts. Back and wings are brownish with darker striations. Hens are duller, having grey underparts and lacking the prominent black area under the throat.

Distribution: Eastern North America, breeding from the vicinity of the Great Lakes and Montana down to Texas and the Gulf coast. Overwinters in parts of Central and northern South America.
Size: 18cm (7in).
Habitat: Treeless areas.
Nest: Cup-shaped.
Eggs: 4–5, pale blue.
Food: Mainly seeds.

Lark bunting

Calamospiza melanocorys

Identification: Cock in breeding condition is primarily black, with prominent white patches on the wings and a white tip to the tail. Out of colour they resemble hens, which have a blackish bib and white underparts speckled with brown markings. The upperparts are brown with darker streaking, and the wings and tail are blackish.

In spite of their name, these birds are finches. The attractive song of the cock lark bunting is similar to that of a canary, making it one of the most distinctive songsters on the plains. Its accompanying display flight is equally spectacular, as it soars up and down off its perch almost vertically. This behaviour is believed to have evolved because there are few trees that can be used as prominent singing sites through this region. Lark buntings live in flocks, which are often seen on the ground alongside roads, seeking seeds and invertebrates. When they do take to the wing they fly in a tight formation, wheeling together through the landscape, making it difficult for a bird of prey to target one particular individual. They breed in groups, with the nests made on the ground often hidden beneath vegetation, and the males compete with each other in song. Flocks leave the breeding grounds during late summer and head south, typically being seen in Mexico from August through to April.

Distribution: Breeds from the prairies of southern Canada to the plains of west-central USA, overwintering in southern parts of the USA and Mexico.
Size: 19cm (7¹/₂in).
Habitat: Prairies and plains.
Nest: Scrape in the ground.
Eggs: 4–5, light blue.
Food: Seeds and invertebrates.

Pyrrhuloxia (Grey cardinal, *Cardinalis sinuatus*): 23cm (9in)
Arizona, New Mexico and Texas, and across the US border to northern Mexico. Prominent red-tipped crest, with a reddish area on the face, extending onto the chest. Rest of the head, back and rump are greyish. Underparts lighter, with brownish areas on the wings. Tail and flight feathers reddish. Down-curved horn-coloured bill. Hens lack red plumage on the face, tail and underparts, which are a brownish grey.

Bronzed cowbird (*Molothrus aeneus*): 23cm (9in)
Breeds in Arizona, New Mexico and Texas (leaves Arizona for winter), ranging through Central America from Mexico south to Panama. Cocks are black with a bronzy-brown on the body and blackish wings. Red eyes, pointed blackish bill. Hens are duller, a dark grey.

Shiny cowbird (*Molothrus bonariensis*): 17cm (6¹/₂in)
Ranges over much of South America, from Bolivia and Paraguay south to Argentina and Uruguay, possibly also Chile. Cock birds mainly a glossy, iridescent black, with brown on the wings and a strong, pointed black bill. Hens are brownish, ranging from pale to almost black.

Bolivian blackbird (*Oreopsar bolivianus*): 23cm (9in)
Occurs in central Bolivia. Shares glossy black plumage with the shiny cowbird, but is larger in size, with a bigger, more sharply curved bill. Hens are slightly smaller than cocks. Young birds have brown primary coverts.

Horned lark

Eremophila alpestris

This is the only true member of the lark family occurring naturally in the Americas. The horned lark is primarily a terrestrial species, walking rather than hopping on the ground. If disturbed it will dart off a short distance before dropping down again. It favours open country where there is little cover. Pairs start nesting early, with hens incubating eggs in February in the northern USA. This can be hazardous if the weather turns bad, since the nest may be buried by snow. Horned larks are prolific breeders, however, and soon start again, with pairs producing up to 15 chicks in a good year. Over summer pairs tend to be solitary, but in fall they come together to form quite large flocks, often with other birds.

Identification: Narrow, raised black feathers on the sides of the head create the impression of horns. Facial colour varies among races, from white to yellow, with variable black markings here. Prominent black stripe across the chest. Underparts whitish with dark flecking on the flanks. Wings a variable brown. Bill and legs blackish. Hens duller with indistinct horns.

Distribution: Breeds as far north as Alaska and the Canadian Arctic, and through much of the USA as far south as Mexico. May occasionally range down to northern Colombia in South America.
Size: 18cm (7in).
Habitat: Fairly arid country.
Nest: Scrape on the ground.
Eggs: 2–5, greyish white with brown markings.
Food: Seeds and invertebrates.

SONGBIRDS OF THE PLAINS

Some birds of the open country draw attention to themselves with their song, particularly at the start of the nesting period, as is the case with thrashers. Others with a relatively dull appearance, such as some of the New World blackbirds found here, may also undergo something of a metamorphosis, with the plumage of the males becoming more brightly coloured.

Western meadowlark

Sturnella neglecta

Distribution: Breeds from British Columbia and Manitoba via Ohio and Missouri to parts of Texas and into northern Mexico. Northern populations move slightly southward in winter.
Size: 25cm (10in).
Habitat: Meadows and grassland.
Nest: Domed cup.
Eggs: 3–7, white with darker markings.
Food: Invertebrates.

Male western meadowlarks are very vocal, especially at the start of the nesting season when they are laying claim to their territories. They will choose a conspicuous site, such as a fence post, and seek not only to attract females but also to drive away rival males. In areas where their distribution overlaps with eastern meadowlarks, even eastern males are perceived as a threat and chased off, since hybridization between these two forms is not unknown. Meadowlarks, which are actually icterids or New World blackbirds, are polygamous in their breeding habits, with a single male mating with several females. Each female constructs a separate and fairly elaborate dome-shaped nest, which takes about a week, before starting to lay. The male plays no part in nest building, but will help to provide food for the young once the eggs have hatched. Western meadowlarks become more social in winter, when they may be observed in small flocks.

Identification:
Brown crown extends back over the top of the head, with a brown stripe running behind the eyes. Pale brown cheeks. Back and wings brown with darker barring. A black band runs across the chest, with lores, throat, and central underparts yellow. Flanks whitish with darker spotting. Sexes alike. Young birds paler with barring rather than a band across the chest.

Bobolink

Dolichonyx oryzivorus

The bobolink's unusual name originates from the sound of the male's song, which is audible through the breeding period. Like many birds found in open country, these icterids often sing in flight. They are known locally in South America as ricebirds, due to the way they have adapted to feeding on this crop. Though found in open country in North America, bobolinks are more likely to be observed in reedy areas of marshland during their winter migration. Remarkably, despite flying such long distances, these birds travel back to the same familiar breeding grounds every spring, with the mature males arriving first. Studies of their unique song patterns have revealed not only local dialects but also that the males use different call notes to communicate with each other, compared with those that are intended to attract females. Although the majority pair individually with a female, some males have more than one partner.

Identification: Cock in breeding condition is primarily black, with pale buff on the hind neck. Prominent white wing bar, with the lower back and rump also white. Hens have a dark crown with a streak down the centre, and a dark streak behind each eye. Their underparts are yellowish, with streaking on the flanks. Young birds have spotting on the throat and upper breast, with no streaking on their underparts.

Distribution: Breeds from British Columbia to Newfoundland south to northern California, Colorado and Pennsylvania. Winters in southern South America, reaching Argentina and southern Brazil, but precise range is unclear.
Size: 18cm (7in).
Habitat: Prairies and open areas.
Nest: Cup-shaped.
Eggs: 4–7, grey with reddish-brown spotting.
Food: Seeds and invertebrates.

Red-winged blackbird

Agelaius phoeniceus

Distribution: Occurs over much of North America, breeding as far north as Alaska, and south into Central America.
Size: 24cm (9¹/₂in).
Habitat: Relatively open country.
Nest: Cup-shaped.
Eggs: 3, pale greenish blue with dark spots.
Food: Seeds and invertebrates.

Unrelated to the European blackbird, the red-winged blackbird is a member of the icterid family. It frequents marshland areas when nesting, but is seen in a much wider range of habitats during winter. In North America, red-winged blackbirds move southward for the winter period, typically travelling distances of about 700km (440 miles). Populations in Central America tend to be sedentary throughout the year, however. There is a quite marked variation in the appearance of these birds through their wide range, and it is also not uncommon for individuals to display pied markings. Both sexes sing, particularly at the start of the nesting period, and some of their call notes are different, so it is possible to tell them apart.

Identification: Only the mature male in breeding plumage displays the typical glossy black feathering and red shoulder patches with a paler buff border. Females have dark streaks running down their bodies, with more solid brownish coloration on the head, sides of the face, and over the wings.

Eastern meadowlark (*Sturnella magna*): 25cm (10in)
South-eastern Canada across eastern USA (resident through much of this area) and west to Nebraska, Arizona and Texas. Also in Mexico, ranging to northern South America. Similar to western meadowlark, with a brownish crown and a lighter central stripe, and a further stripe behind the eyes. Black band across the chest, with yellow central underparts. Flanks are whitish with dark speckling, back and wings are brownish with black barring. Yellow on face varies. Sexes are alike. Young birds are paler.

Brewer's blackbird (*Euphagus cyanocephalus*): 23cm (9in)
Southern British Columbia east to the Great Lakes and down to Baja California and western Texas. Winters south to Central Mexico, sometimes to Guatemala. Cock in breeding colour is iridescent blue with a purplish hue on the head and a greenish suffusion over rest of body and wings. Eyes yellow, pointed bill black. When not breeding, may display darker brownish plumage with black barring and blackish wings. Hens and young birds greyish brown, with slight mottling on the back. Black wings, dark eyes.

Bendire's thrasher (*Toxostoma bendirei*): 25cm (10in)
South-western USA and north-western Mexico. Mainly brown, with mottling on the breast. White tips to the long tail feathers. Undertail coverts are lighter brown. Yellow irides. Relatively long, slightly down-curved beak, with a paler lower bill. Sexes are alike.

Le Conte's thrasher

Toxostoma lecontei

Thrashers are members of the mockingbird family, and as such are talented songsters, even capable of mimicking the songs of other birds. The powerful, melodious song of these particular thrashers is most likely to be heard either at dusk or dawn, when it is most active. At this stage of the day it is easier for the birds to catch the invertebrates that form their diet. Le Conte's thrasher does not appear to be common in any part of its range. Its coloration provides effective camouflage in the sandy desert terrain, and its habits also make it inconspicuous. If disturbed, these mockingbirds generally seek to slip away undetected through the scrub, running with their long tail held upright. During the hottest parts of the day, they hide away in the shade. Their bulky nests consist mainly of twigs and are sited near to the ground, well hidden, in a cactus or shrub.

Distribution: South-western USA (in California, Arizona, Nevada and Utah) and adjacent parts of Mexico, as well as Baja California and Sonora.
Size: 28cm (11in).
Habitat: Arid, open country.
Nest: Made of twigs.
Eggs: 2–4, light bluish green with brown speckling.
Food: Invertebrates.

Identification: Distinguished from other related species by its very pale coloration, having a greyish-brown body and darker tail, with tawny undertail coverts. Dark, strongly down-curved bill, with slight streaking on the throat. Sexes are alike.

INSECT-HUNTING MIGRANTS

Many New World species undertake marked seasonal movements in the course of a year. Though the focus is often on birds from inhospitable northern latitudes flying south for the winter, others in the southern hemisphere also move north toward the equator before the southern winter. Birds found close to or in the Tropics, where food supply is unaffected by the climate, remain as residents.

Groove-billed ani

Crotophaga sulcirostris

These unusual members of the cuckoo clan have a relatively slim body shape and are highly social by nature, living in groups. They even sometimes associate with the slightly larger smooth-billed ani, although they can be distinguished in flight by their more languid flight pattern, as they flap their wings and glide. Neither species is a powerful flier. Groove-billed anis have unusual breeding behaviour. A number of females will lay their eggs in the same location, reflecting their highly social nature. Up to 18 eggs have therefore been recorded in a single nest. Although these birds sometimes take over open nests abandoned by other birds, they may also construct a suitably large receptacle for their eggs from sticks and other vegetation. Groups of groove-billed anis typically feed on the ground by walking along and seizing any prey that comes within reach, which may include lizards.

Identification: Dull black in colour, with a distinctively shaped bill. The culmen (central ridge of the bill) is in the form of a smooth curve from the tip to the forehead. Grooves in the bill leading to the nostrils are apparent on the sides. Iris is blackish. Tail is long, with a rounded tip. Sexes similar, although hens may be slightly smaller in size.

Distribution: South-western USA south through Central America and Colombia, Venezuela, and French Guiana as far as northern Chile and Argentina; also present on Caribbean islands from Aruba to Trinidad.
Size: 30cm (12in).
Habitat: Scrub and pastureland.
Nest: Bowl-shaped, made of vegetation.
Eggs: 4, blue-green with chalky glaze.
Food: Mainly invertebrates.

Smooth-billed ani

Crotophaga ani

This species tends to occur in more humid areas than the groove-billed type, although they are similar in their habits. They are a common sight, partly as a result of their size and also because of their habit of perching in the open, even on fences. In cattle-ranching areas in Colombia, the anis' habit of following the herds has led to them being nicknamed *garrapateros*, meaning "tick eaters," and they are welcomed by ranchers for removing these parasites from their animals. Smooth-billed anis breed communally, like their groove-billed cousins, and can produce many eggs: 29 have been recorded in a single nest.

Identification: Dull, black plumage, with a decidedly rounded shape to the tail. Bill is black, with a distinctive smooth, raised area on the top of the upper bill close to the eyes. Sexes are similar but hens are smaller in size. Recently fledged young of this species lack the raised area on the bill, resembling groove-billed anis at this stage, although the sides of their bills are smooth.

Distribution: Southern Florida through Central America west to Ecuador and east into northern Argentina. Also present in the Caribbean.
Size: 33cm (13in).
Habitat: Brushland and open areas of country.
Nest: Large cup of vegetation.
Eggs: 4, bluish green, with chalk-like glaze.
Food: Invertebrates.

Purple martin (*Progne subis*): 22cm (8¹/₂in)
North America and parts of the Caribbean,
notably the Cayman Islands and Cuba, to
northern South America. Cock bird is an
unmistakable shade of bluish purple overall, with
black flight and tail feathers. Hens are duller,
with a bluish area confined to the top of the
head and the wings. Throat, breast and flanks
are brownish, as are the sides of the neck, with
the lower underparts being white. Young birds
resemble adult hens.

Cave swallow (*Petrochelidon fulva*):
14cm (5¹/₂in)
South-central parts of the USA down through
Mexico and across many islands in the
Caribbean, being permanently resident on Puerto
Rico, Hispaniola and Jamaica. Forehead reddish
brown, dark blue behind with a reddish brown
collar. Reddish brown underparts too. Wings are
blackish. The back is bluish with prominent
white streaking, while the rump is a deep
reddish brown. Sexes are alike.

Tawny-headed swallow (*Alopochelidon fucata*):
12.5cm (4¹/₂in)
Isolated populations in northern South America,
notably in Venezuela and northern Brazil. Occurs
widely in central South America to parts of
Argentina and Uruguay. Distinctive tawny-rufous
head, becoming buff on the sides of the head,
extending down to the breast. Back, wings and
rump are brownish, often with paler edging.
Sexes are alike. Young birds are yellowish and
fawn rather than tawny.

Sand martin

Bank swallow; African sand martin; *Riparia riparia*

In the summer months, sand martins are
usually observed relatively close to lakes and
other stretches of water, often swooping
down to catch invertebrates near the
surface. They are likely to be nesting in
colonies nearby, in tunnels that they
excavate on suitable sandy banks. These can
extend back for up to 1m (3ft), with the
nesting chamber lined with grass, seaweed
or similar material. The eggs are laid on top
of a soft bed of feathers. When the young
birds leave the nest, they stay in groups with
other chicks until their parents return to
feed them, typically bringing about 60
invertebrates back on each visit. Parents
recognize their offspring by their distinctive
calls. If danger threatens, the repetitive
alarm calls of the adult sand martins cause
the young to rush back to the
protection of the nest.

Identification: Predominantly brown,
with white plumage on the throat,
separated from the white underparts
by a brown band across the breast.
Long flight feathers. Small black bill.
Sexes are alike. Immature sand
martins have shorter flight feathers and
are browner than the adults.

Distribution: Throughout
North America, except in the
more arid regions of south-
west USA. Winters in South
America.
Size: 11cm (4in).
Habitat: Open country, close
to water.
Nest: Holes in sandbanks.
Eggs: 3–4, white.
Food: Flying invertebrates.

Northern rough-winged swallow

Stelgidopteryx serripennis

Distribution: Breeds from
southern Alaska down
through British Columbia, the
southern prairies of Canada
and across virtually the entire
USA. Migrates to Central
America, down as far as
Panama.
Size: 5in (13cm).
Habitat: Open country.
Nest: In burrows.
Eggs: 4–8, white.
Food: Invertebrates.

These swallows take their name from the tiny hooks on the feather vane of the outermost
primary feather on each wing, near the shaft. These can only be seen with magnification;
their purpose is unknown. Although they range over a wide area,
northern rough-winged swallows are likely to be seen close to
water, where they hawk insects such as midges on the wing.
They also hunt prey such as caterpillars and spiders near
the ground. Often seen in groups, they
sometimes roost communally in holes
to conserve warmth in cold
weather. Pairs start to nest in
May and adopt a variety of nest
sites, rarely excavating their own
burrows. The nest chamber is
lined with available materials,
from seaweed to pine needles.

Identification: Mainly brown, darker on
head and wings, with long, broad flight
feathers. Tail brown, underparts whitish.
Thin, narrow bill. Sexes are alike. Young
birds have a cinnamon tone to the upperparts.

LONG-DISTANCE TRAVELLERS

A number of small birds undertake two remarkable journeys each year, flying thousands of miles up to the Arctic to breed, and then moving south again for winter. Their nesting cycle has to coincide with the brief Arctic summer, otherwise there will be no food for the young, and the adults too could starve. In summer, however, this area literally teems with insect life, providing vital food for the young.

American pipit

Buff-bellied pipit Anthus rubescens

Identification: Greyish upperparts, with an indistinct whitish stripe passing through each eye, becoming more brownish grey over the back. Wings blackish. Streaking on the reddish-buff underparts, varying according to race. Rump brown, with the tail being black above. Has darker, more brownish upperparts outside the breeding period, and is more heavily streaked overall. Sexes are alike.

American pipits are active birds by nature, tending to walk rather than hop across the ground, bobbing their tails up and down regularly. Their range does not extend to north-eastern parts of the USA, probably because until quite recently this area was heavily forested. The males establish their territories once they reach their breeding grounds in the Arctic tundra. The nest site is carefully chosen to reduce the risk of the eggs becoming chilled: it may be partly buried, or sheltered by a rock, often apparently orientated to catch the warm rays of the sun. It is not uncommon for hens to reuse a nest which has been built previously. The hen sits alone, and the eggs hatch after about 14 days. The chicks fledge after a similar period, and are reared on invertebrates. American pipits leave their breeding grounds in early September, and head south for the winter.

Distribution: Arctic North America and western USA, in parts of northern New Hampshire, California and New Mexico. Winters throughout southern USA, and up to British Columbia in the west and New England in the east.
Size: 17cm (6½in).
Habitat: Tundra, grassland and fields.
Nest: Cup-shaped.
Eggs: 4–5, grey with dark spots and streaks.
Food: Seeds and invertebrates.

Savannah sparrow

Passerculus sandwichensis

These widely distributed birds are as adept at running as they are flying. It is not unusual for them to escape danger by dropping down into vegetation and scampering away. Savannah sparrows can be found in a wide range of habitats, from the tundra of the far north to the grassy sand dunes of Mexico. They breed on the ground, with spiders usually featuring in the diet of the young. Various distinctive races of these sparrows are recognized; some have very limited distributions, none more so than the so-called Ipswich sparrow (*P. s. princeps*), which breeds on a tiny area of land just 32km (20 miles) long on Sable Island, Nova Scotia. It winters more widely along the east coast, including around Ipswich, Massachusetts. Another localized and distinctive form is *P. s. rostratus* from the western side of the USA, which has not only developed a much broader bill but also has a quite different song pattern from all other savannah sparrows.

Identification: Varies through its range, with those from the west coast being darker than those found further east or in Alaska. Streaked appearance, with dark markings running down over the head and on the flanks. Brownish-grey to brownish-black upperparts. Underparts greyish white. Often a yellow or whitish streak above or through the eyes, with a paler stripe on the centre of the crown. Sexes are alike.

Distribution: Breeds throughout Alaska and Canada, extending south across much of the USA (except for part of the south-west) and into northern Mexico.
Size: 14cm (5½in).
Habitat: Grassland and open terrain.
Nest: Cup-shaped.
Eggs: 4–6, blue-green with dark speckling.
Food: Seeds and invertebrates.

Smith's longspur

Calcarius pictus

Its distinctive buff coloration helps to distinguish this member of the bunting family from other longspurs. Smith's longspur is a relatively rare species, however, being far less common on its northern breeding grounds than the Lapland longspur (*C. lapponicus*) arriving in the tundra region up to three weeks later in May. They also tend to prefer a damper, grassy habitat, with the nest often being build on raised areas of ground. The nest is quite bulky in appearance, sometimes incorporating caribou hair as well as feathers as a lining. Smith's longspurs overwinter in grassland areas and remain concealed on the ground, only flying off at the last moment if disturbed. When flushed, these longspurs will frequently take off for only a short distance anyway, zig-zagging in flight close to the ground before dropping down out of sight again in the grass. If pursued however, they will then tend to fly much higher, remaining in the air for several minutes. Once a longspur is disturbed, others nearby may start calling to their companions.

Identification: Cock in breeding plumage has blackish top to the head, with a black area behind the eyes, with a central white spot. Remainder of the head is white. Underparts mainly buff, upperparts buff, with darker centres to the feathers. Small black mark in the shoulder, with white beneath. Bill black above, yellowish below. More dusky, rather than black plumage out of breeding condition. Hens paler, with whitish underparts and buff rather than white spot behind the eyes. Young birds have paler brown legs.

Distribution: Breeds in the far north of North America, from Alaska eastwards to northern Ontario. Overwinters in the USA, in Kansas, Iowa and Illinois, extending south to parts of Arkansas, Mississippi and Tennessee.
Size: 16.5cm (6¹⁄₂in).
Habitat: Tundra and prairie.
Nest: On the ground, made of grass.
Eggs: 4–6, greenish blue with darker markings.
Food: Seeds and invertebrates.

Lincoln's sparrow (*Melospiza lincolnii*): 15cm (6in)
Breeds in northern and western USA, moving farther south for winter. A relatively dull species, greyish brown overall. Broad grey stripe above the eyes, with a dark grey area on the cheeks. Throat is whitish, with streaking continuing from here over the brownish breast and on the flanks, while the lower underparts are whitish. Back and wings are brownish with darker patterning. Sexes are alike. Young birds are paler.

White-crowned sparrow (*Zonotrichia leucophrys*): 18cm (7in)
Found in Central and Eastern Canada, and New England. Distinctive white crown with prominent black border, and a thinner black stripe extending back from the eyes. Sides of the face are grey, and the throat is whitish. Underparts are also grey, becoming whiter in the centre of the abdomen. Wings brownish grey with white edging; back is brown. Pointed bill is orangish with a dark tip. Sexes are alike. Young birds have brownish heads and are duller than adults.

Vesper sparrow (*Pooecetes gramineus*): 15cm (6in)
Breeds across much of the USA, wintering in the southern states. A white moustache-like streak is seen on each side of the head, with a brownish tone to the ear coverts. Upperparts buff with darker streaking, while the underparts are greyish with fine streaking on the breast and flanks. Small black area on the wing edged with white, and chestnut lesser coverts. Sexes alike.

McCown's longspur

Rhynchophanes mccownii

Although named after Captain John McCown, who shot the first recorded specimen in the 1850s, this species was first documented 50 years earlier in Montana by a military expedition led by Captain Meriwether Lewis. These longspurs arrive on their northern breeding grounds in April and cock birds have a very conspicuous display. They fly up to 18m (60ft) off the ground, singing loudly, before falling back down, using their wings rather like a parachute. Their nests are hard to locate on the ground, although they may be parasitized by cowbirds (*Molothrus species*). Hens sit alone, with an incubation of about 12 days. The young are able to fly after a similar interval, although they can run at an even younger age if disturbed.

Identification: Cock in breeding condition has a black area on the top of the head and on the breast, with a black streak running down each side of the lower bill. Greyish area behind the eyes and on the neck, with the rest of the head being whitish. Underparts greyish, prominent chestnut bar on the wings. Back and wings black and brown. Overall less black out of breeding condition. Hens duller, less distinct wing bars. Bill, legs and feet blackish. Young birds resemble hens.

Distribution: Breeds in central-southern Canada and across the US border. Overwinters further south, in parts of Arizona, Colorado Oklahoma and Texas, and across the Mexican border.
Size: 15cm (6in).
Habitat: Grassland plains and fields.
Nest: Depression lined with grass on the ground.
Eggs: 3–6, greenish white with darker markings.
Food: Seeds and invertebrates.

HUNTERS AND SCAVENGERS

Although both corvids and owls are most likely to be seen in wooded terrain, a number of these species inhabit more open areas of country. Their diet varies according to their environment, and in the case of owls it is possible to discover what they have eaten by examining their pellets, which are regurgitated after a meal and contain the undigested remains of their prey.

Chihuahuan raven

White-necked raven *Corvus cryptoleucus*

This relatively small raven is closely tied to its arid habitat. It is found at lower altitudes than the common or northern raven (*Corvus corax*), so the two species tend not to meet where their areas of distribution overlap. Chihuahuan ravens are also more social by nature than their larger cousins, and have a less guttural call. Although they are commonly seen in pairs, much larger groupings can be encountered where food is plentiful, for example around rubbish dumps. They often frequent roadsides too, seeking carrion. With few trees around, pairs will build their nest wherever surroundings are suitable, using sites such as telegraph poles or the roofs of buildings. Chihuahuan ravens engage in a series of soaring and tumbling flights as part of their courtship ritual. This is the time when the white at the base of their neck feathers is most evident.

Distribution: Ranges from south-central USA, being present in parts of Arizona, New Mexico, Colorado, Texas and Nebraska, south to northern-central parts of Mexico.
Size: 50cm (20in).
Habitat: Arid scrubland.
Nest: Stick platform.
Eggs: 3–8, pale blue with brownish markings.
Food: Omnivorous.

Identification: Glossy black, sometimes with a brownish tone. The feathers around the neck are often whitish at the base. Relatively long, stout bill, with very evident nasal bristles extending along two-thirds of its length. Graduated appearance of the tail is evident in flight. Sexes alike. Young birds can be recognized by their bluish irides and duller head and underparts, which are less glossy than their wings.

Burrowing owl

Athene cunicularia

These small owls will hunt during the day, but are most active at dusk. Their small size allows them to nest underground in burrows that may have been dug originally by prairie dogs or other rodents, or may be constructed by the birds themselves. These tunnels can extend over 3m (10ft) in length. Unusually, the owls decorate the entrance with dried cattle dung, and the odour is thought to deter mammalian predators from investigating inside.

Burrowing owls invariably choose an open area for the entrance to their nest site, rather than concealing it in long grass.

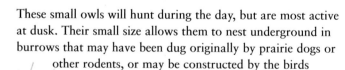

Distribution: North America from British Columbia east to Manitoba and south into Central America. Separate population in Florida and the Caribbean. Also occurs in South America, especially in the east from Brazil south to Tierra del Fuego.
Size: 26cm (10½in).
Habitat: Lightly wooded country.
Nest: Underground burrow.
Eggs: 5–6, white.
Food: Mainly larger invertebrates.

Identification: Brownish edging on the facial disc on the sides of the eyes, with more distinctive brownish stripes beneath the yellowish bill and white eyebrows. Chest and wings are brownish, with generally whiter underparts in the case of the North and Central American race. Burrowing owls seen in Florida and the Caribbean are a darker shade of brown. Sexes are alike. Young birds are buff in colour, with white underparts.

Snowy owl

Bubo scandiacus

The plumage of these owls enables them to blend in well in the tundra region where they commonly occur. In this harsh environment, their numbers are closely related to the availability of their prey, and their population increases rapidly when lemmings are rife. Once the lemming population declines, however, so does that of the snowy owls, and breeding success is greatly reduced, so that pairs may not nest at all in some years. Adult birds are likely to be forced to abandon their usual territories at this time and have to fly south in search of other sources of food. Unusually, snowy owls are active during the daytime.

Distribution: Breeding range extends from northern Alaska across Canada. Typically overwinters in Canada, as far south as northern parts of the USA.
Size: 65cm (25¹/₂in).
Habitat: Woodland, extending to the tundra.
Nest: Scrape on the ground.
Eggs: 3–11, white.
Food: Mainly lemmings but also birds, invertebrates, and fish.

Identification: Cocks are white with yellow eyes and feathering down to the claws. Hens have brown barring all over their bodies apart from their faces, which are white. Young are similar to hens.

Short-eared owl (*Asio flammeus*): 43cm (17in)
Most northerly population extends from Alaska eastward. Also present in north-west South America, across the southern part of the continent and on the Galapagos and Hawaii. Relatively small head, with slight tufts of plumage above the eyes. Variable coloration, brownish with white markings on wings. Pale-streaked chest and black feathering around the eyes. Sexes are alike.

Magellan horned owl (Lesser horned owl, *Bubo magellanicus*): 45cm (18in)
Central Peru south via Bolivia, Chile and Argentina to the tip of South America. Dark stripes evident around sides of the face, with black spotting under the bill. Yellow eyes and prominent ear tufts. Underparts whitish with black vermiculations and brown markings, paler on upper chest. Upperparts darker, with broader banding across the wings. Tail barred. Sexes are alike.

Chaco owl (*Strix chacoensis*): 35cm (14in)
Chaco region in central-southern South America, from Paraguay to Argentina. Pale whitish facial disks with darker rings. Irides brown. Underparts white with brown and buff barring, becoming buff on lower underparts. Wings similar but less white, with grey banding to flight feathers. Tail and buff-coloured legs also banded. Sexes are alike. Young birds have greyish facial disks.

Barn owl

Tyto alba

These owls roost in dark environments, using buildings for this purpose in some areas. They may be seen in open country, swooping over farmland. Some individuals choose to pursue bats where these mammals are common. Males often utter harsh screeches when in flight, which serve as territorial markers, while females make a distinctive snoring sound for food at the nest. They pair for life, which can be more than 20 years. Barn owls have adapted to hunting along roadsides, but here they risk being hit by vehicles.

Distribution: Ranges from southern British Columbia across to New England and southward through Central America into South America.
Size: 39cm (15in).
Habitat: Prefers relatively open countryside.
Nest: Hollow tree or inside a building.
Eggs: 4–7, white.
Food: Voles, amphibians and invertebrates.

Identification: Very pale in colour, with a whitish, heart-shaped face and underparts. In northern, central, and eastern parts of Europe, the underparts have a yellowish-orange tone. Top of the head and wings are greyish, with spots evident. Eyes are black. Males are often paler than females.

BIRDS OF PREY

Agile, aerial predators, falcons are opportunistic hunters, relying on strength and speed to overcome their prey, which frequently includes smaller birds. Caracaras, on the other hand, prefer to seek their quarry on the ground, and have benefited to a certain extent from road-building, which has provided carrion in the guise of animals and birds killed by vehicles.

Southern crested caracara

Common caracara *Caracara plancus*

Distribution: Occurs in southern USA south through Central America and across South America to Tierra del Fuego and the Falkland Islands.
Size: 59cm (23in).
Habitat: Prairies and relatively arid areas.
Nest: Platform of twigs.
Eggs: 2–3, white with brown markings.
Food: Meat-eater.

This predatory species has a wingspan approaching 1.2m (4ft) but tends not to fly, preferring to spend its time on the ground. Crested caracaras can move quickly on their relatively long legs, running through open country in pursuit of prey such as small rodents. They often seek out carrion in the form of road kills along highways, and when feasting on larger casualties even take precedence over vultures. However, their diet does vary according to habitat, and sometimes they will eat invertebrates. On the Falkland Islands they are considered to be a threat to newborn lambs, while in coastal areas they have learnt to harry returning seabirds into dropping their catches. Crested caracaras usually build their nest off the ground, using an untidy framework of twigs with fresh vegetation added to it. The young hatch after an incubation period of around 30 days.

Identification: Blackish cap and crest on the head, with whitish area beneath becoming barred on the back and chest. Wings and abdomen are more blackish. Bare reddish skin on the face. Neck and throat white. Dark band at the tip of the tail. Sexes are alike, but hens are slightly larger in size. Young birds have brown rather than black plumage.

Long-winged harrier

Circus buffoni

These harriers have powerful wings and are believed to fly over the Andes on occasion, and regularly travel long distances when migrating. They are occasionally seen well outside what is usually regarded as their normal range, with individuals having been sighted on the Falkland Islands as well as at Tierra del Fuego. Long-winged harriers are most likely to be encountered in relatively open countryside, often in marshland and similarly wet environments.

Identification: Normal colour form has a whitish area around the eyes and bill, with a further white necklace of markings beneath. Chest and wings are predominantly blackish, with white underparts. Greyish barring on the flight feathers and tail. There is also a melanistic form, in which the white plumage is replaced by black apart from on the rump. Female has brownish rather than black plumage and is significantly larger.

Distribution: South America, from south-west Colombia eastward to French Guiana, through parts of Brazil to Argentina, eastern Bolivia, and central Chile.
Size: 56cm (22in).
Habitat: Relatively open, lowland tropical areas.
Nest: Concealed on the ground in rushes.
Eggs: 2–4, whitish.
Food: Small vertebrates.

Prairie falcon

Falco mexicanus

It has been estimated that the breeding range of these falcons covers about 3.6 million square km (1.4 million square miles), but as with other predatory species the density of the birds in this area varies. Prairie falcons are opportunistic hunters, a key factor in their spread across much of North America. They prey heavily on small birds such as lark buntings, and also rodents. In arid areas greater numbers of reptiles including lizards, snakes and tortoises are caught. Prairie falcons prefer to catch their prey at or just above ground level, but also harry other birds in flight. Breeding occurs from March to July, depending on latitude. With woodland becoming scarce, these falcons have adapted to using cliff faces, laying on the rock rather than building a nest, though pairs may take over nests abandoned by other large birds.

Identification: Brown crown, with white streaking running round each side of the head above the eyes. White area behind each eye, and a dark streak running from below each eye onto the cheeks. Dark brown ear coverts, with a brown and white spotted neck and underparts. Bill pale yellow, darker at its tip. Legs and feet yellow. Sexes are alike. Young birds have greyish legs and feet, with long flight feathers extending back almost as far as the tail feathers.

Distribution: British Columbia eastward through Canada around the southern part of Hudson's Bay to Newfoundland, and through western USA to northern parts of Mexico and east via Texas along the Gulf coast to Florida.
Size: 51cm (20in).
Habitat: Prairies and plains.
Nest: Often lays on a cliff ledge.
Eggs: 4–5, whitish with brownish blotches.
Food: Meat-eater.

Swainson's hawk (*Buteo swainsoni*): 56cm (22in)
From Alaska southward, mainly in the central USA Usually migrates south for the winter to southern Brazil, Argentina and Paraguay via Central America, although some may remain in the southern USA. White area from above the bill to the throat. Chest is brown and underparts are whitish with brown barring. Head and upperparts are dark. Tail is barred. Rarer reddish and black morphs occur, with these colours predominating on the underparts. Hens are larger.

Snail kite (*Rostrhamus sociabilis*): 45cm (18in)
Ranges from the Everglades of Florida south through Central America west of the Andes to Argentina. Also on Cuba. Dark grey with a white area under the tail. The bare skin from the black bill to around the eyes is reddish, becoming more colourful in the breeding season, but yellow in hens, which also have white striping under the throat. Red irises. Feeds mainly on aquatic snails.

Swallow-tailed kite (*Elanoides forficatus*): 62cm (22in)
South-eastern USA, notably Florida, and into Mexico, extending to north-eastern Argentina and Uruguay in South America. Head and underparts are whitish. Black on the back, with purplish and metallic green hues evident on the wings. Long flight feathers and a distinctive V-shaped tail, most apparent in flight. The bill is blackish, the eyes reddish. Sexes are alike. Young birds have shorter tails and sometimes dusky markings on their head.

White-tailed kite

Elanus leucurus

The white-tailed kite has a variable range, influenced by the availability of rodents, which form the bulk of its diet, although it also preys on small birds and invertebrates. The keen eyesight of these kites allows them to spot prey on the ground, even when hovering at heights of 10m (30ft) or more. They tend to hunt in the early morning or around dusk, when rodents are active. White-tailed kites may be seen perched on telegraph poles, though they prefer to nest in trees. Their breeding period is influenced by latitude, occurring during summer in temperate areas, with some pairs raising two broods. By the 1930s, numbers of this kite had fallen steeply in North America, but have increased again. In parts of South America, they have colonized the open terrain resulting from forest clearance, and are fairly common in cereal-growing areas.

Identification: Pale grey crown, neck and back, with prominent black areas on shoulders, and undersides of wings in the carpal region. Black area also around each red eye. Bill blackish with yellow cere. Legs and feet yellow. Sexes alike. Young birds have greyish-brown upperparts and speckling on the breast.

Distribution: Variable, extending as far north as Nebraska, Wisconsin, and Minnesota, south through Central America and much of eastern South America, reaching parts of Chile and Argentina.
Size: 41cm (16in).
Habitat: Grassland and farmland.
Nest: Platform of sticks.
Eggs: 4–5, white with heavy brown spotting.
Food: Meat-eater.

GIANT HUNTERS

These large predatory species occur at low densities and in some cases have suffered heavy persecution. One example, the Californian condor, now ranks as one of the rarest birds in the world. Yet it is not just direct human intervention which can reduce their numbers. Being at the top of the avian food chain, they are also vulnerable to the build-up of toxic chemicals in their bodies.

Andean condor

Vultur gryphus

Andean condors are the only vultures from the New World to show clear sexual dimorphism. With a lifespan often measured in decades, and a correspondingly slow breeding cycle, pairs are only likely to rear a chick in alternate years. In spite of their strong bills, which allow them to rip open carcasses without difficulty, Andean condors are not active hunters. In coastal areas they scour seal colonies, sometimes descending in large numbers to scavenge when food is readily available.

Identification: Massive, vulture-like appearance. The bare skin on the cock's head is red, and black in the larger hen. Cock birds also display a prominent comb on the head, as well as a wattle that is absent in hens. There is a ruff of white feathering below, encircling the neck. The rest of the plumage is predominantly black aside from the greyish-white areas on the wings.

Distribution: Andean region of South America, right down this mountain range from Venezuela to Tierra del Fuego in the far south.
Size: 130cm (51in).
Habitat: Open mountainous terrain, but sometimes near sea level, where these birds seek carcasses of marine animals. Prefers to be well away from human habitation.
Nest: Caves on cliffs.
Eggs: 1, white.
Food: Carrion.

California condor

Gymnogyps californianus (E)

These majestic birds used to soar effortlessly on the thermals, covering huge distances in search of large carcasses in true vulture fashion, but heavy persecution brought them to the very edge of extinction. Collisions with powerlines also reduced their numbers, until the species was virtually extinct. The last remaining wild California condors were caught in 1987 and integrated into a highly expensive captive-breeding programme, carried out at zoological collections at Los Angeles and San Diego. Five years later, the first birds bred in captivity were released back into the wild, and other releases have followed. It takes about eight years for these condors to attain sexual maturity.

Identification: Huge size, predominantly black with white areas on and under the wings. Bare, variable pinkish-orange skin on the head and neck. This entire area of bare skin is grey in young birds. Sexes are alike.

Distribution: Area north of Los Angeles, California. Releases carried out around the San Joaquin Valley in California; birds are fitted with radio telemetry equipment to track their movements.
Size: 134cm (53in).
Habitat: Lightly wooded terrain.
Nest: Usually in caves.
Eggs: 1, white.
Food: Carrion.

Bald eagle

Haliaeetus leucocephalus

Distribution: From the Aleutian Islands and Alaska east across Canada and south across the USA into northern Mexico.
Size: 96cm (38in).
Habitat: Areas where there are large stretches of water.
Nest: Often huge, located in a tree or sometimes on the ground.
Eggs: 1–3, white.
Food: Vertebrates and some carrion, especially in the winter when hunting is more difficult.

The national symbol of the USA, the bald eagle is a highly adaptable species, and is encountered as far north as the freezing tundra of Canada and south to the searing desert heat of Mexico. Feeding habits are diverse; these eagles tend to catch fish during the summer months, switching at other times of the year to birds as large as geese, which are seized in flight. They hunt both by sight and sound, and are drawn to areas where sea otters are feeding by recognizing their calls. The species remains far more common in the northern part of its range, where it has been subject to less habitat disturbance.

Identification: Distinctive white head and tail, yellow bill and talons. Remainder of the plumage is predominantly brown, with lighter edging to some of the feathers on the back and wings. Female is larger, and young birds have dark bills.

Above: Bald eagles may migrate more than 2,000km (1,250 miles).

Variable hawk (Puna hawk, Gurney's hawk, *Geranoaetus polyosoma*): 61cm (24in)
Andean region from southern Colombia south to Chile and Argentina. Exists in both light and dark morphs. Light-coloured cocks have whitish underparts and grey upperparts, with flight feathers blackish at the tips. The tail is white with dark speckling and a black bar. Hens have a chestnut area at the top of the wings. In the dark morph, the entire body except the tail is slate grey. In hens, the chestnut feathering extends over the upper breast, with black-and-white barring on the lower underparts.

Turkey vulture (*Cathartes aura*): 81cm (32in)
Ranges across much of the USA south via Central America to much of South America; also on islands including the Greater Antilles and the Falklands. North American population moves south in winter. Can find carcasses by scent, and feeds mainly on mammals. Bare, reddish-pink head and brownish-black plumage. Varies in size through its range. Sexes are alike.

Black-chested buzzard-eagle (*Geranoaetus melanoleucus*): 80cm (31½in)
Western side of South America, from north-west Venezuela south. Separate population in the east from Brazil to Uruguay. Slaty-grey head, chest, and upperparts. Paler grey area of fine barring on shoulders, with another on whitish undersides of the wings extending to the underparts, depending on race; otherwise these are creamy-white. Tail has pale tip. Bill yellowish with dark tip. Yellow legs and feet. Young birds brown with buff streaking on the underparts.

Golden eagle

Aquila chrysaetos

In spite of their name, the plumage of golden eagles belonging to the subspecies known as *A.c. canadensis* is of a dark blackish-brown shade. Their numbers were once badly affected by hunting pressures through much of North America, but populations have since largely recovered. In some areas, however, they now face new hazards, such as the danger of flying into overhead powerlines. Although this species no longer occurs in the Appalachians, in the eastern part of the USA, this is not as a result of direct persecution, but rather as a consequence of afforestation, which has meant that there is now little open country within which these eagles can hunt.

Distribution: Occurs widely throughout the far north of North America, and also in western areas down into Mexico.
Size: 90cm (35in).
Habitat: Mountainous areas.
Nest: Massive cliff nest made of sticks.
Eggs: 2, white with dark markings.
Food: Mainly birds and mammals.

Identification: Brown overall, with yellowish-brown plumage on the back of the head, extending down the nape. Eagles inhabiting desert areas, such as the Middle East, tend to be slightly paler overall. Bill is yellow with a dark tip. Feet are yellow with black talons. Hens are bigger than cocks.

PIGEONS AND DOVES

Some members of this group have benefited from living in close proximity to people, although their presence is not always welcomed either in the countryside or in cities, because of the damage large flocks can cause to both crops and buildings. Their adaptable nature is further illustrated by the way their numbers can increase rapidly under favourable conditions.

Band-tailed pigeon

Patagioenas fasciata

Distribution: British Columbia and western parts of the USA south through central America and western areas of South America, as far as northern Argentina.
Size: 40cm (16in).
Habitat: Woodland areas.
Nest: Platform of twigs lined with moss.
Eggs: 1, creamy white.
Food: Seeds and vegetation.

Band-tailed pigeons naturally occur in stretches of woodland, although they are now being seen with increasing frequency in suburban areas and even in towns as well. Their favoured food in North America and Mexico is acorns, with seeds and vegetation also featuring prominently in their diet. However, in back gardens, these pigeons will eat fruits and berries, clambering around in trees rather clumsily, as well as feeding from bird tables. The Canadian population of band-tailed pigeons migrates southward at the approach of winter, as do birds from a number of US states, including Arizona and Colorado. Even individuals from south-western Texas may fly south across the border into Mexico, where the influx of northern visitors swells the resident population of pigeons dramatically at this time of year.

Identification: Appearance varies through its range. White band encircling the hind neck, with a variable metallic green area beneath. Wings are greyish. Head and underparts vary from shades of vinous pink to almost purplish pink in South American populations. Tail feathers light grey at their tips, with a dark band near the base of the tail. Legs yellow. Sexes are alike.

White-winged dove

Mesquite dove *Zenaida asiatica*

Flocks of white-winged doves often congregate in crop-growing areas around harvest time, foraging on the ground for cultivated grains. They are very adaptable by nature and can also be found in habitats ranging from semi-desert areas alongside cacti to mangrove swamps, as well as being attracted to backyards. During the breeding season in the USA, pairs of white-winged doves from eastern areas breed in large colonies, while those occurring further west tend to nest individually. Subsequently, many head south for the winter, with birds from Texas, for example, flying as far as Costa Rica. Although they are often hunted, white-winged doves are still common in most areas, and the species is currently expanding its distribution in parts of the Caribbean.

Identification: So-called because of the evident white area on the leading edge of the wings when folded. Wings and tail feathers otherwise mainly brownish, with an adjacent greyer band. The head, neck and upper chest have a pinker tinge. Prominent area of bare blue skin around the eyes. Hens are duller, with less iridescence on the neck.

Distribution: Southern USA and across Mexico, except for the south-east, down to Costa Rica and Panama. Also present in the Caribbean.
Size: 30cm (12in).
Habitat: Relatively open areas, including farmland, parks and backyards.
Nest: Loose platform of twigs.
Eggs: 2, creamy-buff.
Food: Various seeds and grains.

Inca dove

Columbina inca; previously *Scardafella inca*

Identification: Brownish upperparts, with a pinker tinge to the underside of the body. Black scalloping on both wings and body. Finer scalloping on the head, which is greyer. Tail is relatively long and tapering. Rufous underwing coverts seen in flight, with a rufous bar evident when wings are closed. Hens are similar, but underparts less strongly suffused with pink.

Inca doves are typically encountered in open countryside, but can often be found in urban areas throughout the year. The population is largely sedentary through its range, although sometimes these doves may be seen north of their breeding range in the USA, which extends across Oklahoma, Arkansas and Nebraska. They were first recorded there around 1870. Like many doves, pairs will breed two or three times in rapid succession when conditions are favourable, but their limited nest-building skills means that some nests will collapse, resulting in the loss of both eggs and chicks. A well-concealed site in vegetation is usually chosen, with both birds sharing incubation duties: the cock normally sits by day, while the hen takes over in late afternoon. The young grow rapidly and may leave the nest when only 12 days old, although they will not be able to fly strongly at this age.

Distribution: South-western USA south as far as Costa Rica. Range is extending north and south.
Size: 22cm (8¹/₂in).
Habitat: Open areas, including fields, parks and back gardens.
Nest: Fragile platform of twigs and other vegetation.
Eggs: 2, white.
Food: Seeds, fruits, berries.

Long-tailed ground dove (*Uropelia campestris*): 16cm (6¹/₄in)
Two distinct populations, one from Bolivia to central Brazil, the other around the mouth of the Amazon. Grey crown with whitish-grey cheeks and bare reddish skin encircling the eyes. Nape greyish brown, with a black and purple wing patch, edged with white. White area under the wing when seen from below, with the remaining lower surface of the wing being dark. Pale reddish brown on chest, becoming whitish on lower underparts. Long tail tipped with white. Hens have paler pink on the underparts and an ashy-brown crown.

Ring-tailed pigeon (*Patagioenas caribaea*): 46cm (18in)
Restricted to Jamaica. The area from the forehead to the nape is fawn-pink, with a significant area of golden-green iridescence on the hindneck. Underparts are pinkish, greyer on the flanks and near the vent. Wings greyish brown with black flight feathers. There is a broad greyish-brown band on the tail. Hen very similar, but slightly duller overall.

Zenaida dove (*Zenaida aurita*): 30cm (12in)
Occurs widely on Caribbean islands, also the Yucatan Peninsula in Mexico. Considered extinct in the Florida Keys. Coloration varies with race. Grey crown, with browner sides to the face and pinkish underparts. Wings greyish brown, with large black spots. Green iridescence merging into purplish suffusion on sides of neck. Hens generally paler, with less iridescence.

Feral (rock) pigeon

Rock dove *Columba livia*

These birds are not native to America, but were introduced from Europe, where they evolved from rock doves. This helps to explain why they often nest on narrow ledges high above pavements, just as their relatives still do on windswept cliffs. Feral pigeons are common city birds, scavenging from leftovers and having virtually no fear of people. Large flocks of feral pigeons can cause serious damage to buildings, with their droppings and also by pecking away at the mortar, which provides calcium.

Identification: Dark bluish-grey head with slight green iridescence on the neck. Light grey wings with two black bars on each wing. Reddish-purple sides to the upper chest. Rest of plumage grey, with a black band at tip of the tail. Various colour morphs exist, typically displaying orangish red or white areas. Sexes are alike.

Distribution: Much of North America except the far north, through Central America and across most of South America, except for central Amazonia and extreme southern tip; also Caribbean.
Size: 35cm (14in).
Habitat: Narrow ledges of city buildings.
Nest: Loose pile of twigs.
Eggs: 2, white.
Food: Prefers seeds, but highly adaptable.

GRACKLES AND ORIOLES

Some of these conspicuous and often colourful birds are graced with an attractive song. A glimpse of yellowish orange and black plumage, coupled with a pointed bill, is indicative of an oriole sighting. The coloration of grackles is more subdued, although they can display a striking iridescent sheen when sunlight catches their plumage, and are known to put on flamboyant displays to attract a mate.

Common grackle

Quiscalus quiscula

Identification: Variable in colour, with a powerful pointed bill and long tail. The bronze form of northern and western areas has bronze feathering with a blue head, in contrast to the more purplish suffusion that characterizes the purple grackle from the Appalachian region. The southerly Florida race has a more olive-green body with a purplish head. Hens display less iridescence, especially on their underparts.

The song of the common grackle is highly distinctive, allowing individual birds to be distinguished. While singing they perform a so-called "rough out" display, in which they fluff up their plumage. This may be accompanied by dancing on the perch and flashing the eyes, which are a brilliant yellow. Males sometimes react in this way more to other males than females. In flight, they splay out their tail feathers to create a characteristic wedge shape. As autumn approaches the grackles leave northern and western haunts; they only reside all year in southern areas. These can be long-lived birds, surviving to 22 years.

Distribution: Central and eastern North America, from British Colombia to south-eastern USA. Occasionally sighted in Pacific states and Alaska during spring.
Size: 32cm (12½in).
Habitat: Open country, from marshland to suburban areas and parks.
Nest: Large cup-shaped structure.
Eggs: 3–7, pale green to pale rust.
Food: Seeds, invertebrates, fish, small birds.

Great-tailed grackle

Quiscalus mexicanus

The great-tailed grackle is rapidly extending its North American range in a north-westerly direction, nesting for example in Montana for the first time in 1996. It has been suggested that, at their current rate of expansion, these grackles will soon be breeding regularly in Canada. This trend is probably due to their bold, adaptable nature, especially since they thrive in areas where relatively few trees remain. Great-tailed grackles forage on the ground and will feed in large groups, particularly after nesting when pairs split up to form single-sex flocks. At the start of the breeding season males set up a territory in which several hens nest and lay, though under this system the cock does not help to incubate or rear the chicks. Perhaps not surprisingly, populations tend to have a high proportion of females, which mirrors the breeding pattern.

Distribution: From Oregon south and east through Mexico (except Baja California) and into South America, eastward to Venezuela and as far south as northern Peru.
Size: 38–46cm (15–18in).
Habitat: Open areas, including suburbs.
Nest: Cup-shaped, made of twigs lined with grass.
Eggs: 3–4, blue with brownish-black markings.
Food: Seeds, invertebrates, small vertebrates.

Identification: Cock birds are glossy black, with a purplish suffusion on the head, back and underparts. They have keel-shaped tail feathers and yellow eyes. Hens smaller and mainly brown. Young birds resemble hens, but with striped underparts.

Orchard oriole

Icterus spurius

Each year these small orioles fly long distances to and from their northern breeding grounds, often not being sighted in the far north of their range until the end of May. Some head north through Florida, while the majority fly directly across the Gulf of Mexico. Once they reach their breeding grounds pairs tend to be solitary, although they may sometimes associate with eastern kingbirds (*Tyrannus tyrannus*), which defend their nest sites vigorously. Even so, the number of orchard orioles is declining, partly, it is feared, because of nest parasitism by bronzed and brown-headed cowbirds (*Molothrus*). In some areas, over a quarter of orchard oriole nests are host to the young of these species, reducing the rate of survival of their natural offspring. In their wintering quarters hundreds of orchard orioles may congregate together, feeding on the nectar of flowering trees and shrubs.

Identification: Mature male has a black head, back and chest, with the remainder of the body being a distinctive shade of chestnut. Hens in contrast have olive upperparts and are yellowish beneath. Young males are similar to females but with a black bib.

Distribution: South-central Canada down across much of central and eastern USA to Florida and south into Mexico. Occasionally seen in westerly US states. May overwinter in South America.
Size: 18cm (7in).
Habitat: Open woodland close to water, moving into grassland and marshes.
Nest: Hanging cup of grass.
Eggs: 3–7, bluish white with darker blotches.
Food: Fruit, insects, nectar.

Yellow oriole (*Icterus nigrogularis*): 20cm (8in) Occurs in South America, from Colombia eastward to northern Brazil. Also present on offshore islands including Trinidad and the Netherlands Antilles. Predominantly yellow, with black lores and a narrow black throat bib. May have a slight orange cast to the head. Wings black with white edging to some of the feathers. Tail is black. Hens distinguishable by the slight olive cast to the yellow plumage, especially on the head and back, while young birds lack the black markings on the head.

Epaulet oriole (*Icterus cayanensis*): 18cm (7in) Ranges over much of central and eastern South America. Distinguished from other oriole species by its more subdued coloration. Cock bird has a narrow, straight bill that is mainly black, and dark brownish eyes. Plumage is black, apart from the chestnut patches or epaulets in the vicinity of the shoulder, which are not especially conspicuous. Some races have yellow patches there, and may have yellow thighs. Hen resembles the male but is generally smaller.

Hooded oriole (*Icterus cucullatus*): 20cm (8in) Ranges from California southward into Mexico and Belize. Cock bird in breeding plumage varies from yellowish orange in northern parts of the USA through to brilliant orange in Texas, depending on race, offset against a prominent area of black on the throat. The back is black, becoming brown with black barring in winter. Hens have greenish upperparts, with the underparts having a decidedly yellow tone. White edging to the wing feathers is apparent, but not the actual bar seen in cock birds.

Spot-breasted oriole

Icterus pectoralis

The melodic, whistling song of these orioles is heard repeatedly, and though both sexes sing, the call notes of cock birds are more complex. Spot-breasted orioles may be seen in the company of other oriole species, seeking food both on the ground and from flowers. Their nest is tightly woven and secured at the tip of a branch, usually anchored around a convenient fork, making it difficult for potential predators to reach. Mimosa trees are especially favoured since their spiky thorns offer added protection, though the nests may still be parasitized by cowbirds. The population in Florida, which was first recorded breeding in 1949 in the vicinity of Miami, has not spread very far in the intervening decades, occurring today in a radius of some 64km (40 miles) around the city. There are even suggestions that it has recently declined in numbers. Spot-breasted orioles have also been introduced to Cocos Island, Costa Rica.

Identification: Mainly orangish yellow, often most fiery on the head, offset against black lores and throat. Wings black with white barring. Tail also black. Distinctive spotted patterning on the sides of the breast. Sexes are alike. Young birds are olive green over the back and lack spotted markings.

Distribution: Native to central Mexico. Separate introduced population in Florida, ranging from Brevard County southward to Dade County.
Size: 24cm (9½in).
Habitat: Open woodland. Favours suburban gardens in Florida.
Nest: Hanging basket of grass and other vegetation, up to 50cm (20in) long.
Eggs: 3, bluish white with dark markings.
Food: Fruits, invertebrates and nectar.

WOODPECKERS AND WARBLERS

Both these groups of birds are at home in areas close to woodland, which is where the invertebrates that feature prominently in their diets are likely to be numerous. Though woodpeckers are traditionally regarded as bark hunters, like warblers they will also descend to the ground to seek their prey. Both groups also possess distinctive calls.

Red-bellied woodpecker

Melanerpes carolinus

Red-bellied woodpeckers have a variable diet that changes through the year. Over the summer, invertebrates are plentiful and form a high percentage of their food intake. They will also prey on vertebrates, including the nestlings of other species. In the fall, fruits of various kinds start to figure more prominently. During the winter period they sustain themselves largely on nuts and seeds, which have a high energy content, though cock birds will still spend time foraging for insects in the branches of trees (hens less so). Red-bellied woodpeckers prefer to feed off the ground, and are most likely to be sighted in deciduous trees, particularly oaks. Pairs will nest through much of the summer, often raising two or occasionally three broods of chicks. The breeding chamber is usually larger than that used for roosting.

Distribution: Eastern North America, from Ontario southward via South Dakota and southern Minnesota as far as central Texas and Florida.
Size: 24cm (9¹/₂in).
Habitat: Open woodland, parks and suburban areas.
Nest: Tree hollows.
Eggs: 3–8, white.
Food: Omnivorous.

Identification: Cocks have a red top to the head, extending to the back of the neck, whereas only the nape is red in hens. Black and white barring extends over the back and wings, and to central tail feathers. Underparts greyish white, with reddish suffusion to centre of abdomen.

Gila woodpecker

Melanerpes uropygialis

Gila woodpeckers are noisy, conspicuous and also quite aggressive by nature, particularly when close to the nest site, which may be located in a tree. Alternatively, in particularly arid areas, the nest may be sited in the less conventional surroundings of a tall cactus, as high as 7m (23ft) off the ground. This affords good protection from would-be predators, but can only be occupied once the hole has dried up thoroughly and is not leaking sap. Other creatures, including small mammals and even reptiles, may subsequently take over such chambers once they have been vacated by the birds. The breeding period is usually between April and June, although a pair may sometimes nest again in July. Once fledged, the young remain with their parents until the adults begin nesting again. Their bold nature means that gila woodpeckers will readily feed on bird tables, driving off other species such as European or common starlings (*Sturnus vulgaris*) which may otherwise seek to monopolize this food supply.

Identification: Pale greyish head and underparts, with a slightly whiter area above the bill and barring on the flanks. Black and white barring also extends down over the back and wings, and on to the tail feathers too. Cocks can be distinguished by the small red cap of plumage on the top of their head.

Distribution: Ranges from south-western USA to Sonora. Other races occur in Baja California.
Size: 24cm (9¹/₂in).
Habitat: Scrubland and woods, extending into urban areas.
Nest: Tree hollow.
Eggs: 3–6, white.
Food: Invertebrates, seeds and fruits.

Downy woodpecker

Dryobates pubescens

Downy woodpeckers are relatively common and can be found in a variety of habitats. It is possible to attract them to bird tables by offering suet, particularly in the wintertime when other foods are likely to be scarce. They feed largely on wood-boring invertebrates, but are usually forced to seek out plant matter such as nuts through the winter. The breeding period varies across their extensive range, being later in the north, where egg-laying is unlikely to occur before May. Unusually for a woodpecker, the nest site is chosen by the female, and is almost invariably sited in a dead tree. At this time their distinctive drumming sounds can be heard echoing through the forest, as they tap on branches within their territory to keep in touch. Nesting duties are evenly shared, with pairs subsequently splitting up over the winter period to seek food and roost in tree hollows on their own.

Distribution: Ranges widely across much of the wooded region of North America, from south-eastern Alaska to Newfoundland, and southward as far as Florida.
Size: 17cm (6¹/₂in).
Habitat: Forests, orchards, parks and back gardens.
Nest: Tree hollow.
Eggs: 3–6, white.
Food: Mainly invertebrates.

Identification: Black on head and ear coverts, plus a moustachial stripe with intervening white areas. Back and underparts are also white. A band of scalloped white markings in the vicinity of the shoulder, with spots on the black wings and inner tail feathers. Cocks have a bright red area at the back of the head.

White-breasted nuthatch (*Sitta carolinensis*): 15cm (6in)
South-western and eastern Canada down through much of the USA, extending to Florida and Mexico. Characteristic white area on the chest, with black on back of head, and a rufous tinge to underparts. Back bluish grey. Hens may have grey crowns, especially in the northeast.

Pileated woodpecker (*Dryocopus pileatus*): 48cm (19in)
Southern British Columbia across southern Canada to Nova Scotia, and south to the Gulf coast, Florida, northern California in the west, and Idaho and Montana in the east. More widely distributed in eastern than western USA. Distinctively large. Prominent red forehead and crown, with a narrow white stripe beneath. Broad black line runs through the eyes, with a white area beneath and a broad white stripe down the neck. Wings and underparts are blackish, with white scalloping below. Hens have black rather than red moustachial stripes.

Striped woodpecker (*Veniliornis lignarius*): 15cm (6in)
Southern South America, in several isolated populations: west-central and south-western Bolivia, the Andes of southern Chile, and south-west Argentina. Very small in size, with brown on the white-streaked crown, and ear coverts edged by white bands. Brown back and tail are barred with white, with brown streaking and spotting on underparts. Red or reddish-orange patch on the nape of cock birds, sometimes forming a complete band, absent in hens.

American yellow warbler

Setophaga aestiva

The small resident population of mangrove warblers (*S. petechia gundlachi*) in Florida are of Caribbean origin, which helps to explain the distinctive green plumage on their crown. Further south, those found in coastal areas of Mexico are also described as mangrove warblers, *S. petechia*. There is also wide diversity in the plumage of the young birds, which can vary from pale yellow with greener upperparts to a brown shade. Young Florida birds are easily distinguished by their grey coloration, with white underparts. Yellow warblers are popular with people seeking a natural form of pest control in their garden, since they regularly comb the ground for invertebrates. When breeding, their nests are sometimes parasitized by cowbirds. As winter approaches, the warblers head south, to a wide area from southern Mexico down to Peru, and east to French Guiana and Brazil.

Distribution: Northern Alaska east and south across much of northern North America. Ranges down into Central America and through the Caribbean, with a tiny localized population in Florida.
Size: 13cm (5in).
Habitat: Orchards, backyards and open woodland.
Nest: Cup of plant material in a tree fork.
Eggs: 4–5, bluish white with darker speckling.
Food: Mainly invertebrates.

Identification: Coloration varies, especially in young birds. Yellowish, with red streaking on the underparts, and greener upperparts. Adults from northern areas greener than those found further south, while birds from Mexico often have chestnut-brown on the head.

URBAN INSECT-HUNTERS

A number of birds such as swifts and swallows have developed the ability to prey on insects in flight. Their acrobatic agility makes them exciting to observe as they twist and turn. Other insect hunters are more opportunistic, like the cowbirds, whose lifestyles have changed significantly in North America in the course of little more than a century.

Chimney swift

Chaetura pelagica

Distribution: Eastern North America. Migrates through Central America on its way to and from its South American winter quarters in Peru and northern Chile.
Size: 13cm (5in).
Habitat: Urban and agricultural areas.
Nest: Twigs held together with saliva.
Eggs: 2–7, white.
Food: Flying insects.

It is not always easy to identify swifts with certainty as they wheel far overhead in the sky, but the small and quite stocky appearance of this species can help. Chimney swifts have long wings and actively fly rather than glide, flapping their wings fast to stay airborne. When seen at close quarters their square-shaped tails have obvious spines at their tips. Being dependent on flying insects for food, the swifts are forced to head south for the winter, returning north to their breeding grounds in March and April. Just prior to migration, literally thousands of chimney swifts may congregate at favoured roosts. Their habits have changed significantly due to the spread of cities in North America. Instead of the hollow trees that they would formerly have inhabited for roosting, they have switched to using chimneys, barns and similar sites, even breeding in these surroundings.

Identification: Dark brown overall, with a paler area around the throat. Body slightly box-like in bulk, with short tail feathers and long wings. Usually seen in flight from beneath, often at a great height as they soar high. Sexes are similar.

American cliff swallow

Petrochelidon pyrrhonota

Distribution: North America and Mexico, except northern Alaska and the far north-east. Migrates via Central America to southern Brazil, Paraguay, parts of Argentina, and occasionally Chile.
Size: 14cm (5½in).
Habitat: Open areas near buildings.
Nest: Gourd-shaped structure of mud.
Eggs: 3–6, whitish with brown speckling.
Food: Invertebrates.

The cliff swallow has adjusted its habits to benefit from the spread of urbanization in its North American breeding grounds. In the past these swallows built their nests on cliff faces, as their name suggests, but now pairs will breed in barns, bridges and similar structures. They may even decide to use dry, hollowed gourds placed in suitable sites as artificial nests. These swallows may also nest in large colonies. The mud that forms the nest is scooped up in the swallow's bill, and, unlike in related species, is the only building material. The interior is lined with vegetation. Pairs typically take five days to build the nest. In autumn the swallows head south for winter, although a few fly no further than Panama. Their return is greeted as a sign of spring.

Identification: Pale forehead, with a blue top to the head, which is encircled with chestnut plumage. Blackish area at the base of the throat. Upper chest and rump are orangish brown, underparts otherwise whitish, with dark edging to undertail coverts. Back and wings are dark and streaked with white. Young birds have blackish heads.

Western kingbird (*Tyrannus verticalis*):
22.5cm (9in)
Extends from British Columbia and Manitoba south through western USA to northern Texas and New Mexico. May be seen in eastern areas of the USA when migrating. Overwinters in Central America as far south as El Salvador. Ashy-grey head, back and upper breast, with a white area on the cheeks. Underparts yellowish. Wings and tail are a darker brown shade above, with slight scalloping on the wings. Yellow underwing coverts. Sexes are alike.

Eastern kingbird (*Tyrannus tyrannus*):
22.5cm (9in)
Southern Canada across much of the USA to Florida, except for the west coast and inland in the extreme south-west. Overwinters in parts of Central and South America, from Costa Rica eastward as far as French Guiana, and parts of Peru, Bolivia and Brazil as far as north-western Argentina. Jet-black head, with greyer back and white scalloping on the wings. Underparts whitish, with an indistinct greyish band across the chest. Sexes are alike.

Vaux's swift (*Chaetura vauxi*): 12cm (5in)
Breeds from western North America to Venezuela in South America. Smaller in size and with higher-pitched calls than the similar chimney swift, which occurs further east in the USA. Dark plumage overall, but with lighter chest plumage when seen from below. The rump is paler too. Sexes are alike.

Tropical kingbird

Olive-backed kingbird *Tyrannus melancholicus*

It is not unknown for these kingbirds to be seen across the Mexican border in the USA. Pairs have been recorded breeding in parts of Arizona, while some prefer to overwinter in the relatively mild climate of California, where they can hunt for invertebrates in characteristic fashion, swooping down to catch them in flight. Tropical kingbirds are usually most conspicuous toward dusk, as they hawk night-flying insects. They are very agile on the wing, able to drop almost vertically on to a branch from above. Pairs usually build their nests high up, out on a tree limb where they will be relatively safe from predators. The olive plumage on their back may help to conceal their presence when viewed from above during the nesting period. Incubation is carried out by the female alone, and the young will fledge after approximately two weeks.

Distribution: Typically ranges from the extreme south of the USA and Mexico to Argentina, extending west of the Andes to Peru. Also occurs on Trinidad.
Size: 24cm (9½in).
Habitat: Trees, often close to water.
Nest: Cup-shaped, made of vegetation.
Eggs: 3–5, pinkish buff with darker markings.
Food: Invertebrates.

Identification: Greyish head with a blackish eye stripe, whiter on cheeks and throat. Greyish green on the back extends on to the chest, with rest of underparts yellow. Wings dark with scalloping on the shoulders. Coverts of underwings are yellow.

Brown-headed cowbird

Molothrus ater

Cowbirds are so-called because they traditionally followed herds of buffalo (bison) across the plains of North America, seeking the insects that were attracted to these bovids. Bison no longer thunder over the prairies, but brown-headed cowbirds have nonetheless expanded their range. This is partly due to woodland clearance, and also to the abundance of small birds that will rear the cowbirds' chicks. At nesting time, female cowbirds seek out the nests of species such as vireos. They watch and wait until the nest is complete, then deposit their own eggs before the host has laid. The young cowbirds hatch before their unfortunate nestmates, and monopolize the food supply. In some areas they are thought to have caused a great decline in the numbers of their host species.

Left: Young cowbirds grow so fast they can fledge at just nine days old.

Identification: Adult male has a characteristic brown head and metallic green-black body. Hen has greyish-brown upperparts, with paler areas around the eyes and throat. Underparts are streaked with darker markings. Young birds resemble hens but with whitish scalloping on the upperparts and more evident streaking below.

Distribution: Occurs across much of North America except the far north, and south as far as Mexico.
Size: 19cm (7½in).
Habitat: Woodland, open farmland and suburbs.
Nest: Parasitizes those of other birds.
Eggs: 10–12, white with dark speckling.
Food: Feeds on invertebrates, seeds and berries.

HUMMINGBIRDS AND JAYS

Hummingbirds feeding in gardens, either from flowers or special feeders, are one of the unique sights of America. These birds are a source of fascination as they hover in flight and feed, demonstrating their remarkable aerial agility. However, they may not always be resident throughout the year, with some species moving to warmer climes for the winter.

Ruby-throated hummingbird

Archilochus colubris

Distribution: Breeds in eastern North America, moving south to Florida and southwest to Texas through Central America to Panama for the winter. Sometimes seen in the adjoining region of the Caribbean.
Size: 9cm (3½in).
Habitat: Lightly wooded areas with flowering plants.
Nest: Cup built in trees, bound with spiders' silk.
Eggs: 2, white.
Food: Nectar, pollen, sap and invertebrates.

The small size of these hummingbirds is no barrier to flying long distances, which they do back and forth to their wintering grounds each year. Cock birds usually arrive back in their breeding areas about a week before the hens are seen in May. Staying in temperate areas would mean that these birds would have difficulty finding sufficient plant nectar to sustain them through the winter. In fact, ruby-throated hummingbirds are far less specialized in their feeding habits than some members of this family, and have been recorded feeding on more than 31 different types of plant, although they display a preference for red flowers. Hens build their nest alone, binding it with the silk threads of spiders' webs, and are responsible for rearing the chicks on their own. Tiny invertebrates feature prominently in their diet at this stage.

Identification: Metallic, greenish-bronze upperparts. Has a large glossy red area of plumage under the throat. The remainder of the underparts are whitish. Hens are similar in appearance, but they have a dusky white area on their throat instead of the glossy red patch of the cocks.

Anna's hummingbird

Calypte anna

These hummingbirds are sometimes seen feeding at the holes in tree bark drilled by sapsuckers (*Sphyrapicus* species), which results in the plant's sap oozing, providing an accessible source of nutrients. At the outset of the breeding season, males become very territorial. Soon afterwards, hens begin to seek out suitable nest sites, which can include human-made structures, such as electric wires. They gather small lengths of plant fibres and bind them together with silk from spiders' webs. Lichens are used to fill in gaps between the stems, and the cup is lined with feathers. The chicks leave the nest for the first time when only 18 days old.

Identification: Mostly rose-coloured head, with a bronzy-green area behind the eyes and a small white spot evident there as well. Upperparts are a shade of metallic, bronzy green, and underparts are green and whitish. Hens lack the rose-coloured plumage on the head, and have a brownish throat.

Distribution: Western USA, from California and offshore islands south-east to Arizona; may move to southern Oregon during the winter. Sometimes even recorded in Alaska.
Size: 10cm (4in).
Habitat: Generally woodland areas with flowers.
Nest: Cup-shaped.
Eggs: 2, white.
Food: Nectar, pollen, sap and invertebrates.

Steller's jay

Cyanocitta stelleri

Ranging over a vast area, Steller's jay has proved to be a highly adaptable species. In some areas, such as at picnic sites in the Rocky Mountains in Colorado, these jays have become very tame, accepting food from people. Elsewhere, they are much shyer. They eat a varied diet; where food is likely to be hard to find because of snow in winter, they forage for acorns in the autumn, which are then stored for later use. Family groups may remain together over the winter in northern areas, and the young leave in the spring when the adult pair start to nest again. Mud is often used like cement to anchor the bulky nest of twigs together.

Identification: Dark, greyish-blue head and back, with blue underparts. Tail and wings are blue with black barring. North American variety have darker coloration and more prominent crests than those occurring further south, which have a much bluer appearance. Sexes are alike.

Distribution: The largest distribution of all North American jays, extending from Alaska south through Central America to Nicaragua.
Size: 32cm (12½in).
Habitat: Woodland and forest.
Nest: Mound of twigs.
Eggs: 2–6, greenish or bluish with brown spotting.
Food: Omnivorous.

Black-chinned hummingbird (purple-throated hummingbird, *Archilochus alexandri*): 10cm (4in)
Breeding range extends from south-west British Columbia across southern USA. into Mexico. Moves further south over the winter. Black area merging into broader purple area on the sides of the face and throat. Underparts are buffy brown, and upperparts are dull bronzy green. Hen is similar, also with a white stripe behind the eyes, and buffy brown on the sides of the face and throat.

Broad-tailed hummingbird (*Selasphorus platycercus*): 11cm (4½in)
Breeding range from California through Texas into southern Mexico and Guatemala. Winters entirely in Central America. Wide tail feathers. Metallic, deep reddish-purple throat and sides of the face, with buffy-brown underparts and metallic green upperparts. Hens are duller, with brown speckling on the buffy throat plumage.

Rivoli's hummingbird (magnificent hummingbird, *Eugenes fulgens*): 13cm (5in)
Breeding range from southern Arizona and New Mexico in the USA, with these birds wintering in Mexico. A separate population in Central America ranges as far south as western Panama. Deep purple coloration on the head, becoming blackish with a white spot behind the eyes, and a brilliant green throat. Hens have lighter brown underparts. Light green upperparts in both sexes.

Blue jay (*Cyanocitta cristata*): 30cm (12in)
Found extensively in Eastern North America, down to Florida, although southerly populations tend to be smaller. Blue crest, white area on the face, edged by black feathering. Wings are blue with distinctive white markings. Black barring extends from the flight feathers to the tail. Underparts are white. Sexes are alike.

Green jay

Cyanocorax luxuosus

These woodland birds are now a separate species from the more social Inca jays, *C. yncas*, found in South American from Venezuela to Bolivia. One of the most unusual features of these jays is their habit of seeking out smoking areas of woodland, not only in search of small creatures that may be escaping the flames, but also to hold their wings out, allowing the smoke to permeate their plumage. This action is believed to kill off parasites such as lice that may be lurking on their bodies. Young green jays may remain with their parents and help to rear the new chicks before establishing their own territories.

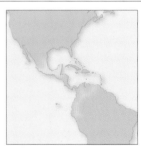

Distribution: Population extends from Texas to Honduras.
Size: 27cm (10½in).
Habitat: Woodland and forest.
Nest: Platform of twigs and similar material.
Eggs: 3–5, greyish lilac with dark speckling.
Food: Omnivorous.

Identification: Green plumage is characteristic. A combination of blue and black plumage on the head, being green elsewhere, and underparts, including the underside of the tail, are yellowish. Iris is black. Sexes are alike.

GARDEN HUNTERS

Predators are not always welcomed in the garden, but these birds at the top of the avian food chain are quite remarkable in the way they hunt and, in many cases, communicate with each other. Their generally bold nature helps them to thrive in the human environment, while their intelligence allows them to profit from environmental changes.

Black-billed magpie

Pica hudsonia

Distinguishable from its European relative by its calls rather than its appearance, the black-billed magpie is a common sight through much of its range. These members of the crow family are quite agile on the ground, holding their tail feathers up as they hop along. They are often blamed for the decline of songbirds because of their habit of raiding nests, taking both eggs and young chicks. These magpies also sometimes chase other birds, particularly gulls, to make them drop their food. They also eat invertebrates and fruit. Bold and garrulous by nature, a pair of black-billed magpies will not hesitate to create a commotion if their nest is threatened by a predator such as a cat. Their calls draw other magpies to the area, who then join in harrying the unfortunate feline. Their nest is a stout and usually large structure, with a protective dome of twigs.

Identification: Black head, upper breast, back, rump and tail, with a broad white patch around the abdomen. When folded, wings have a broad white stripe and dark blue areas below. Black plumage may have a green gloss. Sexes are alike, but cock may have a longer tail.

Distribution: Western North America, extending from Alaska eastward to Ontario down to north-eastern parts of California and northern New Mexico.
Size: 48cm (19in).
Habitat: Trees with surrounding open areas.
Nest: Dome-shaped stick pile.
Eggs: 2–8, bluish green with darker markings.
Food: Omnivorous.

American crow

Common crow *Corvus brachyrhynchos*

Distribution: Occurs across much of North America, from British Columbia to New-foundland and south to Baja California, Colorado and central Texas.
Size: 45cm (17¹/₂in).
Habitat: Ranges widely, including into suburban areas.
Nest: Platform of sticks.
Eggs: 3–7, greenish with brown blotches.
Food: Omnivorous.

Few birds have more highly developed communication skills than these crows. It is almost impossible to approach them without being noticed, since even when feeding they have sentinels keeping a look-out for danger. They are heavily persecuted in farming areas, due to the damage that they can inflict on crops; however the benefits that they bring in foraging for potentially harmful invertebrates are frequently overlooked. American crows are highly adaptable birds, just as likely to be encountered in towns and cities as in open countryside. Noisy by nature, they tend to be much less vocal in the vicinity of their nests, which are sited in tall trees, often in public parks. The height at which they build – 20m (60ft) or more off the ground – keeps them safe from most predators.

Identification: Jet-black plumage, with dark eyes and a large black bill. Sexes are alike. Calls help to distinguish this species from other crows, while the fan-shaped appearance of the tail in flight distinguishes these corvids from ravens.

American kestrel

Falco sparverius

The smallest of the North American falcons, the American kestrel can easily be overlooked unless it is hovering conspicuously along a roadside. Their remarkably keen eyesight allows these birds to spot a mouse or similar prey from as far as 30m (90ft) away. They dive down quickly to seize the unsuspecting quarry, their sharp talons ensuring a secure grip on their prey. After making a kill, the kestrel will fly up to a convenient perch with its meal, or back to the nest site if it has young. Insects such as grasshoppers are also likely to fall victim to these falcons, particularly during the summer months when they are generally more plentiful and can play a vital part in nourishing a growing brood. The vast range of these kestrels means that they need to be adaptable feeders. They have been documented in Peru as preying on both lizards and scorpions, while amphibians will also be caught on occasion.

Distribution: Extends over virtually all of America, from Alaska in the north to Tierra del Fuego at the tip of South America.
Size: 27cm (10^1/$_2$in).
Habitat: Open countryside and urban areas.
Nest: Typically in a hollow tree.
Eggs: 3–7, white with brown blotching.
Food: Insects and small vertebrates.

Identification: Cock has russet back barred with black, and a russet tail with a broad black subterminal bar and whitish feather tips. Top of the head is russet with adjacent greyish-blue area. Wings greyish blue above, with black barring but much paler below, and white circular spots along the rear edge. Two distinctive vertical black stripes on the sides of the face, with an intervening whitish area and chin. Underparts paler. Hens have chestnut wings and a barred tail.

Yellow-billed magpie (*Pica nuttalli*):
42cm (16^1/$_2$in)
Occasionally seen as far north as Oregon, but more typically resides in the Central Valley area of California and in coastal valleys as far south as Santa Barbara County. Similar to the black-billed magpie, with a black head, back and breast. Wings and underparts have white patches. Bill is yellow, with a variable yellow patch of bare skin adjacent to the eyes. Sexes are alike.

Black-winged kite (*Elanus caeruleus*):
41cm (16in)
Mainly occurs through Central and South America. In North America, is sometimes seen as far north as British Columbia, hunting along highways. Greyish crown, back and wings, with prominent black patches at the shoulders. Underparts are white, enabling it to be distinguished from the Mississippi kite (*Ictinia mississippiensis*). Sexes are alike. Young birds have reddish-brownish striations on underparts, with similar suffusion on the head and neck.

Western screech owl (*Megascops kennicottii*):
22cm (8^1/$_2$in)
Western side of North America, from northern Canada down to Mexico. Also occurs in two colour morphs, although reddish individuals are decidedly uncommon outside the humid coastal north-west. The pattern of cross-barring on the plumage of this species is denser, creating an overall impression of a darker-coloured bird, although depth of grey coloration varies.

Eastern screech owl

Megascops asio

The red and grey morphs of these owls are equally common, sometimes even cropping up in the same nest. Habitat appears to play no part in determining coloration. Lightly wooded areas, including back gardens, are favoured by these birds of prey. In true owl fashion, eastern screech owls hunt at night, and despite their size are able to take relatively large quarry, including adult rats. They are opportunists, catching anything from worms to snakes and even moths, which can be seized in flight. In urban areas these owls are even known to plunge into garden ponds at night, seizing unwary fish near the surface. The shape of their wings means that virtually no sound betrays their presence until after they have launched their deadly strike. As with other owls, the study of the pellets regurgitated after meals has allowed ornithologists to confirm their feeding habits.

Distribution: Eastern North America, from eastern Montana and the Great Lakes down via the Gulf states to north-eastern Mexico.
Size: 22cm (8^1/$_2$in).
Habitat: Variable, from forests to suburban areas and parks.
Nest: In a hollow tree.
Eggs: 2–8, white.
Food: Small mammals and invertebrates.

Identification: Red and grey colour morphs. Widely spaced cross-barring on the underparts matches spacing of vertical stripes on a whitish ground. Yellowish-green base to the bill. Ear tufts may be raised or lowered. Lines of white spots with black edging extend diagonally across top of wings. Sexes are alike.

BLUEBIRDS AND OTHER SONGSTERS

One of the most welcome signs of spring in temperate regions is the so-called "dawn chorus," indicating the onset of the breeding period and the return of migrant songbirds. At this hour of day, when the surroundings are relatively quiet, the songs of these birds can be clearly heard in gardens and parks, making this an excellent time at which to spot them too.

Mountain bluebird

Sialia currucoides

Distribution: Western North America, wintering as far south as northern Mexico.
Size: 18cm (7in).
Habitat: Open countryside, including parkland.
Nest: Concealed cup-shaped structure.
Eggs: 4–8, whitish to pale blue.
Food: Invertebrates and berries.

The beautiful song of the mountain bluebird can be heard just before dawn, leading the Navajo people to describe them as "heralds of the rising sun." Almost immediately, when the sun appears, they become quiet again. Pairs seek shelter when they are nesting, building in hollow trees, small caves, or even on cliff faces, although they will also adopt birdhouses. Invertebrates are an important source of food for these bluebirds. However, late frosts can adversely affect the insect population, reducing the likelihood of breeding success if food is scarce when the chicks hatch. The young normally leave the nest at three weeks old, and the adult pair may rear another family before the end of summer. In the autumn and through the winter berries feature more prominently in their diet, with the bluebirds venturing more regularly to birdfeeders in areas where they live.

Identification: Cock is blue overall, being a deeper sky-blue shade on the upperparts. Bills and legs black. Hens are brownish grey, with white on the abdomen, and whitish scalloping seen on the wings. There may be a reddish-orange suffusion on the breast after the autumn moult.

American robin

Turdus migratorius

The return of the American robin to its northern haunts is a long-awaited sign of spring. Adult cock birds usually arrive first, followed by the hens. Last to arrive are the young of the previous year, making their first flight back to the area where they were hatched. American robins are alert hunters, hopping across lawns and pausing at intervals, their head tilted slightly to one side as if listening. It is actually their keen eyesight that allows them to spot earthworms and other invertebrates in the grass. Berries also feature in their diet. Their nest is well-built, with mud serving as cement to hold the vegetation together, and carefully sited in dense vegetation to avoid the attention of predators. It is not uncommon for pale leucistic individuals to occur in this species, and even pure white albinos.

Distribution: All of North America, apart from the central far north, down as far as Mexico. Overwinters in the south of its range, including northern Guatemala, and is also seen in some Caribbean islands, such as Cuba.
Size: 25cm (10in).
Habitat: Woodlands, parks, and suburban areas.
Nest: Cup of vegetation and mud.
Eggs: 3–6, bright blue.
Food: Invertebrates and also fruit.

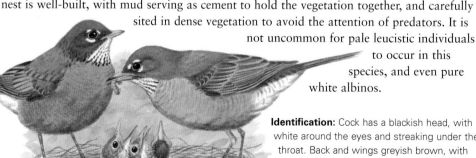

Identification: Cock has a blackish head, with white around the eyes and streaking under the throat. Back and wings greyish brown, with brick red underparts and white under the vent. Hens have browner heads and orangish underparts. The underparts of young birds are speckled. Eastern birds tend to be more brightly coloured than their western counterparts.

Rufous-backed thrush

Rufous-backed robin *Turdus rufopalliatus*

These relatively large thrushes are likely to be found in Mexico at lower altitudes than migrating American robins (*T. migratorius*). Their song is relatively similar, however, being comprised of attractive liquid call notes uttered in a relatively slow style. Rufous-backed thrushes are often seen throughout their range, although those reported around Oaxaca City may well be the descendants of captive individuals, rather than naturally occurring birds. The same may apply to those seen in the Distrito Federal, another part of their range where the species has not been sighted until recently. There is evidence to show that these thrushes regularly move northward, crossing the border into the USA where they are not normally observed; records exist not only for states such as Texas and Arizona but also for sightings further north in California during winter. Outside the breeding season, rufous-backed thrushes are often seen in larger groups rather than as pairs.

Identification: Greyish head, with a white throat streaked with black. Back and wing coverts reddish brown. Wings and rump grey with reddish-brown underparts, becoming white on the lower abdomen. Sexes are alike.

Distribution: Restricted to western Mexico.
Size: 25cm (10in).
Habitat: Trees and shrubbery.
Nest: Cup-shaped.
Eggs: 2–3, whitish with reddish-brown markings.
Food: Invertebrates, berries and fruit.

Eastern bluebird (*Sialia sialis*): 18cm (7in)
Ranges from southern Canada to the Gulf states and Arizona, extending as far south as Nicaragua. Migrates south from northern areas for the winter, occurring no farther north at this stage than southern parts of New England and southern Michigan. Blue head, wings and tail are offset against rusty red breast feathering, becoming whiter on the abdomen. Hens duller, with greyish-blue upperparts. Young birds are brown and speckled, with areas of whitish and some blue plumage.

Eastern slaty thrush (*Turdus subalaris*): 20cm (8in)
Ranges from southern Brazil to the extreme north-east of Argentina. Typical thrush-like appearance. Greyish head and upperparts, with a slight bluish suffusion. The white throat area is heavily streaked with blackish markings, and there is a white crescent at the base of the throat. Underparts are ashy grey, becoming paler on the abdomen. Hens are similar but have a more brownish tinge to their upperparts, with brown rather than blackish streaking on the throat. Bill is yellowish brown, instead of the male's brighter orange-yellow shade.

Austral thrush (*Turdus falcklandii*): 25cm (10in)
Southern South America, occurring widely in Chile and southern Argentina. Also present on the Falkland Islands to the east, being the only resident thrush here. Blackish head, with olive-brown back, wings and tail. Streaked throat with white suffusion, underparts otherwise buff brown. Bill is yellow. Sexes are generally alike, although hens sometimes have slightly browner heads. The mainland population has more contrast in its coloration than individuals from the Falklands, having blacker heads and paler, more yellowish-brown underparts. Young birds are recognizable in either case by their speckled plumage.

Melodious blackbird

Dives dives

Forest clearance in various parts of its range has aided the spread of the melodious blackbird over recent years. This species is often to be seen foraging for food on lawns, pausing occasionally to flick its tail feathers vertically. Although most commonly observed in pairs, much larger groups often congregate in fields. The song of the melodious blackbird is less inspired than its name suggests, consisting mainly of a series of whistles that can be loud and sharp in tone. Pairs may duet with each other on occasions. They become very territorial when breeding, with both members of the pair defending their territory. Working together, it takes these birds nearly two weeks to build their nest, using vegetation of various types and mud or cow dung to bind the fibres together. The hen is responsible for incubating the eggs on her own, although the cock will bring her food during this period. Both adult birds then forage to feed the chicks.

Distribution: Central America, ranging from Mexico south to Costa Rica.
Size: 25cm (10in).
Habitat: Open areas with woodland nearby.
Nest: Open cup in a tree.
Eggs: 3–4, blue with brown blotches.
Food: Invertebrates and berries.

Identification: Black with a slight blue suffusion, depending on the light. Slightly curved black bill, tapering to a point. Legs and feet also black. Long tail feathers, with the wings appearing rounded in flight. Sexes similar in appearance. Young birds are brownish black overall and display no iridescence.

NATIVE INSECT-EATERS AND INVADERS

The present-day distribution of some birds is the direct result of past human interference. The effects of this can be clearly seen in North America, where some introduced European species have now become established across virtually the entire continent. Mimics such as the catbird may even pick up the songs of these feathered invaders.

Brown thrasher

Toxostoma rufum

Distribution: This species is widely distributed in eastern parts of North America, ranging down as far as Florida and the Gulf coast. It has even been recorded in Newfoundland.
Size: 29cm (11½in).
Habitat: Woodland and hedges.
Nest: Cup-shaped.
Eggs: 2–5, being whitish to pale blue with brown speckles.
Food: Invertebrates and berries.

Thrashers are a native American group of birds. Although they are rather shy by nature, hiding away in vegetation, they will venture down to the ground to flick over leaf litter using their long bills, and snatch up any invertebrates disturbed. It has been suggested that the rhythmic movement of the bill in this context bears a resemblance to the cutting action of a scythe, and this may explain the unusual name of this species. At the outset of the breeding season it is difficult to overlook the courtship of the brown thrasher, since the cock bird takes up a prominent position to sing to his would-be mate. He perches with his head up and bill open, although any hint of danger will lead to a cessation of the song. The hen responds by offering a piece of vegetation, which probably marks the start of nest-building. Pairs work together to construct a bulky nest of plant matter, including grass, twigs, and even bark. Incubation and fledging each take about 13 days, which allows two broods of chicks to be reared during a single breeding season.

Identification: Reddish-brown upperparts, with streaking across the wings creating a scalloped appearance. Long chestnut tail feathers. Underparts marked with black streaks arranged in vertical lines running down onto the flanks; plumage is whitish in the vicinity of the throat, becoming fawn on the lower parts of the abdomen. Long, slightly down-curved black bill. Sexes are alike.

Grey catbird

Dumetella carolinensis

The song of these relatives of the mockingbird incorporates a sound like a cat's miaowing, which is the reason for their common name. Grey catbirds also possess a harsher alarm call in their vocal repertoire. They can often be heard singing after dark, especially on moonlit nights. Grey catbirds are quite shy by nature, and their coloration also helps them to blend into the background. Their chestnut underparts are most conspicuous during the cock's courting display, when he chases the hen in the early stages of courtship. When on the move, the grey catbird flicks its long tail repeatedly. Insects are a vital part of the diet of these birds, especially when they are rearing chicks, as the insects provide valuable protein. Grey catbirds may catch their insect prey above water, and these birds are often observed hunting in areas close to ponds and streams.

Identification: This species is slate-grey in colour, with a distinctive black cap. It also has chestnut underparts, which may not be clearly visible. Sexes are alike.

Distribution: Southern Canada south and eastward across the USA, as far down as Florida. Southerly winter range extends as far down as Panama and Cuba.
Size: 23cm (9in).
Habitat: Scrubland, hedgerows and gardens.
Nest: Loosely constructed cup of vegetation.
Eggs: 4–6, glossy blue-green.
Food: Fruit and insects.

Northern mockingbird (*Mimus polyglottos*): 28cm (11in)
Southern Canada through the USA to southern Mexico and the Caribbean. Relatively dull, with grey upperparts, paler on the underparts. Broad white area on the wings, most apparent in flight. Sexes are alike.

Common myna (Common mynah, *Acridotheres tristis*): 25cm (10in)
A member of the starling family, introduced to southern Florida. Blackish head contrasts with long, pointed yellow bill and bare yellow orbital skin around the eyes. Back is brownish. The black wings have a prominent white band across the flight feathers, also evident when the wings are closed. Undertail coverts white, with white tips to the tail feathers. Underparts otherwise brown with a slight reddish tinge. Legs are yellow, matching the bill. Sexes are alike.

Northern shrike (Great grey shrike, *Lanius excubitor*): 25cm (10in)
Widely distributed throughout North America. Ranges up to Alaska but less common in eastern areas, especially the south-east, and not present in Mexico. Grey head and back, with a thin white line running just above the eyes and a broader black stripe running through them. Underparts whitish. White banding running across the otherwise black wings. Long tail, with the central feathers being black and the shorter ones white. Stout, longish and slightly hooked black bill. Sexes are alike. Young birds display brownish markings at first.

House sparrow

Passer domesticus

A common visitor to birdfeeders and city parks, house sparrows have adapted to living close to people. They were originally brought to New York from Europe in 1850, and by 1910 had spread west to California. There are now noticeable differences within the North American population: northern individuals are larger, while those from south-western arid areas are paler. House sparrows form loose flocks, with larger numbers gathering where food is plentiful. They spend much time on the ground, hopping along while watching for predators such as cats. It is not uncommon for them to build nests during winter, to serve as communal roosts. The bills of cock birds turn black at the start of the nesting season in spring. Several males often court a single female in what is known as a "sparrows' wedding."

Identification: Rufous-brown at the back of the head, with grey above. A black stripe runs across the eyes and a broad black bib extends down over the chest. Ear coverts and underparts are greyish, with a whiter area under the tail. Hens are browner overall with a pale stripe prominent behind each eye.

Distribution: Southern Canada southward across the USA and into Central and much of South America.
Size: 15cm (6in).
Habitat: Urban and more rural areas.
Nest: Under roofs and in tree hollows.
Eggs: 3–6, whitish with darker markings.
Food: Seeds and invertebrates.

Common starling

European starling *Sturnus vulgaris*

The common European starling is another New World invader, introduced in 1890 when a small flock of 60 starlings brought from England was set free in New York's Central Park. A further 40 were released there the following year, making the millions of starlings now present in the whole of North America direct descendants of this initial group of 100 birds. (The release came about as part of an unfulfilled plan to introduce all the birds described in the works of British playwright William Shakespeare to North America.) Small groups of starlings are often to be seen feeding in gardens, although occasionally much larger groups comprised of hundreds of birds may visit an area. In flight, European starlings are adept at avoiding predators such as hawks by weaving back and forth in close formation, to confuse a would-be attacker. Their undemanding breeding habits and belligerent nature mean that these starlings will commandeer nest holes from native species for their own use.

Distribution: Occurs widely throughout North America except the far north, just ranging south into Mexico.
Size: 22cm (8¹/₂in).
Habitat: Near houses and buildings.
Nest: Tree hole or birdhouse.
Eggs: 2–9, white to pale blue or green.
Food: Invertebrates, berries, birdfeeder fare.

Identification: Glossy, with purplish-black plumage on the head and a greenish hue on parts of the body overlaid with spots, particularly the neck and back. Dark brown wings and tail. Hens similar, but spotting is larger and base of the tail pinkish rather than blue, as in breeding males. Young birds are duller, being brownish, and lack iridescence.

WRENS

These diminutive, rather stumpy birds are often found in residential areas, especially the aptly named house wren, which has one of the widest distributions of all birds in America, occurring virtually throughout the entire region. Other wrens have more localized distributions, benefiting from birdfeeder offerings to sustain themselves during the cold winter months.

House wren

Troglodytes aedon

The house wren appears a rather nondescript bird, but its lively, jerky movements make it instantly recognizable, even from just a brief glimpse. These wrens often frequent gardens, usually being seen among dense vegetation since they are instinctively reluctant to leave cover for long. Although wrens are small in size, they can be determined and belligerent birds, especially in defence of a chosen nest site such as a woodpecker hole in a tree, and are quite able to force the creator of the chamber to go elsewhere. They will also take occupancy of a birdhouse, particularly when sited in an area of a garden where they feel secure. A pair will collect a jumble of vegetation such as moss and small twigs to line the interior, as well as adding feathers to make a soft pad for their eggs. House wrens are prolific breeders, frequently producing two broods of chicks during the season.

Identification: Brown upperparts, with black barring evident on the wings and tail. Underparts lighter brown, with whitish throat area. Generally indistinct pale eyebrow stripes. Narrow, relatively short bill. Sexes are alike. Young birds have a rufous rump and are a darker shade of buff on the underparts.

Distribution: Present across much of North America except the far north, extending down through Mexico and right across South America.
Size: 12cm (5in).
Habitat: Vegetation in parks and gardens.
Nest: Pile of twigs and sticks.
Eggs: 5–9, white with brown spotting.
Food: Invertebrates.

Carolina wren

Thryothorus ludovicianus

Carolina wrens are relatively easy birds to identify, due partly to their extensive white facial markings. They move with the same jerky movements as other wrens, frequenting bushes and similar dense areas of vegetation through which they can move inconspicuously. Carolina wrens are also quite noisy birds, with a song that is surprisingly loud for a bird of their size. It is uttered throughout the year, rather than just at the start of the breeding season, and sounds in part like the word "wheateater," repeated constantly. Unfortunately, young Carolina wrens often have an instinctive tendency to push northward from their southern homelands. Although in mild years they will find sufficient food to withstand the winter cold, widescale mortality occurs in these northern areas when the ground is blanketed with snow for long periods, almost wiping out the species. In due course, however, their numbers build up again, until the cycle is repeated again at some future stage.

Identification: Chestnut-brown upperparts, with black barring on the wings and tail, and white bands running across the wings. Distinctive white eye stripes, edged with black above and bordered by chestnut below. Black and white speckling on the sides of the face. Throat is white, underparts buff. Sexes are alike.

Distribution: Range extends throughout eastern USA, notably in North Carolina and South Carolina.
Size: 14cm (5¹/₂in).
Habitat: Shrubbery.
Nest: Cup of vegetation.
Eggs: 4–8, whitish with brown spotting.
Food: Invertebrates feature prominently in the diet of this species, with some seeds.

Fasciated wren (*Campylorhynchus fasciatus*):
7.5in (19cm)
Found on the western coast of northern South
America, from Los Rios and Guayas in Ecuador
southwards into northern Peru, extending as far
as Lima, and east to San Martin. Dark greyish
area on the head, with a paler stripe beneath.
Light grey plumage overall, broken by irregular
stripes, blotches and lines, including the back,
underparts and tail, which has a rounded tip.
Two subspecies recognized, with the nominate
race from southern Peru being darker and having
more distinctive markings than *C. f. pallescens*
found elsewhere. Iris colour varies from whitish-
tan to reddish-brown. Upper bill dark grey, lighter
below. Legs and feet are tan. Young birds have a
darker cap, with a grey iris, and paler markings.

Bewick's wren (*Thryomanes bewickii*):
13cm (5in)
This species varies in colour through its range.
It is common and possibly expanding in
western areas of the USA, although numbers in
the east are thought to be falling. The
greyest race (*T. b. eremophilus*) occurs in the
western-central part of their distribution, having
a greyish throat and underparts, with the
characteristic long eye stripe extending back to
the nape of the neck. Upperparts are dark grey.
Nearer to the coast, these wrens display a
brown suffusion to their plumage which
becomes progressively darker in more northerly
populations. Eastern races have rich chestnut-
brown upperparts, with characteristic black
markings on the wings and tail.

Canyon wren

Catherpes mexicanus

As with other wrens it is the powerful,
musical song of this species that attracts
attention, although it can be quite difficult
to spot the songster itself, especially if partly
concealed among a loose outcrop of rocks.
Canyon wrens will occasionally adopt
abandoned buildings as refuges. Their long,
narrow bills allow them to seize
invertebrates from small crevices without
difficulty, their tails often bobbing up and
down as they seek their quarry. Canyon
wrens prefer areas around steep slopes or
cliffs, whereas rock wrens (*Salpinctes
obsoletus*) tend to inhabit flatter areas of
countryside. For breeding they choose a site
in a stone wall or a similarly inaccessible
place such as a chimney. The nest is
fashioned from a jumble of
vegetation on a suitable ledge.

Distribution: Extends from
western parts of the USA
south as far as southern
Mexico.
Size: 15cm (6in).
Habitat: Rocky areas.
Nest: Open cup of
vegetation.
Eggs: 4–7, white with dark
speckling.
Food: Invertebrates.

Identification: Black and white
speckled top to the head, with a
white throat and breast. Black
barring on the wings and tail, with
speckling on the back and
underparts. Characteristic
rufous underparts, with the
red extending across the
back, wings and tail. Sexes are
alike. Long, relatively straight
blackish bill. Young birds lack the
white speckling of the adults.

Cactus wren

Campylorhynchus brunneicapillus

This is a surprisingly large wren that is often seen in the
vicinity of cacti in its arid habitat. It builds a bulky nest of
dried grass within the protective spines of these plants or in
thornbushes. The nest interior is lined with fur or feathers;
the entrance is to one side. Nests near the ground are
concealed so they are less apparent to would-be
predators. The calls of the cactus wren have a
monotonous tone, consisting simply of the
sound "chut" uttered repeatedly. The
cactus wren does not raise its tail
vertically in true wren fashion,
but holds it horizontally. These
birds prefer to remain near
the ground, flying low and
hunting for invertebrates
lurking there.

*Right: Cactus wrens
inhabit arid areas,
including scrublands and deserts.*

Identification: Brown area on the
top of the head extends over the
nape, with a white stripe passing
through the eye, and white
streaking on the back. Prominent
black spotting on the breast,
becoming more streaked on the
pale underparts. Barring is
apparent on the wings and tail.
Sexes are alike.

Distribution: South-western
USA from California
southward as far as
central Mexico.
Size: 22cm (8¹/₂in).
Habitat: Arid areas
and desert.
Nest: Large structure made
of vegetation.
Eggs: 4–7, creamy white with
spots.
Food: Invertebrates.

TITS, TITMICE AND CHICKADEES

These small birds are most likely to be seen in gardens during the winter months, when the absence of leaves on many trees makes them more conspicuous. They often visit bird tables and feeders during colder weather too. Members of this group are very resourceful, clearly displaying their aerobatic skills as they dart about and hang upside down to feed.

Tufted titmouse

Baeolophus bicolor

Distribution: Eastern North America, from southern Ontario south to the Gulf of Mexico, although not present in southern Florida. Range appears to be expanding in some areas of Canada.
Size: 15cm (6in).
Habitat: Light, deciduous woodland.
Nest: Small tree holes and nest boxes.
Eggs: 3–8, creamy white with brown spots.
Food: Invertebrates in summer; seeds during winter.

This is the largest member of the tit family occurring in America. It is quite conspicuous through its range, thanks in part to its noisy nature. The vocal range of male tufted titmice is especially varied, and individuals are able to sing more than 15 different song patterns. Hens also sing, but not to the same extent and mainly during spring and early summer. The range of these titmice has increased northward, largely because bird-table offerings guarantee them food throughout the year. In the south, they have been recorded as hybridizing with black-crested titmice (*B. atricristatus*) in central parts of Texas. The resulting offspring have greyish crests and a pale orange band above the bill. In spite of their small size, these titmice are determined visitors to bird tables, driving off much larger species. They can be equally fierce in defending their nests.

Identification: Characteristic black band immediately above the bill, with grey crest and crown. Cheeks and underparts are whitish, with pale reddish-orange flanks. Sexes are alike. Young birds are duller overall, with less contrast in their plumage.

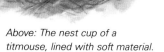

Above: The nest cup of a titmouse, lined with soft material.

Carolina chickadee

Poecile carolinensis

This species is very closely related to the black-capped chickadee (*P. atricapillus*), which occurs further north, and it is not unknown for the birds to hybridize where they overlap. Studies of their song patterns have revealed that the Carolina chickadee has a four-note call, whereas the black-capped type has a two-note whistle. Although pairs have their own territories during the summer, Carolina chickadees form larger groups in the winter months. During cold weather, they spend much longer periods roosting in tree hollows to conserve their body heat, sometimes remaining there for up to 15 hours per day. This is also the time of year when chickadees are most likely to be seen visiting bird tables in search of food.

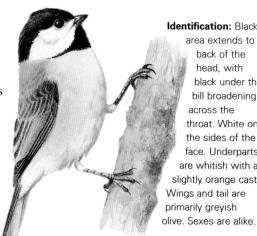

Identification: Black area extends to back of the head, with black under the bill broadening across the throat. White on the sides of the face. Underparts are whitish with a slightly orange cast. Wings and tail are primarily greyish olive. Sexes are alike.

Distribution: Northeastern USA south to Texas and northern Florida. Occasionally recorded in Ontario, Canada.
Size: 12cm (5in).
Habitat: Light, broad-leaved woodland.
Nest: In small holes in trees, also uses nest boxes.
Eggs: 3–9, white with reddish-brown spots.
Food: Invertebrates and seeds.

American bushtit

Psaltriparus minimus

Bushtits are the smallest species of North American tit. These lively birds forage in groups of up to 40 individuals, their movements helping to disturb insects and spiders that might otherwise remain hidden. Bushtits will comb plants in this way, which makes them welcome by gardeners since they can devour unwanted infestations of pests quite rapidly. They are very agile birds, able to hang upside down from a branch when seeking food, and also have a bold nature, so it is often possible to observe them at relatively close quarters. There is a consistent difference in eye coloration between the sexes: the irises of cocks are invariably brown, whereas those of hens may vary from white through to yellow. Remarkably, this change may become apparent within a few days of the young birds fledging, since both sexes have dark eyes at first. Nesting pairs of these tits are also surprisingly tolerant of others of their own kind, to the extent that they may allow them to roost in their nest. Flocks subsequently reform once the breeding season has ended.

Identification: Three groupings exist. Those from northern areas have brownish ear coverts, brown cap, and grey upperparts, with paler, whitish underparts. Hens have greyer throats. Grey coloration extends on to the cap in the lead-coloured variety. In the Central American black-eared form, cock birds have black areas on the sides of the face.

Distribution: Ranges from British Columbia in Canada south and eastward through the USA to parts of Mexico and Guatemala in Central America.
Size: 11cm (4¹/₂in).
Habitat: Scrubland.
Nest: Pendulous mass.
Eggs: 5–13, white.
Food: Mainly invertebrates. Also berries.

Bridled titmouse (*Baeolophus wollweberi*): 13cm (5in)
Southern Arizona and New Mexico south to the uplands of western Mexico. Broad greyish crest, darker at the back, with a blackish stripe running up from the bill. A blackish line runs through the eyes over cheeks, joining a prominent black area on the throat. Yellowish-grey underparts, with wings, back and tail darker grey. Bill blackish, legs and feet grey. Sexes are alike.

Black-crested titmouse (*Baeolophus atricristatus*): 14·5cm (6in)
Restricted to south-western Oklahoma and Texas. Closely related to the tufted titmouse. Pale greyish area above the bill, with black feathering and crest behind. Greyish area around the neck, extending over the back, wings and tail. Paler grey underparts, with rufous area on flanks and a whitish area around the vent. Sexes are alike. Young birds have whitish forehead, with crown a darker grey than rest of upperparts.

Chestnut-backed chickadee (*Poecile rufescens*): 11·5cm (4¹/₂in)
Southern coastal Alaska south via British Columbia and Montana to central California. Sooty-brown cap extends from the bill to the back of the neck, with a white area on the cheeks and a black bib on the throat. Back, flanks and rump generally bright chestnut, with greyish-brown tail feathers. Central underparts whitish. The race *P. r. barlowi* of the coastal region of central California has greyer underparts with a little chestnut. Sexes are alike.

Plain titmouse

Oak titmouse *Baeolophus inornatus*; previously *Parus inornatus*

The dull coloration of the plain titmouse helps it to blend in with its wooded habitat. Pairs maintain distinct territories throughout the year, and form life-long bonds. If one bird dies, the surviving individual may mate with a new partner. Plain titmice breed only once during the year, and the young are driven away by their parents when they are about seven weeks old, being forced to wander in search of their own territory. When feeding, these titmice will often comb branches in search of insects, although during winter acorns feature prominently in their diet – they can open these quite easily with their bill. They are also more frequent visitors to birdfeeders in winter, even picking up edible items from the ground, which are then taken to a more secluded location to be eaten. At night, plain titmice will seek out suitable roosting holes, with pairs using separate locations, although they sometimes prefer a well-hidden perch.

Distribution: Occurs in western parts of the USA extending down to Baja California and other parts of north-western Mexico.
Size: 13cm (5in).
Habitat: Areas of oak woodland.
Nest: Old woodpecker holes, birdhouses.
Eggs: 3–9, white.
Food: Invertebrates, buds and berries.

Identification: Differences in depth of coloration and bill size through its range. Greyish-brown overall, with a small crest at the back of the head. Underparts are a purer shade of grey than the back. Sexes are alike. Formerly classified with the juniper titmouse (*B. ridgwayi*) as a single species.

SPARROWS AND TOWHEES

Although brown predominates in the coloration of these adaptable birds, there can actually be quite a variety of appearance through what is often a wide range. In spite of their relatively small size, a number of sparrows and towhees undertake extensive seasonal migrations to and from their breeding grounds during the spring and autumn.

California towhee

Melozone crissalis

The taxonomy of the towhees can be confusing. In the past, the California towhee and the closely related canyon towhee, which occurs further west, were grouped together under the name brown towhee, although it is now clear that they are, in fact, distinct species. Even so, five distinctive races of California towhee are recognized through its relatively small range. Pairs, which bond for life in many cases, are most likely to spotted in gardens during the breeding season, since this is when the cock bird sings loudly from a prominent perch. Even after egg-laying he continues this behaviour, laying claim to their territory; any intruders will be driven away aggressively. Their nest is hidden low in vegetation, being constructed from a variety of plant material, and the hen incubates alone. Once the chicks have hatched these towhees become largely insectivorous, frequently foraging on the ground, using their feet to scratch around in the hope of discovering invertebrates hiding under leaves or other vegetation.

Identification: Predominantly brown, with the crown being a warmer shade than that of the body. The throat is buff, marked with dark spots that are largest across the upper chest. Cinnamon-brown undertail coverts. Sexes are alike. Young birds are duller with more extensive speckling on their underparts.

Distribution: Coastal western North America, from Oregon down to Baja California, extending east as far as the Cascades and Sierra Nevada Mountains.
Size: 23cm (9in).
Habitat: Chaparral, parks and gardens.
Nest: Cup-shaped.
Eggs: 3–4, bluish green with dark markings.
Food: Seeds and invertebrates.

Chipping sparrow

Spizella passerina

These sparrows are not easy to spot, partly because their coloration provides camouflage, but also because they hide among vegetation. Even when singing, the cock bird often chooses a fairly secluded location. The sound is distinctive, however, being essentially a monotonous "chip"-like call, which explains the species' common name. These sparrows forage mainly on the ground, although they may visit birdfeeders, especially during winter when snow blankets the ground. Each fall, chipping sparrows desert most of their North American range, migrating to southern states and further south in late September. They return to their breeding grounds in the far north the following May. The well-hidden nest is constructed from vegetation, with incubation and fledging each lasting about 12 days. This rapid breeding cycle means that in favourable conditions, they may rear two broods.

Identification: Breeding adults have a chestnut crown with white stripes beneath, and a black stripe running through the eyes. Greyish neck and under-parts, with whitish throat. Wings are black and brown with whitish markings. Dark notched tail. Head coloration is brownish with darker speckling outside the nesting season.

Distribution: Most of North America south of Hudson Bay, except for central-southern USA. Winters along the southern Mexican border and through Central America as far south as northern Nicaragua.
Size: 14cm (5¹/₂in).
Habitat: Parks and wooded gardens.
Nest: Cup-shaped.
Eggs: 3–5, light blue with darker markings.
Food: Seeds and invertebrates.

Lark sparrow

Chondestes grammacus

Lark sparrows have quite a musical song. In common with larks they are rather terrestrial birds, foraging on the ground not just for seeds but also invertebrates and especially grasshoppers during summer, which are used to rear their chicks. They breed on the ground or in a low bush, frequently in scrubland, where the nest can be hidden from predators, and sometimes in loose colonies. Northern populations fly south during late July and August, returning again the following spring. During the winter period they can often be seen in flocks. The range of the lark sparrow has declined over recent years. This may be due to changes in habitat, since their distribution formerly extended up the eastern seaboard to Maryland and New York. Today they are considered to be relatively scarce east of the Mississippi River.

Identification: Black stripe extending up from the bill, with a central white area dividing the chestnut coloration. White bordered with black encircles the chestnut cheek patches. Whitish underparts with very distinctive dark central breast spot. Upperparts greyish brown with black markings. Dark brown wings and tail, showing white edging. Sexes are alike.

Distribution: Across the far south of Canada, and western and central parts of the USA. Winters further south along the Mexican border and the Gulf coast to Florida.
Size: 17cm (6¹/₂in).
Habitat: Roadsides, farms, open country.
Nest: Cup-shaped.
Eggs: 3–5, white with dark spots.
Food: Seeds and invertebrates.

Rufous-sided towhee (Eastern towhee, *Pipilo erythrophthalmus*): 22cm (8¹/₂in)
Most of North America except the far north. Northern populations move south into northern Mexico in the fall. Cock bird has jet-black head, chest and back. White underparts with chestnut flanks. White area at base of primary feathers. Undertail coverts pale yellowish. Iris colour varies with race: usually reddish, but whitish in Florida. Hens have brown rather than black plumage.

White-throated sparrow (*Zonotrichia albicollis*): 17cm (6¹/₂in)
North-central British Columbia to Newfoundland and down to New England. Winters in eastern USA, also in central California, and south to northern Mexico. White throat with greyish chest and whitish underparts. May be white streaking on the head, with yellow bordered by black above the eyes. Dark brown streaks on rufous-brown wings, with white edges to some feathers. Rump brownish. Sexes are alike. Young have brown streaks on chest.

Song sparrow (*Melospiza melodia*): 17cm (6¹/₂in)
The Aleutians and Alaska across to Newfoundland, moving to southern Canada in winter, south to Florida and along the Gulf coast to Mexico. 39 races are described, all with a dark grey stripe above the eyes and dark brownish stripe across the lower cheeks, bordering the white throat. Greyish stripe down the centre of the crown, with adjacent brown plumage often streaked with black. Greyish-brown back and wings. Mainly white underparts, with brown streaking on chest. Sexes are alike. Young birds are more buff overall.

Andean sparrow

Rufous-collared sparrow *Zonotrichia capensis*

As their name suggests, Andean sparrows are most likely to be found in upland areas of South America, where they inhabit relatively open country, and are often seen in villages and towns. At least 25 different races have been identified across their wide area of distribution. The song of the cock bird also varies, although it is usually uttered from a relatively prominent position, aiding identification. Even the nesting habits of these sparrows are not consistent through their range, with those at higher altitudes producing smaller clutches, typically comprised of fewer than three eggs. This may reflect difficulties in obtaining food, or possibly indicate that the level of predation is higher in lowland areas. Breeding pairs are resident throughout the year, with the nesting period varying according to latitude. Insects feature more prominently in the diet when there are chicks to feed, with these occasionally being caught in flight.

Distribution: From Mexico down across South America to Tierra del Fuego. Most common in the Andean region but largely absent from the Amazon basin. Also on Hispaniola in the Caribbean.
Size: 14cm (5¹/₂in).
Habitat: Upland areas.
Nest: Cup-shaped.
Eggs: 2–5, greenish blue with brown markings.
Food: Seeds and invertebrates.

Identification: Red-brown collar. Black crown, slight crest, grey head with black stripes. White throat with some black, pale grey underparts. Blackish wings with brown edges and white-edged barring. Young have streaked underparts and a buff nape.

SONGBIRDS

Many of these birds are a common sight, thanks to their adaptable nature. They often undertake seasonal movements southward to warmer climates in search of more favourable feeding opportunities over the winter period. Their return is keenly anticipated, however, as an indicator of the arrival of spring. Pairs will then breed perhaps twice before returning south again.

Virginian cardinal

Northern cardinal *Cardinalis cardinalis*

The range of these cardinals continues to increase both in northern and western areas, especially since the first breeding record from Canada, which dates back to 1901. This expansion probably results from bird-table offerings. The stout, conical bill of these birds is adapted to crushing seeds, although Virginian cardinals will also hunt invertebrates, particularly when they have chicks in the nest.

Identification: Predominantly red, with a pointed crest. A black mask surrounds the bill extending back to the eyes and down on to the throat. Wings, back and tail are of a slightly duller shade. Hen is predominantly brown, with a slight reddish suffusion over the wings and tail. The bill in adults of both sexes is bright red, whereas that of young birds is blackish, enabling them to be distinguished from adult hens.

Distribution: From southern Ontario, Canada south through the USA to the Gulf of Mexico, and southward as far as Belize.
Size: 23cm (9in).
Habitat: Edges of woodland, parks and gardens.
Nest: Cup-shaped, made of vegetation.
Eggs: 3-4, whitish or greyish white, with darker spots and blotches.
Food: Seeds and invertebrates.

Scarlet tanager

Piranga olivacea

These tanagers undertake long flights each year to and from their breeding grounds. Individuals sometimes venture further afield, and are observed in more northerly and westerly areas than usual, even reaching Alaska on rare occasions. A pair of scarlet tanagers rears only one brood during the summer before returning south. These birds catch invertebrates in the undergrowth and also in flight. More unusually, scarlet tanagers rub live ants onto their plumage. This behaviour, known as anting, results in formic acid being released by the ants among the feathers, which in turn drives out parasites, such as lice, from the plumage. The bright coloration of these birds is linked in part to their diet.

Identification: Mainly yellowish olive, with underparts being more yellowish than upperparts. Cock distinguishable from the hen by having black rather than brownish wings and tail. In breeding plumage, the male has characteristic vivid scarlet plumage. Young cock birds in their first year have more orange rather than scarlet plumage.

Distribution: Migrates north to southeastern Canada and eastern USA, overwintering in Central and South America, east of the Andes to Peru and Bolivia.
Size: 17cm (7in).
Habitat: Light forest and woodland.
Nest: Cup-shaped, made of stems and roots.
Eggs: 2–5, whitish to greenish blue with dark markings.
Food: Mainly invertebrates.

Blue grosbeak

Passerina caerulea

Despite the cock bird's distinctive plumage, the blue grosbeak is not as conspicuous as its coloration would suggest. Indeed, in poor light its feathering can appear so dark that, at a distance, it is sometimes confused with the male common or brown-headed cowbird (*Molothrus ater*). The grosbeak's melodious song is most commonly heard early in the day, although the birds may start singing again at dusk. The song consists largely of short notes interspersed with longer trills. Cock birds usually return from their winter haunts a few days ahead of hens, frequently spending this time searching for food in groups on the ground before splitting up to nest. Pairs are likely to rear two broods of chicks over the summer period before migrating south again during September.

Identification: A dull shade of blue, with a large, greyish bill. The wings are darker, with two distinctive wing bars close to the shoulder. Hens are predominantly brownish, lighter on the underparts, and also display two buff-coloured wing bars. They have some bluish feathering on the rump. Young cock birds display more widespread blue feathering among their plumage.

Distribution: Occurs widely across the USA from California in the west through to New Jersey on the east coast, and south to Costa Rica. Northern populations overwinter in Central America, ranging from Mexico to Panama.
Size: 19cm (7¹/₂in).
Habitat: Brush, often near water.
Nest: Cup-shaped.
Eggs: 3–4, pale blue.
Food: Seeds and invertebrates.

Lesser goldfinch (*Spinus psaltria*): 11cm (4¹/₂in) North-western parts of the USA to parts of Mexico, including the Islas Tres Marias, occurring discontinuously down into Colombia and Venezuela and as far south as Ecuador and northern Peru. Cocks have a black crown, with remaining upperparts varying from black in the western population to green in birds occurring further east. Underparts yellow. Wings are blackish with evident white markings. Hens have a greyish-green head and duller yellow underparts, with brownish rather than black wings. Young birds similar to hens, but males display traces of black above the bill.

Black-chinned siskin (*Spinus barbatus*): 13cm (5in) Southern South America, from southern Chile down to Cape Horn. Also on the Falkland Islands. Cock has black extending from the back of the head over the crown and around the bill on to the throat. Sides of the neck and underparts yellowish. Greenish yellow broken by darker areas on the back. Wings are black with yellow markings. Hens lack the black markings and are more greenish overall, with white area on the belly. Young birds similar to hens but display more streaking, especially on upperparts.

Summer tanager (*Piranga rubra*): 19.5cm (7¹/₂in) Eastern and southern USA, reaching southern California in the west and New Jersey in the east. Winters from Mexico south to southern Peru, Bolivia and French Guiana. Cock is rosy-red overall, darker on the wings, with a prominent pale bill. Hens are generally mustard-yellow, but some display red flecking on their bodies; upperparts are greyer in western birds. Young males resemble hens, but develop a red head in their first spring.

American goldfinch

Spinus tristis

These attractive songbirds are common throughout their range, although those in northern areas move south to warmer areas for the winter. They are often seen in larger flocks at this time, frequently in the company of related birds such as redpolls (*Acanthis* species). Their diet varies through the year, and is influenced by the availability of food. Invertebrates, which provide protein, are important for rearing chicks in the nest. Seeds are consumed through much of the year, while shoots and buds of trees such as spruce and willow will be eaten when other foods are in short supply.

Distribution: Canada southward through much of USA to northern Mexico.
Size: 14cm (5¹/₂in).
Habitat: Wooded or lightly wooded areas.
Nest: Cup-shaped.
Eggs: 2–7, pale blue.
Food: Seeds, other plant matter and invertebrates.

Identification: Brightly coloured yellow plumage, with a black cap and black wings and tail, and white bars on the wings. Duller in winter plumage, being a more olive shade with a less distinct black cap. Hens can be identified by their olive-yellow upperparts and more yellowish underparts, becoming brownish during winter, especially on the upperparts. The white wing barring is still apparent, enabling hens to be distinguished easily from juvenile birds.

FINICHES

Members of this group have actually benefited from human changes to the environment. Along with a greater availability of food, urban areas provide a multitude of nesting sites as people seek to attract these birds into their gardens. Although pairs may establish their own breeding territories, they usually associate in flocks for the remainder of the year.

Purple finch

Haemorhous purpureus

Occurring close to woodland areas, these finches are territorial by nature, especially during the breeding season. Males sing from favoured branches, their song being very evident at this time, and they also undertake display flights to attract a partner. The nest is built on the branch of a conifer, often at a considerable height from the ground. Although some individuals remain on their breeding grounds throughout the year, others move south, where they may be sighted in small flocks. The availability of pine seeds influences their distribution during winter in particular, since in years when the crop fails these finches move to new areas in search of other food. Although their breeding range is continuous, the population splits into distinct western and eastern groups for the duration of the winter. Purple finches are quite bold and conspicuous in a garden setting, often visiting feeders, with oil-rich seeds such as sunflower being favoured foods.

Identification: Cocks are rose-red over much of the body, which is especially pronounced on the head and rump. The back is red with brown streaking, while the lower underparts are whitish in the centre. Hens are brownish, with whitish stripes encircling the eyes and a white area under the throat. Pale underparts heavily streaked with brown.

Distribution: Canada south of Hudson's Bay, most common in the east. Extends to southern California. Winters in the west and through much of eastern USA down along the Gulf coast, and occasionally into northern Mexico.
Size: 15cm (6in).
Habitat: Suburban areas, parks, woodland.
Nest: Cup-shaped.
Eggs: 5–6, pale bluish with dark markings.
Food: Seeds and invertebrates.

House finch

Haemorhous mexicanus

Identification: Cock has a brown cap on the head and brown ear coverts. Remainder of the head and breast are red, sometimes more orange, depending on race. Streaked white underparts, browner on the flanks. Back is streaked, with dark wing feathers typically edged with white. Hens are much duller, being streaked over their entire head and underparts.

Two separate populations of these finches occur in North America: one native to the west and the other in the east. The eastern population is descended from birds released on Long Island, near New York City, during the 1940s. There they bred successfully, but it was not until the 1960s that they began to spread more widely and become established. They appear to have benefited significantly from birdfeeders, though they also forage for berries and other items in gardens. Males have an attractive song, not unlike that of a canary. Nesting pairs are very adaptable and often breed in loose colonies, utilizing nesting baskets fixed up under the eaves of houses. They frequently raise two or more broods of chicks in rapid succession. During the autumn, house finches often associate together in large flocks, and in more rural areas may be seen feeding in the fields. In spring, flocks can cause damage in orchards by pecking at the buds and flowers.

Distribution: South-western Canada through western parts of the USA to Texas and into Mexico. Separate population in eastern USA south of the Great Lakes. Also occurs on Hawaii.
Size: 15cm (6in).
Habitat: Open areas including cities.
Nest: Cup-shaped.
Eggs: 4–5, pale blue with black spots.
Food: Seeds and invertebrates.

Pine grosbeak

Pinicola enucleator

Identification: Cock is mainly reddish, with grey on the sides of the body and along the wings. Wings darker, with variable white edging and grey wing bars. Black forked tail. Hens are grey overall, with a yellowish head, rump and flanks, and a greyish area under the throat. Yellow colour can be more russet in some cases.

As their name suggests, pine grosbeaks are closely associated with coniferous forests, though they move into deciduous woodlands in the autumn. Living in flocks, these finches prefer to feed off the ground, resorting to nibbling buds when seeds and fruit are scarce and snow covers the ground. In some areas, especially the western USA, they are regular birdfeeder visitors. Their winter range is influenced by availability of food, with flocks sometimes moving south of their normal range when berries such as mountain ash fail. Pine grosbeaks are not very active by nature. They are also quite tame, so are fairly easy to observe. The nest is built in a tree, often close to the ground, with the young remaining there for three weeks before fledging.

Distribution: Circumpolar, being present right across northern parts of North America, and in western USA. Overwinters in central parts.
Size: 23cm (9in).
Habitat: Woodland, orchards and gardens.
Nest: Bulky, cup-shaped.
Eggs: 2–5, pale bluish green with dark blotches.
Food: Seeds, berries and invertebrates.

Lesser Antillean bullfinch (*Loxigilla noctis*): 15cm (6in)
Ranges through the Lesser Antilles, though not in the Grenadines, sometimes on Puerto Rico. Cocks are blackish, with a small red area in front of each eye, extending from the chin onto the throat. Undertail coverts may be red. Hens and cocks of the Barbadian race have brownish-olive upperparts, being greyer beneath with orange undertail coverts. Young birds resemble hens.

Hooded grosbeak (*Hesperiphona abeillei*): 18cm (7in)
Mainly Mexico, ranges into central Guatemala and north-western El Salvador. Cock birds have black heads, wings and tail, with mainly yellow underparts and white areas on the wings. Stout bill also yellow. Hens are duller, with olive-green upperparts and greyish rather than white inner greater coverts. Young birds resemble hens, but males more yellowish on their underparts.

Rose-breasted grosbeak (*Pheucticus ludovicianus*): 20cm (8in)
North-eastern British Columbia to the Great Lakes and Canada's east coast down to Georgia. Winters in the Caribbean and Central America, south to Peru and north-east to Guyana. Cocks have a pinkish-red area on the breast bordered by white, extending on to lower underparts. Head and back jet-black, with a white wing bar and other white markings on wings. Rump white with black markings, tail black. Powerful, pale horn-coloured bill. Hens have brownish streaked upperparts, with a white eye stripe and pale area under the chin. Buffy coloured below, with streaked underparts.

Evening grosbeak

Hesperiphona vespertina

When first described in the 1820s it was believed that these birds only emerged from cover at dusk, and although this was completely incorrect they came to be known as evening grosbeaks. Their range has expanded since then. Up until the 19th century these finches were restricted to northern Canada, but suddenly, perhaps because of persistent annual food shortages, evening grosbeaks started travelling further afield to north-eastern parts of the USA Ultimately, they started breeding here, and continued to spread, reaching Maryland by the 1960s, Florida and the Gulf coast a decade later. Pairs build their nest at the very end of a branch, up to 21m (70ft) off the ground, choosing a site where it will be hidden. The hen sits alone, with the chicks hatching after about two weeks. They fledge after a similar interval.

Identification: Large, thick-set finch with a powerful bill. Cocks have yellow forehead and eyebrows. Rest of head is greenish, as is the upper chest, becoming yellow on the underparts. White area on the wings, with black flight feathers and tail. Hens have a grey head and predominantly grey back, with a whitish throat and greyish-tan underparts. Young birds resemble hens.

Distribution: Southern Canada through western parts of the USA to northern Mexico. Extends eastward to Newfoundland and south to south-eastern parts of the USA.
Size: 20cm (8in).
Habitat: Woodland, parks and gardens.
Nest: Cup-shaped.
Eggs: 2–5, bluish green.
Food: Seeds, berries and invertebrates.

VIREOS AND OTHER GARDEN BIRDS

A wide variety of birds can be encountered in garden surroundings, and they are often quite bold in this environment. Some are valuable allies for gardeners, catching invertebrates that would otherwise become pests, particularly in tropical areas. In farmland, however, they may inflict some damage on crops, especially when these are maturing.

Yucatan vireo

Vireo magister

Distribution: Caribbean coast of Mexico and on the southern part of the Yucatan Peninsula, ranging into Belize. Also on nearby Caribbean islands, including Grand Cayman.
Size: 15cm (6in).
Habitat: Scrub and mangrove.
Nest: Cup-shaped.
Eggs: 2–5, white with reddish-brown markings.
Food: Invertebrates and fruit.

Yucatan vireos may appear similar to New World warblers in size, shape and coloration. The family is widely represented in Central America, the Caribbean and adjacent parts of northern South America. The population occurring on the Caribbean island of Grand Cayman is considered sufficiently distinct to be regarded as a separate subspecies, and is known locally as "sweet Bridget" thanks to the sound of its song. The somewhat drab coloration of this species provides camouflage among the mangrove forests and scrubland it frequents. Yucatan vireos are not easy to observe among foliage, and are more often heard than seen. These vireos have an appealing song, however, that has been likened to that of a mockingbird. Invertebrates gleaned from the vegetation feature prominently in their diet, although they also seek out fruit and berries. Breeding usually occurs between April and August. The nest takes the form of a well-woven cup, secured on to a horizontal branch in a tree.

Identification: Greyish top to the head, with broad whitish stripes above the eyes and a dark line beneath running through the eyes. Back and wings olive grey. Underparts are whitish with a buff tinge, and flanks are dusky. Relatively large blackish bill. Sexes are alike.

Bananaquit

Coereba flaveola

Identification: Upperparts vary from dark grey to black, with a prominent white streak above the eyes. Throat is a paler shade of grey. Underparts otherwise yellowish, with white undertail coverts. White wing speculum most apparent when the wings are open. Short, dark, curved bill. Legs and feet dark greyish. Sexes are alike.

Occurring over a wide area, these common honeycreepers vary significantly in colour, with some Caribbean races being completely blackish. Active and lively, bananaquits are also very bold, and some can be tamed to feed from the hand. They will even fly into homes in the Caribbean in the hope of being offered sugar. Their usual feeding method entails puncturing the bases of flowers with their sharp narrow bill to extract nectar. This allows them to gain the sugary solution that they could not reach by probing the flower directly. They may also use their bill as a straw to suck up juice from ripe fruit. Spiders and other invertebrates are eagerly sought, especially when feeding young chicks. Both sexes help to construct the globular-shaped suspended nest, entered near the bottom.

Distribution: Central America and the Caribbean down across much of South America, through eastern Peru, Bolivia and Paraguay to Brazil and north-eastern Argentina.
Size: 10cm (4in).
Habitat: Lowlands and coastal areas.
Nest: Made of plant matter.
Eggs: 2–3, whitish with dark spots.
Food: Nectar, fruit and invertebrates.

Blue-grey tanager

Thraupis episcopus

Distribution: From Central America, reaching north-west Peru and east of the Andes to northern parts of Bolivia.
Size: 16cm (6in).
Habitat: Relatively open areas.
Nest: Made of plant matter.
Eggs: 2–3, creamy to greyish green and spotted.
Food: Fruit and invertebrates.

Blue-grey tanagers are a common sight in many parts of their range. They are rarely observed on the ground, preferring instead to feed in the trees, sometimes even catching insects in flight. Bold by nature, they will become regular visitors to bird tables if fruit is left out for them. Pairs of blue-grey tanagers build their well-disguised nest in a tree up to 10m (30ft) off the ground. The hen sits alone, with the chicks hatching after a period of incubation lasting 14 days. Both members of the pair contribute food for the growing brood, with invertebrates featuring prominently in the diet at this time. The young leave the nest at just two weeks of age, and soon afterward the adult pair will begin nesting again, although the breeding season does vary according to locality. These tanagers are most likely to be encountered at altitudes below 1,500m (5,000ft), but they may sometimes range up to 2,000m (6,500ft).

Identification: Head and body varies from pale blue through to bluish grey, and is lighter on the head and darker across the back. Wings and tail invariably a darker shade of blue. Shoulder area is white in individuals occurring east of the Andes, blue in those further west. Hens may have slightly olive underparts. Young birds are generally duller.

Greyish saltator (*Saltator coerulescens*): 20cm (8in)
Mexico down through lowland South America east of the Andes, also northern Colombia and Trinidad. South through central Brazil into parts of Bolivia, Paraguay, Argentina and Uruguay. Mainly greyish, with a white stripe above the eyes. White throat edged with black streaks. Greyish underparts, paler below and buff undertail coverts. Stocky greyish bill. Sexes are alike.

Orange-crowned euphonia (*Euphonia saturata*): 10cm (4in)
Restricted to south-west Colombia, western Ecuador and the extreme north-west of Peru, typically under 1,000m (3,000ft) Cock has an orangish-yellow crown and underparts; rest of head, throat and body dark violet-blue. Hens have olive upperparts and yellowish underparts.

Common diuca finch (*Diuca diuca*): 18cm (7in)
Southern Bolivia, Chile and Argentina, including Buenos Aires. Grey upperparts, with blacker wings and tail. Grey cheeks and breast, with a white throat patch. Centre of the breast and belly are white. Rufous tinge on the flanks. Grey plumage of hens has a brownish suffusion.

Philadelphia vireo (*Vireo philadelphicus*): 12.5cm (5in)
Breeds in southern Canada and northern USA. Migrates to Central America, rarely northern Colombia. Coloration varies through its range, also brighter in fall. Greyish cap on head, with a black stripe through the eyes edged by white stripes. Upperparts greenish. Underparts yellowish, paler on the belly. Sexes are alike.

Blue-black grassquit

Volatinia jacarina

These birds are often seen in farming areas, foraging for seeds on the ground. They can also be found in towns and gardens, having adapted well to living close to humans. Blue-black grassquits are quite conspicuous despite the male's rather drab coloration, which can nevertheless have a slightly iridescent quality, depending on the light. Young birds only acquire full adult coloration at the start of their second year. When breeding, pairs tend to occupy their own territories, with nests being hidden low down among vegetation. This is the stage at which the male's distinctive buzzy song is most likely to be heard, accompanied by vertical display jumps up and down on a perch. Outside the nesting season, blue-black grassquits associate in much larger flocks of up to several hundred birds, sometimes in the company of similar species. They prefer open country, and are rarely seen in densely forested areas.

Identification: Cock birds have a glossy bluish-black appearance. When molting, their underparts are buff with evident blackish scalloping. Hens are brown overall, with whitish underparts streaked with brown. The bill in both sexes is quite narrow and slender. Young birds have buff wing bars.

Distribution: Mexico south via Panama across virtually all of northern South America, to northern Chile and central Argentina. Also present on some Caribbean islands.
Size: 10cm (4in).
Habitat: Open country.
Nest: Cup-shaped.
Eggs: 2–3, pale bluish with rusty markings.
Food: Seeds and invertebrates.

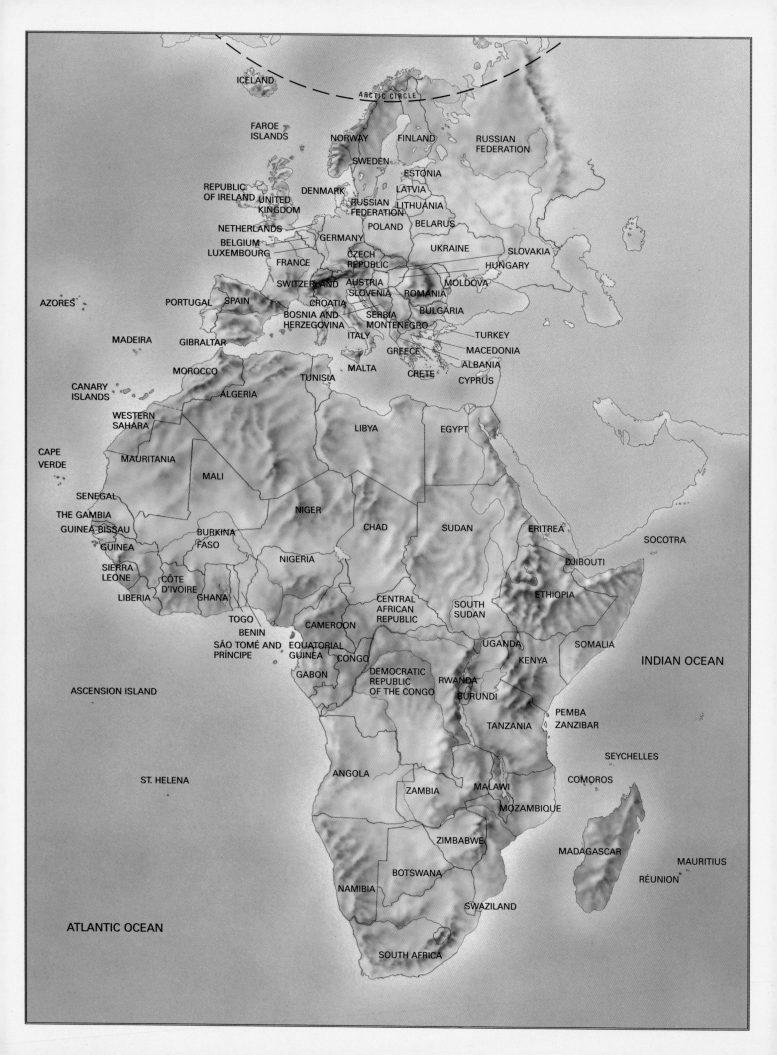

BIRDS OF GREAT BRITAIN, EUROPE AND AFRICA

The distribution of birds occurring on these continents, especially those found in Europe, often extends eastwards into Asia as well. Many northerly species also undergo regular seasonal movements in response to the climate, overwintering in more southerly latitudes, with some even flying as far as southern Africa. Those groups of birds most commonly associated with tropical areas – such as parrots, for example – are poorly represented in this region of the world, partly because of the absence of suitable feeding opportunities in Europe. Urban development has also had a marked impact on the distribution of a number of species, and some have adapted to urban environments better than others. Human involvement has also seen the introduction of avian species into Europe from outside their natural range, often for sporting purposes, as in the case of various species of pheasants and partridges.

Above from left: kestrel *(Falco tinnunculus),* eagle-owl *(Bubo bubo),* malachite kingfisher *(Corythornis cristatus).*

OCEAN WANDERERS

These seabirds typically have a very wide distribution, effortlessly roaming over the oceans far away from the shore. They return to land only in order to nest, though are unlikely to be seen by the casual observer, as they frequently choose remote islands on which to breed. However, they may be attracted to passing ships in search of offerings of food.

Black-browed albatross

Thalassarche melanophris

Distribution: Throughout the entire southern oceanic region, in a broad band extending from just off Antarctica as far north as southern Africa.
Size: 93cm (37in).
Habitat: Over the ocean.
Nest: Earth mound incorporating plant matter.
Eggs: 1, white.
Food: Mainly crustaceans, fish and squid.

This is the most common of the black-backed albatross species seen off the coast of Africa. Despite roaming widely over the ocean, they are also likely to be sighted close to the shore, where they seek out bays and similar stretches of tranquil water when the weather becomes stormy. Here they are easily distinguished in flight from gulls by their much longer wings. These albatrosses will often follow trawlers, seeking offal thrown overboard, and as many as 3000 individuals have been sighted around a single boat. In these circumstances they will descend to the sea to feed, although more commonly they will pick up their prey in flight from the surface of the water, only occasionally venturing beneath the waves. Black-browed albatrosses choose remote islands for their breeding grounds, and ringing studies reveal that many of the birds seen off the coasts of South Africa originate from the population breeding on the island of South Georgia, off the east coast of South America.

Identification: Black upper surface to the body, with relatively dark underwing coloration, especially around the edges. Underside of the body is white, as is the rump. Bill is orangish with a pinkish tip. Sexes are alike.

Shy albatross

Thalassarche cauta

Despite its name the shy albatross is a bold scavenger, swooping down to feed on offal thrown overboard from trawlers and driving away other seabirds. It also feeds by scooping at the surface, sometimes even diving under the water. These albatrosses frequent African waters during the southern winter, although they can be seen off the western Cape throughout the year. Unlike most other albatrosses this species often ventures near to the shoreline. Younger, non-breeding birds may fly further afield than adults, but little is known about their migratory habits. They breed on the smaller islands around Australia and New Zealand, with pairs returning to their breeding grounds in September. Incubation lasts nearly 11 weeks, after which the chick remains in the nest for a further four months.

Identification: Black back and wings, with black edging on the undersides. Underparts white. Pale head with a prominent white cap and a blackish band beneath running through the eyes. Grey area below on the sides of the face. Sexes are alike. Young birds have dark bills, whereas adults are greyish, with a yellowish tip.

Distribution: Occurs widely from the western coast of southern South America via New Zealand and Australia to the southern tip of Africa.
Size: 98cm (38½in).
Habitat: Over the ocean.
Nest: Earth mound incorporating plant matter.
Eggs: 1, white.
Food: Mainly fish and squid.

Dark-mantled sooty albatross

Phoebetria fusca

Distribution: Ranges from the southern Atlantic eastwards to the south of Africa, extending as far as the southern coast of Australia.
Size: 89cm (35in).
Habitat: Open ocean, coming inland to breed.
Nest: Made of mud and plant matter, often on a sloping cliff face.
Eggs: 1, white, may be blotched.
Food: Largely squid, plus some fish and carrion.

Living on the open ocean, these albatrosses return to land every second year to breed, on islands such as Tristan da Cunha and the Kerguelen Islands. They build a raised nest of mud on a sloping area of ground, often on a cliff face. They breed in loose colonies, returning to their traditional nesting grounds around July. The incubation period is protracted, lasting for almost 10 weeks. The chicks hatch with a covering of greyish down, and will be fed by the parents for up to 23 weeks before fledging. It may then take as long as 15 years for the young albatrosses to reach maturity and nest for the first time. During the intervening period, they will fly huge distances, ranging widely through the temperate zone of the southern oceans. Their aerial agility allows them to catch prey easily from the surface of the sea, although they may also follow trawlers in search of food and not uncommonly scavenge on carcasses of other seabirds.

Identification: Blackish in colour, with the upperparts being of a relatively consistent depth of colour. Tail tapers to a point. Pale eyelids, yellow skin along the edge of the black bill. Sexes are alike. Young birds have a paler nape.

Grey-headed albatross (*Thalassarche chrysostoma*): 80cm (31½in) Circumpolar, occurring northwards to the Cape of Good Hope. Characteristic grey head, with blackish back and wings. Wings have black M-shaped pattern when seen from below. Bill is yellow on its upper and lower edges, black on the sides and reddish at the tip, but blackish overall in young birds. Sexes are alike.

Light-mantled albatross (*Phoebetria palpebrata*): 80cm (31½in) Circumpolar, reaching the extreme southern coast of Africa. Moves further north in the southern winter as the pack ice around Antarctica extends. Predominantly blackish overall, apart from a distinctive pale grey area on the mantle. Fairly indistinct yellow eye ring. Sexes are alike.

Campbell albatross (*Thalassarche impavida*): 88cm (35in) Campbell Island and the associated islet of Jeanette Marie, a small New Zealand island group in the South Pacific. It is sometimes considered a subspecies of the black-browed albatross. It is a medium-sized black and white albatross with a pale yellow iris. The adult is very similar to the black-browed albatross, differing in eye colour.

Atlantic yellow-nosed albatross

Thalassarche chlororhynchos

This species was previously thought to encompass two similar birds the grey-headed albatross (*T. chrysostoma*) and the Indian yellow-nosed albatross (*T. carteri*). This white-headed population, which breeds in the Indian Ocean, is most common on the east coast, especially off Natal during the winter months. Their appearance here is linked not just to the end of the nesting period but also the seasonal availability of sardines, which feature prominently in their diet. Breeding grounds of the yellow-nosed albatross include Gough and Prince Edward Islands, with pairs nesting in much looser associations in the former locality. Pairs return to breed annually, constructing large, platform-style nests. Young birds may not nest for the first time until they are about 10 years old, but like others of their kind, these albatrosses have a life expectancy extending over four decades.

Identification: Black wings with prominent black wing tips on the undersides and along the leading edges. Underparts white. Bill is blackish on the sides, with a central yellow stripe and a red tip. Crown white, rest of the head pale grey with a black stripe through the eyes. Sexes are alike. Young birds have white heads and black bills.

Distribution: Extends through the southern oceans, from New Zealand westwards via southern Africa across the southern Atlantic to South America.
Size: 80cm (31in).
Habitat: Over the ocean.
Nest: Earth mound incorporating plant matter.
Eggs: 1, white.
Food: Mainly fish and squid.

STORM PETRELS

Keen eyesight, possibly assisted by a sense of smell, helps these seabirds find food in the oceans. Marine invertebrates feature prominently in their diet, and they will often congregate in areas where krill are to be found, along with other predatory creatures such as whales. They seek out inconspicuous places to nest, such as underground burrows or the crevices in a rocky cliff face.

White-faced storm petrel

Pelagodroma marina

Distribution: Two separate breeding populations present in the Atlantic, either side of the equator. A third area of distribution extends through the Pacific region from the Red Sea to the north-west coast of South America.
Size: 20cm (8in).
Habitat: Over the ocean.
Nest: Underground burrow.
Eggs: 1, white.
Food: Mainly plankton and small fish.

Unlike many storm petrels, these seabirds are rarely attracted to ships seeking offal. They will, however, congregate in the vicinity of whales, since the presence of these creatures often indicates a plentiful source of krill and similar planktonic crustaceans, which feature prominently in their diet. Pairs nest both north and south of the equator, with the breeding period depending on the locality of each individual population, but invariably taking place during the warmer months of the year. Due to their subterrestrial breeding habits in certain locations, these storm petrels are vulnerable to introduced predators that favour similar surroundings, for example mice and rats. These predators not only disturb the sitting bird but may also prey on the egg or chick. There has been a tendency for colonies to adapt though, by moving from the cliffs to offshore rocky stacks away from such danger. Outside the breeding season, white-faced storm petrels are rarely observed near land.

Identification: Characterized by white plumage on the sides of the head, broken by a dark stripe running back through each eye to the neck. Remainder of the upper body is dark brownish-grey, becoming greyer on the rump. The underparts are white. Sexes are alike.

Black-bellied storm petrel

Fregetta tropica

Distribution: Occurs virtually throughout the oceans of the southern hemisphere up to the equator on the western side of Africa and right up to the Red Sea region on the eastern side.
Size: 20cm (8in).
Habitat: Over the ocean.
Nest: Underground burrow or crevice.
Eggs: 1, white.
Food: Small fish and squid.

Widely distributed throughout the southern oceans, these storm petrels are most likely to be sighted off the western Cape when migrating during October and November, and then again during February. At a distance they can be confused with the white-bellied storm petrel (*F. grallaria*), but their behaviour will usually set them apart. Although they will often congregate close to ships in small groups of up to five individuals, they prefer to dart in front of the vessels or fly alongside them, rather than swoop down over the stern as in the case of most other species. They tend not to dive into the water but patter along on the surface, with the movements of their wings keeping them above the waves. When nesting, black-bellied storm petrels do not spend any time brooding their chick once it has hatched. Instead, it relies on the warmth of the burrow and the insulating effect of its thick grey down feathering to maintain its body temperature.

Identification: Seen from beneath, a well-defined and characteristic central black stripe bisects the white plumage on the breast, extending down to the black lower belly and undertail coverts. Whitish areas also present on the undersides of the wings. Sexes are alike.

European storm petrel

Hydrobates pelagicus

Like others of its kind, the European storm petrel prefers to nest on islands, its traditional nesting grounds including the Balearics and similar localities in the Mediterranean region. Unfortunately however, coastal development is having an adverse effect on breeding populations in some areas. The storm petrels may be resident here throughout the year, but the majority of the North Atlantic population moves south for the winter, where they can be seen off Namibia and South Africa. As with other storm petrels, this species is only able to feed on smaller items of food due to its restricted gape. It is thought that they are able to locate food not only by sight but also by smell, which is rare in birds. Their usual diet is comprised of planktonic creatures such as krill, but they have learned to scavenge for edible items thrown overboard from ships, especially trawlers. If threatened at close quarters, they regurgitate their foul-smelling stomach contents as a deterrent.

Identification: Dark brownish-grey in colour overall, with a pale whitish area on the undersides of the wings, and on the sides of the rump. Square-shaped tail, with the legs not extending beyond the tip when in flight.

Distribution: Ranges from Norway and southern Iceland via the western side of Great Britain right down to the Cape of Good Hope. Also present through much of the Mediterranean Sea.
Size: 18cm (7in).
Habitat: Over the ocean.
Nest: Rocky crevice.
Eggs: 1, white.
Food: Small fish, crustaceans and squid.

Grey-backed storm petrel (*Garrodia nereis*): 20cm (8in)
Three isolated breeding populations occur in the southern oceans: one extends from south-eastern South America across towards south-western Africa; the second lies to the east of this; the third population is restricted to the region of Australia and New Zealand. Head and leading edges of the wings are dark, while the remainder of the underparts and wings are white. Grey rump and uppertail coverts, with a black bar edging the tail feathers. Legs are long, extending beyond the tail feathers when in flight. Sexes are alike.

Matsudaira's storm petrel (*Oceanodroma matsudairae*): 25cm (10in)
Ranges from south-east of Japan down through the Indonesian region and across the Indo-Pacific to the eastern side of Africa. Brownish-grey overall, with paler wing bars extending to the leading edges of the wings. This storm petrel is also distinguishable by its more prominent forked tail. White shafts to the outermost primary feathers may also be evident. Sexes are alike.

White-bellied storm petrel
(*Fregetta grallaria*): 20cm (8in)
Ranges mainly over the Southern ocean, but also recorded around the coasts of southern Africa. Similar to the black-bellied storm petrel (*F. tropica*), but can be distinguished by the completely white feathering on the underparts. Also lacks white bars on flight feathers and is greyer overall. Sexes alike.

Leach's storm petrel

Oceanodroma leucorhoa

With an extensive distribution and a population comprised of more than 10 million individuals worldwide, Leach's storm petrel is regarded as a very common species. However, these birds are vulnerable to predators when breeding, even in the isolated locations that they frequent. Their relatively small size means they can suffer attacks by larger seabirds such as gulls, which prey especially on newly fledged chicks. Should they survive this critical early period of their development, the young Leach's storm petrels have a life expectancy of nearly a quarter of a century. Soon after the breeding period has ended, the North Atlantic population moves southwards for the duration of the winter, extending to the coast of South Africa with occasional reports also from the Indian Ocean. As with other storm petrels, they may follow pods of whales, feeding on the food churned up by these cetaceans, and also scavenging on their faeces.

Distribution: Atlantic population extends from Norway southwards around both coasts of Great Britain, being present in the North Sea and the Baltic Sea. Does not range through the Mediterranean. Extends right down to the tip of Africa. There is also a separate, widespread population in the Pacific.
Size: 22cm (9in).
Habitat: Over the ocean.
Nest: Underground burrow or rocky crevice.
Eggs: 1, white.
Food: Mostly small fish, crustaceans and squid.

Identification: Relatively brown head and back. Rump is predominantly white, with a brown stripe running down its centre. Broad, forked tail feathers. Sexes are alike.

SOUTHERN OCEAN PETRELS

Many of the seabirds found in southern African waters have a wide distribution, which can be pan-global, often extending around the southern oceans and sometimes even further afield. Petrels are well adapted to spending virtually their entire lives over these waters, being able to scoop up their food directly from the surface of the ocean and even sleeping on the wing as they glide.

Common diving petrel

Pelecanoides urinatrix

The common diving petrel ranks as one of the most numerous of all seabirds, certainly in the southern hemisphere, although the breeding population on Tristan da Cunha and neighbouring islands off the south-west coast of Africa is smaller than the populations occurring elsewhere in its range. Overall numbers are estimated as being close to 10 million individuals. Pairs nest on remote islands in burrows of up to 1.5m (5ft) in length, the ground underfoot sometimes being a mass of such tunnels. Although the vast majority of young birds will survive through to fledging, which occurs approximately eight weeks after hatching, their mortality rate soars once they take to the water, where few individuals can expect to live for more than 4 years. They do not stray very far from the islands that form their breeding grounds, feeding in these waters too. As their name suggests, common diving petrels will often pursue their quarry underwater, although they may occasionally feed at the surface as well.

Identification: Blackish head and upperparts, with a more whitish area behind the eyes. Underparts, including the undersides of the wings, are also white. Sexes are alike.

Distribution: One population occurs off the south-west African coast, and another can be found further south-east of the Cape. Two other populations exist: one off the eastern coast of southern South America, the second around New Zealand and the south-east Australian coast.
Size: 25cm (10in).
Habitat: Over the ocean.
Nest: Underground burrow.
Eggs: 1, white.
Food: Planktonic crustaceans, including krill.

Kerguelen petrel

Aphrodroma brevirostris

Kerguelen petrels begin nesting in August, when groups form colonies on islands to the south of Africa where conditions are favourable. They seek relatively soft soil in which they can excavate their burrows without great difficulty. Incubation is a fairly lengthy process, taking seven weeks, and it will be a further nine weeks before the young birds are ready to emerge from their burrows. Breeding pairs, especially on Gough Island and Tristan da Cunha, face predation of their young from skuas, which also live in the vicinity, but by nesting together a higher percentage of the young manage to escape these larger, aggressive seabirds. They then have to master the feeding skills that enable them to survive life over the ocean, which is liable to be a harsh environment. Kerguelen petrels generally feed at night, when the squid that feature prominently in their diet move up from deeper water, allowing them to be seized directly from the surface.

Identification: Dark overall, but with a slight iridescence over some areas that can make the plumage appear a little paler, especially over the wings. Sexes are alike, but hens are slightly smaller in size.

Distribution: Circumglobal through the southern oceans, via Cape Horn in southern South America, New Zealand, south Australia and the Cape of Good Hope at Africa's southern tip.
Size: 36cm (14in).
Habitat: Over the ocean.
Nest: Underground tunnel.
Eggs: 1, white.
Food: Squid, plus some krill and small fish.

Cape petrel

Pintado petrel *Daption capense*

Distribution: Circumglobal range throughout the southern oceans, extending from the shore of Antarctica northwards to a line roughly corresponding to the Tropic of Capricorn, including the southern tip of Africa.
Size: 40cm (16in).
Habitat: Over the ocean.
Nest: Often in a crevice on the ground.
Eggs: 1, white.
Food: Krill, squid and fish.

Cape petrels are very common in South African waters over the winter period, when harsher conditions in the Antarctic drive them further north. They are also very bold, with contemporary records describing how they followed whaling ships from the open ocean right into Durban harbour, in the hope of being able to scavenge on offal. Today, they are often seen in large numbers around fishing boats for the same reason, and it is this social side to their nature that has led to them being known rather confusingly as 'Cape pigeons'. They are adept at catching their own food on the wing, however, by flying with heads submerged beneath the waves, sieving water through their partially closed bills. The bill has a series of serrations running down each side, which serve as a filter to trap edible items in the mouth. Cape petrels often settle on the surface of the water when seeking food, which aids identification. Individual birds can also be distinguished by their mottled patterning.

Identification: A combination of brown and white plumage, with the back being speckled brown in the case of subspecies *D.c. capense*, rather than solid brown as in *D.c. australe*, which nests in the vicinity of New Zealand. Rump in both cases is white with brown markings, while the head and neck are also brown. Sexes are alike.

Northern giant petrel (Hall's giant petrel, *Macronectes halli*): 94cm (37in)
Circumglobal in the southern hemisphere, ranging some distance off the coast of Antarctica northwards, reaching the Cape of Good Hope at Africa's southern tip. Variable amount of dark plumage on the head, and relatively dark, more even coloration on the underparts help to distinguish this species from its Southern relative (see right). The pinkish bill tip is another distinguishing feature.

Great-winged petrel (*Pterodroma macroptera*): 40cm (16in)
Distribution extends from east of New Zealand around the Cape of Good Hope and some distance up the western coast of Africa, continuing across the southern Atlantic to an area to the east of the Falkland Islands off the coast of South America. Breeding grounds include islands to the south-west and south-east of Africa. Characterized by its its consistent dark brown coloration. Sexes are similar, but hens are smaller in size.

Soft-plumaged petrel (*Pterodroma mollis*): 37cm (14½in)
Distribution extends from the seas around New Zealand westwards round the southern tip of Africa and a short distance up the west side, and across the southern Atlantic to southern South America. Generally only exists in a light colour phase, although the breadth of the dark throat collar varies in width and definition. Basic coloration similar to related petrels, with dark upperparts and largely white underparts.

White-chinned petrel

Procellaria aequinoctialis

These petrels are often observed around the coast of southern Africa, although their island breeding grounds lie much further to the south. There are two distinct subspecies, and both may sometimes be seen off the western Cape of southern Africa. The form that breeds on the island of Tristan da Cunha is distinguished by more extensive white markings, which extend up the sides of the head to above the eyes. The white patterning displayed by this species is so distinctive that individual birds can be identified by their markings. The presence of these petrels, especially off Natal, is quite seasonal, coinciding with the migration of shoals of sardines during the winter. White-chinned petrels often congregate in the vicinity of trawlers, seeking scraps which they pick up from the surface. A group will frequently draw attention to themselves by calling loudly and squabbling when feeding. They will then return to their breeding grounds by October.

Distribution: Extends throughout the southern oceans, ranging up close to the equator off the western coast of South America. Extends to Namibia on Africa's west coast, but rarely seen further north than Mozambique on the east.
Size: 54cm (21in).
Habitat: Open sea.
Nest: Underground burrows.
Eggs: 1, white.
Food: Fish, crustaceans and squid.

Identification: Dark brown in colour overall, with a variable amount of white plumage on the chin. Has a pale greenish horn-coloured bill, with a blackish area on top, which highlights the tip. Legs and feet dark. Hens slightly paler. Young birds resemble adults.

ISLAND SEABIRDS

Whereas some seabirds have evolved to live largely on the wing, roaming large areas of the ocean, others like the little auk, misleadingly dubbed the "penguin of the north" in spite of its small size, have adapted to a more aquatic lifestyle. A number of seabirds have a very limited distribution, breeding on just a few islands, where their populations are potentially under threat from human interference in the landscape.

Jouanin's petrel

Bulweria fallax

Very little is known about the range, biology and habits of these petrels, although they are not at the moment considered to be endangered, in spite of the fact that they appear to have a relatively restricted area of distribution. Their range seems to extend into the southern part of the Red Sea and north to the coast of Asia, although they have been known to wander much further afield on occasion. One of the mysteries surrounding Jouanin's petrels is where their breeding grounds lie, as at present this is unknown. Ornithologists suspect that these birds might nest either close to the coast of Oman, possibly on the Kuria Muria Islands, or they might breed in colonies even further inland in this part of the Middle East, perhaps in the mountains of the desert. It used to be thought that this species was the same as Bulwer's petrel (*B. bulweri*), differing only in terms of being slightly larger in size. Study of the external parasites of these petrels, however, has revealed that each has a distinctive type of feather louse, indicating that they are far less closely-related than was previously thought.

Identification: Dark brownish coloration overall, sometimes displaying a faint paler upper wing area, prior to a moult. Bill, legs and feet black. Sexes are alike. Young birds are believed to resemble adults.

Distribution: Restricted to the north-western part of the Indian Ocean, ranging into the southern Red Sea, possibly the Kuria Muria Islands and inland in the Middle East.
Size: 32cm (13in).
Habitat: Open sea, possibly breeding inland in the mountains of the desert.
Nest: Unknown.
Eggs: Undescribed.
Food: Probably fish, squid and crustaceans.

Little auk

Alle alle

Despite its relatively restricted distribution, the little auk is considered to be one of the most numerous seabird species in the world. These birds form huge nesting colonies in the Arctic region during the brief summer, before heading south at the approach of winter as the sea begins to freeze. Little auks are often more likely to be spotted at this time of year, frequently flying very low over the waves or even through them on occasion. Sometimes, however, fierce storms make feeding virtually impossible, and in a weakened state little auks are driven into coastal areas, a phenomenon often described as a "wreck".

Identification: In summer plumage, the head and upper part of the chest are black. The back, wings and upper surface of the tail feathers are also black, aside from white streaks apparent over the wings. During the winter, the black on the face is broken by white, leaving a black band across the throat. The bill is small and black. Sexes are alike.

Distribution: Entire coastline of Greenland and Iceland to northern Scandinavia, across the North Sea to the coast of eastern England.
Size: 20cm (8in).
Habitat: Sea, coastal areas.
Nest: Cliff or crevice.
Eggs: 1, pale blue.
Food: Microscopic plankton.

Band-rumped storm petrel

Oceanodroma castro

Distribution: Eastern Atlantic, off the coast of the Iberian peninsula down off the African coast to the Tropic of Capricorn, and out into the mid-Atlantic. There are two other populations in the Pacific, around Japan and also off the west coast of South America.
Size: 20cm (8in).
Habitat: Open sea.
Nest: Underground burrows.
Eggs: 1, white.
Food: Small fish, squid and crustaceans.

Only during the breeding season are these storm petrels likely to be seen near land. Their small size, compared with that of other seabirds, makes them vulnerable to predators at this stage, with western barn owls (*Tyto alba*) preying on colonies breeding in parts of the Cape Verde Islands. The band-rumped storm petrels' habit of nesting underground also leaves them vulnerable to rodents, as well as other introduced predators including domestic cats. These petrels feed largely at the surface of the sea, in flight rather than diving beneath the waves, and they can suffer severe buffeting in storms, causing them to be blown to the coast, sometimes turning up in places well away from their normal range. When nesting, both parents share the task of incubation. In common with other storm petrels, their single egg is resistant to the effects of chilling if left uncovered for any length of time, although the incubation period will be extended accordingly. Hatching typically occurs after an interval of about six weeks, with the young birds then leaving the nest at approximately 10 weeks old.

Identification: Predominantly brown in colour, with lighter wing bars above and a distinctive white band across the slightly forked tail. Sexes are alike. Young birds have greyer wing bars.

Fea's petrel (Cape Verde petrel, *Pterodroma feae*): 36cm (14in)
Restricted to Muddier and Cape Verde Islands in the Atlantic, off north-west Africa. Head is white around the bill, grey extending back and down on to the sides of the neck and over the central areas of the wings. Remainder of wings is black, creating a two-tone effect evident in flight. Black semi-circular areas around the eyes, and a stocky black bill. Sexes are alike.

Zino's petrel (*Pterodroma madeira*): 34cm (13in) (E)
Occurs alongside Fea's petrel on Madeira. Very rare, the population reduced to approximately 20 pairs, making it one of the region's most endangered seabirds. Distinguishable from its relative by paler grey feathering on the head and reduced areas of black on the sides of the face, which are more like streaks running through the eyes than circles. Sexes are alike.

Bulwer's Petrel (*Bulweria bulwerii*): 29cm (11in)
Another Madeiran species, which also occurs on some Canary Islands, but range also extends across the Atlantic to South America. Also represented widely through the Pacific, from off the east coast of Madagascar to near the western seaboard of South America. Dark in colour, with grey underparts and dark leading edges to the wings when seen from below. Paler grey band along the upper surface of the wings. Tail appears narrow in flight. Sexes are alike.

Cape gannet

South African gannet *Morus capensis*

Cape gannets nest between September and April, with five of their six major colonies lying off south-west Africa, where pilchards and anchovies are plentiful. Their young hatch after six weeks, leaving the nest at 14 weeks old, and are occasionally sighted in southern Europe. Adult birds tend to remain closer to their breeding grounds. The young return to breed at three years old. Several thousand tons of their droppings (guano) are still collected annually and sold as a fertilizer.

Distribution: Ranges widely around the African coast, from the Gulf of Guinea on the western side via the Cape of Good Hope to Mozambique on the eastern side. Breeding range is restricted to Namibia and South Africa.
Size: 90cm (35in).
Habitat: Over the sea.
Nest: Flotsam, on the ground.
Eggs: 1, white.
Food: Mainly fish.

Identification: Straw-yellow head, extending down the back of the neck. Body is white, flight feathers black. Black edging to the tail and a more extensive black throat stripe than Gannet. Bill pale yellowish-blue. Legs and feet black. Sexes are alike. Young birds are dark brown.

SKUAS, PRIONS AND FRIGATEBIRDS

It is remarkable how far some seabirds will fly to and from their nesting grounds each year. They may effectively traverse the globe, nesting in the far north and then returning to the Antarctic region by the start of the northern winter, or vice versa. These extensive journeys are made all the more remarkable since they entail little or no rest on land.

Salvin's prion

Pachyptila salvini

Millions of pairs of Salvin's prion may be encountered on their major breeding grounds, which include the Crozet islands, lying to the south-east of Africa. These breeding grounds can be home to as many as eight million pairs of birds. When nesting, the adults tend to return to the islands under cover of darkness, which may afford them some protection against predatory seabirds. The population found on Amsterdam Island is potentially under threat however, from the introduction of domestic cats. Salvin's prions tend not to breed on coastal cliffs, preferring instead inland sites on their chosen islands. Highly social by nature, members of a pair will even share their nesting burrows with other pairs. The young normally fledge by 11 weeks of age, and will then tend to wander over a wider area than the adult birds. Their range may extend out to the eastern side of New Zealand at this stage, and occasionally they may be sighted well away from areas where the species is normally observed, although typically, they associate in groups.

Distribution: Extends from the southern coast of South Africa eastwards to southern Australia and around the coast of New Zealand.
Size: 28cm (11in).
Habitat: Open sea.
Nest: Communal burrows.
Eggs: 1, white.
Food: Crustaceans, some fish and squid.

Identification: Wavy black patterning extending across the wings from the tips of the flight feathers and leading edge across to the rump, with a black tip to the tail. Remainder of the upperparts greyish. Darker stripe runs through and behind the eyes, with the remainder of the underparts being white. There is a faint white stripe above each eye, and a trace of white on the rump. Bill, legs and feet dark. Young birds have more white on the scapulars.

Slender-billed prion

Pachyptila belcheri

The characteristic narrow shape of the bill of these prions is likely to be a reflection of their diet, which is based on small crustaceans, rather than fish. They rarely dive into the water to obtain food, preferring to take it at the surface, holding their position and often treading on the surface of the sea as they feed. Slender-billed prions range over a very wide area, but return each year to their traditional breeding grounds, which include islands to the south-east of Africa, as well as on the Falklands, off the southern tip of South America, where over a million pairs may assemble from October onwards. At this stage, these prions feed relatively close to the shore rather than out over the open ocean. Their habit of nesting in underground burrows leaves them vulnerable to introduced predators, including rats and cats, while more predatory seabirds sharing these islands may also prey on them, with skuas (*Stercorarius* species) using their powerful bills to dig directly into the nests.

Distribution: Ranges from the southern part of South Africa south and eastwards along the southern coastline of Australia to New Zealand. A separate population occurs around the southern part of South America.
Size: 25cm (10in).
Habitat: Open sea.
Nest: Underground burrows.
Eggs: 1, white.
Food: Largely krill.

Identification: Characteristic slender bill, compared with other prions, and a longer white stripe above the eyes. Underparts white, with dark edges to the wings, and to the tip of the tail. Black stripe from the eye for a short distance, broadening behind, with an adjoining grey area on the neck. Bill, legs and feet dark. Sexes are alike. Young birds resemble adults.

Great skua (northern skua, *Stercorarius skua*): 58cm (23in)
Breeds in Iceland, the Faroes and northern Scotland, and to a lesser extent in Norway and north-western Russia. Winters south around the Iberian peninsula, including the western Mediterranean. Some birds migrate further afield to Newfoundland, the Caribbean and northern Brazil. Predominantly brown, with a powerful black bill. Sides and top of the head are entirely dark in colour, with lighter streaking down the neck and on to the chest, broadening out over the wings. Short tail and dark webbed feet. Sexes are alike.

Brown skua (*Stercorarius antarcticus*): 64cm (25in)
Widely distributed through southern latitudes, including off the southern tip of Africa. Breeds further south on islands including Tristan da Cunha and Gough Island. Large size, stocky appearance. Predominantly brown in colour, with paler streaking extending down from the neck around the wings, which tend to be of a darker shade, although there can be considerable variation between individuals. Sexes are alike.

South Polar skua (*Stercorarius maccormicki*): 55cm (22in)
Winters from the Atlantic seaboard off the coast of North America across to the mid-Atlantic, south of Iceland and west of Ireland. Breeds in the Antarctic, notably in the vicinity of the Ross Sea. Two distinctive colour morphs: dark morph (Antarctic Peninsula) is brown, with wings slightly darker than the body; pale morph has brown wings with significantly paler head and underparts. Males are darker overall and smaller.

Antarctic prion

Pachyptila desolata

There are six different species of prion, forming a group within the petrel and shearwater family. The Antarctic prion is the most numerous species, with as many as 44 million birds cramming on to the island of South Georgia, off the coast of South America. Their breeding grounds are scattered on small islands in various parts of their range, with many millions of pairs also occupying the Kerguelen and Crozet groups, lying to the south-east of Africa. The habits of Antarctic prions are similar to those of related species, although they range further south. They are only likely to be observed on land when breeding, wandering widely over the oceans for the remainder of the year. These huge breeding populations are perhaps less stable than may be thought, however, since any fall-off in the supply of krill around their nesting islands could easily trigger a catastrophic population collapse.

Distribution: Ranges from the Tropic of Capricorn down to the Antarctic region, with their distribution extending from the central-southern Pacific Ocean and the coast of South America via southern Africa. Also present around New Zealand.
Size: 27cm (10.5in).
Habitat: Open sea.
Nest: Underground burrow or similar retreat.
Eggs: 1, white.
Food: Mainly krill and fish.

Identification: Black stripe extends around the head, passing through the eyes. Short white line above each eye, with lower cheeks and underparts also white. Upperparts grey; dark band on each wing tip extending back across the wing. Dark tip to tail. Bill, legs and feet dark.

Great frigatebird

Fregata minor

The great frigatebird is an impressive aerial hunter, attracted to shoals of flying fish as well as squid, scooping up their prey from the surface of the water. These large birds are very opportunistic feeders, and will swoop over beaches where turtles nest in order to catch and eat the hatchling reptiles as they head across the sand for the relative safety of the sea. They will also harry other seabirds in skua fashion, forcing them into dropping their catches, which they then take for themselves. Great frigatebirds breed in colonies on remote islands. Their chicks develop very slowly and are cared for by both parents for up to a year and a half after hatching.

Identification: Dark overall with a bright red throat sac. Abdomen is black. Has a long, hooked bill and a streaming tail. Brownish wing bars on the upper side of the wings. Angular wing posture is evident in flight. Black areas of plumage can have a glossy green suffusion. Sexes are similar, but hens are larger with a greyish white throat and white chest.

Left: Great frigatebird with throat sac inflated for displaying.

Distribution: Mainly in the Pacific, from the west coast of South America to the northern coast of Australia and South-east Asia to eastern Africa. A smaller population also occurs in the South Atlantic.
Size: 105cm (41in).
Habitat: Islands and mangroves.
Nest: Platform of sticks.
Eggs: 1, chalky white.
Food: Mainly fish, sometimes squid and carrion.

AGILE AND ADAPTABLE FEEDERS

Seabirds are highly adaptable by nature, as shown by their readiness to scavenge, often following trawlers for miles over the ocean seeking unwanted parts of a catch thrown back overboard. The more agile hunters, such as tropicbirds, are often harried into dropping their catches by other equally resourceful but more aggressive seabirds such as skuas.

Manx shearwater

Puffinus puffinus

In March, large numbers of Manx shearwaters gather to breed in remote coastal areas, typically on islands through their range. Incubation is shared, with both members of a pair sitting individually for up to six days. The eggs hatch after a period of about eight weeks, and the young birds will finally emerge from the nesting chamber at the age of 11 weeks. They mature slowly, and may not start breeding themselves until they are about six years old. Despite their arduous migration they are potentially long-lived birds, surviving for at least 30 years in the wild. While the majority of Manx shearwaters cross the Atlantic to overwinter off South America, a small number head directly south, being recorded along the coasts of Namibia and the Cape, where they can be observed hunting shoals of both anchovies and sardines.

Identification: Sooty-black upperparts, with white plumage beneath, including the undertail coverts. Sexes are alike.

Distribution: Widely distributed from north of Norway and Iceland to the coast of northern Africa during the summer breeding period. Migrates south along the eastern seaboard of South America and across the Atlantic to South Africa.
Size: 35cm (14in).
Habitat: Over the ocean.
Nest: Underground burrow.
Eggs: 1, white.
Food: Small fish, also squid.

Little shearwater

Puffinus assimilis

Distribution: Extends almost circumglobally through the southern oceans, including the southern coasts of Africa, across to the west side of South America. A population also exists off the south-west coast of Europe and north-western Africa.
Size: 30cm (12in).
Habitat: Usually open sea.
Nest: Burrows or similar retreats.
Eggs: 1, white.
Food: Fish and crustaceans.

There are eight distinct races of the little shearwater, differing largely in the extent of their white facial plumage. The small size of these birds enables them to be distinguished easily when in the company of other shearwaters, with whom they regularly associate, particularly when feeding. In the true fashion of members of this group, the little shearwater does indeed shear over the water at times, and yet is also capable of flying fast in short bursts, as well as gliding. Pairs congregate communally to nest on various islands, often creating their own burrows for this purpose. They may venture as far as 15km (9¼ miles) inland at this stage, but mammals such as cats may have a serious impact on local breeding populations. Although the northern Atlantic distribution of the little shearwater is quite separate from the population occurring in the southern oceans, it is nevertheless very similar in its habits. Its nesting grounds in this region include the Cape Verde Islands, the Canary Islands and the Azores.

Identification: Dark brownish upperparts, and top of the head, with the area from the vicinity of the throat to the tail being white. Area of the face encircling the eyes is also white. The under surface of the wings is white, edged with brown, while the undertail coverts are also white. Dark bill, pinkish legs. Sexes are alike. Young birds resemble adults.

Red-billed tropicbird

Phaethon aethereus

These sleek, elegant birds swoop down from their cliff-top roosts and fly out over the sea, catching prey by diving into the water. The red-billed species is the largest of the tropicbirds, its long, streaming white tail distinguishing it from the red-tailed tropicbird (*P. rubricauda*), which has paler wings and ranges further across the Indo-Pacific Ocean to the south. The bill of the Indian Ocean population is less brightly coloured, serving to distinguish these birds from others of the species occurring elsewhere in the world. Islands, rather than mainland areas, are favoured breeding sites, since their isolation means that the birds will be in less danger from predators.

Above: Red-billed tropicbirds nest in crevices in the ground.

Identification: Predominantly white with a black streak surrounding both eyes. Black is clearly visible on the primary flight feathers at the ends of the wings. Black streaking runs over the back and rump down to the base of the tail. Tail streamers are longer in the cock than the hen. Bill is reddish-orange with black edging.

Distribution: The main Atlantic population extends from Brazil to the west coast of Africa between the equator and the Tropic of Capricorn, while a second is centred on the Canary Islands. Another occurs off the north-east coast of Africa in the Red Sea.
Size: 104cm (41in) including streamers of 56cm (22in).
Habitat: Tropical and subtropical seas.
Nest: Rocky crevice or hollow on the ground.
Eggs: 1, pinkish with darker markings.
Food: Fish and squid. Agile enough to catch flying fish.

Yelkouan shearwater (Mediterranean shearwater, *Puffinus yelkouan*): 40cm (16in)
Southern Scandinavia around Great Britain down to the coast of northern Africa. Also through the Mediterranean and the Black Sea. Resembles Manx shearwater but has paler upperparts, resulting in more even coloration, although subspecies *P. y. mauretanicus* (Balearic shearwater) tends to have dark underparts. Relatively short tail, with brown suffusion on the undertail coverts and flanks. Sexes are alike.

Grey petrel (*Procellaria cinerea*): 50cm (20in)
A bird largely of the southern oceans. Silvery-grey upperparts, darker on the head, and instantly recognizable by its completely grey underwing coloration. Rest of underparts are white. Bill is yellowish with a dark tip. Sexes alike.

Great shearwater (*Ardenna gravis*): 50cm (20in)
From Scandinavia and southern Iceland southwards, but absent from the Atlantic off west-central Africa. Dark upperparts and a white band on the uppertail coverts. Underparts below the eyes are whitish, with variable darker mottling on the belly and dark edges to the undersides of the wings. Sexes are alike.

Southern fulmar

Fulmarus glacialoides

These fulmars are social birds by nature, not just breeding colonially, but often feeding together in groups. They take a variety of foods, and often follow ships in the hope of obtaining scraps. When breeding, southern fulmars seek out very inaccessible nesting sites, largely within the Antarctic circle. Incubation lasts about 46 days, with duties being shared. One member of the pair typically sits from three to nine days, before being relieved by its partner. Even after hatching, the chick is brooded for a long period to retain body heat, finally leaving the nest at about eight weeks. Young southern fulmars wander more widely than adults, heading into more northerly latitudes. They are most often seen off the African coast in the vicinity of the Benguela current at this stage, being far less commonly sighted off the south-eastern side of the continent.

Distribution: Extends circumglobally right around Antarctica, northwards to southern parts of the neighbouring continents, including Africa.
Size: 50cm (20in).
Habitat: Open ocean.
Nest: On ledges.
Eggs: 1, white.
Food: Krill, fish.

Identification: Whitish tinge to the head, with the upperparts otherwise being pale grey, aside from the tips of the wings and the rear edge, which are blackish. Bill has a dark tip. Sexes are alike. Young birds similar but have smaller bills.

COASTAL FEEDERS

Most seabirds are not brightly coloured, with white and black as well as hues of grey predominating in their plumage. They are often highly social, especially when breeding, nesting in large colonies on rocky stacks or inaccessible cliffs, which afford them some protection from predators. Food for their offspring is gathered often some distance from the nest site.

Socotra cormorant

Phalacrocorax nigrogularis

Distribution: Extends north to the coast of India from the Horn of Africa, at the entrance to the Red Sea and the nearby island of Socotra, from which it gets its name, via Oman to the Persian Gulf.
Size: 84 cm (33in).
Habitat: Sea.
Nest: Scrape on the ground.
Eggs: 2–4, whitish-blue.
Food: Fish.

These cormorants do not range into freshwater areas, but wander quite widely throughout the ocean, being known to extend down to Somalia and Ethiopia, as well as north-westwards to the coast of India. They feed by diving after fish, and are frequently encountered in flocks, fishing communally, as do a number of other cormorants. Nesting also takes place in colonies, with pairs clustering together on small islands through their range at this stage. Little is recorded about their breeding behaviour, but fears have been expressed about the state of the overall population, based on the fact that some former breeding areas are now no longer occupied. This may be related to an absence of sufficient food in the locality, because elsewhere large colonies comprised of many thousands appear to be thriving. There is no doubt, however, that Socotra cormorants are potentially vulnerable to oil spills caused by tanker disasters, occupying a part of the world that is constantly transected by such vessels.

Identification: Predominantly black in colour, with a distinctive white tuft on each side of the head in breeding condition. There is a prominent bare dark bluish-black area of skin on the sides of the head, with the iris being dark blue. Bill blackish with a lighter edge and hooked tip. Legs and webbed feet black. Hens are smaller in size. Young birds have dull whitish underparts and greyish-brown upperparts.

Black guillemot

Cepphus grylle

These guillemots occur inshore throughout the Arctic Circle. Populations are sedentary, not moving significantly unless forced to do so by expanding ice sheets. They seek food on the sea floor, typically diving to depths of 20m (66ft), remaining submerged for a maximum of around 40 seconds. Pairs generally stay together, breeding each year in the same location. In the far north, colonies may consist of as many as 1,000 pairs, but elsewhere individual pairs may nest on their own. Both sexes share the incubation, which takes about 30 days. Fish is the preferred rearing food for the chicks, who may be fed up to 15 times a day, though during the winter crustaceans feature more prominently in their diet. Black guillemots are common in many parts of their range: the Icelandic population alone is estimated at 50,000 pairs.

Identification: Characteristic jet black coloration, with prominent white patches on the wings. Long, pointed black bill and red feet. In winter, has white underparts and white barring on the back, while retaining its black-and-white wing pattern. Sexes are alike. Young birds have darker upperparts at first, with spotting rather than barring on their wings in winter.

Distribution: Occurs from Iceland around much of the coast of Great Britain, although not typically encountered in the English Channel, via Scandinavia and the Baltic Sea up to the coast of Russia. Circumpolar range continues via Asia to North America.
Size: 32cm (12½in).
Habitat: Sea and rocky cliffs.
Nest: Scrape on cliff.
Eggs: 1–2, whitish-coloured with dark markings.
Food: Fish and invertebrates.

Razorbill

Alca torda

The distinctive broad, flattened shape of the bill, resembling a cut-throat razor, explains the common name of these auks. They can often be observed swimming with their tails held vertically, rather than flat, enabling them to be distinguished from seabirds of similar size and coloration. Razorbills are adaptable feeders, and their diet varys according to location. Pairs display a strong bond and return to their traditional breeding sites, which may sometimes be no more than steep, inaccessible rocky stacks off the coast. They show no tendency to construct a nest of any kind, and the hen will lay her single egg on a narrow ledge directly above the ocean. The pear-like shape of the razorbill's egg helps to prevent it from rolling over the edge if accidentally dislodged. Even so, losses of eggs are fairly high, with predators such as gulls swooping down on unguarded sites.

Identification: Black upperparts, with white edging along the back of the wings and a vertical white stripe across the bill. Black coloration more strongly defined in breeding birds, with a white horizontal stripe reaching from the eyes to the bill. Sexes are alike. Young birds have smaller bills with no white markings.

Distribution: From north of Iceland and Scandinavia south to the Iberian Peninsula and northern Africa, extending into the eastern Mediterranean. Also present throughout the North Atlantic to the American coast.
Size: 39cm (15in).
Habitat: Ocean and shore.
Nest: Cliff-face crevices.
Eggs: 1, whitish-coloured with brown spots.
Food: Fish and crustaceans.

Thick-billed murre (*Uria lomvia*): 43cm (17in)
Right around the northern hemisphere, in the vicinity of the Arctic region. Ranges southwards around Iceland and along the north-western coast of Scandinavia. Resembles the guillemot, but distinguishable by its broader, shorter bill and whitish line extending along the top of the lower mandible. In winter, black head, back and wings with white underparts. In summer, white plumage extends on to the throat and lower part of the face. Young birds resemble adults in winter plumage, but are smaller. Sexes are alike.

Gentoo penguin (*Pygoscelis papua*): 81cm (32in)
Circumpolar throughout the southern oceans, found south of southern Africa. Black upperparts extending down across the throat, with white underparts. White plumage above the eyes, which are also encircled with white. White edging to the flippers, especially evident along the rear edge. The rump also has whitish feathering. Reddish, relatively narrow bill which is dark on its upper surface. White on the head less evident in young birds. Sexes are alike.

Macaroni penguin (*Eudyptes chrysolophus*): 70cm (27¹/₂in)
Confined to southern waters, from the southern tip of South America to below south-eastern Africa, breeding on remote islands in this area. Black on the head, extending to the upper chest and down over the back and wings. Remaining underparts are white. Prominent golden-yellow plumes extend back over the eyes. Iris is red, as are stout bill, legs and feet. Young birds are greyish below the bill, with a less prominent crest. Males are larger than females.

African penguin

Jackass penguin *Spheniscus demersus*

The previous unusual name of these penguins derived from their call, which resembles a braying donkey. They remain close to the coast and are the only penguin species occurring on the African mainland, although their breeding colonies (rookeries) are more often located on small offshore islands. Breeding can occur throughout the year, with both adults sharing the six-week incubation. Young penguins leave the nest from 10 weeks onwards. Numbers of jackass penguins have declined significantly over the past century, and especially over recent years, because overfishing has reduced their food supply. Some populations have also suffered badly from oil spillages and coastal development. These penguins spend much of the day searching for shoals of fish. They may dive to depths as great as 90m (295ft) and can remain submerged for several minutes at a time.

Distribution: From Namibia right around the coast of southern Africa extending up to Mozambique on the eastern seaboard.
Size: 70cm (27¹/₂in).
Habitat: Coastal areas.
Nest: Under rocks; burrows.
Eggs: 2, greenish.
Food: Anchovies and other schooling fish.

Identification: Head, back and wings black. Underparts white, extending up the sides of the face. Black band encircles lower body. Pink area above each eye. Sexes are alike. Bill is black, lighter at the tip. Young have grey heads.

FISH-EATERS

Not surprisingly, birds living close to the coast often catch fish and other forms of aquatic life, though there are differences in their feeding methods. Pelicans, for example, use their large bills to trawl for fish near the surface, whereas snakebirds dive underwater to pursue their quarry. Many of these birds are at risk from overfishing in coastal waters, which deprives them of their food supply.

Pink-backed pelican

Pelecanus rufescens

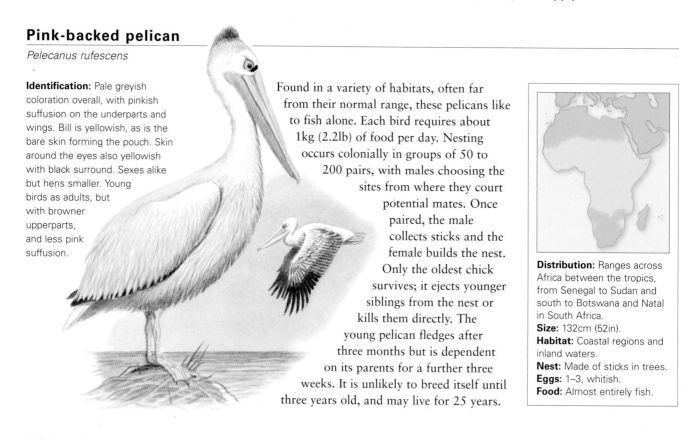

Identification: Pale greyish coloration overall, with pinkish suffusion on the underparts and wings. Bill is yellowish, as is the bare skin forming the pouch. Skin around the eyes also yellowish with black surround. Sexes alike but hens smaller. Young birds as adults, but with browner upperparts, and less pink suffusion.

Found in a variety of habitats, often far from their normal range, these pelicans like to fish alone. Each bird requires about 1kg (2.2lb) of food per day. Nesting occurs colonially in groups of 50 to 200 pairs, with males choosing the sites from where they court potential mates. Once paired, the male collects sticks and the female builds the nest. Only the oldest chick survives; it ejects younger siblings from the nest or kills them directly. The young pelican fledges after three months but is dependent on its parents for a further three weeks. It is unlikely to breed itself until three years old, and may live for 25 years.

Distribution: Ranges across Africa between the tropics, from Senegal to Sudan and south to Botswana and Natal in South Africa.
Size: 132cm (52in).
Habitat: Coastal regions and inland waters.
Nest: Made of sticks in trees.
Eggs: 1–3, whitish.
Food: Almost entirely fish.

African darter

Snakebird *Anhinga rufa*

Distribution: Found right across Africa south of the Sahara, and in Madagascar. Also present in South-east Asia and Australia.
Size: 97cm (38in).
Habitat: Coastal mangroves, inland areas.
Nest: Made of reeds and other aquatic vegetation.
Eggs: 2–6, chalky-white.
Food: Fish and amphibians.

Darters are so called because of their fishing style. Diving in search of prey, their powerful neck muscles enable them to lunge forward and seize quarry with their sharp, pointed bill. African darters swim low in the water, propelled by strong webbed feet, with just their narrow neck visible, hence the characteristic snake-like appearance. Out of water they adopt a cormorant posture, resting with wings held open, which dries their plumage and may also help to maintain body temperature. Darters typically nest off the ground alongside cormorants and other birds. The largest recorded breeding colony was documented in 1962 at Chagana in Tanzania, eastern Africa, and consisted of an estimated 10,000 nests.

Identification: Brownish-black body with a white stripe down each side of the neck. Pale throat with dark-edged whitish plumage over the wings. Hens have pale underparts. Young birds resemble hens, but have buff rather than white markings.

Western reef heron

Egretta gularis

Identification: White in colour, with olive yellow legs and feet. Bill is stocky in shape and yellowish brown in colour. There is also a dark morph, recognizable by its grey plumage overall, with white restricted to the throat and some areas on the primary coverts. Young birds are greyish brown to white, usually mottled.

This species is closely related to the little egret (*E. garzetta*), although it does differ significantly in appearance, and is also essentially confined to coastal haunts. Western reef herons tend to be solitary by nature, and do not generally form very large aggregations, even when they are nesting. Their breeding period extents from April through to July, and some pairs may nest in October as well. They often choose an inaccessible site on cliffs for this purpose, rather than building their nest in amongst vegetation. The incubation period lasts for approximately three weeks, with the young fledging after a further six weeks. Their appearance is surprisingly variable at this stage. Western reef egrets display little tendency to undertake seasonal movements of any kind, remaining resident in their territories throughout the year, searching for crustaceans and fish along the seashore and in rock pools. When not in breeding condition, they lose their distinctive long plumes, which extend downwards at the back of the head.

Distribution: Coastal areas of West Africa, from the vicinity of Senegal to Gabon and on the east coast from Sudan to Mozambique. Occasionally recorded further inland.
Size: 66cm (26in).
Habitat: Rocky beaches and mangroves.
Nest: Platform of twigs.
Eggs: 2–3, pale blue.
Food: Crustaceans, other invertebrates and fish.

Half-collared kingfisher (*Alcedo semitorquata*): 20cm (8in)
A northerly population of this colourful African species is present in Ethiopia, with its more southerly representatives centred on south-eastern Africa. Distinctive, deep blue coloration on the head and cheeks, with a prominent white collar across the nape of the neck. The throat area is also white, although the remainder of the underparts are orangish in colour. The sides of the chest, back and wings are greenish-blue, although plumage is not particularly bright. Adult birds have pinkish feet; in young birds these are black. Bill is black with a small patch of orange either side. Sexes are alike.

Striated heron (Green-backed heron, *Butorides striata*): 40cm (16in)
Widely distributed across all continents, with more than 30 distinctive subspecies recognized. Present across much of Africa south of the Sahara, as well as the Red Sea, apart from the southern tip. Also present on Madagascar and nearby islands. Very variable in appearance. The most widely distributed African race (*B. s. atricapilla*) is predominantly greyish, with white stripes on the face and on the mid-line of the body. White edging to the wing coverts, with green plumage on the back. Bill is blackish above, more yellowish beneath. Legs and feet are yellow. Sexes are alike. Young birds tend to be of a browner shade overall.

Dimorphic egret

Egretta dimorpha

The description "dimorphic egret" refers to two plumage phases. White birds are more common, but there is also a grey morph distinguishable from that of the western reef heron (*E. gularis*) by the colour of its legs. Although occurring primarily in coastal areas, these egrets may also be encountered inland, in relatively arid surroundings, especially in Madagascar. Here they use their feet to probe for insects, reptiles and amphibians lurking in the grass. In coastal areas, they feed largely on fish and crustaceans. Dimorphic egrets may be seen in small groups, although frequently they are observed on their own when not nesting. They are sedentary by nature, displaying no urge to migrate after the breeding season.

Identification: Most are predominantly white, with breeding plumes on the back of the head. Bill yellowish at the base and black at the tip, with the feet being yellow and the legs black. Yellow on the toes extends up the front of the legs. Sexes are alike. Young birds greyish, with variable brown on the upperparts and a white throat.

Distribution: Madagascar and surrounding islands. Also sighted on the East African coast, from Kenya to Mozambique.
Size: 65cm (25½in).
Habitat: Coastal and further inland.
Nest: Platform of sticks.
Eggs: 2, pale blue.
Food: Invertebrates and vertebrates.

SEA DUCKS AND COASTAL WATERFOWL

Although more commonly encountered on inland waters, a number of waterfowl species have adapted to life in coastal waters, and some will even venture far out to sea. These include the eider ducks, whose plumage was once highly sought-after to make eiderdown, before artificial substitutes for stuffing pillows became available. These ducks will insulate their nests with their own feathers once eggs are laid.

King eider

Somateria spectabilis

Like most birds from the far north, the king eider has a circumpolar distribution that reaches right around the top of the globe. Seasonal movements of these sea ducks tend to be more widespread than in other eiders. They are remarkably common, with the North American population estimated at two million individuals. Huge groups of up to 100,000 birds congregate when moulting, although for the breeding season they split up and pairs nest individually across the Arctic tundra. King eiders are very powerful swimmers and generally dive to obtain their food.

Identification: Drakes in breeding condition have an orange area edged with black above a reddish bill. Light grey head plumage extends down the neck. Chest is pale pinkish-white, with black wings and underparts. Ducks are mainly a speckled shade of brown, with the pale underside of their wings visible in flight. In eclipse plumage, drakes are a darker shade of brown, with an orangish-yellow bill and white plumage on the back.

Distribution: From the coast of Iceland westwards around the British Isles and along northern Scandinavia. Also present in northern latitudes of eastern Asia and on both coasts of North America, as well as Greenland.
Size: 63cm (25in).
Habitat: Tundra and ocean.
Nest: Hollow on the ground lined with down.
Eggs: 4–7, olive-buff.
Food: Mainly crustaceans and marine invertebrates.

Common eider

Somateria mollissima

This is the most common European sea duck. Along the Norwegian coast the population is estimated at some two million individuals, and may even be increasing. Common eiders occur in large flocks and nest in colonies on islands, where they are safe from predators such as Arctic foxes (*Alopex lagopus*). The start of the breeding period depends on latitude, often not commencing until June in the far north. The nest is lined with their dense down, which safeguards the eggs from being chilled. While the ducks are incubating, drakes congregate to moult out of their breeding plumage. Outside the nesting period, common eiders are most likely to be observed close to shore. They do not generally migrate far, although ducks and young birds disperse further than drakes. They usually forage for food underwater.

Identification: Drake in colour has a black cap to the head, with black underparts and flight feathers. Rest of the body is white, and the bill is greyish. Out of colour, drakes are blackish-brown, lacking the barring seen in ducks, and have white upperwing coverts. Ducks are predominantly a combination of black and brown in colour, with a dark bill and legs.

Distribution: Northern and north-western parts of Europe extending to Siberia. Also from eastern Asia to both Pacific and Atlantic coasts of North America.
Size: 70cm (27¹/₂in).
Habitat: Coastal areas.
Nest: Hollow on the ground lined with down.
Eggs: 1–8, yellowish-olive.
Food: Mainly invertebrates.

Long-tailed duck

Oldsquaw *Clangula hyemalis*

These sea ducks often congregate in large numbers, although in winter females and young birds tend to migrate further south in flocks than do adult drakes. They spend most of their time on the water, obtaining food by diving under the waves. They come ashore to nest on the tundra, where the ducks lay their eggs directly on to the ground under cover. The drakes soon return to the ocean to moult. When migrating, oldsquaws fly low in lines, rather than in any more organized formation.

Identification: Black head, neck and chest, with white around the eyes and white underparts. Head becomes white across the top outside the breeding season, with patches of black evident on the sides. Grey rather than brown predominates on the wings. Long tail plumes present throughout the year. The smaller ducks undergo a similar change in appearance, with the sides of the face becoming white rather than blackish.

Distribution: Circumpolar, breeding in Northern Europe and the Arctic. Winters further south.
Size: 47cm (18½in).
Habitat: Coasts and bays.
Nest: Hidden in vegetation or under a rock.
Eggs: 5–7, olive-buff.
Food: Mainly crustaceans and marine invertebrates.

South African shelduck (*Tadorna cana*): 64cm (25in)
Southern Africa north into Namibia, occurring in freshwater and coastal areas. Drake is golden-brown overall, lighter on the upper chest, with a grey neck and head. Tail and flight feathers are dark brown. Mature ducks have prominent white plumage over much of the head and face, except for a dark crown. Young females display less white here, the white largely confined to around the eyes. Young drakes are similar but duller in coloration than adult drakes.

Cape teal (*Anas capensis*): 46cm (18in)
Namibia southwards, though more restricted in south-eastern southern Africa. Also found inland on salt marshes. Able to excrete salt through specially-adapted tear glands. Brown overall, with the feathers typically having dark centres, which are especially apparent on the flanks. Prominent white and dark green wing speculum, most evident in flight. Bill is pinkish, dark at its base. Legs and feet blackish. Sexes are alike.

Barnacle goose (*Branta leucopsis*): 71cm (28in)
Breeds in the far north, overwintering in the British Isles and north-western Europe. Broad white area on the forehead, extending across the face to the throat. Rest of the head, neck, upper back and chest are black. Black stripe runs back from the bill to the eyes. Underparts are whitish, becoming greyer with more distinct barring on the flanks. Wings have alternating broad grey bars and narrow black bars edged with white. Bill, legs and feet are black. Young birds have brownish suffusion to the upperparts. Sexes are alike but males generally larger.

Brent goose

Brant goose *Branta bernicla*

Brent geese start breeding in June. A site close to the tundra shoreline is favoured, with pairs lining the scrape with plant matter and down. It takes nine weeks from egg-laying to the young geese leaving the nest, after which they head south with their parents. Goslings may not breed until they are three years old. On the tundra, brent geese graze on lichens, moss and other terrestrial vegetation, while in winter they feed mainly on aquatic plants like seaweed, which is plucked from under the water as the geese up-end their bodies. On land, they graze by nibbling the shoots of plants.

Identification:
Black head and neck, with trace of white on lower neck. Wings grey-black. White flanks with barring. Abdomen is white in the American brant (*B. b. hrota*) from the east, but often dark in its western relative, the black brant (*B. b. nigricans*). Sexes are alike. Young geese may lack white neck patches.

Distribution: Breeds in the Arctic, overwintering in Ireland and parts of north-western Europe. Other populations overwinter in eastern Asia and along both coasts of North America.
Size: 66cm (26in).
Habitat: Bays and estuaries.
Nest: Scrape on the ground.
Eggs: 1–10, whitish.
Food: Plant matter.

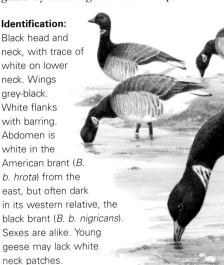

GULLS

Many of these gulls have adapted to feed inland, and have become a common sight near farms and city parks, where they will forage on anything from earthworms and grubs in ploughed fields to scraps of food and refuse left behind by humans. The exception is the white-eyed gull, which spends most of its life at sea, and is now registered as a near-threatened species in its east African range.

European herring gull

Larus argentatus

These large gulls are often seen on fishing jetties and around harbours, searching for scraps. They have also moved inland and can be seen in areas such as rubbish dumps, where they scavenge for food, often in quite large groups. Herring gulls are noisy by nature, especially when breeding. They frequently nest on rooftops in coastal towns and cities, a trend that began in Britain as recently as the 1940s. Pairs can become very aggressive at breeding time, swooping menacingly on people who venture too close to the nest site (and even including the chicks once they have fledged).

Left: The herring gull's pink legs are a distinctive feature.

Identification: White head and underparts, with grey on the back and wings. Prominent large, white spots on the black flight feathers. Distinctive pink feet. Reddish spot towards the tip of the lower bill. Some dark streaking on the head and neck in winter. Sexes are alike. Young birds are mainly brown, with dark bills and prominent barring on their wings.

Distribution: The northern Atlantic north of Iceland and south to northern Africa and the Mediterranean. Also the North Sea and Baltic areas to northern Scandinavia and Arctic Russia.
Size: 60cm (24in)
Habitat: Coasts and inland.
Nest: Small pile of vegetation.
Eggs: 2–3, pale blue to brown with darker markings.
Food: Fish and carrion.

Black-headed gull

Chroicocephalus ridibundus

These gulls are a common sight not only in coastal areas but also in town parks with lakes. They move inland during the winter, where they can often be seen following ploughing tractors searching for worms and grubs disturbed in the soil. Black-headed gulls nest close to water in what can be quite large colonies. Like many gulls, they are noisy birds, even calling at night. On warm, summer evenings they can sometimes be seen hawking flying ants and similar insects in flight, demonstrating their airborne agility.

Identification: Throughout the summer, distinctive black head with a white collar beneath and white under-parts. The wings are grey and the flight feathers mainly black. In the winter, the head is mainly white except for black ear coverts and a black smudge above each eye, while the bill is red at its base and dark at the tip.

Above: The black feathering on the head is a transient characteristic, appearing only in the summer (above right).

Distribution: Greenland and throughout Europe, south along the coast of north-western Africa and into Asia.
Size: 39cm (15in).
Habitat: Coastal areas.
Nest: Scrape on the ground lined with plant matter.
Eggs: 2–3, pale blue to brown with darker markings.
Food: Typically molluscs, crustaceans and small fish.

White-eyed gull

Ichthyaetus leucophthalmus

These gulls, with their restricted distribution through one of the world's busiest shipping lanes, are far less numerous than other members of this group, because of their vulnerability to oil spillages. Their population is thought to be around 13,000. White-eyed gulls spend much of their time at sea outside the nesting period. They seek food in small groups, diving under the waves to catch prey rather than scavenging. The breeding season begins in July, with pairs often nesting on small offshore islands, using little nesting material apart from seaweed to create a simple lining on which the eggs are laid. They frequently breed in colonies, concentrating largely on nesting grounds located at the entrance to the Red Sea, after which many will disperse further afield.

Identification: Black head, extending to the upper chest, with an area of white forming a collar, and light grey plumage on the chest. Remainder of the underparts white, with a white, crescent-shaped area above and below the eyes. Wings largely dark grey, flight feathers black. Bill red with a black tip, legs and feet yellow. Sexes are alike. Young birds have dark greyish-brown heads.

Distribution: From the Gulf of Suez throughout the Red Sea, as far as the Gulf of Aden, being observed on the surrounding coastline of north-west Africa and the Arabian Peninsula.
Size: 43cm (17in).
Habitat: Sea and coast.
Nest: Scrape on the ground.
Eggs: 2–3, pale bluish to brown, with dark markings.

Lesser black-backed gull (*Larus fuscus*): 56cm (22in)
Breeds around the shores of the extreme north of Europe, moving as far south as parts of northern Africa in the winter. Similar to the great black-backed but smaller and lacks the prominent white seen on the flight feathers when the wings are closed. Legs are yellow rather than dull pink. Much smaller area of white on the outstretched upper surface of the wings in flight. Sexes are alike.

Glaucous gull (*Larus hyperboreus*): 68cm (27in)
Coastal areas of northern Europe, including Iceland. Very pale bluish-grey wings with white edges. Head and underparts white in summer, developing grey streaks in winter. Sexes are alike. As with other species, young birds are more mottled overall.

Yellow-legged gull (*Larus michahellis*): 58cm (23in)
Found in coastal areas of southern England and mainland Europe to northern Africa, and also around the Black and Caspian seas. It has a white head and underparts, grey back and wings, and small white spots on the black flight feathers. The wings have large black areas towards the tips. The bill and legs are yellow, and there is a red spot on the lower bill. Grey suffusion on the head in winter. Sexes are alike. Was recognized as a form of the herring gull (*L. argentatus*) but now considered a separate species.

Hartlaub's gull (*Chroicocephalus hartlaubii*): 38cm (15in)
Restricted to the western seaboard of southern Africa, from Walvis Bay in Namibia south to Cape Agulhas. White head, chest and underparts, with grey on the back of the neck becoming darker on the wings. White tips to the black flight feathers. Bill blackish with a slight reddish hue. Sexes are alike. Young birds have brown areas on the wings, and a similar band across the tail.

Common gull

Mew gull *Larus canus*

Common gulls often range inland over considerable distances, searching for earthworms and other invertebrates to feed on. In sandy coastal areas they will seek out shellfish as well. There is a distinct seasonal variation in the range of these gulls. At the end of the summer they leave their Scandinavian and Russian breeding grounds and head further south in Europe, to France and various other locations in the Mediterranean. Here they overwinter before migrating north again in the spring. In spite of its rather meek appearance, this species will bully smaller gulls such as the black-headed gull and take food from them. Common and black-headed gulls are often found in the same kind of inland environment, both showing a preference for agricultural areas and grassland.

Distribution: Iceland and throughout Europe, with the main breeding grounds in Scandinavia and Russia. Extends across Asia to western North America.
Size: 46cm (18in).
Habitat: Coasts and inland areas close to water.
Nest: Raised nest of twigs and other debris.
Eggs: 2–3, pale blue to brownish-olive in colour, with dark markings.
Food: Shellfish, small fish and invertebrates.

Identification: White head and underparts with yellow bill and yellowish-green legs. Wings are greyish with white markings at the tips, which are most visible in flight. Flight feathers are black with white spots. Tail is white. Dark eyes. Greyish streaking on the head in winter plumage. Sexes are alike. Young birds have brown mottled plumage, and it takes them more than two years to obtain adult coloration.

WIDE-RANGING GULLS

The adaptability of gulls ensures that the group has a worldwide representation, and there is evidence that some species are starting to colonize new areas, even moving across the Atlantic in the case of the ring-billed gull. While a number of species are sedentary through the year, others undertake regular seasonal movements, depending partly on the individual population concerned.

Kelp gull

Larus dominicanus

These gulls have a wide global distribution, present in the southern hemisphere along the shores of southern Africa, Australia and New Zealand, and South America. Birds from the latter population may venture inland, sometimes being found on lakes in the Andean region. The kelp gulls' extensive range is matched by their opportunistic feeding habits. In addition to taking fish and crustaceans they may attack other creatures ranging from geese and lambs to whales. Those gulls found in the Antarctic, below Tierra del Fuego, remain there all year, frequenting open water away from the pack ice. They breed between October and December. Pairs construct a relatively bulky nest from seaweed and similar material gathered on the shore, often concealed by rocks or trees, which offer some security. The young fledge when they are seven weeks old.

Identification: A large, black-winged species with a white area at the rear of the flight feathers (most evident in flight). A red spot is present near the tip of the lower mandible. Sexes are alike. Dark area mottled brown in maturing young birds.

Distribution: Southern Africa, from Cape Cross in Namibia to Cape Province in South Africa, and also on southern Madagascar. Represented on the other southern continents.
Size: 65cm (26in).
Habitat: Ocean and shore.
Nest: Pile of vegetation.
Eggs: 3, olive-brown in colour and speckled.
Food: Animal matter.

Sabine's gull

Xema sabini

Identification: Dark, slaty grey head, with a black band at the rear, broad white collar extending down to white underparts. Wings greyish, with white edging. Flight feathers black with white tips. Bill dark grey at the base, pale yellow at the tip. Legs and feet grey. Sexes are alike. Young birds have greyish-brown heads, extending down the lower back.

Few gulls undergo such a dramatic shift in lifestyle as Sabine's gull. It breeds on the Arctic tundra during the summer, arriving on its breeding grounds in May, when the area is usually still blanketed with snow. Courtship begins, with laying starting once the snow thaws. Sabine's gulls build their nests close to standing areas of water, where their young are chaperoned within a few days of hatching. They catch their prey in flight close to the ground at this stage, and will also seize eggs and chicks from other birds nesting in the region, especially those of Arctic terns (*Sterna paradisaea*). Sabine's gulls occurring in western areas then head south to South America, whereas the population nesting in eastern Canada, Greenland and Iceland flies over the Atlantic to reach the shores off southern Africa. Here they feed on fish, and also scavenge, particularly close to sewage outflows. If the weather is particularly bad on migration, numbers of Sabine's gulls may be observed in coastal districts of western Europe in the autumn.

Distribution: Breeds in the far north, typically from Asia across North America, with populations also present in Greenland and Iceland. Migrates south to overwinter offshore along the south-western coast of Africa. Another population overwinters off north-western parts of South America.
Size: 30cm (12in).
Habitat: Tundra and open ocean.
Nest: Grass-lined scrape on the ground.
Eggs: 1–3, bluish to brownish with dark markings.

Little gull (*Hydrocoloeus minutus*): 28cm (11in) Distribution extends through north-eastern parts of Europe and into Asia during the summer. Overwinters around the shores of western Europe, including the British Isles, down to the Mediterranean region. Pale grey back and wings. Black head, with the black extending right down on to the neck. Red legs and feet. In winter, has a dark spot towards the rear of the head, which is otherwise whitish apart from a mottled area on the crown. Sexes are alike.

Audouin's gull (*Ichthyaetus audouinii*): 52cm (20½in) Restricted to parts of the Mediterranean, and the western coast of northern Africa. Adults are predominantly whitish. Wings are grey, with a white edge along the back, and black flight feathers tipped with white markings. Bill is relatively short and reddish, with a black band towards its tip. Eyes are dark, as are the legs. Sexes are alike. Young birds are mottled brown, gaining grey on the wings first.

Bonaparte's gull (*Chroicocephalus crassirostris*): 34cm (14in) Essentially a North American species; European sightings are birds from the Atlantic population, which normally winters from New England down to the Gulf Coast. Identified by its black head, with a white collar on the neck. pale grey wings and underparts. The bil is black throughout the year, but the black plumage on the head can be reduced to a spot beneath each eye. Legs and feet are red. Sexes are alike.

Iceland gull

Larus glaucoides

The name of this gull is misleading, since it is only present on Iceland (and in Europe) outside the breeding season. The gulls found here are those that breed in north-eastern Greenland; birds further south on Greenland are resident throughout the year. Young birds travel further afield, and are often seen with other gulls, frequently scavenging for food in coastal waters and inland at rubbish dumps. Iceland gulls will consume almost anything edible. At sea they prefer to feed on the surface, although they may dive to catch fish or invertebrates. Breeding typically starts on Greenland around the middle of May, with pairs nesting on steep, inaccessible cliffs, often in the company of other seabirds, whose eggs and chicks may be preyed upon by the Iceland gulls.

Identification: Predominantly white, with pale grey coloration on the wings. Bill is yellowish, with a red spot near the tip of the lower bill. Legs and feet pink. Sexes are alike. Out of breeding condition, adult birds display brownish markings on the head, extending on to the breast. Young birds are very pale in colour, with a brownish bill.

Distribution: The Greenland population overwinters on Iceland, around the British Isles and in parts of Scandinavia. North-eastern Canadian population overwinters south to Virginia in the US and inland to the Great Lakes.
Size: 64cm (25in).
Habitat: Typically near cliffs adjoining sea coasts.
Nest: Made from seaweed and other vegetation.
Eggs: 2–3, olive-brownish in colour.
Food: Fish and other edible items.

Slender-billed gull

Chroicocephalus genei

Identification: White head and underparts. The wings are pale grey, with some white areas here. Flight feathers black. Relatively narrow, reddish-black bill. Legs and feet reddish pink. May display a dark spot by the eye when not in breeding condition. Sexes are alike. Young birds have a light bill with a dark tip, and orange legs.

The slender-billed is a highly social gull, particularly when nesting. Large numbers may then crowd together, with as little as 20cm (8in) separating neighbouring nests, often being mixed in alongside those of various terns (*Sterna* species) as well. These gulls frequent inland areas, such as river deltas, when nesting and rely largely on catching their own food at this stage, rather than scavenging. They employ a variety of techniques for this purpose, sometimes simply up-ending themselves in water, or diving briefly out of sight. They will also catch insects such as swarming ants in the air. After the breeding season some populations, typically those found around the Black Sea and further east in Asia, tend to migrate southwards, heading to the Mediterranean region and the Persian Gulf respectively, overwintering as far south as the Horn of Africa. Slender-billed gulls in West Africa are mainly resident there throughout the year, however, although they will move to the coast for the winter.

Distribution: Ranges widely through parts of the Mediterranean, through the Red Sea and the Persian Gulf, and also occurs in West Africa. Seen in various Asian localities too, again often depending on the season.
Size: 43cm (17in).
Habitat: Frequents wetlands when breeding, and coastal areas.
Nest: Scrape on mud.
Eggs: 2–3, pale bluish to brown with some darker markings.
Food: Fish and invertebrates.

TERNS

Terns are easily distinguished, even from gulls, by their relatively elongated shape. Their long, pointed wings are an indication of their aerial ability. Some terns regularly fly great distances on migration, further than most other birds. Not surprisingly, their flight appears to be almost effortless. When breeding, terns prefer to nest in colonies.

Common tern

Sterna hirundo

These graceful birds are only likely to be encountered in northern parts of their range between April and October, after which time they head south to warmer climes for the duration of the winter period. Travelling such long distances means that they are powerful in flight, and yet are also very agile. Their strongly-forked tail helps them to hover effectively, allowing them to adjust their position before diving into the water in search of quarry. They are very versatile feeders and may also hawk food on the wing. Common terns are represented on all the continents, their long bills providing a simple way of distinguishing them from gulls.

Identification: Long body shape, with black on the top of the head extending down the back of the neck. Rest of the face and underparts whitish-grey. Back and wings greyish, with long flight feathers. Narrow white streamers on the tail. Bill is red with a dark tip, which becomes completely black in the winter. The plumage in front of the eyes becomes white during winter. Legs and feet are red. Sexes are alike.

Distribution: Great Britain, Scandinavia and much of Central Europe during the summer. Migrates south to parts of eastern and southern Africa for the winter.
Size: 36cm (14in).
Habitat: Near water.
Nest: Scrape on the ground.
Eggs: 3, pale brown with dark spots.
Food: Mainly fish, but also eats crustaceans.

Sandwich tern

Thalasseus sandvicensis

A summer visitor to northern Europe, this species is often sighted slightly earlier than the common tern, and also leaves just before its relative. The sandwich tern is significantly larger and is surprisingly noisy, with the sounds of its calls having been likened to a grating cartwheel. Although these terns will skim over the water surface seeking food, they can also dive spectacularly from heights of up to 10m (33ft). Sandwich terns usually breed in high-density colonies in the open on sand bars and similarly exposed coastal sites, although they may sometimes nest on islands in lakes.

Identification: Shaggy black crest evident at the back of the head. The entire top of the head is black during the summer, while a white forehead is characteristic of the winter plumage. The bill is long and black with a yellow tip. Rest of the head and underparts are white, and the wings are grey. Sexes are alike.

Distribution: Around the shores of Great Britain and northern Europe, as well as the Caspian and Black seas. Winters further south in the Mediterranean region and northern Africa. Also found in South-east Asia, the Caribbean and South America.
Size: 43cm (17in).
Habitat: Coastal areas.
Nest: Scrape on the ground.
Eggs: 1–2, brownish-white with darker markings.
Food: Fish and especially sand eels.

Roseate tern

Sterna dougallii

In northern parts of their range these terns are brief summer visitors, only likely to be present from about the middle of May until the end of August. Their distribution is quite localized. They are most likely to be seen where the shore is shallow and sandy, providing them with better fishing opportunities. They dive into the water to catch their prey from heights of no more than 2m (7ft), and may also take fish from other terns. Their shorter wings and quicker wing beats make them incredibly agile in flight. Roseate terns avoid open areas when nesting, preferring sites that are concealed among rocks or vegetation.

Identification: This tern gets its name from the slight pinkish suffusion on its whitish underparts. Compared to other terns, it has relatively long tail streamers and quite short wings. The bill is primarily blackish with a red base in the summer. Entire top of the head is black in summer, and the forehead turns white in winter. Sexes are alike. Subspecies differ in both wing and bill length.

Distribution: From the British Isles south to Spain and north-western Africa. Winters along the west African coast.
Size: 36cm (14in).
Habitat: Coastal areas.
Nest: Scrape on the ground.
Eggs: 1–2, cream or buff with reddish-brown markings.
Food: Mainly fish.

Caspian tern (*Hydroprogne caspia*): 55cm (22in)
Baltic region, overwintering in western Africa. Sometimes seen in the Mediterranean. Black top to the head becoming streaked in winter. Grey wings, with a white chest and underparts. Large red bill with a black tip. Sexes are alike.

Black-naped tern (*Sterna sumatrana*): 35cm (14in)
Western Indian Ocean, from the horn of Africa to Mozambique, and across the Indo-Pacific to western India. Separate population occurs off South-east Asia, on islands to the north and east of Australia. Mostly white, with a silvery back and strongly-forked tail. Distinctive black area extending back from the eyes around the nape. Bill also black. Sexes are alike.

Saunders's tern (*Sternula saundersi*): 28cm (11in)
Red Sea to Tanzania, and southern Madagascar. Also in the Indo-Pacific, including Sri Lanka, to South-east Asia. Black streaks from the sides of the bill to the eyes, with a white crown. Black above the eyes to the nape of the neck. Back, rump and wings are grey, with darker flight feathers. Underparts are white. Non-breeding plumage is darker. Bill is yellow with a blackish tip. Legs and feet greyish-yellow. Young have blackish areas over the wings. Sexes are alike.

White-cheeked tern (*Sterna repressa*): 35cm (14in)
Red Sea to Kenya. Also further east, along the Asian coast to south-western India. Black from the upper bill back over the head to the neck, encompassing the eyes, with white cheeks. Throat, underparts, back and wings all grey. Bill is reddish with a dark tip. Legs and feet also reddish. Non-breeding: white on the head more extensive, and dark areas confined to around the eyes. Young have brownish upperparts.

Arctic tern

Sterna paradisaea

It can be very difficult to distinguish this species from the common tern, but the Arctic tern's bill is shorter and does not have a black tip in the summer. The tail too is longer, and the tail streamers are very evident in flight. Arctic terns undertake the most extensive migration of all birds, flying virtually from one end of the globe to the other. After breeding in the vicinity of the Arctic Circle the birds head south, often beyond Africa to Antarctica, before repeating the journey the following year, though it appears that at least some of the young birds stay in the Antarctic for their first full year. Arctic terns nest communally, often choosing islands on which to breed. They will react aggressively to any potential predators in their midst, with a number of individuals turning on and mobbing an intruder. Arctic terns may steal food from other birds, for example from puffins in the Faroe Islands.

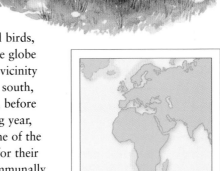

Identification: Black area covering the entire top of the head, with white chest and underparts. Wings grey. Bill is dark red, becoming black in the winter, when the forehead is white. Sexes are alike.

Distribution: Breeds in the Arctic and northern Europe. Migrates south to overwinter in southern Africa.
Size: 38cm (15in).
Habitat: Sea and fresh water.
Nest: Hollow on the ground, lined with vegetation.
Eggs: 2, can be brownish, bluish or greenish in colour, with dark markings.
Food: Fish and invertebrates.

LONG-DISTANCE TRAVELLERS

Many terns have a very wide distribution through the world's oceans, with individual populations ranging across large areas. By nature they are quite adaptable, and may sometimes modify their feeding habits depending on the type of food available. Their breeding grounds are often small, remote islands, where the terns can nest in relative safety on the ground.

Bridled tern

Onychoprion anaethetus

This tern has a pantropical distribution, but rarely ventures further than 50km (30 miles) from the shore. It feeds mainly on small fish that school near the surface, swooping down to seize them in its bill. Breeding birds typically return to the same beach each year, and will attempt to conceal the nest site among rocks or vegetation. Bridled terns often associate with related species, such as sooty terns, when nesting. Incubation lasts about a month. The young stay in the nest for seven weeks, and remain with the colony a further month or so after fledging. They are unlikely to nest themselves until four years old. Bridled terns live for about 18 years.

Identification: Long, narrow wings are brownish-black with a white collar. A black patch towards the back of the head narrows to a stripe connecting the eyes and bill. White patch above the eye. White underparts and underwing coverts with black flight feathers. Deeply-forked tail. Young have white edging to dark plumage on back and wings, and black area on head is mottled.

Distribution: Separate African populations, on the west and east coasts. Also in Australasia and on both sides of Central America.
Size: 38cm (15in).
Habitat: Ocean and shore.
Nest: Scrape on the ground.
Eggs: 1, brownish with darker markings.
Food: Mostly fish, also squid and crustaceans.

Gull-billed tern

Gelochelidon nilotica

Although more commonly sighted around coastal areas, these terns can also be found some considerable distance inland, for example when overwintering in the vicinity of the River Niger in West Africa, as well as through the Rift Valley lakes of eastern Africa. Gull-billed terns are adaptable and highly opportunistic feeders, with terrestrial invertebrates ranging from grasshoppers to spiders frequently making up a significant part of their diet. The terns may congregate in large numbers in areas where food is plentiful. When hunting over grassland, the terns will fly low and swoop down quickly to seize their quarry, a technique similar to the one used when hunting for fish over the water. Small mammals such as voles may also fall prey to them in this fashion, as may reptiles including lizards, which are killed by blows from the terns' short but strong bill. Gull-billed terns prefer to nest in colonies, and their overall success rate is significantly higher when they associate in large groups. This is because collectively the terns are more able to drive off gulls and other predatory species seeking to seize their eggs and chicks.

Identification: Black cap on the head extends down to the nape of the neck. Frosty grey wings, back and tail feathers, the latter having white edges. Remainder of the plumage is white. In winter plumage the black cap is replaced by blackish ear coverts. Bill is relatively short and black. Sexes are alike.

Distribution: Ranges along the southern coasts of mainland Europe to the Mediterranean, extending east into Asia. Overwinters in Africa. Other populations present through southern Asia to Australia, and from the USA down to Argentina in South America.
Size: 42cm (16½in).
Habitat: Coastal areas and inland lakes.
Nest: Scrape on the shore.
Eggs: 1–5, pale-coloured with darker blotches.
Food: Invertebrates and small vertebrates.

Lesser crested tern

Thalasseus bengalensis

The lesser crested tern's northern range extends as far as the Mediterranean, though its main centre of distribution is located within the tropics. It is less migratory than many tern species, with northern populations overwintering along the northern and north-western coast of Africa. Those terns encountered on the eastern coast of Africa, occurring as far south as Natal, migrate to this region from the Middle East. Outside the Mediterranean, breeding often occurs on coral islands, where the birds will be relatively safe from predators. Here, their large nesting colonies may comprise as many as 20,000 individuals. During breeding, lesser crested terns sometimes associate with other related species, and have even been recorded as hybridizing with sandwich terns (*Thalasseus sandvicensis*) on their European breeding grounds. They prefer to seek their food in sheltered bays rather than over the open sea, and will sometimes venture into estuarine waters.

Identification: Black top to the head, with a crest. Wings, rump and upper tail are grey, and the remainder of the plumage is white. Bill is slender and yellow in colour, while the legs are black. In winter plumage, the area of black on the head is reduced. Sexes are alike.

Distribution: Found along the north African coast and less commonly in the Gulf of Suez and the Red Sea, extending through the Indo-Pacific region to Australia. Occasionally seen in Europe.
Size: 40cm (16in).
Habitat: Mainly tropical areas of coast.
Nest: Scrape on the shore.
Eggs: 1–2, brownish with dark markings.
Food: Fish and crustaceans.

Black noddy (white-capped noddy, *Anous minutus*): 39cm (15in)
From the Gulf of Guinea, off Africa's west coast, across the Atlantic to the northern coast of South America and the eastern Caribbean. Also in the Pacific, north and east of Australia. All *Anous* noddies, which are members of the tern family, are similar in appearance. Whitish plumage extends from the bill across the crown. Remainder of the body is dark greyish, and the flight feathers are blackish. Sexes are alike.

Brown noddy (noddy tern, common noddy, *Anous stolidus*): 45cm (18in)
From the Gulf of Guinea across the Atlantic to the Caribbean. Also throughout the Indian Ocean and the Pacific, from the east coast of Africa to Hawaii and East Island. Dark chocolate-brown, with greyish-white on the crown and a narrow broken area of white plumage encircling the eyes. Long, pointed black bill, with black legs and feet. Young birds have a brown crown. Sexes are alike.

Lesser noddy (*Anous tenuirostris*): 34cm (13in)
Restricted to the Indian Ocean and Pacific, but mainly around Madagascar. Breeds on the Seychelles and Mascarene Islands, the Maldives, and the Houtman Abrolhos Islands, off the western coast of Australia. Relatively small, with a more extensive whitish area on the head, which extends down beneath the eyes. Greyish hindcrown and nape. Blackish-brown elsewhere. Young birds have more prominent white area on the head, and brownish bodies. Sexes are alike.

Little tern

Sternula albifrons

Little terns are adaptable breeders, nesting both on the coast and at some distance inland, where they choose spits and even grassy areas. They prefer mainland breeding sites rather than more isolated islands, and will associate in small groups of just a few pairs. Their diet is varied, with terrestrial invertebrates featuring significantly when breeding inland. Little terns undertake long migrations, with western European populations overwintering on the western coast of Africa, and eastern European birds heading to the opposite coast. They have a characteristic way of hovering when hunting over water, while on land they can hawk invertebrates directly off branches. They will also pick up worms from sandbanks or soil.

Identification: Prominent white forehead with black edges, which form a black cap that extends down the nape of the neck. The chest and underparts are white and the wings are grey, except for the black edges to the primary feathers. The bill is yellow with a black tip, and the legs are orangish-yellow. Sexes are alike.

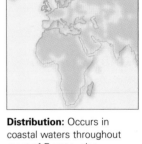

Distribution: Occurs in coastal waters throughout most of Europe, also breeding inland in central Europe. Overwinters in Africa. Present too in parts of southern Asia, ranging to Australia and New Zealand.
Size: 25cm (10in).
Habitat: Coastal areas and inland rivers.
Nest: Usually a bare scrape.
Eggs: 2–3, often brownish with darker markings.
Food: Fish and invertebrates.

SOUTHERN TERNS

Although terns are generally widespread around the globe, and often particularly well-travelled on migration, some are confined mainly to the southern hemisphere, rarely crossing the equator. Occasionally, breeding colonies of southern terns may include odd pairs of related species, which have joined up with them for the nesting period.

White tern

Gygis alba

These unmistakable terns have long flight feathers that reach to the tip of the tail when the wings are folded. They rarely venture to mainland areas, preferring to nest on remote tropical islands. Unlike most terns they do not choose a site on the ground, selecting instead a large leaf, such as that of a banana plant, often close to the trunk, where the egg will be relatively secure. This unusual behaviour in island-nesting birds, which instinctively lay on the ground, helps to protect their nests from introduced predators such as rats. In some parts of their range, notably on Ascension Island, where vegetation is scarce, pairs will breed on cliffs. Hatching takes about five weeks, and the single chick is equipped with strong claws that anchor it to its insecure nest site. It is reared mainly on small fish.

Identification: Predominantly pure white, but the African subspecies *G. a. candida* has a bluish-grey base to its otherwise black bill. Legs and feet are greyish. Sexes are alike.

Distribution: A population occurs in the vicinity of the Seychelles and Mascarenes, extending to the Indo-Pacific region. Also present off the coast of South-east Asia out across the Pacific, past Hawaii reaching western Mexico, and possibly extending down as far as western Colombia.
Size: 30cm (12in).
Habitat: Coral islands.
Nest: Lays on branches.
Eggs: 1, greyish-white with dark markings.
Food: Mainly eats fish and marine invertebrates.

Antarctic tern

Sterna vittata

Confined to the far south as their name suggests, Antarctic terns nest on remote islands during the brief summer, flying north to the southern coastal tip of Africa, where they will overwinter. Here they are most likely to be observed along craggy stretches of coastline. Ringing studies have helped to unravel the movements of the different populations of Antarctic tern, and have also revealed them to be relatively long-lived birds. One individual rung on the south-western Cape was eventually recaptured by ornithologists on Gough Island, close to the Antarctic, around 18 years later. Their survival may be due in part to their adaptability, since their feeding habits alter depending on the prevailing weather conditions. Antarctic terns avoid diving when the sea is rough, preferring instead to scoop up food from the surface.

Identification: Black cap, from the base of the upper bill over the head to the nape of the neck, including the eyes. White forehead (white streaking on the crown in non-breeding). Rest of the face is white. Lower back and forked tail are white, as are the lower underparts. Throat, chest and wings pale grey. Bill bright red, with darker legs and feet. Sexes are alike. Young birds have a black bill and legs, with barring when seen from below.

Distribution: Extends from the Antarctic north to the southern tip of South Africa. Other populations extend from Antarctica north to the Falklands and south-eastern South America, and also to New Zealand.
Size: 40cm (16in).
Habitat: Mostly rocky areas, including cliffs.
Nest: Scrape on the ground.
Eggs: 1–2, whitish-coloured with dark markings.
Food: Fish and crustaceans.

Sooty tern

Onychoprion fuscatus

Throughout their range, sooty terns seek out inaccessible islands on which to breed, where they can nest in relative safety. They congregate in large colonies, with nesting pairs often less than 50cm (20in) apart. The breeding period varies according to location, typically beginning in June in the Seychelles but not until November further north. Pairs and offspring subsequently leave their island breeding grounds and spend up to three months over the oceans, before the adult terns head back to the colonies. It will be at least six years before the young return to breed. Remarkably, these terns cannot swim, and so are confined to an aerial existence, even to the extent of sleeping in flight. They often feed at night, scooping prey out of the water, but will also catch flying fish as they leap over the waves. Sooty terns have been known to live for over 30 years.

Identification: Black plumage extends from the base of the bill through the eyes, joining the black cap on the head which extends over the back and wings. The tail is black too, and deeply forked. The underparts are white, and the bill and legs are black. Young birds have blackish-brown upperparts, and are greyish-brown below. Sexes are alike.

Distribution: Two separate populations exist. One extends from the Caribbean right across the Atlantic Ocean to the west coast of Africa, while the other is present along the eastern side of the continent from the Horn of Africa to below Madagascar. Also ranges from South-east Asia into the Pacific Ocean.
Size: 45cm (18in).
Habitat: Oceanic islands.
Nest: Lays on the ground.
Eggs: 1, whitish-coloured with dark markings.
Food: Fish and squid.

Whiskered tern (*Chlidonias hybrida*): 27cm (11in)
Southern Africa to Asia, south to Australia. Cock has a black cap and grey body, except for white on the sides of the face. In non-breeding, this area is speckled, and the underparts are white. Sexes are alike, but hens smaller. Young are buff on the sides of the face, grey on the hindneck.

Kerguelen tern (*Sterna virgata*): 33cm (13in)
Restricted to Kerguelen, Marion, Prince Edward and Crozet Islands in the southern Indian Ocean. Similar to Antarctic tern, but has pale grey rather than white tail, and white on the upperparts is confined to the lower back. Grey on the body, the chest especially being darker.

Damara tern (*Sternula balaenarum*): 23cm (9in)
Endemic to south-western Africa, from Namibia to the eastern Cape. Similar to little tern, with a black cap on the head in breeding plumage. Wings are pale grey and the underparts white. Black bill, legs and feet. Sexes are alike.

Royal tern (*Thalasseus maximus*): 51cm (20in)
East African coast, winters in Namibia, breeds in the Gulf of Guinea. Separate population in the Americas, centred on Central America and the Caribbean. Large, with black on the head encompassing the eyes, and plumes on the nape of the neck. Underparts white, back and wings light grey. Bill orange-red. Black legs and feet. Sexes are alike. Young have a grey hindcrown, yellow legs and feet.

Black tern

Chlidonias niger

The change in coloration between this species' breeding and non-breeding plumage is unique among terns. In Europe they breed in wetland areas far from the coast, with nesting colonies often comprising fewer than 20 pairs. The nest is made of vegetation, built on a bed of reeds, directly above the water. If a sitting bird is disturbed by a predator, other members of the colony will make no attempt to swoop down and harry the intruder. Black terns feed largely on insects while nesting, though will also catch fish and other vertebrates, usually without diving into the water. In August the terns migrate south, the majority heading to the west coast of Africa. Young birds remain behind another month, building up their strength before undertaking the journey.

Distribution: From southern Scandinavia to Spain, with the mainland European population extending into Asia. Mostly winters along the west coast of Africa. Also found inland in the Nile valley. Distinct American population.
Size: 28cm (11in).
Habitat: Coastal areas, marshland and lakes.
Nest: Made of vegetation.
Eggs: 2–3, olive-brown with dark markings.
Food: Both vertebrates and invertebrates.

Identification: Black head and chest, greyer back and wings, with a white vent. Hens may be greyer overall. Bill black, legs and feet reddish-black. Non-breeding: much of the head is white, as are the underparts, with black on the sides of the breast. Young have a brownish forehead suffusion.

CORMORANTS AND SHAGS

Widely distributed around the world, and particularly in the southern hemisphere, these coastal seabirds are not only restricted to the marine environment. A few species inhabit freshwater, and some will move inland if fishing opportunities are better, which has brought them into conflict with anglers. Others are found only on tiny islands lying to the south of Africa.

Cormorant

Great cormorant *Phalacrocorax carbo*

This is the most common species, although there are disagreements about certain races. The isolated South African form *P. c. lucidus* ('white-breasted cormorant') is often regarded as a distinct species since it differs markedly in appearance, with a more extensive white throat extending on to the upper chest, and dark, greenish-black wing plumage. Cormorants can be seen in habitats ranging from the open sea to inland freshwater lakes, where they are despised by fishermen, as they prey on their quarry, diving and chasing the fish underwater. Although they nest colonially in a wide variety of sites, it is not uncommon to see odd individuals perched on groynes and similar places. While human persecution and oil spillages represent dangers, these cormorants can have a life-expectancy approaching 20 years.

Identification: Predominantly black once adult, with a white throat area. A white patch is present at the top of each leg in birds in breeding condition. Some regional variations. Bluish skin around the eyes. Bill is horn-coloured at its base and dark at the tip. Sexes are alike. Young birds are brownish with paler underparts.

Distribution: Scandinavia and the British Isles southwards via the Iberian peninsula, through the Mediterranean, and on to north-western Africa. May occur in southern Africa. Range also extends to North America, southern Asia and Australia.
Size: 94cm (37in).
Habitat: Mainly coastal, sometimes inland.
Nest: Made of seaweed and other flotsam.
Eggs: 3–4, chalky white.
Food: Largely fish.

Common shag

European shag Green cormorant *Phalacrocorax aristotelis*

These shorebirds range over a wide area, but in contrast to the more common cormorant they very rarely venture into reservoirs or other freshwater areas. They also shy away from artificial structures such as harbour piers, roosting instead on cliffs and rocky stacks. Young birds may disperse far from where they hatched, especially those of the more northerly populations, but are likely to return in due course to breed in the same area. However, younger birds command only the less favourable sites, often around the perimeter of the nesting colony. The common shag's breeding season varies according to latitude, typically not commencing until March in the far north of its range, by which time the northern African population will have almost ceased nesting. The number and size of colonies fluctuates quite significantly, depending on the availability of food. Common shags catch fish underwater, diving to pursue their quarry, but unlike some cormorants never appear to hunt co-operatively.

Identification: Black with a slight greenish suffusion to the plumage, and an upturned crest on the head. Iris is blue. The bill is dark grey with a bare yellowish area of skin at its base. Legs dark grey. Non-breeding adults lose their crest and display mottled brown coloration on the throat. Sexes are alike. Young birds are entirely brown.

Distribution: Ranges around much of coastal Iceland and eastwards along the northern Scandinavian coast, south around the British Isles and the North Sea, around coastal Europe and through the Mediterranean to the Black Sea and northern Africa.
Size: 80cm (32in).
Habitat: Coastal areas.
Nest: Made of seaweed with a grass lining.
Eggs: 3–5, a chalky, bluish-white colour.
Food: Mainly fish.

Crowned cormorant

Microcarbo coronatus

The crowned cormorant's distribution falls within that of the Cape cormorant (*Phalacrocorax capensis*), and both populations are sustained by the food-rich Benguela current which nourishes fish stocks in this region, some 10km (6.25 miles) offshore. There are very distinct differences in their feeding preferences however, since the crowned cormorants prefer to catch slower-swimming fish and a higher percentage of marine invertebrates, often quite close to the shoreline in the tidal zone, making them much easier to observe. They also breed in far smaller groups than Cape cormorants, with colonies usually comprising fewer than 150 pairs. This means they can occupy smaller sites, and will even take the opportunity to nest on wrecked ships close to this treacherous stretch of the African coastline. Crowned cormorants are relatively scarce birds, and their population probably consists of no more than 6,000 individuals, although there is no evidence that they have declined in numbers over recent years.

Identification: Relatively conspicuous crest above the bill. Overall body plumage is blackish, with no lighter areas over the wings. Reddish eyes and facial skin. Sexes are alike in colour, but hens are smaller. Young birds are a browner shade.

Distribution: Restricted to the south-western coast of Africa, extending from Namibia down to Cape Agulhas in South Africa.
Size: 55cm (22in).
Habitat: Coasts, especially rocky areas.
Nest: Made from seaweed and flotsam.
Eggs: 2–4, chalky-white.
Food: Fish and invertebrates.

Pygmy cormorant (*Microcarbo pygmeus*): 55cm (22in)
Restricted to parts of south-eastern Europe and adjacent areas of Asia, including parts of Italy and Turkey, extending to the Aral Sea. Still recorded occasionally in Israel but extinct in Algeria. Relatively small. Predominantly black with a fairly indistinct crest and a long neck. Browner overall out of breeding condition, with paler, silvery coloration across the wings. Yellow bill. Sexes are alike but hens smaller. Young birds have whitish underparts.

Crozet shag (*Leucocarbo melanogenis*): 70cm (27¹/₂in)
Confined to Crozet and nearby Prince Edward Island, lying to the south-east of Africa in the southern Indian Ocean. Black and white, with a black crest in breeding condition. White extends from the throat down the sides of the neck to the underparts and vent. Narrow white band evident across each wing, with black on the sides of the flanks, extending to the legs. Legs are pink, as are the feet. Blue skin encircles the eyes, with white plumes on the sides of head. Sexes are alike. Young birds are brownish rather than black, with no white on the wings.

Heard Island shag (*Leucocarbo nivalis*): 77cm (30in)
Present only on Heard Island, which lies south-east of mainland Africa. Piebald, with similar patterning to the Crozet shag (above), but is much larger and has broad white wing patches. Also has more extensive white plumage on the sides of the face. Crest absent in non-breeding birds. Sexes are alike. Young birds have brownish upperparts.

Cape cormorant

Phalacrocorax capensis

These highly social cormorants generally nest in the southern spring, commencing in September, with pairs occupying cliffs and breeding at very high densities. The largest colonies may consist of over 100,000 pairs. This species is the most common of all cormorants occurring off the coasts of southern Africa. However, in the past the population has plummeted in some years, due to a collapse in pilchard stocks, which are a major source of food for them. Fortunately, there are now signs that the birds are taking other pelagic fish and invertebrates, and so are less dependent on this one food source. Cape cormorants feed in large flocks, sometimes consisting of hundreds if not thousands of individuals, diving underwater to catch their quarry. In some areas their numbers have increased following the provision of suitable platforms that the cormorants use for nesting. Like their neighbour, the Cape gannet, the bird's droppings, or *guano*, are then collected and processed into fertilizer.

Distribution: From Namibia around the Cape, reaching Algoa Bay. May extend north to Angola on the west coast, and up to Mozambique outside the breeding period.
Size: 65cm (25¹/₂in).
Habitat: Coastal areas, but rarely inland.
Nest: Made from seaweed and flotsam.
Eggs: 2–5, chalky-white.
Food: Predominantly fish.

Identification: Black overall, with distinctive bright blue eyes and a short tail. The skin at the base of the bill is a bright shade of yellow, while the bill itself is greyish. Legs are dark grey. Non-breeding adults have greyer plumage, with paler head feathering. Sexes are alike.

COASTAL WANDERERS

Some wading birds undertake regular migrations from Europe to Africa, usually following the land rather than flying across the ocean. Others occasionally crop up unexpectedly, typically having crossed the Atlantic from North America, perhaps having been blown off course. Such individuals are described as vagrants, since their presence cannot be guaranteed.

Red-necked phalarope

Northern phalarope *Phalaropus lobatus*

Distribution: Circumpolar, breeding throughout the Arctic, with the European population overwintering further south in the Arabian Sea region.
Size: 20cm (8in)
Habitat: Tundra and shore.
Nest: Scrape on the ground.
Eggs: 3-4, buff-coloured with brown spots.
Food: Mostly plankton and invertebrates.

These long-distance migrants fly north to breed in the Arctic region from late May onwards, frequently choosing sites well away from the coast. The ground here is boggy at this time of year, since only the top layer of soil thaws out and the meltwater is unable to drain away. Insects reproduce readily in these standing pools, providing a ready source of food for the phalaropes on which they can rear their chicks. Unusually, both incubation and rearing are undertaken by the male alone. Having laid their eggs, the hens depart the breeding grounds soon afterwards, followed by the males about a month later, once the chicks are independent. The young will be the last to leave. Red-necked phalaropes head south across Europe to their wintering grounds, breaking their journey by stopping off in Kazakhstan and around the Caspian Sea, where they can be observed feeding on lakes, before flying on through the Gulf of Oman to the Arabian sea.

Identification: Cocks duller than hens, with reduced chestnut-orange to the chest and whiter throat. Underparts whitish, grey barring on the flanks. Dark wings (less streaked in cocks). Long, pointed bill. Blackish legs and feet. Young birds have brown rather than black crowns.

Red phalarope

Grey phalarope *Phalaropus fulicarius*

Identification: Breeding hens have reddish underparts, black on top of head, and white cheek patches. Cocks are less vivid. In winter, the head is mainly white with black near the eyes, and the back is grey with a black strip reaching to the tail. Young have orangish chest band.

This phalarope is tied very closely to the ocean, but may be seen on inland water after severe storms. Unlike all other waders, it always migrates over the oceans rather than land. In its North American range it occurs predominantly along the Pacific coast, with peak numbers being seen here in the fall. They are often sighted in the company of whales, feeding on the skin parasites of these marine mammals. Red phalaropes congregate in areas where plankton is present, which provides them with rich feeding. They feed close to the water surface, sometimes dipping down with their strong bills to obtain food. In their breeding grounds in the far north the female leaves after egg-laying, sometimes seeking another partner. Male red phalaropes hatch and rear the young alone.

Distribution: Breeds in Iceland. Migrates south with other populations from Greenland and eastern North America, either to the west African coast or right down to the south-western coast.
Size: 22cm (8½in).
Habitat: Arctic tundra, coast and ocean.
Nest: Scrape on the ground.
Eggs: 2–4, buff-olive with dark spots.
Food: Invertebrates and fish.

Slender-billed curlew (*Numenius tenuirostris*): 41cm (16in) (E)
Now extremely rare, possibly due to changes in habitat. Formerly overwintered in north-western Africa, having migrated there from Siberia. Now occasionally sighted in Morocco, although vagrants are appearing in Italy. Shorter in stature than the curlew, with more evident white plumage on the underparts. A white stripe may also be present on the head. Characteristic short, slender bill. Young birds have mottled, rather than streaked, flanks. Sexes are alike.

Lesser yellowlegs (*Tringa flavipes*): 27cm (10¹/₂in)
Typically breeds in the far north of North America, wintering in Florida and further south in Central America, but vagrants are recorded annually off the British Isles. Narrow black bill, with dark streaking on the chest and white underparts. The back and wings are mottled and the flight feathers are dark. Characteristic yellow legs. Young birds have buff spotting on brown upperparts. Sexes are alike.

Greater yellowlegs (*Tringa melanoleuca*): 36cm (14in)
Another northern American vagrant sighted around the British Isles, usually during the winter. Larger than the lesser yellowlegs, with a longer, darker bill that curves slightly upwards towards its tip. More barring also evident on the underparts in breeding plumage. Young birds have darker backs. Sexes are alike.

Whimbrel

Numenius phaeopus

The relatively large size of the whimbrel makes it conspicuous among smaller waders. Although it may probe for food, it often snatches crabs scampering across the sand. In their tundra nesting grounds whimbrels have a more varied diet, eating berries and insects too. Both adults help to incubate and raise the young. They begin their migration journey south in July, when they can often be seen flying over land, seeking out inland grassy areas, such as golf courses, in search of food. Unusually, some whimbrels may avoid land, flying directly from Iceland to Africa over the Atlantic Ocean. It is not uncommon for young birds to remain here for their first year, before returning north again.

Distribution: In Europe, breeds mainly in Iceland and Scandinavia. Overwinters from the western Mediterranean and around the coast of Africa, including Madagascar, and on smaller islands in the Indian Ocean.
Size: 45cm (17¹/₂in).
Habitat: Tundra and shore.
Nest: Grass-lined scrape.
Eggs: 4, olive-coloured with dark blotches.
Food: Mostly invertebrates and berries.

Identification: Brown crown with lighter central stripe. Fainter brown line through eyes. Brown streaks on silvery background on rest of body. Back and wings darker brown. Long, down-curving bill. Sexes are alike. Young have shorter, straighter bill.

Curlew

Eurasian curlew *Numenius arquata*

The distinctive call-note of the curlew, which gives rise to its name, is audible from some distance away. This wader's large size and its long, narrow bill also help to distinguish it from other shorebirds, and its legs are so long that the toes protrude beyond the tip of the tail in flight. Curlews are most likely to be seen in coastal areas outside the breeding season, where they feed by probing in the sand with their bills. They return to the same wintering grounds each year, and can live for more than 30 years.

Identification: Streaked plumage, with lighter ground colour on the throat and buff chest. Larger dark patterning on the wings. Underparts and rump are white. Cocks have plain-coloured heads, but hens' heads usually show a trace of a white stripe running down over the crown. Hens are also distinguished by their longer bills, which can be up to 15cm (6in) in length. When not breeding, the curlew has grey rather than buff plumage.

Distribution: Present throughout the year in the British Isles and adjacent areas of northern Europe. Also breeds widely elsewhere in Europe and Asia, migrating south to the Mediterranean and Africa in winter.
Size: 57cm (22in).
Habitat: Marshland, moorland and coastal areas.
Nest: Scrape on the ground concealed by vegetation.
Eggs: 4, greenish-brown with darker spots.
Food: Omnivorous.

NORTHERN WADERS

Many waders that breed in northern parts of Europe are only temporary residents. They fly south in the winter, when their nesting grounds are likely to be covered in snow. Having bred inland in many cases, this is when they can be sighted on the shoreline. Some however, such as the crab-plover, choose to move within their more southerly ranges without being subjected to climatic pressures.

Crab-plover

Dromas ardeola

This aberrant plover is the only member of its family, and displays a number of unusual habits. It uses its heavy bill to catch the crabs that form the bulk of its diet, often grabbing them out of their burrows and killing them with blows from its bill. The bill has another important function: it is also used as a digging tool to construct their underground nesting burrow. The tunnel sometimes extends back as far as 2.5m (8ft) before widening into the nesting chamber. Crab-plovers are the only waders to nest underground. Young crab-plovers remain dependent on the adults for food, not only while they are in the nest but also for some time after leaving. This is probably a reflection of their very specialized diet. Adults have to be very adept at catching crabs, and this is a skill that the young have to learn if they are to survive. This level of parental care helps to explain why they usually lay only a single egg.

Identification: White body with an area of black down the back, even when the wings are closed. Flight feathers also black. Long legs are greyish, and the large, heavy bill is black. Young birds are brownish on the head and over the wing coverts. Sexes are alike.

Distribution: African distribution centred on the continent's east coast, breeding as far south as Tanzania, in coastal areas of Madagascar and on smaller islands. Also present to the Red Sea region and western India, migrating eastwards as far as Thailand.
Size: 40cm (16in).
Habitat: Coastal areas.
Nest: Underground tunnel.
Eggs: 1-2, white.
Food: Crustaceans, but particularly crabs.

Ringed plover

Common ringed plover *Charadrius hiaticula*

In spite of their relatively small size, these waders have strong migratory instincts. They are most likely to be seen in Europe during May, en route to their breeding grounds in the far north, and then again from the middle of August for about a month, before finally leaving European shores to make their way south to Africa for the winter. Ringed plovers typically breed on beaches and on the tundra, the mottled appearance of their eggs and the absence of an elaborate nest providing camouflage. They can be seen in reasonably large flocks outside the nesting season, often seeking food in tidal areas.

Identification: Black mask extends over the forehead and down across the eyes. There is a white patch above the bill and just behind the eyes. A broad black band extends across the chest. The underparts are otherwise white. The wings are greyish-brown and the bill is orange with a black tip. In winter plumage the black areas are reduced, apart from the bill, which becomes entirely blackish. White areas extend from the forehead to above the eyes. Cheek patches are greyish-brown, and there is a similar band on the upper chest. Sexes are alike.

Distribution: Along most of western and northern coastal Europe, and North America. Winters around much of continental Africa. Also recorded in parts of Asia.
Size: 19cm (7¹/₂in).
Habitat: Coasts and tundra.
Nest: Scrape on the ground.
Eggs: 4, stone-buff with black markings.
Food: Freshwater and marine invertebrates.

Terek sandpiper

Xenus cinereus

From April onwards, these small sandpipers can be seen on their northern breeding grounds, where the ground is boggy and there is an abundance of midges which form the bulk of their diet. Pairs normally produce a single clutch of eggs, with their offspring developing rapidly and becoming independent just two weeks after hatching. The exodus south to their winter coastal areas begins in July. It is thought that the Finnish population, at the western edge of their breeding range, fly directly to the south-western coast of Africa. Here, Terek sandpipers are to be seen darting around the shoreline, and enjoying a much more varied diet. They use their bills both to grab and to probe for invertebrates, on land and in shallow water, preferring to feed when the tide is out. They are very agile, able to move quickly to snap up prey before it can escape. Their unusual name derives from the Terek River, which flows into the Caspian Sea.

Identification: Brownish head and back, darker streaking on the breast. Underparts white, with contrasting black markings on the wings. Greyer tone to the upperparts in non-breeding. Bill long, brownish and upturned. Legs and feet slightly orange, more yellowish in young birds. Sexes are alike.

Distribution: Isolated population in Finland. Winters around much of coastal Africa and Madagascar, extending to parts of Asia and Australia. Also breeds throughout Asia.
Size: 25cm (10in).
Habitat: Inland and coasts.
Nest: Scrape on the ground lined with vegetation.
Eggs: 2–5, greenish-brown with dark spots.
Food: Midges and other invertebrates.

Black-winged stilt (*Himantopus himantopus*): 36cm (14in)
Southern Europe, overwinters in Africa. Top of the head to the nape is blackish. Ear coverts are black. Back and wings jet black, underparts are white. Long black bill. Legs are very long and red. Sexes are similar, but hens lack dark head markings and the back is more brownish.

Sanderling (*Calidris alba*): 20cm (8in)
Breeds in the Arctic. Seen in Europe on migration and during the winter. Breast is rufous with black speckling. Underparts white. Back and wings are grey with black and buff markings. In winter, rufous markings less evident, but a broad wing bar with black edging is seen in flight. Sexes alike.

Red knot (*Calidris canutus*): 25cm (10in)
Breeds in the Arctic, migrates south to northern Africa. Distinctive rufous underparts, with black and rufous speckling on the wings offset against areas of grey. Black legs and grey upperparts. In winter, has streaking on the head, chest and flanks, greyish-white underparts and grey-green legs. Sexes are alike.

Purple sandpiper (*Calidris maritima*): 22cm (9in)
Iceland to Scandinavia and further north. Winters around the British Isles and from Scandinavia to the Iberian peninsula. Whitish stripe above each eye, with a dark brown area behind. Chestnut and brown markings on the dark wings. Brown streaking extending down the neck and over the underparts, which become whiter. Slightly down-curving, dark bill and yellowish legs. Young birds have brownish-grey breast with spots. In non-breeding, distinctive purplish suffusion over the back. Sexes are alike but hens are larger.

Stone-curlew

Thick-knee *Burhinus oedicnemus*

The stone-curlew is a wader that has adapted to a relatively dry environment, and its mottled plumage enables it to blend in well against a stony background. When frightened, it drops to the ground in an attempt to conceal its presence. These birds are frequently active after dark, when they will be much more difficult to observe. However, their loud call-notes, which sound rather like "curlee", are audible over distances of 2.5km (1.5 miles) when the surroundings are quiet. Occasionally, stone-curlews living close to coastal areas fly to mudflats, feeding when the flats are exposed by the sea.

Distribution: Breeds in various locations throughout western and southern Europe, but not as far as Scandinavia. Ranges into southern Asia and south to parts of northern Africa.
Size: 45cm (18in).
Habitat: Open and relatively dry countryside.
Nest: Scrape on the ground.
Eggs: 2, pale buff with dark markings.
Food: Invertebrates, typically caught at night.

Identification: Streaked plumage on the neck, upper breast and wings, with prominent white stripes above and below the eyes. White wing bars edged with black are also apparent on the wings. Abdomen and throat are whitish. Long, thick yellowish legs. Bill is mainly blackish, but yellow at the base. Sexes are alike. There is variation among races, with some having a greyer tint to their feathers.

OYSTERCATCHERS AND OTHER WADERS

Identifying waders is not always straightforward since a number of species moult into breeding plumage, transforming their appearance. While it may be possible to determine the sexes visually during the nesting period, it may be very difficult after a further moult. The situation becomes even more confusing as the young typically have different plumage from the adult birds.

Eurasian oystercatcher

Haematopus ostralegus

Their large size and noisy nature ensure these waders are quite conspicuous. The Eurasian oystercatcher's powerful bill is a surprisingly adaptable tool, enabling the birds not only to force mussel shells apart but also to hammer limpets off groynes and even prey on crabs. When feeding inland, the oystercatchers use their bills to catch earthworms in the soil without any difficulty. Individuals will defend favoured feeding sites such as mussel beds from others of their own kind, although they sometimes form large flocks numbering thousands of birds, especially during the winter.

Identification: The head, upper chest and wings are black. Underparts are white, and there is a white stripe on the wings. It has a prominent, straight orangish-red bill, which may be shorter and thicker in cock birds. Legs are reddish. In winter plumage, adults have a white throat and collar, and pale pink legs. Sexes are alike.

Distribution: Shores of Europe, especially Great Britain, extending to Asia and down the north-western and Red Sea coasts of Africa.
Size: 44cm (17in).
Habitat: Tidal mudflats, sometimes in fields.
Nest: Scrape on the ground.
Eggs: 2–4, light buff with blackish-brown markings.
Food: Cockles, mussels and similar prey.

Avocet

Pied avocet *Recurvirostra avosetta*

The unique shape of the avocet's long, thin, upward-curving bill enables these birds to feed by sweeping the bill from side to side in the water, locating their prey predominantly by touch. Pairs can display very aggressive behaviour when breeding, and in some areas may gather in very large numbers, nesting at high densities. Although they usually move about by wading, avocets can swim well and will place their heads under water when seeking food. On migration, avocets fly quite low in loose lines. Birds from western areas tend to be quite sedentary, while those occurring further east will usually overwinter in Africa as well as the Mediterranean region.

Identification: Slender, with long, pale blue legs. White overall, with black plumage on the top of the head extending down to the nape of the neck. Black stripes extend over the shoulder area and around the sides of the wings. Flight feathers are black. Long, thin black bill curves upwards at the tip. Hens often have shorter bills and a brownish tinge to their black markings.

Distribution: Throughout Europe (except in the far north) and northern Africa, often close to the coast. Range extends into western Asia. Some winter in Africa.
Size: 46cm (18in).
Habitat: Mostly lagoons and mudflats.
Nest: Scrape on the ground lined with vegetation.
Eggs: 4, pale brown with faint markings.
Food: Small crustaceans and other invertebrates.

Black-tailed godwit

Limosa limosa

Grassland areas are favoured by these godwits for breeding. Egg-laying begins in April, with established pairs returning to the same nesting sites, which are out in the open rather than concealed in tall grass. The adults share incubation, which lasts about three weeks, but the chicks are largely brooded by the female. They fledge within five weeks, after which the godwits migrate to their winter quarters, where the young may remain until their second year. Black-tailed godwits can adapt to habitat change, and in the 20th century returned to breed in Britain, where they were formerly extinct. When feeding in water they may vibrate their feet to disturb aquatic invertebrates, including larvae, and in muddy water snails may be found by touch. In Africa they often feed mainly on vegetation.

Identification: Dark stripe runs through each eye, with a white streak above. Pale sides to the face. Chestnut on the neck and upper breast, becoming mottled with black streaks on the lower chest. Underparts white, but some regional variation. Wings brownish-grey with individual blackish markings. Long, narrow bill, pinkish at the base and dark at the tip. Legs are black. Chestnut is missing from both sexes in non-breeding plumage. Hens are less brightly-coloured than cocks. Young birds have no barring across their underparts.

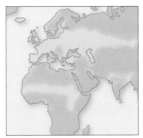

Distribution: Breeding range extends from Iceland and southern Scandinavia through much of western and central Europe into Asia. Western population overwinters in parts of the British Isles and the Iberian Peninsula. Others move further south into Africa, Asia and Australia.
Size: 44cm (17in).
Habitat: Coast and marshes.
Nest: Pad of vegetation.
Eggs: 3–5, greenish-brown with dark blotches.
Food: Mainly invertebrates.

African oystercatcher (*Haematopus moquini*): 45cm (18in)
Lobito Bay, Angola southwards as far as Natal. Jet black, with a bare red area of skin encircling each eye. Long, relatively narrow red bill. Legs and feet also red. Sexes are alike, but hen's bill is slightly longer. Young birds are browner overall.

Common redshank (*Tringa totanus*): 27cm (10½in)
Iceland, Scandinavia, British Isles and central Europe. Migrates to the Mediterranean. Greyish head and wings, with striations and mottling on the chest, back and wings. White area in front of each eye. Bill is red with a dark tip. Legs bright red. Non-breeding: body a more even shade of brownish-grey. Sexes are alike. Young birds have yellowish-orange legs and feet.

Broad-billed sandpiper (*Calidris falcinellus*): 17cm (7in)
Scandinavia, wintering in eastern Africa. Rare sightings in western Europe. Asian population winters along the southern coast of Asia, reaching Australia. Black spot in front of the eyes, with streaking on the crown. Dark plumage with pale edging on the wings. Triangular-shaped streaking on the sides of the body. Rest of underparts white. In non-breeding, much paler grey. Bill is blackish. Legs and feet yellowish-grey. Sexes are alike. Young birds are brownish on the back.

Bar-tailed godwit

Limosa lapponica

These godwits fly long distances to and from their breeding grounds. Studies have shown that birds observed in western Europe during the winter are most likely to have come from as far east as the Yamal peninsula. Those overwintering in southern Africa will have originated from further into Asia, their journey entailing crossing the Caspian sea. It is estimated that nearly three-quarters of a million bar-tailed godwits undertake this annual journey to Africa, after the end of the breeding season in late July or August. It is possible to gain an insight into the gender of individual birds by watching a flock feeding on an outgoing tide, as hens, with their longer bills, are better equipped to feed in deeper water. The godwits favour estuarine rather than freshwater areas. Young birds remain on the wintering grounds for their first year, while the adult birds head back north again in May.

Distribution: Scandinavia and northern Asia to Alaska. Winters in British Isles and western Europe to Africa.
Size: 16cm (6in).
Habitat: Tundra and coasts.
Nest: Lined scrape.
Eggs: 2–5, greenish-brown with dark blotches.
Food: Mainly invertebrates.

Identification: Chestnut. Back has shades of brown with pale edging. Dark stripe runs through each eye; crown is also dark. Long, up-curved bill, paler at its base. Legs and feet grey. Hens have whitish underparts, with fine brownish striations on the chest and flanks. Both have barred tail and greyer underparts in non-breeding. Females are larger. Young birds have buff suffusion to the neck and upper breast.

DIVERS AND GREBES

These species are better known from northern latitudes. Divers as a group are not represented in Africa, whereas grebes range right down to the tip of South Africa. They are suited to their aquatic existence, preferring to swim rather than fly. It is not uncommon for them to carry their young on their backs, affording them some protection from predatory fish such as pike (Esox lucius).

Madagascan grebe

Tachybaptus pelzelni

Distribution: Restricted to the island of Madagascar, mainly in northern and western areas.
Size: 25cm (10in).
Habitat: Largely freshwater, with aquatic vegetation.
Nest: Platform of floating plant matter.
Eggs: 3–4, white, soon becoming stained.
Food: Fish and insects.

These grebes probably used to be more widely-distributed through their native island than is the case today, with the population now most common in northern and western areas. Assessing their numbers can be rather difficult, however, because they will spread out to occupy temporary areas of water, especially when breeding at the end of the wet season, from February onwards. They do face a number of threats to their existence, including the effects of water pollution, the conversion of some wetland areas into paddy fields, and fish farms where their presence is unwanted. Fears have also been expressed over the introduction of exotic and more aggressive fish to parts of the island, notably the black bass (*Micropterus salmoides*), as it is though that large individuals will prey on young grebes. Fish forms a far less significant part of their diet compared with other related species: the Madagascan grebes are much more insectivorous by nature.

Identification: Black on the top of the head, the back of the neck, down on to the chest and along the back. Whitish area on the lower cheeks with chestnut sides to the neck. Paler when not in breeding plumage. Bill yellowish, legs and feet greyish. Sexes are alike. Young birds have greyish-brown stripes on the head and neck.

Black-throated diver

Black-throated loon *Gavia arctica*

This species occurs in slightly more southerly locations than its red-throated relative, preferring the taiga (forested) area of northern Europe rather than the treeless tundra zone. However, it still has a circumpolar distribution, and is present in North America, but absent from Iceland and Greenland. The British Isles marks the southerly extent of the black-throated diver's breeding range. An estimated 150 pairs nest here during the summer, and numbers can rise significantly when they are joined by overwintering birds that have bred further north in Scandinavia. Solitary by nature, these divers seem especially vulnerable to any disturbance on their breeding grounds. As their name suggests, they seek their food largely underwater, diving to depths of up to 6m (20ft) in search of fish, including freshwater species such as sticklebacks and marine species such as herring.

Identification: In breeding condition, has a distinctive grey head and neck, and a black throat with conspicuous white stripes running down the sides of the neck. Underparts are white, with finer black striping on the sides of the upper breast. Back and wings are predominantly black, with prominent areas of white barring and spotting. Bill, legs and feet black. Remaining upperparts are brownish-grey with a white area on the flanks. Sexes are alike. Young birds resemble adults out of colour.

Distribution: Scandinavia and the far north of Europe and Asia. Overwinters to northern Scandinavia, the British Isles and down to northern Spain. Also in the northern Mediterranean, and in the Black and Caspian seas.
Size: 65cm (25½in).
Habitat: Freshwater lakes and sheltered coastal areas.
Nest: Plant matter by water.
Eggs: 1–3, olive-brown with darker spots.
Food: Fish, some invertebrates and vegetation.

Black-necked grebe

Podiceps nigricollis

Black-necked grebes are frequently observed over the winter period on large stretches of water. They are especially social at this time of year, and can often be found in the company of other birds such as black-headed gulls (*Chroicocephalus ridibundus*). They also associate with their own kind during the breeding season. Although mostly seen on lakes, black-necked grebes also frequent similar habitats with dense aquatic vegetation around the edges of the water, which provides them with nesting cover. Their floating nests afford protection from land-based animals such as foxes (*Vulpes vulpes*), but the young chicks are still vulnerable to other dangers on fledging, including large predatory fish. Their down feathering is particularly dark on hatching, helping to distinguish them from related species. When migrating after the breeding season, black-necked grebes often associate in large groups, and may sometimes be seen in places where they are not regularly observed, such as the Canary Islands and Madeira.

Identification: Unmistakable in summer plumage, with a black head, neck and back and contrasting chestnut underparts. Golden ear tufts adjacent to the red eyes. Much duller in winter plumage, when chestnut areas are replaced by blackish-white coloration. A white area is present on the throat and sides of the neck. Sexes are alike. Young birds are similar, but have duller eyes and a faint yellowish hue at the rear of the neck.

Distribution: Migratory birds breed in Ireland, the Scottish borders and southern Scandinavia, wintering in western Europe. Others are resident further south, and through eastern Europe. Also in North America and Asia.
Size: 34cm (13in).
Habitat: Ponds and lakes, often coastal areas in winter.
Nest: Floating plant material.
Eggs: 3–4, brownish with darker markings.
Food: Invertebrates and fish.

Great crested grebe

Podiceps cristatus

Great crested grebes are primarily aquatic birds, and their flying ability is compromised by their short wings. They can dive very effectively, however, and often disappear underwater when they feel threatened. Rarely observed on land, these grebes are relatively cumbersome since their legs are located far back on the body, limiting their ability to move fast across open ground. Their toes are not fully webbed, unlike those of waterfowl, but they can swim quickly due to their streamlined body shape. They use their ruff-type facial feathers during display.

Distribution: Eastern parts of Europe, overwintering further south. Generally resident in western Europe. Occurs in parts of northern, eastern and southern Africa, and into Asia.
Size: 51cm (20in).
Habitat: Extensive reedy stretches of water.
Nest: Mound of reeds.
Eggs: 3–6, chalky-white.
Food: Fish and invertebrates.

Identification: Black from top of the head to the back. Brownish sides to the body in winter. In summer, has an extensive black crest, with a chestnut ruff at rear of head edged with black. Bill reddish pink. Sexes are alike.

Great northern diver (common loon, *Gavia immer*): 88cm (35in)
Icelandic and British coasts. Also North America and Greenland. Black head, with barring on the neck and throat. The back is patterned black and white, with white spots. Underparts are white. There is less contrast in the winter plumage, with white extending from the lower bill and throat down over the underparts. In winter, the eyes are dark rather than red. Sexes are alike.

Little grebe (*Tachybaptus ruficollis*): 29cm (11in)
Found in most of Europe on a line from southern Scotland southwards. Also in North Africa and the Middle East. Black head, chestnut patches on the neck and a yellow gape at the corners of the bill. Dark feathering on the back and wings, with brown flanks. In the winter, light buff plumage replaces darker areas. Sexes are alike.

Red-necked grebe (*Podiceps grisegena*): 46cm (18in)
Breeds in eastern Europe, and as far west as parts of Scandinavia. Overwinters primarily in coastal areas around the North Sea, and in the eastern Mediterranean. Black extends over the top of the head to the hind neck, forming a small crest. There is a narrow white band below this, with a prominent grey area on the throat. Sides of the neck and chest are chestnut-red. Back and wings blackish. Grey flanks and underparts. Bill black, yellow at the base. Out of colour, reddish plumage is greyish-white, with the grey of the throat reduced. Sexes are alike. Young birds display blackish streaking here.

LARGER WATERBIRDS

Although generally considered to be among the most spectacular of all of Africa's avifauna, the flamingos and pelicans found on this continent have distributions that actually extend further north into parts of Europe. They are conspicuous birds due to their large size and massive bills, and pelicans in particular have relatively bold natures, happily living alongside people.

Glossy ibis

Plegadis falcinellus

Groups of these ibises can be encountered in a wide range of environments, from rice fields to river estuaries, and they will often undertake extensive seasonal movements. They prefer to feed by probing into the mud with the tips of their sensitive bills, enabling them to grab prey easily even if the water is muddy. Occasionally they will dip their head under water when feeding. These birds may also use their long legs to pursue prey, such as snakes, on the ground. Glossy ibises nest colonially. The nest site is located low over the water, and fledglings sometimes fall victim to crocodiles lurking nearby as they leave the nest.

Identification: Dark brown overall, but with some white streaking on the head. The wings and rump are green. Legs and bill are dark. They are duller in colour when in non-breeding condition. Sexes are alike.

Distribution: Ranges over much of Africa. Extends from the Red Sea via northern India to eastern Asia. Also present in Australia, the Philippines and Indonesia.
Size: 66cm (26in).
Habitat: Shallow water.
Nest: Platform of sticks, built above water.
Eggs: 2–6, deep green to blue.
Food: Invertebrates, small vertebrates and crustaceans.

African sacred ibis

Threskiornis aethiopicus

These ibises are relatively bold by nature, and are not uncommonly seen in areas close to humans. During the breeding season, large numbers of African sacred ibises may congregate in suitable locations, building their bulky, platform-shaped nests in trees, often in the company of other birds. In more remote areas with dense vegetation they may occasionally nest on the ground. They are adaptable feeders, able to probe the mud in search of worms or seize small mammals running through the grass. They may even help to control plagues of locusts. Flocks of African sacred ibises may be observed scavenging on rubbish dumps, and will even raid the nests of crocodiles to feed on the eggs of these reptiles. Populations tend to be fairly sedentary, with breeding occurring during the wet season. In Egyptian mythology they were reputed to save the country from plagues and serpents.

Identification: Bare black head and neck. White body with fine black plumes extending over the lower back. Depending on race, flight feathers may have black tips and eye colour may vary. Legs, feet and bill black. Sexes are alike. Young birds are mottled black and white on the head.

Distribution: Most of Africa south of the Sahara, except for parts of the south-west. Also present on the Aldabras and Madagascar. .
Size: 75cm (29½in).
Habitat: Usually found close to water.
Nest: Made of vegetation off the ground.
Eggs: 2–3, greenish-white.
Food: Invertebrates, small mammals and carrion.

Greater flamingo

Phoenicopterus roseus

Occurring in huge flocks, these flamingos provide one of the most spectacular sights in the avian world. Even in flight they are unmistakable, flying in lines with their long necks and legs held horizontally (such groups are often referred to as "skeins"). At this time their calls are similar to the honking notes of geese. Flamingos feed by sieving microscopic crustaceans from the salt water using plates in their bills. It is this food source that gives the birds their distinctive reddish coloration. Greater flamingos breed communally on these salt pans, with the female constructing the raised, cone-shaped nest above the water. Their young hatch covered in greyish down, and are chaperoned in groups by the adult birds. Although usually seen wading, flamingos are able to swim if necessary. To get airborne, they run on the water's surface while beating their wings.

Distribution: Range extends from parts of France and southern Spain down through suitable habitat in Africa and the Red Sea region, and eastwards into Asia.
Size: 145cm (57in).
Habitat: Saline lagoons.
Nest: Built of mud.
Eggs: 1–2, white.
Food: Tiny crustaceans and other plankton.

Identification: The tallest of all flamingos. Relatively pale pink overall, with a pinkish bill with a dark tip. Flight feathers are of a more pronounced pinkish shade. Hens are significantly smaller, with shorter legs. Young birds change from brown to pink plumage over approximately three years.

Great white pelican

Pelecanus onocrotalus

Large and sociable, these pelicans are found on open stretches of water where they can fish easily. Each individual needs to catch about 1.2kg (2.6lb) of fish per day. The largest colony, comprising 80,000 birds on Tanzania's Lake Rukwa, requires approximately 35,000 tonnes per annum from this lake alone. The great white pelican is migratory in northern areas, breeding in Europe and overwintering in Africa. Pairs arrive in the Danube Delta from March, departing again by November. About 7,000 pelicans make this journey. They are vulnerable to pollution and overfishing, but may regularly fly long distances in search of food.

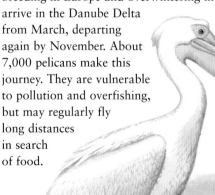

Distribution: Breeds from northern to eastern Europe. Present through much of eastern Europe, and south of the Sahara, but absent from south-eastern parts of the continent. Also present in parts of Asia.
Size: Males 175cm (69in); females 145cm (57in).
Habitat: Freshwater and brackish lakes.
Nest: Pile of vegetation on the ground.
Eggs: 1–2, chalky-white.
Food: Mainly fish.

Identification: Large stature. White plumage with black flight feathers. Yellow tinge to the breast when breeding, and a pinkish suffusion overall. Bare eye skin also becomes more pinkish in the male, and orange in the hen. Upper bill dark, yellow pouch beneath. Young birds are mostly greyish-brown.

Spot-breasted ibis (*Bostrychia rara*): 50cm (20in)
Central-western Africa, found in Liberia, Cameroon, Gabon and extending to Zaire and north-eastern Angola. Three very distinctive bluish areas adjacent to the base of the upper and lower bill and behind the eyes. Characteristic cinnamon-buff streaking, from the neck down to the underparts. The remaining plumage is dark, with a greenish iridescence over the wings. Relatively narrow red bill, legs and feet. Hen similar, but with a less brightly-coloured bill and facial spots. Young birds are similar to hens, but duller.

Olive ibis (*Bostrychia olivacea*): 70cm (27¹/₂in)
Scattered localities right across Africa, on each side of the Equator, from Sierra Leone and Liberia to Kenya and Tanzania. Distinctive black facial skin coloration, extending around the eyes to the base of the bill. Remainder of the head and neck greyish, with a shaggy crest at the back of the head, which is less prominent in young birds. Prominent iridescent green wing patches, with olive coloration evident here as well. Relatively short reddish bill, legs and feet. Sexes are alike.

RARER WETLAND BIRDS

In Europe especially, there has been increasing pressure over the years to drain marshland areas for agriculture or housing. This has had a severe effect on the avian species found in this habitat, greatly curtailing their numbers, and explains why such species are now often rarer in western rather than eastern Europe, where their habitat remains more intact.

White stork

Ciconia ciconia

Distribution: Summer visitor to much of mainland Europe. Winters in western and eastern parts of North Africa, depending on the flight path. Also occurs in Asia.
Size: 110cm (43in).
Habitat: Wetland areas.
Nest: Large platform of sticks off the ground.
Eggs: 3–5, chalky-white.
Food: Amphibians, fish, small mammals and invertebrates.

Considered a harbinger of good fortune, these birds often return each year to the same site, adding annually to their nest, which can become bulky. The return of the storks in April from their African wintering grounds helped to foster the widespread myth of the link between storks and babies. Their migration – over the Strait of Gibraltar and further east over the Bosphorus – is a spectacular sight. They fly with necks extended and legs trailing behind their bodies. The journey back to Africa begins in August.

Identification: Large, tall, mainly white bird with prominent black areas on the back and wings. Long red bill and red legs. Sexes are alike. Young birds are smaller and have a dark tip to the bill.

Great bittern

Eurasian bittern *Botaurus stellaris*

Bitterns are shy by nature, more likely to be heard than seen, thanks to the loud booming calls of cock birds at night as they try to attract mates. They are very patient hunters, relying on stealth to avoid detection before striking fast once their quarry is within reach.

Great bitterns are largely solitary by nature and form no strong pair bond, only coming together to mate. The female is solely responsible for incubating the eggs and rearing the chicks. Hatching takes 26 days, with the chicks fledging after eight weeks. In freezing weather northern bitterns will head to warmer latitudes, where they may be more conspicuous. The isolated South African race (*B. s. capensis*) is slightly darker in colour than its northern relative.

Identification: Relatively light, yellowish-brown colour overall, with variable black markings. A white streak is present under the throat, with dark areas on the top of the head and along the sides of the bill, which is yellowish, as are the legs and feet. Adult hens are paler than cocks. Markings of young birds are less defined on the upperparts.

Distribution: Breeds widely in eastern Europe, and is present in various parts of western Europe where suitable habitat exists. Also found in north-east and central Africa, with a separate population in southern Africa.
Size: 80cm (31in).
Habitat: Reedbeds.
Nest: Mat of vegetation in the reeds.
Eggs: 4–5, pale blue.
Food: Fish and other aquatic creatures.

Hamerkop

Scopus umbretta

The hamerkop's nest is an amazing structure. Usually built in a sturdy tree (although it may sometimes be located on the ground) it consists of up to 8,000 different components, all of which the birds collect locally. The construction process averages three to six weeks. Almost anything may be used for building the nest, including rubbish, plastic and discarded pieces of clothing. It is assembled very carefully, beginning with a platform that is then domed over with sticks and held in place by mud, acting rather like cement. A further covering of vegetation on top ensures that the inner chamber is largely impregnable. The hamerkops enter through a tunnel. Even more remarkably, studies have revealed that pairs routinely build three to five such nests every year. The reason is unclear, but other birds, especially waterfowl such as the African pygmy goose (*Nettapus auritus*), will often adopt the sites.

Distribution: Throughout the whole of Africa south of the Sahara, with the range extending to the south-west Arabian peninsula. Also present on Madagascar
Size: 56cm (22in).
Habitat: Wetland areas with nearby trees.
Nest: A massive mound of vegetation.
Eggs: 3–6, white.
Food: Primarily amphibians such as frogs, but also other aquatic creatures.

Identification: Greyish or brownish-grey overall, with a shaggy crest at the back of the head. Slight iridescence on the wings. Stocky, pointed black bill with similarly coloured legs and feet. Sexes are alike.

African openbill (*Anastomus lamelligerus*): 94cm (37in)
Occurs across Africa south of the Sahara, but absent from central-western and southern parts. Present on western Madagascar. Dark, greyish-black overall, with a greenish suffusion across the mantle and on the breast, appearing more purple or brown in some cases. Distinctive gap between the upper and lower bill can measure up to 6mm (0.2in) in adults, but not apparent in young birds. Dark greyish bill, legs and feet. Sexes are alike but cock birds larger.

Woolly-necked stork (*Ciconia episcopus*): 85cm (33½in)
Tropical Africa south of the Sahara. Absent from Madagascar. Dense white plumage on the neck, with a black area on top of the head. Grey sides to the face. Underparts, back and wings are blackish, with a purplish gloss. Bill dark at the base, red towards the tip. Legs and feet partially or wholly dark, depending on race. Sexes alike, but males are larger. Young birds dull brown.

Black stork (*Ciconia nigra*): 100cm (39in)
Breeds on the Iberian Peninsula and through eastern Europe to Asia. Overwinters in a band across Africa south of the Sahara, and also in southern Africa, where there is a resident population. Predominantly black, with purplish-green iridescence. White chest and underparts. Bare skin around the eyes; bill, legs and feet are red. Sexes alike, but cock birds are larger. Young birds have greenish bill, and are browner.

African jacana

Actophilornis africanus

The African jacana's long toes enable it to walk across aquatic vegetation. Unusually, it is the male that incubates the eggs and cares for the young. Hens mate and lay in the nest of one partner, before moving on to the next. The reason for this is unclear, but it may help to maximise the number of chicks reared. The jacanas' nests are at risk from flooding and predators during incubation, which lasts just over three weeks. The young will begin feeding themselves soon after hatching; however, it may be about seven weeks before they fly. During this time, they may be carried under the wing of the male parent, as shown here.

Distribution: Range extends throughout Africa south of the Sahara, although absent from the Horn.
Size: 30cm (12in).
Habitat: Wetlands such as lakes and ponds; occasionally the banks of sluggish rivers.
Nest: Platform made from floating vegetation.
Eggs: 2–5, tan-coloured with black markings.
Food: Invertebrates.

Identification: Chestnut body with a yellow area on the breast. The neck is white with a black streak running from the base of the bill to the crown and then down the back of the neck. Brilliant blue bill and frontal shield. Legs and feet are greyish. Hens larger than cocks. Young birds have white under-parts and no frontal shield.

SHY AND LONG-LIVED WATERBIRDS

Although waterbirds such as herons feed in a similar fashion to waders, probing with their bills, their larger size allows them to wander into deeper water in search of food. This affords them greater feeding opportunities, as well as enabling them to prey on larger fish. They are opportunistic feeders, however, and will take amphibians just as readily as fish.

Slaty egret

Egretta vinaceigula

Identification: Primarily greyish black, with a chestnut-red throat, and similar coloration at the top of the yellow legs. Bill blackish. Orange iris. Longer plumes on the back of the head in breeding condition. Sexes are alike. Young birds unknown.

The range and population of these egrets in southern Africa is not well-documented. The species formerly occurred in South Africa, but appears to have become extinct there, although there could be populations in both eastern parts of Angola and southern Zaire.

Whether they are resident birds is unclear, because slaty egrets may disperse over a wider area when faced with unfavourable environmental conditions. They hunt for food during the day, often on their own but sometimes in groups. They frequently breed in small colonies, often sharing with related species. Their nests may be in the branches of fig trees, or hidden in reedbeds, depending on the locality. They can be vulnerable to predators at this stage: African fish eagles (*Haliaeetus vocifer*) have been observed wiping out a relatively large breeding colony of these egrets in Namibia.

Distribution: Centred on the Okavango Delta, in Botswana, ranging into north-eastern Namibia. Also extends through northern Zimbabwe as far as Zambia's Bangweulu swamp.
Size: 60cm (24in).
Habitat: Swamp and marshland.
Nest: Made of sticks.
Eggs: 2–3, pale blue.
Food: Small fish, some invertebrates.

Eurasian spoonbill

Platalea leucorodia

Distribution: Breeds in northern temperate parts of Europe and Asia, as far east as China. Winters further south in tropical parts of Africa and South-east Asia. Indian birds are sedentary.
Size: 93cm (37in).
Habitat: Mudflats, marshes and shallow water.
Nest: Platform of sticks off the ground.
Eggs: 3–4, white with brown markings.
Food: Fish, other aquatic creatures and vegetation.

The enlarged surface area of these birds' bills enables them to feed more easily as they move their heads from side to side in the water. Young spoonbills, however, have a much narrower, light-coloured bill with no enlargement at the tip. They can also be identified in flight by the black tips to their outer flight feathers. It may be up to four years before they start nesting. Spoonbills can swim if they need to, but usually prefer to inhabit calm, shallow stretches of water. When resting, they may perch on one leg and tuck their bills over their backs, while in flight they will extend their necks. Spoonbills can live for nearly 30 years.

Identification: Highly distinctive and enlarged, yellow-edged, spoon-like tip to the black bill. Crest of feathers on the back of the neck, longer in the male, and an orange patch on the chest at breeding time. The rest of the feathering is white. Black legs.

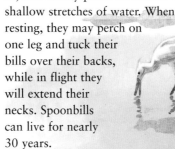

Grey heron

Ardea cinerea

These large, opportunistic hunters are often shy on the ground and can be difficult to spot. They are usually seen in flight, with their long necks tucked back on to their shoulders and their legs held out behind their bodies. They fly with relatively slow, quite noisy wing beats. Grey herons are very patient predators. They stand motionless, looking closely for any sign of movement in the water around them, then lunge quickly with their powerful bills to grab any fish or frog that swims within reach. During the winter, when their freshwater habitats are frozen, grey herons will often move to river estuaries in search of food. These birds frequently nest in colonies, and some breeding sites may be used for centuries by successive generations.

Identification: Powerful yellow bill. White head, with black above the eyes extending to long plumes off the back of the head. Long neck and chest are whitish with a black stripe running down the centre. Grey wings and black shoulders. Underparts are lighter grey. Long yellowish legs. Sexes are alike.

Distribution: Throughout most of Europe into Asia, except for the far north. Also in Africa, but absent from the Sahara and the Horn.
Size: 100cm (39in).
Habitat: Water with reeds.
Nest: Platform of sticks built off the ground.
Eggs: 3–5, chalky-blue.
Food: Fish and any other aquatic vertebrates.

Little egret (*Egretta garzetta*): 65cm (26in)
Southern Europe, overwintering mainly in Africa and the Middle East. White plumage, with blue-grey area at the base of the bill. Long, white nuptial plumes when breeding. Legs blackish, with very unusual yellow toes. Sexes are alike.

Black egret (Black heron, *Egretta ardesiaca*): 52cm (20½in)
Eastern Africa south of the Sahara. Present on Madagascar. Jet black. Long plumes on the nape of the neck and chest. Narrow black bill, yellow irides. Legs black. Feet yellow, becoming red at the start of the breeding period. Sexes are alike. Young birds brownish, with no long plumes.

Black-crowned night heron (*Nycticorax nycticorax*): 64cm (25in)
Breeds in southern Europe, overwintering in Africa, where there are resident populations. Present on Madagascar. Also occurs in Asia and the Americas. Predominantly grey. Black crown and black plumage extending down the back. Bill is black. Legs and feet yellow, becoming redder at the onset of breeding. White plumes at the back of the neck. Females are smaller than males. Young birds have brownish streaking.

Malagasy pond heron (*Ardeola idae*): 48cm (19in)
Migrates from central and eastern Africa to its breeding grounds on Madagascar and Aldabra. Pure, snow white coloration. Sky blue bill with a black tip. Legs and feet pinkish, the latter turning green in the breeding season. Eyes yellow with surrounding bare bluish-green skin. Has a black nape outside breeding period. Young birds have brown coloration on their tail and flight feathers. Sexes are alike.

African rail

Rallus caerulescens

Like others of its kind, the African rail is a very shy bird, relying on its slim body shape to slip undetected through reeds and similar vegetation. Its toes are sufficiently agile to enable it to climb reed stems in search of insects, but it will also feed on aquatic creatures such as tadpoles, often emerging into the open in the process. African rails have a distinctive, jerky gait, and their short tails twitch constantly as they move. Pairs become very territorial when breeding, calling repeatedly to reinforce their claim to their chosen nesting area. The nest is often built directly above the water. Both adults share the incubation, which lasts about three weeks. Although the young are able to follow the adults as soon as they hatch, they remain dependent on them for food for up to two months. It will be at least a year before the young rails nest for the first time.

Distribution: Centred mainly on the eastern side of Africa, south of the Sahara, but species is also occasionally sighted in western parts of the continent.
Size: 35cm (14in).
Habitat: Wetlands with aquatic vegetation.
Nest: Cup-shaped, made from vegetation.
Eggs: 2–6, pinkish-cream with darker markings.
Food: Mainly invertebrates.

Identification: Back and wings are dark brownish. Grey plumage extends from the head down to the breast, except for a white area on the throat. Prominent white barring on the flanks. Long red bill and legs. Young birds are recognizable by the brown coloration of their breast and bill. Sexes are alike.

CRAKES

This group of birds can often be observed out in the open, but when frightened will usually scuttle away to the safety of the reeds or vegetation along the water's edge. They can all be recognized by their relatively long legs and toes, short stubby tail and narrow body shape, which enables them to slip easily and quietly through their waterside habitat.

Water rail

Rallus aquaticus

Being naturally very adaptable, these rails have an extensive distribution, and are even recorded as foraging in tidal areas surrounded by seaweed in the Scilly Isles off south-west England. In some parts of their range they migrate to warmer climates for the winter. Water rails survive in Iceland during the winter thanks to the hot thermal springs, which never freeze. They are very territorial when breeding and, as in other related species, their chicks hatch in a precocial state.

Identification: Prominent, long, reddish bill with bluish-grey breast and sides to the head. Narrow brownish line extending over the top of the head down the back and wings, which have black markings. Black-and-white barring on the flanks and underparts. Short tail with pale buff underparts. Sexes are alike.

Distribution: Extensive, from Iceland throughout most of Europe, south to northern Africa and east across Asia to Siberia, China and Japan.
Size: 26cm (10in).
Habitat: Usually reedbeds and sedge.
Nest: Cup-shaped, made from vegetation.
Eggs: 5–16, whitish with reddish-brown spotting.
Food: Mainly animal matter, but also some vegetation.

Coot

Eurasian coot *Fulica atra*

Open stretches of water are important to coots, enabling them to dive in search of food. During the winter, these birds may sometimes assemble in flocks on larger stretches of waters that are unlikely to freeze over. Coots may find their food on land or in the water, although they will dive only briefly in relatively shallow water. Pairs are very territorial during the breeding season, attacking the chicks of other coots that venture too close and even their own chicks, which they grab by the neck. Such behaviour is often described as "tousling". The young usually respond by feigning death, and this results in them being left alone.

Identification: Plump, sooty-grey body with a black neck and head. Bill is white with a white frontal plate. The iris is a dark brownish colour. White trailing edges of the wings evident in flight. Long toes have no webbing. Sexes are alike.

Distribution: From Great Britain eastwards throughout Europe, except the far north, south into northern Africa and east to Asia. Also present in Australia and New Zealand.
Size: 42cm (16¹/₂in).
Habitat: Slow-flowing and still stretches of water.
Nest: Pile of reeds at the water's edge.
Eggs: 1–14, buff to brown with dark markings.
Food: Various kinds of plant and animal matter.

Spotted crake (*Porzana porzana*): 22cm (9in)
Found in western and central parts of Eurasia as far east as southern Siberia and north-west China. Winters in northen Africa and southwards from Ethiopia. Has a distinctive, heavily white-spotted breast, although the abdomen is more streaky. Prominent brown ear coverts, with a bluish-grey stripe above, and black markings on the wings. The undertail area is pale buff and whiter at the tip, but may show dark spots in some cases. The bill is yellow, although red at the base. Sexes are alike.

Little crake (*Porzana parva*): 19cm (7¹/₂in)
Present in areas of Spain and Portugal, the range extending eastwards through Europe to China. Overwinters in southern Asia and northern parts of Africa. Slaty-blue head and underparts. Black markings are found predominantly across the top of the wings. The remainder of the back is brown. Has a black-and-white speckled undertail area. The bill is yellow with a red base. Adult hens are easily distinguished by their white chest area, which turns buff on the underparts. Sexes are alike.

Baillon's crake (*Porzana pusilla*): 18cm (7in)
Has a sporadic distribution through Europe and overwinters in North Africa. Also occurs further south, in Africa and on Madagascar. Ranges through Asia to parts of Australia and New Zealand. Slaty-blue head and underparts. Can be distinguished from little crake by the far more extensive barring on the flanks and heavier white speckling on the wings. The bill is dull with no red area. Hens may have paler plumage on the throat.

Lesser moorhen

Paragallinula angulata

These moorhens often follow the rains in search of suitable aquatic habitat, tending only to be seen in South Africa at this time of year, although they often prefer to remain in areas that are constantly flooded. Their breeding season varies widely according to locality, with pairs becoming quite territorial at this stage. The nest is built above the water surface to avoid flooding, but with a ramp to allow easy access. It is invariably well-concealed in dense vegetation. Incubation duties, shared by both sexes, last approximately three weeks and the chicks leave the nest at about five weeks of age. When seeking food, lesser moorhens grab invertebrates when swimming, or when walking, either on the bank or across aquatic vegetation, with their long toes helping to support their weight. They are not conspicuous birds by nature, retreating rapidly and quietly to the relative safety of reedbeds if disturbed.

Identification: Cock has a dark bluish-black head with lighter underparts. Upperparts brownish, becoming greyer on the wings, with a white edge and white undertail coverts. Facial shield and upper bill scarlet-red, yellow below. Legs and feet greenish-yellow. Hen are similar but much paler overall. Young birds have olive-brown upperparts and brownish-yellow bills.

Distribution: Ranges across most of mainland Africa, south of the Sahara, although absent from Horn of Africa and the surrounding area, as well as the south-west coastal region, and some distance inland.
Size: 23cm (9in).
Habitat: Wetlands with vegetation.
Nest: Cup-shaped, built of vegetation.
Eggs: 3–9, buff, with brown markings.
Food: Invertebrates and vegetable matter.

Western swamphen

Purple swamphen *Porphyrio porphyrio*

The European population of the Western swamphen has become more scarce over recent years due to changes in its habitat, specifically drainage of wetland areas. In some other localities, however, such as the Nile Valley of Egypt, the species has expanded its range thanks to the greater availability of suitable habitat created by irrigation schemes. Western swamphens are most likely to be observed late in the day, when they venture out in search of food. These birds are rather clumsy on short flights, literally running across the surface of the water to take off, and flying with their legs hanging down rather than being held against the body. They are unable to fly when moulting.

Identification: Relatively large, with vivid blue and purplish shades predominating in the plumage, and prominent white undertail coverts. The wings especially may have a greenish hue in some cases. Bill is dull red with brighter frontal plate. Long legs are pinkish red. Sexes alike.

Distribution: Southern parts of Europe. Sporadic locations in northern Africa and southern parts of that continent. Also present in Asia and Australiasia.
Size: 50cm (20in).
Habitat: Reedy lakes and marshes, river banks.
Nest: Platform of vegetation just above the water.
Eggs: 2–7, whitish to green with dark spots.
Food: Mostly vegetarian.

FEEDERS OF WOODLANDS AND WETLANDS

A variety of birds have adapted to living and breeding in close proximity to water. Some, such as the water pipit, are from families normally associated with other types of terrain. Not all actually venture onto the water, but are instead drawn by the availability of food, seeking not fish but rather the host of invertebrates that are associated with the aquatic environment.

Greater painted-snipe

Rostratula benghalensis

These waders feed in water by moving their bills from side to side, and may also probe the earth in search of worms or pick up seeds from the ground. They are shy by nature, only emerging to feed at dusk, when they may venture into fields. Breeding is frequently triggered by rainfall. The incubation period may last only 15 days, and the young are dependent on their parents for just the first few days after hatching, enabling the adult pair to start nesting again soon afterwards. Hens have been recorded as laying up to four clutches of eggs in rapid succession, when conditions are favourable. If scared, greater painted-snipe freeze in position, and an incubating bird will slip quietly into the vegetation rather than fly away and reveal the nest site. These painted-snipe can swim well from an early age.

Identification: Male has a white streak around each eye. Remainder of the head is greyish with white speckling. A white band extends around the sides of the neck, and the underparts are white. Yellowish-grey sides to the wings, grey elsewhere broken with spots and barring. Yellow V-shaped area on the mantle. Long yellow bill with a dark tip. Young birds resemble adult males. Hens have dark brown rather than grey head and neck.

Distribution: Found in various locations throughout Africa, notably in western and south-eastern parts of the continent. Also present on Madagascar. Range extends to Asia and Australia.
Size: 28cm (11in).
Habitat: Swampy areas.
Nest: Hidden on the ground.
Eggs: 2–5, pale yellow.
Food: Invertebrates, seeds.

Water pipit

Anthus spinoletta

These pipits undertake regular seasonal movements, nesting at higher altitudes in the spring, where they often frequent fast-flowing streams. Pairs nest nearby, choosing a well-concealed location. Subsequently they will retreat to lower altitudes for the winter months, and are not averse to moving into areas of cultivation, such as watercress beds in southern Britain. These aquatic pipits are lively birds, and are sometimes encountered in small flocks. They can often be observed on the ground, searching for invertebrates, and will readily make use of cover to conceal their presence should there be any hint of danger. Their song is attractive, and rather similar to that of the closely related rock pipit (*A. petrosus*), with studies of their song pattern revealing regional variations between different populations. Water pipits, like others of their kind, often utter their song in flight, and this is most likely to be heard at the start of the nesting period.

Identification: In breeding plumage, has a white stripe above the eye, a white throat with a distinctly pinkish tone to the breast, and a white abdomen. Slight streaking evident on the flanks. The head is greyish and the back and wings are brownish. During winter, the breast becomes whitish with very obvious streaking. Wings are lighter brown overall. Regional variations apply. Sexes are alike.

Distribution: Southern England and much of western Europe, extending to the northern African coast and into South-east Asia.
Size: 17cm (7in).
Habitat: Marshes, still water areas. Nests by streams.
Nest: Made of vegetation.
Eggs: 3–5, greenish with darker markings.
Food: Largely insectivorous.

African finfoot

Podica senegalensis

Few birds show greater variation in appearance than the African finfoot. Its name stems from the lobes on its feet, likened to fins, which undoubtedly enhance this species' swimming ability. They are equally adept out of the water, able to climb around in branches. Another unusual feature is their stiffened tail, which is held flat when swimming. Even more surprising, however, is the presence of a claw at the end of each wing, located on a mobile first digit. This may help prevent finfoots from losing their grip when clambering in vegetation. They are solitary birds and difficult to observe, often remaining close to the shore, especially alongside waterways overgrown by vegetation. If disturbed in open water they will freeze, lowering their body down in the hope of avoiding detection. Even when breeding, African finfoots are unusual in having a remarkably short incubation period of just 12 days.

Identification: Considerable variation in appearance through its range, with the Cameroon race (*P. s. camerunensis*) having blackish upperparts and chest, brown feathering edged with white on the lower underparts, and a brown rump. Other forms have a white stripe down each the side of neck, speckling on the wings, and variable barring across the underparts. Males are much larger in size. Red bill, legs and feet.

Distribution: Africa south of the Sahara, largely absent from much of the south-west of the continent.
Size: 39cm (15in).
Habitat: Forested stretches of water.
Nest: Mass of vegetation.
Eggs: 2–3, cream-coloured with dark streaks.
Food: Mainly invertebrates.

Pacific golden plover (*Pluvialis fulva*):
25cm (10in)
Iceland and the far north of Europe, wintering as far south as northern Africa. Black sides of the face extend to the chest and underparts, bordered by white feathering and barring from above the bill down the sides of the body. Coarse, mottled pattern of brown, black and white over the wings. Very upright stance on grey legs. In winter, underparts become mottled with black-and-white feathering. Sexes are alike.

Little ringed plover (*Charadrius dubius*):
18cm (7in)
Southern Scandinavia across Europe, wintering in northern Africa. Also in Asia. Broad black lines across the top of the forehead and from the bill back around the eyes, with a broader black band across the chest. Brown crown edged white. White neck collar. Underparts entirely white. In winter the entire head is brownish, with a pale buff area from the bill to above the eyes, and the black chest band turns brownish-grey. Legs pinkish-brown, bill black. Sexes are alike.

Snipe (common snipe, *Gallinago gallinago*):
28cm (11in)
Iceland eastwards through Europe into Asia, and often into northern Africa in winter. Pale buff streak down the centre of the crown, with buff stripes above and below the eyes. Dark mottled chest and wings. White underparts. White stripes run down the wings, with a white border to the rear of the wings. Long bill, often larger in hens. Sexes otherwise alike.

Egyptian plover

Crocodile bird *Pluvianus aegyptius*

Despite its name, this plover is no longer present in Egypt, where it was common along the River Nile until the early 20th century. Egyptian plovers have bold natures, but there is little evidence to confirm the belief that they will pick food morsels from the open mouths of resting crocodiles. Their prey normally consists of small aquatic creatures, hunted by careful stalking or probing in the sand. Pairs nest on their own on sandbars, where their eggs can be partly buried if the adult birds are away from the nest. The incubating bird will soak its breast feathers if the eggs are in danger of overheating. Even the chicks may be buried until almost a month old, to help conceal their presence, although they can begin feeding themselves when a week old.

Identification: Black head and back, with a white streak above each eye. Black extends down the sides of the neck to form a band across the chest, bordered below by a white band. Throat is white, becoming buff on the chest. Underparts are buff. Grey wings. Bill is black, legs and feet grey. Young birds have brownish edges to the feathers on their backs.

Distribution: Ranges in a broad band across the whole of central Africa south of the Sahara, extending as far as northern Angola.
Size: 20cm (8in).
Habitat: Sandy river banks.
Nest: Scrape on a sandbank.
Eggs: 1–4, cream-coloured with dark markings.
Food: Invertebrates.

HABITAT SPECIALISTS

The adaptability of birds as a group is reflected by the diversity which exists among those associated with freshwater areas. While the dipper is at home by a fast-flowing mountain stream, aquatic warblers and a number of similar species thrive in a more sluggish aquatic environment where reedbeds proliferate, although observing them in this habitat can be difficult.

White-throated dipper

European dipper *Cinclus cinclus*

The dipper's name comes from the way in which it bows, or "dips" its body, often on a boulder in the middle of a stream, rather than describing the way it dives into the water. Dippers are very adept at steering underwater with their wings, and can even elude birds of prey by plunging in and disappearing from view, before surfacing again further downstream. They feed mainly on aquatic invertebrates caught underwater, sometimes emerging with caddisfly larvae and hammering them out of their protective casings on land. Pairs work together to construct their nest, which may be concealed in a bridge or a hole in a rock. The hen usually sits alone, and the youngsters will fledge after about three weeks. Norway's dipper population is increasing as streams in the southern mountains remain free of ice, possibly due to global warming.

Identification: Prominent white throat and chest. Brown on head extends below the eyes, rest of the plumage is dark. Young birds are greyish with mottling on their underparts. Some regional variation, usually relating to the extent of chestnut below the white of the chest. Dark bill, legs and feet. Sexes are alike.

Distribution: Present in much of Scandinavia but only irregularly through the rest of Europe. Absent from central and eastern England and much of north-west Europe. Range extends south to parts of northern Africa. Also present in Asia.
Size: 20cm (8in).
Habitat: Stretches of fast-flowing water.
Nest: Domed mass made from vegetation.
Eggs: 1–7, white.
Food: Aquatic invertebrates and small fish.

Aquatic warbler

Acrocephalus paludicola

Distribution: Mainland Europe. Few remaining strongholds in eastern Europe, notably in Poland, ranging into Asia. Migrates south to western Africa.
Size: 13cm (5in).
Habitat: Waterlogged areas, with sedge.
Nest: In tussocks of sedge.
Eggs: 4–6, greenish-coloured with dark markings.
Food: Invertebrates.

Identification: Black areas on the head, with a central yellow-buff streak and broader areas above the eyes. Similar markings also at the top of the wings. The remaining wing plumage is brownish with black markings, with marked streaking over the lower back. Underparts are paler and have variable fine streaking. Sexes are similar. Young birds less brightly coloured.

The aquatic warbler's range has contracted significantly over recent years, as the sedgeland areas that these birds favour have been increasingly drained for agriculture. However, they are seen more widely on migration, when they take a westerly route down over the Strait of Gibraltar. During the autumn in particular, they can even be seen in southern parts of England. They remain in Africa from November through to April, before heading north again, where they occur in a number of scattered locations in areas of suitable habitat, including flooded grassland. Aquatic warblers may be difficult to observe since they tend not to utter any calls away from their breeding grounds. When nesting, they will usually sing most frequently towards dusk, from a suitable perch rather than in flight. They are shy birds by nature, and prefer to search for food near the base of reedbeds. They are also very agile, often perching on two adjacent reeds rather than grasping the same stem with both feet.

Grauer's swamp warbler (*Bradypterus graueri*): 15cm (6in) (E)
Eastern Africa, confined to the Albertine Rift region centred on Rwanda, where it is endangered by drainage of its habitat. Prominent white stripe above the eye, with a dark stripe running through the eye beneath. Whitish underparts, heavily streaked especially on the throat and upper breast, becoming browner on the sides of flanks and lower underparts. Upperparts dark. Sexes are alike.

Eurasian reed warbler (*Acrocephalus scirpaceus*): 13cm (5in)
Southern parts of Scandinavia and the British Isles. Also in northern Africa, overwintering south of the Sahara, particularly in parts of East Africa. Brown head, back and wings, with a rufous suffusion to the plumage on the rump. There is a paler brown streak above each eye. Lower cheeks, breast and underparts are whitish, with a brown suffusion across the chest and on the flanks. Pointed bill, darker on the upper bill and paler beneath. Legs and feet are pinkish-grey. Sexes are alike.

Marsh warbler (*Acrocephalus palustris*): 13cm (5in)
Central Europe into Asia, north to southern Scandinavia. Rare in the British Isles. Winters through much of East Africa. Similar to Eurasian reed warbler, but with a slightly greyer tone to the brown upperparts. Underparts also whitish, with brownish suffusion on the chest and flanks. Identified by its shorter bill and longer wings, the tips of which clearly extend behind the rump when the bird is perched. Sexes are alike.

Great reed warbler

Acrocephalus arundinaceus

Great reed warblers return to their northern breeding grounds from April onwards, with their distinctive and sometimes harsh calls betraying their presence in the reedbeds. However, they are notoriously difficult to spot, due to the colour of their plumage. They sing from the tops of reed stems, and this provides the best opportunity to spot them. They are very agile, able to clamber between the reed stems with ease. In flight, great reed warblers stay close to the water's surface, with their tail feathers held out. The female constructs the nest in May, which is suspended from several adjacent reed stems, about half-way up their length. Incubation lasts around two weeks and is shared by both members of the pair, as is the rearing of the young. They leave the nest after about 12 days. Both young and adult birds migrate south as early as September.

Distribution: Most of Europe, but restricted to the extreme south in both Scandinavia and the British Isles. Overwinters in Africa south of the Sahara, except the far south and the Horn of Africa. Resident population in northern Africa.
Size: 20cm (8in).
Habitat: Reedbeds.
Nest: Vegetation woven into a basket shape.
Eggs: 4–6, bluish-green with dark markings.
Food: Invertebrates.

Identification: Upperparts are dark brown, with darker areas on the wings and a pale stripe running through the eyes. Whitish underparts, becoming more buff in colour on the flanks. Some greyish streaking evident across the breast. Bill is blackish, lighter below, while the legs and feet are typically greyish. Sexes are alike. Young birds are rusty-brown above, with buff underparts.

Bearded reedling

Bearded tit *Panurus biarmicus*

This species' distribution is directly affected by the availability of marshland with extensive reedbeds. Contrary to their name they are members of the babbler family, rather than tits, although their lively nature and jerky tail movements, coupled with their overall appearance, are more suggestive of the latter group. In addition to providing a source of insects, the reeds also produce seeds which the bearded reedlings eat over the winter, when invertebrates are less common. Nevertheless, these small birds can suffer a high mortality rate when the weather is harsh. They are more social at this time of year, and may associate in groups of up to 50 individuals. Pairs breed alone, and the male is largely responsible for nest-building, choosing a well-concealed site hidden in the reeds. Both birds incubate and care for the chicks, which may fledge at just nine days old. Pairs may rear up to three broods in a year.

Identification: Reddish-brown overall, with a relatively long tail which tapers to its tip. Some white patches on the wings. Cocks have a mainly grey head, with a prominent black area beneath each eye, and a white throat. Hens have a brownish head, with a greyish-white throat. Young birds similar to hens, but with a distinctive black area on their backs. Bill is yellowish-orange, legs and feet are black.

Distribution: Localised distribution from southern parts of Scandinavia and England through areas of Europe and parts of Asia.
Size: 15cm (6in).
Habitat: Reedbeds.
Nest: Made of vegetation.
Eggs: 5–7, white with dark markings.
Food: Invertebrates, seeds.

DUCKS

Waterfowl are generally conspicuous birds on water, but their appearance and distribution can differ markedly through the year. Drakes often resemble hens outside the breeding season, when their plumage is much plainer. Some species are migratory, heading south to escape freezing conditions, while others are to be found on stretches of water that may at times be covered in ice.

Red-billed teal

Anas erythrorhyncha

Distribution: Eastern and southern Africa, from Sudan and Ethiopia through southern South Africa. Typically absent further north in the west, apart from Angola. Also occurs on Madagascar.
Size: 48cm (19in).
Habitat: Lakes and marshes.
Nest: Made of vegetation.
Eggs: 5–12, buff to greyish green.
Food: Vegetable matter and aquatic invertebrates.

The red-billed teal is easily identified in the field, because it is the only species of African duck with a bill of this colour. These waterfowl are most conspicuous outside the breeding season, usually forming large flocks at this stage. The nesting period varies significantly through their range, however, depending largely on the water level, with pairs generally starting to breed towards the end of the rainy season. They may spread out in areas that are temporarily flooded as well. The nest itself is built near water, in a well-concealed locality. Incubation lasts approximately a month, with the young ducklings being camouflaged on hatching by the dark brown down covering their upperparts. Red-billed teal take a wide range of foods, feeding both in shallow water, even partially submerging themselves in search of molluscs, and on land, where they will graze on vegetation. Although heavily hunted in many parts of their range, these adaptable waterfowl remain relatively common.

Identification: Dark brown top to the head, extending to below the eyes, with the sides of the face whitish, becoming brownish on the neck. Remainder of plumage on the body is dark brown, with whitish edging to the underparts, becoming buff above. Pale buff area at the back of the wings, with a narrow stripe in front. Reddish bill, duller in females. Young birds less brightly coloured with a brownish-pink bill.

Ruddy shelduck

Tadorna ferruginea

Although ruddy shelducks are resident throughout the year in some parts of their range, they are more often migratory. Occasionally, they may be encountered well outside their natural range, and there have been verified sightings reported from countries as far apart as Iceland, Oman and Kenya. They are quite noisy birds by nature, and the calls of drakes are of a higher pitch than those of hens. These shelducks favour stretches of water surrounded by open countryside, allowing them to graze on the surrounding vegetation. After the breeding season, huge flocks may assemble in areas where conditions are favourable for feeding.

Identification: Cinnamon shade to the head, with paler whitish area around the eyes. Black neck ring. Remainder of the body is orange-brown. Greenish gloss to black feathering on the rump. Tail and flight feathers are black. Bill, legs and feet are also black. White plumage under the wings. Hens lack the neck collar, which is less apparent in drakes outside the breeding season.

Distribution: North-western Africa, south-eastern Europe extending into Asia. Over-winters in eastern Africa.
Size: 70cm (27¹/₂in).
Habitat: Inland, can be some distance from water.
Nest: Under cover, lined with down feathers.
Eggs: 8–15, creamy-white.
Food: Aquatic creatures and plant matter.

Red-crested pochard

Netta rufina

The largest of the pochards, the red-billed nests primarily in eastern Europe, but may breed further north, including Denmark and the British Isles. There have been no reported sightings in North Africa in recent years, however. The sexes live separately for part of the year, as males depart from their breeding grounds just before the ducklings hatch, leaving the hens to care for the young. It is not unknown for female red-crested pochards to lay in the nests of other waterfowl, thus avoiding having to rear their own ducklings, although this behaviour is not common. The young pochards are able to fly by the time that they are about seven weeks old, and can breed themselves in the following year.

Identification: Drake has a rusty-brown head, with a black neck and chest. White on the flanks and as a wing bar, with the upperparts otherwise being brownish. Bill, legs and feet reddish. Hens are brownish, darker above with white patches below the eyes on each side of the face. White undertail coverts and under the wings. Bill brownish, pale red at the tip. Legs and feet dark. Drakes resemble hens when in eclipse plumage, but retain their red bills. Young birds are like hens, with a blackish bill.

Distribution: Southern Europe, but occasionally further north, to the eastern end of the Mediterranean and parts of central and southern Asia.
Size: 57cm (22in).
Habitat: Large lakes and also rivers.
Nest: Made of vegetation, on the ground.
Eggs: 6–10, creamy white.
Food: Invertebrates and plant matter.

Eurasian teal (*Anas crecca*): 38cm (15in)
Found throughout Europe. Resident in the west, migrating south to parts of northern Africa. Also found in Asia and North America. Brown head with broad green stripes running across the eyes and yellow stripes above and below. Chest is pale yellow with black dots. Body and wings are greyish with a yellow area under the tail, and a white edge to the sides of the wings. Hens are mottled brown, with a pale whitish area beneath the tail and a green area on the wing. Bill is dark. Drakes in eclipse plumage resemble hens.

Garganey (*Anas querquedula*): 41cm (16in)
Ranges from England and France eastwards across Europe, overwintering south of the Sahara. Present in Asia. Prominent white stripe from the eyes down along the neck. Remainder of the face and breast area are brown with black barring. Greyish area on the body. Wings are greyish-black. Brown mottling over the hindquarters. Hens have mottled plumage with a distinctive buff-white area under the chin. Drakes in eclipse plumage resemble hens but with greyish areas on the wings.

Ferruginous duck (*Aythya nyroca*): 42cm (16½in)
Occurs throughout much of eastern Europe and into Asia, overwintering around the Mediterranean and further south in Africa, as well as in parts of South-East Asia. Chestnut plumage, lighter on the flanks than the back, with white eyes. Very obvious white wing stripe. Whitish belly, underwing and undertail area. Greyish bill, black at the tip. Hens are similar but have a pale band across the bill and brown eyes (which distinguishes them from drakes in eclipse plumage).

Pintail (Northern pintail, *Anas acuta*): 62cm (24in)
Throughout the Northern Hemisphere, migrating south for the winter to central Africa. Long, narrow black tail. Head is blackish, with white stripes on the neck down to the breast and underparts. Grey flanks. Wings are greyish with prominent wing stripes. Hens are brown, with darker patterning on the plumage and a long, pointed tail with a white edge to the wings in flight.

Common pochard

Aythya ferina

These ducks are most likely to be found on open water, where they can often be seen diving for food. Islands are favoured as breeding grounds since they provide relatively secure nesting sites, particularly where there is overhanging vegetation. Pairs will stay together for the duration of the nesting period. Subsequently the pochards form large flocks, sometimes moving away from the lakes and other still-water areas to nearby rivers, especially in winter when ice is likely to form on the water's surface.

Distribution: Resident in parts of western Europe, extending eastwards into Asia. Overwinters further south, in parts of western and central Africa.
Size: 49cm (19in).
Habitat: Marshland, lakes.
Nest: Under cover, lined with down feathers.
Eggs: 6–14, greenish-grey.
Food: Aquatic creatures and plant matter.

Identification: Chestnut-brown head and neck, with black chest and a broad grey band encircling the wings and body. Black feathering surrounds the hindquarters. Eyes are reddish. Black is replaced by a greyish tone in eclipse plumage. Hens are significantly duller in coloration, having a brownish head with buff areas and a noticable stripe extending back from the eyes. Brown also replaces the drake's black plumage.

WATERFOWL

Waterfowl are occasionally sighted well outside their natural range, suggesting the bird in question may be an exotic escapee from a wildfowl collection. Some endemic African waterfowl, which are found nowhere else in the world, appear to have no close European relatives, while a number, for example the Hottentot teal, are clearly related to European species.

African black duck

Anas sparsa

These ducks are often encountered in wooded upland areas, on fast-flowing stretches of water, although sometimes they may also be found in more open countryside at lower altitudes. The breeding period varies through their extensive range, but usually takes place during the dry season. The nest site is well-hidden among rocks or debris left by flooding. Incubation lasts approximately four weeks, and the young hatch covered in black down with pale buffy-white underparts. The dark coloration of these ducks makes them difficult to spot in the relative gloom of the forest, particularly as they will remain stationary if disturbed, rather than fly off immediately. When they do fly in this terrain they instinctively follow the path of the waterway, skimming low over the surface. African black ducks feed by dabbling, upending and even occasionally diving beneath the surface of the water.

Identification: Dark, blackish-brown coloration with relatively broad, lighter barring on the wings, back and tail. Bill is completely or partially black, depending on the race. Legs and feet are pinkish-red. Ducks are smaller than drakes. Young have narrow barring and a white abdomen.

Distribution: Two separate populations exist. The most widespread extends from near the Red Sea in East Africa to much of the southern region, while a smaller one is present in western equatorial Africa.
Size: 58cm (23in).
Habitat: Flowing and still stretches of water.
Nest: Vegetation lined with down feathers.
Eggs: 4–8, buffy-grey.
Food: Aquatic plants, invertebrates, small fish.

Knob-billed duck

African comb duck *Sarkidiornis melanotos*

Distribution: Occurs widely throughout Africa south of the Sahara, and is also present on Madagascar. Occurs in South America and southern Asia.
Size: 76cm (30in).
Habitat: Fairly open country with lakes and rivers.
Nest: Made of vegetation.
Eggs: 6–20, yellowish-white.
Food: Grass and vegetation, some invertebrates.

It is unusual for waterfowl to occur naturally both in Africa and South America, therefore the comb duck species has been split. Knob-billed ducks are likely to be found in relatively open countryside, where they can leave the water and graze on grasses and other vegetation, but they also seek out aquatic invertebrates in the shallows. They may associate in groups of 40 individuals or more, which will disperse at the start of the breeding season. The comb on the bill of the drakes becomes much more conspicuous at this stage. Knob-billed ducks are tree-nesting by nature, but may also adopt large nests abandoned by birds such as hamerkops (*Scopus umbretta*), or even abandoned buildings. Incubation lasts a month. The young can take to the water almost immediately but must first tumble down from the nest site, since it will be nearly 10 weeks before they are able to fly well.

Identification: Black area on the head extending down the back of the neck, with speckling on the sides of the face and throat. Nape of the neck is white, underparts predominantly white. Back and wings are metallic green. Only the drake has the massive, comb-like protrusion on the upper bill, along with a slight yellowish suffusion on the head, grey flanks and a black area around the vent. Hen in contrast has some relatively faint brownish barring on the flanks. Young birds are less varied in colour, with brownish plumage.

Eurasian wigeon

Anas penelope

Identification: Drakes in breeding plumage have chestnut heads, with yellow stripe extending above bill. Paler, more pinkish tone to breast with grey on sides of body and wings. White band evident in flight, green wingbar beneath. White central area and rump. Bill, legs and feet greyish. Hens vary from brown to grey, with dirty whitish areas under the throat. Central area of abdomen white. Cocks out of colour resemble hens. Young resemble hens.

Pairs typically undertake a long migration north to their breeding grounds each year, arriving from April onwards. The incubation period lasts for 24 days, with the young ducklings being able to fly at 6 weeks. After egg-laying the drakes leave their partners and congregate together to moult into their eclipse plumage before flying south to their winter quarters from the end of August. They are very social at this stage, congregating in large flocks. Eurasian wigeon may often venture into coastal districts, feeding in estuaries by dabbling, although more commonly they will graze in groups on vegetation adjacent to water. Some populations, such as those found in the British Isles, are quite sedentary by nature and tend to be seen in the same localities throughout the year. It is also not unknown for some Eurasian wigeon, probably those of the Icelandic population, to migrate to the eastern coast of North America for the winter.

Distribution: Breeds in parts of Iceland, throughout Scandinavia and right across northern Asia. Overwinters in the British Isles, on both sides of the Mediterranean and in various parts of Africa, including the Nile Valley.
Size: 50cm (20in).
Habitat: Shallow areas of water, often close to the coast.
Nest: Scrape on the ground, lined with down.
Eggs: 6–12, greenish.
Food: Mainly vegetation.

Maccoa duck (*Oxyura maccoa*): 51cm (20in)
Two separate African populations exist, one in the central-eastern region and one in the south. The drake in breeding plumage is chestnut overall, with a black head and a broad blue bill. The tail, which is very stiff and is often held just above the water, distinguishes this species from all other African ducks. Ducks and males out of colour are dark brown overall, with a paler stripe below each eye. The throat is also paler, and the bill is a much duller yellowish-black shade. Young birds are similar in colour to hens, but can be easily identified by the narrower shape and more spiky appearance of their tail feathers.

Cape shoveler (*Anas smithii*): 53cm (21in)
Distribution is restricted to southern Africa. The plumage of the drake is a much paler grey than that of the duck, and this coloration is especially apparent on the head and neck. Sky blue wing pattern with a white band behind, which is most apparent in flight. The iris in the drake is pale yellow, darker in ducks. Ducks and young birds are much browner overall, with a slightly lighter black bill. Legs and feet are orange-yellow, but brighter in drakes.

Hottentot teal (*Anas hottentota*): 35cm (14in)
Distribution extends from central-eastern parts of Africa southwards, and is also present on Madagascar. Black area on top of the head, encompassing the eyes, with a white area beneath, broadening out over the hind neck. Creamy cheek patches. Black speckling across the chest and down the sides of the body. The sides of the lower neck and the wings are predominantly blackish. The bill is bluish, and the brighter green wing speculum of the male is very evident in flight.

Yellow-billed duck

Anas undulata

These ducks are the only African species with yellow on the bill, which is a richer, deeper shade in birds from northern parts of their range. These individuals also appear darker overall, displaying a much narrower white edging to their plumage. Yellow-billed ducks frequent a wide range of habitats, especially during the rainy season, when the large flocks split up and pairs head off to breed individually. Although there is virtually no visual difference between the sexes, the whistling call of the drake is often more apparent at this stage, compared with the quacking note of the duck. Yellow-billed ducks often remain close to the bank when not feeding, being shy by nature. They feed both in the water and on land, grazing on vegetation as well as diving beneath the water on occasion, to obtain snails and crustaceans.

Identification: The feathering on the head is dark, with whitish streaks evident here. White edging to the plumage on the back and wings, as well as the underparts, with a green speculum evident in the wing. Bill yellow, with a brown central area, legs and feet pinkish. Sexes alike, but females smaller. Young birds display less evident whitish edging to the plumage.

Distribution: Through much of eastern and southern parts of Africa, from southern Sudan and Ethiopia down to Cape Province.
Size: 58cm (23in).
Habitat: Wetland habitats, including coastal lagoons.
Nest: Hidden on the ground in dense vegetation.
Eggs: 4–12, creamy white.
Food: Vegetation and invertebrates.

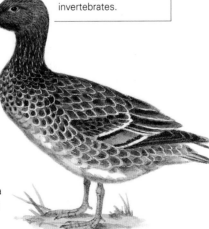

SWANS AND GEESE

Many of these large, unmistakable birds regularly fly long distances to and from their breeding grounds. They also rank among the longest-lived of all waterfowl, with a possible life expectancy of 20 years or more. Young birds are unlikely to breed until they are three or four years old. Both geese and swans can be aggressive, so caution is advised when observing them.

Spur-winged goose

Plectropterus gambensis

Distribution: Occurs across most of Africa south of the Sahara, apart from the rainforest and much of the south-east. Also not present on Madagascar.
Size: 100cm (39in).
Habitat: Lakes and rivers.
Nest: Made of vegetation.
Eggs: 6–14, cream.
Food: Largely vegetarian.

These large geese use the prominent spurs on their wings to batter an attacker or a rival, and are capable of inflicting painful blows. They are social by nature, typically occurring in flocks of more than 50 individuals. Spur-winged geese prefer to graze on ground close to the shore, but are able to swim well if necessary. Their large size makes them appear ponderous in flight. Flocks are most commonly seen flying at dusk and dawn in a V-shaped formation, heading to and from their roosting grounds. The breeding season varies according to the locality, and they sometimes breed off the ground in an existing nest build by another bird, or in a tree cavity. Pairs have even been known to utilise the nests of arboreal termites. Moulting takes place during the dry season, with large groups congregating together at this stage.

Identification: Glossy blackish plumage covering much of the head, throat and upperparts, with a small white area on the sides of the face and throat. Underparts white. White area prominent at the front edge of the wings in flight, extending beneath. May be a knob present on the forehead, which is more prominent in males, lying adjacent to the reddish-pink area on the sides of the face and the bill. Legs and feet pinkish. Sexes are alike but males are larger. Young birds are browner overall.

Mute swan

Cygnus olor

These graceful birds can be seen in a wide range of habitats and may occasionally even venture out on to the sea, although they will not stray very far from the shore. They prefer to feed on aquatic vegetation, but can sometimes be found grazing on short grass. In town and city parks mute swans often eat a greater variety of foods, such as grain and bread provided for them by people. They rarely dive, but instead use their long necks to dabble under the surface of the water to obtain food. Pairs are very territorial when breeding and the male swan, known as a cob, will actively try to drive away people with fierce movements of its wings if they venture too close.

Identification: Mainly white, with a black area extending from the eyes to the base of the orange bill. A swollen knob protrudes over the upper part of the bill. The legs and feet are blackish. Hens are smaller with a less pronounced knob on the bill. Traces of staining are often evident on the head and neck. Young birds are browner.

Distribution: Resident throughout the British Isles and adjacent areas of western Europe, often living in a semi-domesticated state. Also occurs in the north-west Black Sea area and in parts of Asia. Localized introduced populations also found in other areas including South Africa, the eastern USA, Australia and New Zealand.
Size: 160cm (63in).
Habitat: Larger stretches of fresh water and estuaries.
Nest: Large pile of heaped-up aquatic vegetation.
Eggs: 5–7, pale green.
Food: Mainly vegetation.

Whooper swan

Cygnus cygnus

Although some Icelandic whooper swans are sedentary throughout the year, the majority of these birds undertake regular migrations, so they are likely to be observed in southern Europe only during the winter months. At this time they often frequent areas around inland waterways, such as the Black and Caspian seas. Pairs nest on their own, and the young chicks fly alongside their parents on the journey south. In the winter, whooper swans may sometimes invade agricultural areas, where they eat a range of foods varying from potatoes to acorns, although generally they prefer to feed on aquatic vegetation.

Identification: Body plumage is white, although sometimes it may be stained. The base of the bill is yellow, extending as far as the nostrils, and the tip is black. Legs and feet are grey. Hens are a little smaller, while young birds have pinkish rather than yellow bases to their bills.

Above left: These swans fly in a V-shaped formation when migrating. Huge numbers may congregate together at their wintering grounds.

Distribution: Iceland and north-western parts of Europe. Northern Scandinavia eastwards to Siberia. Overwinters further south.
Size: 165cm (65in).
Habitat: Wooded ponds and lakes. Winters near the coast.
Nest: Mounds of plant matter, often moss.
Eggs: 3–7, pale green.
Food: Vegetation.

Pink-footed goose (*Anser brachyrhynchus*): 75cm (29½in)
Found in eastern Greenland, Iceland and Spitzbergen. Overwinters in northern Britain and Denmark southwards. Has a brown head with white streaking on the neck, and more prominent markings on the wings and underparts. Bill is pinkish but dark at its base. Legs and feet are pinkish. Sexes are alike.

African pygmy goose (*Nettapus auritus*): 33cm (13in)
Most of Africa, south of the Sahara, except for the south-west. Present on Madagascar. Face and throat are white in the male, with an extensive green patch on the back of the head, edged with black. Central area of the underparts is white, with chestnut on the remainder, except for dark feathering around the vent and on the undertail coverts. Bill bright yellow with a dark tip. Legs and feet black. Hens and young birds lack the prominent green neck patch, having a mottled whitish head and a much duller bill.

Blue-winged goose (*Cyanochen cyanoptera*): 75cm (29in)
Restricted to the highland region of Ethiopia, where these geese are found near to lakes and rivers at altitudes above 1800m (6000ft). Grey coloration overall; browner on the underparts, with a white area surrounding the vent. White edging is apparent on the down covering the flanks. Distinctive light blue upperwing coverts, which are evident in flight when the wings are open. Young birds are similar to adults, but lack the glossy sheen on the flight feathers.

Bewick's swan

Tundra swan *Cygnus bewickii*

Bewick's swan is sometimes regarded as a separate species from the tundra swan (*C. columbianus*), which occurs at similar latitudes in North America. They differ most noticeably on the bill, since Bewick's has more yellow coloration, but share identical lifestyles. Both breed in the Arctic during the brief summer, taking advantage of the pools of water that form above the permafrost. Breeding starts in May, with the life-long pairs heaping up vegetation to form their bulky nests. The eggs hatch after about a month, and the young cygnets are able to fly when six weeks old. They travel with their parents on the southward migration during September, but it may be four years before they are ready to nest themselves. If they can avoid the hunters, Bewick's swans may live for over 20 years.

Distribution: Breeding grounds extend along the north Russian coast to Siberia. Overwinters in southern British Isles and parts of north-western Europe, and also in Asia south of the Caspian Sea across to Japan.
Size: 127cm (50in).
Habitat: Pools, marshland.
Nest: A heaped-up pile of aquatic vegetation.
Eggs: 3–5, pale greenish.
Food: Mainly vegetation.

Identification: White overall with a restricted area of yellow on the bill that does not extend as far as the nostrils. Cobs (male swans) are larger than females (known as pens). Young birds are greyish with a pinkish bill.

KINGFISHERS AND WETLAND OWLS

Although renowned for catching fish, a number of kingfisher species do not actually venture near standing water on a regular basis, preferring instead forests or more open areas of country and feeding on invertebrates. Conversely, owls as a group are better-known for hunting rodents, but in Africa several species have adapted to catching fish with their talons.

Kingfisher

Common kingfisher *Alcedo atthis*

These birds are surprisingly difficult to spot, as they perch motionlessly while scanning the water beneath them for fish. Once its prey has been identified, the kingfisher dives down in a flash of colour. A protective membrane covers its eyes as it enters the water. Its wings provide propulsion, and having seized the fish in its bill the bird darts out of the water and back onto its perch with its catch. The whole sequence happens incredibly fast, taking just a few seconds. The kingfisher then stuns the fish by hitting it against the perch, before swallowing it head first. It regurgitates the bones and indigestible parts of its meal later.

Left: Kingfishers dive at speed into the water, aiming to catch their intended quarry unawares.

Identification: Bluish-green extending over the head and wings. The back is pale blue, and a blue flash is also present on the cheeks. The throat area is white, and there are white areas below the orange cheek patches. The underparts are also orange, and the bill is black. In hens, the bill is reddish at the base of the lower bill.

Distribution: Occurs across most of Europe, but absent from much of Scandinavia. Also present in northern Africa, ranging eastwards through the Arabian peninsula and South-East Asia as far as the Solomon Islands.
Size: 18cm (7in).
Habitat: Slow-flowing water.
Nest: Tunnel excavated in a sandy bank.
Eggs: 6–10, white.
Food: Small fish. Also preys on aquatic insects, molluscs and crustaceans.

Giant kingfisher

Megaceryle maximus

Distribution: Present across much of Africa south of the Sahara, except for the south-west of the continent. Also absent from the Horn of Africa and a large part of adjacent eastern Africa.
Size: 43cm (17in).
Habitat: Wooded waterways, rivers and estuaries.
Nest: Long tunnel excavated in a suitable bank.
Eggs: 2–3, white.
Food: Mainly fish and crabs.

These large kingfishers are shy by nature, and are not often seen in the open. They perch quietly, often as high as 4m (13ft) above the water, looking for potential quarry beneath them. They may even occasionally fish out over the sea. Their diet varies through their range, with crabs proving more significant than fish in some parts of South Africa. The breeding season is also variable. A tunnel is excavated in a suitable bank, which can be some distance from water, although mostly it is located in a riverbank, and constructed high enough to avoid any risk of flooding. The tunnel is usually around 2m (6½ft) long, but can sometimes be up to 8.5m (28ft). The young emerge when about five weeks old and are able to dive soon afterwards, although they will not be fully independent for at least a further three weeks.

Identification: Black head with some white markings, notably below the large black bill. Speckled black-and-white patterning on the wings, back and tail. Rufous chest, with white lower underparts. Shaggy crest on the back of the head. In the adult female, the chest is streaked and the underparts are rufous. Young cocks have black-and-white speckled chest, with rufous areas on the flanks, while females have a white chest.

Pel's fishing owl

Scotopelia peli

Like many owls, this species is not easy to observe since it is largely nocturnal. Perching directly above the water, and recognizing the presence of fish below by the ripples they create at the surface, the owl glides down as quietly as possible and scoops up its quarry with its sharp talons. Such is their overall strength that Pel's fishing owls can lift fish weighing as much as 2kg (4.4lb). Only rarely do they enter the water directly, such as when seeking relatively immobile prey like mussels, or seizing crabs in the shallows. These owls favour old forests because they provide plenty of large tree hollows, which make suitable nesting sites. Egg-laying is closely co-ordinated with the seasons, so that when the eggs hatch after about 32 days the water level is falling back. The young owls thus hatch during the dry season, and the declining water level makes it easier for their parents to hunt for food.

Identification: Considerable variation exists in the markings of these owls. Reddish-brown overall, with paler, buff-coloured underparts displaying darker, tear-like droplets. These contrast with the barring evident elsewhere on the body. Bill is blackish. Sexes are alike. Females have a higher-pitched call. Young birds are paler overall.

Distribution: Has a variable distribution in Africa, mostly in western-central and south-eastern regions, but also in other parts where suitable habitat exists.
Size: 60cm (24in).
Habitat: Swamps and old riverine forests
Nest: Tree hollow.
Eggs: 1–2, white.
Food: Fish, crabs, amphibians and invertebrates.

Malachite Kingfisher (*Corythornis cristatus*): 13cm (5in)
Widely distributed in Africa south of the Sahara. General colour of the upper parts of the adult bird is bright metallic blue. The head has a short crest of black and blue feathers. The face, cheeks, and underparts are rufous and there are white patches are on the throat and rear neck sides. The bill is black in young birds and reddish-orange in adults; the legs are bright red. Sexes are similar. The São Tomé kingfisher was sometimes considered as a distinct species but a study published in 2008 showed that it is a subspecies of the malachite kingfisher.

Pied kingfisher (*Ceryle rudis*): 25cm (10in)
Widely distributed across much of Africa south of the Sahara. Prominent black area on the sides of the head and also extending partially across the chest, while the remainder of the underparts are white. Males can be distinguished by the additional presence of a narrower black band across the lower chest. Back and wings are mottled black and white, while the underside of the wings are pure white.

Shining-blue kingfisher (*Alcedo quadribrachys*): 16cm (6in)
Restricted to western and central parts of Africa. Brilliant cobalt blue, with a white area on the neck and under the throat. The remainder of the underparts are rufous, apart from a small blue area at the top of the wings. Bill is black, legs and feet red. Sexes are alike. Young birds display light barring on the chest.

Marsh owl

Asio capensis

These owls are unusual since they rest on the ground during the daytime, rather than perch in a tree. This probably reflects their countryside habitat, where few trees are available. Even when hunting, marsh owls swoop low over the ground in search of likely prey. They are opportunistic feeders, prepared to eat whatever is available, and have been observed catching insects attracted by street lamps at night. The nest site is chosen carefully and is screened by vegetation on all sides, while the hen conceals her presence even further by propping up a layer of overhead vegetation from below. She sits alone, and is fed by her mate during this period. The young hatch after about four weeks, and may sometimes leave the nest within 10 days. They are found and fed individually by their parents, who track them by their calls. The young owls will be able to start flying when they are five weeks old.

Distribution: Main African distribution is in the eastern-central region southwards, but several other isolated populations occur, notably in the north-west, west, south-west and on Madagascar.
Size: 38cm (15in).
Habitat: Open country, including marshland.
Nest: Made from vegetation, on the ground.
Eggs: 2–6, white.
Food: Invertebrates and vertebrates.

Identification: Some regional variation. Buff face with black edging to the facial disc and eyes. Dark, rufous-brown body, paler underparts broken by barring. Bill and feet greyish. Sexes are alike.

WETLAND HUNTERS

A number of large birds of prey hunt fish and small vertebrates in wetland areas, but being at the top of the food chain has resulted in some populations suffering a build-up of pollutants in their bodies, which have been passed on from their prey. However, most birds of prey are opportunistic hunters rather than specialists, and this has aided their survival.

African marsh harrier

Circus ranivorus

Habitat loss is a serious threat to these harriers, especially in Kenya, where populations have declined over recent years. They survive in relatively small areas, venturing out to hunt for mice or swooping down over open stretches of water in the marshes to catch small ducks. The breeding season varies through their range, with the nest site itself being well-concealed. There is a strong and lasting pair bond, with aerial displays featuring prominently in courtship. The male hunts while the female incubates alone, with the chicks hatching after just over a month. They grow quite fast, fledging by six weeks old, but it will take three years for them to attain adult plumage.

Identification: Similar to the Eurasian marsh harrier, which overlaps in parts of its range, but distinguishable by the barring extending across both the flight feathers and the tail, which is clearly apparent when viewed from below. Also head coloration is darker, with more white speckling across the wings. Sexes are alike. Young birds are easily recognizable thanks to the white band across the lower breast.

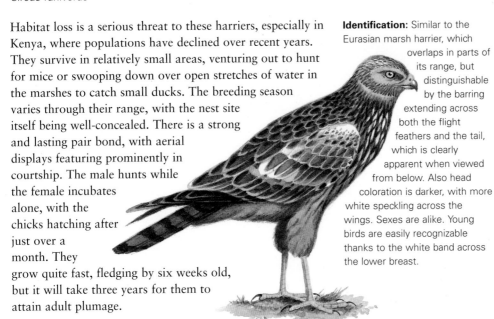

Distribution: Various separate localities mainly through eastern and southern Africa, right down to Cape Province. An isolated population also present in Namibia.
Size: 50cm (20in).
Habitat: Areas of marshland.
Nest: Pile of vegetation, often on the ground.
Eggs: 3–6, white, sometimes with reddish blotching.
Food: Vertebrates, largely small mammals.

Long-crested eagle

Lophaetus occipitalis

Distribution: Across Africa in a broad band below the Sahara, then continuing from Mozambique largely through the coastal region down to the south-eastern area of South Africa.
Size: 55cm (22in).
Habitat: Close to rivers, in wooded areas.
Nest: Platform of sticks and twigs.
Eggs: 1–2, white with reddish-brown blotches.

These eagles often prove nomadic in some areas, with pairs establishing a breeding territory after a period of heavy rainfall. The nest itself is relatively small in size, measuring as little as 50cm (20in) in diameter. During dry years, they may not breed at all, although when conditions are favourable, pairs may nest twice in a year. These eagles often congregate at the site of grassland fires, seizing rodents and other prey seeking to escape the flames. Long-crested eagles catch their prey entirely on the ground, typically by relying on their keen eyesight to spot potential quarry. They will sometimes soar up to a great height as part of their courtship ritual. When feeding young at the nest, food is regurgitated from the crop, rather than being carried in the eagle's sharp talons. The cock bird undertakes much of the task of hunting on his own, bringing back food for his mate at the nest, who in turns feeds their offspring once they have hatched. The young fledge at about two months.

Identification: Dark chocolate-brown coloration, with white plumage on thighs, although this area is occasionally brown. Very evident white wing bars in flight, with tail barred black and white. Distinctive long crest, sloping towards back of head. Yellow cere, legs and feet, with grey bill. Sexes are alike. Young birds have much shorter crests.

African fish eagle

Haliaeetus vocifer

These large eagles are fearsome predators. Although fish feature most prominently in their diet they take a wide range of aquatic life, even killing birds up to the size of a flamingo. They also feed on bullfrogs, young crocodiles and monitor lizards (*Varanus* species), and monkeys caught in or near the water. They only rarely feed on carrion, usually when migrating across dry country or in the case of young birds who have not fully mastered the necessary hunting skills. African fish eagles can fly with prey weighing up to 1.5kg (3.3lb), but will tackle heavier creatures, which they drag up on to the shore. Noisy and conspicuous, these eagles are not easily overlooked, particularly when they swoop down over the water with talons outstretched, hoping for a catch. On average, they are successful only once in every eight attempts.

Identification: White extends from head to neck and on to the breast. Tail feathers also white, with the remainder of the underparts brown. The wings are black, with prominent brown shoulder patches. Prominent area of yellow at the base of the bill, which is black at the tip. Cock birds have a higher-pitched call than females and may also display more prominent white on the breast. Young birds have dark brown markings on the crown, and similar streaking on the white of the back and chest.

Distribution: Occurs south of the Sahara, except in the east towards the Horn and throughout much of south-west and central Africa.
Size: 73cm (29in).
Habitat: Prefers stretches of open water.
Nest: Constructed from sticks and reeds.
Eggs: 2–3, whitish.
Food: Fish and any other aquatic creatures.

Western banded snake eagle (Smaller banded snake eagle, *Circaetus cinerascens*): 60cm (24in) Occurs across much of Africa, especially in western and central parts, not overlapping with the southern species (see below). Darker and heavier, with a greyish chest and abdomen. Broad white band across the tail. Young birds are dark brown, with streaking on the head down to the breast and the tail band becoming grey. Hens may display more prominent barring on the lower underparts, and are a darker shade of brown overall.

Southern banded snake eagle (East African snake eagle, *Circaetus fasciolatus*): 60cm (24in) South-eastern areas of Africa, typically close to water in wooded countryside. Greyish head and breast, with barring extending across the remaining underparts and the undersides of the wings. Barred tail, darker on the upper surface. Back and wings dark brownish with some paler edging. Young birds have dark brown upperparts, with paler underwing patterning. Sexes are alike.

Sooty falcon (*Falco concolor*): 33cm (13in) Widely-distributed in north-eastern Africa and also occurring further south along the coastal strip down to South Africa. Breeds on islands in the Red Sea. Adults are grey, with long wings that extend further than the tail when closed. Cere, legs and feet yellow. Young birds dark grey above with cream throat and buff underparts, streaked on the chest, with similar patterning across the underside of the wings. Tail barred on the underside, but abdomen largely unmarked.

White-tailed fish eagle

White-tailed sea eagle *Haliaeetus albicilla*

The white-tailed fish eagle is reviving once again after human persecution and pollution contracted its range significantly in the 20th century. Successful reintroductions have now established 15 pairs in Scotland, where it formerly occurred. They are highly effective predators, with both members of a pair hunting co-operatively to achieve a kill, although carrion also features prominently in their diet. These sea eagles will harry other predatory species, including otters and even other birds of prey such as ospreys, into giving up their catches.

Identification: Brown, lighter and creamier on the head and upper body. Darker wings and rump; tail is white. Pale yellow bill, legs and feet. Young are darker, with white on the tail confined to the centre and a blackish bill.

Distribution: From Iceland east to northern Scandinavia and across Russia. Various other countries, particularly in eastern Europe.
Size: 92cm (36in).
Habitat: Large stretches of water, often coastal.
Nest: Bulky, made of sticks.
Eggs: 1–3, whitish.
Food: Vertebrates and carrion.

INSECT-HUNTERS

While trees provide birds with fruits, berries and seeds, they also attract a wide range of invertebrates.
Different species have developed different hunting techniques in order to locate and catch these insects.
Many simply comb the trees, but others use the branches as vantage points, from where they can
swoop down directly and seize their prey in flight.

Common scimitarbill

Scimitar-billed wood hoopoe *Rhinopomastus cyanomelas*

Distribution: Ranges from Kenya and parts of Somalia southwards in a broad band across much of southern Africa, reaching central parts of South Africa and extending as far as Namibia in the south-west.
Size: 25cm (10in).
Habitat: Dry woodland areas.
Nest: Tree holes.
Eggs: 3–4, blue.
Food: Mainly invertebrates.

Restricted to Africa, scimitarbills were formerly grouped with wood hoopoes but are now usually regarded as a separate entity. This is based partly on their habits, since they occur in individual pairs rather than in flocks, although they can sometimes be encountered in family parties once the breeding season has ended. They probe into nooks and crannies with their curved bills, extracting grubs and insects lurking in the bark of trees. Common scimitarbills will also occasionally descend to the ground in their search for invertebrate prey, and here they will often raid ants' nests, using their bills to break into the nest. Their breeding period starts towards the end of the dry season, with the hen locating a suitable cavity in a tree, which may have been created by another bird such as a barbet. The chicks hatch after an incubation period of around 16 days. The male continues to roost on his own, but both members of the pair will feed their growing brood.

Identification: Cock bird is dark in colour, with white bands across the outer edges of the open wings and white tips to the undersides of the shorter tail feathers. Glossy purple suffusion over much of the body, with greenish hues apparent also, especially on the sides of the head. Distinctive, narrow, curved black bill is longer in the male. Young birds and hens have brownish coloration on the head.

Bar-throated apalis

Apalis thoracica

These warblers vary in coloration through their range, although the basic patterning of their feathers remains constant. More than 20 different races are recognized in eastern-southern Africa, with upperparts ranging from greyish-brown to green and underparts ranging from white to greenish-yellow. A number of these subspecies are very localized, such as *A. t. spelonkensis*, which occurs in the northern Transvaal. Originating from the Soutpansberg and Woodbush region, this most colourful race of bar-throated apalis has green upperparts contrasting with extensive yellow plumage on the underparts. Their breeding season also varies depending on location, and usually extends over a longer period in more northerly parts of their range. Once paired, the adults generally stay together throughout the year. Bar-throated apalis often hunt insects in the company of other small birds, either catching them among the vegetation or on the wing, but they rarely feed at ground level.

Identification: Upperparts dark greyish-brown. Greyish-white throat and underparts, broken by a prominent black band across the chest. Greenish-yellow flanks. Black bill, dark pinkish legs. White outer tail feathers. Hen less brightly coloured, often with a narrower breast band. Young birds as adults, but underparts have more buff.

Distribution: Present in parts of eastern to southern Africa, extending from Kenya southwards through Tanzania, Zambia, Malawi and Zimbabwe right down to South Africa. Absent from coastal areas except in South Africa.
Size: 12cm (4³⁄₄in).
Habitat: Forest and thickets.
Nest: An oval dome made from vegetation.
Eggs: 2–4, bluish-white with reddish markings.
Food: Invertebrates.

Eurasian treecreeper

Certhia familiaris

These treecreepers can be distinguished from the southerly short-toed species (*C. brachydactyla*) by their longer hind toes, which assist them in climbing vertically up tree trunks. Having reached the top of the trunk, the treecreeper flies down to the base of a neighbouring tree and begins again, circling the bark, probing likely nooks and crannies with its bill. The pointed tips of the tail feathers provide extra support. Pairs start nesting in the spring, with the cock bird chasing after his intended mate. They seek out a small, hidden cavity where a cup-shaped nest can be constructed. The hen incubates mainly on her own for two weeks, and the young fledge after a similar interval. It is not uncommon, especially in southern parts of their range, for pairs to breed twice in succession.

Left: Small crevices in a trunk may be used as a nesting site.

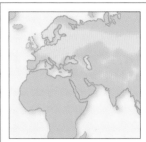

Distribution: Much of northern Europe, except for the far north of Scandinavia. Sporadic distribution through France and northern Spain, not occurring further south on the Iberian peninsula. Not present in northern Africa, but extends into Asia.
Size: 14cm (5^1/$_2$in).
Habitat: Dense woodland.
Nest: Small hollow.
Eggs: 5–7, white with reddish-brown markings.
Food: Assorted invertebrates.

Identification: Mottled brownish upperparts, with a variable white stripe above the eyes, depending on race. Underparts whitish. Narrow, slightly curved bill. Sexes alike. Young birds resemble adults.

Violet wood hoopoe (*Phoeniculus damarensis*): 40cm (15^3/$_4$in)
Restricted to south-western Angola and north-western Namibia. Metallic violet coloration overall, with white areas on the wings and on the underside of the shorter tail feathers. Long, slightly down-curving red bill, tapering along its length. Pinkish legs and feet. The hen is distinguishable by its shorter, duller and less curved bill. Young birds have dark bills and either brown throat patches (males) or black throat patches (females).

Green wood hoopoe (*Phoeniculus purpureus*): 36cm (14in)
Ranges widely in a band across Africa south of the Sahara, extending down the eastern side and across southern parts of the continent. Dark greenish head and underparts, with bright blue on the wings and tail. White patches apparent on the open wings, and close to the tips of the shorter tail feathers. Bill strongly down-curved and bright red in the cock, shorter and less curved in the hen. Young birds recognizable by their black bills in their first year.

Chapin's apalis (chestnut-headed apalis, *Apalis chapini*): 12cm (4^3/$_4$in)
Restricted to eastern Africa, occurring in the forests of southern Tanzania and extending to Malawi and Zambia. Distinctive chestnut-red plumage runs from the base of the bill just above the eyes, down across the breast to the centre of the abdomen. The lower underparts are light grey. Chin is white in the northern race. Upperparts are dark brownish-grey. Sexes are alike. Young birds resemble adults.

Tree pipit

Anthus trivialis

Tree pipits sing with increasing frequency at the start of the breeding period. Their nest is constructed close to the ground in open countryside, well-hidden from predators. This need for camouflage may explain the variable coloration of their eggs. These long-distance migrants overwinter in Africa, reaching southern parts towards the end of October. Tree pipits feed on the ground, moving jauntily and pausing to flick their tails up and down, flying to the safety of a nearby branch at any hint of danger. As well as invertebrates they may also eat seeds. Solitary and quiet, these pipits are not easily observed away from their breeding grounds. They begin returning to Europe in April.

Distribution: Occurs widely through much of Europe up into Scandinavia and eastwards into Asia. Overwinters across Africa south of the Sahara, continuing down the eastern side of the continent, with isolated populations in Namibia and South Africa.
Size: 15cm (6in).
Habitat: Woodland.
Nest: Made of grass.
Eggs: 4–6, greyish with variable markings.
Food: Mainly invertebrates.

Identification: Brownish upperparts with dark streaking. White edging to the wing feathers. Buff stripe above each eye, darker brown stripes through and below them. Throat whitish. Underparts pale yellowish with brownish streaking. Bill dark, especially at the tip. Legs and feet pinkish. Sexes are alike. Young birds are more buff overall.

FOREST FINCHES

Many seed-eating birds are to be found in open country, but a number prefer to live in woodland, at least for part of the year in temperate areas. Here the trees offer a reliable source of food, especially during the winter, when fruit and berries are in short supply. Some species, such as the crossbills, have evolved very distinctive bills to enable them to extract their seeds more easily.

Forest weaver

Dark-backed weaver *Ploceus bicolor*

Unlike many weavers, this species is quite solitary, usually encountered in individual pairs rather than in flocks. Studies of their song pattern have revealed not only regional differences but that members of a pair learn to attune their song patterns exactly, so that they sound identical. Their subsequent duetting is believed to help reinforce the bond between them, and may also enable the birds to keep in touch with each other in the dense woodland. Forest weavers construct a fairly typical weaver nest suspended off a branch, with both members of the pair collecting material, although it is thought the cock bird alone is responsible for building the structure. Another point of distinction is that male forest weavers do not moult into breeding plumage at the onset of the nesting season.

Identification: Chocolate-brown head, back, wings and tail. The throat is brownish with yellow markings, and the underparts are a rich shade of golden-yellow. Bill is brownish, especially on the upper bill, and pinkish-brown below. Legs also pinkish-brown. Young birds have paler throats. Sexes are alike.

Distribution: From northern Angola across Africa to Tanzania and Mozambique. Extends down the eastern coast to South Africa, and as far as Somalia in the north. Isolated populations also in Cameroon, Gabon and islands in the Gulf of Guinea.
Size: 16cm (6¹⁄₄in).
Habitat: Forest areas, often near streams.
Nest: Suspended, made out of vegetation.
Eggs: 2–4, pinkish-white with brownish markings.
Food: Invertebrates, nectar.

Red-faced crimsonwing

Cryptospiza reichenovii

These colourful forest waxbills are shy by nature, and their small size makes them difficult to observe in the dense undergrowth. They fly relatively short distances, rarely emerging out into the open, although occasionally small groups may be spotted in fields of ripening millet. Red-faced crimsonwings often associate with other finches in mixed flocks, feeding mainly on the ground. The seeds of pine cones are a significant source of food in Zimbabwe. Little is known about their breeding habits, but it is thought that invertebrates feature more prominently in their diet when they are rearing young. The nest is a large and untidy structure, with the birds going back and forth through a side entrance. Young cock birds soon develop the characteristic red facial feathering after fledging. Pairs appear to favour the same tree for nesting, and there are often nests from previous years alongside the current one.

Identification: Cock bird easily distinguishable by the presence of prominent red patches around the eyes. The body plumage is mainly olive, slightly lighter at the base of the bill. Back and rump are reddish, with red areas also on the lower flanks. Flight and tail feathers are black. Bill is black, legs and feet grey. Hens are similar, but with yellowish-buff patches surrounding the eyes. Young birds are a dull shade of olive-brown, with no distinctive facial patches, and a brownish-green shade on the wings.

Distribution: Separate areas of distribution occurring in Uganda, Kenya and Tanzania, Mozambique and Zimbabwe, Angola, and south-western Nigeria and neighbouring islands in the Gulf of Guinea.
Size: 12cm (4³⁄₄in).
Habitat: Dense forest.
Nest: Ball of vegetation.
Eggs: 3–5, white.
Food: Mainly seeds.

Common crossbill

Red crossbill *Loxia curvirostra*

The crossbill's highly distinctive bill can crack the hard casing of conifer seeds, enabling the bird to extract the inner kernel with its tongue. These finches also eat the pips of various fruits, and will prey on invertebrates, particularly when they have young to feed. The breeding season varies through their wide range, starting later in the north. Both members of the pair build the nest, which is constructed in a conifer, sometimes more than 18m (60ft) high. Common crossbills only rarely descend to the ground, usually to drink, unless the pine crop is very poor. When faced with a shortage of food, they move to areas far outside their normal range. This phenomenon, known as an irruption, occurs once a decade in Europe.

Identification: Males are reddish with darker blackish feathering on the top of the head, more evident on the wings. Underparts reddish, paler towards the vent. Upper and lower parts of the distinctive blackish bill are curved at the tip. Hens are olive-green, darker over the back and wings, and have a paler rump. Young birds resemble hens, but have evident streaking on their bodies.

Distribution: Resident throughout much of Scandinavia and northern Europe, extending into Asia. Found elsewhere in Europe, usually in areas of coniferous forest, extending as far as northern Africa.
Size: 15cm (6in).
Habitat: Coniferous forests.
Nest: Cup-shaped, made from vegetation.
Eggs: 3–4, whitish-blue with reddish-brown markings.
Food: Mainly the seeds of pine cones.

Scottish crossbill (*Loxia scotica*): 17cm (6³⁄₄in)
Restricted to the pine forests of the Caledonian region of northern Scotland. Similar to the male common crossbill (*Loxia curvirostra*) but with a larger head. The bill is also bulkier and the lower bill is not so pronounced. Hens and juveniles also resemble this species, except for the differences in their bills.

Dusky crimsonwing (*Cryptospiza jacksoni*): 12cm (4³⁄₄in)
Restricted to a small area of eastern Dem. Rep. Congo, extending to Rwanda and south-western Uganda. Cock has a predominantly red head, with a grey collar extending up the hindneck. Back and rump are also red, and there are some red markings on the flanks. Remainder of the body is dark grey. Wings, tail and bill blackish. Legs and feet greyish. Hens are similar, but the red on the head is restricted to the area surrounding the eyes. Young birds display no red on their head or flanks, and the red on their back is reduced in extent.

Black-bellied seedcracker (*Pyrenestes ostrinus*): 15cm (6in)
Central Africa, ranging from the Ivory Coast east to Uganda and south to northern parts of Angola and Zambia. Red head and chest, extending to the flanks. Rump and tail are also red, and the remainder of the body is black. Stocky greyish-black bill. Legs and feet pinkish. Hens have red restricted to the head and upper breast, as well as from the rump to the tail. Remainder of the body is olive-brown. Young birds are duller, with red only on the rump and tail.

Brambling

Fringilla montifringilla

After breeding in northern parts of Europe, the harsh winter weather forces bramblings to migrate to more southerly latitudes in search of food. Here they can be seen in fields and other open areas of countryside. These finches feed largely on beech nuts, relying heavily on the forests of central Europe to sustain them over the winter period. Although normally occurring in small flocks, millions of individuals may occasionally congregate in the forests. Bramblings have a rather jerky walk when on the ground, sometimes hopping as well when searching for food. Their diet is much more varied during the summer months, when they are nesting. Caterpillars of moths in particular are eagerly devoured at this time and used as a rearing food for their young. Bramblings have a relatively rapid breeding cycle. The hen incubates the eggs on her own, and they will hatch after about a fortnight. The young birds leave the nest after a similar interval.

Distribution: Breeds in the far north of Europe, through most of Scandinavia into Russia, extending eastwards into Asia. Overwinters further south throughout Europe, extending to parts of north-western Africa.
Size: 18cm (7in).
Habitat: Woodland.
Nest: Cup-shaped, made from vegetation.
Eggs: 5–7, a dark greenish-blue colour.
Food: Seeds and nuts.

Identification: Black head and bill. Orange underparts, white rump and white wing bars. Underparts whitish, blackish markings on the orange flanks. Duller in winter, with pale head markings and yellowish bill. Hens like winter males, but have greyer sides to the face and duller scapulars. Young birds like hens but are brown, with a yellowish rump.

WOODLAND-DEPENDENT FINCHES

Many finches associated with woodland in northern latitudes have a wide area of distribution, extending not just into Asia but also sometimes to North America. Conversely, there are other species that have very localized distributions. What links them all is that they are dependent on woodland, with large-scale deforestation posing a severe threat to their survival, locally and globally.

Tenerife blue chaffinch

Fringilla teydea

The Tenerife blue chaffinch, now separated from the Gran Canaria blue chaffinch (*F. polatzeki*), is found almost exclusively in the Canarian pine (*Pinus canariensis*) forests of Tenerife. The shape of their bills allow these finches to easily crack conifer seeds, but they also hunt invertebrates, seeking beetles and caterpillars as well as butterflies, which are caught in flight. Their breeding period begins in May, with pairs usually only rearing one brood per year. The young remain with the adults after fledging, forming family parties through the autumn. Flocks may sometimes be seen at lower altitudes during the winter, if the weather is especially severe. Inter-island movements appear unlikely, although there is a reliable record of one blue chaffinch being sighted in north-western Lanzarote. On Tenerife, large areas of the pine forest were replanted during the 1950s, and since the chaffinches are legally protected their future seems reasonably assured there.

Identification: Cock bird is slaty-blue, slightly darker over the head and wings. Pale bluish-white wingbars and white undertail coverts, with a bluish-grey bill. Hens are brown with pale buff wingbars, greyish underparts and a brownish bill. Young birds resemble adult hens but are a darker shade of brown.

Distribution: Restricted to the western Canary Islands, off north-west Africa.
Size: 17cm (6½in).
Habitat: Pine forests.
Nest: Cup-shaped, made from vegetation.
Eggs: 4–5, bluish-brown with darker markings.
Food: Mainly pine seeds, some invertebrates.

Forest canary

Crithagra scotops

Distribution: Restricted to South Africa, occurring from eastern Transvaal to Natal and into Cape Province.
Size: 13cm (5in).
Habitat: Upland forest.
Nest: Cup-shaped, made from vegetation.
Eggs: 3–4, whitish-blue with reddish speckling.
Food: Mainly seeds, but also some fruit.

The relatively dark, streaked plumage of these canaries helps them to blend in with their woodland habitat. Other, similar species are to be found further north in Africa, extending as far as Ethiopia. The song of cock birds, uttered largely just before and during the breeding season, is quite musical, but does not compare to that of domesticated canaries – it is not as loud, although sufficiently distinctive to draw attention to their presence. Forest canaries are not especially social by nature. Cocks are quite territorial, and are most likely to be encountered in pairs or family groups rather than in flocks. The breeding season varies through their range, depending on location and other factors including rainfall. The nest is concealed in a tree or brush, and the hen lines the cup with insulating material such as feathers or wool. She sits alone, with incubation lasting approximately two weeks. The young birds fledge after a similar period.

Identification: Cock birds have a variable blackish area on the sides of the face, extending from the sides of the bill, with a yellow streak above the eyes. Yellow bib and small wingbars. The head, back and wings are otherwise greenish with dark streaking, becoming more yellow on the underparts and rump. Hens have greyish rather than black faces. Young birds are paler than adult hens, with more pinkish feet.

Hawfinch

Coccothraustes coccothraustes

With their characteristic stocky, powerful bills, hawfinches are able to crack open cherry stones and the hard kernels of similar fruits and feed on the seeds within. They usually feed off the ground, but may sometimes descend to pick up fallen fruits. In the spring they will also eat emerging buds, as well as feeding on invertebrates, with their bill strength enabling them to prey on even hard-bodied beetles without difficulty. Pairs are formed during the spring, with the cock bird harrying the female for a period beforehand. She will then start to build the nest, which can be located in the fork of a tree more than 22m (75ft) above the ground. The incubation period lasts approximately 12 days, and the young leave the nest after a similar interval. Hawfinches are most likely to be observed in small flocks over the winter period, with populations occurring in more northern areas usually moving southwards at this time.

Identification: Adult male in breeding condition has a black area around the bill and eyes, with a brown crown and grey around the neck. Whitish area on the wings and black flight feathers. Underparts are brownish. Bill is black, paler in non-breeding, as is the head. Hens have paler and greyer heads, and greyer secondary flight feathers. Young birds have distinct streaking on their underparts.

Distribution: Resident in most of Europe, although absent from Ireland. Breeds in the south of Scandinavia and further east into Asia, where these populations are only summer visitors. Some reported sightings on various Mediterranean islands and parts of northwestern Africa.
Size: 16½cm (6½in).
Habitat: Mixed woodland.
Nest: Cup-shaped, made of plant matter.
Eggs: 3–6, bluish-white to green, with dark markings.
Food: Seeds, invertebrates.

Warsangli linnet (*Linaria johannis*): 13cm (5in)
Juniper forest and upland in northern Somalia. White area above the bill, forming a streak above the eyes, with white extending to the sides of the face and on to the breast and underparts. Head and back greyish. Wings are blackish with a white wing bar. Rufous-brown flanks extending to the rump. Bill silvery-grey, as are the legs and feet. Hens are similar but with streaking on the grey upperparts, especially on the back. Young are browner with more definite streaking, which extends to the underparts.

Grant's bluebill (*Spermophaga poliogenys*): 14cm (5½in)
North-central Dem. Rep. Congo east to western Uganda. Red head and breast, narrowing to the sides of the flanks, with the rump also red. Remainder of plumage is black. Bill red with bluish markings at its base. Legs and feet blackish. Hens have red restricted to the breast and rump, and the head, back and wings are greyish-black. Underparts spotted with white. Young birds have red restricted to the rump and are darker overall, with more blue on the bill.

Grey-headed nigrita (Grey-headed negrobird, *Nigrita canicapilla*): 15cm (6in)
Guinea east to Sudan, Kenya and Tanzania, and south to Dem. Rep. Congo and Angola. Grey on the rear of the head, extending over the back, and black on the face, underparts and across the wings. Narrow white line often apparent on the head, depending on race, with white spots on the wings. Yellow iris, black bill and greyish legs. Young are dark grey overall. Sexes are alike.

Pine grosbeak

Pinicola enucleator

These northern grosbeaks may sometimes be encountered further south, particularly in years when food is scarce. They were first recorded in France as recently as 1992, and have been observed in countries bordering the Mediterranean, including Spain and Italy. The pine grosbeak's song is quite loud, although they are not especially conspicuous birds, particularly when perched – their coloration actually helps them to merge into the shadows. Agile by nature, they feed by climbing around in branches or hopping along on the ground. Various invertebrates including mosquitoes feature in their diet during the summer, while seeds are more significant in the winter.

Identification: Cock is pinkish with grey on the face, wings and underparts, and white on the wings. Greyish-black bill. Hens are olive-green and grey, with a pale base to the bill. Young similar to hens but greyer, buff not white on their wings.

Distribution: The extreme north of Scandinavia and Russia, extending into Asia. Moves south in the winter, sometimes well away from their usual haunts. Also present in North America.
Size: 25cm (10in).
Habitat: Coniferous forest.
Nest: Bulky, cup-shaped, made from vegetation.
Eggs: 2–5, pale bluish-green.
Food: Seeds, fruit and invertebrates.

CUCKOOS AND SHRIKES

Predatory by nature, these two groups of birds also display unusual breeding behaviour. They typically rely on other birds, either of a different species or helpers of their own kind, to raise their chicks. However, although well-known for their parasitic habits, not all cuckoo species neglect their parental duties – some do raise their own offspring.

Cuckoo

Common cuckoo *Cuculus canorus*

The distinctive call of the cuckoo, heard when these birds return from their African wintering grounds, has traditionally been regarded in Europe as one of the earliest signs of spring. Typically, they are only resident in Europe between April and September. Adult cuckoos have an unusual ability to feed on hairy caterpillars, which are plentiful in woodlands throughout the summer. Common cuckoos are parasitic breeders – the hens lay single eggs in the nests of smaller birds such as hedge sparrows (dunnock, *Prunella modularis*), meadow pipits (*Anthus pratensis*) and wagtails (*Motacilla* species). The unsuspecting hosts hatch a monster, with the cuckoo chick ejecting other eggs or potential rivals from the nest in order to monopolize the food supply.

Right: The young cuckoo lifts eggs on its back to eject them from the nest.

Identification: Grey head, upper chest, wings and tail, and black edging to the white feathers of the underparts. In hens this barring extends almost to the throat, offset against a more yellowish background. Some hens belong to a brown colour morph, with rufous feathering replacing the grey, and black barring apparent on the upperparts.

Distribution: Throughout the whole of Europe, ranging eastwards into Asia. Also present in northern Africa. Populations in Northern Europe overwinter in eastern and southern parts of Africa, while Asiatic birds migrate as far as the Philippines.
Size: 36cm (14in).
Habitat: Various.
Nest: None – lays directly in other birds' nests.
Eggs: 1 per nest, resembling those of its host.
Food: Mainly invertebrates, including caterpillars.

Great spotted cuckoo

Clamator glandarius

These lively cuckoos hunt for invertebrates in trees and on the ground, hopping along in a rather clumsy fashion. Great spotted cuckoos are bold birds by nature. When breeding, they parasitize the nests of magpies and similar corvids, and in Africa will sometimes lay in the nests of starlings. The hen usually removes any eggs already present in the host bird's nest before laying, but if any do remain and hatch, the nestlings are reared alongside the young cuckoo. Their relatively large size and noisy nature make these cuckoos quite conspicuous, particularly after the breeding period, when they form flocks.

Identification: Silvery-grey top to the head, with a slight crest. Darker grey neck, back and wings, with white spots over the wings. Pale yellow plumage under the throat extending to the upper breast. The remainder of the underparts are white. Sexes are alike, although their song notes are different. Young birds are much darker in colour – black rather than grey, with rusty-brown flight feathers.

Distribution: Southern Europe, from Spain to Turkey and into Asia as far as Iran. Migrates to Africa, mainly south of the Sahara.
Size: 39cm (15in).
Habitat: Prefers relatively open country.
Nest: None – lays directly in other birds' nests.
Eggs: 1 per nest, resembling those of its host.
Food: Invertebrates.

Black cuckoo (*Cuculus clamosus*): 30cm (12in)
Much of Africa south of the Sahara. Absent from southern Dem. Rep. Congo, eastern Tanzania and much of the south-east. Occurs in Cape Province. Black overall, with relatively long wings. The Gabon race (*C. c. gabonensis*) is more colourful, with a rufous-brown upper breast, white on the lower breast and abdomen, and black barring on the underparts. Undertail coverts are yellow.

Senegal coucal (*Centropus senegalensis*):
40cm (16in)
Senegal to Sudan and Tanzania. Also present in Egypt and southern Africa. Strong bill. Black over the head and down the neck. Lemon underparts. Back is dark brown, wings are rusty-brown and the tail is long and black. Sexes are alike.

São Tomé fiscal (Newton's fiscal, *Lanius newtoni*): 23cm (9in)
Restricted to Sao Tome, in the Gulf of Guinea. Slightly glossy black head, back, wings and tail. Underparts are whitish-yellow, paler on the throat. Distinctive whitish-yellow patches across the top of each wing. Bill, legs and feet are black. Sexes are alike.

Red-eyed puffback (*Dryoscopus senegalensis*):
18cm (7in)
Parts of western and central Africa. Distinctive red irides. Cock is white below and glossy black above, with the rump also white. Hens have more greyish upperparts, and a distinctive white streak from the upper bill to each eye. Young birds are duller. Bill, legs and feet blackish.

Magpie shrike

African long-tailed shrike *Urolestes melanoleucus*

The calls of the magpie shrike consist of a series of noisy whistles, some of which may reflect the dominance of an individual within a flock. These shrikes are very social by nature, even during nesting, when the members of a breeding pair may have up to three helpers to assist in collecting food for their growing brood. Older hens rank highest in the social structure, which may explain why the helper birds are normally males. The eggs are laid in a large nest usually constructed in a thorn tree, its branches holding the structure together as well as affording some protection from would-be predators. When hunting, magpie shrikes rely heavily on their keen eyesight, remaining alert to movement around them before quickly swooping to seize their quarry. They will also sometimes catch invertebrates in flight.

Distribution: Two African populations. One is centred on Tanzania, while another extends from southern Angola to Mozambique and northern South Africa.
Size: 50cm (20in).
Habitat: Woodland.
Nest: Cup-shaped, made from vegetation.
Eggs: 3–5, buff with brownish spotting.
Food: Small vertebrates, insects.

Identification: Mainly black. White area across the top of the wings, creating a broad band. A white area is also largely hidden in the folded wing, on the outer flight feathers. Feathers adjacent to the back also edged white. Long, elegant tail, shorter in the Tanzanian (*U. m. aequatorialis*) race. Bill, legs and feet black. Hens have white on the flanks. Young browner with shorter tails.

White-crested helmetshrike

White-helmeted shrike *Prionops plumatus*

The white-crested helmetshrikes' nest-building skills are highly developed. Instead of assembling a jumble of material, they use a combination of grass and bark to make a very tidy cup. Spiders' webs are placed on the outside to bind the structure together, and to the branch, serving to anchor it firmly in place. A variety of trees may be chosen for the nesting site, but the positioning of the nest is of more significance. It is normally located around 5m (16ft) off the ground, usually at some distance along a branch, rather than adjacent to the main trunk. Pairs may nest on their own, but frequently have several non-breeding helpers assisting them in finding food. Occasionally, two hens may lay in the same nest, but the dimensions of the cup mean that a number of the eggs will be lost over the rim if piled on top of each other, falling to the ground below. The young subsequently join the group once they are three weeks old.

Identification: Distinctive white crown and forehead, with blackish stripes on the sides of the neck and variable grey plumage on the hindneck. Underparts are whitish. Young birds have whiter faces, lack the dark plumage on the hindneck and have brownish rather than black bills. Sexes are alike.

Distribution: Across Africa south of the Sahara, from Senegal to Ethiopia. Ranges down the eastern side of the continent to northern South Africa, and across to Angola.
Size: 25cm (10in).
Habitat: Dry woodland.
Nest: Cup-shaped, usually anchored to a branch.
Eggs: 2–5, creamy-white with dark markings.
Food: Invertebrates, fruit.

TURACOS AND FLYCATCHERS

*Turacos or touracos are now confined to Africa, although fossilized remains unearthed in Bavaria,
Germany indicate that these birds once occurred in Europe. Greens, blues and purples predominate
in their plumage, although go-away birds (so called because of their calls)
and certain plantain-eaters are grey in colour.*

Ross's turaco

Lady Ross's touraco *Musophaga rossae*

These turacos have adapted well to living in trees, and are able to run and jump among the branches with great agility. Their toes are flexible, enabling them to grip the perch either with three toes pointing forward or with two forward and two gripping from behind. Ross's turacos feed on a variety of fruit and berries, congregating in small groups of up to a dozen birds where such food is plentiful. At other times, especially when breeding, they are territorial and surprisingly aggressive, and will even harry birds of prey. The nest site is usually secluded, often hidden by creepers, and both members of the pair work together to build it. This takes just over a week on average. Incubation is also shared, with the birds swapping over several times during the day. The young hatch after about 25 days, and are initially covered in thick, dark brown down feathering.

Identification: Predominantly purplish-blue, with characteristic crimson-red primary flight feathers and a red crest. Yellow bill and frontal shield, with a bare yellow area around the eyes. Legs and feet black. Sexes are alike. Young birds duller, with no frontal shield and a blackish bill.

Distribution: Centred on Dem. Rep. Congo, extending to adjacent countries including Angola, Zambia, Malawi and Tanzania. Believed to occur in isolated areas to the north, including north-eastern Gabon and parts of Cameroon.
Size: 52cm (20½in).
Habitat: Dense forest.
Nest: Platform of twigs.
Eggs: 1–2, creamy-white.
Food: Berries, plant matter.

Great blue turaco

Blue plantain-eater *Corythaeola cristata*

This is the largest member of the turaco family, and is most likely to be seen in small groups. Great blue turacos are not powerful fliers but they are agile, and able to climb easily among the branches. Along with fruits and berries, leaves feature prominently in their diet, as do flowers. Where possible, small fruits that can be swallowed whole are preferred. Members of a group leave a fruiting tree individually rather than flying off as a flock, flapping their wings to get airborne and gliding to another nearby tree. At dusk they return to their roosting site, which is normally a tall tree – such sites are known to be used consistently by the same group of birds for more than a decade. Pairs separate from the rest of the flock at the start of the breeding period, which varies markedly through their range, and may be accompanied by a youngster from a previous clutch, whose task is to aid the adult turacos in providing food for their new offspring.

Distribution: Range extends from Guinea on the western coast of Africa across through Nigeria and Cameroon to southern Sudan, Dem. Rep. Congo and south as far as parts of Angola.
Size: 75cm (29½in).
Habitat: Forest.
Nest: Platform of sticks.
Eggs: 1–3, whitish or pale bluish-green.
Food: Vegetarian.

Identification: Predominantly turquoise-blue, with a curved black crest extending right across the top of the head. Underparts are greenish-yellow, lower underparts and vent area are brownish. Prominent black area at the ends of the tail feathers. Bill is yellow, becoming red at the tip. Legs and feet are greyish. Sexes are alike. Young birds have shorter crest feathers, and are greyer on the breast.

Hartlaub's turaco

Tauraco hartlaubi

The brilliant red coloration present in the flight feathers of these and most other turacos is the result of a copper-based colour pigment called turacin, which is unique to this group of birds. Although agile in the trees, Hartlaub's turacos drop significant numbers of fruits when feeding. They can eat fruits that are known to be toxic, and suffer no apparent side effects as a result. In some areas they have adapted to take food from non-native plants, and may also prey on invertebrates such as moths. They are rarely seen on the ground, however, usually descending only to drink. Hartlaub's turacos are opportunistic breeders, nesting repeatedly under favourable conditions. Incubation is quite short, lasting a maximum of 18 days. In common with other turacos, the parent massages the chick's vent area until it produces a dropping, which the adult swallows, keeping the nest clean.

Identification: Metallic blue head and comb-like crest. White area in front of and white stripe below each eye. Underparts and upper back are greenish, becoming bluish-purple on the wings and lower back. Tail also dark bluish-purple. Crimson-red on the flight feathers. Bare red skin encircles each eye. Bill orange-red, darker on the upper bill. Legs and feet blackish. Sexes are alike. Young birds resemble adults.

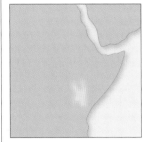

Distribution: Restricted to an area in eastern Africa, occurring in Tanzania, Kenya and Uganda.
Size: 43cm (17in).
Habitat: Forested areas.
Nest: Platform-type, made of sticks.
Eggs: 1–2, whitish.
Food: Wide variety of berries and fruits, and some other plant matter. Will occasionally take invertebrates.

Bannerman's turaco (*Tauraco bannermani*, E): 40cm (15¾in)
Restricted to south-western Cameroon, in the Bamenda highlands. Very distinctive, short reddish-orange crest, with dark grey patches on the sides of the face. Lighter green on the hindneck and down on to the chest. Darker green underparts, back and tail, with red patches evident in the wings. Bill yellow, legs and feet grey. Sexes are alike.

Ruspoli's turaco (*Tauraco ruspolii*): 40cm (15¾in)
Confined to southern parts of Ethiopia. Mostly green, darker on the back and lower upperparts. Low creamy-pink crest, with a red patch behind. Bill reddish, legs and feet greyish. Young birds resemble adults. Sexes are alike.

Grey go-away-bird (*Corythaixoides concolor*): 48cm (19in)
From parts of Angola and Namibia east to southern Tanzania and northern South Africa. Entirely grey, with a tall, fairly broad crest. Sexes are alike. Young birds are more buff and have a small crest.

Western plantain-eater (*Crinifer piscator*): 50cm (20in)
From Senegal to the Central African Republic. Also an apparently isolated population in south-western Dem. Rep. Congo. Greyish, with pale edging on the upperparts and spotting on the white underparts. Tall, shaggy crest, shorter in young birds. Yellow bill. Legs and feet grey.

Black-and-white shrike-flycatcher

Vanga flycatcher *Bias musicus*

These flycatchers are very lively birds. There is a strong bond between pairs and they stay together throughout the year, becoming increasingly territorial at the start of the breeding season. Cocks start to sing more frequently at this time, especially in flight, and a male will challenge a rival by raising his crest and extending his neck. Females may also drive off other hens venturing into their territory. Their breeding period tends to begin during March in western Africa, but does not commence until October in more southerly areas. The cup-shaped nest is shallow but well constructed, and may be bound by the sticky protein of spiders' webs. The hen sits alone, while the cock remains nearby, deterring potential nest raiders, such as monkeys. Young birds fledge at about 18 days old.

Identification: Cock has a black head with a crest at the rear, and black plumage extending down over the back and wings. Black feathering is also present on the upper chest. Tail feathers are black, as is the bill, and the legs and feet are yellow. Blackish plumage in hens is largely restricted to the head, with chestnut plumage on the back, wings and tail, and mottling the flanks. Young birds are duller, and tend to have more brownish heads.

Distribution: Ranges down the western coast of Africa, in Kenya in the centre, and down the south-east coast to Mozambique.
Size: 15cm (6in).
Habitat: Forested areas.
Nest: Open, made of vegetation.
Eggs: 2–3, whitish with dark markings.
Food: Mainly Invertebrates.

TROGONS, PITTAS AND BROADBILLS

Trogons are colourful birds, but even their bright hues merge into the gloom of the forest. Three species occur in Africa, although the family is more widespread in Asia. African trogons differ from their Asiatic relatives in having more powerful bills and feet, which may be linked to their predatory lifestyle. Pittas and broadbills are also widespread in Asia, particularly in the south-eastern region.

Narina trogon

Apaloderma narina

Narina trogons are not easily observed, since their sedentary nature helps them to blend in against the forest background. They are most likely to be seen at the forest edge, perched quietly with their heads drawn down, resting on their shoulders. They remain watchful for potential prey, however, and will dart off to seize invertebrate quarry such as spiders and tree grasshoppers, but especially butterfly caterpillars. Occasionally, small vertebrates such as lizards, including young chameleons, may also be caught, but as far as is known narina trogons never eat fruits or berries of any kind. They breed through much of the year, certainly in the Kenyan part of their range. The incubation period lasts for approximately 18 days, with the young leaving the nest once they are a month old. They remain dependent on the adults to provide them with food for at least a further month, until they are able to fly well themselves.

Identification: The head, breast, shoulders, back and rump are a vivid deep green colour. Wings are otherwise greyish, while the underparts are bright red. Hens have brownish-red on the face and breast, with green encircling each eye. The bill is pale yellow with a darker tip. Young resemble hens but are paler.

Distribution: Extends across Africa from Sierra Leone in the west to Ethiopia and Somalia in the east, although not to the Horn of Africa. Ranges down as far as the eastern coast of South Africa, but largely absent from Namibia, Botswana and the rest of South Africa.
Size: 34cm (13in).
Habitat: Rainforest and gallery forest.
Nest: Tree hollow, no lining.
Eggs: 1–4, white.
Food: Mostly invertebrates.

Bar-tailed trogon

Apaloderma vittatum

Distribution: Scattered populations in various parts of Nigeria and adjacent areas of Cameroon. Also present in western Angola and eastern Africa, mainly in Tanzania, Kenya and Uganda.
Size: 30cm (12in).
Habitat: Mountainous areas of woodland.
Nest: Hollow tree.
Eggs: 2–3, white.
Food: Invertebrates.

Quiet by nature, these trogons usually roost in pairs in the forest for much of the day. Occasionally however, they can be detected by the sound of their wings as they hunt insects, darting in among foliage and seizing caterpillars from the leaves of trees. Bar-tailed trogons are highly arboreal and rarely descend from the upper layers of the forest. Resident in Africa throughout the year, there appears to be no mixing of the populations through their widely-scattered range. Pairs choose a small cavity for nesting, often located in a dead tree, and the hen simply lays on the floor of the chamber. This is the only stage at which the "wup"-like call of these birds, which is uttered repeatedly and grows to a crescendo, will be heard, as they stake their claim to the surrounding territory. Any intruders will be fiercely driven away. Incubation is shared, with the cock bird sitting for much of the day.

Identification: Cock bird has a blackish head and chest, with green shoulders, back and rump, and two bare yellowish areas below the eyes. Head and upper breast are dark green. The breast is a bluish bar, and the remaining underparts are bright red. Wings are dark, as is the upper surface of the tail, which has fine, horizontal black-and-white barring underneath. Hens are similar but duller, with a brownish head and rose-coloured underparts. Young birds resemble adult females, but with some spotting on the wings.

African pitta

Angolan pitta *Pitta angolensis*

These dumpy, short-tailed birds spend most of their time on the forest floor, although they will fly up and perch on a branch if disturbed, remaining frozen until the danger has passed. Populations in western Africa are sedentary, but pittas occurring elsewhere in their range migrate, sometimes ending up in areas far outside their normal distribution. They fly at night, and for reasons that remain unclear are attracted to lights in buildings, sometimes being killed after attempting to fly through the windows. When breeding, the display of the male African pitta is quite unusual in that it is accompanied by a purring sound made by the wings. The pitta flutters up to a perch, then simply jumps down to the ground in free fall. At this stage the short tail feathers are raised to display the red lower underparts. Their bulky, domed nest is built off the ground and measures about 20cm (8in) in height and diameter, with the pittas entering the site through a side entrance hole.

Identification: Black cap on the crown and a broad black streak running through each eye, with an area of buff plumage between. Underparts also buff, becoming reddish on the lower abdomen. Back and wings predominantly green, with bluish rump and areas on the wings. Remainder of the wings are black, with white patches evident when open. The bill is blackish (orangish in younger birds) and the legs and feet are brownish-yellow.

Distribution: Sporadic distribution through western parts of Africa as far south as Angola, with the major range extending from the Central African Republic down to Tanzania and Mozambique. Also reported from various locations outside the normal range, including Ethiopia and South Africa.
Size: 22cm (8³/₄in).
Habitat: Forested areas.
Nest: Dome-shaped, made from vegetation.
Eggs: 2–4, whitish with darker, reddish markings.
Food: Invertebrates.

Bare-cheeked trogon (*Apaloderma aequatoriale*): 34cm (13in)
Western Africa, from Nigeria to Gabon. An isolated population is present in north-eastern Dem. Rep. Congo; also recorded once in the south of this country. Cock has green upperparts and breast, with bare yellowish areas of skin close to the eyes. Underside of the tail is white. Hen has green restricted to the top of the head, and the area above the bill and the underparts are rufous-brown, becoming redder below. Young cock birds have brown on the upper breast, while young hens are duller than adults.

Green-breasted pitta (*Pitta reichenowi*): 20cm (8in)
From Cameroon and Gabon eastwards through Dem. Rep. Congo to western Uganda. Head entirely black, except for buff-coloured stripes above the eyes, joining at the back of the head. Throat is white with a small black area beneath. Chest and back are dark green, and the underparts are red. Wing patterning similar to that of the African pitta (*Pitta angolensis*).

African green broadbill (Grauer's broadbill, *Pseudocalyptomena graueri*): 12cm (4³/₄in)
Found in eastern Africa, in the Albertine Rift area, centred on Rwanda and Burundi. Predominantly bright grass-green, with a short tail. Pale buff on the head, with dark speckling which extends down to below the eye. The throat is whitish, and the chest is pale blue. Bill is black, as are the legs and feet. Sexes are alike. Young birds are duller overall.

African broadbill

Smithornis capensis

African broadbills construct a distinctive, bag-like nest, hung off a young tree or bush and typically no more than 2.5m (8ft) above the ground. The nest varies depending on location and the availability of material, but is held together using strands of a fungus. Spiders' webs may also be incorporated. In southern parts of its range it is often made from a type of lichen. Once complete, the nest is about 9cm (3¹/₂in) deep. Both sexes undertake specific, elliptical display flights, particularly just prior to nesting, with the cock bird fluffing up white feathers on his back. The breeding season varies, but egg-laying generally begins just before the onset of the rainy season. African broadbills' nests may be parasitized by barred long-tailed cuckoos (*Cercococcyx montanus*).

Distribution: Various parts of western Africa, from Sierra Leone to Ghana, and also sporadically from Cameroon to northern Angola. More extensive distribution on the eastern side, from Uganda and Dem. Rep. Congo down as far as South Africa.
Size: 14cm (5¹/₂in).
Habitat: Forested areas.
Nest: Made of vegetation, suspended off a branch.
Eggs: 2–3, white.
Food: Invertebrates.

Identification: Black cap and brown lores. Brown back, with some streaking, and white rump. Throat is whitish. Underparts are buff, becoming whiter lower down, with dark brown streaking evident here too. Bill, legs and feet are blackish. Hens have a dark brown rather than black cap, with some streaking. Young birds resemble hens.

WOOD DOVES AND FOREST PIGEONS

Numerous pigeons and doves inhabit woodland. The islands lying off the south-eastern coast of Africa are home to some of the most unusual pigeons in the world, although habitat destruction still threatens their future, in spite of determined conservation efforts. Fruit figures prominently in the diets of those birds occurring in tropical areas, since it is readily available throughout the year.

Bruce's green pigeon

Treron waalia

Distribution: Range extends right across Africa south of the Sahara Desert, from Senegal in the west through to Sudan, Ethiopia and Somalia in the east. Also present on the adjacent part of the Arabian peninsula.
Size: 30cm (12in).
Habitat: Woodland.
Nest: Platform of twigs.
Eggs: 1–2, white.
Food: Mainly fruit, but especially figs.

Bruce's green pigeons congregate in relatively large numbers where trees are fruiting, which can sometimes be quite close to settlements. They are arboreal by nature, being sighted on the ground only very rarely, usually when seeking water. Their grey-green coloration helps them to blend in against the wooded background. In some parts of their range, where their distributions overlap, they may associate with African green pigeons (*Treron calvus*), but there is no evidence that these two species hybridize. The breeding season varies widely through their range, and is most extensive in western Africa, where nesting has been recorded from December right through until the following September. The choice of nest site also varies according to location – date palms are used on Socotra, while in the sub-Saharan region acacia trees are favoured. Both members of the pair share the task of incubation.

Identification: Grey head, neck and breast, with a yellow abdomen and a green area around the vent with white markings. Lesser wing coverts are mauve, and the remainder of the back and wings are green, except for the black flight feathers. Tail is mauvish towards its tip. Bill pale grey, reddish at the base, with legs and feet also reddish. Sexes alike. Young birds are less brightly coloured, especially on the purple wing patches.

Blue-spotted wood dove

Turtur afer

These doves do not form large flocks, preferring instead to associate as pairs or in small groups. Although they are naturally woodland inhabitants, blue-spotted wood doves have adapted to areas where tree cover has been reduced. They will readily venture down to the ground in search of grass seed, which forms the basis of their diet, although they will sometimes feed on invertebrates too. In some parts of their range the doves are migratory – this depends on rainfall, since they generally prefer more humid habitats. Their breeding season varies. The male engages in a head-bobbing display, and also preens the hen's head as part of the courtship ritual. They construct a typical platform nest, which may measure up to 20cm (8in) in diameter, although occasionally pairs have been known to take over the abandoned cup-shaped nests of thrushes. Both the incubation and rearing periods last approximately 13 days. In addition to the blue-spotted there are four other related wood doves, all of which occur in Africa.

Identification: Bluish-grey crown. Reddish-brown underparts. Wings darker brown with blue spots. Two black bands on the rump. Bare whitish-grey skin surrounds each eye. Bill reddish-black, legs and feet pinkish. Sexes are alike. Young duller, with small wing spots.

Distribution: Much of Africa south of the Sahara Desert, extending as far as Ethiopia. Ranges south to Angola in the west and down as far as South Africa on the eastern side of the continent.
Size: 22cm (9in).
Habitat: Woodland.
Nest: Platform made from small twigs.
Eggs: 2, whitish.
Food: Mainly seeds.

Madagascan blue pigeon

Alectroenas madagascariensis

The distinctive blue pigeons are confined to islands in the Indian Ocean, off the eastern coast of Africa. Today there are only four surviving species – a fifth is now extinct. They appear to share a common ancestry with the fruit-eating pigeons and doves found in Asia, rather than those birds occurring on the African mainland. The Madagascan blue pigeon is a typical representative of the group. Like others of its kind it remains vulnerable to forest clearance on its native island, although fortunately it is relatively common within the boundaries of Madagascar's national parks, which should help to safeguard its future. These blue pigeons are normally seen in pairs, but will sometimes associate in larger groups numbering up to a dozen individuals. Their breeding season extends from October to December, and the nest is built in the fork of a tree often well above the ground, at heights of up to 20m (66ft). However, virtually nothing else is currently known about the breeding behaviour of these unusual pigeons.

Distribution: Range extends along the eastern side of Madagascar, off the south-east coast of Africa.
Size: 28cm (11in).
Habitat: Rainforest.
Nest: Platform of twigs.
Eggs: 1, white.
Food: Mainly fruits.

Identification: Dark bluish feathering on the head extending down the back of the neck, with a loose crest here. Rest of the head, and sides of neck and chest, are silvery bluish-grey. Back, wings and upperparts dark blue. Red undertail coverts and tail feathers. Red skin around the eyes. Legs and feet also red. Dark greenish bill with a lighter tip. Sexes are alike. Young birds have darker facial skin and are duller overall.

African green pigeon (*Treron calvus*): 30cm (12in)
Ranges largely south of Bruce's green pigeon (*T. waalia*), although absent from much of the southern area. Also islands in the Gulf of Guinea, including Principe. Predominantly green overall, with dull mauve wing coverts, yellow edging on the black flight feathers, and yellow-and-white barring under the tail, which is greyish above. Base of the bill coral-red, the tip pale horn. Legs and feet vary from red to yellow, depending on race. Hens smaller, with less prominent ceres. Young birds are duller, less purple on the wings.

Blue-headed wood dove (*Turtur brehmeri*): 25cm (10in)
From Sierra Leone and Liberia to north-west Angola and east across Dem. Rep. Congo. Cock bird has a bluish head, with rich chestnut-red plumage on the remainder of the body. Browner on the wings, with greenish wing spots. Bill has a dark reddish base and lighter tip. Legs and feet purplish. Sexes are alike. Young birds duller, with barring on the back of the neck.

Afep pigeon (Congo wood pigeon, *Columba unicincta*): 30cm (12in)
Isolated areas of western Africa, the main range extending from Cameroon and Gabon to Dem. Rep. Congo. Cock is predominantly greyish, darker on the wings, where the plumage is edged with white. Breast has a slight pinkish wash. A prominent, broad greyish band extends across the tail. Bill dark at the base, pale yellow at the tip. Legs and feet greyish. Hens lack the pinkish breast suffusion. Young birds are darker overall, with browner underparts.

Pink pigeon

Nesoenas mayeri (E)

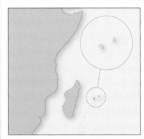

Pink pigeon numbers have plummeted over the past century, partly due to deforestation and hunting. More recently, cyclone damage on Mauritius has further reduced their numbers, and introduced animals such as monkeys and rats have interfered with their nesting. In 1976, with the population having fallen to just 18, the Jersey-based Durrell Wildlife Conservation Trust began a captive-breeding project, which has grown to involve more than forty zoos worldwide. The wild population is now estimated at around 250, with a breeding stock of 180 in zoos, reflecting a remarkable transformation in its fortunes. Furthermore, in the wild these pigeons now favour the introduced Japanese cedar (*Cryptomeria japonica*), which has sharp needles and a very sticky resin that deters rats from preying on their nests.

Distribution: Restricted to the south-west of Mauritius, in the Indian Ocean. Formerly occurred over almost the entire island.
Size: 40cm (16in).
Habitat: Montane forest.
Nest: Platform, made from twigs.
Eggs: 2, white.
Food: Fruits, and seeds.

Identification: Pinkish head, back and underparts, with brown wings and a rufous-brown tail. Bare red skin around the eyes and at the base of the bill, as well as the legs and feet. Sexes are alike. Young birds are duller, with ashy-brown wings and a greyish suffusion to the pink areas; red skin more purplish.

BARBETS AND TINKERBIRDS

These dumpy, short-tailed birds, all with fairly stumpy bills, are restricted to Africa, with none occurring in Europe. Other members of this group can be found in Asia and the Americas, and appear similar in profile to their African relatives. They use their stubby bills to bore into tree trunks in order to excavate their nesting cavities, rather like woodpeckers. Many have quite loud calls.

Green barbet

Stactolaema olivacea

Distribution: Occurs in isolated areas of eastern Africa, including Kenya and northern Tanzania, and Malawi and Mozambique. Isolated population also present in South Africa.
Size: 17cm (6¾in).
Habitat: Forested areas.
Nest: Tree hollow.
Eggs: 3–6, whitish.
Food: Fruits, particularly figs, and some invertebrates.

Green barbets are lively birds. They are often to be encountered in small groups, particularly in the vicinity of fig trees, the fruits of which feature prominently in their diet. They will also hunt invertebrates, regurgitating the indigestible harder parts of their bodies, along with fruit stones. The breeding period is variable through their range. A dead tree is often chosen as the nesting site, and the barbets use their powerful, stocky bills to tunnel into the rotten wood, removing any material they excavate in their bills. The chamber itself extends down as much as 60cm (2ft) into the tree. These hollows are also used for roosting outside the breeding season, and can accommodate as many as eight birds at a time. During the breeding season, other barbets may act as helpers to the breeding pair. They will collect food for the young once they have hatched, but it is unlikely that they take part in incubating the eggs. The young birds leave the nest when they are about a month old.

Identification: A number of races are recognized, varying largely in head coloration. Mainly olive-green overall, and lighter below. Blackish plumage on the top of the head extends to the breast in subspecies Thyolo green barbet (*S. o. belcheri*), distinguishing it from Woodward's barbet (*S. o. woodwardi*), which also has greenish-yellow ear coverts. The Tanzanian race (*S. o. rungweensis*) may have either buffy ear coverts or a uniform head, as in the nominate race from the north. Bill, legs and feet are black. Sexes are alike. Young birds are less brightly coloured.

Naked-faced barbet

Gymnobucco calvus

The lack of feathering on the heads of these barbets may help to prevent their plumage from becoming stained and matted by fruit juices. Young birds leave the nest with their heads almost fully feathered, but this plumage is shed as they grow older and not replaced. Social and noisy by nature, naked-faced barbets are very conspicuous birds, encountered predominantly in lowland areas. They nest in colonies, often seeking out dead trees since in these the nesting chambers are more easily created. Using their powerful bills, they excavate chambers that typically extend 23cm (9in) below the entrance. As many as 30 pairs have been reported occupying a single tree.

Identification: Predominantly brown, with significantly darker upperparts and tail. Underparts are light brown. Large, powerful bill, with beard of longer brown feathers at its base. Bare blackish-brown skin on the head. The bare ear holes at the back of the head are clearly evident. Sexes are alike.

Distribution: Range extends from Guinea in western Africa eastwards and southwards following the coastline, reaching as far as northern Angola.
Size: 18cm (7in).
Habitat: Wooded areas.
Nest: Tree hollow.
Eggs: 3, white.
Food: Invertebrates and fruit.

Double-toothed barbet

Lybius bidentatus

The unusual coloration of these barbets, along with shape of their bills, aids identification in the field. The notch on the bill, which looks like a tooth, may help the birds to grasp their food. Double-toothed barbets have a reputation for attacking ripening bananas, and their diet may feature more fruit than barbets inhabiting more open areas of country. They are most likely to be seen in pairs, rather than in larger groups, and may breed throughout much of the year in some parts of their range. They use their strong bills to excavate a nesting site in a tree by hammering at the trunk. Even so, a dead tree or branch is usually preferred since the wood is softer and easier for tunnelling.

Identification: Predominantly black upperparts and red underparts. The rump and an area on each side of the body are white. There is a blackish area around the eyes, and a red wing bar. The prominent, toothed bill is whitish. Sexes are alike.

Distribution: Western-central Africa, from Senegal around to Angola and eastwards to parts of Sudan, Ethiopia, Kenya and Tanzania.
Size: 23cm (9in).
Habitat: Woodland, although not rainforest.
Nest: Tree hollow. Nesting chamber usually lined with wood chips.
Eggs: 3–4, white.
Food: Invertebrates, fruits and berries.

Banded barbet (*Lybius undatus*): 18cm (7in)
Restricted to highland areas of Eritrea and Ethiopia. Races quite variable in coloration. Red plumage from the base of the bill to above the eyes, with a white streak extending back from behind each eye. Remainder of the head and breast blackish, browner over the back, with the plumage often having a slight silvery edging. Underparts white becoming yellow towards the vent, with black barring. Irides yellow. Large bill is black, as are the legs and feet. Sexes are alike.

Black-collared barbet (*Lybius torquatus*): 20cm (8in)
Southern Africa from Tanzania southwards. Absent from much of Namibia and Botswana, except the far north, and the neighbouring area of South Africa. Bright red face and upper breast, with a black band beneath extending up to the back of the head and encircling the neck. Lower underparts yellowish-white. Back and wings brownish, with yellowish edging to the flight feathers. Stocky bill is black, as are the legs and feet. Sexes are alike. Young birds have a brown head and throat with orangish-red streaks. There is also a rare yellow morph, which has a yellow rather than a red face.

Green tinkerbird (*Pogoniulus simplex*): 10cm (4in)
Eastern coastal forests of Africa, from Kenya to Mozambique. Dull green upperparts, greyer on the underparts. Rump yellow, with some yellow edging to the wing feathers. Bill is black with black whiskers. Sexes are alike. Young birds have a paler base to the bill. Legs and feet black.

Red-fronted tinkerbird

Pogoniulus pusillus

These are noisy tinkerbirds, producing a variety of calls from trills to croaking notes that have been likened to the sound of snoring. They are seen individually or in pairs rather than groups, frequently on the bark of trees hunting for invertebrates. They also catch insects in flight, darting down from a perch, but rarely emerge into the open for long, keeping out of sight as far as possible. When foraging separately, both members of the pair will call frequently to each other. Singing is used as a preliminary to courtship by the male, who also retains fruits or berries in his beak that he passes directly to the hen. The well-concealed nest can be up to 55cm (22in) deep, with the entrance hole often measuring no more than 2.5cm (1in) in diameter. It is thought that the incubation period lasts about 12 days, with the young leaving the nest for the first time when they are just over three weeks old.

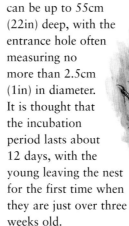

Distribution: Two widely-spaced populations, one in eastern Africa, from Ethiopia to Tanzania, and another in eastern South Africa.
Size: 10cm (4in).
Habitat: Forest and more open woodland.
Nest: Tree hollow.
Eggs: 2–4, white.
Food: Invertebrates, fruits and berries.

Identification: Characteristic red forehead, with a black stripe in front running through each eye. Parallel white band, and another black stripe from the base of the bill. Largely white behind the eyes, except for another black stripe. Rest of the head, back and wings black with yellowish streaking, and more evident golden-yellow barring above the flight feathers. Underparts pale lemony-white. Bill, legs and feet black. Sexes are alike. Young birds lack the red on the head.

HORNBILLS

This family of rather unusual, often large birds has a distribution that extends from Africa through the forests of Asia. It is thought that they may assist the spread of forest plants, by passing the seeds out of their bodies or by regurgitating them. Hornbills are vulnerable to forest clearance, as they require large territories in order to obtain sufficient food, and mature trees that can be used as nesting sites.

Long-tailed hornbill

White-crested hornbill *Horizocerus albocristatus*

Distribution: Western Africa, from Sierra Leone to Dem. Rep. Congo. Apparently absent from the border district between Rep. Congo and Dem. Rep. Congo.
Size: 75cm (29¹/₂in).
Habitat: Forested areas.
Nest: Tree hollow.
Eggs: 2, white.
Food: Mainly invertebrates, some fruit.

The distinctive calls of these hornbills echoing through the forest have been likened to the sound of wailing hyenas. Long-tailed hornbills often associate with bands of monkeys moving through the trees, pouncing to seize any prey disturbed by the troupe's presence. This is not only a one-way relationship however, since the hornbills' sharp alarm calls in turn alert the monkeys to approaching danger and they can react accordingly, taking evasive active. These hornbills hunt large invertebrates such as mantids and cicadas, but they will also catch small vertebrates including rodents and lizards, and raid the nests of other birds. Occasionally, they may descend to the ground to feed on fallen fruit. A pair will choose a nest site in a tree hollow, usually around 10–15m (32–48ft) above the ground. Here the hen will seal herself in, using her droppings to plaster over the entrance to the nesting chamber. She will leave a small hole, through which the male can pass her food for the duration of her incarceration.

Identification: Black overall. White crest with black markings. Long tail feathers tipped with white. Coloration around the eyes grey or whitish, depending on race. Blackish bill, pink at the base of the lower mandible. The casque is more prominent in males. Young birds have a greenish bill and no casque, with pale blue rather than cream eyes.

Black-casqued wattled hornbill

Ceratogymna atrata

The braying calls of these hornbills are audible from 2km (1¹/₄ miles) away, with cocks having a deeper tone than hens. The noise of their wings in flight may also help them to keep in touch with each other. Black-casqued wattled hornbills live mainly in pairs, although they can be observed in family groups. They seek food in the canopy, but may descend to the ground to feed on seeds fallen from ruptured seed pods. The nuts of oil palms feature prominently in their diet, but these hornbills will occasionally take invertebrates and have been recorded raiding the nests of village weavers (*Ploceus cucullatus*). However, they are less predatory than many hornbills. Pairs nest in suitable trees, at heights of up to 20m (66ft).

Identification: Predominantly black overall, with white areas on the tips of the tail feathers. Dark greyish area of bare skin around each eye, with a blue area under the lower bill. Iris red. Bill is black, with a very tall, long casque. Hens easily distinguished by their brownish head and much smaller casque. Young birds have no casque or blue throat wattles, and the bill is olive-coloured rather than black.

Distribution: Main area of distribution is from southern Nigeria to Angola eastwards to Dem. Rep. Congo. Also further west in Liberia, Ivory Coast, Ghana and Togo.
Size: 80cm (31¹/₂in).
Habitat: Forested areas.
Nest: Tree hollow.
Eggs: 2, white.
Food: Mainly fruit.

African crowned hornbill
Lophoceros alboterminatus

These hornbills establish territories, although in some parts of their range, notably South Africa, drought forces them to migrate. Pairs have a number of roosting sites, which are well screened from birds of prey, and their chosen nesting site is often used for a number of years. The female begins to seal the nest from the outside, then retreats inside to continue until only a slit remains. This is believed to protect the occupants from snakes. She will spend about nine weeks confined to the nest, during which she will moult while incubating the eggs and raising her brood. The young birds reseal the entrance after her departure, and remain inside for a further two weeks, with both the adult birds feeding them. They will start to develop their casques at around four months old.

Identification: Predominantly dark brown in colour, with paler scalloping on the wings and similar streaking over the head and neck. White underparts and tip to the tail. Bill red, with cock birds displaying a pronounced casque running along the top of the upper bill. Hens have a greatly reduced casque and turquoise-blue rather than black facial skin. Legs and feet blackish. Young birds have orange bills with no casque.

Distribution: Present mainly in eastern-central Africa, from Kenya down as far as the southern coastal region of South Africa. Extends to Rep. Congo and Angola in the west. There is also an isolated northern population in Ethiopia.
Size: 54cm (21in).
Habitat: Forested areas.
Nest: Tree hollow.
Eggs: 2–5, white.
Food: Invertebrates and fruit.

Brown-cheeked hornbill (*Bycanistes cylindricus*): 75cm (29½in)
Restricted to the forested area from Sierra Leone to Ghana in western Africa. Black head, neck and top of the wings, with a black band across the tail feathers. The back, flight feathers and tip of the tail are white. Bare reddish skin encircling the eyes. Bill and casque are yellowish, ivory in young birds. Young also have much smaller casques than cocks, as do hens.

Piping hornbill (white-tailed hornbill, *Bycanistes fistulator*): 50cm (20in)
Senegal in western Africa around to northern Angola and eastwards to the Central African Republic and Dem. Rep. Congo. Black and white, with white on the underparts extending down from the lower breast. White also evident in the wings and tail. Cocks have a small yellow casque, and the tip of the bill and its base are yellowish. Hens have darker bills with a smaller casque. Young birds distinguishable by their black bills and the absence of any casque.

Yellow-casqued wattled hornbill (*Ceratogymna elata*): 90cm (35½in)
Coastal area of western Africa extending from Guinea Bissau to Cameroon. Predominantly black, except for the mostly white tail feathers, which have a central area of black, and the cream streaks evident on the neck, adjacent to the blue wattle. Iris is red, with an area of grey skin around the eyes. Bill blackish, with a prominent yellow casque. Hens have brown heads and a much smaller casque. Young birds similar to adult hens, but have darker brown plumage on the neck.

Silvery-cheeked hornbill
Bycanistes brevis

Groups of 100 or more silvery-cheeked hornbills congregate where food is plentiful, pursuing plagues of locusts, for example. They are agile in the treetops, bouncing from branch to branch in pursuit of prey. More commonly, they are observed in pairs. At the start of the breeding period the nest opening is reduced to a narrow slit by the hen, from pellets of mud mixed with saliva regurgitated by the cock. He collects the food, regurgitating small fruits for the hen. During this period he will collect around 24,000 fruits from some 1,600 forays. Usually only one chick is reared successfully, breaking out of the nest with its mother when 11 weeks old.

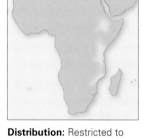

Distribution: Restricted to the eastern African region, occurring in several distinct populations. The northerly population occurs in Ethiopia, while the others are found in Kenya and Tanzania, and in Mozambique and Zimbabwe.
Size: 75cm (29½in).
Habitat: Prefers upland and coastal forests.
Nest: Tree hollow.
Eggs: 1–2, white.
Food: Mainly fruit.

Identification: Predominantly black, but with white on the back, lower underparts and the tip of the tail. There is also a white area on the underwing coverts. The feathers on the sides of the face are tipped with silver. Cocks have a very tall, curved casque that extends along much of the bill. Hens have much shorter, lower casques, as do young birds.

PARROTS OF THE FOREST

Although there are fewer parrot species in Africa than in Asia or the Americas, their ranges extend to many of Africa's offshore islands. These are home to some of the most unusual parrots in the world, such as the vasa parrot (Coracopsis vasa). Like many other forest birds, parrots do not occur naturally in Europe, since the climate would restrict their food supply.

Grey parrot

Psittacus erithacus

The highly distinctive coloration of these parrots enables them to be identified without difficulty, although they are not always easy to spot in their forest habitat. They are more conspicuous in the early morning and evening, when they fly above the trees in flocks to and from their feeding grounds, often calling loudly. These parrots roost in mature trees, giving them a good view of the surrounding area. They are not easy to approach and often fly off at the first hint of danger. When feeding, at least one bird acts as a sentinel, calling loudly to warn the others of any approaching threat.

Identification: Mainly grey (silvery-grey in some cases) with bright red tail feathers. The timneh subspecies (*P. e. timneh*) from western Africa is not only smaller but has a maroon tail and a horn-coloured, rather than black, upper bill. Sexes are alike.

Distribution: Ranges across much of central Africa, from Guinea eastwards to Ethiopia and Somalia, extending south to Namibia.
Size: 33cm (13in).
Habitat: Woodland areas, including rainforest, savanna and mangroves.
Nest: Tree hollow, often 10m (33ft) or higher.
Eggs: 2–3, white.
Food: Fruits, nuts and seeds, often sought in trees.

Greater vasa parrot

Coracopsis vasa

These unusual parrots have a very drab appearance, quite unlike that of other members of the family. Another characteristic is their habit of sunbathing, lying at an unusual angle on a perch with one or both wings raised, in similar fashion to pigeons. Although they occur primarily in woodland, vasa parrots also venture into open country, and have come into conflict with farmers on their native islands due to the damage they cause to growing crops, especially rice. The breeding period, which extends from October to December, also brings changes to the parrots' appearance. As well as their bills turning pink, cock birds also develop pronounced swellings adjacent to the vent area, while hens often lose some or all of their head plumage. Exposed to light, the hens' skin becomes yellowish or even orange, but the plumage regrows after the breeding season.

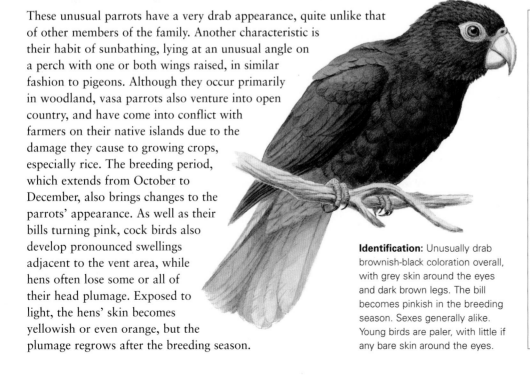

Identification: Unusually drab brownish-black coloration overall, with grey skin around the eyes and dark brown legs. The bill becomes pinkish in the breeding season. Sexes generally alike. Young birds are paler, with little if any bare skin around the eyes.

Distribution: Range extends throughout Madagascar, off the south-east coast of Africa. Also present on Grand Comoro, Anjouan and Moheli in the nearby Comoros Islands, located mid-way between the northern tip of Madagascar and the northern coast of Mozambique.
Size: 45cm (18in).
Habitat: Forested areas.
Nest: Tree hole.
Eggs: 2–3, white.
Food: Seeds and fruit.

Cape parrot

Brown-necked parrot *Poicephalus robustus*

The classification of the Cape parrot is controversial. In addition to its South African range there are populations in western and south-central Africa, each of which are distinctive in appearance and thus often regarded as separate species. Cape parrots cause crop damage in some areas, but usually feed on *Podocarpus* fruits, and favour these trees as nesting sites. They may be semi-nomadic, wandering widely through their range, but are not encountered in large groups. Some areas have large roosts, but these divide into smaller groups that may fly over 80km (50 miles) in search of food. Cape parrots also have regular early morning drinking sites. Their breeding season in South Africa is between August and October. The hen sits alone, and the eggs hatch after 28 days. The young leave the nest after a further two months.

Identification: Brownish mottled head, with green underparts and rump. Wings are dark blackish-green, with the plumage here having lighter green edging. The flight and tail feathers are dark. Prominent reddish-orange area on the shoulders and at the tops of the legs (young birds lack these red areas). Hens are red on the forehead, although this is a variable feature.

Distribution: The species illustrated here is restricted to South Africa, occurring from north-eastern Transvaal down to the eastern Cape Province. **Size:** 35cm (13¾in). Other populations occur in west and southern-central Africa. **Habitat:** Forest. **Nest:** Tree hollow. **Eggs:** 2–4, white. **Food:** Seeds and fruit.

Lesser vasa parrot (Black parrot, *Coracopsis nigra*): 40cm (15¾in)
Madagascar. Grand Comoro and Anjouan in the Comoros Islands, and Praslin in the Seychelles. Blackish-brown, smaller and darker than the vasa parrot (*Coracopsis vasa*). Bill greyish, lighter in the breeding season. Sexes are alike. Young birds have a paler bill and paler undertail coverts.

Yellow-fronted parrot (*Poicephalus flavifrons*): 25cm (10in)
Central Ethiopia. Greenish. Bright yellow head with an an occasional orange. Yellow on the edges of the wings and thighs. Bill, legs and feet are black. Sexes are alike. Young birds duller, with an olive-green head suffused with yellow.

Red-fronted parrot (*Poicephalus gulielmi*): 27cm (11in)
Several forms. Discontinuous distribution from Ivory Coast to northern Angola, east to Kenya and Tanzania. Dark green, blackish on the head and wings. Reddish-orange above the bill and over the crown, and on the leading edges of the wings and the tops of the thighs. Sexes are alike. Young birds lack the red coloration.

Black-collared lovebird (*Agapornis swindernianus*): 13cm (5in)
Isolated areas from Sierra Leone to Gabon and Dem. Rep. Congo. Green head. Black collar, with a similar orangish area below broadening out to the chest. Underparts green, with darker upperparts. Rump is mauve. Bill, legs and feet are black. Sexes are alike. Young birds duller.

Madagascan lovebird

Grey-headed lovebird *Agapornis canus*

Unlike most parrots, lovebirds use nesting material, carrying the leaves and grass to the nest site in the bill, rather than in among the feathers of the rump. Their nest is not an elaborate structure, and consists of a simple lining in the nesting hollow on which the eggs are laid. Incubation lasts 23 days, and the chicks leave the nest at about six weeks old. Madagascan lovebirds are normally observed in flocks, and generally seek their food on the ground. They will often attack rice crops when the seed is ripening, in the company of red fodies (*Foudia madagascariensis*), a native weaver finch. Not all attempts to introduce these lovebirds to other Indian Ocean islands have proved successful, with the species having failed to establish itself on Mauritius and Zanzibar, but they are now numerous on the Comoros Islands.

Distribution: Naturally occurs on the island of Madagascar, off the south-eastern coast of Africa. Introduced to various neighbouring islands, such as the Comoros. **Size:** 15cm (6in). **Habitat:** Forest and surrounding open country. **Nest:** Tree hole. **Eggs:** 3–6, white. **Food:** Seeds and fruit.

Identification: Grey head and upper breast. Dark green wings and lighter underparts. Dark band on the short tail. Hens entirely green. Bill, legs and feet are greyish. Young birds as adults but with a yellowish bill, and the heads of cocks are suffused with green.

FOREST WOODPECKERS

Few groups of birds are more closely associated with trees than woodpeckers. They are well-equipped to thrive in these surroundings, with their powerful bills serving as tools to obtain food and also to create nesting chambers. Many species occur in dense woodland. However, not all are exclusively arboreal, since a number of species forage for food on the ground.

Great spotted woodpecker

Dendrocopos major

Great spotted woodpeckers can be found in both coniferous and deciduous woodland, especially in areas where the trees are mature enough for the birds to excavate roosting and nesting chambers. Their powerful bills enable them to extract grubs hidden under bark and to wrest the seeds from pine cones – the birds use so-called "anvils", which may be existing tree holes, as vices to hold the cones fast, so as to gain more leverage for their bills.

Identification: Black top to the head. Black areas also from the sides of the bill around the neck, linking with a red area at the back of the head. Wings and upperside of the tail are predominantly black, although there is a white area on the wings and white barring on the flight feathers. Underside of the tail mostly white. Deep red around the vent. Hens are similar but lack the red on the hindcrown.

Distribution: Throughout most of Europe except for Ireland, the far north of Scandinavia and much of south-eastern Europe. Also found in North Africa. Ranges eastwards into Asia.
Size: 25cm (10in).
Habitat: Woodland.
Nest: Tree hollow.
Eggs: 5–7, white.
Food: Invertebrates, eggs and seeds.

Black woodpecker

Dryocopus martius

Distribution: Throughout most of Europe, from parts of Spain, the Pyrenees and France up into much of Scandinavia and eastwards across Asia. Absent from Italy and the British Isles, but present in Greece.
Size: 55cm (21³/₄in).
Habitat: Mature forest.
Nest: Tree hole.
Eggs: 3–5, white.
Food: Mostly invertebrates, some seeds.

Black woodpeckers are found in a range of forest types, especially areas with dead trees. They forage on the trunks, but also seek out the nests of wood ants on the ground, which they raid regularly. Territorial by nature, they rely on their ability to find the ants' nests even under a blanket of snow. Seeds of various kinds, such as beech mast, also help to sustain them over the winter, and they may even attack bees' nests too. Breeding behaviour is evident as pairs are formed at this time of year, but egg-laying will not occur until the spring. They often excavate a new nest hole, rather than reuse an old site. Incubation is shared and, unusually, the cock bird sits through the night. The chicks hatch after two weeks, and the young emerge from the nest when they are about a month old.

Identification: Cock birds are predominantly black, with prominent crimson-red plumage extending over the top of the head. Bill is greyish, as are the legs and feet. Iris whitish. Hens easily distinguished by the much reduced red on the top of the head, which is restricted to a band on the nape. Young birds are duller, less glossy overall, and are more of a sooty-black shade.

Lesser spotted woodpecker (*Dryobates minor*): 16cm (6in)
Most of Europe. South to Algeria and Tunisia, and east into Asia. Buff above the bill. Males have a red area on the crown, hens black. Black tail, white barring on the wings. Barring on the underparts, with a reddish area around the vent. Black stripes on the sides of the face.

Stierling's woodpecker (*Dendropicos stierlingi*): 18cm (7in)
Confined largely to Mozambique. Cock has a bright red area extending over the back of the head; back, wings and tail are olive. Barred underparts. Area behind the eyes is dark, and the remainder of the face is whitish. Young birds are duller overall.

African piculet (*Sasia africana*): 8cm (3in)
Cameroon to Dem. Rep. Congo and Angola, and isolated areas in western Africa. Small. Greyish overall. White stripe above the eyes and bare red skin around the eyes. Cock has a rufous area on the forehead. Back and wings olive-green. Young birds have a rufous hue to the underparts.

Mombasa woodpecker (*Campethera mombassica*): 20cm (8in).
Mainly coastal Kenya, including Mombasa. Red over the head to the neck, with red stripes from the base of the bill. Back and wings greenish, with spotting. Tail barred. Sides of the face and breast greyish with black markings, yellower on the abdomen. Hens red only on the hindcrown, with a white-spotted black top to the head. Young like hens, but are more heavily marked.

Eastern grey woodpecker

Dendropicos spodocephalus

This species is closely related to the African grey woodpecker (*D. goertae*), which ranges in a band across Africa south of the Sahara. They can be distinguished by their belly colour, which in the grey-headed is more extensive and always red, never orange or yellow as in its near relative. However, both species have very similar calls, particularly the drawn-out rattle used to indicate territory. They become especially vocal prior to breeding, although they are rarely heard drumming at the nest site. This is always located in a dead tree, sometimes close to the ground but more usually up to 20m (66ft) high. The chamber extends down about 30cm (1ft). Both adults incubate the eggs, changing over at least once every 30 minutes during the day, although the cock sits alone through the night.

Distribution: Two distinct populations in eastern Africa, one occurring largely in western Ethiopia, the other present on the border of Kenya and Tanzania.
Size: 20cm (8in).
Habitat: Forest areas, often near rivers.
Nest: Tree hollow.
Eggs: 2–4, white.
Food: Invertebrates.

Identification: Cock bird has a bright red area of plumage on the crown, with red in the centre of the underparts extending down to the vent. Rump is also red. Remainder of the body is grey except for the back and wings, which are yellowish-green, with spotting on the flight feathers and barring on the tail. Hens have grey heads. Young birds are duller, usually with some barring on the underparts, and have greyish-brown irides.

Eurasian three-toed woodpecker

Picoides tridactylus

Largely arboreal by nature, three-toed woodpeckers rarely descend to the ground. Cocks forage on trees at lower levels than hens, often venturing quite near to the base. These woodpeckers rely on their pointed bills both to probe into crevices for invertebrates and also as a chisel to strip off bark, especially from dead trees. Their diet consists mainly of beetles and their larvae, although they also bore into the bark to create "sap wells", which offer an additional source of nutrients. Although not easily spotted in the forest, their slow drumming will confirm their presence. They nest in a dead tree, with the incubation period lasting about 12 days. The young fledge after a further four weeks, and will be fed by their parents for another month.

Distribution: Range extends through Scandinavia and across to the eastern coast of Asia. Populations also found in south-eastern Europe. Present in a broad band across North America.
Size: 24cm (9 1/2in).
Habitat: Conifer woodland.
Nest: Tree hollow.
Eggs: 3–6, white.
Food: Mainly invertebrates.

Identification: Cock bird is predominantly black and white, except for a yellow area on the crown. Black stripe running back from each eye, bordered by white stripes. Wings are black with white markings, as is the tail. Underparts are white with black markings on the flanks. Bill, legs and feet greyish. Hens lack the yellow area on the crown. Young birds are brownish-black, and duller overall. A number of distinctive races of this species are recognized through its wide range.

FLYCATCHERS, BOUBOUS AND SHRIKES

These predatory birds benefit from the insect life that thrives in the woodland. Shrikes will even hunt small vertebrates as well. Many of these often shy species have relatively subdued coloration, which helps them to merge into the background. Others moult into display plumage prior to the breeding season, but observing them in these surroundings can still be difficult.

African paradise flycatcher

Terpsiphone viridis

African paradise flycatchers are summer visitors to South Africa, migrating closer to the equator during April and not usually returning until September. In suburban gardens, the increased planting of trees has provided them with additional habitat, and they may even breed close to buildings. A site up to 6m (20ft) off the ground is usually chosen, and the nest is made from vegetation and spiders' webs. Lichens are added around the outside by way of disguise. Both members of the pair incubate the eggs. Hatching takes 13 days, with the young fledging at just 11 days old. It is not uncommon for African paradise flycatchers to breed twice or even three times over the summer. The cock then moults his tail plumes, which can measure 30cm (12in) or more.

Identification: Cock birds are quite variable in appearance, but usually have greyish underparts and a distinctive crest. The back is rufous in some cases, occasionally with white wing bars and dark flight feathers. Tail is rufous as well, with very long tail plumes during the breeding period. There is also a white form, which may have white wing bars in addition to long white tail feathers. Young birds are less brightly coloured. Hens lack the long tail streamers, and have a paler blue bill and periophthalmic skin.

Distribution: Ranges widely throughout Africa south of the Sahara, but absent notably from the Horn of Africa and from parts of the south-west.
Size: 20cm (8in).
Habitat: Forest, woodland.
Nest: Cup-shaped, made from vegetation.
Eggs: 1–4, creamy with reddish spots.
Food: Invertebrates.

Wattle-eyed flycatcher

Black-throated wattle-eye *Platysteira peltata*

Distribution: Eastern Africa, from Somalia to South Africa. Range extends westwards to Angola, but absent from Namibia, Botswana and much of South Africa.
Size: 18cm (7in).
Habitat: Coastal forests and near rivers.
Nest: Cup-shaped, made from vegetation.
Eggs: 2, cream-coloured with brown spotting.
Food: Invertebrates.

Wattle-eyed flycatchers are very agile birds, able to seize insects both in flight and directly off trees and bushes. They are generally seen in pairs, and in family groups after the breeding period, which in southern parts of their range extends from September to November. Their nest, usually located close to the ground in the fork of a bush, is firmly anchored in place and bound together with spiders' webs. The incubation period lasts about 18 days, and the chicks leave the nest when they are just two weeks old. However, they will not be fully independent of their parents for another three months, and will not develop the characteristic red wattles above their eyes until approximately six months old. Young birds may breed the following year, by the time they are 12 months old. Wattle-eyed flycatchers are relatively quiet by nature, but they have a rapid alarm call that is employed as a warning when they encounter snakes lurking off the ground.

Identification: Named after the red wattles of skin above the eyes. Cock bird has black upperparts, with a black band extending across the chest. Remainder of the underparts are white. Hens have a largely black chest. Young birds have brown mottling on their throats.

São Tomé paradise flycatcher (*Terpsiphone atrochalybeia*): 18cm (7in)
Found only on the island of São Tomé, in the Gulf of Guinea, off the western coast of central Africa. Cock bird is bluish-black, with glossy plumage and tail plumes measuring about 11cm (4¼in) long. The bill is blackish, as are the legs and feet. Hens have chestnut upperparts and a similarly-coloured short tail, with greyish underparts. Young birds are duller.

Bedford's paradise flycatcher (*Terpsiphone bedfordi*): 20cm (8in)
Restricted to lowland rainforest on the north-eastern Dem. Rep. Congo border. Entirely grey, usually slightly darker on the head and back. The skin around the eye is bluish, as is the bill. Young birds are browner. Sexes are alike.

Mountain sooty boubou (*Laniarius poensis*): 20cm (8in)
Found in the Albertine Rift area, like the preceding species (*Terpsiphone bedfordi*). There is also a separate population in the south-west of Cameroon. Entirely black, with a relatively stocky bill. Sexes are alike. Young birds are more brownish-black.

Slate-coloured boubou (*Laniarius funebris*): 20cm (8in)
Range restricted to north-east Africa, from Ethiopia and Somalia to Tanzania. Dark grey overall, and more of a matt shade than glossy shade. Sexes are alike. Young birds are browner, with barred underparts.

Woodchat shrike

Lanius senator

These migratory shrikes return to their European breeding grounds in the spring. Established pairs choose a nest site in a tree or bush, within 5m (16ft) of the ground. Their nest can be built in four days, but egg-laying may not occur for several weeks. The hen sits alone, with incubation lasting about 15 days. Once hatched, she broods the chicks for another 10 days, while the male continues to bring food to the nest. The young leave the nest at nearly three weeks old, remaining with their parents through the summer, and only become fully independent just before their southward migration. Woodchat shrikes leave their breeding grounds relatively early, typically between July and August, arriving back in Africa between August and October.

Identification: Pale yellow area above the bill, with a black mask above encompassing the eyes. Top of the head is a rich brown, extending back to form a collar. Underparts whitish with a hint of orange on the flanks. Wings mainly black with white wing bars. Greyish rump. Hens less vividly coloured, with a greyer back and often a slight barring on the flanks. Bill, legs and feet blackish. Young birds have brownish upperparts, greyish underparts and evident markings on the flanks.

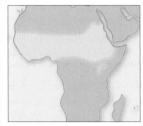

Distribution: Breeds through much of southern Europe bordering the Mediterranean. Overwinters in a broad band across Africa south of the Sahara, with an isolated population in Tanzania.
Size: 19cm (7½in).
Habitat: Wooded areas in the breeding season.
Nest: Cup-shaped, made of vegetation.
Eggs: 1–8, olive-green or yellowish with dark markings.
Food: Largely invertebrates.

Southern boubou

Laniarius ferrugineus

Identification: Jet black head, back and tail, with narrow white wing bars. The throat area is pure white, becoming rusty-orange on the lower underparts. Bill, legs and feet are black. Hens have greyer upperparts and more rufous underparts. Young birds buff-brown above, with barring on their underparts.

Relatively shy by nature, southern boubous are difficult shrikes to observe, typically remaining hidden in the undergrowth, although their song helps to confirm their presence. Members of a pair duet with each other in close unison, and it can sometimes sound as if one bird is singing from two separate places. Their song pattern is highly individual, even varying between neighbouring pairs. The frequency of singing increases with the advent of the rainy season, which usually also marks the start of the breeding period. The nest, constructed by both members of the pair, is a relatively loose structure often anchored together with spiders' webs. Incubation is also shared by both birds, and lasts approximately 16 days, with the young birds leaving the nest after a similar interval. Adult southern boubous hunt for food among trees and bushes as well as on the ground. The nests of other birds may be raided too, and small lizards and similar creatures are also occasionally caught and eaten.

Distribution: Range extends from Mozambique down along eastern and southern parts of South Africa, as far as Cape Province. Present also in parts of Botswana and Zimbabwe.
Size: 22cm (9in).
Habitat: Wooded areas.
Nest: Generally a loose, bowl-shaped platform.
Eggs: 2–3, greenish-white with darker speckling.
Food: Mainly invertebrates.

WOODLAND INSECT-EATERS

Many birds rely on invertebrates to form a significant part of their diet. Those species resident in Europe may be forced to fly south to warmer climes for the winter, where such food will be more readily available. In Africa however, members of such families are largely resident through the year, although they too may occasionally undertake seasonal movements.

Woodlark

Lullula arborea

The attractive whistling call of these larks, characterized by a distinctive yodelling tone, is mainly heard at sunrise or even on a starry night, rather than during the daytime. They are not easy birds to spot, since their plumage provides them with excellent camouflage. Woodlarks spend long periods on the ground, but sometimes fly up to perch, and this is when they are most conspicuous. Nesting also often occurs on the ground, with both members of the pair building the nest in a suitable hollow, although they may prefer to utilize a shrub or young sapling. The hen sits alone, and the chicks hatch about two weeks later. The young woodlarks develop quickly, and may leave the nest at only 10 days old, emerging on foot since they are not able to fly well at this stage. In the autumn, those birds occurring in more easterly parts head to south-west Europe to overwinter. Some fly further afield, over the Strait of Gibraltar to north-western Africa.

Identification: A white stripe above each eye. Top of the head streaked black and brown, ear coverts brownish. Streaked back, white tip to short tail. Underparts streaked, white on the abdomen. Yellowish-brown bill, yellowish legs and feet. Young have blacker crown, more spotted underparts. Sexes are alike.

Distribution: Range extends throughout much of Europe, but resident only in more westerly areas. Restricted to the south in England. Breeds right across the continent as far as southern parts of Scandinavia. Also extends to north-west Africa.
Size: 15cm (6in).
Habitat: Open woodland.
Nest: Deep and cup-shaped, made of vegetation.
Eggs: 1–6, white with some brown speckling.
Food: Mostly invertebrates, seeds in winter.

Terrestrial bulbul

Terrestrial brownbul *Phyllastrephus terrestris*

Identification: Upperparts dark brown, underparts whitish. Dark bill, grey legs and feet. Sexes are alike, but males larger. Young birds paler, with a yellowish tone to the underparts and a rufous rump and tail.

As their name suggests, terrestrial bulbuls spend their lives close to the forest floor. Social by nature, these brownbuls are usually observed in small, noisy groups, calling almost constantly to each other while on the move. Their main feeding technique consists of flicking over dry leaves with their bills as they comb the forest floor, seizing any invertebrates that are uncovered, although they will also eat fruit and berries. An unusual breeding characteristic of the terrestrial bulbul is that every year a pair will return to the vicinity of their previous nest, although they will construct a new nest here each time. In southern Africa, breeding occurs during the summer months, but it is likely to be more variable in other parts of their range. The nest itself, which may be located in branches or disguised among creepers, is made using a variety of vegetation ranging from leaves to seed pods. The incubation period lasts for around two weeks, with the young bulbuls leaving the nest after a similar interval.

Distribution: Isolated populations in southern Somalia, Kenya and southern Angola. Main range largely centred on Zimbabwe, extending from Tanzania down to Cape Province.
Size: 19cm (7$\frac{1}{2}$in).
Habitat: Forest.
Nest: Loose, cup-shaped.
Eggs: 2–3, greenish-white with dark streaks.
Food: Mostly invertebrates.

African yellow white-eye

Zosterops senegalensis

Some taxonomists recognize more than a dozen different subspecies of African yellow white-eye through its wide range, which differ from each other in their depth of coloration. Groups of yellow white-eyes wander through the forest, seeking insects among the foliage, often squabbling between themselves. A dominant individual will challenge one of its companions by opening its bill and crouching on the perch. The weaker individual stays still and fluffs up its plumage, keeping its eyes partially closed as well. This causes the surrounding white feathering to form an oval, and also makes it more conspicuous. Such is their natural agility that yellow white-eyes can forage successfully both above and below the leaves, in rather tit-like fashion. They will also take nectar, along with fruit and berries. Pairs nest on their own, choosing a well-hidden site. The hen is largely responsible for incubation, and hatching takes 11 days. The young birds leave the nest when they are just two weeks old.

Identification:
Upperparts are dark olive-yellow, with the underparts a pure shade of yellow. Distinctive white band of feathering encircles each eye, with a thinner, darker streak connecting from here to the base of the bill. Slender blackish bill, dark grey feet and legs. Sexes are alike. Young birds resemble adults.

Distribution: Occurs in a band across Africa south of the Sahara, from Senegal to Ethiopia. Also ranges south to northern Namibia and southern Mozambique, but largely absent from Rep. Congo and Dem. Rep. Congo.
Size: 12cm (4.75in).
Habitat: Woodland areas.
Nest: Cup-shaped, made from vegetation.
Eggs: 1–4, whitish-turquoise.
Food: Mainly invertebrates, some nectar.

Cape white-eye (*Zosterops virens*): 12cm (4³/₄in)
Restricted to eastern and southern parts of South Africa. Dark olive-green upperparts, with a characteristic yellow area on the throat and under the tail. Two distinctive forms, varying in colour on their underparts: *Z. c. capensis* from the south-west has grey underparts, whereas those of *Z. c. virens* are green. Sexes are alike. Young birds duller, developing white feathering around the eyes at about five weeks old.

Montane white-eye (*Zosterops poliogastrus kulalensis*): 12cm (4³/₄in)
Range is restricted to northern Kenya, found only in the forested region of Mount Kulal. Dark olive-green above, with yellowish areas above the bill extending below the eyes and on the underparts. Flanks and lower underparts are grey. Relatively broad white eye ring. Young birds resemble adults. Sexes are alike. Bill, legs and feet black.

Johanna's sunbird (Madame Verreaux's sunbird, *Cinnyris johannae*): 14cm (5¹/₂in)
Various isolated locations from Sierra Leone in West Africa. Cock bird has a metallic green head and upper back, while the throat area is purplish, merging into red, with some barring. Wings and lower underparts are black. Rump dark blue. Hens have dark olive-green upperparts, with a pale whitish streak extending above the eye and from the base of the lower bill; underparts becoming more yellowish, heavily streaked overall with green. Bill, legs and feet blackish-grey. Young birds resemble adults, with young cocks having heavier grey streaking.

Superb sunbird

Cinnyris superba

These colourful sunbirds are surprisingly difficult to spot in the gloomy forest. They also forage high up in the canopy, where the trees flower in the sunlight. As well as nectar, superb sunbirds will also feed on invertebrates such as spiders or midges, taking them off leaves or even seizing them in flight. They are also attracted to banana plantations, not only for food but also for breeding. Their nest is suspended off a branch, anchored in place largely by grass. A distinctive tail extends beneath which, along with pieces of lichen attached to the exterior, may help to disguise its presence. The hen builds the nest alone, which can take from a day to a month to complete.

Distribution: Western-central Africa. Range extends from Sierra Leone across central Africa to Uganda, Kenya and Tanzania, and down as far as western Angola.
Size: 15cm (6in).
Habitat: Areas of forest.
Nest: Suspended from a tree branch.
Eggs: 1–2, creamy-white with darker markings.
Food: Mostly nectar, and invertebrates.

Identification: Metallic blue crown, with green sides to the face and back. Throat is metallic purple, with dark red underparts. Wings and tail are black. Hens have olive-green upperparts, a pale stripe above the eyes, dusky yellow throat and golden yellow underparts. Long, down-curved blackish bill. Black legs and feet. Young as adult females, but young cocks have a greenish suffusion on their back.

WOODLAND TITS AND WARBLERS

These small, lively birds are quite bold and aggressive by nature, often associating in mixed groups which forage for food through the woodland. Tits frequently construct elaborate nests, with hens laying relatively large clutches of eggs, and they sometimes nest more than once in a season. While tits remain resident in northern climes through the winter, warblers generally migrate to Africa.

Long-tailed tit

Aegithalos caudatus

The tail feathers of these tits can account for nearly half their total length. Those birds occurring in northern Europe have a completely white head and underparts. The Turkish race (*A. c. tephronotus*) in contrast displays more black feathering, including a bib, with evident streaking on its cheeks. Long-tailed tits are lively birds, usually seen in small parties, and frequently in the company of other tits. They are often most conspicuous during the winter, when the branches are without leaves. Long-tailed tits will roost together, which helps to conserve their body heat – sometimes as many as 50 birds may be clustered together. Groups can be quite noisy when foraging during the day. Their breeding period starts early, in late February, and may extend right through until June.

Identification: Dumpy and long-tailed. Black stripe above each eye extends back to form a collar. Head and upper breast otherwise whitish. Underparts rose-pink. Reddish-brown shoulders, white edges to the flight feathers. Sexes are alike. Young have brown colouring on their heads.

Long-tailed tits build a large nest with a side entrance.

Distribution: Resident throughout virtually the whole of Europe, but absent from central and northern parts of Scandinavia. Extends into Asia, but not found in Africa.
Size: 15cm (6in).
Habitat: Deciduous and mixed woodland.
Nest: Ball-shaped, usually incorporating moss.
Eggs: 7–12, white with reddish speckling.
Food: Invertebrates, seeds.

European crested tit

Lophophanes cristatus

Although these tits can lower their crest feathers slightly, the crest itself is always visible. This makes European crested tits easy to distinguish, even when they are foraging with other groups of tits, which happens especially during the winter period. They rarely venture high up, preferring to seek food on or near the ground. Invertebrates such as spiders are preferred, although they often resort to eating conifer seeds during the winter. European crested tits frequently create food stores, particularly during the autumn, to help them survive through the harsher months when the ground may be blanketed with snow. Seeds are gathered and secreted in holes in the bark, and among lichens, while invertebrates are decapitated and stored on a shorter-term basis. Nesting begins in March, with a pair choosing a hole, usually in rotten wood, which they can enlarge before constructing a cup-shaped lining for their eggs. In more southerly areas, two broods of chicks may be reared in succession.

Identification: Triangular-shaped, blackish-white crest. Sides of the face are also blackish-white, with a blackish line running through each eye and curling round the hind cheeks. Black collar joins to a bib under the bill. Upperparts brownish. Underparts paler buff, more rufous on the flanks. Young as adults but have brown rather than reddish irides. Sexes are alike.

Distribution: Resident from Spain across to Scandinavia (although not the far north) and Russia. Present in the British Isles only in northern Scotland. Absent from Italy.
Size: 12cm (4³⁄₄in).
Habitat: Conifer woodland.
Nest: In a rotten tree stump.
Eggs: 5–8, white with reddish markings.
Food: Mainly invertebrates, seeds in winter.

Grey penduline tit

African penduline tit *Anthoscopus caroli*

These small birds can be hard to spot in their woodland habitat, thanks to their inconspicuous coloration, although they are relatively common through their range, with five separate races now recognised. These tits are most likely to be observed in pairs or family groups, keeping in touch with each other via their calls. Agile by nature, they will comb branches in a typical tit-like fashion, searching for invertebrates and sometimes venturing down very close to the ground. They build distinctive nests, which are so carefully constructed that they remain intact long after being vacated. Suspended off a branch, the nest is made of plant fibres and has the texture of felt. The pair enter through a disguised horizontal slit on the side, which they prize apart with their foot.

Identification: Variable through its range. May have pale buff patches on the sides of the face, extending above the bill, with a faint black stripe running through the eyes. Back, wings and tail are grey, sometimes greyish-green. Throat, chest and underparts are buff. Narrow, pointed greyish bill. Sexes are alike.

Distribution: Occurs in southern and central parts of Africa, centred mainly on eastern Angola, extending east and southwards to northern South Africa. Also found in Uganda.
Size: 9cm (3¹⁄₂in).
Habitat: Woodland areas.
Nest: Hanging pouch of plant matter.
Eggs: 4–6, white.
Food: Mainly invertebrates.

Dusky tit (*Melaniparus funereus*): 14cm (5¹⁄₂in)
Patchy distribution through numerous parts of western and central Africa. Guinea south to Angola and east to Sudan and Uganda. Cocks completely black, with a black bill, legs and feet. Red eyes. Hens are similar but greyer, especially on the underparts. Young birds have white wing bars (white tips to the wing coverts).

White-backed black tit (*Melaniparus leuconotus*): 14cm (5¹⁄₂in)
Highland forest areas of Ethiopia. Cock birds are predominantly black, except for a triangular-shaped white area on the mantle. Hens have a more creamy patch here. Bill, legs and feet are black. Young birds are similar to hens.

Stripe-breasted tit (*Melaniparus fasciiventer*): 14cm (5¹⁄₂in)
Confined to the border area of western Uganda known as the Albertine Rift. Black head and upper chest, with a black stripe extending down the centre of the abdomen. Belly whitish, with more buff coloration on the flanks. The back is greenish-grey. Black wings with a prominent white wing bar. Bill is black, legs and feet grey. Sexes are alike. Young birds are duller.

Cape penduline tit (*Anthoscopus minutus*): 8cm (3in)
Southern Africa, mainly Namibia, Botswana, Zimbabwe and western South Africa. Greyish upperparts, with a black area around the bill, extending to the eyes. White on the cheeks and pale yellowish below. Bill, legs and feet black. Sexes are alike. Young have paler underparts.

Icterine warbler

Hippolais icterina

These warblers reach the southernmost parts of their winter range in November, where they are most likely to be found in acacia woodland. Solitary by nature, they remain hidden in vegetation, although will venture into the open to catch flying insects. Small berries and larger fruits are also eaten. Icterine warblers leave their wintering grounds from late February, after moulting. Most head north over the Strait of Gibraltar, rather than crossing further east as occurs on their southward passage. Prior to setting off, male icterine warblers begin to sing more frequently in anticipation of the breeding season, which starts in May. The nest is often built in a bush, and the hen sits alone. The eggs hatch after 12 days, with the young fledging after a similar interval.

Distribution: Ranges widely across much of central and northern Europe into Asia. Overwinters in Africa south of the Sahara, although absent from parts of western Africa, some easterly regions, and the far south.
Size: 14cm (5¹⁄₂in).
Habitat: Woodland.
Nest: Cup-shaped, made out of grass.
Eggs: 4–5, pinkish with darker spots.
Food: Invertebrates, fruit.

Identification: Upperparts olive-green, with blackish wings. Sides of the face, underparts and flanks mainly yellowish, while the abdomen is white. In brown morph, underparts are white and upperparts brownish-grey. Bill is brown, greyish legs and feet. Sexes are alike. Young birds have paler underparts.

THRUSHES AND ORIOLES

The attractive song of these birds forms part of the dawn chorus in woodland areas, and is especially conspicuous in spring when the birds are on their breeding grounds. A number of the more common species are actually migratory, nesting in Europe but overwintering in Africa, where food is more plentiful. Some African species have very restricted areas of distribution.

Common redstart

Phoenicurus phoenicurus

This member of the thrush family seeks cover when building its nest. It is often constructed inside a tree hollow, but sometimes an abandoned building or even an underground tunnel is chosen. The hen incubates alone for two weeks until the eggs hatch, with both parents subsequently providing food for their growing brood. Fledging takes place around two weeks later. The pair may sometimes nest again, particularly if food is plentiful. When migrating south, birds from much of Europe take a westerly route through the Iberian Peninsula, whereas those passing further east through Libya and Egypt are believed to originate from Russia. The return journey back north begins in late March. Males generally leave first, enabling them to establish their breeding territories by the time they are joined by the hens.

Identification: Cock birds have a prominent white area above the bill extending back above the eyes. Remainder of the face is black, and the head and back are grey. Chest is rufous, becoming paler on the underparts. Hens are duller, with a greyish-brown head and buff-white underparts. Young birds have brown heads and rufous tails.

Distribution: Breeding range extends across virtually the whole of Europe, including Scandinavia, and eastwards into Asia. Absent from Ireland. Also occurs in parts of north-west Africa, and overwinters in a band south of the Sahara.
Size: 15cm (6in).
Habitat: Woodland.
Nest: Built in a suitable hole.
Eggs: 5–7, bluish with slight red spotting.
Food: Mainly invertebrates and berries.

Natal robin

Red-capped robin-chat *Cossypha natalensis*

Opportunistic hunters, these robin-chats will follow ant columns, darting in to seize fleeing invertebrates, as well as seeking food under leaves on the forest floor. Males are talented mimics and determined songsters – one individual was revealed as mimicking the calls of 17 other birds while singing continuously over a period of 20 minutes. They have even been recorded yapping like dogs. Having mastered an unusual call, other cock birds in the vicinity start to mimic the sound, creating regional song variants. Natal robins are highly territorial by nature, and pairs nest in their own territory. In addition to the more typical materials such as leaves and grasses, they have even been recorded smearing hippopotamus dung on their nests, which are constructed on or close to the ground. Their eggs are surprisingly variable in colour – the majority are an olive shade, but some are bright blue.

Identification: Rufous face and underparts, becoming reddish-brown over the crown and down to the nape. Back and wings slaty-blue, and the tail is dark on its upper surface. Bill, legs and feet are blackish. Sexes are alike. Young birds have black upperparts and wings coverts with rufous spotting.

Distribution: Isolated northern populations in Nigeria, Central African Republic and Ethiopia. The main area of distribution ranges across Africa from Angola to Tanzania and down to eastern South Africa.
Size: 18cm (7in).
Habitat: Forested areas.
Nest: Cup-shaped, close to the ground.
Eggs: 2–4, variable in colour, but usually olive.
Food: Mainly invertebrates, some fruit.

Eurasian golden oriole

Oriolus oriolus

Despite their bright coloration, golden orioles are quite inconspicuous birds, preferring to hide away in the upper reaches of the woodland, although they will sometimes descend to the ground in search of food and water. Their diet varies, consisting mainly of invertebrates from spring onwards, with fruits and berries more significant later in the year. Migrants arrive at the southern tip of Africa by November, and by March will have set off on the long journey back to Europe. It is unclear where the small north-west African population disperses to after breeding, but they head south also, returning by the middle of April. Males establish territories on arrival at their breeding grounds. There is no lasting pair bond between orioles.

Identification: Yellow. Black wings with a yellow patch. Red bill. Hens have greenish-yellow upperparts, streaked underparts mainly white, yellow flanks and blackish wings. Young are more greyish-green, white underparts only slight yellow.

Distribution: Breeds right across mainland Europe, to the southernmost parts of Scandinavia, extending east into Asia. In the British Isles, restricted to eastern England. Also present in north-west Africa, overwintering throughout the continent.
Size: 25cm (10in).
Habitat: Prefers deciduous woodland areas.
Nest: Cup-shaped.
Eggs: 3–4, creamy-buff with dark spotting.
Food: Invertebrates, berries and fruits.

Snowy-crowned robin-chat (*Cossypha niveicapilla*): 22cm (8¹/₂in)
Senegal to Kenya and Tanzania. Also in Ethiopia and southern Dem. Rep. Congo. White crown, black patches on the sides of the head. Rufous throat, underparts and sides of the neck. Back and wings are blackish. Black bill, legs and feet. Sexes are alike. Young birds are duller.

Western forest robin (*Stiphrornis erythrothorax*): 11cm (4¹/₄in)
Sierra Leone to Togo. Also in southern Nigeria. Blackish-brown sides to the face, with a white spot in front of each eye. Olive-brown back, a bright orange chest and white underparts. Sexes are alike. Young birds have spotted plumage, and fledge without the eye spots.

East Coast akalat (Gunning's akalat, *Sheppardia gunningi*): 12cm (4³/₄in)
Three populations, occurring in Kenya, Malawi and Mozambique. Brownish head and back, with greyer tone on the sides of the face, and a white spot in front of each eye. Underparts orange, white on the lower abdomen. Bill is black, legs and feet pinkish-grey. Young birds have spotted plumage. Sexes are alike.

Somali thrush (Somali blackbird, *Turdus ludoviciae*): 23cm (9in)
Highland forests of northern Somalia. Black head and breast, with greyer underparts and slightly darker wings. Hens have blackish streaking on the throat. Bill is yellow. Young birds are more brownish and have dark bills.

Eastern black-headed oriole

Oriolus larvatus

Often seen individually or in pairs, these orioles also congregate in larger numbers where food is plentiful. They eat a range of berries and small fruits, and will take nectar and pollen from flowers. Invertebrates such as caterpillars may be caught on the ground. Their nest is relatively large, usually built towards the end of a main branch where it forks into several side-branches. Plant fibres such as lichens are used to anchor it tightly in place, a task that is undertaken by the female. It is a slow process that takes at least three days and can last for over a fortnight. Having laid her eggs the hen will incubate alone, with the chicks hatching after two weeks. Both parents feed their brood, and the cock continues to provide food to his mate. The young will leave the nest when they are 18 days old.

Distribution: Ranges down through most of east Africa, from Somalia southwards to South Africa. Also extends westwards through Zambia, Zimbabwe and Dem. Rep. Congo to Angola.
Size: 20cm (8in).
Habitat: Broad-leafed forest.
Nest: Cradle-shaped.
Eggs: 1–3, pinkish-buff with darker markings.
Food: Invertebrates and fruit.

Identification: Black head and chest, with red eyes and bill. Yellow collar and underparts, becoming more yellowish-green across the back and the tail. Wings blackish with white tips to the outer secondary feathers. Sexes are alike. Young have brownish-black streaking extending from the throat to the chest, and a dark bill.

CORVIDS

Studies suggest that corvids rank among the most intelligent of avian species. Many of these birds display an instinctive desire to hoard food such as nuts, to help sustain them through the winter months. Their plumage is often predominantly black, sometimes broken with grey and white areas. Corvids are generally noisy and quite aggressive by nature, but are often quite social as well.

Siberian jay

Perisoreus infaustus

The appearance of these jays varies through their range, essentially in depth of coloration. They are opportunistic feeders, and in some locations will leave the woodland to seek scraps at picnic sites. Virtually anything edible is likely to be eaten, including carrion. They will raid the nests of other birds, seizing their eggs and chicks, and will prey on small mammals and invertebrates. Siberian jays have salivary glands, which enable them to produce food balls for storing over the winter when food is scarce, especially if the ground is covered by snow. Their breeding season starts in March, and chicks may hatch before the spring thaw is complete. They will leave the nest when just over three weeks old, but the young jays may remain with their parents almost until the start of the following breeding season.

Identification: Brownish-black head. Upper breast greyish, back greyish-brown. Rust-red rump, wing patches and tail (central feathers grey). Blackish bill, legs, feet. Sexes are alike.

Distribution: The far north of Europe, ranging from Scandinavia eastwards through Russia right across Asia to the Pacific coast.
Size: 30cm (12in).
Habitat: Coniferous forest.
Nest: Platform of twigs.
Eggs: 3–5, greenish with darker markings.
Food: Omnivorous.

Carrion crow (*Corvus corone*): 51cm (20in)
Western and south-western parts of Europe. Black overall, sometimes slightly glossy. Broad, blunt bill is curved on its upper surface, with no bare skin at the base and feathering around the nostrils. Sexes are alike. Young birds duller overall, less glossy than adults.

Piapiac (*Ptilostomus afer*):
36cm (14in)
Western and central Africa south of the Sahara, from Senegal to Ethiopia and Uganda. Glossy black, with unusually long tail feathers that taper slightly along their length. Stout black bill. Relatively long legs and feet are black. Reddish iris, often a deeper shade in hens. Young birds have a pinkish bill and dark irides.

Stresemann's bushcrow (*Zavattariornis stresemanni*): 30cm (12in)
Restricted to southern Ethiopia. Predominantly grey on the top of the head and back, with blackish wings and tail. Underparts paler grey, virtually whitish, but sometimes may appear reddish owing to staining by the soil. Prominent area of pale blue skin extending from the bill, encompassing the eyes. Bill, legs and feet are blackish. Sexes are alike. Young birds duller, with the plumage on the upperparts a more brownish-grey shade.

Jay

Eurasian jay *Garrulus glandarius*

Throughout their wide range, there is some local variation in the appearance of these jays, both in the depth of colour and the amount of black on the top of the head. However, their harsh call, which resembles a hoarse scream, coupled with a flash of colour, help to identify them. Jays are shy by nature and rarely allow a close approach. In the autumn they store acorns and other nuts and seeds, with these caches helping to sustain them through the winter, when the ground may be covered in snow and other feeding opportunities limited. During the summer, jays may raid the nests of other birds, taking both eggs and chicks.

Distribution: Range extends throughout the whole of Europe, except for Scotland and much of Norway. Also present in north-western Africa and Asia.
Size: 35cm (14in).
Habitat: Woodland.
Nest: Platform of twigs.
Eggs: 3–7, bluish-green with dense speckling.
Food: Omnivorous.

Identification: Pinkish-brown, with a greyer shade on the wings and streaking on the head. Broad, black moustachial stripe, and a whitish throat. White rump and undertail area. Tail is dark. White stripe on the wings, with black-and-blue markings on the sides of the wings. Sexes are alike.

Raven

Common raven Northern raven *Corvus corax*

Distribution: From northern Africa and south-western Europe to Scandinavia, and eastwards throughout most of northern Asia. Also present in North America, Greenland, Iceland and the British Isles.
Size: 67cm (26in).
Habitat: Prefers relatively open country.
Nest: Bulky, made of sticks.
Eggs: 3–7, bluish with some darker spots.
Food: Carrion.

The croaking calls of the raven are a foolproof way of identifying this bird, and its size is also a good indicator. Ravens are the largest members of the crow family occurring in the Northern Hemisphere. The impression of bulk conveyed by these birds is reinforced by their shaggy throat feathers, which do not lie sleekly. There is a recognized decline in size across their range, with ravens found in the far north larger than those occurring further south. Pairs occupy relatively large territories, and even outside the breeding season ravens do not usually associate in large flocks. When searching for food, they are able to fly quite effortlessly over long distances, flapping their wings slowly.

Identification: Very large in size, with a powerful, curved bill. Entirely black plumage. Wedge-shaped tail in flight, when the flight feathers stand out, creating a fingered appearance at the tips. Males often larger than females.

Nutcracker

Spotted nutcracker *Nucifraga caryocatactes*

As their name suggests, nuts feature prominently in the diet of these distinctive corvids, particularly hazel and pine nuts, although they will take other items such as invertebrates and berries when available. They use their powerful bills to crack open hard-shelled nuts without difficulty, holding them with their feet or wedging them in a convenient hollow. Nutcrackers lay down large food stores in the autumn, to sustain them through the winter months. In years when the nut crops fail, however, they are forced to leave their traditional winter haunts and seek food elsewhere, often moving much further into western Europe. These irruptions typically occur on average about once every ten years, and usually involve those birds of the Siberian race (*N. c. macrorhynchos*), which are generally restricted to a region east of the Ural Mountains. Thousands of nutcrackers can be involved, with some of them flying as far as the Iberian Peninsula and North Africa. Subsequently, these birds are likely to be encountered in a very wide range of habitats, including gardens, and will prove to be quite bold visitors.

Identification: A dark brown cap extends across the top of the head. The back, sides of the face and underparts are heavily spotted with white markings. Wings are a dark blackish-grey, as is the rump. The vent area is white, as are the tips of the tail feathers. The dark greyish bill is thick and pointed, and the lores behind are white. Legs and feet are also greyish. Sexes are alike, but males may be slightly larger. Young birds are similar to adults.

Distribution: Range is generally restricted to central and south-eastern parts of mainland Europe. Also found in southern parts of Scandinavia and through the Baltic region into Asia.
Size: 35cm (13¾in).
Habitat: Prefers mainly coniferous forest.
Nest: A well-constructed platform of sticks.
Eggs: 2–5, bluish with some brown speckling.
Food: Omnivorous. Mostly nuts, also invertebrates and some berries.

HUNTERS OF THE NIGHT

Most owls become more active after dark, and so are more likely to be heard than seen. They are predatory birds, and it is possible to determine their diet by examining their pellets, which are the indigestible remains of their prey regurgitated after a meal. These pellets are often found near their nests or at favoured roosting sites, indicating their presence.

Tawny owl

Strix aluco

The distinctive double call notes of these owls reveal their presence, even though their dark coloration makes them difficult to spot. Tawny owls prefer ancient woodland, where trees are large enough to provide hollow nesting cavities. They will, however, adapt to using nest boxes, which has helped to increase their numbers in some areas. Nocturnal by nature, these owls may nevertheless occasionally hunt during the daytime, especially when they have chicks in the nest. They usually sit quietly on a perch, waiting to swoop down on their quarry. Young tawny owls are unable to fly when they first leave the nest, and at this time the adults can become very aggressive in protecting their offspring.

Identification: Tawny-brown, with white markings across the wings and darker striations over the wings and body. Slight barring on the tail. Distinctive white stripes above the facial disc, which is almost plain brown. Some individuals have a greyer tone to their plumage, while others are more rufous. The bill is yellowish-brown. Sexes are similar, although females are generally larger and heavier. Females are also distinguished by their higher-pitched song.

Distribution: Across Europe (not Ireland) to Scandinavia and eastwards into Asia. Also occurs in North Africa.
Size: 43cm (17in).
Habitat: Favours ancient temperate woodland.
Nest: Tree hole.
Eggs: 2–9, white.
Food: Small mammals, birds and invertebrates.

African wood owl

Woodford's owl *Strix woodfordii*

These owls can be encountered in a range of different woodland types, from mountainous areas right down to coastal forests, and can also be observed in agricultural plantations. They are relatively common throughout their range, although their nocturnal nature ensures they are inconspicuous. African wood owls take a wide variety of prey, but typically hunt in a similar fashion irrespective of location. They perch on a relatively low branch, often no more than 2m (6.5ft) off the ground, and proceed to drop down on their unsuspecting target from above, although occasionally they will also catch insects in flight. As well as invertebrates, numerous small vertebrates may also be caught, ranging from amphibians and reptiles to small mammals such as shrews. Breeding pairs will establish their own territory and choose a nest site, which is likely to be reused annually. The hen sits alone, with incubation lasting approximately 31 days, and the young will leave the nest after a similar interval, before they are able to fly well.

Identification: Pale whitish area above and beneath the eyes, with fine brown barring over the face. Variable dark brown head and back, with white spotting. Spotting especially evident on the wings, extending in a line from the shoulders. White and brownish barring on the underparts. Alternating dark and light barring across the tail too. Some individuals are a more russet shade. No ear tufts. Dark irides and yellow bill. Hens are larger in size. Young birds are paler with white barring.

Distribution: From Senegal in western Africa eastwards across central Africa to Kenya and southern Somalia. Also extends north into Ethiopia and down the east coast to South Africa, but absent from Namibia and surrounding areas of the south.
Size: 34cm (13in).
Habitat: Forested areas.
Nest: Tree cavity.
Eggs: 1–3, white.
Food: Mainly invertebrates.

Long-eared owl (*Asio otus*): 37cm (14¹/₂in)
Ranges through Europe and across Asia. Found also in north-western Africa and North America. Characteristic tufts on the head are only raised when the owl is alert. Facial area is an orangish-yellow, with a white central area extending between the orange eyes and around the bill. Underparts are pale yellow with black streaking. Hens have more rusty-buff faces, otherwise sexes are alike.

Shelley's eagle-owl (*Bubo shelleyi*):
60cm (24in)
Restricted to West Africa, notably Sierra Leone, ranging to Gabon and Dem. Rep. Congo. Large and dark, with brown patches surrounding the characteristic dark eyes. Underparts are blackish-brown, with alternating white barring. Tall ear tufts and brown barring on the tail. Females are larger. Young birds are paler than adults, with more evident white areas of plumage.

Maned owl (Akun scops owl, *Jubula lettii*):
40cm (15³/₄in)
West Africa, from Liberia to Ghana, with a separate population between Cameroon and Gabon extending eastwards across Dem. Rep. Congo. Distinctive shaggy feathers, creating a mane-like appearance on the nape. White eyebrows edged with black, and a rufous area around the eyes. Characteristic rufous chest, becoming buff with streaks on the underparts. Back also rufous, with some white markings. Light and dark barring on the wings and tail. Eyes and bill yellow. Hens are darker and more heavily marked. Young birds are paler.

Ural owl

Ural wood owl *Strix uralensis*

Ural owls often hunt on the fringes of the woodland, occasionally straying near to villages, particularly in winter. Here they are able to catch birds such as pigeons and sparrows more easily. Traditionally, small mammals such as voles are their main prey. Hunting at night, these owls rely largely on their keen sense of hearing, and can even detect quarry under 30cm (1ft) of snow. Their breeding season begins in February. A tree cavity is normally chosen, but the abandoned nests of other birds of prey may be used. They will also adopt nest boxes, which has helped to increase their numbers in some areas. Mature when three years old, banding studies reveal Ural owls may live for over 20 years.

Distribution: Ranges through the Baltic region, Finland and much of Sweden into Russia, and across Asia to Japan. Also occurs in separate locations in central and south-eastern Europe.
Size: 60cm (24in).
Habitat: Prefers lowland forest.
Nest: Tree cavity.
Eggs: 2–4, white.
Food: Mainly small mammals and birds.

Identification: Relatively plain greyish facial disc. Remainder of the plumage is white, heavily streaked on the underparts, with a greyer tone barred with brown markings over the back and tail. Bill yellowish, irides dark brown. Hens are larger. Young birds are paler, and have white markings on the head.

Giant eagle-owl

Verreaux's eagle-owl *Bubo lacteus*

Distribution: Eastern and southern Africa; also present in some areas of West Africa, south of the Sahara.
Size: 65cm (25³/₄in).
Habitat: Most common in savanna.
Nest: Large, abandoned stick nest.
Eggs: 2, white.
Food: Mammals, birds, some carrion.

These eagle-owls are the largest species on the African continent and can be distinguished from their relatives by their dark brown eyes. They are territorial by nature, living in pairs, although cock and hen may forage individually, keeping in touch with each other by their individual calls, which may echo for over 5km (3 miles). Giant eagle-owls hunt by swooping down low to seize prey, such as hedgehogs. They use their sharp bills to rip the protective spines off the hedgehog's back, undeterred by this protective covering. Their strength is such that they can lift prey weighing nearly 2kg (4.4lb), with various birds, including waterfowl and the nestlings of other predatory species such as secretarybirds (*Sagittarius serpentarius*) being seized.

Identification: A pale shade of greyish brown, with black edging to the sides of the whitish face, and pinkish areas above the eyes. White markings run in a line from the shoulder, with white tips on the wing coverts here too. Dark vermiculations on the plumage on the underparts. Bill yellowish horn, legs and feet similar, with dark claws. Sexes are alike. Young birds are much greyer overall at first.

DAYLIGHT PREDATORS

Numerous birds of prey whose relatives are more commonly seen over open country have adapted to living and hunting in forests. They range from large eagles to the smaller, more agile goshawks and sparrowhawks. Some hunt in the forest understorey, while others glide above the canopy, ever watchful for movements of prey in the trees beneath them.

Goshawk

Northern goshawk *Accipiter gentilis*

Goshawks are opportunistic hunters. In the far north, birds such as grouse (*Phasianidae*) are significant in their diet, but in central Europe they prey more on pigeons and rabbits. The Spanish population hunts lizards, although larger quarry is preferred. Appearance is equally variable through their range, with birds from the far north paler than those further south. Breeding starts in April, with pairs seeking out tall trees as nesting sites, each occupying a large territory. The bulky nest is made from sticks with a softer lining of leaves. Incubation lasts five weeks.

Young cock goshawks leave the nest after a similar interval, about a week before their female siblings.

Identification: Dark cap, pale around the eyes. Grey ear coverts, lighter wings. White underparts finely barred with grey. Broad, light-and-dark grey tail banding. Iris orange. Yellow cere, dark tip to the bill. Hens slaty-grey, cocks bluish-grey. Young brownish above, with brownish streaking on buff-coloured underparts.

Distribution: Throughout mainland Europe, except for the far north of Scandinavia and southern parts of the Iberian Peninsula. Localized in British Isles (absent from Ireland). Small population present in north-west Africa, opposite the Strait of Gibraltar. Extends across Asia. Also found in North America down to Mexico.
Size: 68cm (26³/₄in).
Habitat: Forested areas.
Nest: Platform made from sticks and leaves.
Eggs: 1–5, bluish-white.
Food: Mammals and birds.

African cuckoo-hawk

Aviceda cuculoides

Cuckoo-hawks are so named not because they prey on cuckoos but simply because their barred patterning is similar to that of many cuckoos (*Cuculidae*). They are shy birds by nature, perching quietly for long periods before darting down to seize prey such as a chameleon climbing along a branch, or taking quarry directly from the ground. African cuckoo-hawks have even been recorded as catching fish and crabs, and they may also catch flying insects. The breeding period varies through their range, but is usually linked to the onset of the rainy season. The nest is located as high as 30m (100ft) above the ground, and measures up to 30cm (1ft) in diameter. The young hatch after about 30 days, and will fledge up to six weeks later. After the breeding period, African cuckoo-hawks disperse and may be recorded in areas where they are not normally seen. They themselves can also fall victim to larger birds of prey.

Identification: Bluish-grey head and chest, becoming darker grey over the wings. A paler streak is present above the eyes. Small crest at the back of the head. The tail has alternating bands of dark and light grey, and the underparts are white with rufous bands. Cocks have reddish-brown irides, while hens have yellow. Young birds have brown upperparts and brown mottling on the breast.

Distribution: Roughly south of a line from Senegal in western Africa to Kenya in the east, although absent from much of Tanzania. Absent also from much of Namibia, Botswana and western South Africa.
Size: 40cm (15³/₄in).
Habitat: Woodland.
Nest: Platform of sticks.
Eggs: 2–3, greenish-blue with darker markings.
Food: Mostly invertebrates and lizards.

Palm-nut vulture

Gypohierax angolensis

Up to two-thirds of the diet of these raptors consists of palm-nuts and similar food such as dates, although they are not entirely frugivorous. They will also catch fish and crabs, especially in the eastern part of their range. In more typical vulture-style, they will scavenge on carrion, frequently being attracted to road kills. Usually quite solitary birds, palm-nut vultures occasionally associate in groups, particularly where food is plentiful, and will drive away birds such as hornbills (*Bucerotidae*) as well as monkeys attracted to the palm trees. Pairs become very territorial when breeding. The nest is large and bulky, measuring up to 90cm (3ft) in diameter, although only a single egg is laid. Their chick grows slowly, and will not fledge until it is approximately three months old. Both adults share the incubation and rearing.

Identification: Black and white, with the black plumage extending over the back and wings, and also at the base of the tail, which is short and rounded. Bare reddish-pink areas of skin on the face. Large horn-coloured bill, and yellowish legs. Hens are significantly heavier than cocks. Young birds are brownish and black, with greyish skin on the face and a dark bill and legs; white plumage only evident as a band in front of the black flight feathers under the wings.

Distribution: Western and central Africa, from Senegal to southern Sudan, south to Angola and northern Zambia. Occasionally reported further south. Also occurs in some eastern coastal areas from Kenya to Mozambique.
Size: 60cm (23³/₄in).
Habitat: Forested areas, often close to palms.
Nest: Large platform made from sticks.
Eggs: 1, white with dark brown and lilac markings.
Food: Mainly fruit, some animal food.

Crowned eagle (*Stephanoaetus coronatus*): 98cm (38³/₄in)
Western-central Africa, and down the eastern side to South Africa. Dark grey upperparts. Whitish lower chest and abdomen heavily barred with black, with a rufous suffusion. Barring on the tail. Iris, legs and feet yellow, bill black. Slight crest at the back of the head. Hens have fewer wing bars. Young have white head and underparts, dark iris, and speckling on the legs.

Forest buzzard (*Buteo trizonatus*): 50cm (19³/₄in)
Southern South Africa. Also from Zimbabwe to Lesotho. Brownish head, back and wings, whitish above the eyes and on the cheeks. Tail rufous with darker brown barring. Whitish breast band, with brown streaking on the underparts and rufous markings around the thighs. Wings dark at their tips when seen from beneath, with brown markings, especially on the leading edge. Rest of the wings white. Cere yellow, bill dark at its tip. Young birds lack the broad sub-terminal tail band, and have paler underparts.

Red-thighed sparrowhawk (*Accipiter erythropus*): 30cm (12in)
Sierra Leone to Dem. Rep. Congo. Population in Senegal. Dark greyish-black upperparts and tail. White rump, white spots on the tail underside. Whitish throat, greyer underparts. Rufous suffusion on the flanks. Hens have browner upperparts and barring on the breast. Iris and cere orange-red, bill black. Young have brown upperparts, dark rump, yellow iris and often barring on the breast.

Lesser spotted eagle

Clanga pomarina

Lesser spotted eagles catch a wide variety of prey, from amphibians to small mammals, depending on location. In Greece they take snakes, whereas in Africa they prey on red-billed quelea (*Quelea quelea*) and termites. Pairs return annually to their chosen nest site. The youngest chick fails to survive since it is deprived of food by its older sibling, which fledges after eight weeks. It can be five years before the young bird attains full plumage. European birds head to Africa during September, flying east over the Bosphorus and Israel.

Distribution: Breeds in eastern and central parts of Europe, reaching the Caspian Sea. Overwinters in eastern and southern parts of Africa. Also occurs in India.
Size: 65cm (25¹/₂in).
Habitat: Forested areas.
Nest: A platform made from sticks.
Eggs: 1–2, dull white with variable dark markings.
Food: Takes a wide range of prey.

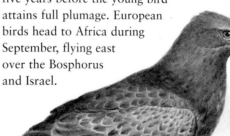

Identification: Brown body and dark greyish flight feathers. Slightly paler head and neck. Relatively small bill, yellow at the base and dark at the tip. Feet yellow with black claws. Hens are larger. Young birds usually display white edging to the flight feathers, often with a rufous patch at the back of the head.

GIANTS OF THE PLAINS

The spread of open grassland afforded some birds the opportunity to grow much larger. Although this left them unable to fly, their pace, physical stature and lethally-strong legs meant they could defend themselves against predators. The ostrich is the only member of this ancient group surviving in Africa today, but other large birds live in groups on the plains too.

Ostrich

Common ostrich *Struthio camelus*

The ostrich is the tallest and one of the heaviest birds in the world, with males weighing up to 150kg (330lb). They have just two toes on each foot, and can run at 50kph (31mph) – even faster over short distances. They will eat almost anything, from plant matter and carrion to lizards and even small tortoises. Ostriches live in groups, headed by a dominant male. He pairs with one of the females, known as the major hen, who lays her eggs in a scrape. Other hens also lay here, but the major hen concentrates on her own eggs, rolling any surplus out of the nest. The young ostriches will all hatch six weeks later.

Identification: Blackish, with a white tail, white wing feathers and white neck band. Hens smaller and greyish-brown, with no white. Legs dark pink. Young are smaller, light brown and striped.

Distribution: Ranges across Africa in a band south of the Sahara, and also through much of eastern Africa. Separate population found in the south of the continent.
Size: 275cm (108in).
Habitat: Open country, including semi-desert.
Nest: Scrape on the ground.
Eggs: 7–10, glossy white.
Food: Omnivorous.

Secretarybird

Sagittarius serpentarius

Distribution: Found in a broad band across Africa south of the Sahara, through eastern Africa, and across the south of the continent.
Size: 140cm (55in).
Habitat: Open grassland.
Nest: Platform of sticks.
Eggs: 1–3, whitish to bluish-green in colour.
Food: Invertebrates, snakes, small animals.

These unusual birds of prey have no close relatives. Although capable of soaring on their large wings like vultures, secretarybirds spend most of the time walking across the plains on the look-out for prey, covering about 20km (12½ miles) a day. Their long legs are useful for tackling venomous snakes, which they will literally stamp to death, without being bitten. They may catch small birds, and raid their nests, and have been observed trying to eat golf balls thinking they are eggs. Inedible items are, however, ejected as pellets after a meal. Pairs build a large, bulky platform nest, sometimes over several months, and both adults incubate and raise their offspring. Chicks spend about 10 weeks in the nest, although their growth is influenced by the food supply.

Identification: Whitish head, with prominent red skin around the eyes. Darker, trailing crest. Chest, neck, upper back and wings, rump and tail are all grey. Flight feathers and the rest of the wings are black, as are the thighs. Black tip to the tail. Long, yellowish legs and grey bill. Sexes are alike. Young birds have yellow skin and a short tail.

Black crowned crane (*Balearica pavonina*): 100cm (39in)
Range is restricted to a band across Africa south of the Sahara (more patchily distributed in western parts and more common in Sudan and Ethiopia). Golden crown on the head, with a reddish area beneath. Predominantly dark grey, with white on the wings and a golden area towards the brown tail. Prominent reddish throat wattle. Bill, legs and feet are blackish. Sexes are alike. Young birds display brown mottling on their plumage.

Blue crane (*Grus paradiseus*): 100cm (39in)
Range is mainly confined to eastern and southern parts of South Africa, with a separate population in northern Namibia. White cap over the broad head. Remainder of the plumage is greyish, darker on the back, flight feathers and tail. The bill and legs are yellowish-grey. Sexes are alike. Young birds are paler overall, especially on the head.

Demoiselle crane (*Grus virgo*): 90cm (35in)
Distribution extends from Egypt southwards, to Chad in the west across to eastern Ethiopia. Greyish-black head and upper neck, with a light grey patch extending from behind the eyes to form a tuft of feathers at the back of the neck. Dark plumage otherwise restricted to the underside of the throat and the flight feathers. Sexes are alike. Young birds easily recognized by the absence of blackish markings on the head and throat.

Grey crowned crane

Balearica regulorum

With a population estimated at 90,000 individuals, these are the most common cranes in Africa. They have adapted well to increased farming, moving into agricultural areas, especially adjacent to wetlands. Crowned cranes will sometimes associate with herds of grazing herbivores, such as zebras, looking for insects and small animals disturbed by the herd. In wetland areas, amphibians such as frogs form a significant part of their diet. Frequently quite solitary, grey crowned cranes may form large flocks during the dry season. Their breeding period is closely linked to rainfall. Incubation lasts about a month, and the young birds, which are brownish at first, may remain in the nest for nine weeks or more. They become sexually mature during their second year.

Identification: Prominent golden crown, with a black area in front. White skin on the cheeks with a thin black line behind, and a red wattle on the throat. Grey neck and upper breast. Back and underparts dark grey, with prominent white and golden areas on the wings. Tail brown. Bill, legs and feet greyish. Young birds have small cheek patches, with a less prominent crown.

Distribution: Eastern Africa, from Kenya to Mozambique and westwards to southern Angola and northern Namibia. Also present in the eastern part of South Africa.
Size: 110cm (43in).
Habitat: Grassland and agricultural areas.
Nest: On the ground, made from vegetation.
Eggs: 1–4, dirty white with brown spots.
Food: Omnivorous.

Wattled crane

Grus carunculata

These cranes are most likely to be encountered in wetland areas. They use their large bills to dig in the wet soil for the tubers of water-lilies and other roots. They also feed on amphibians and invertebrates such as water snails, and will forage over agricultural land. Their breeding period is linked to the rainy season. Wattled cranes construct a bulky nest from vegetable matter, normally surrounded by about 4m (13ft) of water, which protects them from predators. Incubation can last nearly five weeks, and the young cranes develop slowly. They are unlikely to leave the nest before three months of age, and sometimes not until they are 4½ months old. Development is influenced by the available food supply.

Identification: Tall, elegant bird with a prominent area of red skin at the base of the bill, and an adjacent wattle. Bare greyish-black crown. Hind part of the head and the neck are white, while the underparts are black. Back and wings grey. Bill is light grey, legs and feet darker. Sexes are alike. Young birds have a whitish crown.

Distribution: Isolated populations in Ethiopia, Angola and Namibia, and South Africa. Main range is centred on Zambia and surroundings countries. Also occasionally recorded from elsewhere in Africa.
Size: 120cm (47in).
Habitat: Grassland adjacent to wetlands.
Nest: Pile of vegetation.
Eggs: 1–2, sandy-cream, with darker markings.
Food: Mainly vegetation, some invertebrates.

STORKS AND IBISES

While some large African birds have moved into grassland areas, storks still retain a close affinity with water. Different species have developed distinctive feeding habits suited to their particular diet and environment, perhaps none more so than the unmistakable shoebill. Ibises are smaller, but they too are most likely to be encountered near water.

Shoebill

Whale-headed stork *Balaeniceps rex*

Identification: Unmistakable. Huge greyish-yellow bill. Plumage greyish overall, slightly darker on the back and wings, with a slight crest on the back of the head. Blackish legs and feet. Sexes are alike. Young darker grey, with a pink tip to the bill.

These bizarre birds are very distinctive thanks to their massive bill, which measures nearly 20cm (8in) long and almost as wide. This enables them to catch larger fish and other aquatic prey such as small crocodiles. Quarry is decapitated using the sharp ridges along the edge of the bill. The shoebill's hunting technique is also quite distinctive. It relies primarily on stealth, waiting with head pointing downwards and seizing prey that comes within reach, toppling forwards as it lunges. It has just a single opportunity to strike, since its intended prey is likely to be out of reach once it has regained its balance. Such is the difficulty of feeding in this fashion that shoebills may have to wait several days to make a catch. They are solitary birds by nature, even when breeding.

Distribution: Eastern Africa, from Ethiopia and Sudan to Uganda. Scattered distribution in Tanzania, Dem. Rep. Congo and Zambia.
Size: 120cm (47in).
Habitat: Open country, close to water and swampland.
Nest: Platform of vegetation.
Eggs: 1–3, a chalky bluish-white colour.
Food: Aquatic vertebrates, especially fish.

Saddle-billed stork

Saddlebill *Ephippiorhynchus senegalensis*

Distribution: Ranges in a narrow band across Africa south of the Sahara, up to north-eastern Sudan. Also occurs south across much of the continent, except for the far south.
Size: 145cm (57in).
Habitat: Open country, close to water.
Nest: Tree platform of sticks.
Eggs: 2–3, dull white.
Food: Small vertebrates.

Like other storks, saddlebills are found near wetland and feed mainly on fish, but they also prey on other aquatic creatures, including water beetles and amphibians, as well as small birds. They will usually seize their quarry directly, but in muddy water or among reeds will probe with their long bills to detect prey. Unlike most storks, however, the saddlebill and other members of its genus display clear sexual dimorphism. Nesting generally begins towards the end of the rainy season, so that water levels will be falling once the young have hatched, making it easier to find food for them. Pairs of saddlebills are normally solitary by nature and often choose an isolated nesting site, occasionally adopting a cliff-face rather than a tree. The young are unlikely to reach maturity until they are at least three years old, and have a potential life expectancy of 30 years or more.

Identification: Cock has a black head and neck, with a small wattle, and a white area encircling the upper body, extending down on to the underparts. Central areas of the wings are black, as is the tail. Multi-coloured bill, maroon at the base with a yellow area on top, black in the middle, and the terminal half dull red. Brown irides. Legs black with prominent red joints and feet. Hens are smaller, with yellow eyes and no wattle. Bills of young birds are greyish, with a black band down their length.

Marabou stork

Leptoptilos crumenifer

These storks are frequent scavengers, often to be seen seeking scraps near human habitation, and drawn to road kills of animals too. They will also hunt for their food, both on land and in water. Marabous sometimes mingle with herds of herbivores, seizing snakes and other animals flushed out into the open by the presence of the herd. They will wade into water to hunt fish and other aquatic creatures, both by probing in the shallows and by watching and waiting. Here, they can be seen in groups. Marabou storks breed in colonies, often nesting in association with other storks, and in suitable locations there can be thousands of nesting pairs. They may sometimes nest colonially on the fringes of towns, where there are good opportunities for scavenging on nearby rubbish dumps. However, the majority of birds do not breed on an annual basis, and this may be linked to their long life expectancy – marabous can live for several decades.

Identification: Largely unfeathered reddish head, with a white area behind and on the underparts. Back and wings dark greyish-black. Very prominent, pendulous, pinkish wattle hangs down over the chest. Large, dull-coloured bill. Sexes are alike, but males larger. Young birds have a covering of down on their heads. Legs and feet are greyish.

Distribution: Ranges across Africa south of the Sahara, from Senegal in the west to north-eastern Sudan and Ethiopia. Extends southwards through much of eastern and central parts of the continent, reaching the west side in Rep. Congo and Gabon, and again in southern Angola and northern Namibia.
Size: 150cm (59in).
Habitat: Grassland, especially near wetlands.
Nest: Platform made from sticks, in a tree.
Eggs: 1–4, white.
Food: Vertebrates, carrion.

Abdim's stork (white-bellied stork, *Ciconia abdimii*): 80cm (31in)
Across most of Africa south of the Sahara, except for the western coastal region, much of Mozambique, Namibia and the far south. Predominantly blackish, with a dark bluish face. White plumage on the lower underparts extends beneath the wings, and the lower back and rump are also white. Greenish-grey legs, with pinkish feet. Sexes are alike, but male larger. Young birds are duller, especially on the face.

Wattled ibis (*Bostrychia carunculata*): 80cm (31in)
Restricted to the highland areas of Ethiopia and southern Eritrea. Plumage of the head is greyish, with faint white edging to the untidy crest at the back of the head. Wings are darker, with more prominent white patches running down from the shoulders. Bill reddish, with a wattle at the base. Feet also reddish. Sexes are alike. Young birds are duller, with no wattle.

São Tomé ibis (dwarf olive ibis, *Bostrychia bocagei*): 62cm (24in)
Found only on the island of São Tomé, in the Gulf of Guinea off Africa's west coast. Dull greenish head and underparts, with traces of white edging to the crest at the back of the head. The area around the eyes is dark, with a whitish streak extending a short distance back from here. Metallic green coloration on the wings. Iris orangish. Bill, legs and feet reddish. Sexes are alike. Young birds have shorter crests.

Southern bald ibis

Geronticus calvus

These ibises hunt for invertebrates in short grass grazed by livestock. Their breeding cycle is linked to the grassland fire season, which results from lightning strikes. The young leave the cliff-face colony at eight weeks, but fledging success depends on rainfall. Unlike the northern bald ibis (*G. eremita*), which is critically endangered, this species is relatively common and has a population of up to 5000 individuals. A few new colonies have also been discovered in recent years.

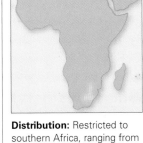

Distribution: Restricted to southern Africa, ranging from north-east Botswana down to South Africa and eastwards to Lesotho and the coast.
Size: 80cm (31in).
Habitat: Grassland.
Nest: Platform of sticks.
Eggs: 1–5, bluish-white with dark markings.
Food: Mainly invertebrates.

Identification: Glossy blackish overall, with coppery-purple patches on the shoulders. Top of the bare head has a reddish crown, and the face itself is pinkish. The bill, legs and feet are pinkish-red. Young birds are significantly duller, lacking the coppery feathering on the wings; head has a covering of brownish feathers, and the bill, legs and feet are mainly greyish.

ADAPTABLE INSECT-HUNTERS

Open countryside can take a number of forms, ranging from huge expanses of grassland to inaccessible upland areas where trees are largely absent. Birds have adapted to living in both types of terrain. For example, rock nuthatches nest and hunt for invertebrates on exposed crags and hillsides, whereas all other species of nuthatch are at home in woodland areas.

Rock nuthatch

Western rock nuthatch *Sitta neumayer*

Distribution: Resident in south-eastern parts of Europe into Asia, from along the eastern Adriatic down to Greece and through much of Turkey into Iran.
Size: 15cm (6in).
Habitat: Rocky country.
Nest: Made of mud.
Eggs: 6–9, white with heavy dark markings.
Food: Largely invertebrates.

Ranging to altitudes of around 900m (3,000ft), these nuthatches occur most commonly in limestone areas, and are quite at home on steep slopes. They hunt avidly for small invertebrates such as spiders, probing into crevices and among vegetation in search of food. Their breeding season starts in the spring, and the nest is made from wet mud hardened into a bottle-shaped chamber. It is well-hidden, out of sight at the base of a cliff overhang or in a cleft in the rocks. The interior of the nest is lined with soft material including feathers and plant matter. The hen incubates the eggs on her own, with the chicks hatching after about two weeks. Both members of the pair will forage for food for their offspring, who fledge when they are 25 days old.

Identification: Narrow black eye stripe from the base of the bill back through each eye and down the sides of the neck. The cheeks and remainder of the underparts are pure white, but with a very indistinct buff suffusion on the lower underparts. Upperparts are grey. Bill, legs and feet are all blackish-grey. Sexes are alike. Young birds are similar to adults.

Wallcreeper

Tichodroma muraria

Grouped together with nuthatches, wallcreepers are similarly agile, able to climb vertical surfaces and dart up rock faces without difficulty, although they are very rarely observed in trees. However, wallcreepers also spend a significant amount of time foraging for food on the ground. They are lively birds, with a fluttering flight pattern not dissimilar to that of a butterfly. Even when sedentary, they often flick their wings repeatedly. In the Alps they reach altitudes of 2,300m (7,500ft), but may venture to more than double this height in the Himalayas. They move to lower altitudes during the winter. In Europe, breeding begins in May. A variety of material gathered by both adults is used to make the nest, which is hidden in a small hole in a cliff face, although they have also been found in buildings.

Identification: In summer, cocks have a black throat and black sides to the face, with dark grey underparts and upperparts. Wings have very evident reddish patches, with white tips to the darker feathers here and on the tail. Hens have a pale greyish-white throat and chest, with the grey on the wings lighter; they also develop a blackish patch on the throat during the summer. Narrow, slightly curved black bill. Legs are also black. Young birds are generally duller in colour.

Distribution: Resident in southern parts of Europe, from northern Spain and the Pyrenees through to parts of Italy and along the eastern Adriatic to Greece. Also present in Asia.
Size: 17cm (6³⁄₄in).
Habitat: Rocky areas.
Nest: Made of vegetation.
Eggs: 4, white with reddish-brown markings.
Food: Invertebrates.

Eastern rock nuthatch (*Sitta tephronota*): 18cm (7in)
Extreme south-eastern Europe, into Asia. Broad black stripe through and behind the eyes. Grey upperparts. Sides of the face and breast are whitish, with the abdomen showing a very clear buff suffusion. Grey bill, legs and feet. Sexes are alike. Young birds are similar to adults.

Black-headed lapwing (*Vanellus tectus*): 25cm (10in)
Across Africa south of the Sahara, from Senegal to Somalia. Head is black above, with a white stripe through the eyes and black below, on to the chest. Buff back and wings, with white and black areas. Rump white, tail black. Pale buff underparts. Reddish wattles at the base of the black-tipped bill. Legs and feet reddish. Sexes are alike. Young birds duller, with small wattles.

Senegal lapwing (*Vanellus lugubris*): 25cm (10in)
Senegal to Nigeria. Also across central-eastern Africa to South Africa. Isolated population in Angola. Dull whitish forehead and throat, with greyish-black over the head and breast; a black band separates this from the white underparts. Wings and back dark brownish-grey. Rump and back of the wings in flight are white. Tail black. Reddish skin encircles the eyes. Bill is greyish, as are the legs and feet. Sexes are alike. Young birds browner on the back, with buff fringes.

Eurasian wryneck

Jynx torquilla

Wrynecks return to their breeding grounds by April, when pairs are very territorial. They seek a suitable hollow, which may be in a tree, on the ground or in a bank. When displaying, pairs face each other and shake their heads, opening their bills to reveal pink gapes. The two-week incubation is shared, and both adults care for their young, who fledge after three weeks. They are independent in a further two weeks. Two broods may be reared. If disturbed on the nest, a sitting adult will stretch out its head and neck, before suddenly withdrawing it, hissing like a snake. Wrynecks use their long, sticky tongues to rapidly pick up ants, and will eat other invertebrates such as spiders.

Identification: Mottled grey on the upperparts, browner over the wings. Broad, tapering tail. Dark stripe through each eye, narrower adjacent white stripe above. Throat and chest are buff with streaking. Abdomen barred, mainly white with buff near the vent. Sexes are alike. Young birds are duller.

Distribution: Breeds through most of mainland Europe, extending eastwards into northern Asia. Absent from Ireland, and the only British breeding population is in Scotland. Overwinters in Africa in a broad band south of the Sahara, with a resident population also in the north-west.
Size: 16.5cm (6½in).
Habitat: Open country.
Nest: Suitable hole.
Eggs: 7–10, white.
Food: Mainly ants.

Blacksmith plover

Blacksmith lapwing *Vanellus armatus*

Identification: White crown. Head black, extending over the breast and on to the back. White back to the neck, underparts also white. Wings greyish with black flight feathers. Lower back and rump white, with black on the tail. Bill, legs and feet black. Sexes are alike. Young have a brownish head, with greyish-brown flight feathers.

Far right: Blacksmith plovers seek invertebrates disturbed by herds.

These plovers are named after their calls, which sound like a hammer hitting a blacksmith's anvil. They are usually found in small groups, but larger numbers may be seen where food is plentiful – such flocks are often mainly immature birds. Their breeding period varies, starting in April in the north but sometimes not until September in the south. They nest near water, and both adults share the incubation, which lasts about a month. The dark markings apparent on the eggs are mirrored in the chicks when they hatch. The young blacksmith plovers fledge when they are six weeks old, but will not breed themselves until their second year. Breeding pairs can become surprisingly aggressive, dive-bombing people who venture too close to the nest site.

Distribution: Range extends from Kenya on the eastern side and Angola in the west down across virtually the whole of southern Africa. Largely absent from the south and the eastern coastal area of Tanzania, and almost all of Mozambique.
Size: 30cm (12in).
Habitat: Grassland with nearby wetland.
Nest: Scrape on the ground lined with vegetation.
Eggs: 2–4, buff-brown with darker markings.
Food: Invertebrates.

BEE-EATERS AND ROLLERS

Colourful and athletic in flight, these birds are well-known migrants between Europe and Africa. Some Asian populations also head to Africa for the winter, and within Africa itself there are more sedentary species occupying relatively restricted ranges throughout the year. Bee-eaters do hunt bees, carefully removing the stings before swallowing their prey.

Bee-eater

European bee-eater *Merops apiaster*

In spite of their name, European bee-eaters hawk a much wider range of prey in the air than simply bees. More than 300 different invertebrates have been identified in their diet, including dragonflies and butterflies. They have even been known to swoop on spiders, seizing the arachnids from their webs. Although individual birds hunt on their own, European bee-eaters nest in colonies of up to eight pairs. Sandy cliffs, where they can excavate their breeding tunnels with relative ease, are favoured nesting sites. Outside the breeding season, groups roost huddled together on branches.

Identification: Whitish band above the black bill, merging into blue above the eyes. Black band extends from the bill through each eye. The throat is yellow, with a black band separating it from the bluish underparts. Chestnut-brown extends from the top of the head, over the back and across the wings. Golden scapulars and rump. Hens have more green on their wings and scapulars.

Distribution: Ranges across much of southern and south-eastern Europe, extending into adjacent parts of Asia and into North Africa. Overwinters in western and southern Africa.
Size: 25cm (10in).
Habitat: Open country.
Nest: Tunnel in a bank or cliff.
Eggs: 4–10, white.
Food: Flying invertebrates.

Blue-cheeked bee-eater

Merops persicus

These social and predominantly Asiatic bee-eaters may migrate alongside European bee-eaters, flying at high altitude to their African wintering grounds. They head over north-west Somalia and the Rift Valley region of Ethiopia, with those birds travelling right down to South Africa arriving here from November. Large numbers may be observed in some locations – as many as 1,500 bee-eaters were observed in a single tree in Mauritania. When seeking flying insects, they will often use vantage points in the open, such as telegraph poles, and so are relatively conspicuous. In direct contrast to their arid breeding habitat, however, blue-cheeked bee-eaters favour wintering grounds close to water, where they are able to catch dragonflies, an important item in their diet. They may even trawl large invertebrates on the water's surface, flying back to a perch to hammer the unfortunate creature before eating it.

Identification: Broad black stripe running through each eye, edged with a border of white, with light blue stripes above and below. Throat yellowish-orange. The back of the head and wings are green, as is the tail, which terminates in narrow streamers. Chest greenish, underparts blue. Reddish undersides to the wings. Young birds are duller. Hens have shorter tail streamers.

Distribution: Breeds in north-west Africa, and the extreme south-east of Europe through into Asia. Winters in western Africa, from Senegal to Central African Republic, and also through central and eastern parts of the continent south to northern Namibia and northern South Africa.
Size: 25cm (10in).
Habitat: Open country.
Nest: Bank or ground burrow.
Eggs: 4–8, white.
Food: Bees, flying insects.

European roller

Coracias garrulus

European rollers may occupy an old woodpecker nest site, and will even tunnel into a suitable bank. The hen sits alone during incubation, which lasts 18 days, and the young fledge after a further month. Although solitary at this stage, the European roller's northward migration in early April is a spectacular sight. Tens of thousands of birds can be observed flying in massive columns more than 2km (1¼ miles) wide through the coastal regions of Tanzania and Kenya. They leave Africa via Somalia and head to Oman, which is used as a staging post before they continue northwards to their breeding grounds. The journey covers some 10,000km (6,250 miles) and lasts just over three months. Their southerly migration is less evident, and takes even longer.

Identification: Vivid turquoise-blue head and breast, with more lilac stripes around the sides of the head. Underparts slightly greener. Wings also vivid blue on the edges, and the back and inner area are reddish-brown. Mainly black flight feathers. Tail bluish, with greyish central feathers. Young are much duller and paler, with pale blue streaked underparts and brown on the wings. Sexes are alike.

Distribution: Summer visitor to Europe, breeding through much of the Iberian peninsula and the Mediterranean region into Asia, and through much of eastern Europe north to the Baltic. Also breeds in north-west Africa. Migrates mainly to eastern and southern parts of Africa, but also western Africa.
Size: 30cm (12in).
Habitat: Arid open country.
Nest: Usually a tree hole.
Eggs: 2–6, white.
Food: Largely invertebrates.

Red-throated bee-eater (*Merops bulocki*): 22cm (8¾in)
Extends across western Africa, from Senegal to Chad. A separate population ranges from Ethiopia to northern parts of Uganda and Dem. Rep. Congo. Bright green head with a broad blackish eye stripe. Red throat, with an orange breast becoming yellower on the abdomen. Undertail coverts and rump are blue. Dark black edging along the flight feathers. Narrow, slightly down-curved dark bill. Black legs and feet. Sexes are alike. Young birds are duller.

Little green bee-eater (*Merops orientalis*): 20cm (8in)
Range extends across Africa south of the Sahara. Also present in the Middle East. Predominantly green overall, lighter and decidedly more yellowish on the cheeks, throat and underparts. A black stripe passes through each eye, with blue beneath. Narrow black stripe across the throat. The flight feathers are greenish-brown with black tips. Long tail streamers. Black bill, legs and feet. Sexes are alike. Young birds lack the throat marking and are less brightly coloured than the adults.

Somali bee-eater (*Merops revoilii*): 15cm (6in)
Restricted to Somalia and neighbouring parts of Ethiopia and Kenya. Black eye stripe, with a blue line above. Prominent area of white plumage on the throat. Pinkish-buff collar and underparts. Blue lower back and rump, the upperparts otherwise greenish. Blue undertail coverts. Bill, legs and feet are black. Sexes are alike. Young birds are slightly duller.

Racket-tailed roller

Coracias spatulatus

As with related species, male racket-tailed rollers have a dramatic display flight. This entails them flying vertically to 10m (33ft) and tumbling down with wings closed, calling loudly, then rolling as they begin to fly up again. Unlike many rollers, however, these birds are sedentary, although they may undertake local movements outside the breeding season. Racket-tailed rollers often rest on and hunt off low perches, darting down to the ground to grab a range of invertebrates. Nesting occurs between September and December. Pairs seek out a bare chamber, which may have been created by a woodpecker or a barbet, around 7m (23ft) off the ground. Here they are very territorial, but outside the breeding season may be seen in small groups – possibly family parties – of up to seven birds.

Distribution: Range extends through part of southern Africa, from southern Angola on the western side of the continent across to northern Tanzania and southern Mozambique in the east.
Size: 30cm (12in).
Habitat: Open country.
Nest: Tree hollow.
Eggs: 2–4, white.
Food: Invertebrates.

Identification: Black stripe runs through each eye, with white above and brown on the crown extending back over the wings. Sky blue cheeks and slightly greenish underparts. Violet-blue shoulders, rump and flight feathers. Dark upper tail feathers with a pair of enlarged "rackets" at their tips, which are absent in young birds. Bill, legs and feet black. Sexes are alike. Young are duller overall, as are moulting adults.

SMALLER BIRDS OF THE PLAINS

Camouflage is an important element of survival in the grassland, since there is much less natural cover here for birds. It is no coincidence that shades of brown, black and white are very common in the coloration of birds occurring in this type of habitat, rather than the vibrant reds and purples typically associated with ground-dwelling species found in forested areas.

Small buttonquail

Common buttonquail *Turnix sylvaticus*

Identification: Cock bird has a speckled head, with a whitish throat and a rufous-brown chest. Black spots evident on the sides of the breast, and the underparts are a buff shade. Upperparts brownish-black with white edging to the plumage. Hens are larger, with buff around their eyes extending down and around the throat, and are more brightly coloured overall. Young birds are spotted and speckled, and have white abdomens.

In spite of their similarity both in appearance and behaviour to true quail, buttonquail as a group are anatomically more closely related to rails – in lacking a hind toe, for example. The hen's call is noticeably louder than that the cock bird. Having mated with a particular male she will leave him to incubate the eggs and rear the chicks on his own, moving on to find other partners to mate with. Breeding can take place throughout the year, but is most common during the summer months. The chicks hatch after a period of two weeks, and have developed sufficiently to fly by the time they are 10 days old. Small buttonquail favour dry conditions for breeding, and in years when rainfall is excessive they will irrupt westwards in search of drier terrain. They were formerly called Kurrichane buttonquail – which was pronounced "currycane" – and was derived from a place known as Kaditshwene, in the western Transvaal, where it was originally documented by Sir Andrew Smith in 1834.

Distribution: In Europe, a small population is present in southern Spain. Main range extends across Africa south of the Sahara, though largely absent from Somalia and much of Ethiopia, the central area from southern Nigeria to Dem. Rep. Congo, and southern Namibia to western South Africa. Extends to Asia.
Size: 15cm (6in).
Habitat: Grassland areas.
Nest: Scrape on the ground.
Eggs: 3–4, cream-coloured with darker speckling.
Food: Seeds, invertebrates.

Whinchat

Saxicola rubetra

Whinchats hunt for food largely on the wing, catching their insect prey in the air or swooping low over the ground. They arrive in Europe by April, and in agricultural areas can be seen perching on field fences in the open. They often flick their tail feathers upwards when they land on a perch. These chats have a protracted song which is often audible at night, although it is not as fluid as those of true thrushes. The female builds the nest on her own, choosing a site which is relatively hidden. She uses a variety of material to create the basic structure, including grass, and lines the inside with softer material such as feathers. The hen also incubates alone, while her partner remains in attendance nearby. The eggs hatch about two weeks later and both members of the pair will feed their young chicks, who grow rapidly and may leave the nest when they are just 12 days old. Pairs often rear two broods. They begin the southbound migration to their African wintering grounds by October.

Identification: Cock bird has a white stripe above each eye. Another white stripe separates the blackish cheeks from the reddish-orange breast, while the abdomen is whitish. Upperparts have brown and black speckling, and the tail has a prominent black tip. Black bill, legs and feet. Hens have buff rather than white eye stripes, and buffy cheek markings. Young birds resemble hens but have black spotting on the breast.

Distribution: Breeds through most of Europe including Scandinavia, except for parts of Ireland, southern England and much of the Iberian Peninsula. Overwinters in western Africa to Cameroon, and from Sudan to Zambia. Present across Asia to Japan.
Size: 14cm (5¹/₂in).
Habitat: Breeds in open, uncultivated areas.
Nest: Close to the ground.
Eggs: 5–6, pale blue with reddish-brown markings.
Food: Invertebrates.

African stonechat (*saxicola torquatus*): 13cm (5in)
Resident in south-west arabian peninsula and sub-saharan Africa. Migratory populations breed further east, across Asia to Japan. Overwinters in northern, south-eastern and central Africa. Black head, white collar. Dark wings with a white streak. Underparts reddish-orange, with white around the vent and spotting on the rump. Hens are brownish rather than black, with paler underparts. Young birds have lighter, more buff upperparts.

Blackstart (*Oenanthe melanura*): 15cm (6in)
South-eastern Europe. Overwinters in Africa, from eastern Mali and Niger across to Somalia. Whitish throat, with an ash-grey head, chest and wings, and white underparts. Lower back, rump and tail are black. Relatively slender bill is black, as are the legs and feet. Young birds resemble adults. Sexes are alike.

Cream-coloured courser (*Cursorius cursor*): 23cm (9in)
Across Africa, from Mauritania to Sudan. Upright stance. Small area of grey on the hindcrown, with a white stripe extending from the bill above the eyes down the back of the neck. Black lines extend back from behind the eyes. Sandy body, darker on the wings. Black under the wings, with a small white area at the rear, adjacent to the body. Narrow, dark, slightly down-curved bill, and greyish legs. Sexes are alike. Young birds have mottled upperparts.

Black-winged pratincole

Glareola nordmanni

These pratincoles are most active soon after dawn, when the air is cool, and then again towards dusk. Fast runners, they search for insects on the ground as well as hawking them in flight. Pairs breed in large flocks on steppelands close to water, before starting to moult in July. The southward migration to Africa begins the following month, with the birds usually flying directly over Arabia and the Red Sea. Their winter range may extend as far south as the Kalahari region, where they often help to control the plagues of locusts that arise in this part of the continent (although in South Africa locust control may have led to a decline in numbers). These birds are quite nomadic, moving on to new locations quite unexpectedly.

Distribution: Typically breeds around the Black and Caspian Sea area, extending north-eastwards into northern Asia. Migrates to Africa for the winter, to south-eastern Dem. Rep Congo, Zambia, northern Namibia, Botswana and northern South Africa.
Size: 25cm (10in).
Habitat: Grassland.
Nest: Scrape.
Eggs: 2–3, buff to stone-coloured, dark markings.
Food: Invertebrates.

Identification: Breeding: white throat, underparts and rump. Brownish upperparts, buff chest. Bill base reddish. Duller out of breeding. Sexes alike. Upperparts scalloped in young birds.

Rufous-bellied heron

Ardeola rufiventris

Distribution: Main area of distribution extends from Tanzania to the eastern corner of Angola and Namibia. Ranges south-west to southern Mozambique and northern South Africa. There are also reports of sightings in south-western parts of Africa, as far north as Kenya.
Size: 40cm (15¾in).
Habitat: Floodplains.
Nest: Made of twigs.
Eggs: 1–4, plain blue.
Food: Amphibians, fish and aquatic invertebrates.

These herons are found in flooded areas through their range, with populations often moving seasonally, in response to the local rainfall pattern. Large concentrations occur in Zambia's Bangweulu swamp, from December to July, breeding here during this period in large aggregations consisting of as many 800 pairs. They are often to be seen nesting in mixed colonies as well, alongside other herons, as well as storks, with their nests generally being concentrated at the outer edges of the colony. The young grow quite rapidly, fledging in some cases when they are just over three weeks old. These herons are otherwise quite shy by nature, although they will retreat to a nearby tree if flushed. When hunting, they keep their bodies low, stretching out their necks horizontally, and move slowly through the aquatic vegetation, listening and looking for potential feeding opportunities. They may hunt in groups, and sometimes associate with other herons at this stage as well.

Identification: Dark greyish-black head, neck and chest, with chestnut plumage extending down from the shoulders to the rump. Remainder of the underparts are also chestnut. Bill dark, with adjacent yellow skin around the eyes. Legs and feet yellow. Hens have a buff stripe at the front of the neck. Young birds similar to hens but with streaking on the head and neck.

SMALLER THRUSHES

Many thrushes are migratory by nature, breeding in Europe before flying south to overwinter in Africa. This is partly a reflection of their diet, since thrushes consume large numbers of invertebrates, which are more difficult to obtain during the European winter. Some display marked regional variations in plumage from one part of Europe to another, such as the bluethroat.

Bluethroat

Luscinia svecica

Bluethroats have a powerful and mellifluous song. They arrive in their northern breeding grounds from April onwards, with the loud song of the cock bird betraying its presence, although they are quite shy by nature and not easily observed. Bluethroats are also talented mimics, and in some areas may incorporate other birds' song passages into their own song. Breeding starts at the beginning of May in more southerly parts of their range, while further north it usually commences about a month later. The hen builds the nest on her own, which is carefully concealed close to ground level, hidden among the vegetation. She incubates the eggs for about two weeks, but once the chicks have hatched both members of the pair forage for food for their offspring. The young birds fledge around two weeks after hatching. Bluethroats hunt largely on the ground, seeking worms, snails and other invertebrates. They will also eat berries when they ripen in the autumn.

Identification: Blue throat with a red or white spot, black bib and a reddish band beneath. Underparts greyish-white. Broad white stripe above each eye, brownish-grey cheeks. Upperparts greyish. Inner tail rusty, base black. Bill, legs and feet black. Hens have a white throat. Young birds are spotted.

Distribution: Resident in parts of Iberian Peninsula and east of the Caspian Sea. Breeds in parts of western Europe, but mainly in central and north-eastern Europe across into Asia. Overwinters in Africa south of the Sahara, from Senegal to Somalia.
Size: 14cm (5¹/₂in).
Habitat: Breeds in wetlands and sparse woodland.
Nest: Made of vegetation.
Eggs: 4–7, green to reddish-cream, with darker markings.
Food: Mainly invertebrates.

Northern wheatear

Oenanthe oenanthe

Distribution: Breeding range extends throughout virtually all of Europe and parts of north-west Africa, although more patchily distributed in western areas. Overwinters across central Africa north to Egypt, joined by populations from North America.
Size: 15cm (6in).
Habitat: Open countryside.
Nest: Built in a hole.
Eggs: 5–6, pale blue.
Food: Invertebrates.

Found throughout the far north but overwintering in Africa, some wheatears undertake a migration journey of around 12,000km (7,500 miles). Young birds head further south than adults, even reaching South Africa. The wheatear's name is derived from the sound of its calls, rather than its feeding habits. Various types of insects as well as spiders make up the bulk of their diet, although they occasionally eat grass seeds too. Pairs start nesting in April. The hen builds the nest on her own, sometimes in a wall but usually well-hidden and close to the ground. She incubates the eggs largely on her own for two weeks, though both members of the pair hunt for food for their chicks. The young fledge after about 15 days in the nest. A pair may breed twice in succession, especially in southern parts of their breeding range, before migrating south for the winter.

Identification: Cock bird has a white stripe above and a black stripe running through each eye. Remainder of the head and back is grey in breeding condition. The wings and tip of the tail are black. Underparts are white, but with a buff suffusion on the throat and chest. Grey areas become much browner in the autumn. Hens easily separated as their wings are brown not black, and they have no black on the head. Young birds are similar to hens.

Black wheatear

Oenanthe leucura

These wheatears are encountered in rocky areas, often with very little vegetation, usually individually or in pairs rather than as larger groups. Cock birds initiate the breeding cycle, and their distinctive song can be heard more frequently from February onwards. The male seeks out potential nesting sites, but the hen subsequently builds the nest and incubates the eggs largely on her own. The nest is a bulky structure, and the birds use stones weighing up to 28g (1oz), not only at the entrance, where they serve as a barrier against predators, but also as a marker outside. Large accumulations of stones, totalling in excess of 2kg (4¹/₂lb), have been recorded at some nests, although these may have been built over more than one breeding season. The young leave the nest at approximately two weeks of age, before they are able to fly well, and retreat under larger rocks and other cover. It may be a further two weeks before they are fully independent.

Identification: The cock bird is a dull shade of black, with white plumage restricted to an area behind the legs, including the vent and rump. The base of the tail feathers is black, and the central tail feathers are all black. Hens are a more sooty-brown shade overall, rather than black. Bill, legs and feet also black. Young birds similar to hens, but have dark brown underparts.

Distribution: In Europe, range extends throughout the Iberian Peninsula. Also present through the adjacent region of north-west Africa, extending into Libya.
Size: 14.5cm (5³/₄in).
Habitat: Arid slopes.
Nest: Built in a hole.
Eggs: 3–5, whitish to greenish-blue, with some reddish spotting.
Food: Mainly invertebrates.

White-crowned wheatear (*Oenanthe leucopyga*): 18cm (7in)
Resident in scattered locations throughout northern parts of Africa, especially in the north-west, in Morocco and Algeria. Predominantly black overall. Prominent white area on the head from just above the bill, extending back over the crown to the nape. The area behind the legs is white, and the tail is also largely white, with a very definite black central stripe. Bill, legs and feet are black. Sexes are alike. Young birds have blackish crowns, often with just a few white feathers.

Cyprus wheatear (*Oenanthe cypriaca*): 15cm (6in)
Breeding range restricted to the Mediterranean island of Cyprus. Overwinters further south in Africa, in southern Sudan and Ethiopia, migrating via the Middle East. Cock in breeding plumage has a white crown that extends from the bill above the eyes and over the nape of the neck. Remainder of head and upper breast is black, as are the wings. Tips of the tail feathers are also black, with a black central tail stripe. Underparts, rump and lower back are white, with a slight buff suffusion on the breast. Hens have duller plumage overall. In the autumn, the white on the head is replaced by grey, with a buff streak above the eye extending down the sides of the neck; the black plumage becomes greyer with buff edging, and the underparts are more yellowish-ochre. Hens have browner upperparts at this stage. Young birds are similar but have browner upperparts.

Desert wheatear

Oenanthe deserti

As their name suggests, desert wheatears are found in arid areas, although not in areas of shifting sand and dunes. Resident pairs occupy breeding territories and are quite conspicuous, running across the ground and perching in the open, often flicking their tails. They are agile in flight, able to hover and dive down on prey. Eurasian birds leave their African wintering grounds by March, as do birds from north-western Africa, having overwintered up to 1,000km (625 miles) further south. The cock bird's song announces their return, and the hen builds a nest for her eggs made largely of dry grass lined with softer material such as feathers.

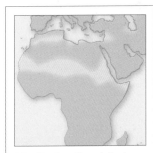

Distribution: Breeds in the far eastern Mediterranean region, and also in Asia. Overwinters in Africa from northern Senegal and Mauritania across to Sudan and Somalia. A migratory population occurs in north-western Africa, but resident there at lower latitudes.
Size: 15cm (6in).
Habitat: Dry, open country.
Nest: Bulky, in a hollow.
Eggs: 3–5, greenish-blue with reddish-brown markings.
Food: Invertebrates.

Identification: Cock has a buff-brown top to the head and upper back. A white stripe runs back through each eye and around on to the upper chest, separating the black throat and lower face from the adjacent buff-brown feathering. Underparts whitish, with a slight buff suffusion on the chest and flanks. Tail is predominantly black, as are the bill, legs and feet. Hens are duller, with brownish ear coverts and no black on the face or at the top of the wings. Young birds have browner wings.

LARGER THRUSHES

This group of birds is well-known for its song. Cock birds become especially vocal at the start of the breeding period, as they lay claim to their territories. Although their bills are not particularly strong, thrushes are adept ground feeders, able to smash snails out of their shells by banging them on rocks, and sometimes even overpowering small vertebrates in this way.

Cape rock thrush

Monticola rupestris

Strongly territorial throughout the year, Cape rock thrushes are only likely to be seen in groups after the breeding period, before the young birds disperse. They are not always easy to observe, being both rather shy and also relatively inactive by nature. These thrushes usually forage on the ground, although occasionally they will take fruit from trees. Their breeding period extends from September to February. Pairs choose a well-concealed site among boulders for their nest, although occasionally they may prefer the protection offered by the leaves of plants such as large aloes. The cock bird has a special call for alerting the hen to danger while she is on the nest – she will fly off quietly, returning only when the male indicates the threat has passed.

Identification: Cock bird has a bluish-grey head, while the breast and underparts are orangish-red, particularly rich on the breast. Back and wings are rufous-brown. Bill, legs and feet are black. Hens have a brownish head, with a pale throat and a pale white streak on the side of the face; back and wings rufous-brown and underparts orangish-red, but paler than in the cock. Young birds have black scalloping on their underparts and buff spotting above.

Distribution: Range is restricted to eastern and southern parts of South Africa, including Swaziland and Lesotho.
Size: 20cm (8in).
Habitat: Rocky grassland.
Nest: Cup-shaped, made from vegetation.
Eggs: 2–4, bluish-cream with darker markings.
Food: Largely invertebrates.

Groundscraper thrush

Turdus litsitsirupa

Distribution: Found in Eritrea and Ethiopia. Also patchily distributed in southern parts of Africa, from Dem. Rep. Congo, Angola and Tanzania to South Africa.
Size: 24cm (9¹/₂in).
Habitat: Mountain grassland and savanna.
Nest: Cup-shaped, made from vegetation.
Eggs: 1–4, pale bluish with darker markings.
Food: Largely invertebrates.

These thrushes are relatively social by nature, and may be seen in groups for much of the year. Even when breeding, young from a previous brood may remain with their parents and help to feed the new chicks. Groundscraper thrushes hunt for food on the ground. They are often attracted to bushfires, seeking out creatures attempting to escape from the flames, sometimes even preying here on small lizards. More commonly however, groundscraper thrushes seek their food by turning over leaves and other debris, seizing invertebrates lurking beneath. Their breeding season varies according to location, but typically occurs outside the main rainy season. The nest can be located as high as 7m (23ft) above the ground, with the thrushes often nesting in association with fork-tailed drongos (*Dicrurus adsimilis*); this may give the thrushes protection against predators, since these colonial drongos are highly aggressive in defence of their nest sites.

Identification: Upright posture. Greyish head, back and wings. Chestnut wing bars seen in flight. Face and underparts white. Black streaking through and around the eyes, and speckling on the throat becoming larger over the chest, flanks and upper abdomen. Upper bill blackish, lower bill yellowish with a dark tip. Legs and feet yellowish. Sexes are alike. Young as adults, with whitish speckling on the head and back.

Rufous-tailed scrub robin

Rufous bush robin *Cercotrichas galactotes*

Rufous-tailed scrub robins spend much of their time on the ground, hopping rather than flying, often flaring out their tail feathers and fanning them up and down. Cock birds have a very powerful song, usually uttered from a branch, and rivals challenge each other by displaying in intimidating fashion with their wings and tail. The nest is constructed by both members of the pair, and though it is largely made of dry grass, other items, including wool, may also be used. In Tunisia, they often incorporate shed snakeskin, possibly to deter would-be predators. A concealed site is normally chosen, often in a cactus or palm. The hen incubates alone, and the chicks hatch after about thirteen days, with both parents providing food for their offspring. The young birds grow quickly and may leave the nest when just 10 days old, before they can fly well.

Identification: White stripe above and below each eye, with a black stripe running through. Top of the head, sides of the face and neck are a variable shade of brown, as are the wings. Underparts whitish but with a slight brownish suffusion, especially across the chest. Rufous extends from the lower back down to the tail, which terminates in a black and white tip. The upper bill is dark, paler at the base of the lower bill. Sexes are alike. Young birds are a slightly greyer shade of brown.

Distribution: Southern part of the Iberian Peninsula and the southern Mediterranean coast in summer, also in the eastern Mediterranean to Asia. Overwinters largely south of the Sahara, from south-western Mauritania right across Africa to Sudan, Somalia and Kenya.
Size: 15cm (6in).
Habitat: Dry areas of scrub.
Nest: Cup-shaped nest of vegetation.
Eggs: 3–5, whitish or pale bluish with dark markings.
Food: Mainly invertebrates. Some fruit.

Benson's rock thrush (*Monticola sharpei bensoni*): 16cm (6¹/₂in)
Western-central region of Madagascar, typically in boulder-strewn habitat. Cock has a slaty-grey head and back; wings are darker. Underparts are orange-red. Bill is black, legs and feet are grey. Hen has greyish-brown upperparts, with white on the throat and brown streaking evident on the chest, plus dirty buff-white underparts. Young cocks have grey spotting on the head, whereas hens are completely grey in breeding.

Sentinel rock thrush (*Monticola explorator*): 18cm (7in)
Restricted to eastern and southern parts of South Africa, including Lesotho. Cock has a light, ash-grey head and back, with darker wings. Underparts rufous-orange. Hens have a brown head, back and wings; whitish on the throat and at the base of the bill, with brownish streaks on the sides of the head extending over the breast. Pale rufous-orange on the upper abdomen, with a white area around the vent. Tail is rufous-orange below, brown above. Young have buff spotting on the upperparts.

Black scrub robin (*Cercotrichas podobe*): 20cm (8in)
Western Mauritania and Senegal eastwards in a band across to Eritrea, and down the coast to Somalia. Predominantly black, but with white edging to the feathers of the vent. Long tail feathers have white tips. Rufous area evident on the wings in flight. Bill, long legs and feet are black. Sexes alike. Young birds brownish-black.

Common rock thrush

Rufous-tailed rock thrush *Monticola saxatilis*

These rock thrushes return to their northern breeding grounds in March. They are seen in a wide range of habitats, including ruined buildings. Cliff faces with ledges are often adopted as breeding sites, and nests may be built in walls. The incubation period lasts about two weeks, and the young fledge after a similar interval. Pairs in northern areas tend to reproduce just once a year, and may begin to depart Europe as early as August. In their African wintering grounds, they are encountered in virtually any type of open country, including coastal sand dunes, but not forested areas. These thrushes frequently seek food on the ground, watching for potential prey from a low perch, although they are also adept at catching winged insects in flight.

Identification: Cock in breeding condition has a bluish-grey head, and a white patch on the back. Wings are slate-grey and underparts rufous. Hens and cocks out of colour are similar; brownish overall, lighter on the underparts, with barred markings and a paler bill.

Distribution: Throughout the north Mediterranean and Asia on a similar latitude. Winters in Africa, ranging extensively through northern parts, and to Tanzania in the east.
Size: 20cm (8in).
Habitat: Open rocky areas.
Nest: Cup-shaped.
Eggs: 3–6, pale blue with some speckling.
Food: Invertebrates, fruit and seeds.

HORNBILLS OF OPEN COUNTRY

These hornbills are generally smaller than their forest-dwelling cousins, with the notable exception of the ground hornbills, which have adapted to living terrestrially and foraging in groups. Hornbills have clearly defined social structures, and individuals often work collectively to ensure that breeding is successful. Many male hornbills have a swelling on the upper bill, known as a casque.

Northern red-billed hornbill

Tockus erythrorhynchus

These hornbills are often observed in small groups foraging on the ground. They will seek out the droppings of large herbivores, digging with their bills in search of grubs. They also prey on small reptiles such as geckos, and may raid the communal nests of red-billed quelea (*Quelea quelea*). Pairs become more territorial at the start of the nesting period. A suitable tree hollow is sought, although they may adopt a cavity created by a woodpecker or barbet, and the nest is lined with fresh vegetation. The hen seals herself in the nest with mud, leaving just a slit through which the male will feed her. She remains here until the chicks have hatched and are about three weeks old, before breaking her way out and helping the male to feed their brood. The chicks reseal the nest behind her, emerging when they are approximately six weeks old.

Identification: Blackish stripe running down the centre of the head, from above the bill to the back of the neck. Sides of the head and underparts are whitish. Back and wings blackish, with white spots extending from the shoulders. Upper tail feathers also dark. Bare red skin encircles each eye and also present at the base of the lower bill. Bill reddish, with a darker marking near the base of the lower bill. Young birds have smaller, brownish-yellow bills. Cocks have larger and blacker bills than hens. Blackish legs and feet.

Distribution: Range extends across Africa south of the Sahara, from Senegal to Somalia and south as far as Tanzania. Also further south, from Angola and Namibia eastwards to Mozambique.
Size: 48cm (19in).
Habitat: Savanna.
Nest: Tree hole.
Eggs: 3–5, white.
Food: Invertebrates, fruits, some seeds.

Eastern yellow-billed hornbill

Tockus flavirostris

Distribution: Range is restricted to the eastern side of Africa, from Eritrea in the north down through Ethiopia, Somalia and Kenya as far as northern Tanzania.
Size: 50cm (20in).
Habitat: Savanna.
Nest: Tree hollow.
Eggs: 2–3, white.
Food: Mainly invertebrates, some fruit.

These hornbills hunt invertebrates on the ground, especially locusts and termites. They have a remarkable relationship with the dwarf mongoose (*Helogale parvula*) – these small mammals help the hornbills find food by flushing locusts out of the grass. In return, the hornbills alert the mongooses to birds of prey flying overhead. Their breeding season extends from February to May, although in Ethiopia pairs may nest again in October. Courtship involves the male passing items of food to his partner. Hollows in acacia trees are often chosen as nesting sites, and the floor of the nest is lined with bark chips. The hen is sealed-in for much of the nesting period, with the cock bird feeding her through a vertical slit measuring 1.7cm ($7/10$in) wide. Incubation lasts approximately 24 days, and the young birds break out when they are around six weeks old.

Identification: Blackish crown stripe and dark ear coverts. Rest of the head and top of the back are white. Underparts also white, with black streaking on the chest. Wings are black, with large white spots and a stripe. Long tail, dark above and white below. Yellow bill, cock is reddish at the base of the lower bill. Hens have shorter bills, with a less evident casque. Young birds have smaller, mottled bills and dark eyes.

Tanzanian red-billed hornbill (*Tockus ruahae*): 48cm (19in)
Central Tanzania. Black stripe across the head, with white spots on the blackish wings. Whitish underparts. Blackish area surrounds the yellow iris. Base of the lower bill blackish. Down-curved bill otherwise red, larger in males. Young birds have smaller, less brightly coloured bills.

Von der Decken's hornbill (*Tockus deckeni*): 47cm (18½in)
Southern Ethiopia, Somalia, Kenya and Tanzania. Black crown stripe, with another through the eyes. Wings and tail black, with a white patch on the wings evident in flight. Rest of the body whitish. Cock bird has a distinctive casque which is red and yellow, with a dark tip. Hens lack the large casque and have a predominantly black bill. Young birds have paler bills than hens, with spotting on the wing coverts.

Southern yellow-billed hornbill (*Tockus leucomelas*): 55cm (21¾in)
Range extends from western Angola and northern Namibia eastwards to the southern tip of Malawi, down to northern parts of South Africa. Black crown, with extensive blackish markings on the neck and breast. Narrow white area extending down the back, and large pale spots on the wings. Characteristic area of red skin around the eyes, with a patch each side of the lower bill too. Cock bird has a bright yellow bill with an evident casque. Hens have pinker skin, with a smaller, often paler bill. Young birds have grey irides and mottled bills.

African grey hornbill

Lophoceros nasutus

These hornbills catch winged insects such as bees in flight, removing their stings prior to swallowing them. They also hunt tree frogs and reptiles such as lizards, and will raid the nests of weavers. They are can be observed around large herbivores and troupes of monkeys, always watchful for disturbed prey. Grey hornbills may be forced into different areas in times of drought. They can fly quite fast, at speeds of around 30kph (18¾mph), and have a distinctive, dipping flight. As with other hornbills, the female will not begin to lay until she is confined to the nesting cavity. She will add to her clutch on alternate days.

Distribution: Range extends across Africa in a band south of the Sahara, from Senegal in the west to Sudan in the east, and down the eastern side as far as northern South Africa. Also extends west to parts of Angola and Namibia.
Size: 50cm (20in).
Habitat: Savanna.
Nest: Tree hollow.
Eggs: 2–5, white in colour.
Food: Various.

Identification: Upperparts grey-brown. White stripe on each side of the crown. Underparts white. Bill is black with a yellowish stripe. Hens' upper bill is white, tip maroon, no casque. Young have grey bill and no casque.

Southern ground hornbill

Bucorvus leadbeateri

These large hornbills live in groups of up to 11 individuals. There is always a dominant pair, and often more than one mature male along with a number of immature birds, but rarely more than one adult female. They can be aggressive, attacking their reflections in windows, smashing the glass with repeated blows of their powerful bills. They can catch hares, snakes, large tortoises and locusts, and will feed on carrion and even take honey from bees' nests. Although terrestrial, members of a group will roost in trees at dusk. Members also assist the breeding pair in finding food. Mating occurs on a branch. The young develop quite slowly and fledge when three months old.

Distribution: South-eastern Africa, from southern Kenya down to eastern South Africa and across to Angola and northern Namibia.
Size: 100cm (39in).
Habitat: Open country near woodland areas.
Nest: Hole in large tree.
Eggs: 1–3, white.
Food: Largely carnivorous.

Identification: Prominent area of red skin around each eye and a red wattle under the throat. Remainder of the plumage jet black, except for the white wing tips (most evident in flight). Cock has a low casque on the upper bill, which is also black. Hens lack the casque, and have blue on the throat and a reduced wattle. The facial skin of young birds is a duller brownish-yellow.

LOVEBIRDS AND PARAKEETS

Lovebirds occur only in Africa, and are distinguishable by their small size and short-tailed appearance. In contrast, rose-ringed is the only parakeet found on mainland Africa – of its relatives occurring on islands off the south-east coast, only the echo parakeet (Psittacula eques) still survives, in a critically-endangered state on Mauritius. Others such as Newton's parakeet (P. exsul) are now extinct.

Black-cheeked lovebird

Agapornis nigrigenis

Distribution: Range is restricted to an area of southern Africa, in the south-west of Zambia.
Size: 14cm (5¹/₂in).
Habitat: Fields with nearby woodland areas.
Nest: Tree hollow.
Eggs: 3–8, white.
Food: Mainly seeds but also eats berries.

These small members of the parrot family have a very restricted area of distribution, which may explain why they were not discovered until 1904. Their breeding period extends through November and December. Hens collect nesting material such as dry grass, which they carry back to their chosen nest sites in their bills, and make a bulky, domed nest that they line with softer material such as feathers. Incubation lasts approximately 23 days, and the young birds fledge after around five weeks in the nest. The total population of black-cheeked lovebirds is estimated at about 10,000 birds, and seems relatively stable. Luckily, they occur in a region with little possibility of further agricultural development, since the land is generally poor. However, drought is a potential hazard they face, which could have a serious impact on their numbers, as these lovebirds rarely stray far from water.

Identification: Blackish-brown head, white skin around each eye and at the base of the upper bill. Throat is orangish, and the back of the head is brownish-orange. Back and wings greenish, with darker flight feathers, green underparts and a paler yellowish-green rump. Bill red, legs and feet greyish. Sexes are alike. Young birds have paler bills.

Abyssinian lovebird

Black-winged lovebird *Agapornis taranta*

Relatively little is known about these lovebirds, although they will associate in small flocks when not breeding, particularly in areas where food is plentiful. They are not always easy to observe due to their small size and green coloration. Abyssinian lovebirds are typically encountered in grassland areas with nearby woodland, although occasionally they will venture into gardens in Ethiopia's capital, Addis Ababa. Juniper (*Juniperus communis*) berries are a favoured item in their diet, and figs (*Ficus carica*) are also eaten regularly too. Unlike other lovebirds, they will sometimes use their feet to hold food. Abyssinian lovebirds also build a less elaborate nest than other species, often constructing little more than a pad of feathers on which the hen lays her eggs. This is usually located in a tree hollow, but sometimes other locations may be chosen, including the disused nests of weaver finches and suitable hollows in walls. They have no fixed breeding season, with pairs nesting throughout the year.

Identification: Cock birds are bright green overall, slightly darker on the back and wings. Underwing coverts are black. Evident red plumage above the bill, which is also red. Legs and feet are grey. Hens lack the red plumage on the head and also have green underwing coverts. Young have pale bills.

Distribution: Range is restricted to a small region in eastern Africa, largely in the highland areas of Ethiopia but also ranging north into neighbouring Eritrea.
Size: 15cm (6in).
Habitat: Savanna.
Nest: Pad of feathers, in a suitable hollow.
Eggs: 3–8, white.
Food: Various seeds and also some berries.

Peach-faced lovebird

Rosy-faced lovebird *Agapornis roseicollis*

Living and breeding in flocks, these small parrots are encountered from sea level to altitudes of 1,600m (5,250ft). They may be present in large numbers in agricultural areas when crops are ripening – a time when flocks will join together. For breeding, they may take over the abandoned nests of weaver birds, which enables them to nest in colonies. Peach-faced lovebirds have an unusual way of building their own nests: hens collect strips of nesting material and carry it back to the nest site folded and tucked into the plumage on the rump. The nest may be sited in a range of locations, from cliff-faces to the eaves of buildings.

Identification: Predominantly green, although darker on the wings. Has a blue rump, a reddish forehead and rose-pink facial feathering that extends onto the upper breast. Rosy coloration less pronounced in young birds, who may show traces of darker markings on their bill, when fledging. Sexes are alike, but pinkish coloration may sometimes be paler in hens (this is not usually apparent). The Angolan race (*A. r. catumbella*) is more lightly coloured overall.

Distribution: Ranges from northern Angola southwards to South Africa.
Size: 15cm (6in).
Habitat: Dry woodland and agricultural areas.
Nest: Tree hollow or disused weaver nest.
Eggs: 4–6, white.
Food: Seeds, including cultivated crops such as millet and sunflower.

Masked lovebird (Yellow-collared lovebird, *Agapornis personata*): 14cm (5½in)
Present in northern and central parts of Tanzania. Blackish head merging into a yellow collar and underparts. The wings and abdomen are green. Prominent white areas encircle the eyes. Bill is red, legs and feet greyish. Sexes are alike.

Fischer's lovebird (*Agapornis fischeri*): 14cm (5½in)
Found in eastern Africa, mainly in northern Tanzania. Reddish-orange head becoming paler around the throat and the back of the neck, where there is also a yellowish area. Underparts are light green, wings are dark green and the rump is mauve. Prominent white eye ring of bare skin. The bill is red and the legs and feet are grey. Sexes are alike.

Nyasa lovebird (Lilian's lovebird, *Agapornis lilianae*): 14cm (5½in)
Restricted to Zambia, particularly in the south, and also neighbouring Malawi. Orangish-red head with a prominent white eye ring, becoming yellow across the neck and on the chest. Underparts are yellowish-green, and the back and wings are a darker shade. Bill is red. Sexes are alike. Young birds are duller, have darker bills and lack the eye ring.

Red-headed lovebird (*Agapornis pullarius*): 15cm (6in)
Isolated areas of western Africa. Main range extends from Nigeria eastwards to Kenya and Uganda. Also extends to Angola in the west. Cock bird has a bright red face, with green upperparts and more yellowish underparts. Rump is blue, with a dark band across the tail feathers. Bill red, legs and feet greyish. Hens are similar but with more orange facial colouring, whereas young birds are more yellowish.

Rose-ringed parakeet

Psittacula krameri

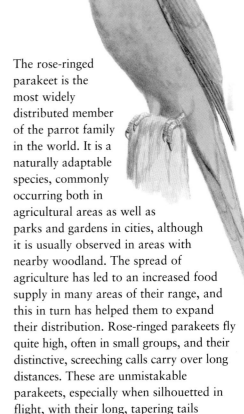

Distribution: Found across Africa in a band south of the Sahara, from Mauritania and Senegal eastwards to Sudan and Ethiopia. Also extends further eastwards through the Arabian Peninsula and Asia to China.
Size: 40cm (16in).
Habitat: Light woodland.
Nest: Tree cavity high off the ground, sometimes on a rocky ledge.
Eggs: 3–6, white.
Food: Cereals, fruit, seeds.

Identification: The African race (*P. k. krameri*) has black on the bill and is more yellowish-green than the Asiatic form (*illustrated*), which is now established in various locations including parts of England, well outside its natural range. Hens and young birds of both sexes lack the distinctive neck collar seen in cocks, which is a combination of black and pink.

The rose-ringed parakeet is the most widely distributed member of the parrot family in the world. It is a naturally adaptable species, commonly occurring both in agricultural areas as well as parks and gardens in cities, although it is usually observed in areas with nearby woodland. The spread of agriculture has led to an increased food supply in many areas of their range, and this in turn has helped them to expand their distribution. Rose-ringed parakeets fly quite high, often in small groups, and their distinctive, screeching calls carry over long distances. These are unmistakable parakeets, especially when silhouetted in flight, with their long, tapering tails streaming behind their bodies.

PARROTS

Poicephalus parrots are the most widely distributed group of parrots in Africa, although they are found only on the mainland and not on offshore islands. Some species have quite localized distributions, whereas others range more widely across the continent. They occur most commonly in small groups, sometimes causing crop damage in agricultural areas.

Senegal parrot

Yellow-bellied parrot *Poicephalus senegalus*

These parrots are usually only observed in small groups, although much larger flocks may congregate in areas where food is plentiful, for example agricultural areas when crops are ripening. Groundnuts are a particular favourite food. In some areas seasonal movements have been reported, such as in southern Mali, where the parrots head further south as water becomes more scarce during the dry season. These are shy birds by nature, difficult to observe when perched and ready to fly off rapidly when disturbed; at such times their calls, which frequently consist of whistling notes, become more raucous.

Identification: Greyish head and bill, with a green back and wings. Distinctive V-shaped green area on the chest, with orangish-yellow plumage on the underparts. The distinctive western subspecies (*P. s. versteri*) has more reddish underparts and darker green plumage. Sexes are alike.

Distribution: Ranges from western to central Africa, from Senegal through Nigeria and northern Cameroon to south-west Sudan.
Size: 23cm (9in).
Habitat: Open countryside and forest.
Nest: Tree hollow, typically 10m (33ft) above the ground.
Eggs: 2–4, white.
Food: Fruit, greenery, seeds and cultivated crops, notably groundnuts and millet.

Red-bellied parrot

Poicephalus rufiventris

Unlike their relatives, these *Poicephalus* parrots can easily be sexed from a distance. They occur in arid country, often in the vicinity of baobab trees, and in some areas may be encountered at altitudes of up to 2,000m (6,500ft). In Somalia, they seek out ripening figs in the summer, retreating to lower altitudes in the winter. Acacia seeds also feature regularly in their diet, and they will sometimes raid maize fields too.
Red-bellied parrots are normally seen in pairs or small groups, but are not very conspicuous. When breeding, as many as six pairs have been observed using baobab trees (*Adansonia digitata*) in the same area. The nesting period varys widely through their range. Pairs occasionally adopt arboreal termite mounds in preference to tree holes, presumably benefiting from the protection the termites afford.

Distribution: North-eastern Africa, extending from Djibouti through western Somalia, Ethiopia and Kenya to northern Tanzania.
Size: 24cm (9½in).
Habitat: Sparse woodland.
Nest: Tree hole.
Eggs: 1–2, white.
Food: Fruit, seeds.

Identification: Cock bird has brown head, back and wings. The lower chest and upper abdomen are orange, and the lower underparts are green. Irides red. Bill is black, legs and feet dark grey. In hens, underparts are green rather than red. Young birds are similar to hens, but cocks have some orange-red plumage on the abdomen.

Meyer's parrot

Poicephalus meyeri

Meyer's parrot is the most widely distributed member of its genus, with six distinct races recognized through its range. These parrots generally feed on seeds rather than fruit, although they may occasionally also eat caterpillars and other invertebrates. Their habit of invading maize fields and orange groves has led to them being considered serious crop pests in some parts of their range. Meyer's parrots breed during the dry season, with pairs preferring to nest on their own rather than colonially. They often seek out tree holes created by other birds such as woodpeckers, usually at least 3m (10ft) above the ground, although once a suitable site is found it may be reused over a number of years. The interior of the nest is lined simply with wood chips, rather than any material collected by the parrots themselves. The hen sits alone, and the eggs hatch around 30 days after laying. The fledging period can be quite variable, with the young birds leaving the nest between 8½ and 12 weeks of age.

Identification: Variable. Underparts generally bluish-green. Yellow areas on the shoulders and head, which is mainly brownish, as are the back and wings. Dark bill, legs and feet. Sexes are alike. Young birds are duller, with less yellow.

Distribution: Ranges widely across central and southern Africa, from Nigeria to Ethiopia in the north down to the Botswana-South African border in the south. Extends westwards to Angola and northern Namibia
Size: 23cm (9in).
Habitat: Savanna.
Nest: Tree hollow.
Eggs: 2–4, white.
Food: Seeds and fruit.

Brown-headed parrot (*Poicephalus cryptoxanthus*): 25cm (10in)
South-eastern Africa, from Kenya to northern South Africa. Dark brown head and a green body. Dark flight feathers contrast with yellow underwing coverts, evident in flight. Undertail coverts a yellowish-green shade. Dark upper bill, yellow lower bill. Pale yellow irides. Sexes are alike. Young birds are duller, with dark irides.

Niam-niam parrot (*Poicephalus crassus*): 25cm (10in)
Restricted to central Africa, from Cameroon through the Central African Republic to south-western Sudan. Brownish head and breast, with brownish wings edged green. Lower breast, underparts and rump bright green. Blackish area of bare skin around the eyes. Irides bright red. Upper bill dark, lower bill pale yellowish. Grey legs and feet. Sexes are alike. Young birds have olive-yellow markings on greyish heads.

Grey-headed parrot (*Poicephalus fuscicollis suahelicus*): 36cm (14in)
Subspecies of brown-necked parrot. Mainly south-eastern Africa, extending from Tanzania to northern South Africa. Greyish head with pale edging to the individual feathers, especially over the head and back. Bright orange-red shoulder patches, with similar plumage also at the top of the legs. Chest is greyish and the underparts are green. Large bill is light grey. Legs and feet dark grey. Hens are similar but have a slight reddish suffusion above the bill, absent in cocks. Young birds lack the orange-red coloration seen in adults.

Rüppell's parrot

Poicephalus rueppellii

A rather short, square-tailed and relatively compact appearance is characteristic of Rüppell's and other *Poicephalus* parrots. Although naturally inhabiting dry country, these parrots are most likely to be encountered near water. They can sometimes be observed in small flocks comprising 20 or more birds, particularly in areas where figs are plentiful. They will actually feed on a wide range of vegetable matter, including shoots, buds and flowers, as well as seeking out nectar, especially that of flowering mistletoe. Their main breeding period usually begins in February and extends through until May, though some pairs nest later – this is possibly linked to the onset of the rainy period. Breeding pairs will generally remain together, and favoured nesting sites may be reused in successive years. Rüppell's parrots are not uncommon birds in Angola, while further south in Namibia their population consists of an estimated 9,000 individuals.

Distribution: Range is confined to the western side of southern Africa, occurring from western Angola south to central Namibia.
Size: 22cm (8½in).
Habitat: Dry country.
Nest: Tree hollow.
Eggs: 3–5, white.
Food: Seeds and fruit, also plant matter.

Identification: Greyish overall, more silvery on the ear coverts, with yellow plumage at the shoulders extending under the wings. Lower underparts, back and rump are blue. Irides red. Bill, legs and feet black. Hens have a larger area of blue on their underparts. Young birds are duller.

BARBETS, HOOPOES AND OXPECKERS

Barbets found in open country are more insectivorous than those species living in the forest, often probing into ant and termite nests with their strong bills. Hunting techniques of birds living in this type of habitat vary greatly, however, as reflected by the oxpecker, which has formed a remarkable partnership with other animals to obtain its food.

Levaillant's barbet

Crested barbet *Trachyphonus vaillantii*

Distribution: Southern Africa, from northern Angola and Tanzania southwards, though absent from much of southern Angola, Namibia and southern South Africa.
Size: 22cm (9in).
Habitat: Open country.
Nest: Hollow chamber.
Eggs: 3–5, white.
Food: Mainly invertebrates, but also fruit and berries.

Although there are slight variations in the patterning of these barbets, it is not possible to distinguish between the sexes. Levaillant's barbets are quite conspicuous birds, and can be observed perching in trees or searching for food on the ground, often near termite mounds. When breeding, they will sometimes seek the relative security offered by the termite mounds, tunnelling in to create a safe nesting chamber. Their intrusion is apparently not resisted by the insects, who would normally deter potential predators. One advantage of nesting in a termite mound is that the heat generated by their surroundings will keep the eggs warm enough for the adult birds to leave the nest.

Identification: Reddish-orange area on the top of the head and lores. Tall black crest. The wings are predominantly blackish with white markings. A black band with white spots extends across the chest. Underparts are yellowish with some reddish streaks, becoming paler with fewer markings on the abdomen. The rump is yellow, red at the base, and the tail feathers have white tips. The bill is pale greenish-yellow. Sexes are alike.

Hoopoe

Eurasian hoopoe *Upupa epops*

The distinctive appearance of these birds helps to identify them with relative ease, especially as they are most likely to be observed in open country. When in flight, the broad shape of the wings is clearly visible and the tall crest is held flat over the back of the head. Hoopoes often raise their crest on landing, however. They use their long bills to probe for worms in the ground, or to grab prey such as lizards scurrying through the grass. They can also often be observed dust-bathing, which keeps their plumage in good condition. Hoopoes are not especially shy of people, and pairs will sometimes nest in buildings. Their common name is derived from the sound of their "hoo, hoo" call.

Identification: Mainly pale buff, although more orange on the crown and with black edging to the feathers. Alternate bands of black-and-white coloration on the wings. Long, narrow, downward-curving bill. Sexes are alike.

Above: The hoopoe's black-and-white barring is also present on the underside of the wings, shown to best effect in flight.

Distribution: Range extends throughout most of Europe, although usually absent from Scandinavia and the British Isles. Overwinters in Africa south of the equator. Also occurs in parts of north Africa and much of central Africa, extending to the Arabian Peninsula and Asia.
Size: 29cm (11in).
Habitat: Open country.
Nest: Secluded hole.
Eggs: 5–8, whitish to yellowish-olive.
Food: Mainly invertebrates, especially worms.

D'Arnaud's barbet (*Trachyphonus darnaudii*): 17cm (7in)
Ranges in eastern parts of Africa, from Sudan, Ethiopia and Somalia through Uganda and Kenya to south-west Tanzania. Black crown that is often spotted with yellow, although yellow is usually more evident on the sides of the face. Variable black markings present on the throat and breast. The underparts are mainly pale yellow in colour. Under-tail coverts are red and the upperparts are brown with white spotting. Individuals differ from each other slightly in the pattern of their markings. Sexes are alike.

Acacia pied barbet (*Tricholaema leucomelas*): 16cm (6in)
Distributed in southern parts of Africa, where it can be found in Zimbabwe, Botswana and South Africa. Deep red forehead with black plumage behind. Adjacent white stripes with some yellow suffusion extend to the back of the neck. An irregularly-shaped black area runs from below the bill down on to the chest. The remainder of the underparts are white. The wings are black, except for some white markings which have a sporadic yellow suffusion. Sexes are alike.

Red-faced barbet (*Lybius rubrifacies*): 15cm (6in)
Present in only a small area of eastern Africa, in southern Uganda and north-western Tanzania. An area of red plumage above the pale greyish bill extends to the sides of the face, but not on to the crown or throat. The remainder of the plumage is blackish, and there is a yellow edging to the wings. Sexes are alike.

Yellow-fronted tinkerbird

Pogoniulus chrysoconus

These small and relatively slim members of the barbet family will sit for long periods during the day on well-concealed branches, uttering their monotonous-sounding call. However, it can be surprisingly difficult to locate them by their sound alone. Their lively, agile nature becomes evident when seeking food. They hover and pick insects off branches, and hop up tree trunks like woodpeckers, seeking grubs. They will also eat fruit, especially the berries of mistletoe and other similar plants. Once eaten, yellow-fronted tinkerbirds help to distribute these plants around their environment by passing the seeds in their droppings.

Distribution: Across much of central and southern Africa, from Senegal to Ethiopia and down as far as South Africa.
Size: 11cm (4in).
Habitat: Savanna.
Nest: Tree hole.
Eggs: 2–3, white.
Food: Invertebrates and fruit.

Identification: Prominent yellow plumage above the upper bill, appearing almost orange in some cases, with alternating black-and-white stripes on the sides of the head. A similar, mottled colour combination extends over the wings, with yellow coloration evident on the flight feathers. The rump is sulphur-yellow. Underparts are whitish with a yellowish suffusion. Legs and the long, stout bill are black. Sexes are alike.

Red-billed oxpecker

Buphagus erythrorhynchus

These starlings have formed a close association with large grazing mammals including rhinoceroses, elephants, antelopes and buffalo. Perching on their bodies, the oxpeckers hunt for ticks by scissoring, which entails pushing the bill into the coat and snapping it open and shut in the hope of locating a parasite. They also use the animals as vantage points from which to hawk insects. As specialist feeders, red-billed oxpeckers are at risk from any decline in the number of large animals, and they are also threatened by cattle-dipping, which wipes out parasites. Not all animals appreciate their intentions either, and will shake their bodies to dislodge the birds. When breeding, oxpeckers use hair collected from animals, especially impala, to make a soft lining for their nest, with dung often being added too.

Distribution: From Eritrea and Ethiopia in eastern Africa south-westwards to southern Angola and down to northern South Africa.
Size: 20cm (8in).
Habitat: Savanna.
Nest: Tree holes.
Eggs: 2–5, creamy-white with darker markings.
Food: Invertebrates, mainly ticks and other parasites.

Identification: Olive-brown head, back and wings. Underparts and chest paler. Pale skin around red iris. Stocky bill red. Legs and feet grey. Young birds duller, irides and bill brown. Sexes are alike.

GRASSLAND BIRDS

Although grassland birds tend to have relatively subdued coloration, enabling them to blend into the background, larks are well known for their song and the display flight of cock birds, which makes them conspicuous. Less musical, but equally distinctive, are the calls of the corncrake, which was formerly a common summer sound in northern meadows and fields.

Dupont's lark

Chersophilus duponti

Dupont's larks are found in open country, usually with tussocks of grass which provide them with cover and nesting cover. The eastern North African race (*C. d. margaritae*), which extends from southern Algeria to Egypt, is noticeably lighter in colour and more of a cinnamon-brown shade than the nominate race. These larks are shy by nature and difficult to spot on the ground, retreating out of sight by running rather than flying if approached. They extend their necks cautiously above the grass to check for possible danger before emerging from cover. Their song can often be heard after dark, although it is commonly uttered at both ends of the day, especially during the breeding period. The display flight of Dupont's lark is a spectacular sight, with birds flying almost vertically to a height of around 150m (500ft), remaining in the air while singing for up to an hour before dropping straight down to the ground again. They sometimes engage in wing-clapping as part of their display too.

Identification: Birds occurring in Europe and north-west Africa have a whitish area bordering dark brownish ear coverts. The breast is white with dark brown streaking. Top of the head is dark, as are the back and wings, with the wing feathers having pale edging. Lower underparts are white. Relatively long brownish bill, yellowish legs and feet. Sexes are alike. Young birds are paler overall.

Distribution: Ranges through central and eastern parts of the Iberian Peninsula. Also sporadically seen in North Africa, through the southern Mediterranean region.
Size: 18cm (7in).
Habitat: Dry sandy areas, including coastal plains.
Nest: Scrape on the ground.
Eggs: 3–4, pinkish-white with dark spots.
Food: Invertebrates, seeds.

Desert lark

Ammomanes deserti

There are marked differences in the depth of coloration of desert larks – some races are much paler than others, which may be linked to their habitat. They are rarely seen in large groups, and if flushed tend to fly low, weaving from side to side, before returning to the ground some distance away. Invertebrates are caught on the ground and in flight, and animal dung may be broken up as the larks search for undigested seeds. Breeding starts around March. Both members of the pair collect material to build their nest, which is concealed on the ground, often with stones deposited around it. The hen incubates on her own. The young larks may leave the nest before they are able to fly properly, but the birds will remain in family groups for some time. It would appear that desert larks have a low requirement for water, since they are rarely observed drinking and have been spotted as far as 6km (3¾ miles) from the nearest water source. It is thought they obtain much of their water requirement from their food.

Identification: Dark brownish upperparts, with a paler area around the eye and on the throat, which has slight black streaking. The breast is more prominently streaked with black and the belly is rufous, as is the tail. Bill is pale with a dark tip, and the legs and feet are greyish. Sexes are alike. Young have mottled upperparts.

Distribution: North-western Africa, including western Sahara and Mauritania east to Niger, the border of Niger, Algeria and Libya, and northern Chad. Also ranges southwards from Egypt to Somalia and into Sudan.
Size: 15cm (6in).
Habitat: Rocky areas, desert.
Nest: Cup-shaped, made from vegetation.
Eggs: 2–3, white with some dark speckling.
Food: Invertebrates, seeds, plant matter.

Common skylark

Eurasian skylark *Alauda arvensis*

The skylark's drab coloration and patterning help it to remain hidden on the ground, where it sometimes freezes to escape detection. If disturbed at close quarters, however, it takes off almost vertically. Skylarks are talented songsters, and frequently reveal their presence by singing. Their distinctive, rounded song can be heard throughout most of the year, even in the depths of winter. Their song flight entails fluttering their wings and rising slowly through the air to a height of 100m (330ft) or so, then hovering before plunging back down, singing the whole time. During the breeding period, a sitting hen may draw attention away from her nest site by feigning injury, dragging one wing along the ground and taking off only as a last resort.

Above: Skylarks build their nests on the ground, hidden in the grass.

Identification: Greyish-brown plumage over the back and wings, with speckling becoming paler on the flanks. Underparts are mainly white. Whitish stripe above each eye extends around the ear coverts, which are greyish. Short crest on the crown, not always visible. Hens are similar but lack the crest.

Distribution: Resident throughout much of western Europe from Denmark southwards. Also occurs in northern Africa. Breeding range extends further north to Scandinavia and through eastern Europe into Asia.
Size: 18cm (7in).
Habitat: Open countryside, especially farmland.
Nest: On the ground, hidden in grass.
Eggs: 3–5, greyish in colour and darkly spotted.
Food: Invertebrates, also plant matter.

Greater hoopoe-lark (*Alaemon alaudipes*): 23cm (9in)
North Africa and the Middle East. A black stripe runs through the eyes, with similar moustached patterning adjacent to the bill. Whiter stripe above each eye. Throat and underparts white, with a darker streaked area on the breast. Back of the head and neck greyish. Wings a browner shade becoming black with white edging; broad central white area bordered by black, evident in flight. Long tail black below, browner above. Bill black, legs and feet grey. Hens are more buffy-grey. Young birds are paler and more yellowish.

Gray's lark (*Ammomanopsis grayi*): 13cm (5in)
Southern coastal Angola to adjacent Namibia. Light sandy brown upperparts. Pale brownish speckling on the breast at the shoulders; throat, sides of the neck and underparts otherwise white. Short dark bill, greyish legs and feet. Northern Namibian race (*A. g. hoeschi*) identical but significantly darker brown. Sexes are alike. Young birds have slightly mottled upperparts.

Cape long-billed lark (*Certhilauda curvirostris*): 24cm (9½in)
Western coastal South Africa. Pale greyish-white streak over the eyes. Upperparts greyish overall, with paler edging to the plumage over the wings. Throat is whitish, with slight dark streaking; remaining underparts are more heavily streaked. The blackish bill is long and curves slightly downwards to a point. Hens have smaller bills. Young birds have mottled upperparts, and less streaking on their underparts.

Corncrake

Crex crex

Similar in appearance to quails, corncrakes are actually members of the rail family. Agricultural practices have led to a fall-off in numbers – entire broods are wiped out when cornfields are harvested. The corncrake's distinctive "crek, crek" call explains its scientific name, and is also the reason why rails are known as "crakes". Corncrakes hide among vegetation, running to escape danger rather than flying. Pairs begin nesting in May. The hen incubates for 14 days, and the young fledge at five weeks old. They will be fully grown three weeks later.

Identification: Bluish-grey sides to the head, with a brown stripe running back through each eye. Rufous flanks with vertical white striping. Flight feathers also rufous. Back brownish with prominent black spotting and streaking. Bill pinkish, legs and feet yellowish. Hens have less bluish-grey on the flanks. Young birds have greyer legs and feet.

Distribution: Breeding range extends across much of central Europe, but absent from the Iberian Peninsula, Italy and most of Scandinavia (except the south). Scarce in England. Overwinters in central and down eastern parts of Africa.
Size: 25cm (10in).
Habitat: Fields, meadows.
Nest: Scrape on the ground.
Eggs: 6–14, greenish-grey to buff, with some darker markings.
Food: Mainly invertebrates, some seeds.

DRY COUNTRY OPPORTUNISTS

Living in areas with low and irregular rainfall creates difficulties for birds, especially during the breeding season, as their young require water as well as food. In areas with few trees for nesting they may even be forced to breed on the ground, where both eggs and chicks will be more vulnerable to predators. Even so, a range of species flourish in such relatively inhospitable surroundings.

Temminck's courser

Cursorius temminckii

Distribution: Western Africa, from Mauritania to Nigeria and Chad. Also over much of southern Africa, reaching as far as northern Ethiopia.
Size: 20cm (8in).
Habitat: Grassland.
Nest: Lays on bare ground.
Eggs: 1–2, yellowish-buff with dense black markings.
Food: Invertebrates, seeds.

Coursers are aberrant waders found in dry country, and Temminck's is the smallest species. They prefer to run on their long legs if disturbed, rather than flying off, although they can fly well if necessary. Their upright stance affords them good visibility, while their coloration helps them to blend in against the background. Temminck's coursers often hunt in areas that are being swept by fire, catching fleeing invertebrate prey, and are rather nomadic in their habits – it is thought that they are drawn to such areas by the smoke. They may also be active after dark, and can usually be encountered in small parties outside the breeding period. Pairs are territorial when nesting, however, and will drive away young from the previous season who have remained with them up until this stage. The eggs blend in very well with the bare soil, and their brown plumage camouflages the adult birds on the nest. Incubation lasts approximately 30 days.

Identification: Broad black stripe through each eye extending to the back of the neck. White stripe above, linking at the back of the head. Top of the head is rufous, as is the belly, with a paler rufous area on the cheeks. Throat is white, with white on the lower underparts. Remainder of the body is brownish, and the flight feathers are black. Sexes are alike. Young birds have dark brown crowns and mottled upperparts, with a brownish-black rather than black patch on the underparts.

Speckled pigeon

Triangular-spotted pigeon, rock pigeon *Columba guinea*

These social pigeons are often seen in flocks comprised of hundreds of individuals. They breed in loose colonies where conditions are favourable, such as rocky cliff-faces or caves. In the extreme south of their range pairs will even nest under boulders on the ground, adjacent to colonies of African penguins (*Spheniscus demersus*). They are now becoming more common in cities, breeding on tall buildings, and will sometimes take over nests of other birds such as storks. Incubation is shared, with the cock bird usually sitting for much of the day and the hen taking over at dusk. The chicks hatch just over two weeks later, and are initially reared on a special high-protein food known as pigeon milk, which is produced by glands in the crops of the adult birds. They grow quickly, and may leave the nest at three weeks old.

Identification: Greyish head, with a prominent area of red skin around each eye. Streaked neck. Underparts are grey. Back and wings are vinous, with greyish-black flight feathers and rump. Distinctive, triangular-shaped white markings extend across the wings in rows. Bill blackish, legs and feet pinkish. Tail is blackish with a grey band. Young birds are duller and browner, notably on the breast, where there is no white patterning. Sexes are alike.

Distribution: Two separate populations, the northern one extending in a band across sub-Saharan Africa, east to Somalia and south to Tanzania. The southern Africa population ranges from southern Angola to South Africa, extending north as far as Zimbabwe.
Size: 34cm (13in).
Habitat: Open country, including farmland.
Nest: Platform of sticks.
Eggs: 1–3, white.
Food: Seeds and fruit.

Lichtenstein's sandgrouse

Pterocles lichtensteinii

The barred plumage of these sandgrouse creates what is described as "disruptive camouflage" – breaking up their appearance so they are more difficult to recognize, especially in stony areas. However, they often forage at night to avoid the intense heat of the desert. Their breeding period varies but usually peaks between May and July. A sheltered site is preferred, partly to prevent the eggs being exposed to the hot sun. The hen incubates during the day and the cock bird takes over at dusk, sitting overnight. The young hatch after 23 days and are patterned to blend in with their surroundings. They develop rapidly, eating seeds when just a day old.

Identification: Cock bird has two black bands across the top of the head, reaching down to the base of the upper bill and the eye on each side, with intervening white plumage that extends back towards the neck. Two black bands also extend across the breast, with a sandy-yellow strip of plumage in between and above. The underparts are otherwise yellowish-white, with fine black vermiculations, while the upperparts display similar mottling but on a more prominent yellow background. Hens are plainer, lacking the evident barring on the head and lower breast of cocks, and their bills are brownish rather than brightly coloured. Legs and feet yellowish. Young birds are similar to adult hens.

Distribution: Scattered locations from north-west Africa to Somalia, and along the Red Sea coast to Egypt. Also across southern Arabian Peninsula to Pakistan.
Size: 28cm (11in).
Habitat: Relatively arid areas.
Nest: Scrape on the ground.
Eggs: 2–3, stone-coloured with darker markings.
Food: Largely seeds.

Somali courser (*Cursorius somalensis*): 22cm (9in)
Eritrea, eastern Ethiopia and Somalia to Kenya. Black stripe through each eye, white stripe above joining on the hindcrown. Top of the crown brown. Abdomen white, remainder of the plumage fawn-brown, except for the black flight feathers. Bill blackish, legs and feet yellowish-grey. Sexes are alike. Young birds have mottled upperparts and barring on the tail.

White-collared pigeon (*Columba albitorques*): 32cm (12½in)
Highland areas of Eritrea and Ethiopia. Brownish-grey overall. Crown and face dark grey, with a white band encircling the back of the head. Whitish edging and longer feathers also on the back of the head, often with green iridescence. Pale grey band across the tail. Black markings across the wings, and white plumage seen when the wings are open. Bill greyish, legs and feet red. Sexes are alike. Young are browner and duller, with lighter edging to the crown feathers.

Yellow-throated sandgrouse (*Pterocles gutturalis*): 30cm (12in)
Sporadically from Eritrea and Ethiopia south via Tanzania. Southern population centred on Botswana. Large. Pale yellow head, greyish crown and a broad black neck collar. Diffuse golden area beneath, merging into grey on the body. Back greyish with some darker markings, and chestnut on the wings and underparts. Hens are heavily mottled and lack the black band. Young birds as hens, but with smaller spots and more intense barring on the upperparts.

Pin-tailed sandgrouse

Pterocles alchata

Male pin-tailed sandgrouse wade into pools of water before flying back to the nest, where the chicks instinctively suck droplets of water from their saturated plumage. (First reported in 1896, it took zoologists until 1960 to become convinced of this behaviour.) However, studies suggest that in spite of their efforts, the nesting success of these birds is poor, with the majority of young chicks falling victim to predators. If eggs are taken, a pair may nest again soon afterwards. Pin-tailed sandgrouse remain relatively common in Morocco and Spain, but elsewhere in Europe their numbers have fallen markedly over recent years.

Identification: Black throat and stripe through each eye. Greyish crown, neck and chest. Orangish breast (bordered black) and sides of the head. Underparts white, yellow spots over the back and wings. Black-and-buff barring on the rump and characteristic long tail. Hens are paler, have a shorter tail and mottled wings, and lack the yellow spots. Young paler too, with no upper black breast line and only a trace of the lower.

Distribution: Resident in south-west Europe and in the Caspian region. Migratory in some parts of Asia. Also found in northern Africa.
Size: 32cm (12½in).
Habitat: Open, dry country.
Nest: Scrape on the ground.
Eggs: 3, stone-coloured with darker mottling.
Food: Seeds, plant material.

GAME BIRDS AND SONGSTERS

Game birds as a group are commonly associated with woodland areas, but francolins have adapted successfully to live in more open country. However, they may not always be resident throughout the year in these areas, often undertaking regular migrations or sometimes even irregular seasonal movements influenced by rainfall or the availability of food.

Red-necked francolin

Red-necked spurfowl *Pternistis afer*

The red-necked francolin's head markings differ markedly through its range, with the feathering on the sides of the head sometimes whitish rather than predominantly blackish. The patterning of the underparts also differs in the nominate race, *P. a. afer*, from western Angola and adjacent parts of Namibia, which has white underparts with black markings. In total, there are five distinct races recognized through its range. Red-necked francolins are found in areas of higher rainfall than Swainson's francolin or spurfowl (*Pternistis swainsonii*), since here there is more vegetation to provide cover. They are most likely to be encountered in the early morning and towards dusk, seeking shade when the sun is at its hottest. Red-necked francolins rarely fly, although if being chased they may fly low over the ground for a short distance, before dipping back down into vegetation and continuing on foot; they may sometimes take to a tree for a short time. They also roost in trees.

Identification: Prominent bare red skin around each eye and on the throat. Fine white streaking on the black neck, becoming longer on the underparts. Back and wings brown. Bill, legs and feet red. Sexes are alike. Young birds are browner, with a dark bill, yellowish legs and down partly obscuring the bare throat skin.

Distribution: Ranges in a band across southern Africa, from Rep. Congo and Angola in the west across to Tanzania and down the eastern side of the continent to southern South Africa.
Size: 41cm (16in).
Habitat: Grassland, often near scrub.
Nest: Scrape on the ground lined with vegetation.
Eggs: 3–9, buff to pale brown.
Food: Plant matter.

Swainson's francolin

Swainson's spurfowl *Pternistis swainsonii*

Distribution: Southern parts of Africa, extending from Zambia to southern Angola and northern Namibia in the west, and down to northern South Africa.
Size: 38cm (15in).
Habitat: Arid savanna.
Nest: Scrape on the ground lined with vegetation.
Eggs: 4–8, creamy-buff.
Food: Mainly plant matter.

These francolins can sometimes be observed in small groups, which are described as coveys, as well as in the company of other related species. They are also known as spurfowl because of the presence of one or two spurs which are evident on the legs of cock birds. Pairs nest individually, usually choosing a site hidden in grass and protected from above by a bush. Hatching typically takes about 21 days, with the young birds able to fly shortly afterwards. In some parts of their range they may nest twice during the year. In agricultural areas, Swainson's francolin will invade freshly-sown maize fields, digging up the seeds. They often forage in this way, unearthing edible plant items from the ground, as well as eating invertebrates. If disturbed in the open, these francolins will fly off and drop down out of sight in the nearest available cover. Especially during periods of heavy rainfall, they may also be seen perching in suitable trees. They have loud, harsh calls that frequently betray their presence.

Identification: Predominantly dark brown, with black markings evident on the underparts. Bare red skin around the eyes and under the throat. Bill, legs and feet are blackish. Sexes are alike. Young birds are duller, lack the red on the head and have paler markings on the flanks.

Tawny pipit

Anthus campestris

The tawny pipit's breeding season begins in Europe in April, with cock birds engaging in song flights, fluttering upwards almost vertically to a height of around 30m (100ft) before plunging back down, singing especially loudly at this stage. The cock will also chase his mate frantically until egg-laying commences. She constructs the nest on her own, usually hiding it behind a tussock of grass. Incubation lasts about two weeks, with the young pipits leaving the nest after a similar period. It is not uncommon for pairs to rear two broods. Like many young birds however, a significant proportion will die in the first few weeks following fledging, but those which survive will migrate south to their African wintering grounds from September onwards. Tawny pipits may be observed in small flocks of up to 30 individuals when migrating. A relatively small number of pairs also nest in north-west Africa.

Identification: Black stripe through each eye, with a white stripe above. Upperparts mainly plain, slightly greyish, with buff-white underparts. Row of darker markings across the median coverts, and also slight streaks at the sides of the chest. Bill is darker at the tip. Legs and feet are pale pink, with a short hind claw. Sexes are alike. Young birds display more heavily marked upperparts, with streaking over the head and on the back.

Distribution: Ranges through Europe as a breeding visitor. Absent from the British Isles and Scandinavia (except for the extreme south-west). Overwinters in Africa, from southern Mauritania and Senegal across to Somalia and Kenya. Present in Asia.
Size: 18cm (7in).
Habitat: Sandy areas and gravel pits.
Nest: Cup-shaped, made from vegetation.
Eggs: 4–6, white, spotted.
Food: Largely invertebrates.

Yellow-necked francolin (Yellow-necked spurfowl, *Pternistis leucoscepus*): 40cm (15³⁄₄in) Eastern Africa, with an isolated population in Eritrea. Also ranges from Somalia to parts of Ethiopia, Kenya, Uganda and Tanzania. Recognizable by its distinctive bare yellow throat patch and predominantly brown plumage with very evident white streaking, especially on the underparts. Sexes are alike. Young birds have paler throats.

Moorland francolin (*Scleroptila psilolaema*): 35cm (13³⁄₄in)
East Africa, occurring in areas of Ethiopia and Kenya, ranging to Uganda. Mottled brown upperparts, with a white throat. Ethiopian race (*S. p. psilolaema*) has buff underparts, with wavy black lines across the chest and speckling on the underparts. Underparts become more rufous in the southerly race (*S. p. elgonensis*). Sexes are alike. Young birds yet to be described.

Quail-plover (*Ortyxelos meiffrenii*): 13cm (5in) Sub-Saharan Africa, in a band from Mauritania to Sudan. Also Ethiopia south to Kenya. Isolated areas elsewhere, including Ghana. Looks like a miniature courser, but exact relationship unclear. Cheeks and sides of the neck are pale yellow. Rufous ear coverts. Mottled brownish markings on the back and across the chest. White is evident on the underparts and across the wings, which are predominantly black when seen from above. Bill greyish with a dark tip. Legs are yellowish. Hens have more rufous coloration on the breast. Young birds are paler, with more intense spotting on the upperparts.

Grasshopper warbler

Locustella naevia

Difficult to observe, these warblers are very adept at clambering through grass and low vegetation. They may be spotted running across open ground, flying low if disturbed and seeking vegetation as cover. Their song, which is usually heard at dusk, may also betray their presence. They sing in bursts of up to a minute in duration, and their calls incorporate ringing notes that have been likened to the sound of a muffled alarm clock. Grasshopper warblers migrate largely without stopping, and have been observed in West Africa from August onwards. They undertake the return journey to their breeding grounds in Europe and Asia between March and May, flying in a more easterly direction, often crossing the Mediterranean from Algeria. The breeding period extends from May until July, with the bulky nest built close to the ground. The chicks hatch after two weeks, and are reared by both adults before leaving the nest as early as 10 days old.

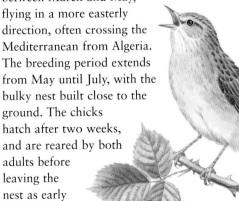

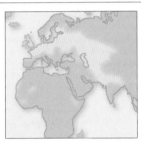

Distribution: Breeds through central and northern parts of Europe as far as southern Scandinavia. Present in much of the British Isles. Absent from the Mediterranean region. Overwinters in parts of Africa, especially on the western side.
Size: 12.5cm (5in).
Habitat: Marshland and grassland areas.
Nest: Made of vegetation.
Eggs: 6, creamy with brownish-red spotting.
Food: Invertebrates.

Identification: Olive-brown upperparts. Streaked head, back and undertail coverts. Faint eye stripe. Underparts whitish, more yellowish-green on the breast. Variable chest markings. Narrow, pointed bill. Pink legs and feet. Sexes are alike. Young birds have yellowish underparts.

PHEASANTS AND PARTRIDGES

A number of pheasant and partridge species have been selectively bred and released for sport, so that sightings far outside their usual areas of distribution are not unusual. In Europe, these game birds are most likely to be observed during the winter months, when there is less natural cover available and groups may be forced to forage more widely.

Common pheasant

Ring-necked pheasant *Phasianus colchicus*

Common pheasants show considerable individual variation in appearance throughout their European range. This is due to hybridization between races, resulting in the loss of distinguishing characteristics. Even odd black-feathered (melanistic) examples are not uncommon. This situation has arisen largely because of widespread breeding of these pheasants and their subsequent release into the wild for shooting. They occur naturally in Asia. Common pheasants usually live in groups comprised of a cock bird with several hens. They forage on the ground, flying noisily and somewhat clumsily when disturbed, and may choose to roost off the ground.

Right: Its mottled plumage provides the common pheasant hen with good camouflage.

Identification: Cock bird has prominent areas of bare red skin on each side of the face, surrounded by metallic dark greenish plumage. Variable white area at the base of the neck. The remainder of the plumage is predominantly brown, with the underparts a more chestnut shade with dark blotching. Hens are lighter brown overall, with darker mottling, especially on the back and wings.

Distribution: Range now extends throughout most of western Europe, except for much of the Iberian Peninsula, and in a band eastwards through central Asia as far as Japan. Has also been introduced to the United States, Australia, Tasmania and New Zealand.
Size: Cock 89cm (35in); hen 62cm (24in).
Habitat: Light woodland.
Nest: Scrape on the ground.
Eggs: 7–15, olive-brown.
Food: Plant matter including seeds, berries and young shoots, also invertebrates.

Red-legged partridge

Alectoris rufa

The red-legged partridge was brought to England as long ago as the late 1600s for shooting, and its adaptable nature ensured that its range steadily expanded. However, during the 20th century the chukar partridge, which hybridizes with the red-legged variety, was also introduced to the British Isles. Today it can be difficult to determine whether partridges are pure or cross-bred red-legged individuals, even in their natural range, thanks to their similarity in appearance to chukars. Red-legged partidges form individual pairs when breeding. The cock bird chooses and then prepares the nest site.

Identification: Prominent black collar with disctinctive black streaks extending around the sides of the neck to the eye. Black stripe continues through the eye to the bill, with a white stripe above and white below around the throat. Bluish-grey above the bill, and on the breast and barred flanks. Brownish abdomen. Hens are smaller and lack the tarsal spurs on the legs.

Distribution: Found naturally in Europe from the Iberian Peninsula to Italy. Introduced to the rest of Europe.
Size: 38cm (15in).
Habitat: Open countryside.
Nest: Scrape on the ground.
Eggs: 9–12, pale yellowish-brown with dark spotting.
Food: Mainly plant matter, some invertebrates.

Rock partridge

Alectoris graeca

Rock partridges take their name from the rocky slopes on which they can frequently be observed, which in Italy range to altitudes as high as 2,700m (8,850ft). They often move down to lower levels in the winter, when snow collects on the slopes, and they avoid north-facing slopes altogether. Throughout the year, rock partridges are rarely sighted far from water, and are most likely to be seen in flocks. Their coloration provides excellent camouflage when foraging on the ground. When flushed, their flight is quite low and fast, and they will dip down into nearby cover again as soon as they are out of danger. Rock partridges nest as individual pairs, and their chicks will be fully grown when they are three months old.

Distribution: Central southern Europe, from southeast France to Italy and along the eastern Adriatic coast to Greece. Present on Sicily.
Size: 36cm (14in).
Habitat: Rocky alpine areas.
Nest: Scrape on the ground.
Eggs: 8–14, yellowish-brown with some darker spotting.
Food: Mainly plant matter, some invertebrates.

Identification: Grey crown. Thick black stripe running from around the red bill through each eye and down onto the chest, encircling the white lower face and throat area. Breast is greyish-blue, becoming fawn on the underparts, with black-and-white barring on the flanks. Brownish suffusion over the back. Sexes are alike.

Helmeted guineafowl

Numida meleagris

Helmeted guineafowl vary considerably in appearance throughout their wide range. In the past, taxonomists have recognized more than 30 different races, but this figure has now been whittled down to approximately nine. The various subspecies can be distinguished by the shape of their casques and wattles, as well as by the depth of blue coloration on the sides of their head. These guineafowl prey readily on invertebrates, even to the extent of picking off ticks from warthogs. They scratch around on the ground using their powerful toes, searching for seeds, invertebrates and other edible items. Young helmeted guineafowl are able to fly just 14 days after hatching, and family groups link up with the main flock again after a month or so.

Distribution: Much of Africa south of the Sahara, except some western and eastern areas. Introduced elsewhere, including Saudi Arabia and the Caribbean.
Size: 53–63cm (21–25in).
Habitat: Open country, especially savanna.
Nest: Scrape on the ground, often hidden in long grass.
Eggs: 6–12, creamy-buff with brown-and-white speckling.
Food: Mostly plant matter and invertebrates.

Identification: Distinctive, horn-coloured casque on the top of the head, often with an adjoining area of red skin. Blue areas on the sides of the face extending down the neck. The head is largely bare, although traces of fine down feathering may be visible. Plumage is predominantly dark, broken by variable white spots. Sexes are similar, but hens are smaller than cocks.

Chukar partridge (*Alectoris chukar*): 35cm (14in)
Found in southern Europe eastwards to Asia. Introduced to the British Isles and elsewhere. Very similar in appearance to the rock partridge (*Alectoris graeca*) but has a cream rather than white area on the sides of the face and chest, a broader white stripe above each eye, and black only on the side of the lower mandible rather than on the whole bill. Numerous races are recognized through its wide range. Hens lack the tarsal swelling of cocks, and their head patterning is less colourful.

Grey partridge (*Perdix perdix*): 32cm (12½in)
Occurs in a broad band across central Europe, from Ireland eastwards to Asia. Orange-brown face, with faint grey stripes extending back on the sides of the head. Crown, neck and much of the underparts are greyish, with dark edging to the plumage. Prominent dark brown feathering on the belly is largely absent or reduced in size in hens. The flanks are barred with brown, while the wings are brown with black speckling. Tail is reddish brown.

Barbary partridge (*Alectoris barbara*): 35cm (14in)
Natural range is in North Africa. Introduced to southern Spain and also present on Sardinia. Dark stripe on the crown, with a greyish-white area beneath and a lighter fawn stripe extending through each eye. The remainder of the head and throat area are greyish-white. Reddish-brown border to the bib, with black-and-white speckling behind. The chest is otherwise greyish and the abdomen is fawn. Back and wings are greyish with a fawn suffusion. Brown and black markings on the flanks on a whitish background. Sexes are alike.

BUSTARDS AND GROUSE

This group of birds may be encountered in a range of different landscapes, from arid, desert-like terrain to the frozen north, but they all rely heavily on cryptic plumage to avoid detection. Grouse, whose range extends into the tundra region, have plumage that extends right down their legs and over their toes to minimize heat loss and guard against frostbite.

Great bustard

Otis tarda

These massive birds have declined greatly in number over recent years owing to a combination of hunting and habitat change. They still flourish in undisturbed areas, where they are seen in groups throughout the year. The display of the cock is an amazing sight as he bends forwards, raising his wings and inflating his throat sac. His head disappears from view, creating what has been likened to a foam bath. Great bustards are quiet birds by nature, uttering a short call resembling a bark only if alarmed. They will hunt voles, but invertebrates are favoured for rearing the chicks, which is accomplished by the hen alone.

Identification: Grey head and neck, with a rufous area at the base. Black-and-chestnut markings over the wings, with prominent white areas. Underparts and tips of tail feathers are also white. Hens have more extensive but paler rufous coloration on the neck, and less white on the wings.

Distribution: Scattered locations through the Iberian Peninsula and adjacent parts of north-west Africa. Also present in eastern Europe, ranging eastwards into Asia.
Size: Cock 105cm (41in); hen 75cm (29½in).
Habitat: Open steppes and agricultural land.
Nest: Flattened area, made of vegetation.
Eggs: 2–4, greenish or olive-brown in colour.
Food: Invertebrates, plant matter and small mammals.

Southern black korhaan

Black bustard *Afrotis afra*

Distribution: Southern Africa, extending from the Cape north across much of Namibia and Botswana.
Size: 52cm (20½in).
Habitat: Grassland, savanna.
Nest: Lays on bare ground.
Eggs: 1, olive-green with darker brown markings.
Food: Mostly invertebrates and plant matter.

Male black korhaan bustards are bold and conspicuous by nature, whereas hens are much shyer. Highly territorial, the male's call, from a vantage point such as a termite mound, can travel over 1km (⅝ mile). He will also fly regularly over his territory, and may end up in aerial conflict with one or more neighbouring cock birds. Males display throughout the year, and hens may mate at any stage too, hatching and rearing their offspring alone. The chick follows its mother almost immediately. Taxonomists have reclassified the black korhaan as two separate species: the northern form (*A. afraoides*) has white centres to its flight feathers and white underwing coverts, while its southern relative (*A. afra*) is characterized by its black underwing coverts.

Identification: Black head, white patches behind the eyes, white neck collar. Underparts black. Brown-and-black mottling on the back. White sides to the wings. Bill is red, tip greyish-black. Legs and feet yellow. Hens have a paler bill and a mottled head and neck; whiter on the lower chest, with black confined to the lower underparts. Young resemble hens.

Willow ptarmigan (Willow grouse, red grouse, *Lagopus lagopus*): 35–43cm (14–17in)
Circumpolar distribution, including northern areas of the British Isles (where the race concerned is called red grouse) and Scandinavia. Brownish head and upperparts, and white underparts. Plumage becomes pure white during the winter months. Hens are similar but have much more speckled upperparts, and also become pure white in winter.

Black grouse (*Lyrurus tetrix*): Cock 58cm (23in); hen 45cm (18in)
Present in Scotland and northern England. Extends from Belgium north to Scandinavia and eastwards across northern Asia. Also occurs in the Alpine region. Predominantly jet black, with scarlet combs above the eyes. White wing bar, white undertail coverts and a white spot at the shoulder area. The tail feathers are decidedly curved. The hen is predominantly brown, speckled with black barring, and has a narrow white wing bar.

Hazel grouse (*Tetrastes bonasia*): 40cm (16in)
Occurs in north-eastern France, Belgium and Germany north to Scandinavia and eastwards across Asia. Distinctive-looking solid black throat patch, outlined in white, and a tall crest. The back, vent and legs are greyish. Darker abdominal markings are highlighted on a white background. Rufous patches appear on the sides of the chest. Hens have a speckled throat patch and a smaller crest.

Caucasian grouse (*Lyrurus mlokosiewiczi*): 55cm (22in)
Present in parts of Turkey and the adjoining Caucasus mountain range between the Black and Caspian seas. Almost entirely black, except for a small white patch at the shoulder area of the wings and a prominent red stripe above each eye. Relatively long, slightly curved tail. Hens are greyish-brown overall, with fine barring over the body and dark ear coverts.

Capercaillie

Western capercaillie *Tetrao urogallus*

Like New World turkeys (*Meleagris* species), male capercaillies adopt a display pose with tail feathers fanned out in a circle. They display communally to hens at sites known as "leks". After mating with her chosen partner, the hen nests and rears the young alone. The weather in the critical post-hatching period has a major impact on the survival rate of chicks – in wet springs, many become fatally chilled. Hens are about a third of the weight of cocks. Both sexes have strong, hooked bills, which enable them to easily nip off pieces of tough vegetation such as Scots pine (*Pinus sylvestris*) shoots. This helps them to survive when the ground is covered by snow.

Distribution: Present in Scotland and other mountainous regions in western Europe. Range extends through much of Scandinavia and eastwards through northern Asia.
Size: 80–115cm (31–45in).
Habitat: Coniferous and deciduous areas.
Nest: A shallow scrape on the ground.
Eggs: 6–10, yellow with light brown blotches.
Food: Buds and shoots.

Left: Male capercaillies fan their tail feathers when displaying to hens at leks.

Identification: Greyish-black head with an obvious red stripe above each eye. Green area on the chest. Wings are chestnut, the rump and tail blackish. Underparts are variable, ranging from predominantly white to black. Legs are covered with brown feathers, toes are exposed. Hens have an orangish patch on the sides of the face and chest, brown mottled upperparts and whiter underparts.

COLD COUNTRY INHABITANTS

Many birds have adapted to living through the winter period, while some can survive in this kind of habitat throughout the year thanks to their dense plumage, which provides insulation against the cold. Some species also grow larger than close relatives found at lower altitudes, with their increased body mass helping to counter the freezing temperatures.

Snow bunting

Plectrophenax nivalis

This bunting breeds closer to the North Pole than any other passerine. The cock has an attractive display flight, rising to about 10m (30ft) before starting to sing, then slowly fluttering down again. The nest is often sited among rocks, which provide shelter against cold winds. The hen incubates alone for about 12 days, with the young fledging after a similar period. Outside the breeding season, snow buntings are social and can be seen in flocks, searching for food on the ground, often in coastal areas. They are usually quite wary, flying away to prevent a close approach. These buntings have a varied diet comprised of seeds and berries when invertebrates are scarce over the winter.

Identification: Breeding males are mainly white, with black on the back, wings, tail and flight feathers. Bill and legs black. Hens have dark brown streaking on the head, buff ear coverts and brown on the wings. Non-breeding males resemble hens but with a white rump and whiter wings. Young birds are greyish and streaked.

Distribution: Breeds in Iceland, northern Scandinavia and the far north of Europe eastwards into Asia. Overwinters further south in Europe and Asia. Also present in North America. Populations from Greenland often overwinter in the British Isles.
Size: 17cm (6³/₄in).
Habitat: Tundra, grassland.
Nest: Scrape on the ground.
Eggs: 4–6, white with reddish-brown spots.
Food: Seeds, invertebrates.

Lapland longspur

Calcarius lapponicus

The nest of the Lapland longspur is set into the ground and lined with feathers, giving the hen some protection against the cold as well as helping to conceal her from predators while she is at her most vulnerable. The breeding period is short, taking advantage of the brief thaw in the tundra ice during the Arctic summer. This leads to a profusion of midges and other insects hatching in the surface meltwater, which cannot drain away because of the permanently frozen soil beneath. This abundance of insect life is available to the young Lapland longspurs once they have hatched. They grow and fledge rapidly, leaving the nest at just ten days old, and then begin to hunt themselves. Longspurs are so called because of their elongated rear claws, which may help them to maintain their balance, since they move either by walking or running instead of hopping on the ground like most birds.

Identification: Breeding males have a black head and upper breast, with white behind each eye extending down along the edge of the wings, bordered by a chestnut collar. Lower underparts are white, with black streaking on the flanks. Wings are a variable blackish-brown pattern. Tail black. Hens are less striking, with black-edged brown ear coverts, a black-streaked rufous collar, and black speckling on the chest. Males in eclipse plumage resemble females, except for a broad brownish area at the back of the neck, while hens gain a brownish suffusion on the chest and flanks. Young birds have distinctive speckling on the face.

Distribution: Breeds in northern Scandinavia and in the far north of Europe, extending eastwards into northern Asia. Overwinters in coastal areas of eastern England and along adjacent coasts of mainland Europe. Also overwinters around the Caspian Sea region and eastwards into Asia.
Size: 16cm (6¹/₄in).
Habitat: Tundra, grassland.
Nest: Cup-shaped.
Eggs: 3–7, greenish-buff with dark spots.
Food: Seeds, invertebrates.

White-winged snowfinch (*Montifringilla nivalis*): 19cm (7½in)
Northern Spain to the Alps and along the northern Mediterranean to the Red Sea. Main distribution is in central Asia. Breeding cock has a greyish head with a black throat, and white underparts. Brownish-grey back, with white on the sides of the wings, visible in flight. Tail black above, white below. In winter, bill is ivory rather than black. Hens are paler. Young birds resemble hens, but with buff on the sides of the head.

Caucasian snowcock (*Tetraogallus caucasicus*): 60cm (24in)
Caucasus Mountains. Head and sides of the face yellowish-grey, with orange encircling the eye. White throat, with a rufous streak and a white band behind. Rufous on the back of the neck. Vermiculations on the neck and breast, extending over the back and wings, which have orangish markings. Broad white bands across the open wings. Underparts have reddish-brown streaking. Undertail white. Bill greyish, legs and feet yellowish. Hens have narrower streaking on the flanks. Young birds are smaller and duller, with indistinct streaking on the flanks.

Güldenstädt's redstart (*Phoenicurus erythrogastrus*): 15cm (6in)
Breeds in the Caucasus, moving lower in the winter. Cock has a white crown, with a broad white area on the wings. Head, throat, upper back and wings are black, lower back, rump and rest of the body chestnut-red. Bill, legs and feet blackish. Hens are greyish, with a yellowish tinge to the lower parts and slightly rufous on the tail. Young birds are duller.

Rock ptarmigan

Lagopus muta

These grouse live in a region where natural cover is very scarce, and undergo a stunning transformation in appearance through the year. Their summer plumage is mottled brown and their winter plumage is white, enabling them to merge into the snowy landscape. When snow is on the ground, rock ptarmigans feed on buds and twigs of shrubs such as willow, which manage to grow in this treeless region. Pairs nest in the brief Arctic summer, often choosing a site protected by shrubs. The cock stays nearby while the hen incubates alone. The chicks are covered in down and can move easily, but are not able to fly until their flight feathers have emerged fully, at about ten days old.

Distribution: Circumpolar. Present in Iceland, Scotland, northern Scandinavia and in the Alps and Pyrenees. Also in the far north of Asia, North America and Greenland.
Size: 38cm (15in).
Habitat: Tundra.
Nest: Scrape on the ground, lined with vegetation.
Eggs: 6–9, creamy-buff, heavily blotched and spotted with blackish-brown.
Food: Buds, leaves, berries and other plant matter.

Identification: Head is mottled and brownish, with red above each eye. Similar patterning across the body, which becomes white in the winter. Blackish stripes on the face, lacking in hens.

Caspian snowcock

Tetraogallus caspius

This snowcock occurs in mountainous areas and is the most southerly representative of its genus. It is normally encountered in pairs or in small groups. Most active in the early morning, Caspian snowcocks then hide away among the rocks until late in the afternoon, when they venture out to feed again. Seeds form an important part of their diet, but they will also dig up bulbs and pull off leaves with their stocky bills. Unfortunately, in some parts of their range overgrazing by sheep and goats is depriving them of food. In the winter they may move down to lower altitudes, although are still often to be encountered well above the treeline at this time of year. Their plumage is very dense – individual feathers have down at their bases which helps to trap warm air next to the skin, insulating the birds against the bitter cold.

Identification: White head and throat, grey down the sides of the face. Orange skin encircling each eye. Back and chest grey, darker spotting on the chest. Underparts bluish-grey with orange streaks. Vent area white. Wings bluish-grey with orangish spotting, and dark tips to the flight feathers. Bill is greyish, legs and feet orangish. Hens are similar but smaller and duller. Young are smaller and duller than hens.

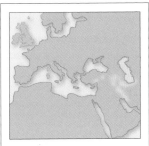

Distribution: Extreme south-east of Europe. Present around the Caspian Sea area, in central and eastern parts of Turkey to north-western Iran, extending south as far as the Persian Gulf.
Size: 60cm (24in).
Habitat: Bare mountains.
Nest: Scrape on the ground, lined with vegetation.
Eggs: 6–9, pale greenish-brown, with some reddish-brown markings.
Food: Plant matter.

MOUNTAIN-DWELLERS

Mountainous areas such as the Alps have a harsh climate, particularly during the winter months. In this bleak landscape, birds make use of whatever cover is available, which often means roosting and breeding in caves. Some mountain birds have become surprisingly tame, especially around alpine campsites and similar areas where they are regularly fed.

Alpine chough

Yellow-billed chough *Pyrrhocorax graculus*

Identification: Blackish overall, with a slight gloss to the plumage. Relatively short yellow bill, and red legs and feet. Sexes are alike. Young birds are duller and more brownish, with grey feet and a duller yellow bill.

These choughs eat snails and similar invertebrates, which they dig from the ground with their powerful bills, and from late summer onwards will forage for berries. In areas popular with walkers and skiers, these bold and intelligent corvids have learnt to take scraps from visitors. Alpine choughs are social by nature, and can be seen in flocks of 100 or more birds. They are very agile in flight. They roost communally when not nesting, often in caves, where they will be protected from the worst of the weather. Breeding starts in late spring. Incubation lasts 19 days, and the chicks leave the nest 30 days later. The family party joins a larger flock, and the young choughs are fed by the group until they are fully independent.

Distribution: The Pyrenees, Alps and mountainous areas through the northern and eastern Mediterranean, and into Asia to the Himalayas. Also ranges to parts of north-west Africa.
Size: 38cm (15in).
Habitat: Mountain regions.
Nest: Made of twigs, roots and similar material.
Eggs: 3–6, cream to pale green, with dark markings.
Food: Omnivorous.

White-necked raven

Corvus albicollis

These large corvids weigh as much as 1kg (2$^{1}/_{5}$lb), and have a wingspan of 1.5m (5ft), which enables them to glide effortlessly. They are most often seen in pairs, but flocks of up to 800 individuals may be encountered where food is plentiful. White-necked ravens are primarily scavengers, attracted to road kills, although they are considered a menace by sheep-farmers in South Africa for attacking young lambs and sick ewes. They also catch reptiles and small mammals, and will steal the eggs and chicks of other birds, even those of the Cape vulture (*Gyps coprotheres*), which may share the same nesting cliffs. Their powerful bills can hammer open eggs and even the shells of young tortoises. The breeding period extends from August to December, and the hen incubates alone for three weeks.

Distribution: Range extends through highland areas of eastern and southern Africa, from Kenya and Tanzania right down to the coastal regions of South Africa.
Size: 54cm (21$^{1}/_{4}$in).
Habitat: Mountain regions.
Nest: Bulky pile of sticks.
Eggs: 1–6, greenish with olive spots.
Food: Omnivorous.

Identification: Predominantly black, more glossy on the upperparts, with a very broad white collar around the back of the neck. Occasionally there may be signs of a pale area across the breast as well. Upper bill is broad and down-curved, and the bill overall is black with a white tip. Very short tail. Sexes are alike. Young birds are more of a brownish-black shade.

Rock sparrow (*Petronia petronia*): 17cm (6^1/$_2$in)
Iberian peninsula, southern Italy and the eastern
Mediterranean north-eastwards into Asia. Also
north-west Africa. Broad white stripe from the
eyes down the sides of the neck. Blackish-brown
above, grey central crown. Underparts white
with irregular brown streaks down the sides and
across the chest. Faint yellow spot at the base
of the throat. Upperparts light brown with darker
markings. Bill dull brown, paler on the lower bill.
Pinkish legs and feet. Sexes are alike. Young
birds warmer buff above and greyer below, with
no yellow spot.

Rock bunting (*Emberiza cia*): 15cm (6in)
Northern Mediterranean, including the Iberian
Peninsula. Also north-west Africa. Greyish head
and upper chest, broken with black stripes over
the crown, through the eyes and around the
cheeks. Underparts and back rusty-brown, black
lines down back. Two narrow white wing bars,
the wings blackish and brown. Tail dark at the
tip, white beneath. Hens similar, less black head
patterning. Young have orange-buff underparts.

Grey-necked bunting (*Emberiza buchanani*):
15cm (6in)
Eastern Turkey, overwintering in India. Grey
head, whitish throat patch and moustachial
stripe. Underparts reddish-brown with pale
fringes, becoming whitish near the vent. Grey
shoulders, with an adjacent band of rufous.
Wing feathers blackish with light brown edging.
Hens are duller, with less distinct red wing bars,
and streaking on the breast. Bill, legs and feet
pinkish. Young birds similar to hens.

Crag martin

Eurasian crag martin *Ptyonoprogne rupestris*

These martins appear uniformly brown from
a distance. They fly relatively low, usually
alongside the crags and mountainsides
rather than above them, and as with other
related species spend most of their time in
the air. They often remain close to cliff-faces
when these are in sunlight, which may help
them to capture insects in flight, and will
forage as far as 16km (10 miles) from their
roosts. Crag martins have a varied diet
including flying beetles, butterflies and
wasps, and feed almost entirely on the wing,
although very occasionally they will feed on
the ground. Pairs nest on their own or in
small colonies, and are strongly territorial.
Both members of the pair construct their
distinctive nest, which can take up to three
weeks. Caves are traditionally used, but
crag martins may also
breed in buildings.
Their young can
fly at four
weeks old.

Distribution: Through much
of the Iberian Peninsula and
the northern Mediterranean
region to Turkey, and east
into Asia. Also present in
north-west Africa. European
birds overwinter in Senegal
and Gambia, while those in
the east travel through the
Rift Valley, occurring in Egypt,
Sudan and Ethiopia.
Size: 15cm (6in).
Habitat: Craggy landscapes,
sometimes cliffs.
Nest: Cup made of mud,
lined with grass.
Eggs: 1–5, white with slight
red-and-grey spotting.
Food: Invertebrates.

Identification: Dull brown head,
back and upperparts. Lighter on
the cheeks and down over the
breast onto the abdomen. Slight
speckling on the throat. Blackish
underwing coverts. Bill is black,
legs and feet paler. Sexes are
alike. Young birds have pale buff
edging on their upperparts.

Alpine accentor

Prunella collaris

Although only recorded in Europe at altitudes up to 3,000m
(9,850ft), reaching the snowline, Alpine accentors have been
observed as high as 8,000m (26,250ft) in the Asiatic part of
their range. They seek out the warmest areas and forage on
the ground, using their feet to hold on to rocks, probing
small openings for invertebrates such as spiders. They are
also able to catch insects in flight. Males engage in short
display flights to gain the attention of their mates, although
mating itself takes less than a quarter of a second.
Both members of the pair share the incubation,
and the chicks hatch after two weeks. The
adults may be joined by other Alpine
accentors, who act as helpers
in providing food for the
brood. The young fledge
after approximately 16 days, and will be
independent in a further two weeks. They
may subsequently remain with the adult birds,
forming larger flocks over the winter.

Identification: Dark greyish head
with brown ear coverts. Throat is
white with heavy barring. Dull
greyish-yellow underparts, with
evident rufous streaking. Back is
brownish with black streaking.
Two narrow white wing bars, the
area in between
blackish, forming
a distinct band
in flight. Narrow
bill is dark at the tip
and orange-yellow
at the base. Legs
and feet are pinkish.
Sexes alike. Young birds
have mostly brown heads.

Distribution: Range extends
through mountainous areas
of the Iberian Peninsula and
northern Mediterranean,
including the Pyrenees and
Alps, east to the Caucasus
and into Asia. Also present in
north-west Africa.
Size: 17cm (6^3/$_4$in).
Habitat: Prefers barren and
stony ground.
Nest: Among boulders, or in
a crevice.
Eggs: 3–4, pale blue.
Food: Mainly invertebrates
and seeds.

SWIFTS, SWALLOWS AND MARTINS

This group of birds spend most of their lives in flight. They undertake long journeys, with European populations migrating south to Africa at the approach of winter, and returning to breed the following spring. Pairs frequently return to the same nest site they had occupied previously – a remarkable feat of navigation after a journey covering thousands of kilometres.

Swift

Common swift *Apus apus*

Distribution: Found across virtually the whole of Europe, extending to northern Africa and Asia. Overwinters in southern Africa.
Size: 16.5cm (6½in).
Habitat: In the air.
Nest: Cup-shaped, built under cover.
Eggs: 2–3, white.
Food: Flying invertebrates, such as midges and moths.

Flocks of swifts are most noticeable when uttering their distinctive, screaming calls, flying low overhead in search of winged insects. At other times they may appear little more than distant specks in the sky, wheeling around at heights of 1,000m (3,300ft) or more. Their flight pattern is quite distinctive, consisting of a series of rapid wingbeats followed by gliding into the wind. Their tiny feet do not allow them to perch, although they can cling to vertical surfaces. Except when breeding, swifts spend their entire lives in the air, and are apparently able to sleep and mate in flight too. If hunting conditions are unfavourable, such as during a cool summer, nestling swifts respond by growing more slowly, while the adults can undergo short periods of torpidity to avoid starvation.

Identification: Dark overall, with relatively long, pointed wings and a forked tail. Pale whitish throat. Sexes are alike.

Swallow

Barn swallow *Hirundo rustica*

The swallows' return to their European breeding grounds is one of the most welcome signs of spring. Although pairs return to the same nest site every year, they do not migrate together. Cock birds arrive back before their partners and jealously guard the site from would-be rivals. Cocks fight with surprising ferocity if one of the birds does not back down. Although swallows may use traditional nesting sites such as caves or hollow trees, they more commonly build their nests inside buildings such as barns, choosing a site close to the eaves. It can take up to a thousand trips to collect enough damp mud, carried back in the bill, to complete a new nest.

Identification: Chestnut forehead and throat, dark blue head and back, and a narrow dark blue band across the chest. The wings are blackish and the underparts are white. Long tail streamers. Sexes are alike.

Distribution: Throughout virtually the entire Northern Hemisphere. European populations overwinter in Africa south of the Sahara.
Size: 19cm (7½in).
Habitat: Open country, close to water.
Nest: Made of mud, built off the ground.
Eggs: 4–5, white with reddish-and-grey spotting.
Food: Flying invertebrates.

Alpine swift (*Tachymarptis melba*): 23cm (9in)
Found throughout southern Europe and North
Africa. Overwinters in southern Africa. Plain brown
upperparts, with a black collar around the neck.
Throat, chest and upper abdomen are white. Lower
underparts brown. Tail is short. Sexes are alike.

Red-rumped swallow (*Cecropis daurica*):
17cm (7in)
Southern Europe, the Mediterranean and North
Africa. Overwinters in sub-Saharan Africa. Dark
bluish area on the head and back, separated by a
wide chestnut collar. Wings are blackish. Pale
chestnut rump with narrow streaking; streaking
also on the underparts. Sexes are alike.

Rock martin (*Ptyonoprogne fuligula*):
13cm (5in)
Occurs in Africa, except for the central region.
Also extends into south-western Asia. Brownish
upperparts, rufous-brown underparts. Northern
birds are lighter and greyer. Sexes are alike.

Brown-throated martin (Brown-throated sand
martin, *Riparia paludicola*): 12cm (5in)
Sporadic distribution in north-western and sub-
Saharan Africa. Also occurs on Madagascar.
Predominantly brown overall, with a greyish-
brown tinge to the throat and breast. Remainder
of the underparts are white. Sexes are alike.

Congo martin (Congo sand martin, *Riparia
congica*): 11cm (4¹⁄₂in)
Confined to three regions of the Congo River,
hence its common name. Similar to the sand
martin (*Riparia riparia*), but the brown breast
band is less defined. Sexes are alike.

House martin

Common house martin *Delichon urbicum*

The house martin's breeding habits have
changed significantly due to an increase in
the number of buildings in rural areas. They
traditionally nested on cliff faces, but over
the past century began to prefer the walls of
houses and farm structures as sites, as well
as beneath bridges and even on street lamps,
where a ready supply of nocturnal insects
are attracted to the light. The nest is usually
spherical and normally made of mud. The
base is built first, followed by the sides. On
average, the whole process can take up to
two weeks to complete. House martins are
highly social by nature, nesting in huge
colonies made up of thousands of pairs
where conditions are suitable. Even
outside the breeding
period, they will
associate in large
flocks comprising
of hundreds of
individuals.

Distribution: Throughout the
whole of Europe, extending
eastwards across much of
Asia. Overwinters in Africa
south of the Sahara.
Size: 13cm (5in).
Habitat: Open country, close
to water.
Nest: Cup made of mud.
Eggs: 4–5, white.
Food: Flying invertebrates.

Identification: Dark
bluish head and back.
Black wings with white
underwing coverts. The
underparts and rump are
also white. Forked tail is dark
blue. Sexes are alike.

Banded martin

Riparia cincta

The banded martin is a relatively solitary species when
nesting, tending to prefer areas near water. Their breeding
season varies through their range, often being linked to the
rainy season. A pair will excavate a nesting tunnel which
can extend up to 90cm (3ft) into a bank, ending in a
rounded chamber that is lined with dry
vegetation and feathers. Although they may
sometimes be observed in small groups at this
stage, larger numbers join together when they
are migrating. The major movements see
banded martins leave their southern breeding
grounds, heading north and west to West Africa,
whereas in parts of Central and Eastern Africa,
they are present throughout the year. Outside
the breeding period, banded martins often
frequent reedbeds, where they are likely to be seen in
larger numbers. These martins feed on insects in flight,
and will also seize other invertebrates off plants.

Identification: Brown head and
sides of the face, across the back
and wings, with a white throat
and lower cheeks. There is a
very evident brown band across
the chest, with the lower
underparts being white. Tail
feathers are square. Bill,
legs and feet are dark.
Young birds have a
pale band on the
breast, with cream
and rufous edges
to the feathers
over the back.

Distribution: Ranges over
much of Africa, south of the
Sahara.
Size: 17cm (7in).
Habitat: Open country.
Nest: Tunnel dug in sandbank
with vegetation-lined nesting
chamber.
Eggs: 3–5, white.
Food: Winged insects and
other invertebrates.

SUNBIRDS AND SUGARBIRDS

These nectar-feeding birds are not encountered north of the Mediterranean, and both sugarbird species occur only in southern Africa. Metallic plumage is a common feature of male sunbirds in breeding condition. Their relatively small size does not indicate a placid nature however – these lively and bold birds can be very aggressive towards their own kind.

Giant sunbird

Dreptes thomensis

Distribution: Found only on the island of São Tomé in the Gulf of Guinea, off the west coast of Africa.
Size: 23cm (9in).
Habitat: Open country and forest areas.
Nest: Pouch-shaped, made from vegetation.
Eggs: 2, white with some red spotting.
Food: Nectar, soft fruit and also invertebrates.

The sole member of its genus, the giant sunbird is the largest sunbird of all. They can usually be encountered in upland areas on their native island, but will also fly further afield and may be found in more open agricultural areas. Giant sunbirds probe flowers – often the flowers of banana trees – with their long bill, but will also clamber over the bark of trees rather like a treecreeper (*Certhia* species), searching for invertebrates in a similar fashion. They catch invertebrates in flight too, and use their bills to suck up the juicy pulp of ripe fruits. Their nesting period on São Tomé extends from September to January, at which time males become very territorial. It is thought that breeding trios comprised of a cock bird and two hens are not unusual in this species, but relatively little is known about their breeding habits. The nest is suspended off the end of a narrow branch, and may be located as much as 10m (32ft) above the ground.

Identification: Predominantly dark, appearing blackish in colour, with greenish-yellow plumage around the vent. The longest tail feathers are entirely black but those beneath have white tips. Bill, legs and feet are black. Hens are similar but smaller. Young birds are also smaller.

Scarlet-tufted sunbird

Nectarinia johnstoni

These distinctive sunbirds can be found in mountainous areas of Africa, such as Mount Kilimanjaro in Tanzania, where the temperature drops considerably at night despite being close to the Equator. These sunbirds seek flowering plants, which provide them with nectar, and are often seen near flowering *Protea* bushes. They usually occur in pairs or small parties, although cock birds are often very aggressive towards each other, particularly during the breeding season. Their bulky nests are constructed from a wide variety of materials bound together with cobwebs, and lined with feathers.

Distribution: Ranges through the eastern side of Africa, from parts of Kenya, Uganda and Tanzania south as far as Malawi and eastern parts of Zambia.
Size: Cock 30cm (12in); hen 15cm (6in).
Habitat: Open country.
Nest: Suspended in bushes.
Eggs: 2–3, cream-coloured with dark streaks.
Food: Mostly nectar and small invertebrates.

Identification: A rich shade of dark green, with red pectoral tufts at the top of the wings. Non-breeding cock's body feathers are blackish-brown. The tail is square, with two much longer narrow tail plumes extending beyond it, accounting for half the bird's total length. Hens are dark brown, paler in the centre of their bellies, and lack the long tail feathers.

Orange-breasted sunbird

Violet-headed sunbird *Anthobaphes violacea*

These sunbirds move from area to area, tracking the flowering periods of the heather on the mountain heathland, the blooms of which provide the nectar that forms the basis of their diet. Unlike many sunbirds, the orange-breasted is often encountered in loose flocks, although cocks become territorial at the start of the breeding season. The nest, which may be reused each year, is built by the hen on her own, although she is often accompanied on her forays to find suitable material by the cock. It is constructed near to the ground and made of roots, pieces of heather and similar items, while the interior is lined with soft material gathered from *Protea* flowers growing alongside the heather. Incubation lasts approximately two weeks, and the chicks spend three weeks in the nest. They are closely supervised after fledging by the hen, and will not be independent for another three weeks.

Identification: Cock has brilliant metallic green plumage on the head and upper back. Purple band across the breast and golden-orange beneath. Olive-brown back and elongated central tail feathers. Plainer in non-breeding condition, with an olive head, purple band more indistinct and the abdomen less brightly coloured; also lacks the longer central tail feathers. Hens are olive-green above and greenish-yellow below, becoming yellow on the abdomen. Bill, legs and feet are black. Young birds resemble hens, but upperparts are browner.

Distribution: Occurs at the southern tip of Africa, in the Cape Province region in southern South Africa.
Size: 15cm (6in).
Habitat: Mountain heathland.
Nest: Made of vegetation.
Eggs: 2, creamy with some dark streaks.
Food: Nectar, invertebrates.

Tacazze sunbird (*Nectarinia tacazze*): 15–22cm (6–8¹/₂in)
Eritrea to Ethiopia and parts of Kenya, Tanzania and Uganda. Dull bronzy-green head, with a reddish or purple iridescence across the chest and back, extending over the rump. Tail feathers are black, with long, narrow extensions to the upper pair. Hens lack extensions and have dark upperparts, more yellowish underparts, and yellowish streaks above and below the eyes. Young birds have a black throat, and are greyer above and yellower below.

Pemba sunbird (*Cinnyris pembae*): 10cm (4in)
Restricted to Pemba Island, off the coast of Tanzania. Dark metallic green head and back. Narrow violet breast band extending to the shoulders. Blackish underparts and wings. Bill, legs and feet black. Hens have greyish-green upperparts, pale stripe above the eyes and a greyish-brown tail. Underparts creamy-white. Young birds resemble hens, but have grey mottling on the underparts.

Gurney's sugarbird (*Promerops gurneyi*): 23–29cm (9–11¹/₂in)
Eastern Zimbabwe to northern and eastern South Africa. Rufous-brown crown. White stripe below, behind the eyes, and a black streak through the eyes. Ear coverts, back, rump and tail grey. Throat is white. Broad chestnut band across the chest, with darker brown speckling over the white underparts, particularly the flanks. Undertail coverts bright yellow. Bill, legs and feet black. Hens are similar, but have a small tail. Young birds have a dark brown breast and crown, with greenish-yellow undertail coverts.

Cape sugarbird

Promerops cafer

These sugarbirds may sometimes appear to have a yellow crown, but this is just pollen which has rubbed off the *Protea* flowers on which they feed. Consequently, sugarbirds play quite an important part in the pollination of these shrubs. Although there are similarities between sugarbirds and sunbirds, there are differences too, not least in their flight pattern, which in sugarbirds is much more direct. Sugarbirds catch large insects on the wing in similar fashion to flycatchers, battering them against a perch in order to kill them. Pairs remain together throughout the year, becoming more territorial at the start of the breeding period, which extends between March and August. Interestingly, the tail length of males is very important, since this is the major factor in attracting females. Furthermore, these hens lay more eggs per clutch on average than hens mating with cock birds with shorter tails.

Distribution: Occurs at the southern tip of Africa, in the Cape Province region of South Africa, extending up towards Namibia.
Size: 28–44cm (11–17in).
Habitat: *Protea* heathlands: the fynbos.
Nest: Cup-shaped, made of twigs.
Eggs: 1–2, buff with darker spots.
Food: Mainly nectar, but also invertebrates.

Identification: Brown head, back and chest. Brown stripe on white throat. Darker mottling on underparts. Vent area yellow. Back and long tail dark brown. Bill, legs and feet are black. Hens have a white breast, shorter tail. Young greyer, no yellow, and no brown on the breast.

AFRICAN FINCHES

Many finches, particularly members of the waxbill or estrildidae family, live in the more arid regions of Africa. They feed largely on seeds, although also take small invertebrates as well, especially as a rearing food for nestlings. The spread of agriculture has assisted their population growth, with flocks increasingly becoming pests as they raid ripening crops such as millet.

Quailfinch

Ortygospiza atricollis

As their name suggests, these unusual members of the waxbill family spend most of their time on the ground, never normally perching. If flushed, they fly up vertically like a quail, before gliding back down into the grass some distance away. They build their nest on the ground too, using grass to create a well-hidden, ball-like structure with a clear area in front. It is invariably sited carefully, on a well-drained piece of ground to prevent flooding, since quailfinches normally breed during the rainy period. The incubation, which lasts two weeks, is shared by both members of the pair. Invertebrates as well as seeds feature in the diet of the young birds, who leave the nest by the time they are three weeks old. Although they do not live in tight-knit flocks, these finches do form loose groupings, with up to two hundred individuals present in some locations. They are often encountered in South Africa in the grass borders alongside rural airstrips.

Identification: Cock bird has a mostly blackish face and throat, with a white bib under the bill. Top of the head is greyish, and in southern populations there are white spectacles around the eyes; the head is brownish in quailfinches found further north. Black-and-white barring across the breast and down the flanks. The underparts are pale orangish. Bill is red, legs and feet are pinkish-grey. Hens are less brightly coloured, and have a darker upper bill. Young birds have dark bills and very little barring on the flanks.

Distribution: Range extends in Africa south of the Sahara. Various locations in western Africa and across to Ethiopia, extending down through Kenya and Tanzania and over much of the southern half of the continent.
Size: 9cm (3¹/₂in).
Habitat: Grassland.
Nest: Made of vegetation.
Eggs: 4–6, white.
Food: Mainly seeds.

Red-billed firefinch

Common firefinch *Lagonosticta senegala*

Distribution: From the Cape Verde Islands across Africa south of the Sahara, and down the eastern side of the continent to South Africa, reaching Angola and northern Namibia in the west.
Size: 10cm (4in).
Habitat: Grassland.
Nest: Made of vegetation.
Eggs: 3–4, white.
Food: Seeds.

Firefinches are so named because of their red coloration, which is most evident in adult cock birds. Red-billed is the smallest and the most widely distributed species, occurring through most of sub-Saharan Africa. These finches are often encountered in small flocks, and members of a group stay in close contact with each other. They feed on seeds gathered on the ground, and in the vicinity of homes can become quite tame. They may also be seen in agricultural areas, feeding on ripening millet seedheads. Flocks generally split up during the breeding season.
Red-billed firefinches construct the typical, bulky nest associated with waxbills, using mainly dried grasses and lining the interior with softer material. The adult birds enter through a side opening, which may afford some protection from predators. The incubation period normally lasts around 12 days, and the young firefinches will leave the nest after a further 18 days.

Identification: Cock bird has a reddish head, back and breast, becoming browner on the underparts. The wings and tail feathers are also brown, and the lower back is red. There are some faint white spots on the sides of the chest and flanks. Bill, legs and feet are reddish. Hens have spots on their chest and are brownish overall, except for their pinkish-red rump area and lores, between the bill and the eyes; bill is also duller than in cocks. Young birds are plain brown, with a dark bill.

Red-billed quailfinch (black-chinned quailfinch, *Ortygospiza atricolis gabonensis*): 9cm (3½in)
Subspecies of O. atricolis. Equatorial Guinea and Gabon to southern Angola and Namibia, east to Uganda. Black around the base of the bill. Ear coverts chestnut-brown, remainder of the head brownish with black flecking, as are the wings. Chest barred black-and-white, as are the flanks. Underparts pale orange, becoming whiter beneath. Hens have grey cheeks and no black surrounding the bill. Young birds have dark bills and display little barring on the underparts.

Red-headed finch (*Amadina erythrocephala*): 13cm (5in)
Coast of Angola across Namibia and South Africa. Bright red head. Scalloping on the underparts, becoming reddish-brown on the flanks and paler around the vent. Upperparts brown, with dark edging and white tips creating two wing bars. Bill pale, legs and feet pinkish. Hens have brown heads. Young birds are paler than hens, with faint barring on the rump.

Reichenow's firefinch (Chad firefinch, *Lagonosticta umbrinodorsalis*): 10cm (4in)
Localized, restricted mainly to Chad but also north-east Cameroon. Distinctive greyish crown and nape, reddish on the mantle, becoming rufous-brown over the back and wings. Sides of the face and underparts red, with faint white spotting at the shoulder. Tail reddish, darker towards the tip. Vent and undertail coverts blackish. Bill, legs and feet greyish. Hens have brown upperparts, paler and more orange below. Young birds are browner overall.

Cut-throat finch

Amadina fasciata

Depth of coloration varies in cut-throat finches through their range; birds ranging in eastern Africa show more prominent black markings compared with those originating further south. Breeding occurs mainly during the dry season, when pairs will often adopt nests originally built by weavers, which are vacated at the end of the wet season. However, they may sometimes build their own nests in a range of different locations, including among bushes and even in suitable cavities in buildings. There is a tunnel leading into the nest, which is lined with soft material such as feathers. Outside the breeding season, cut-throat finches may form large flocks, often associating with various weavers and the related red-headed finch (*A. erythrocephala*), where their distributions overlap. They feed on the ground, eating mainly grass seeds, but will also hunt for invertebrates such as termites.

Identification: Distinctive red throat area from the ear coverts, with white above. Head white with black markings. Back brownish with darker brown markings. White wing bars. Underparts warm brown, becoming whiter below, with dark markings. Bill is pale, legs and feet pinkish. Hens lack the red throat area and have completely mottled heads. Young birds resemble hens.

Distribution: Occurs in a band across Africa south of the Sahara, extending down in the east as far as Tanzania. A second population extends from the Namibian-Angolan border region to Mozambique and into northern parts of South Africa.
Size: 10cm (4in).
Habitat: Arid areas.
Nest: Made of grass.
Eggs: 4–9, chalky-white.
Food: Mainly seeds, also eats invertebrates.

Violet-eared waxbill

Common grenadier *Uraeginthus granatinus*

Shy by nature and difficult to approach, these colourful dry country waxbills visit waterholes in the middle of morning to drink and forage on the ground. As well as eating seeds, they will hunt for invertebrates, particularly termites, and – unusually for waxbills – will also eat ripe fruits. They breed between December and April, and the nest is made of dry grasses often sited quite low down in a thornbush. Incubation takes around 13 days, with the young waxbills leaving the nest when they are 16 days old. Their distinctive violet facial coloration develops quite rapidly, around three weeks later. Occasionally, shaft-tailed whydah hens (*Vidua regia*) may enter the waxbills' nests and lay, with pairs rearing the young whydah chicks alongside their own.

Identification: Bluish above the bill, violet patches on each side of the head, and a narrow black band from the base of the bill to the eyes. Underthroat area is black. Dark chestnut back and body, browner wings. Blue lower back and rump. Bill is red, legs and feet blackish. Hens have creamy-buff underparts, lighter brown above. Young birds have black bills, and tan-coloured faces.

Distribution: Ranges in southern Africa, extending from southern Angola and northern Namibia across to Zimbabwe and Mozambique, and south to northern parts of South Africa.
Size: 15cm (6in).
Habitat: Savanna.
Nest: Made of grasses.
Eggs: 3–6, white.
Food: Seeds, invertebrates.

WHYDAHS AND WEAVERS

These birds have fascinating breeding cycles, with cocks often undergoing a remarkable transformation from their dull, sparrow-like non-breeding appearance. Black predominates in the coloration of whydahs, which is why they are sometimes known as widowbirds. They do not usually rear their own chicks, although those birds known as indigobirds may do so on occasions.

Long-tailed paradise whydah

Eastern paradise whydah *Vidua paradisaea*

Distribution: Mainly eastern Africa, extending from Eritrea and Ethiopia down to South Africa, and via Botswana and Namibia to the coastal region of Angola.
Size: 12cm (4³⁄₄in); breeding cocks 36cm (14in).
Habitat: Savanna.
Nest: Lays in green-winged pytilia (*Pytilia melba*) nests.
Eggs: Unknown.
Food: Seeds.

Five paradise whydah species are recognized in Africa, with breeding cocks differing in their nape and chest colouring and in the length and shape of their majestic tail plumes. They perform elaborate, acrobatic flights to attract the attention of the hens, although they come together only briefly to mate. Hens lay in the nests of green-winged pytilias (*Pytilia melba*), which is the only host species used by these whydahs. The markings inside the mouths of the hatchling whydahs are identical to those of the young melba finches, so the adults rear them unsuspectingly alongside their own chicks. The whydahs' incubation is slightly shorter, so they hatch simultaneously.

Identification: Breeding cock has a black head and upper breast. Ochre on the breast and neck. Yellowish underparts turning buff on the abdomen. Back and wings blackish, with broad, down-curving central tail feathers. Bill, legs and feet black. Hens have black-and-white striping on the head and greyish-brown streaked upperparts; plain, pale buff below. Non-breeding cocks resemble females. Young birds are brown with a pale belly.

Pin-tailed whydah

Vidua macroura

The finery and display of the cock pin-tailed whydah attracts a harem of hens during the breeding period. After mating however, the females lay individual eggs in the nests of waxbills, rather than constructing their own nests. This species ranks among the most adaptable of all birds displaying parasitic breeding behaviour – as many as 19 different species have been recorded as playing host to a pin-tailed whydah chick. However, unlike the common cuckoo for example, the young whydahs do not kill their fellow nestlings but are reared alongside them. They even develop similar mouth markings on hatching, which fool their hosts into believing the whydah is one of their own.

Identification: Breeding cocks have a black cap, with a white collar, sides of the face and underparts. Remainder of the upperparts are black, except for the white wing bars. Very long tail plumes. Hens and out-of-colour cocks have black stripes from the sides of the bill through the eyes, a black area on the crown, and speckling over the back and wings. Underparts are a lighter shade of fawn.

Distribution: Occurs widely throughout Africa south of the Sahara.
Size: 11cm (4in) excluding male's tail plumes, which reach 25cm (10in).
Habitat: Open country.
Nest: Lays in those of other species, mainly waxbills.
Eggs: 3, whitish.
Food: Mainly seeds, but also some invertebrates.

Straw-tailed whydah (*Vidua fischeri*): 10cm (4in); breeding cocks 28cm (11in)
North-east Africa, extending from Djibouti and Somalia to Ethiopia, Kenya and Tanzania. Cock bird in breeding colour has a buff cap, while the head, chest and wings are black. The lower chest and abdomen are buff, as are the long, slender, straw-like tail plumes. Bill is reddish, legs and feet pinkish. Hens have a broad brownish streak above the eyes, with a pale central area. Back and wings streaked brown, with pale edging to the plumage. Young birds are brown with dark bills.

Quailfinch indigobird (*Vidua nigeriae*): 12cm (4³/₄in)
Western Africa, restricted to Nigeria and Cameroon. Cock birds in breeding condition are black, with a greenish suffusion to their plumage. The wings are pale brown, with white edging to the flight feathers. Bill is silvery, legs and feet dark. Males out of breeding colour resemble hens, who have black streaking on the head, and brown plumage over the back with lighter edges. Underparts whitish, with a pale brown suffusion on the breast. Young birds are brown, with a paler abdomen and eye stripe.

Cape weaver (*Ploceus capensis*): 17cm (6³/₄in)
Ranges in South Africa, except for the central part of the country. Cock birds have a chestnut suffusion on the face, while the sides of the head and underparts are yellower. Upperparts olive-yellow, with dark plumage on the wings. Pale irides. Long, pointed black bill, and pinkish feet. Hens are a more olive-green shade overall, but have dark eyes, which distinguishes them from out-of-colour cock birds. Young birds are duller overall.

Red-billed quelea

Black-faced dioch, red-billed weaver *Quelea quelea*

This weaver is considered to be the most numerous bird in the world, with the total population estimated at ten billion individuals. It lives in large flocks which can inflict massive damage on ripening crops of millet and other seeds. To reflect this, red-billed weavers are often known as feathered locusts. They are communal breeders – nests are built close together in thorn trees, which helps to deter any potential predators, while the thorns also serve as fixing points for the nests.

Distribution: Ranges widely across Africa in a band south of the Sahara, to Sudan and Ethiopia. Extends down the eastern side as far as South Africa, and in the west to Namibia and western Angola.
Size: 13cm (5in).
Habitat: Often stays close to reedbeds.
Nest: Made of grasses.
Eggs: 2–4, pale blue.
Food: Seeds, invertebrates.

Identification: Both sexes have brown-and-black streaked plumage outside the breeding season. Cocks in breeding colour have a black mask, with pinkish plumage on the head extending across the underparts. Dark brown-and-black wings. The tail feathers are also dark.

Southern red bishop

Red bishop *Euplectes orix*

As well as cracking open the seeds that form the basis of their diet, the stocky bills of these weavers also make highly effective needles, enabling the birds to weave their elaborate nests. This is a learnt skill which improves with practice, and young cocks, with their clumsily-constructed nests, are far less likely to attract mates than the more experienced males. Cocks are polygamous, with each mature male mating with several hens and providing each one with a nesting site, although he takes no direct role in hatching the eggs or rearing the chicks.

Above: By weaving their nests, southern red bishops can site them in areas where they are more likely to be out of reach of predators.

Distribution: Across Africa south of the Sahara reaching Ethiopia, extending south as far as Zimbabwe.
Size: 13cm (5in).
Habitat: Grasslands.
Nest: Woven from grasses.
Eggs: 3–4, pale blue.
Food: Seeds, vegetation and some invertebrates.

Identification: Orangish-red ruff around the head. Face, lower breast and upper abdomen are black. Blackish-red mantle, orangish-red lower back and abdomen. Brown flight feathers. Hens and out-of-colour cocks (left) have brownish-black streaked upperparts, a pale yellowish stripe above each eye, and buff underparts with light streaking on the breast sides.

MIGRATORY INSECT-EATERS

In temperate areas, obtaining sufficient invertebrate prey throughout the year can be difficult. During the winter, winged insects such as butterflies, bees and flies either hibernate or die, and frozen ground can make it impossible to find food such as earthworms. Not surprisingly, many birds migrate south in the autumn in search of a more dependable food supply.

Nightjar

European nightjar *Caprimulgus europaeus*

Nightjars are regular summertime visitors to Europe. These birds are nocturnal by nature, which makes them relatively difficult to observe. However, they have very distinctive calls, likened both to the croaking of a frog and the noise of a machine, which are uttered for long periods and carry over a distance of 1km (⁵/₈ mile). During the daytime, nightjars spend much of their time resting on the ground, where their mottled, cryptic plumage provides them with excellent camouflage, especially in woodland. Additionally, they narrow their eyes to slits, which makes them even less conspicuous. Nightjars are sufficiently agile in flight to catch moths and other nocturnal invertebrates, flying silently and trawling with their large gapes open. If food is plentiful, pairs may rear two broods in succession, before beginning the long journey south to their African wintering grounds.

Identification: Very small bill and long wings. Greyish-brown and mottled in overall appearance, with some black areas, especially near the shoulders. There are white areas below the eyes and on the wings, although the white spots on the wings are seen only in cock birds.

Distribution: Most of Europe and north-west Africa, east to Asia. Northern European birds overwinter in south-eastern parts of Africa, while southern European birds migrate to western Africa.
Size: 28cm (11in).
Habitat: Heathland and relatively open country.
Nest: Scrape on the ground.
Eggs: 2, buff-coloured, with darker markings.
Food: Invertebrates.

Pied flycatcher

European pied flycatcher *Ficedula hypoleuca*

These flycatchers hawk invertebrates in flight, and will also catch slower-moving prey such as caterpillars by plucking them off vegetation. They can frequently be seen in oak woodlands in Europe during the summer, though may range north to the taiga, where mosquitoes hatching in pools of water during the brief Arctic summer provide an almost constant supply of food. Pied flycatchers are closely related to collared flycatchers (*F. albicollis*), and the two species may sometimes hybridize. It is usually possible to identify the male offspring of these pairings by the narrow area of black plumage evident on the nape of the neck.

Identification: Summer plumage is a combination of black and white. White patches are present above the bill and on the wings. The underparts are white, and the remainder of the plumage is black. Hens also have whitish underparts and white areas on the wings, while their upperparts are brownish. Cocks in non-breeding plumage resemble adult hens, but retain the blackish wings and uppertail coverts.

Distribution: Summer visitor to Europe. Breeding range extends throughout virtually the whole of Europe including Scandinavia, although not the far north. Overwinters in Africa north of a line from coastal Nigeria to Djibouti.
Size: 13cm (5in).
Habitat: Most areas where insects are common.
Nest: Hole in a tree.
Eggs: 5–9, pale blue.
Food: Invertebrates.

Greater short-toed lark (*Calandrella brachydactyla*): 16cm (6in)
Breeds in southern Europe and North Africa, sometimes seen as far north as the British Isles. Overwinters in Africa and the Middle East. Largely unmarked white underparts. Dark patch on each side of the throat. Dark wing bar, wings otherwise brownish and streaked. The eye stripes are white and the ear coverts are a darker brownish colour. Sexes are alike.

Bar-tailed lark (Bar-tailed desert lark, *Ammomanes cinctura*): 14cm (5½in)
Extends from north-western Africa into parts of the Middle East. Pale sandy-brown overall, with brownish wings, darker at the tips of the flight feathers. Black bar across the tail feathers, clearly visible in flight. Sexes are alike.

Meadow pipit (*Anthus pratensis*): 15cm (6in)
Resident in the British Isles and neighbouring parts of western Europe east to Denmark. Individuals from more northerly and easterly areas overwinter around the Mediterranean. Brownish head and wings with darker markings. Dark streaking on the breast and flanks, which are a darker shade of buff. Underparts become whiter in the summer. Sexes are alike.

Collared flycatcher (*Ficedula albicollis*): 13cm (5in)
Occurs as a summer breeding visitor in central-eastern parts of Europe, overwintering in Africa. Similar to the pied flycatcher (*F. hypoleuca*), but cocks are usually identified by the white collar encircling the neck and the white area on the rump. Hens have greyer upperparts and a distinct white patch on the edge of the wings.

Lapwing

Northern lapwing *Vanellus vanellus*

These birds are also known as peewits in some areas due to the sound of their calls. Flocks of lapwings are a common sight in farmland areas, where they comb the ploughed soil for invertebrates. They are easily recognized even from a distance by their distinctive crests. Lapwings may breed in loose groups, and their scrapes are lined with what often becomes quite a substantial pile of vegetation. Lapwings may move long distances during prolonged spells of severe winter weather, sometimes congregating in huge flocks in estuaries when freshwater areas become frozen.

Distribution: Occurs from southern Scandinavia south across the whole of Europe to the Mediterranean. Migrates eastwards across Asia as far as Japan. Also occurs in North Africa, and may even be seen in areas further south.
Size: 30cm (12in).
Habitat: Marshland, farmland.
Nest: Scrape on the ground.
Eggs: 4, light brown with dark markings.
Food: Mainly invertebrates.

Identification: Long, narrow, backward-curving black crest, with black on the face which is separated by a white streak in hens. Underparts are white, except for the chestnut undertail coverts. Wings are dark green, with a greyer green area on the neck. The white cheek patches behind the eyes are broken by a black line. Outside the breeding period the facial plumage is buff, and white areas are restricted to the chin and throat.

Dartford warbler

Sylvia undata

These small warblers have been recorded from Sweden, but their most northerly breeding outpost is in southern Britain, where they maintain a tenuous foothold – numbers become severely depleted in harsh winters. They roost in groups, which helps conserve body heat. Dartford warblers forage low down in shrubbery, sometimes venturing to the ground, where they can run surprisingly quickly. Berries feature more significantly in their diet during the winter, certainly in northern areas. Males establish breeding territories in the autumn. They sing more loudly and frequently during the spring, raising the grey feathers on the sides of their faces as part of the courtship ritual. The nest is built by both adults, hidden in a shrub. The hen incubates mainly on her own, for two weeks, and the chicks fledge after a similar interval.

Identification: Cock bird has a greyish head, back and wings. White spots on the throat, reddish chest and a grey central area to the underparts. Red area of skin encircles each eye. The bill is yellowish with a dark tip, and the legs and feet are yellowish-brown. Hens are paler with white throats. Young birds have grey-buff underparts, with no orbital skin and dark irides.

Distribution: Range extends through western parts of Europe, including the Iberian Peninsula, the western Mediterranean region and western parts of North Africa. Also present in southern parts of England.
Size: 14cm (5½in).
Habitat: Heathland.
Nest: Cup-shaped, made from vegetation.
Eggs: 3–5, whitish with darker markings.
Food: Mostly invertebrates, but some berries.

CORVIDS AND SHRIKES

These two groups of predatory birds frequently associate in flocks with others of their kind, and display relatively well-developed social awareness. Breeding shrikes are often assisted by "helpers" in caring for their young while they are still in the nest. As well as increasing the likelihood of the chicks receiving sufficient food, this may also develop the helpers' nesting skills.

Pied crow

Corvus albus

These corvids are characteristically versatile feeders. They scavenge near human settlements, especially on rubbish tips, and watch for road kills, carrying off surplus food which they store in a cache to be eaten later. Pied crows have even been observed washing dirty food before eating it. Their strong bills are used to crack shells, as well as for digging up crops of grain. Vegetable matter often features in their diet alongside carrion, and the birds will hunt too, catching small birds and even pulling ticks off cattle. Bold by nature, they have profited from the development of towns across Africa, where large numbers often congregate on the outskirts at suitable roosts. Pairs are equally versatile when breeding, nesting not only on cliffs and in trees but also on telegraph poles. The young crows fledge from the age of five weeks onwards.

Identification: Plumage is a glossy black, except for the thick white collar broadening out across the lower breast and abdomen. Bill, legs and feet are black. Sexes are alike. Young birds are duller, with faint black tips to the white areas of plumage.

Distribution: Much of Africa, south of the Sahara, except for central and eastern areas. Isolated locations elsewhere, notably in rainforest. Also occurs on Madagascar.
Size: 50cm (20in).
Habitat: Open country.
Nest: Large pile of sticks.
Eggs: 3–7, bluish-green with darker markings.
Food: Omnivorous.

Brown-necked raven

Desert raven *Corvus ruficollis*

Distribution: Across much of northern Africa and through the Arabian Peninsula into Asia. Separate population in central Asia, to the east of the Caspian Sea.
Size: 56cm (22in).
Habitat: Arid, desert country.
Nest: Pile of sticks.
Eggs: 2–7, bluish with brownish markings.
Food: Omnivorous.

In some parts of the Middle East, brown-necked raven roosts comprise over 1,000 individuals, although typically these birds are seen in small groups. Like the larger birds of prey, they sometimes soar on upcurrents of warm air, known as thermals. Opportunistic feeders, brown-necked ravens will eat locusts as well as carrion, and have even been observed ripping open sacks with their powerful bills to plunder supplies of grain. They will also readily eat dates. Pairs generally breed on their own, seeking out remote locations in the desert rather than nesting near settlements, although they may use abandoned oil drums here as nesting platforms. Material discarded by people, for example rags, may also be collected and used to line the nest. The young ravens leave the nest by the age of six weeks, and will remain as part of the family group with their parents for perhaps a month or more.

Identification: Black back and relatively short wings. Brownish-black head and underparts, the brown suffusion being more pronounced prior to a moult. Bill, legs and feet black. Sexes alike. Young birds similar to adults.

Southern fiscal (Fiscal shrike, *Lanius collaris*): 23cm (9in)
Two populations, one from sub-Saharan western Africa eastwards, the other over much of southern Africa. Black upperparts with a prominent white bar. The underparts are white. Hens have rufous flanks.

Somali crow (Dwarf raven, *Corvus edithae*): 46cm (18in)
From Eritrea to Somalia and Ethiopia, south into northern Kenya. Dark overall, except the base of the neck is white, evident when displaying. Brownish suffusion to the head and underparts, with wedge-shaped tail feathers. Bill, legs and feet black. Sexes are alike. Young birds are duller overall.

Fan-tailed raven (*Corvus rhipidurus*): 47cm (18¹/₂in)
Mountainous areas in western and central sub-Saharan Africa, and from Egypt southwards to Uganda and Kenya. Also in parts of the Middle East, especially eastern and southern Arabian Peninsula. Black overall, with a very distinctive short tail, the feathers of which look fan-shaped when spread open. Sexes are alike. Young birds are duller.

Cape crow (Black crow, *Corvus capensis*): 50cm (20in)
One population from Eritrea through parts of Sudan, Ethiopia and Somalia, with scattered populations as far south as Tanzania. Another population from southern Angola right down to the Cape, ranging eastwards to Zimbabwe. Glossy black plumage, with a fairly long, narrow black bill. Sexes are alike. Young birds are less glossy overall.

Red-backed shrike

Lanius collurio

In common with many insectivorous species, the red-backed shrike migrates south each autumn, spending the winter in savanna where food is more plentiful. In some parts of this shrike's breeding range, its nests are parasitized by the common cuckoo. However, unlike many host species, pairs learn to recognize cuckoo eggs laid alongside their own and discard them from the nest. Cock birds often impale their prey during the breeding season, and this behaviour ensures a more constant supply of food for the chicks, although there is always a risk that such stores will be raided by scavengers.

Distribution: Mainland Europe, except for much of the Iberian Peninsula and northern Scandinavia. Extends eastwards to the Caspian Sea. Overwinters in southern parts of Africa.
Size: 18cm (7in).
Habitat: Open country.
Nest: Cup-shaped, in the fork of a bush or tree.
Eggs: 5–9, variable coloration.
Food: Invertebrates.

Identification: Light grey crown. Black stripe extends through each eye from the bill. Underparts pinkish, reddish-brown back and wings. Hens have a brownish area at the front of the crown, grey behind, and dark brown wings; underparts white with darker edging to the feathers, brown patches behind the eyes.

Southern white-crowned shrike

Eurocephalus anguitimens

These shrikes are highly social by nature, and are usually encountered in groups of up to ten individuals, leapfrogging over each other in turn as they move through the branches. They hunt invertebrates, often on the ground and sometimes in the company of other birds, especially *Tockus* hornbills, preferring larger quarry including locusts and termites. Southern white-crowned shrikes show no tendency to cache surplus prey by impaling it on thorns. Breeding is carried out collectively, with nesting pairs frequently being assisted by up to five helpers. The nest is usually constructed on a horizontal branch, using a combination of dry grass and bark anchored together with spiders' webs, which give it a silvery appearance. Occasionally, a second hen may lay here unannounced, but the limited space available in the nest means that a number of the eggs will fall out onto the ground below. The incubation period lasts for up to 20 days, with the young shrikes fledging after a similar interval.

Identification: A black stripe extends from the bill through each eye to the sides of the neck, and the crown above is white. The throat and upper breast are white, and the underparts are pale greyish. A thin white collar is evident on both sides of the neck. The back is completely greyish and the wings are blackish, as is the tail. Bill, legs and feet black. Sexes are alike. Young birds are paler, and mottled on the crown.

Distribution: Ranges in a band across southern Africa, from western Angola and northern Namibia eastwards via Botswana and Zimbabwe to north-eastern parts of South Africa.
Size: 25cm (10in).
Habitat: Arid country.
Nest: Cup-shaped, made of grass and bark.
Eggs: 3–4, white with some darker blotches.
Food: Largely invertebrates.

FALCONS

Agile, aerial predators, these opportunistic birds of prey rely on strength and speed to overcome their prey, which frequently includes smaller birds. In the past, falcon populations were adversely affected by organochlorine pesticides such as DDT, but there has been a resurgence in their numbers in many areas, with populations occasionally even moving into urban areas.

Kestrel

Common kestrel *Falco tinnunculus*

These common birds of prey can frequently be seen hovering at the side of busy roads, largely undisturbed by the traffic thundering close by. Roadsides provide them with good hunting opportunities, and their keen eyesight enables them to spot even quite small quarry such as grasshoppers on the ground. In the winter, they may resort to hunting earthworms drawn to the surface by heavy rainfall. Kestrels also venture into towns, hunting in parks.

Identification: Bluish-grey head, with a black stripe under each eye and a whitish throat. Dense black spotting on the pale brownish chest, extending to the abdomen. Wings are chestnut-brown with black markings. Rump and tail feathers are grey with black tips. Hens are similar but have browner heads and distinct barring across the tail feathers.

Distribution: Range extends throughout western Europe across to South-east Asia and North Africa. Also breeds in Scandinavia.
Size: 37cm (14¹⁄₂in).
Habitat: Open countryside.
Nest: Platform of sticks in a tree or farm building.
Eggs: 3–7, pale pink with dark brown markings.
Food: Invertebrates and small mammals.

Peregrine falcon

Falco peregrinus

Peregrine falcons are powerful aerial predators, swooping down incredibly quickly on unsuspecting birds from above. Indeed, it is thought that they can dive at speeds of up to 350km/h (217mph). The impact made by their feet when they strike is so great that their quarry is frequently killed instantaneously. Pigeons are generally favoured as prey, although they may also hunt waterfowl. Peregrine falcons are highly adaptable hunters and can very occasionally be sighted in cities, where apartment blocks replace the crags from which they would normally fly on hunting excursions.

Identification: Dark grey upperparts. A broad blackish stripe extends down below each eye, and the surrounding white area extends right around the throat. The barring on the chest is lighter than on the abdomen. Darker markings are apparent on the grey feathers of the back and wings. The tail is barred, with paler grey feathering at the base. The legs and feet are yellow. Wings appear relatively narrow when seen in flight. Hens are much larger than male birds.

Distribution: Resident throughout most of western Europe and much of Africa, except for the Sahara Desert and the central rainforest band. One of the most adaptable and widely distributed birds of prey, occurring on all continents.
Size: 38–51cm (15–20in).
Habitat: Usually near cliffs, sometimes open ground.
Nest: Cliff ledges.
Eggs: 3–4, whitish with red-brown markings.
Food: Birds.

Red-footed falcon (*Falco vespertinus*): 34cm (13in)
Eastern Europe and Asia. Sighted in western Europe including the British Isles. Bluish-grey overall, with red lower abdomen and undertail coverts. Legs bright red. Hens are rufous-brown, with white cheeks and throat, blue-grey wings with black barring, and pinkish legs.

Hobby (Eurasian hobby, *Falco subbuteo*): 35cm (14in)
Mainland Europe to southern Scandinavia, east to Asia and south to North Africa. Overwinters in southern Africa. Long, pointed, dark bluish-grey wings. White band around the sides of the face. White underparts with barring. Reddish on the lower abdomen. Barred underside to the tail. Sexes are alike.

Lanner falcon (*Falco biarmicus*): 50cm (20in)
South-eastern Europe, Arabia and much of Africa except the central rainforests. Upperparts slaty- or brownish-grey (North African birds are more bluish). Dark stripe below each eye extends into a whitish area across the cheeks and throat. Underparts white with dark barring. Legs and feet yellow. Sexes are alike but hens larger.

Saker falcon (*Falco cherrug*): 55cm (22in)
Central Europe eastwards across South-east Asia to China. Westerly populations migrate to the eastern Mediterranean and North Africa; also observed in Arabia and eastern Africa. Brown overall, with a paler head. Heavily streaked on the breast, with darker areas on the flanks. Dark underwing coverts broken by whitish markings. Sexes are alike. A rare grey morph also exists.

African pygmy falcon

Polihierax semitorquatus

These small birds of prey are bold and conspicuous, frequently perching in the open. They hunt lizards, including skinks and agamids, as well as larger invertebrates. When a target is spotted from its vantage point, the African pygmy falcon bobs its head then flies down to seize it. Rodents are caught in this way too. The determining factor affecting their distribution is not the availability of prey however, but rather that of suitable nesting sites. These falcons seek out nests built by weavers, such as the social weaver (*Philetairus socius*), occasionally preying not only on the weaver chicks but the adult birds as well. The incubation period lasts four weeks, and the young leave the nest for the first time about a month later. The adult pair may soon nest again, but it is not unusual for the young to remain in the area for up to a year after fledging.

Distribution: Two African populations. One occurs in eastern Africa, from Djibouti, Ethiopia and Somalia south as far as northern Tanzania. The other is in the south-west, from Namibia to northern South Africa.
Size: 20cm (8in).
Habitat: Arid country.
Nest: Adopts those built by weaver birds.
Eggs: 2–4, white.
Food: Mainly lizards and larger invertebrates.

Identification: Cock bird has a greyish head, back and wings. Pale facial area, with a pale area also across the back of the neck. Pale underparts and rump. Black flight feathers and tail with white spots. Bare reddish skin around each eye. The bill is greyish with a dark tip. Legs and feet are pinkish. Hens are easily recognized by the chestnut plumage on the back. Young birds have brown backs.

Gyrfalcon

Falco rusticolus

The gyrfalcon is the largest member of its genus. It has adapted well to surviving life in the far north, where its coloration helps to conceal its presence, even in areas with little tree cover. These impressive falcons can often be sighted in coastal regions, where they prey on seabirds. They fly low when hunting in open countryside, taking grouse and similar birds as well as small rodents, preferring to catch their quarry on the ground rather than in flight. When breeding, pairs may adopt artificial nest sites, in buildings associated with oil pipelines, for example.

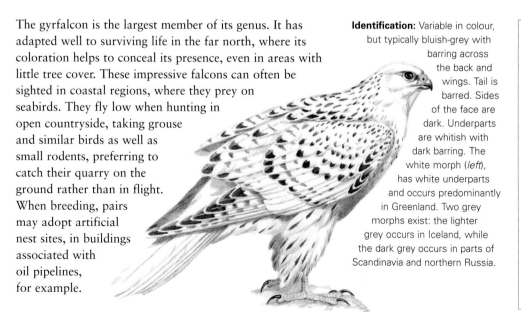

Identification: Variable in colour, but typically bluish-grey with barring across the back and wings. Tail is barred. Sides of the face are dark. Underparts are whitish with dark barring. The white morph (*left*), has white underparts and occurs predominantly in Greenland. Two grey morphs exist: the lighter grey occurs in Iceland, while the dark grey occurs in parts of Scandinavia and northern Russia.

Distribution: Through Iceland and Scandinavia. An annual vagrant in the British Isles.
Size: 63cm (25in)
Habitat: Mainly taiga and tundra regions.
Nest: On cliff ledges.
Eggs: 3–4, buff with dense reddish speckling.
Food: Mostly takes small birds and mammals.

AGILE AERIAL HUNTERS

Aerial agility is a feature associated with birds of prey, particularly those that hunt other birds. Some are equally adept at pursuing terrestrial prey. Many species have developed specialized hunting techniques, and the young of these birds have to remain with the adults for some time after fledging in order to learn the skills they will need to feed themselves.

Red kite

Milvus milvus

Distribution: Range includes Wales, the Iberian Peninsula and the adjacent area of North Africa. Extends north-eastwards across Europe to southern Sweden, and also found in Russia.
Size: 66cm (26in).
Habitat: Light woodland.
Nest: Platform of sticks, built in a tree.
Eggs: 1–4, white with reddish-brown markings.
Food: Small birds, mammals and carrion.

Although very agile hunters, red kites also seek carrion such as dead sheep. This behaviour has resulted in their persecution in some areas because of misplaced fears that the kites actually kill lambs. When seeking prey, red kites circle repeatedly overhead, relying on their keen eyesight to spot any movement on the ground. They will then drop and sweep low, homing in on their target. Up until the 1700s, flocks of red kites were common scavengers on the streets of London, where they were sufficiently tame to swoop down and steal food from children. It was their willingness to scavenge that led to a dramatic reduction in their numbers, however they have now recovered and been successfully reintroduced in many regions.

Identification: Predominantly reddish-brown, with a greyish head streaked with darker markings. Darker mottling over the wings, with some variable streaking on the underparts as well. Feet are yellowish with black talons. White areas under the wings and forked tail can be clearly seen in flight. Sexes are alike.

Hen harrier

Circus cyaneus

Hen harriers are very distinctive hunters, flying low over moorland, seeking not only small mammals but also birds. Their preference for hunting grouse has led to persecution by gamekeepers in various parts of their range. However, over the winter months these harriers may be forced to feed largely on carrion. Their range extends further north than those of related species, into the tundra region, but they are not resident in far northern areas throughout the year, and will head further south before the start of winter. Hen harriers are unusual in not only roosting on the ground but also breeding on the ground. Once the breeding season is over they will often congregate at communal sites, which may be used for several generations.

Identification: Mainly chestnut overall, streaked with white. Darker over the wings. Narrow white band around each eye, with a solid brown area beneath. Tail is barred. The bill is dark, and the legs are yellow. Hens are larger.

Distribution: Throughout much of the Northern Hemisphere. Extends across most of Europe, including Scandinavia, east to Asia. Often moves south for the winter as far as North Africa.
Size: 52cm (20in).
Habitat: Moorland.
Nest: On the ground, hidden in vegetation.
Eggs: 3–5, whitish.
Food: Mainly small mammals and birds.

Pale chanting goshawk

Melierax canorus

The so-called chanting of these goshawks is only audible during the breeding season, and consists of a series of similar call notes repeated persistently. They breed from June to March, with the nest itself built near the top of a tree or even on a telegraph pole. The hen incubates largely on her own for five weeks, and the young leave the nest when they are two months old. Pale chanting goshawks hunt from a perch, swooping down to the ground, but will also scavenge at road kills. They are adept hunters, and have struck up a remarkable relationship with mongooses (*Galerella*) and honey-badgers (*Mellivora*). They follow these mammals closely, waiting patiently on the ground while they excavate in the hope of catching disturbed rodents or lizards. If necessary, the goshawks are able to run fast across the ground to capture fleeing quarry.

Identification: Grey head, chest and back, with grey barring on a white background on the abdomen. The rump and inner flight feathers are white, outer flight feathers black. Tail dark above, banded grey-and-white below. Red base to the bill, tip dark. Legs and feet reddish. Sexes are alike, but male is slightly smaller. Young birds are distinctive: brown overall, darker on the crown, back and wings, with a white throat; underparts streaked with black above, displaying brown-and-white barring below; bill dark, legs and feet orangish.

Distribution: Range is restricted to south-western Africa. Extends from south-west Angola and northern Namibia through Botswana to western parts of Zimbabwe, and occurs over much of South Africa except for the eastern side.
Size: 54cm (21in).
Habitat: Arid country.
Nest: Pile of twigs, usually built in a tree.
Eggs: 1–2, bluish-white.
Food: Lizards, rodents and other terrestrial vertebrates.

Black kite (*Milvus migrans*): 60cm (24in) Present on much of mainland Europe to Asia and Australia. Also occurs in North Africa and overwinters south of the Sahara. Mainly brown but darker on the wings. The underparts are decidedly rufous. Barring on the tail. Some grey markings on the head. Sexes are alike.

Black-winged kite (*Elanus caeruleus*): 30cm (12in) Present in North Africa and widely distributed south of the Sahara. Grey head, extending down the back over the wings. Whitish sides to the face and white underparts. Prominent black area on each wing extending from the shoulders. Sexes are alike.

Montagu's harrier (*Circus pygargus*): 50cm (20in) Found in Europe and North Africa, east to Asia. Overwinters in central and eastern Africa south of the Sahara. Predominantly grey, with barring on the lower underparts. Narrow white rump. Hens are larger, with brown plumage replacing the grey. In the dark morph, males are blackish and hens are a dark chocolate-brown.

Black harrier (*Circus maurus*): 52½cm (21in) Restricted to southern Africa, including parts of Namibia and South Africa. Cock is brownish-black, with white feathering on the rump, grey flight feathers and grey bands on the tail, which also has a white tip. Black bill, yellow cere, and yellowish legs and feet. Sexes are alike. Young birds have rufous-brown edging on the wings, and buff underparts also streaked with brown.

Sparrowhawk

Eurasian sparrowhawk *Accipiter nisus*

These hawks favour preying on groundfeeding birds, and males generally take smaller quarry than females, reflecting the difference in their respective sizes. Even females rarely take birds much larger than pigeons, although they will prey on thrushes. Pairs nest later in the year than many songbirds, so there are plenty of nestlings to prey on and feed to their own chicks. Sparrowhawks have short wings and are very agile in flight, able to manoeuvre easily in wooded areas. They approach quietly with the aim of catching their target unawares, seizing their prey using their powerful feet.

Identification: Grey head, back and wings, with darker barring on the grey tail. The underparts are also barred. Bare yellow legs and feet, with long toes. Cock birds are smaller than hens and have pale rufous areas on the lower sides of the face, extending to the chest, while the barring on their underparts is browner.

Left: Young male sparrowhawks fledge several days before their heavier siblings.

Distribution: Resident in most of Europe (except the far north of Scandinavia), North Africa and the Canary Islands. Migratory birds overwinter around the Red Sea. Extends east to Asia.
Size: 28cm (11in).
Habitat: Light woodland.
Nest: Made of sticks.
Eggs: 4–6, pale blue with reddish-brown markings.
Food: Mainly birds.

BUZZARDS

These predatory birds possess sharp, pointed bills and powerful talons. They feed on other birds as well as mammals, while some also resort to eating carrion and invertebrates. Buzzards can sometimes occur in recognized colour morphs, with their plumage being either lighter or darker than usual. Individuals of this type occur alongside those with normal coloration.

Common buzzard

Eurasian buzzard *Buteo buteo*

With its rather broad and stocky appearance, the common buzzard's silhouette in flight helps to confirm its identity. Buzzards are capable of soaring for long periods, before suddenly swooping down to seize a rabbit – their traditional prey, particularly in many parts of Europe. On the other hand, buzzards can sometimes be observed hunting invertebrates, walking purposefully on the ground in search of their quarry. They may occasionally be spotted on roads too, feeding on road kill, even placing themselves in danger from the passing traffic. However, buzzards remain one of the most common raptors in Europe, thanks largely to their adaptable feeding habits.

Identification: Mainly dark brown, with a variable amount of white plumage around the bill and on the underparts. The tail is barred, with paler plumage around the vent. Legs and feet are yellow, and the bill is yellow with a dark tip. White predominates in the pale morph. Hens are often larger.

Distribution: Resident in western Europe. Summer visitor to parts of Scandinavia and across Asia. Migratory European birds overwinter in southern and eastern Africa.
Size: 57cm (22in).
Habitat: Areas with trees.
Nest: Platform of sticks, usually in a tree.
Eggs: 2–4, white.
Food: Small mammals and other prey.

Jackal buzzard

Buteo rufofuscus

Although carrion features in their diet, these buzzards do not scavenge as much as some vultures. Jackal buzzards are active and efficient hunters, scanning the ground below from prominent perches overlooking open ground, which often includes nearby roads. This is a productive strategy for reptile-hunters, since lizards and snakes often bask on warm tarmac in the morning, to raise their body temperature. Jackal buzzards also hunt on the wing, soaring and hovering over the ground. Pairs remain in their breeding territories throughout the year, and will often reuse the same nest annually, lining it with green leaves at the start of the breeding period. A cliff face is often favoured as a nest site, but trees may also be used. According to ringing studies, young birds may disperse over distances of up to 640km (400 miles) from the nest site.

Distribution: Southern Africa, from Namibia in the west and Zimbabwe in the east down across virtually all of South Africa.
Size: 55cm (22in).
Habitat: Grassland.
Nest: Made of sticks.
Eggs: 1–3, white with reddish-brown markings.
Food: Mainly small mammals and reptiles.

Identification: Predominantly black head, back and wings, usually with a chestnut breast. Black underparts, with white edging to the plumage. Prominent white underwing areas, with chestnut undertail coverts and tail. Bill yellow at the base, black at the tip. Legs and feet yellowish. A rare white-breasted morph also exists, with almost totally white underparts. Sexes are alike. Young birds are easily distinguished by their brown coloration, darker on the wings with pale edging; tail lightly barred with darker brown stripes.

Long-legged buzzard

Buteo rufinus

These buzzards vary in depth of coloration, with some a much darker shade of brown than others. European birds migrate south in August, with most heading no further than Kenya, though some are seen in South Africa. They start returning in February, and the male may be joined by his partner in aerial display, rising and circling each other in the sky. The nest measures about 80cm (32in) in diameter, and is usually built on a cliff face or an inaccessible site at ground level. Incubation lasts a month, and the young fledge after six weeks. For a while they may stay together in a family group, but long-legged buzzards are generally solitary birds by nature.

Identification: Whitish head, streaking on the back of the neck and breast. Otherwise brownish, with blackish centres to the plumage on the back and wings. Flight feathers dark at the tips. White areas spotted brown on the undersides of the wings. Tail more rufous. Bill base yellow, tip dark. Legs and feet yellowish. Sexes alike but females larger. Young are browner, especially on the head, and the tail is lightly barred.

Distribution: Ranges through extreme south-eastern parts of Europe, extending into Asia and to the Arabian Peninsula. Migrates across northern parts of Africa, where it is also resident, with a more extensive range in eastern Africa, extending from northern Sudan to Kenya. Also occasionally recorded in other locations in southern Africa.
Size: 65cm (26in).
Habitat: Grassland.
Nest: Bulky pile of sticks.
Eggs: 2–5, whitish with darker markings.
Food: Small vertebrates.

Steppe buzzard (*Buteo buteo vulpinus*): 58cm (23in)
Subspecies of common buzzard. Present throughout Europe, extending to central Asia. Overall coloration is brownish, noticeably darker in some individuals than in others. Lightly barred rufous tail. Bill is yellow at the base, dark at the tip. Legs and feet are yellow. Sexes are similar.

Grasshopper buzzard (*Butastur rufipennis*): 44cm (17in)
Occurs across Africa south of the Sahara, extending down the eastern coast to northern Tanzania. Greyish head and a white throat, with rufous underparts displaying dark streaking on the breast. Undertail coverts are whitish. Back and wings are greyish, the wings showing distinctive rufous patches in flight. Bill is yellow at the base, dark at the tip. Legs and feet are yellowish. Sexes are alike. Young birds have browner upperparts, with grey restricted to the ear coverts.

Augur buzzard (*Buteo augur*): 55cm (22in)
Largely confined to eastern parts of Africa, from Sudan to Zimbabwe, with a separate population extending from southern Angola to northern Namibia. Dark blackish head and back, with black speckling in a band across the wings. Short rufous tail. Largely white when seen from below, with dark edging to the flight feathers. Bill is yellow at the base, black at the tip. Legs and feet are yellow. Young birds are dark brown rather than black above, with a lighter brown barred tail.

Rough-legged buzzard

Buteo lagopus

These buzzards hunt lemmings and voles, but, when rodent populations undergo their regular cyclical collapse, take birds including snow buntings and grouse. In winter, wood pigeons are frequently targeted. Insects and spiders may also be caught, along with fish, and carrion may be scavenged. Pairs return to their breeding grounds in mid-April, reusing a nest built previously, lining the inside with fresh greenery. Like many species nesting in the far north, the number of chicks reared is directly correlated to the availability of food.

Identification: Brownish head and upperparts, with darker brown chest markings and barring on the white underparts. Tail white, with a broad brown tip. Whitish wings edged dark when seen from below. Bill base is yellow, tip dark. Legs are feathered, feet yellow. Sexes similar, but hens heavier with fewer tail bars. Young paler.

Distribution: Circumpolar. Breeds throughout the far north of Europe, extending to Asia. Migrates southwards to eastern England and across much of central Europe and South-east Asia. Absent from much of France, the Iberian Peninsula, Italy and Africa.
Size: 59cm (23in).
Habitat: Open country.
Nest: Pile of sticks.
Eggs: 3–5.
Food: Rodents, birds.

EAGLES

These large predatory birds are most conspicuous when seen in flight. They range over wide areas, although do not occur at high densities unless food is plentiful. A number of species have developed specialized feeding habits, for example snake eagles, but all tend to be relatively opportunistic feeders, prepared to scavenge on carrion of all types.

Bateleur

Terathopius ecaudatus

Bateleur is the French word for tight rope walker, and describes this bird's wings-outstretched display flight. They are adept at locating carrion, but also hunt prey including larger birds such as bustards (*Otididae*) and eagle-owls (*Bubo*), and even small antelopes. Bateleurs spend much of the day on the wing, covering distances of more than 500km (300 miles) in search of food. Their young develop slowly, spending nearly 16 weeks in the nest. After fledging, they spend a similar period learning to hunt with their parents. It will take up to eight years to acquire full adult plumage. Bateleurs are usually solitary, but may congregate in larger numbers where food is plentiful.

Identification: Black head and underparts. Brown V-shaped area on the back, edged black. Grey shoulders. Long, narrow wings, white underneath. Short brown tail. Bare red skin around the eyes to the base of the bill, which is black at its tip. Legs and feet red. Hens similar but have another, more silvery area on the wings. Young birds much duller, brown overall, with a brownish-yellow bill and red only on the feet and legs.

Distribution: Occurs in a band across Africa south of the Sahara, and down the eastern side of the continent to northern South Africa. Ranges westwards to Gabon, Angola and Namibia.
Size: 70cm (28in).
Habitat: Savanna.
Nest: Stick platform in a tree.
Eggs: 1, white.
Food: Mainly vertebrates.

Verreaux's eagle

Black eagle *Aquila verreauxii*

Verreaux's eagles are specialist hunters of rock hyraxes (*Heterohyrax* and *Procavia*), which look like guinea pigs but are considered small ungulates, rather than rodents. Studies in the Matobo Hills of Zimbabwe have revealed more than 18,000 are killled every year by these eagles. Their range closely mirrors that of the rock hyrax itself, although the birds also feed on a range of other prey, and carrion too. Pairs establish territories and are resident year-round, staying in close contact even to the point of sharing kills. Usually only one chick is reared successfully, since the younger nestling will be attacked and killed by its older sibling.

Identification: Black overall, white rump. Underwings speckled, whiter nearer the tips. Base of the bill yellowish, tip dark. Legs and feet yellow. Hens similar but slightly larger. Young birds browner, wings edged white, underparts blackish mottled brown.

Distribution: Occurs mainly along eastern and southern parts of Africa. Isolated northern population on the Chad-Sudanese border. Patchily distributed from southern Sudan down to South Africa, and up the western side of the continent to western Angola.
Size: 95cm (37in).
Habitat: Mountainous and rocky country.
Nest: Large pile of sticks.
Eggs: 2, white, sometimes with speckles.
Food: Small mammals.

Short-toed snake eagle

Circaetus gallicus

As their name suggests, snakes feature prominently in the diet of these eagles. They are able to catch snakes measuring over 1.5m (5ft) in length, holding down and overpowering even venomous ones with their powerful feet and sharp bills. Once dead, the reptile is swallowed head first, often on the ground but sometimes in flight, depending on size. Other reptiles, notably lizards, may also be caught occasionally, along with small mammals up to the size of hares. Pairs establish their own breeding territories, becoming more conspicuous during this period, with males especially calling loudly.

The single chick grows rapidly, and is capable of eating whole snakes measuring up to 9cm (3½in) long when just three weeks old.

Identification: Dark brownish upperparts, with paler edging to the wing coverts. Tail is banded with four brown bars. Underwings whitish with regular rows of dark brown markings, also running across the body. Head and chest dark brown. Greyish bill, legs and feet. Sexes are alike, but female slightly larger. Young birds have paler underparts, and the undersides of their wings are largely unmarked.

Distribution: Breeds in the Iberian Peninsula and through southern Europe, extending into north-west Africa, the Middle East and Asia. Birds from Europe and North Africa migrate to a fairly narrow band across Africa south of the Sahara, east as far as Sudan, with a number of reports from Kenya.
Size: 67cm (26in).
Habitat: Arid country.
Nest: Stick platform in a tree.
Eggs: 1, white.
Food: Mainly vertebrates.

Martial eagle (*Polemaetus bellicosus*): 85cm (34in)
The largest African eagle. Ranges down eastern and throughout southern Africa, from Dem. Rep. Congo to the Cape. Dark brown head, breast and upperparts, with a short crest at the back of the head. Underparts white with brown spots. Tail is barred, as are the flight feathers when seen from below. Irides yellow, bill black. Legs feathered, feet are yellow. Sexes are similar, but hens often slightly larger, with bigger feet. Young birds are lighter overall, with whitish underparts and sides of the face.

Beaudouin's snake eagle (*Circaetus beaudouini*): 65cm (26in)
Ranges from Senegal to Kenya. Dark blackish upperparts. Whitish area under the bill. Breast is dark, with vermiculated lower underparts and whitish undertail coverts. Banding across the flight feathers when seen from below, and on the tail. Bill is greyish, black at the tip. Legs and feet also greyish. Sexes are alike. Young birds have brown bodies and less distinct barring across the wings.

Bonelli's eagle (*Aquila fasciata*): 65cm (26in)
Wide range encompasses the Iberian peninsula, southern France, north-west Africa, the Middle East, southern China and parts of Indonesia. Regional variations in colour occur. Has a dark brown head and upperparts. Underparts are white, often with dark brown streaking. Pale grey tail with a broad, black band at tip. Black bill; yellow cere and feet. Hens are a little larger.

Black-chested snake eagle

Circaetus pectoralis

These snake eagles differ from their close relatives by spending longer on the wing searching for food, hovering in flight. In Zimbabwe, large and potentially deadly cobras form a significant part of their diet. Their small nest is built in a tree, on top of the canopy. The chick hatches after seven weeks, and spends long periods alone in the nest while its parents are hunting for food. Returning adults will regurgitate a partially swallowed snake, aided by the youngster, who helps to pull it from its parent's mouth. The chick then swallows the snake while rhythmically rotating its head, which presumably helps to transport the reptile along its digestive system. Fledging takes place once the young snake eagle is about three months of age.

Identification: Blackish upperparts, with the black extending onto the chest. Underparts white. Underwings white with three rows of black barring, and black tips to the flight feathers. Tail is greyish below with black barring. Bill, legs and feet are greyish. Sexes are alike, but hens slightly larger. Young birds are mostly brown overall, with a barred tail and black flight feathers.

Distribution: Eastern and southern parts of Africa. From Sudan down to northern South Africa in the east, and from Rep. Congo southwards in the west.
Size: 68cm (27in).
Habitat: Open areas, woods.
Nest: Platform of sticks.
Eggs: 1, white.
Food: Largely snakes.

OTHER EAGLES AND VULTURES

Soaring overhead, these eagles and vultures are usually quite conspicuous. Unfortunately, they have suffered intense persecution by people due to fears that they will attack domestic stock, and their readiness to feed on carrion has meant they can be easily poisoned. Many species are therefore quite scarce, and are only observed in more remote areas of country.

Golden eagle

Aquila chrysaetos

Identification: Brown overall, with yellowish-brown plumage on the back of the head extending down the nape of the neck. Those eagles inhabiting desert areas, such as the Middle East, are slightly paler overall. The bill is yellow with a dark tip. Feet are also yellow, with black talons. Hens are larger in size than cocks.

These majestic eagles generally inhabit remote areas away from people, where they are likely to be left undisturbed. When seen in flight, the golden eagle's head looks relatively small compared to its broad tail and large, square-ended wings. It has some yapping call notes not unlike those of a dog, but generally its calls are quite shrill. Golden eagles have adapted their hunting skills to suit their environment. For instance, in some areas they take tortoises, dropping the reptiles from a great height in order to smash their shells before eating them; in other areas, they may prey on cats. They prefer to capture their quarry on the ground, swooping down low, rather than catching birds in the air.

Distribution: Ranges sporadically through the Mediterranean region and eastwards into Asia. Present in Scotland and Scandinavia. Also occurs in parts of northern Africa.
Size: 90cm (35in).
Habitat: Mountainous areas.
Nest: Massive cliff nest made of sticks.
Eggs: 2, white with some dark markings.
Food: Birds and mammals.

Imperial eagle

Eastern imperial eagle *Aquila heliaca* (E)

The imperial eagle population declined dramatically during the 20th century due to persecution by humans. However, thanks to effective protection there are now signs that numbers are increasing again in countries such as Hungary. Here they can frequent areas of open countryside, rather than being forced into retreating to the relative safety of the mountain forests. Imperial eagles, like others of their kind, are potentially long-lived birds, having few natural enemies other than people. Their longevity is measured not in years but decades, and is mirrored in the pace of their development: young imperial eagles may not breed for the first time until they are six years old, before they have even attained their full adult plumage.

Identification: Predominantly dark brown. Pale buff on the back of the head extending down around the neck. Patches of white at the shoulders. The bill is yellow with a dark tip. Feet also yellow. Sexes are alike. This species is now regarded as distinct from the Spanish imperial eagle (*A. adalberti*), which has small white shoulder patches.

Distribution: Eastern parts of Europe and Turkey eastwards across much of central Asia. Overwinters in Africa, from Egypt southwards, and also in Arabia and southern parts of Asia.
Size: 84cm (33in).
Habitat: Open country.
Nest: Made of sticks and other vegetation.
Eggs: 2, white with some dark markings.
Food: Small mammals, birds and carrion.

Griffon vulture

Eurasian griffon *Gyps fulvus*

These vultures are most likely to be seen in areas of relatively open countryside with surrounding cliffs, which are used for nesting and roosting. They glide over plains, using their keen eyesight to locate carcasses, although nowadays groups of griffon vultures can often be found scavenging at rubbish dumps. Hot currents of air, known as thermals, enable them to soar with very little effort and remain airborne for long periods. Griffon vultures nest in colonies that have been known to consist of as many as 150 pairs. Their chicks develop slowly, often not embarking on their first flight until they are nearly 20 weeks old. Young birds are unlikely to breed until they are at least four years old.

Identification: Dark brown around the eyes, with the top of the head and neck whitish. Light brown body, back and wings. Darker flight feathers and tail. Relatively elongated horn-coloured bill, curved on the upper tip. Legs and feet grey, whitish on the inner thighs. Sexes are alike. Young birds have a darker brown back and a brown neck collar. Distinguished from African white-backed vulture (*G. africanus*) by its larger size and paler plumage.

Distribution: North-western Africa, the Iberian Peninsula and the Caucasus eastwards into Asia. Young birds may migrate further south to western and eastern Africa.
Size: 110cm (43in).
Habitat: Mountain country.
Nest: Sticks on rocky crag.
Eggs: 1, white with reddish-brown markings.
Food: Carrion.

Rüppell's vulture (*Gyps rueppellii*): 105cm (41in)
Ranges across Africa south of the Sahara in a band to Somalia, extending further south here than in the west, down through Uganda and Kenya to Tanzania. Vagrants also occasionally recorded further south. Blackish, with creamy-white edging to the feathers on the body and wings, creating a scaly appearance. Covering of whitish, down-like feathering on the back of the head; skin is bluish-grey. Bill pale horn-coloured at its tip, grey at the base. Legs and feet grey. Dark flight feathers when viewed from beneath, with white banding evident. Sexes are alike. Young birds are very distinctive: predominantly brown, darker across the wings, with the feathers here having buff edging; bill, legs and feet greyish. Young obtain adult plumage slowly, over the course of successive moults, with this process typically taking seven years.

Cinereous vulture (Eurasian black vulture, *Aegypius monachus*): 107cm (42in)
Range extends from Spain and the Balearic Islands eastwards to the Balkans, and from Turkey across Asia. Some birds overwinter in north-eastern Africa. Pale bluish skin encircles the nostrils. Bald head with a brownish area around the eyes. Plumage is a dark sooty black. Sexes are alike.

Egyptian vulture (*Neophron percnopterus*): 70cm (27½in)
Distributed around the Mediterranean into Asia. Also the Canary Islands and across Africa south of the Sahara to Tanzania and Arabia. Pale whitish plumage with brown markings prominent over the wings and flight feathers. Bald, bright yellow area of skin on the sides of the face and along the bill, which may have a dark tip. Sexes are alike.

Lappet-faced vulture

Nubian vulture *Torgos tracheliotus*

These massive scavengers have a wingspan of 3m (10ft), weigh 7kg (15½lb) and can carry up to 1.45kg (3lb) of food in their crops. They are dominant at a kill, which is why they are known as king vultures. They also hunt small mammals. Pairs mate for life, and build the largest nest of any vulture – up to 2m (6½ft) in diameter. Hens normally lay a single egg, incubated by both adults, which hatches after 55 days. The chick grows slowly and is unlikely to fledge until it is 18 weeks old. The vultures remain in a family group for over a year, and the young birds are fed by the adults throughout this period.

Distribution: Scattered locations in Africa, largely south of the Sahara. Main range extends eastwards to Somalia. Also down many parts of eastern Africa. Southern range extends from western Angola through Namibia and Botswana as far as northern South Africa
Size: 115cm (45in).
Habitat: Arid savanna.
Nest: Made of sticks.
Eggs: 1–2, white.
Food: Largely carrion.

Identification: Pinkish and blue skin on the head and throat, which varys depending on distribution. Back is black. Whitish areas extend down the sides of the underparts and the thighs. White markings under the wings, near the leading edge, close to the body. Bill is horn-coloured at its tip, greyish at the base in southern areas but darker further north. Legs and feet greyish. Hens can be larger. Young birds are brown, with whitish streaking on the mantle, pale heads and greyer bills.

OWLS OF OPEN COUNTRY

Although often considered forest birds, a number of owl species are encountered in areas of open country, ranging from the Arctic through temperate latitudes to the tropics. They generally hunt from dusk onwards, having keen eyesight and hearing which enables them to home in on their quarry very accurately. Owls pursue a wide range of prey, catching it on the ground.

Pharaoh eagle-owl

Bubo ascalaphus

Identification: Individuals have a whitish facial disc, with blackish markings on the forehead and ear tufts. Upperparts buff with darker markings, becoming whiter over the wings. Tail banded. Chest has some dark markings, paler below. Varies in depth of colour through its range. Bill dark, as are the claws, with an orange iris. Sexes are alike, females often larger. Young birds have more barring on the upperparts.

These owls are exclusively nocturnal in their habit, roosting in a well-concealed locality during the day, protected from the heat of the sun. At night, they are most likely to be heard rather than seen. The cock pharaoh eagle-owl has a higher-pitched call than that of its Eurasian relative, enabling them to be distinguished in the Atlas Mountains of Algeria, where the range of both species overlaps. Desert rodents such as gerbils (*Gerbillus*) feature prominently in their diet, but they may occasionally take larger quarry such as desert foxes (*Vulpes*). The nest is usually hidden away on the ground, although where there are stunted trees pairs may prefer to breed in hollows or by taking over abandoned nests built by other birds of similar size. The hen is responsible for incubating the eggs on her own, and is fed by her mate. The young take two years to attain sexual maturity.

Distribution: Much of northern Africa, across much of the central and eastern Sahara, along the northern and eastern edge of the Arabian peninsula.
Size: 50cm (20in).
Habitat: Arid, desert and rocky areas.
Nest: Scrape in amongst rocks.
Eggs: 2–4, white.
Food: Small vertebrates and larger invertebrates.

Omani owl

Hume's owl *Strix butleri*

Areas with low-growing vegetation, rocky terrain and desert oases characterize the typical habitat of these owls, whose range is not fully documented at present. There is a suggestion that they may extend more widely through the Middle East, reaching as far east as Pakistan. Omani owls are opportunistic hunters, taking whatever quarry is available, ranging from rodents, especially gerbils which are relatively common, to lizards and flying insects. They have also been observed hawking night-flying invertebrates drawn to street lights, and frequently hunt along roads, which can result in them becoming casualties themselves. A secluded site is chosen for nesting, which is believed to take place in the early spring, starting in February. There is no nest preparation and the eggs are laid directly on the ground, with the hen incubating on her own. The young hatch after a period of about 5 weeks, and will vacate the nest site after a similar interval, at the time of fledging.

Identification: Distinctive silky texture to the plumage. Relatively pale in colour, with few markings on the buff-white underparts. Facial disc lightly coloured, with a darker streak between the eyes, and buff elsewhere. Upperparts darker, brownish and grey. Iris is orange, bill horn-yellow, whitish plumage on the legs. Toes and claws dark. Hens are larger. Young birds have yellowish eyes.

Distribution: Far eastern Mediterranean to north-east Egypt and eastern side of the Red Sea; other areas of the Arabian Peninsula.
Size: 33cm (12½in).
Habitat: Open country, typically rocky terrain.
Nest: Bare hollow in a cave.
Eggs: 5, white.
Food: Small vertebrates and invertebrates.

African scops owl

Otus senegalensis

The calls of these small owls, which may be uttered quite frequently, have been likened to those of a frog. African scops owls are difficult to observe during the daytime, since their cryptic coloration proves excellent camouflage. They are often attracted to lights at night, in order to catch the flying insects which feature prominently in their diet. They will also take prey from the ground, as has been revealed by the remains of scorpions found in their pellets, which are regurgitated after a meal and contain the indigestible remains of their prey. These owls may take small vertebrates occasionally too. During the breeding period the hen sits alone, but her partner remains in the vicinity and may alert her to any danger. He will also bring food to the nest for her, although she may occasionally hunt for herself during the incubation, which lasts around 22 days. The young owls will leave the nest when they are about four weeks old.

Identification: Greyish overall, with prominent ear tufts. Some variable brown feathering, with black streaks and white areas too, especially on the wings. A variable blackish border is evident around the facial disc. Irides yellow, bill black. Legs and feet feathered whitish. Sexes are alike. Young birds are similar to adults.

Distribution: Range extends in a band across Africa south of the Sahara, and widely in eastern Africa. Extends down along the Dem. Rep. Congo border to cover most of southern Africa, but largely absent from the coastal areas of southern Angola, Namibia and western South Africa.
Size: 17cm (6³/₄in).
Habitat: Savanna.
Nest: Tree hole.
Eggs: 2–4, white.
Food: Largely insectivorous.

African grass owl (*Tyto capensis*): 38cm (15in) Rep. Congo to Mozambique. Also in eastern and southern South Africa, along the Kenyan-Ugandan border, and in Nigeria. White, heart-shaped face surrounded by dark brown, faintly spotted white over the back of the neck. Underparts pale buff. Bill grey, legs and feet feathered. Sexes alike. Young birds are darker on the underparts, with rufous facial feathering.

Cape eagle-owl (*Bubo capensis*): 54cm (21¹/₄in) Eastern Africa, notably in central Ethiopia, Kenya and Zimbabwe. Main range in southern Africa. Grey face with black edging, and a white bib. Prominent ear tufts speckled black-and-brown. White mottling on the wings and underparts. Tail is barred black-and-brown. Irides bright orange, bill blackish. Legs and feet feathered. Mostly whitish underwings, with some rows of darker markings. Sexes alike, females usually larger. Young birds lack ear tufts until six months old.

Southern white-faced owl (*Ptilopsis granti*): 28cm (11in)
Gabon to Kenya and down to Lesotho. Absent from north-eastern South Africa. Whitish face, greyish around the bill. Black on the sides of the face. Head, back and wings bluish-grey with vertical dark streaking. Oblique white bands across each wing. Chest white, greyer below, streaked black. White vent. Prominent ear tufts. Barred tail feathers. Irides bright orange, bill grey, legs whitish. Sexes alike, but hens heavier. Young birds browner overall, with yellow irides.

Eagle-owl

Eurasian eagle-owl *Bubo bubo*

The eagle-owl's scientific name reflects the sound of its loud calls, which are clearly audible on still nights even from quite a distance. Pairs will call alternately before mating, and the call notes of the female are higher-pitched than the male's. In spite of their large size, these owls fly quietly and may sometimes be seen soaring. Formidable hunters, they will occasionally take large, potentially dangerous quarry such as buzzards and herons. eagle-owls are adaptable in their feeding habits, and may sometimes resort to catching earthworms and fish, as well as eating carrion when hunting opportunities are limited.

Distribution: Throughout southern Europe, Scandinavia and eastwards across Asia. Small populations in parts of western Europe and western North Africa.
Size: 73cm (29in).
Habitat: Rocky areas and relatively open country.
Nest: Cliff ledges, or occasionally on the ground.
Eggs: 1–4, white.
Food: Mammals and birds.

Identification: Brownish with dark markings on the wings. Underparts are buff-brown with streaking, most evident on the breast. Prominent ear tufts. Black bil, orange irides. Hens are often slightly larger. There may be great variation in appearance through their wide range, and at least 16 different races are recognized.

WARBLERS AND OTHER SMALL GARDEN VISITORS

Spotting these birds in a garden is not always easy since their neutral coloration merges in well against the foliage. They generally favour overgrown areas where there will be a good supply of invertebrates. Some are resident in northern latitudes throughout the year, while others migrate to Africa for the winter.

Wren

Eurasian wren *Troglodytes troglodytes*

Although often difficult to spot due to their size and drab coloration, these tiny birds have a remarkably loud song which usually betrays their presence. Wrens can be found in areas where there is plenty of cover, such as ivy-clad walls, scurrying under the vegetation in search of spiders and similar prey. During the winter, when their small size could make them vulnerable to hypothermia, the wrens huddle together in roosts overnight to keep warm. However, populations are often badly affected by prolonged spells of severe weather. In the spring, the hen chooses one of several nests that the male has constructed, lining it with feathers to form a soft base for her eggs. Wrens are surprisingly common, although not always conspicuous, with the British population alone made up of an estimated ten million birds.

Identification: Reddish-brown back and wings with visible barring. Lighter brown underparts and a narrow eye stripe. Short tail, often held vertically, which is greyish on its underside. Bill is long and relatively narrow. Sexes are alike.

Distribution: Resident throughout Europe, except in Scandinavia and neighbouring parts of Russia during the winter. European wrens move south in the winter. Present in northern Africa.
Size: 10cm (4in).
Habitat: Overgrown gardens and woodland.
Nest: Ball-shaped.
Eggs: 5–6, white with reddish-brown markings.
Food: Mainly invertebrates.

Eurasian nuthatch

Sitta europaea

With relatively large, strong feet and very powerful claws, Eurasian nuthatches are adept at scampering up and down tree trunks. They hunt for invertebrates, which they extract from the bark with their narrow bills, but their compact and powerful beak also enables them to feed easily on nuts. The nuthatches first wedge the nut into a suitable crevice in the bark, then hammer at the shell, breaking it open so they can extract the kernel. They will also store nuts, which they will eat when other food is in short supply. The bill is also useful as a tool for plastering over the entrance hole of their nest in the spring. The opening, just small enough to allow the adult birds to squeeze in and out, helps to protect them from predators. Eurasian nuthatches are most likely to be encountered in areas with broadleaved trees, as these provide food such as acorns and hazelnuts.

Distribution: Found throughout most of Europe, except for Ireland, northern England and Scotland. Also restricted to southern parts of Scandinavia. Occurs in northern Africa opposite the Strait of Gibraltar.
Size: 14cm (5¹/₂in).
Habitat: Gardens and parks with mature trees.
Nest: In a secluded spot.
Eggs: 6–9, white with heavy reddish-brown speckling.
Food: Invertebrates, nuts and seeds.

Identification: Bluish-grey upperparts from head to tail. Distinctive black stripes running from the base of the bill down the sides of the head, encompassing the eyes. Underparts vary in colour from white through to a rusty shade of buff, depending on the race. Dark reddish-brown vent area, more brightly coloured in cocks.

Willow warbler

Phylloscopus trochilus

Distribution: Occurs in the summer from the British Isles right across most of Europe. Overwinters in Africa.
Size: 12cm (5in).
Habitat: Wooded areas.
Nest: Dome-shaped, built on the ground.
Eggs: 6–7, pale pink with reddish spotting.
Food: Small invertebrates.

Identification: Greyish-green upperparts, with a pale yellowish streak running across each eye. Pale yellow throat and chest, with whitish underparts. The yellow plumage is much whiter in birds from more northern areas.

The subdued coloration of these small birds is so effective that, despite being one of Europe's most common species, willow warblers are very inconspicuous. Difficult to observe in their wooded habitat, it is their song, which heralds their arrival in woodland areas in early spring, that usually betrays their presence. In the British Isles, the willow species is the most numerous of all warblers, with a population estimated at around three million pairs. These warblers are typically resident in Europe between April and September. Their nest is hidden among the vegetation and features a low entry point. In late summer, willow warblers can often be seen in loose association with various tits, before they head off to their African wintering grounds.

Eurasian blackcap (*Sylvia atricapilla*): 15cm (6in)
Resident population is restricted to southern parts of the British Isles (including Ireland), France, the Iberian Peninsula and Italy; also north-western Africa. Jet black area on the crown, extending just above the eye and bordered by grey above the bill. Remainder of the head and breast is greyish. White plumage under the throat. Back, wings and underparts are olive-grey. Sexes are alike. Young birds have a reddish-brown cap.

Spotted flycatcher (*Muscicapa striata*): 15cm (6in)
Occurs throughout Europe during the summer, wintering in Africa. Greyish-brown upperparts, with darker streaking on the head extending to the whitish underparts. Area above the bill is also white. Relatively long wings and long, distinctive, square-tipped tail that can be spread to aid hovering. Bill, legs and feet are blackish. Sexes are alike. Young birds have dull yellowish markings extending from the head down over the wings, rump and tail.

Chattering cisticola (*Cisticola anonymus*) 12.5cm (5in)
This African warbler ranges from Nigeria west across Dem. Rep. Congo, and south as far as the Angolan border. Rufous crown, with a dark stripe from the base of the bill to the eyes, and a narrow dusky white area above and below, extending over the throat. Neck, back and wings are dark brownish. Slender, blackish bill, pinkish legs and feet. Sexes are alike, although cocks may be identified by their song.

Garden warbler

Sylvia borin

Rather dull coloration, coupled with their small size, ensures these warblers are relatively inconspicuous, particularly when darting among foliage. However, their attractive song and call notes may help identify them in the undergrowth. Garden warblers arrive on their breeding grounds from middle of April onwards, and construct a fairly large nest using a variety of plant matter, usually including stems of grass, and lining it with softer material. The hen sits alone through the incubation period, which lasts approximately 12 days, but subsequently both parents will seek food for their rapidly-growing brood. The young quickly leave the nest, sometimes when just 9 days old, and may be forced to scrabble among the vegetation to escape would-be predators until they are able to fly from danger. In more southern parts of their breeding range, pairs of garden warblers may produce two successive broods of chicks. They return to Africa in September.

Distribution: Summer range extends from Scandinavia southwards across virtually all of Europe. Migrates south for the winter, ranging over much of Africa except the Horn and the south-west.
Size: 14cm (5¹/₂in).
Habitat: Gardens with trees, also parks.
Nest: Made of vegetation.
Eggs: 4–5, buff with brown spots.
Food: Mainly invertebrates.

Identification: Olive-brown head and upperparts, with a greyish area present at each side of the neck. Underparts are greyish-white, buffer along the flanks. Bill and legs are dark greyish. Sexes are alike. Young birds similar to adults.

TITS

Thanks to their small size, most tits are most likely to be spotted in gardens during the winter months, when the absence of leaves on trees makes these birds more conspicuous. They are also more frequent visitors to bird feeders and tables during this period. Tits are very resourceful when seeking food, clearly displaying their aerobatic skills as they dart about, even feeding upside down.

Coal tit

Periparus ater

These tits are often to be seen in gardens feeding on bird tables, sometimes taking food which they will then store in a variety of locations, ranging from caches on the ground to suitable hollows in trees. The urge to store food in this way becomes strongest in the late summer and during the autumn, and helps the birds to maintain a food supply through the coldest months of the year. This hoarding strategy appears to be very successful, since coal tit populations rarely crash like many other small birds following a particularly harsh winter. In fact, these tits have increased their breeding range significantly over recent years, with their distribution now extending to various islands off the British coast, including the Isles of Scilly. During the winter, in their natural habitat of coniferous forest, they may form flocks comprised of many thousands of individuals, yet in gardens they are only usually seen in quite small numbers.

Identification: Jet black head, with white patches on the sides of the face and a similar area on the nape. Greyish-olive upperparts, with white wing bars, and brownish-white underparts, although some marked regional variations. Young birds have pale yellowish cheek patches. Sexes very similar, but the female's head markings may be duller. The bill is black. Legs are greyish.

Distribution: Resident throughout the whole of Europe, although absent from northern parts of Scandinavia. Range extends south to north-western parts of Africa, and spreads right across Asia to Japan.
Size: 11cm (4¹⁄₂in).
Habitat: Wooded areas.
Nest: Cup-shaped, made from vegetation.
Eggs: 8–11, white with reddish markings.
Food: Mostly invertebrates and seeds.

Great tit

Parus major

Distribution: Found through all of Europe except in parts of northern Scandinavia, and ranges south as far as northern Africa. Also extends widely across much of Asia.
Size: 14cm (5¹⁄₂in).
Habitat: Woodland.
Nest: Cup-shaped, made from vegetation.
Eggs: 5–12, white with reddish spotting.
Food: Invertebrates, seeds.

There is a marked difference in appearance between great tits throughout their wide range. They form groups after the breeding season, often associating with other small birds, foraging for food through woodland as well as visiting bird tables, where their bold, jaunty nature makes them conspicuous. Although they do not hoard food like some tits, they are able to lower their body temperature significant overnight when roosting, effectively lessening the amount of energy they need. Great tits become much more territorial at the start of the breeding season, which in Europe typically starts during March. They build their nest in a tree hollow, but readily use garden nestboxes where provided. Studies have shown that the male seeks out potential nesting sites within the pair's territory, but it is the female who has the final choice. Pairs may nest twice during the breeding period, which lasts until July.

Identification: Cock has a black head with white cheek patches. Broad band of black feathering extends down the centre of the body, with yellow plumage on either side. Wings are olive-green at the top, becoming bluish on the sides and on the flight feathers and tail. Hens are similar but display a narrower, uneven vertical black band. Young birds significantly paler overall, with yellowish cheeks and little of the vertical band seen in adults.

Blue tit

Eurasian blue tit *Cyanistes caeruleus*

Distribution: Throughout Europe except the far north of Scandinavia. Also present in north-western Africa.
Size: 12cm (5in).
Habitat: Wooded areas, parks and gardens.
Nest: Tree holes.
Eggs: 7–16, white with reddish-brown markings.
Food: Invertebrates, seeds and nuts.

A common visitor to bird tables, blue tits are lively, active birds by nature, and are welcomed by gardeners because they eat aphids. Their small size allows them to hop up the stems of thin plants and, hanging upside down, seek these pests under leaves. Blue tits are well-adapted to garden life and readily adopt nest boxes supplied for them. Their young leave the nest before they are able to fly properly, and are therefore vulnerable to predators such as cats. Those that do survive the critical early weeks can be easily distinguished by the presence of yellow rather than white cheek patches.

Identification: Has a distinctive blue crown edged with white, and a narrow black stripe running back through each eye. The cheeks are white. Underparts are yellowish, and the back is greyish-green. There is a whitish bar across the top of the blue wings. The tail is also blue. Sexes are similar but hens duller.

Mouse-coloured penduline tit (*Anthoscopus musculus*): 8cm (3in)
Restricted to north-eastern Africa, from Somalia and Djibouti to the border between Kenya and Tanzania. Olive-grey upperparts, with a darker streak running through the eye. Wings and tail greyer. Faint spotting on the forehead. Underparts whitish, becoming slightly brownish on the flanks. Short, pointed, blackish bill. Legs and feet also dark. Sexes alike. Young birds browner.

Marsh tit (*Poecile palustris*): 13cm (6in)
Widely distributed in a central band across Europe, but largely absent from the Iberian peninsula and much of Scandinavia, as well as areas of the British Isles. There is also a separate Asian population. Black cap extends right over the top of the head, and there is usually a small area of black plumage below the bill. Broad whitish area on the cheeks, while the back and wings are brown. The underparts are paler, being whitish in colour. Bill black, legs greyish. Young birds whiter on the underparts. Sexes are alike.

White-bellied tit (*Melaniparus albiventris*): 15cm (6in)
Scattered throughout Cameroon, western Africa, but occurs more consistently in the east, from Sudan southwards to Tanzania. Cock bird has black, slightly glossy plumage over the head, chest and back. A striking white bar extends down across each wing from the shoulders; adjacent feathers, including the flight feathers, and also the tail, are white. Underparts are also white. Bill, legs and feet are dark. Hens are similar, but more sooty-grey than black, with these areas being browner in young birds.

Southern grey tit

Melaniparus afer

These tits are most commonly observed in pairs, or larger family groups after the breeding season, which extends from August through until October. The nest is usually hidden in a tree but can be at ground level in a suitable bank, or even in buildings, with open pipework being especially favoured. The incubation period lasts approximately two weeks. It is thought that the young from a previous brood may assist the adults in rearing their chicks. Southern grey tits hunt a wide variety of invertebrates, including beetles and wasps, as well as various types of insect larvae. Their natural agility means they can obtain food upside down, holding themselves in position with their claws. Although they usually forage on their own they will occasionally join up with other birds, including various warblers, and this may make it easier for them to disturb and catch their prey.

Identification: Prominent jet black cap extending over the top of the head, and a broad black area extending down from the throat on to the breast. Upperparts are dark brown, while the underparts are a more buff shade. Sexes are similar, but hens have a much smaller area of black on the breast. Young birds are duller overall.

Distribution: Two distinct populations are present in southern Africa: one in South Africa, reaching southern parts of Namibia, the other in Namibia, extending into western Botswana.
Size: 13cm (5¼in).
Habitat: Open scrubland.
Nest: Cup-shaped, usually in a tree hole.
Eggs: 3–4, white with reddish markings.
Food: Mainly invertebrates.

FINCHES

By feeding mainly on seeds but adopting different feeding strategies, finches can exploit a wide variety of food sources without competing with each other. Goldfinches, for example, probe for and eat small seeds such as teasel, whereas the stout-billed hawfinch can crack tougher seeds such as cherry, exerting a force equivalent to 50kg (110lb) to reach the kernel within.

Chaffinch

Common chaffinch *Fringilla coelebs*

The behaviour of the chaffinch changes significantly during the year. These birds can be seen in groups during the winter, but at the onset of spring, and the breeding season, cock birds become very territorial, driving away any rivals. While resident chaffinches remain in gardens and similar settings throughout the year, large groups of migrants seeking refuge from harsh winter weather associate in large flocks in farmland areas. Chaffinches usually prefer to feed on the ground, hopping and walking along in search of seeds. They seek invertebrates almost exclusively for rearing their chicks.

Identification: Black band above the bill, with grey over the head and neck. Cheeks and underparts are pinkish. The back is brown, and there are two distinctive white wing bars. Cocks are less brightly coloured in winter plumage. Hens have dull grey cheek patches and dark greyish-green upperparts, while their underparts are a buff shade of greyish-white.

Distribution: Resident in the British Isles and western Europe, and a summer visitor to Scandinavia and eastern Europe. Also resident in the west of northern Africa and at the south-western tip.
Size: 16cm (6in).
Habitat: Woodland, parks and gardens.
Nest: Cup-shaped, usually in a tree fork.
Eggs: 4–5, light brown or blue with dark, very often smudgy, markings.
Food: Mostly seeds, but some invertebrates.

European goldfinch

Carduelis carduelis

The long, narrow bill of the goldfinch enables it to prise kernels out of seeds, and these birds often congregate in the winter to feed on stands of thistle heads and teasel. Alder cones are also a favoured food at this time of year. Goldfinches are very agile birds, capable of clinging on to narrow stems when feeding. They are social by nature, usually mixing in small flocks in areas where food is plentiful, although they are usually shy when feeding on the ground. They have a relatively loud, attractive, twittering song. Pairs usually prefer to build their nest in the fork of a tree rather than concealing it in a hedge.

Identification: Bright red face with black lores. Black area across the top of the crown that broadens to a collar on the neck. White extends around the throat, and a brown necklace separates the white on the throat from the paler underparts. Brown back and flanks, underparts otherwise white. The bill is narrow and pointed. Wings are black with white spotting and yellow barring. Tail is black with white markings. Hens display duller coloration with yellow less apparent.

Distribution: Occurs throughout much of the British Isles and mainland Europe, including Denmark but confined to the extreme south of Scandinavia. Also present in northern Africa.
Size: 13cm (5in).
Habitat: Woodland and more open areas.
Nest: Cup-shaped, made from vegetation.
Eggs: 5–6, bluish-white with darker markings.
Food: Mainly seeds, but some invertebrates.

Syrian serin (*Serinus syriacus*): 13cm (6in)
Occurs north-eastern Africa, and eastern Mediterranean.
Cock displays a band of deep yellow plumage above the
bill, encircling the eyes and also on the throat. Ear
coverts and top of the head are greyish, as are the
flanks. Remainder of the underparts have a yellowish
suffusion. Bill greyish, legs and feet pinkish-grey. Hens
are less colourful on the head, with definite streaking on
the grey of the flanks and back. Young birds are pale buff
rather than grey.

Common linnet (*Linaria cannabina*): 14cm (5¹⁄₂in)
Resident throughout western Europe and in parts of
north-western Africa. Summer resident in north-eastern
Europe, but absent from much of Scandinavia. Grey
head with a red crown. Back and wings are brown. The
sides of the chest are red, becoming paler on the flanks
with a white area on the breast. Hens are much duller
with a short grey bill.

Common redpoll (*Acanthis flammea*): 14cm (5¹⁄₂in)
Occurs in northern Europe, including Iceland, moving
further south in the winter. Crimson-red cap and black
lores contrast with the yellowish bill. The brownish
upperparts are quite streaked. Red chest fades to white
on the steaked abdomen. White wing bar. Hens are
similar but lack the red on the chest.

Common rosefinch (*Carpodacus erythrinus*): 15cm (6in)
Now breeding as far west as southern Scandinavia.
Cock has a deep pinkish-red head, breast and rump.
Lower underparts are whitish. The lores and area behind
the eyes are brown, as are the wings and tail. Dark
stocky bill, pinkish-brown legs and feet. Hens are
brownish overall, with streaking on the head and back,
and on the underparts. Young birds resemble hens, but
are a warmer olive brown in colour.

European greenfinch

Chloris chloris

Greenfinches have quite stout bills
that enable them to easily crack open
tough seed casings to reach the edible
kernels inside. These birds are most
likely to be observed in areas where
there are trees and bushes, which
provide nesting cover. In the winter,
European greenfinches visit bird
tables, readily taking peanuts as well
as foraging in gardens. Groups of
greenfinches are also sighted in more
open areas of countryside, such as
farmland, searching for weed seeds
and grains that may have
been dropped during
harvesting. Pairs will
often nest two or
three times in
succession during the
summer, and when there
are chicks in the nest the
birds consume invertebrates
in much larger quantities.

Identification: Greenish head, with greyer
areas on the sides of the face and wings.
Yellowish-green breast, with yellow also
evident on the flight feathers. Relatively
large, conical bill. Hen is duller, with
greyer tone overall, brownish mantle
and less yellow on the wings.

Distribution: Throughout
Europe and much of northern
Africa, but absent from more
northern parts of Scandinavia.
Size: 16cm (6in).
Habitat: Edges of woodland
and more open areas.
Nest: Bulky, cup-shaped.
Eggs: 4–6, whitish to pale
blue with darker markings.
Food: Largely seeds and
some invertebrates.

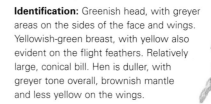

European serin

Serinus serinus

Although mainly confined to relatively southerly latitudes,
these serins are occasionally seen in the British Isles and
have even bred successfully in southern England. It
appears that serins are slowly extending their northerly
distribution, with ornithological records revealing they
had spread to central Europe by 1875 and had
started to colonize France within another 50
years. Serins often seek out stands of conifers,
where they nest, although they also frequent
citrus groves further south in their range.
Young birds differ from adults in that they
are predominantly brown and lack any
yellow in their plumage.

Identification: Bright yellow forehead extends
to a stripe above each eye, encircling the
cheeks and joining with the yellow breast. Back
is yellow and streaked with brown, as are the white flanks.
Hens are duller in coloration, with a pale yellow rump.

Distribution: Resident in
coastal areas of France
south through the Iberian
Peninsula to northern Africa
and around the northern
Mediterranean area. A
summer visitor elsewhere
in mainland Europe.
Size: 12cm (5in).
Habitat: Parks and gardens.
Nest: Cup-shaped, in a tree.
Eggs: 3–5, pale blue with
darker markings.
Food: Mostly seeds and
some invertebrates.

WAXBILLS AND MANNIKINS

Occurring in Africa rather than Europe, these finches are highly social by nature. They often associate in relatively large flocks, especially in agricultural areas, where they may inflict considerable damage on millet crops. Waxbills are so called because the red coloration of their bills resembles sealing wax. They are also more colourful overall than mannikins (which are sometimes called munias).

Orange-breasted waxbill

Golden-breasted waxbill, zebra waxbill *Amandava subflava*

The striped patterning on the sides of their bodies explain why this species is also known as the zebra waxbill. They are the smallest of all waxbills and have a very confiding nature. They can be observed in areas near reedbeds, since these provide the birds with roosting and breeding sites. Occasionally though, and particularly in southern areas, the waxbills will take over abandoned nests constructed by birds such as the southern red bishop (*Euplectes orix*). In open country they are more likely to construct their own nests, usually near the ground. Breeding coincides with the end of the rainy season, commencing in January in South Africa, and pairs often rear two broods. Invertebrates feature more prominently in their diet at this stage. The chicks can fledge just 2½ weeks after hatching.

Identification: Cock bird has a bright red eye stripe, and yellowish underparts becoming decidedly orange on the breast. Darker greenish-grey barring on the flanks corresponds to the coloration of the upperparts. Rump reddish. Hens lack the red eye stripe and the orange on the underparts. Young birds are very plain, greenish-grey with more yellowish underparts and dark bills.

Distribution: Extends from Senegal in western Africa across to Sudan and Ethiopia in the east, and from here south across much of central Africa down to the eastern side of South Africa.
Size: 10cm (4in).
Habitat: Grasslands, fields.
Nest: Large domed structure made from grass.
Eggs: 4–6, white.
Food: Mostly small seeds, but also invertebrates.

St Helena waxbill

Common waxbill *Estrilda astrild*

A highly adaptable species, these waxbills are commonly encountered not only in Africa but also in other parts of the world, including the island of St Helena, where they have been introduced. Populations are also established on the islands of Rodriquez, Seychelles and Reunion, close to Africa, as well as places further afield such as Hawaii and Brazil. St Helena waxbills are most likely to be observed in flocks in areas where there are relatively tall grasses, although they rarely stray far from water. Grass seeds feature prominently in their diet, and the birds can be seen grasping on to the stems and feeding from the ripening seedheads. They often roost alongside each other. While in proximity to people, whether in gardens or villages, they can become quite tame.

Distribution: Occurs across much of Africa from a line south of the Sahara, although is absent from the more heavily-forested areas
Size: 12cm (4½in).
Habitat: Grassland, gardens.
Nest: Bulky, pear-shaped structure made from grass.
Eggs: 4–8, pink.
Food: Seeds, invertebrates.

Identification: Grey forehead and prominent red eye stripes. Chest is pale. The wings are dark grey and barred, with heavy barring also on the underparts, including the flanks. Displays faint red markings in the centre of the abdomen. Sexes are alike.

Orange-cheeked waxbill (*Estrilda melpoda*): 10cm (4in)
From Senegal in western Africa down to the Dem. Rep. Congo, Angola and Zambia. Large orange cheek patches. The surrounding plumage is greyish but the head is darker. Wings are chestnut brown. The rump is reddish. Sexes are generally alike, although hens may be slightly paler than the cock.

African silverbill (*Euodice cantans*): 10cm (4in)
Extends in a broad band across Africa south of the Sahara, from Mauritania in western Africa eastwards to Somalia and Tanzania. Also ranges further east, from Saudi Arabia to Oman. The top of the head is dark brown, continuing down over the back and wings. The chest and cheeks are pale buff, becoming darker on the abdomen. Silvery bill and black rump. Sexes are similar, but hens may be a little smaller.

Madagascan mannikin (*Lepidopygia nana*): 10cm (4in)
Present only on Madagascar, often in the vicinity of villages. Black stripe extends from the bill to the lores. Black bib. Rest of the head is greyish with blackish speckling, merging into the brown of the back and wings. Underparts pinkish-buff with darker speckling, evident also on the rump. Tail is dark. The bill is black above and greyish below. Legs and feet are pinkish. Young birds are brown above, paler brown below. Bill is dark. Sexes are alike.

Magpie mannikin

Lonchura fringilloides

Mannikins as a group are relatively dull in colour, with black, brown and white mostly predominating in their plumage. The magpie mannikin is no different in this respect from Asiatic members of the group. It lives in small flocks, but is not especially common through much of its range when compared to other African mannikins overlapping its area of distribution. Tall grasses, reeds and bamboos are all favoured for roosting, feeding and breeding, whether in close proximity to people or further afield. Magpie mannikins prefer to feed on ripening seeds, and use their spindly claws to anchor themselves to narrow stems.

Distribution: Ranges from Senegal in western Africa eastwards across to Kenya, and down as far as Angola in the west; also to South Africa in the east.
Size: 13cm (5in).
Habitat: Grassland and woodland clearings.
Nest: Ball of dried grass and similar material.
Eggs: 5–6, white.
Food: Seeds, invertebrates.

Identification: Head is a glossy bluish-black, with a powerful, conical greyish-black bill. The underparts are entirely white except for black and brown barring on the flanks. Back and wings are dark brown, broken by some lighter markings, especially on the back. Rump and tail are black. Sexes are alike.

Bronze mannikin

Lonchura cucullata

These mannikins are common throughout their extensive range, living in flocks and often being sighted in the company of other related species. They are opportunistic breeders, with pairs nesting several times each year under favourable conditions. The social structure of the group appears to be reinforced by nest-building activity, in which most members of the flock participate. The birds may construct a fresh nest for communal roosting almost on a daily basis, using sprigs of dry grass and similar material. Although the sexes are identical in appearance, males are easily recognisable by the way in which they bob and display to females, as well as by their singing, during which performance the male may sometimes twist his body round towards his intended mate. He will also initiate nest building although this task will ultimately be taken over by his partner. The bulky nest constructed for breeding is typically comprised of more than 600 separate strands of grass, and is lined inside with feathers.

Identification: Dark brown head. Purplish suffusion on the upper chest, becoming a lighter shade of brown over the back and wings. The underparts are white with individual dark metallic green markings on the flanks, and a more prominent greenish patch at the top of each wing. Bill greyish, darker on the upper mandible. Legs black. Young birds brownish, with paler underparts and a dark grey bill. Sexes are alike.

Distribution: Has a similar range to magpie mannikin. Distribution extends through much of central Africa, from Senegal in the west across to Ethiopia in the east, though not as far as the coast, and down as far as Angola and eastern South Africa.
Size: 10cm (4in).
Habitat: Open countryside.
Nest: Domed-shaped, made from grass.
Eggs: 4–8, white.
Food: Mainly seeds, but some invertebrates.

SPARROWS AND OTHER SEED-EATERS

A variety of sparrows are to be found across Africa. The majority can be easily identified by the predominance of brown, black and grey tones in their plumage, although there are exceptions, typified by the golden sparrows, so called due to the appearance of the cock birds. Yet other small seed-eaters are brightly coloured too, for example the cordon-bleus.

Abyssinian waxbill

Estrilda ochrogaster

These waxbills used to be grouped with the fawn-breasted waxbill (*E. paludicola*), but are now regarded as a separate species, occurring at the northern end of the particular species' range. They are most commonly observed in pairs or small flocks, seeking food on the ground, sometimes in the company of other waxbills. They construct a typically bulky nest of grasses, with a false entry point above to deter would-be predators, who see the nest is apparently empty, while the true nest is concealed below, with the entry point beneath. Although they subsist on seeds for most of the year, insects become much more significant in their diet when they are rearing their chicks, providing the necessary protein to sustain their rapid growth. The young may leave the nest by the time they are two weeks of age, and will generally breed themselves in the following year. Waxbills are relatively short-lived, with a typical average life expectancy of just two or three years.

Identification: Distinctive yellowish-brown coloration extends from the sides of the face over the entire underparts, with a slight pinkish hue around the vent. Darker on the top of the head, becoming browner over the back and wings. The rump is reddish and the tail is black. Bill red, legs and feet black. Hens are similar but without any pink on the belly. Young birds have a white throat, and are paler on the underparts, with a black bill.

Distribution: Restricted to the highlands extending from the Baro River to the Boma hills of eastern Sudan, extending to Ethiopia in north-eastern Africa.
Size: 11.5cm (4^1/$_2$in).
Habitat: Grassland and swamps.
Nest: Made of grasses.
Eggs: 4–6, pinkish.
Food: Seeds, some insects.

Cape sparrow

Passer melanurus

Like others of its kind, the Cape sparrow has proved to be a highly adaptable species. These birds are often to be found close to people, and can be frequent visitors to bird tables. As with the house sparrow (*P. domesticus*), the bill of the cock bird is black only for the duration the nesting period, being brown like the hen's for the remainder of the year. Pairs may sometimes nest communally, in trees or even deserted buildings, but where they choose to establish their own territories the cock bird actively seeks to drive away any would-be rivals. The nest itself is a bulky, untidy pile of vegetation, which may incorporate torn strips of paper and other rubbish, with an entry point near the top. When the young chicks hatch the adult birds raise them largely on invertebrates, until they fledge at about three weeks old. After the breeding season, pairs join together into flocks numbering as many as 200 individuals.

Distribution: Southern Africa, reaching up to Angola in the west and Zimbabwe in the east.
Size: 15cm (6in).
Habitat: Scrubland and more open country.
Nest: Bulky, domed mass of vegetation and other material.
Eggs: 2–5, greenish-white with darker markings.
Food: Invertebrates and seeds, also a regular visitor to bird tables.

Identification: Cock bird has a black face, crown and chest, with a silvery area behind the eyes forming a collar. Underparts pale brownish-grey. Prominent chestnut area at the top of the wings, with a white band below and similar edging on the wing coverts. The back is dark brown, as are the flight feathers. Bill is black, legs and feet dark grey. Hens are similar, but with much duller facial coloration. Young birds are similar to hens.

Tree sparrow (*Passer montanus*): 14cm (5¹/₂in)
Present in Europe except for northern Scandinavia, western England, northern Scotland and central Ireland. Top of the head is reddish-brown. Black bib beneath the bill. White area on the cheeks below the eyes extends back around the neck and is broken by central black patches. Grey chest. The wings are light brown and black, broken by a white wing bar edged by black. Sexes are alike.

Black-crowned waxbill (Blackcap waxbill, *Estrilda nonnula*): 12cm (4¹/₂in)
From Nigeria to Sudan and south to Dem. Rep. Congo in the west and Tanzania in the east. Black cap. Upperparts white, except for red on the flanks. Greyish back and wings with fine barring. Red rump and black tail. Bill reddish with dark markings. Black legs. Hens greyish-brown, with reduced red on the flanks. Young birds are buffer overall, with black bills.

Blue-breasted cordon-bleu (Blue waxbill, *Uraeginthus angolensis*): 13cm (5in)
Rep. Congo east to southern Kenya, south to Angola, Botswana, Zambia and Zimbabwe, extending to northern Namibia and to Natal and neighbouring parts of South Africa. Sky blue plumage from the bill down over the sides of the face and chest to the flanks. Upperparts and wings dark brown. Sky blue tail. Lighter fawn from the centre of the abdomen to the vent. Bill blackish, legs and feet pinkish. Blue plumage is restricted to the breast in hens. Young birds resemble hens, with paler blue coloration.

Golden song sparrow

Sudan golden sparrrow *Passer luteus*

In spite of their name, these birds are not talented songsters, uttering little more than a series of chirping notes, even during the breeding season. Cocks undergo an unusual change at this time, however, as their bills are transformed from a pinkish shade to black. The depth of their yellow coloration can also vary, in some cases being paler, often reflecting slight regional variations. Although golden song sparrows tend not to feed in towns, they frequently roost there in large flocks. They are often nomadic when not breeding, with flocks typically of more than 100 birds wandering widely in search of favourable conditions. They breed communally too, and the young are reared primarily on invertebrates.

Identification:
Yellow head and underparts. Chestnut-coloured feathering runs over the back and wings, merging with black. Hens are a dull brown and have paler, more buff-coloured underparts.

Distribution: Extends in a broad band from Mauritania in western Africa eastwards right across the continent to northern parts of Sudan and Ethiopia.
Size: 13cm (5in).
Habitat: Scrub, cropland and urban areas.
Nest: Bulky.
Eggs: 3–6, off-white with darker irregular markings.
Food: Seeds and some invertebrates.

Red-cheeked cordon-bleu

Uraeginthus bengalus

Distribution: Ranges across Africa south of the Sahara Desert, extending to eastern Angola, Zambia and southern parts of the Dem. Rep. Congo. Also thought to be in existence on the Cape Verde Islands.
Size: 13cm (5in).
Habitat: Villages, gardens and grasslands.
Nest: Bulky, usually an oval or spherical structure.
Eggs: 4–5, white.
Food: Seeds, invertebrates.

The depth of this species' sky blue coloration varies through its range, particularly among males. These colourful finches have adapted well to the spread of human settlement, and can often be sighted in villages. They seek their food primarily on the ground, hopping along in search of seeds as well as invertebrates, which are used to feed chicks in the nest. These so-called blue waxbills are also sufficiently agile to catch flying ants. Pairs are relatively solitary when nesting, but once the breeding season is over they will reunite to form quite large flocks. The red-cheeked cordon-bleu's natural environment is open country, and although they may wander through their range they are unlikely to be encountered in the more densely forested areas.

Identification: Greyish-brown plumage extends from the top of the bill down over the back and wings. The plumage from around the eyes down on to the chest and flanks is sky blue, and the abdomen is light buff. Sexes are similar, except hens lack the dark red ear coverts and have less blue on their underparts.

BULLFINCHES, CANARIES AND BULBULS

While bullfinches are birds of northern climates, canaries as a group have a more southern range, reaching right to the tip of Africa. Caged canaries are of course known for their attractive song, the result of a domestication process that began about 500 years ago. Although less well known, bulbuls are also talented songsters and are common garden visitors in Africa.

Common bullfinch

Eurasian bullfinch *Pyrrhula pyrrhula*

Distribution: Ranges widely across Europe, except the far north of Scandinavia and the southern half of the Iberian Peninsula, and extending eastwards through Asia. Also present on the Azores.
Size: 16cm (6¼in).
Habitat: Woodland areas.
Nest: Cup-shaped, made from vegetation.
Eggs: 4–6, greenish-blue with dark brownish markings.
Food: Seeds, invertebrates

These birds are unmistakable thanks to their stocky appearance and the bright pink coloration of the males. They are often seen in gardens but may also be encountered in woodland. Bullfinches are regarded as a potential pest by fruit farmers since they will eat the emerging buds in the early spring. Tree seeds, such as those of ash and beech, form a significant part of their diet in the winter, and they can also be beneficial to farmers by eating a range of invertebrates, particularly when rearing their young. Breeding starts from mid-April onwards, with a pair constructing their nest using twigs and lining the interior with softer material. The hen sits alone, with incubation lasting 14 days, after which both adults feed their growing brood. The chicks leave the nest when about 2½ weeks old.

Identification: Cock has a black face and top to the head, with deep rosy-pink underparts, lighter around the vent. Grey back, black wings and tail with a white area on the rump. The bill, legs and feet are all black. Hen is similar but with brownish rather than pink underparts. Young birds lack the black cap seen in hens, and show brownish coloration on the wing coverts.

Canary

Atlantic canary, Island canary *Serinus canaria*

These small and relatively plain finches are the original ancestors of the millions of domestic canaries now kept throughout the world by bird-fanciers. Domestication has affected not just the canary's appearance but also its singing prowess. Wild canaries lack their domestic counterparts' vocal range, but the song of the cock bird is still most likely to be heard through the breeding period, from spring onwards. They are often observed in open country, sometimes associating in large flocks during the winter alongside *Linaria* species, such as linnets (*L. cannabina*). The hen constructs a tidy nest using a variety of vegetation, usually choosing a location in a tree or bush, and incubates the eggs on her own for two weeks. She may not begin sitting immediately, which effectively extends the incubation period of those eggs laid first. This results in the chicks hatching closer together, improving the chances of survival of the youngest.

Identification: Yellowish sides to the face extending to the throat, and also on the rump and the lower underparts, merging into greyer plumage especially on the chest. Head is greyish with streaking, which becomes more prominent over the wings. Hens are similar but less yellow. Young birds are browner.

Distribution: Restricted to the western Canary Islands, off the north-west coast of Africa, Madeira and the Azores. Also introduced to the islands of Bermuda, Puerto Rico and Midway, part of the Hawaiian group.
Size: 12.5cm (5in).
Habitat: Open country.
Nest: Cup-shaped, made from vegetation.
Eggs: 3–5, bluish with reddish-brown markings.
Food: Mainly seeds.

Common bulbul

Pycnonotus barbatus

Common bulbuls range widely over much of the continent, and the southern population is sometimes recognized as a separate species (known as the dark-capped bulbul, *P. tricolor*) thanks to its yellow undertail coverts. They are noisy birds, congregating in groups as dusk falls and calling loudly to each other, although they do not form true flocks. They are agile in flight, able to catch flying insects, and may also venture on to lawns to search for invertebrates. Fruit also figures prominently in their diet, and they can cause serious damage in fruit-growing areas. Their nests sometimes attract the attentions of Jacobin cuckoo (*Clamator jacobinus*), which adds an egg alongside those of the bulbuls. Instead of throwing out the eggs or young chicks the cuckoo chick suffocates its companions, and, with calls mimicing theirs, the intruder is reared by its foster parents.

Identification: Relatively dull brown coloration, darker on the head and becoming paler on the underparts, with white undertail coverts. Back and wings are brown. Sexes alike. Young birds may have shorter tail feathers.

Distribution: Ranges in a broad band across Africa, south of the Sahara, widely distributed throughout western Africa south as far as Rep. Congo. In the east, extends from Egypt down as far as South Africa. Also present in north-west Africa.
Size: 22cm (8¹/₂in).
Habitat: Areas with trees.
Nest: Cup-shaped, made from vegetation.
Eggs: 2–4, pinkish-white with darker markings.
Food: Fruit and invertebrates.

Black-headed canary (*Serinus alario*): 15cm (6in)
Namibia, Botswana and South Africa. Cock has a black head and chest (broken by white in *S. a. leucolaemus*), with a white area around the nape extending over the underparts. Brownish and black markings on the flanks. Back and tail are chestnut. Black flight feathers. Hens are greyish on the head, with streaking extending back over the head. Underparts paler, with chestnut and black areas on the wings. Young birds similar to hens, but paler with streaking on the underparts.

Cape canary (*Serinus canicollis*): 12cm (5in)
Sporadic, parts of eastern Africa to South Africa, with a population in central Angola. Cock has yellowish-green underparts with a greyish crown and mantle. Some races are more yellow than others. Hens have prominent streaking on their head and back, with duller underparts. Young birds have more prominent streaking overall, with less yellow coloration.

African citril (*Crithagra citrinelloides*): 12cm (4³/₄in)
From Ethiopia south to Zimbabwe and northern Mozambique. Cock has a black mask around the bill, encompassing the eyes. The underparts are otherwise yellowish, with slight streaking on the flanks. Yellow streak above each eye, upperparts otherwise greenish with darker streaking and two narrow yellow wing bars. Hens much duller, with prominent streaking on the underparts. Young birds resemble hens but are greyer, with brownish-buff rather than yellow wing bars.

African red-eyed bulbul

Pycnonotus nigricans

Bold and lively birds, with a small crest on their heads, which is usually raised when singing. They often sing from a conspicuous branch soon after sunrise, making them easy to observe. They are not easily intimidated, even by predators such as smaller birds of prey, which they may mob. Breeding is from September to March, with the nest located in a tree and protected by thorns, as high as 3.65m (12ft). The female incubates alone and the chicks hatch after about 12 days, leaving the nest after a similar interval. Red-eyed bulbuls feed mainly off the ground, seeking insects such as grasshoppers, particularly when chicks are being reared, as well as plucking fruits and berries off the branches. They will also probe flowers for nectar, but can easily be attracted to bird tables.

Distribution: Present in south-western Africa. Occurs through Namibia and in Botswana and South Africa, extending north as far as southern Angola
Size: 21cm (8in).
Habitat: Open country.
Nest: Cup-shaped, made from vegetation.
Eggs: 3, pinkish-white with darker markings.
Food: Fruit, invertebrates.

Identification: Black head. Bare red skin encircles the eyes. Dark brown back and wings. Upper breast greyish-brown, underparts turning whitish. Undertail coverts yellow. Bill, legs and feet black. Young have a paler eye ring. Sexes alike.

SMALL INSECT-EATERS AND MOUSEBIRDS

The presence of neighbouring trees greatly increases the variety of birds likely to be spotted in a garden. Shrubs, too, can be of benefit, providing cover, food and nesting opportunities. Many avian visitors are relatively small in size, but they can be quite bold by nature, as shown by the chiffchaff and the various sunbirds that can be encountered in these surroundings.

Chiffchaff

Phylloscopus collybita

The chiffchaff is a lively warbler, generally common through its range and often seen in gardens, particularly those with trees nearby. There are regional differences in appearance, with individuals found in western and central areas having brighter yellow coloration than those birds occurring further north and east. Its unusual name reflects its common two-note song pattern. Pairs are likely to start nesting from April onwards, with the female building the nest on her own. This is positioned relatively close to the ground in a suitable bush or shrub that provides good cover, typically an evergreen such as rhododendron, or sometimes in among brambles, offering protection against predators. The chiffchaffs slip in and out of the nest itself via a side entrance. The hen undertakes the incubation on her own, and this lasts for about 13 days, with the young chicks subsequently fledging after a similar interval. Chiffchaffs may rear two broods during the course of the summer.

Identification: Yellowish stripe above each eye, with a black stripe passing through the centre. Underparts whitish, with variable yellow on the sides of the face and flanks. Rest of the upperparts dark brownish-green. Pointed bill is dark. Legs and feet are black. Sexes are alike.

Distribution: Occurs through most of Europe during the summer but absent from parts of northern Scandinavia and Scotland. Resident in parts of southern Britain and Ireland and further south, near the Mediterranean. Overwinters in northern Africa and south of the Sahara. Also found in Asia.
Size: 12cm (4in).
Habitat: Wooded areas.
Nest: Dome-shaped, made from vegetation.
Eggs: 6, white in colour with brownish spotting.
Food: Invertebrates.

Goldcrest

Regulus regulus

These warblers are the smallest birds in Europe and are surprisingly bold, drawing attention to themselves with their high-pitched calls and the way they jerkily flit from branch to branch. They can be easily distinguished from the slightly larger firecrest (*R. ignicapilla*) by the absence of a white streak above the eyes. Goldcrests associate in groups both of their own kind and also with other small birds such as tits, seeking food relatively high up in the branches rather than at ground level. Pairs split off to breed in the early spring, with both sexes collecting moss and other material to construct their nest. This may be hung off a conifer branch, up to 12m (40ft) off the ground, although it may also be concealed among ivy or similar vegetation. Cobwebs act as thread to anchor the nest together, and the interior is lined with feathers. The young will have fledged by three weeks old, and the adults may nest again soon afterwards and rear a second brood.

Distribution: Resident through much of Europe, except for northern Scotland and northern Scandinavia, where pairs spend the summer. Often moves south to the Mediterranean for the winter. Range also extends eastwards into Asia.
Size: 8.5cm (3¹/₄in).
Habitat: Wooded areas.
Nest: Suspended basket made of moss.
Eggs: 7–8, buffy-white with brown markings.
Food: Mainly invertebrates.

Identification: Dumpy appearance, with cock birds having an orange streak (yellow in hens) running down the centre of the head, bordered by black stripes on each side. Prominent area of white encircling the eyes, with much of the rest of the head pale grey. White wing bars. The plumage on the back is greyish-green. Underparts are paler in colour. Bill is black, legs and feet greyish. Young birds have greyish heads and pale bills.

Eastern double-collared sunbird

Cinnyris mediocris

There are a number different species of double-collared sunbird, and their distributions overlap. For this reason it can be difficult to tell them apart, though much depends on the altitude at which sightings are made. The eastern double-collared sunbird is seen only at relatively high altitudes, above 1,500m (5,000ft), hence it is quite locally distributed through its range. Like other sunbirds, this species allows a relatively close approach when feeding, especially in flower gardens, which they visit regularly. Red flowers hold a particular attraction for them, especially the blooms of red hot pokers (*Kniphofia* species), which are native to Africa.

Identification: Iridescent green plumage on the head, chest and back. The rump is blue. Lower chest is scarlet, with yellow edging of longer feathers (known as pectoral tufts). Remainder of the underparts are olive. Wings and tail black. Bill is relatively short and narrow, curving down at its tip. Hens are a dusky shade of olive-green overall.

Distribution: Eastern side of Africa, ranging through parts of Kenya and Tanzania southwards into Malawi and Zambia.
Size: 10cm (4in).
Habitat: Forest and gardens.
Nest: Bulky, built off a branch.
Eggs: 2.
Food: Mostly nectar and small invertebrates.

Scarlet-chested sunbird (*Chalcomitra senegalensis*): 15cm (6in)
Widely distributed through western Africa, ranging from Senegal and The Gambia eastwards to Cameroon and the Central African Republic. Iridescent green crown and chin, with scarlet-red plumage on the throat and breast. Remainder of the plumage is blackish-brown, often a lighter shade on the wings. Hens are duller, having a mottled dark brown throat with yellowish underparts, and brown elsewhere.

White-backed mousebird (*Colius colius*): 33cm (13in)
Restricted to southern Africa, with a range extending from Namibia and Botswana down to western parts of South Africa. Predominantly ashy-grey in colour over the head and back. The rump area is maroon and the underparts are more of a buffy shade. Rufous on the breast. A distinctive white stripe runs down the back. The bill is grey with a black tip. Sexes are alike. Young birds display more evenly-spread buff colouring on their underparts.

Red-faced cisticola (*Cisticola erythrops*): 13cm (5½in)
These African warblers have a wide distribution in western parts of the continent, and are also present on the eastern side, extending here down as far as northern parts of South Africa. Orange-brown facial coloration, with a brown crown, back and wings. More of an olive-grey shade in the summer, compared with the winter plumage. The underparts are a creamy shade, and the flanks are browner. Young birds resemble adults in winter plumage, but have a more yellowish suffusion. The upper bill is dark, yellower beneath, and the legs and feet are pinkish-grey. Sexes are alike, but cocks are slightly larger in size.

Red-faced mousebird

Urocolius indicus

Occurring only in Africa, mousebirds take their name not only from their coloration and narrow tails but also from the way they move through vegetation, climbing in a similar fashion to mice. Yet they can also fly strongly, in a straight line rather than the undulating flight pattern of many birds. Typical representatives of their group, red-faced mousebirds are highly social by nature and usually observed in groups consisting of up to 10 individuals. They will often come down to the ground in order to dust bathe, which helps to keep their plumage in good condition and free from parasites. Unfortunately, the young are not as agile as the adults. They will leave the nest when about 17 days old, before they are able to fly properly, and will often fall straight to the ground. Unable to clamber back up to the nest, they face starvation. The number of chicks that are reared successfully by these mousebirds is correspondingly low, with just one in four on average surviving to become independent.

Distribution: Confined to southern parts of Africa, extending up the coast of Angola in the west. An isolated population exists along the coast of Mozambique, extending as far as Tanzania.
Size: 33cm (13in).
Habitat: Prefers relatively open country.
Nest: Cup-shaped, made from vegetation.
Eggs: 3–5, whitish-coloured with red markings.
Food: Largely berries and other fruit.

Identification: Prominent red area of skin around the eyes, extending to the top of the bill. Brownish-grey overall, with a greenish suffusion. Crest on the head. Long tail feathers. Sexes are alike. Young birds have greener colouring on the face.

PIGEONS AND DOVES

The columbiformes have adapted well to living in close association with people, although their presence is frequently unwelcome. Large flocks of feral pigeons can cause serious damage to buildings in urban areas, not just with their droppings but also by pecking at the mortar, which is a source of calcium. Their adaptability is demonstrated by their readiness to breed throughout much of the year.

Mourning collared dove

African mourning dove *Streptopelia decipiens*

Identification: Greyish top to the head and broad back collar edged with a narrow band of white on the back of the neck. Pinkish breast, lighter on the underparts. Sandy-brown upperparts, with dark flight feathers. Bill black, legs and feet red. Sexes are alike. Young birds dull overall, with evident pinkish suffusion on the underparts.

The long mournful coos of this dove help to explain its common name. Its range has increased over recent years, thanks to more widespread irrigation in agricultural areas, as it tends to stray no more than about 10km (6¹/4 miles) from water.

Although roosting together in relatively large groups, these doves tend to split up into small parties to forage for food on the ground. They will eat a variety of seeds as well as fruit, and they may also eat termites. The availability of suitable foods in agricultural areas, where crops such as millet are being grown, means that they are becoming more numerous in these places. Pairs tend to nest individually, however, often choosing garden trees, or thornbushes which afford protection against would-be predators. The nest itself is often a more stable structure than that built by related species. Both members of the pair take turns at incubating, with the chicks hatching after a period of two weeks.

Distribution: Ranges widely across Africa in a band to the south of the Sahara. Also extends down through eastern and central areas of the continent, with a separate population on the border between Angola and Namibia.
Size: 28cm (11in).
Habitat: Open country, usually close to water.
Nest: Platform of twigs in trees or thorn bushes.
Eggs: 2, white.
Food: Largely seeds, but also fruit and termites.

Wood pigeon

Columba palumbus

Distribution: Throughout most of Europe except for northern Scandinavia and Iceland, ranging eastwards into Asia. Also present in north-western Africa.
Size: 43cm (17in).
Habitat: Areas with tall trees.
Nest: Platform of twigs.
Eggs: 2, white.
Food: Seeds, plant matter and invertebrates.

Identification: Grey head, with a reflective metallic-green area at the nape of the neck and characteristic white patches on the sides. Bill is reddish at the base, becoming yellow towards the top. Purplish breast becoming paler on the underparts. Tip of tail is black. White edging to the wings most evident in flight, forming a distinct band. Sexes alike.

These pigeons can be significant agricultural pests in arable farming areas. In towns they will often frequent parks with established stands of trees, descending into nearby gardens and allotments to raid growing crops. However, they also occasionally eat potential crop pests such as snails. Pairs sometimes nest on buildings, although they usually prefer a suitable tree fork. Their calls are surprisingly loud and are often uttered soon after dawn. Outside the breeding season these birds will often congregate in large numbers. If danger threatens, they can appear quite clumsy when taking off thanks to their relatively large size.

Collared dove

Streptopelia decaocto

The westerly spread of these doves during the second half of the 20th century was one of the most dramatic examples of the changing patterns of distribution among bird species. In this case, the triggers for the distribution change are unclear. Collared doves had been recorded in Hungary in the 1930s, and they moved rapidly over the next decade across Austria and Germany to France, and also headed north to the Netherlands and Denmark. The species was first sighted in eastern England during 1952, and a pair bred there three years later. The earliest Irish record was reported in 1959, and by the mid-1960s the collared dove had colonized almost all of the UK. No other bird species has spread so far and so rapidly in recent times, to the extent that the collared dove's range now extends right across Europe and Asia.

Above: The collared dove is a frequent visitor to towns and will happily build its nest on the roof tops.

Identification: Pale greyish-fawn with a narrow black half-collar around the back of the neck. Dark flight feathers, with white along the leading edges of the wings. White tips to tail feathers, visible when spread. Depth of individual coloration can vary. Sexes are alike.

Distribution: Across much of Europe but not including the far north of Scandinavia and the Alps, ranging eastwards into Asia. More localized on the Iberian Peninsula and in northern Africa particularly.
Size: 34cm (13in).
Habitat: Parks and gardens.
Nest: Platform of twigs.
Eggs: 2, white.
Food: Mostly eats seeds and plant matter.

Laughing dove

Spilopelia senegalensis

These very adaptable doves are often seen in urban habitats, particularly in areas where they are expanding their range. In Australia, for example, bird-table offerings have afforded them a constant supply of suitable food, allowing them to become established here well away from their natural range. In northern Africa, these doves are frequently encountered near oases, which has led to them becoming known as palm doves. Their fast breeding cycle, with chicks hatching and leaving the nest within a month of the eggs being laid, means that they can rapidly increase their numbers under favourable conditions. Pairs may also attempt to breed throughout much of the year, rather than having a prescribed breeding period like most bird species, particularly those occurring outside the tropics.

Distribution: Ranges widely throughout most of Africa, both north and south of the Sahara Desert, although is absent from western-central parts. Also extends through the Middle East into Asia. Has been introduced to Western Australia.
Size: 26cm (10in).
Habitat: Acacia woodland, oases and open country.
Nest: Loose platform made from twigs.
Eggs: 2, white.
Food: Mainly seeds and invertebrates.

Identification: Reddish-brown, with a brown-and-black speckled collar under the neck. Grey bar on the leading edges of the wings. Underparts are pale. Long, relatively dark tail. Sexes are alike.

Stock pigeon (Stock dove, *Columba oenas*): 32cm (12¹/₂in)
Throughout Europe, but absent from much of Scotland, northern Scandinavia and most of the mountainous central region. Range extends to north-western Africa and east to Asia. Grey head with green iridescence on the neck. The wings are dark grey with black markings. Black band across the tips of the tail feathers. Pale grey rump and lower underparts. The chest is pinkish-grey.

European turtle dove (*Streptopelia turtur*): 27cm (10¹/₂in)
Much of Europe but not common in Ireland, Scotland or Scandinavia. Present in northern Africa. More brightly coloured on the wings than its East Asian cousin, having orange-brown feathers with darker centres. Black-and-white barring on the sides of the neck. Head is greyish. Underparts are pale with a slight pinkish hue. White edge to the tail feathers.

Cape dove (Namaqua dove, *Oena capensis*): 26cm (10in)
Found in Africa south of the Sahara, including Madagascar. Also present in southern Israel and Arabia. Black area from the forehead down on to the chest, with bluish-grey behind. Long, narrow tail. Dark flight feathers and black markings on the wings, with rufous underwing areas. Upperparts are light grey, whiter on the underparts. Hens lack the black area on the face, displaying only a narrow stripe extending from the bill to the eye.

STARLINGS

Starlings are well represented in Europe and Africa, although they display greater diversity on the latter continent. Generally quite distinctive, sometimes with spectacular plumage, many starlings, including even the common starling, have an attractive metallic iridescence which gives them a sleek, attractive appearance that changes according to the light.

Pied starling

Lamprotornis bicolor

Identification: Predominantly black overall, with a little gloss on the plumage. White area on the lower underparts in the vicinity of the vent. Iris whitish. Bill dark above, with yellow on the lower bill, legs and feet blackish. Sexes are alike. Young birds display no trace of gloss on their plumage, and have dark irises. The bill also tends to be darker.

These starlings are often seen in agricultural areas, where they are generally welcomed for eating locusts and other harmful invertebrates such as caterpillars, as well as removing parasites from cattle. However, they may also sometimes feed on ripening crops of grapes and other fruits. They are highly adaptable birds, even scavenging on beaches in some areas, and are not averse to feeding on road-kill on occasion either. Congregating in small flocks, they often breed co-operatively, with a pair being assisted by others of their own kind in obtaining food to rear their nestlings. It may be that these are young birds from an earlier round, which remain as helpers, as they are generally immature birds. In spite of this attention at the nest site, however, both greater honeyguides (*Indicator indicator*) and great spotted cuckoos (*Clamator glandarius*) frequently manage to parasitize their nests. African pied starlings have been recorded nesting in a wide range of covered localities, even breeding well offshore in a wrecked ship.

Distribution: Confined to South Africa, being present here throughout the country, with the exception of the east and the north-west.
Size: 25cm (10in).
Habitat: Grassland.
Nest: Tunnels of river banks.
Eggs: 2–6, blue-green, sometimes spotted red.
Food: Mainly insects such as locusts and cattle parasites, other invertebrates, some seeds and fruits.

Spotless starling

Sturnus unicolor

Pairs of spotless starlings may breed close to people, beneath roof tiles or in a suitable hole in a wall. They may also adopt nest cavities constructed by other birds, such as European green woodpeckers (*Picus viridis*). The nest is built from dried grasses and other items including yellow flowers, and both members of the pair collect material to line the chamber. Spotless starlings seek food on the ground and in trees and bushes. Small amphibians such as young frogs may be eaten, and during the breeding period earthworms and caterpillars feature more prominently. In autumn and winter, fruits and seeds are eaten, and they may cause damage to ripening crops such as grapes. At this time of year they are more likely to be observed in mixed flocks with common starlings (*Sturnus vulgaris*), with roosts numbering as many as 100,000 individuals.

Identification: Predominantly glossy black with long feathers on the throat when in breeding plumage. In the winter, fine white spotting is evident over the head and extending down on to the chest. Bill is yellow, becoming darker in the winter, when the plumage is greyer overall. Young birds are relatively dark brown overall. Hens resemble cocks in breeding plumage, but have shorter neck feathers and less iridescence.

Distribution: Ranges through the Iberian Peninsula and adjacent areas of northern Africa. Also found on the Mediterranean islands of Sicily, Corsica and Sardinia.
Size: 22cm (8¹/₂in).
Habitat: Open woodland.
Nest: Hole or cavity lined with vegetation.
Eggs: 2–9, pale blue.
Food: Invertebrates and fruit.

Purple glossy starling

Lamprotornis purpureus

Like many of its relatives, the purple glossy starling is a very adaptable bird, able to feed both in trees and on the ground. They will descend to search for food in the aftermath of a grassland fire, and have even been known to grab invertebrates that are retreating from the flames. Although the starlings' traditional nest site is a tree hole, they have adapted to nesting under the roofs of buildings and may even use drainpipes. The hen incubates alone, but the cock bird helps to rear the chicks, which are fed mainly on invertebrates in the early stages after hatching. Invertebrates in the diet help to meet the chicks' need for protein in order to grow rapidly. Outside the breeding season in particular, these starlings can be seen in large groups, made up of as many as several thousand individuals. In such numbers, they readily drive off solitary birds of prey which are drawn to the colony.

Identification: Upperparts are bluish-green. Sides of the face and the underparts are a deep purple. Iridescence is most marked on the wings and in the vicinity of the neck. Tail feathers are purple. Iris is bright yellow in adults, but grey in young birds. Sexes are alike.

Distribution: Extends across Africa south of the Sahara, from Senegal in the west eastwards to parts of Sudan, Kenya and Uganda.
Size: 27cm (10¹/₂in).
Habitat: Light woodland and parkland areas.
Nest: Sticks in a tree hole.
Eggs: 3–4, blue-green with darker markings.
Food: Invertebrates, also fruit and berries.

Cape glossy starling (*Lamprotornis nitens*): 10in (25cm)
Extends across most of Angola and southern Zaire southwards through Namibia, and across Zimbabwe, Botswana and southern Mozambique to the southern coast of Africa. Glossy blue-green shade over most of the body, with a glossier blue on the back of the head which may appear blackish in shaded areas. Bright orange-yellow iris. Bill, legs and feet black. Young birds have little gloss on their feathers and dark irides.

White-crowned starling (*Lamprotornis albicapillus*): 23cm (9in)
Present in eastern Africa, ranging from northern parts of Kenya up into southern Ethiopia and western Somalia. Prominent whitish cap extends right across the top of the head. Back and wings are bronzy-black, with white evident on the flight feathers. Underparts are dark grey with white streaking, and the lower underparts are white. Iris is yellow. Bill, legs and feet are black. Sexes are alike. Young birds are duller, with greyish-white plumage on the crown and dark irides.

Red-winged starling (*Onychognathus morio*): 30cm (12in)
Widely distributed through East Africa, from eastern Sudan and Ethiopia right down to the southern tip of South Africa. Cock bird is metallic black overall, with black bill, legs and feet. Flight feathers are reddish and the iris is red. Hens have greyish coloration over the head, nape and upper chest. Young birds resemble adult males but have dark irides and are less glossy overall.

Superb starling

Lamprotornis superbus

Like other birds from this part of Africa, superb starlings roost quietly during the heat of the day, which means they are hard to spot in spite of their bright coloration. They are most easily observed either early in the morning or late in the afternoon, often near water. Superb starlings have recognized that tourists are a likely source of food, so in some areas they will frequent safari camps. Few birds are more adaptable when it comes to selecting a nest site. Pairs may build in the thatched roofs of village huts or take over the nests of weaver birds, often with the addition of thorny branches around the entrance hole to give protection from predators while the nest is occupied.

Identification: Glossy black head merging into shiny blue nape and breast. Distinctive white band extends across breast. Belly is chestnut, and vent and undertail coverts are white. Wings are metallic bluish-green. Pale yellowish-white iris. Sexes are alike.

Distribution: Occurs on the eastern side of Africa, from northern Ethiopia southwards to Kenya, Somalia, western Uganda and Tanzania.
Size: 18cm (7in).
Habitat: Open country.
Nest: Variable, self-built or lines a tree hole.
Eggs: 4, dark blue.
Food: Invertebrates, fruits and berries.

THRUSHES

Although overall not brightly coloured, some members of this group are excellent songsters. Their long, powerful bills enable them to prey on a range of invertebrates, and they also feed on berries and fruit. Some thrushes are migratory, either moving within Europe or flying further afield when the weather becomes unfavourable, often descending in large numbers.

Robin

European robin *Erithacus rubecula*

The robin's colourful appearance belies its strong aggressive streak, for these birds are highly territorial. In the garden, robins can become very tame, regularly hopping down alongside the gardener's fork or spade to snatch invertebrates such as earthworms that come to the surface. Young, recently-fledged robins look very different from mature individuals – they are almost entirely brown, with dense spotting on the head and chest. Robins are not musical birds, and their calls consist largely of a tick-like note which is often drawn-out and repeated, particularly when they are alarmed by the presence of a nearby predator such as a cat. Since robins usually feed on the ground, they can be very vulnerable to these predators.

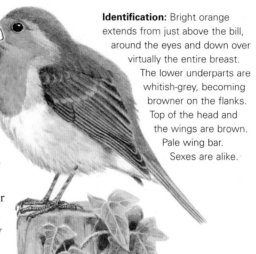

Identification: Bright orange extends from just above the bill, around the eyes and down over virtually the entire breast. The lower underparts are whitish-grey, becoming browner on the flanks. Top of the head and the wings are brown. Pale wing bar. Sexes are alike.

Distribution: Resident in the British Isles, western Europe and parts of northern Africa. Scandinavian and eastern European populations winter further south.
Size: 14cm (5½in).
Habitat: Gardens, parks and woodland areas.
Nest: Under cover, often near the ground.
Eggs: 5–7, bluish-white with red markings.
Food: Invertebrates, berries, fruit and seeds.

Song thrush

Turdus philomelos

Identification: Brown back and wings, with some black areas evident, and a yellow-buff area across the chest. Dark markings that extend over the chest and abdomen are shaped like arrows, rather than circular. Sexes are alike. Young birds have smaller spots, which are likely to be less numerous on their underparts.

The song of these thrushes is both powerful and musical. It can be heard particularly in the spring at the start of the breeding season, and is usually uttered from a relatively high branch. Song thrushes are welcomed by gardeners as they readily hunt and eat snails and other pests on the ground. Having grabbed a snail, the birds choose a special site known as an anvil where they smash it against a rock to break the shell and dislodge the mollusc within. These thrushes are excellent runners, and this allows them to pursue quarry such as leatherjackets (the larvae of certain species of crane fly, *Tipula* species). When breeding, song thrushes build a typical cup-shaped nest, which the hen is mainly or even solely responsible for constructing.

Distribution: Ranges widely throughout the whole of Europe. Eastern populations head to the Mediterranean region for the winter. Also present in northern Africa, even as far south as the Sudan.
Size: 22cm (8½in).
Habitat: Woodland areas, parks and gardens.
Nest: Cup-shaped.
Eggs: 5–6, greenish-blue with reddish-brown markings.
Food: Invertebrates, berries.

Common blackbird

Turdus merula

Blackbirds frequently descend on lawns to search for invertebrates. Earthworms, which feature prominently in their diet, are most likely to be drawn to the surface after rain, and slugs and snails also emerge in wet conditions. In the 19th century, blackbirds were rarely seen in gardens, but today they have become commonplace. They are quite vocal and have a variety of calls. Cocks are talented songsters, and both sexes will utter an urgent, harsh alarm call. Although blackbirds do not associate in flocks, pairs can be seen foraging together. As with other thrushes, their tails are surprisingly flexible and can be raised or lowered at will. It is not unusual to see pied blackbirds, with variable amounts of white among the black plumage. The majority of these birds, especially those with the most extensive white areas, are cocks.

Identification: Jet black plumage contrasts with the bright yellow bill, which becomes a deeper yellow during the winter. Hens are drab in comparison, brownish overall with some streaking, notably on the breast, and have a darker bill.

Left: The hen alone is usually responsible for incubating the eggs, although very occasionally the cock may share the task.

Distribution: Resident throughout virtually the whole of Europe, except the far north of Scandinavia. Also present in northern Africa. The majority of Scandinavian and eastern European populations are migratory.
Size: 29cm (11½in).
Habitat: Woodland, gardens and parkland.
Nest: Cup-shaped, hidden in a bush or tree.
Eggs: 3–5, greenish-blue with reddish-brown markings.
Food: Invertebrates, fruit and berries.

Karoo thrush (*Turdus smithi*): 22cm (9in)
Occurs in much of South Africa, apart from the east and southern coastal areas. Greyish-brown overall, darker over the wings and lighter on the underparts. Throat displays black rows of spots, but is otherwise whitish. A restricted area of rufous coloration is evident on the belly. The bill is yellowish, becoming redder at the tip. Legs and feet are pinkish. Sexes are alike. Young tend to display black spotting on their underparts, and red speckling on their upperparts.

Mistle thrush (*Turdus viscivorus*): 29cm (11½in)
Resident throughout most of western Europe south to northern Africa. Breeds as far north as Scandinavia and also further east. Relatively large thrush. White underparts, often smudged with an area of grey on the upper breast, and displaying a variable black spotted patterning. Pale sides to the head. Back and wings are grey. Sexes are alike.

Fieldfare (*Turdus pilaris*): 27cm (10½in)
Occurs in central parts of Europe, overwintering in the British Isles and south to the northern Mediterranean. White eye stripe and grey on the sides of the head. Brown band joins the wings across the back. The rump is grey. Rusty-yellow band across the breast with darker markings, especially on the flanks. Underparts otherwise white. Sexes are alike.

Common nightingale

Luscinia megarhynchos

The arrival of the common nightingale in Europe is seen as heralding the start of spring. However, these birds are often difficult to spot, since they utter their musical calls towards dusk and even after dark on moonlit nights. Their relatively large eyes indicate that these members of the thrush family are crepuscular, becoming active around dusk. Their drab, subdued coloration enables them to blend easily into the dense shrubbery or woodland vegetation that they favour. The common nightingale is only present in Europe from April to September, when it breeds, before it once again heads back to Africa for the winter.

Identification: Brown plumage extends from above the bill down over the back of the head and wings, becoming reddish-brown on the rump and tail. A sandy-buff area extends across the breast, while the lower underparts are whitish. The large eyes are dark and highlighted by a light eye ring. Sexes are alike.

Distribution: From southern England and mainland Europe on a similar latitude south to north-western Africa. Over-winters further south in Africa.
Size: 16cm (6in).
Habitat: Woodlands, gardens.
Nest: Cup-shaped.
Eggs: 4–5, greyish-green to reddish-buff.
Food: Mainly invertebrates.

GARDEN PREDATORS

A diverse range of birds may be encountered in the confines of a garden, preying on invertebrates and other vertebrates. Their hunting strategies may vary but they are all to some extent opportunistic, adapting to the prevailing conditions and the availability of food. The same applies to their breeding habits, with a number of these species often nesting in buildings.

European green woodpecker

Picus viridis

Distribution: Range extends across most of Europe, although absent from much of Scandinavia, Ireland, Scotland and various islands in the Mediterranean. Also present in parts of north-western Africa.
Size: 33cm (13in).
Habitat: Open woodland.
Nest: Tree hole.
Eggs: 5–8, white.
Food: Mainly invertebrates.

Unlike many of its kind, green woodpeckers hunt for food mainly on the ground, using their powerful bills and long tongues to break open ants' nests. They are equally equipped to prey on earthworms, which are drawn to the surface of lawns after rain, and may catch small creatures such as lizards. In the autumn, fruit forms a more significant part of their diet, but they avoid seeds, and so are not drawn to bird feeders. Pairing begins during the winter, with excavation of the nesting chamber taking two weeks to a month to complete. Unlike many woodpeckers they do not drum loudly with their bills to advertise their presence, but pairs can be quite vocal. Incubation is shared, with the hen sitting during the day. Hatching takes just over a fortnight, with the young fledging when a month old.

Identification: Red crown, with red below the eyes and blackish in between. Regional variations. Underparts greyish to green. Back and wings darker green, with yellow spotting. Yellowish rump. Hens often have black rather than red stripes below the eyes. Young are heavily spotted and barred, with a greyer crown.

Little owl

Athene noctua

Little owls can be seen resting during the daytime, on telegraph poles and similar perches in the open. Introduced to Britain in the 1800s, they have since spread right across southern England. They hover in flight, but are rather ungainly when walking on the ground. One factor which has assisted their spread is their adaptability in choosing a nest site – disused factories and even rabbit warrens may be used. The hen sits alone for the incubation, which lasts 24 days. Both adults feed the young, who fledge after five weeks. They will be independent within a further two months.

Identification: White spotting on the head, white above the eyes and a whitish moustache. Heavy brown streaking on a white chest. Larger whiter spots on the wings, barring on the flight feathers and banding across the tail. Whitish legs and feet. Bill yellowish, irides yellow. Sexes alike, but hens usually larger. Young lack white spotting on the forehead.

Distribution: Range extends from southern Britain and throughout most of Europe at a similar latitude (not as far as Scandinavia) eastwards into Asia. Also present in northern parts of Africa, extending to parts of the Middle East.
Size: 25cm (10in).
Habitat: Prefers relatively open country.
Nest: Tree hole or a cliff hole.
Eggs: 3–5, white.
Food: Invertebrates and small vertebrates.

Thick-billed raven (*Corvus crassirostris*): 64cm (25in)
Restricted largely to the highland areas of Ethiopia. An unmistakable corvid – the largest member of the family – which is predominantly glossy black in colour, except for a small white patch at the back of the head. The glossy sheen is most marked over the back and wings. The black bill is greatly enlarged, with a raised ridge running down the centre of the curved upper bill. The bill also has a paler tip. Legs and feet are black. Sexes are alike, but cocks are slightly larger. Young birds have a slightly browner hue to their plumage.

Bokmakierie (*Telophorus zeylonus*): 22.5cm (9in)
This bush shrike ranges from the western coast of southern Angola, spreading out across southern Namibia and into South Africa. Isolated population exists in eastern Zimbabwe. Greyish head and neck, with a yellow stripe above the eyes and a black area beneath, which extends downwards to form a bib on the lower chest. Upper chest is bright yellow, with the remainder of the underparts orangish-yellow. Greyish on the flanks. Back, wings and tail are olive-green. Sexes are alike. Young birds lack black markings.

Rock kestrel (*Falco rupicolus*): 33cm (13in)
Restricted to southern Africa, extending north as far as Tanzania, although absent from much of the eastern coast. Cock birds have a greyish head with a yellowish throat. The wings are brown with black markings, and the flight feathers are black. The rump is grey, as is the tail, which is barred with black markings and ends in a white tip. Underparts are paler and more rufous than the wings, with variable black markings. White undersides of the wings display grey markings. Hens have more heavily barred tails. Young birds have rufous heads.

Jackdaw

Western jackdaw *Coloeus monedula*

These corvids are very adaptable birds, just as likely to be seen foraging on rubbish dumps as visiting garden bird tables. When ants swarm on warm summer days, they are sufficiently agile to catch these flying insects on the wing. In agricultural areas, jackdaws soon learn to pull ticks off the backs of grazing animals such as sheep, as well as stealing their wool, which they use to line their nests. Pairs rarely nest in the open, however, preferring instead the relative security of an enclosed area, often utilising buildings or even chimneys or church steeples. The hen incubates the eggs alone, and hatching takes place after about 19 days. The young chicks are ready to leave the nest after a further five weeks. Relatively social at all times, jackdaws will often associate in large groups during the winter months, not infrequently being seen in the company of rooks (*Corvus frugilegus*) in agricultural areas. Jackdaws are also to be found in coastal areas, and will even breed on cliffs.

Distribution: Resident throughout virtually the whole of Europe, although absent from large parts of Scandinavia. Range extends eastwards into Asia. Also occurs in various parts of north-western Africa.
Size: 39cm (15$\frac{1}{4}$in).
Habitat: Prefers relatively open country.
Nest: Made from sticks, sited in a hole.
Eggs: 3–8, pale bluish-green with darker markings.
Food: Omnivorous.

Identification: Glossy blackish overall, darker on the crown, around the eyes and down on to the throat. Back of the head and neck are lighter, almost silvery, depending on the race. Black bill, legs and feet. Distinctive pale bluish irides. Young birds have blackish irides and darker, less glossy feathering.

Magpie

Eurasian magpie *Pica pica*

Bold and garrulous, magpies are a common sight throughout much of their wide range. They are often blamed for the decline of songbirds because of their habit of raiding the nests of other birds. Magpies are usually seen in small groups, although pairs will nest on their own. If a predator such as a cat ventures close to the nest there will be a considerable commotion, and the nesting magpies will be joined by others in the neighbourhood to harry the unfortunate feline. Magpies sometimes take an equally direct approach when seeking food, chasing other birds – gulls in particular – to make them drop their food. Magpies are quite agile when walking, holding their long tails up as they move.

Identification: Black head, upper breast, back, rump and tail, with a broad white patch around the abdomen. Broad white wing stripe and dark blue areas evident below on folded wings. Depending on the light, there may be a green gloss to the black plumage. Sexes are alike, but the cock may have a longer tail.

Distribution: Virtually the whole of Europe south to north Africa. Present in parts of Asia and North America.
Size: 51cm (20in).
Habitat: Open and lightly wooded areas.
Nest: Dome-shaped stick pile.
Eggs: 2–8, bluish-green with darker markings.
Food: Omnivorous.

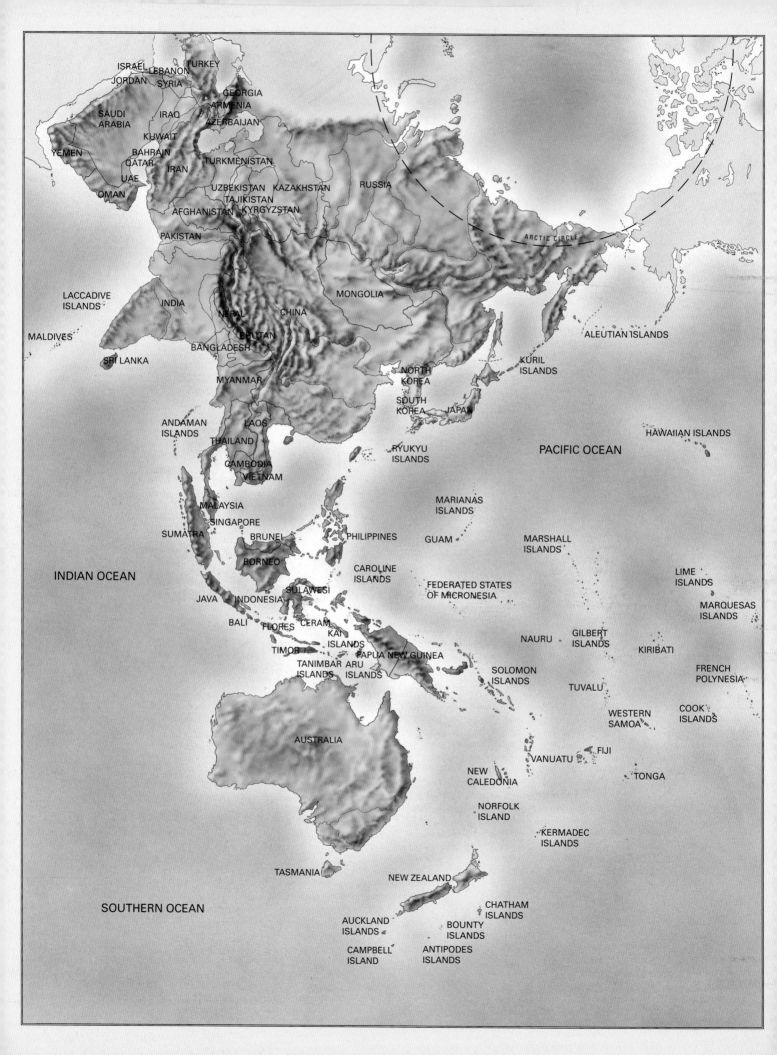

BIRDS OF ASIA, AUSTRALIA AND NEW ZEALAND

Nowhere else in the world is there such a striking division between avian distributions as there is in this region. Although some of the birds occurring on the Asiatic mainland are also present further west in Europe, avian distributions found off the coast of the former are less likely to range as widely. Many of the species that inhabit the islands to the east and south for instance, such as cockatoos, are restricted to this region, and do not occur on the mainland. There can be seasonal movements to some of these islands, however, with birds migrating southwards in Asia. The avifauna of New Zealand is particularly unusual, as birds have evolved here in the absence of mammalian predators over the course of many millions of years. While the giant moas – once the dominant avian group – are now extinct, a number of other bizarre birds, such as the flightless kiwi, are still to be found on these islands.

Above from left: Rainbow lorikeet (Trichoglossus moluccanus), *yellow-crested cockatoo* (Cacatua sulphurea), *great hornbill* (Buceros bicornis).

OCEAN WANDERERS

Many of the seabirds found in Asiatic and Australian waters have a wide distribution, which can be pan-global, often extending around the southern oceans and sometimes even further afield. Birds such as albatrosses are well adapted to spending virtually their entire lives on the wing, even to the extent of scooping their food from the surface of the sea and sleeping on the wing as they glide.

Red-tailed tropicbird

Phaethon rubricauda

This species spends longer over the open ocean than the other two species of tropicbird, and ringing studies have shown that they may travel huge distances in some parts of their range, with Hawaiian birds recorded some 5,000km (3,125 miles) away from where they were banded. They catch their prey by diving into the sea from a height of up to 50m (164ft) and they are also agile enough to catch flying fish in the air. The breeding season is variable through their range, with cliff-top sites being preferred, where the birds will be relatively safe from predators. It takes about six weeks for the chick to hatch, and a further three months before fledging occurs.

Above: Nesting birds try to find a safe concealed locality.

Identification: Distinguishable from other tropicbirds by red tail streamers. Also paler, being predominantly white with hints of black on the outer flight feathers and adjacent to the rump. Black stripe extends through each eye. Bill red, legs and feet dark. Sexes are alike. Young birds have blackish bills and lack the streamers, which can measure up to 35cm (14in) long.

Distribution: Ranges from the south-eastern coast of Africa, south of the Equator to Australia, apart from the southern coast, then extending northwards up to the Asian coast down to the south Pacific, close to the coast of South America.
Size: 80cm (31 1/2in).
Habitat: Open sea.
Nest: Under a rocky crevice, or sheltered locality.
Eggs: 1, pinkish with darker markings.
Food: Mainly fish.

Masked booby

Blue-faced booby *Sula dactylatra*

Distribution: This bird is pan-tropical – both north and south of the Equator – as it is found right around northern Australia.
Size: 92cm (36in).
Habitat: Sea.
Nest: On the ground or on a cliff top.
Eggs: 2, bluish white.
Food: Mainly fish.

Island habitats are favoured by the masked booby, allowing these birds to fly long distances out over the sea in search of prey, stopping off to rest on the islands as they do so. They catch fish by plunging into the middle of a shoal, swimming well underwater to achieve a catch. Apart from fish, other marine creatures, such as squid, feature less prominently in their diet. They live in colonies and individuals may sometimes be badly harried by frigatebirds (*Fregata* species), which rob the masked boobies of their catch before they reach land. They lay their eggs on bare rock, and although two chicks may hatch, only one is likely to be reared successfully, unless food is freely available.

Identification: Large, white head, back and underparts. Dark areas around the eyes and the base of the bill. Black areas on the wings are apparent at rest and in flight. Tail feathers are black. The bill is yellowish in cock birds and greenish in hens. Legs and feet are greyish.

Wilson's storm petrel (*Oceanites oceanicus*): 19cm (7¹/₂in)
Extends from Antarctica throughout the southern oceans into northern latitudes. Brownish overall, with a prominent white rump. Paler buff barring on the upper and underwing coverts. Sexes alike.

Sooty albatross (*Phoebetria fusca*): 89cm (35in)
Ranges across oceans from the west coast of Tasmania westwards almost as far as the Falkland Islands. A distinctive uniform shade of sooty black with a black bill. Its wings are long and pointed. Tail feathers are long and wedge-shaped. Sexes alike.

Fairy prion (*Pachyptila turtur*): 28cm (11in)
Found in three separate colonies in the southern oceans: one extends from south-east Australia to New Zealand. Grey crown, wings and back with white underparts and a dark tip to the tail. Blackish patterning across the wings. Sexes alike.

Streaked shearwater (white-fronted shearwater, *Calonectris leucomelas*): 48cm (19in)
Extends from eastern Asia from the Ryuku Islands and north-eastern Japan to Korea. Migrates south to Australia via New Guinea. Whitish underparts. Brown mottling on the sides of the head. Brown edging to the undersides of the wings. Upperparts are brown. Bill is silvery grey. Sexes alike.

Southern giant petrel

Macronectes giganteus

These aerial giants, with a wingspan of more than 2m (78in) and weighing as much as 5kg (11lb), can cover huge distances over the oceans around the southern hemisphere. They feed on the carcasses of marine mammals, such as seals, left on the shoreline, as well as dead seabirds. They may be sighted close to trawlers, seeking offal and fish thrown overboard, which they scoop up from the sea's surface. These petrels nest on grassy islands in colonies of up to 300 pairs. The single chick develops slowly and may not fledge until it is nearly 20 weeks old. It is unlikely to breed for the first time until it is seven years old.

Identification: Brownish overall although darker on the lower underparts towards the vent. Paler greyish-brown head and neck. Bill yellow. The white morph of this species displays odd speckled brownish feathering on a white background. Hens smaller.

Distribution: Circumpolar in the southern ocean, occurring off the southern half of the Australian coastline and right around New Zealand.
Size: 99cm (39in).
Habitat: Sea.
Nest: Grassy mound or pile of stones.
Eggs: 1, white.
Food: Carrion.

Wandering albatross

Snowy albatross *Diomedea exulans*

Distribution: The range is circumpolar, extending from southern parts of Australia and New Zealand southwards. Also occurs on numerous smaller islands, such as Antipodes Island, all south-east of New Zealand.
Size: 135cm (53in).
Habitat: Sea.
Nest: Piles of mud and grass.
Eggs: 1, white with reddish-brown speckling.
Food: Mainly squid, but also fish, crustaceans and carrion.

As their name suggests, these albatrosses range widely over the southern oceans, often following ships and scavenging on galley scraps thrown overboard. They are also active hunters, however, scooping squid from the sea after dark, when these cephalopods come closer to the surface. Pairs separate at the end of the breeding period, but then some will reunite later on the breeding grounds. They breed only every second year because it takes nearly 40 weeks for a newly hatched chick to grow large enough to leave the nest.

Identification: Predominantly white. Black areas over much of the wings, although the areas closest to the body have only a black edging. There is often a pinkish area near the ear coverts, and there may be a greyish area on the crown. Bill is pink with a yellowish, hooked tip. Hens are slightly smaller, and may display a light greyish band around the chest and black on the edges of the tail feathers.

PENGUINS, PELICANS AND OTHER COASTAL BIRDS

Although these birds are not closely related, they all depend on the marine environment for food in the form of fish or marine invertebrates. While some groups, such as plovers, have a broad distribution around the world, penguins in particular are confined to relatively cold areas of the southern hemisphere.

Fiordland penguin

Eudyptes pachyrhynchus

Distribution: Ranges from the south-eastern coast of Australia around the shores of Tasmania, eastwards on around the coast of New Zealand.
Size: 70cm (27½in).
Habitat: Sea., but nesting in rainforest.
Nest: Scrape under bushes, well concealed.
Eggs: 2, bluish-white.
Food: Small fish and cephalopods.

These penguins remain at sea throughout the year, apart from when they are nesting. They return to their traditional sites for this purpose in June, and lay soon afterwards. They do not frequent coastal areas like many penguins at this stage, however, but head instead to nearby areas of rainforest, where the hen lays either in the roots of an old tree, or a similarly well-hidden locality. Although they nest colonially, the nests of the Victoria penguin are well-spaced in this type of terrain. Both birds share the task of incubation, each one sitting for periods of up to 13 days before being relieved by their partner. It takes approximately five weeks for the eggs to hatch, and then, once they are a month old, the young penguins are shepherded together to form a crèche. They are relatively slow to develop, and will not be ready to make their way to the sea until they are about 10 weeks old. The colony then splits up until the following breeding season, with the young themselves not being mature until they are at least five years old.

Identification: Black on the crown, with golden feathering extending from the base of the bill above each eye. Brownish ear coverts, with white speckling on the cheeks below the eyes. Remainder of the upperparts are black, with white below. Stocky red bill, pinkish feet. Sexes are alike but hens are smaller. Young birds have brown bills, less evident golden feathering above the eyes.

Spot-billed pelican

Grey pelican *Pelecanus philippensis*

This particular species is thought to be the rarest member of the pelican family and its range is now greatly reduced. Indeed, it is extinct in the Philippines despite also being known as the Philippine pelican. The use of pesticides may have contributed to this decline, along with habitat changes. These large birds weigh about 5kg (11lb) and need to catch roughly a fifth of their body weight in food every day, so easy access to food is imperative to their survival. Widespread destruction of forests is also believed to have had an adverse effect on their numbers, as these pelicans require large trees in which to build their nests.

Above: These pelicans fish by trawling the water with their bills.

Identification: Predominantly a silvery-grey colour. Darker over the wings. A short, brownish crest extends down the neck. The bill and pouch are pinkish with darker blotching. Greyish legs and feet. Sexes are alike.

Distribution: South-east India and Sri Lanka east to Myanmar (Burma) and south-eastern parts of China. Overwinters further south reaching Sumatra and Java.
Size: 150cm (59in).
Habitat: Ranges from coastal bays to lakes.
Nest: Made of vegetation.
Eggs: 2–3, chalky white.
Food: Fish.

Lesser frigatebird

Fregata ariel

These frigatebirds are the smallest members of the family. They are well-adapted to their oceanic lifestyle, being able to catch fish close to the surface of the sea in flight, and they can even seize flying fish above the waves. Pairs breed in colonies on remote islands, often in mangrove areas, where they construct their nests in trees up to 15m (49ft) from the ground. In some treeless areas, however, they nest further inland on the ground. The breeding cycle is very long, with incubation taking 45 days. It may then be six months before the young fledge, and they remain dependent on their parents for a similar interval. This means that pairs breed only every second year. The Pacific population remains healthy, however, with over 15,000 pairs nesting on islands in the vicinity of Australia.

Identification: Cock birds black with sheens of green and purple. Small areas of white on sides of body when wings are closed. Red gular pouch under the chin. Bill black, legs and feet red. Hens lack the pouch, have a broad white area across the body from chest to abdomen, light-edged wing panels and a red bill.

Distribution: Ranges widely through the Indian Ocean, from east coast of Africa through the Indo-Pacific region and out into the central Pacific. Separate, rarer population on a similar latitude in the southern Atlantic, off the eastern coast of South America.
Size: 80cm (31½in).
Habitat: Open sea, breeding on islands.
Nest: Platform of sticks.
Eggs: 1, chalky white.
Food: Largely fish and squid.

Royal penguin (*Eudyptes schlegeli*): 76cm (30in)
Distribution centred on Mocker Island, south of New Zealand and Campbell Island. Sometimes found on the southern coast of New Zealand. Crested, but with a distinctive white face. Black plumage on the crown, back and wings. Underparts are white. Has a greyish band across the throat. Hens smaller, with a less robust bill.

King penguin (*Aptenodytes patagonicus*): 95cm (37in)
This penguin is almost circumpolar, breeding on sub-Antarctic and Antarctic islands. Has a black head with a relatively narrow orange collar around the side of the head. Upperparts are greyish. On the upper chest, underparts are white with an orange suffusion. Long bill which is pale red near the base of the lower mandible. Sexes are alike. These large penguins weigh up to 15kg (33lb).

Little penguin (Fairy penguin, *Eudyptula minor*): 45cm (18in)
Found on southern coasts of Australia, extending from Perth and east to Tasmania, New Zealand and the Chatham Islands. Has dark greyish-black upperparts and white underparts. Dull pinkish black bill. Pink feet. Sexes alike. Weighing barely 1kg (2.2lb), this is the smallest of the penguins.

Crab-plover (*Dromas ardeola*): 40cm (16in)
Confined to the Indian Ocean coastline. White body with areas of black feathering on the top and edges of the wing. Legs are greyish. Large, heavy, blackish bill is used for crushing crabs. Sexes alike. It is the only wader that nests in underground tunnels over 1.5m (5ft) in length.

Milky stork

Mycteria cinerea (E)

The name of these storks originates from the milky white shade of their plumage when they are in breeding condition. Milky storks have become much rarer through their range for a variety of reasons, which include habitat destruction. In Vietnam, the widespread use of defoliant chemicals in mangrove swamps during the Vietnam War is thought to have affected their numbers to the extent that there is only a single breeding colony left in the country. The largest remaining population occurs on the eastern part of the Indonesian island of Sumatra. There is some movement of these storks after breeding, which takes place during the dry season. They use their long bill to probe for food in often muddy water, grabbing fish and small vertebrates that come within reach.

Identification: Predominantly white, but has a bald, reddish area of skin over much of the face and a black patch by the base of the bill. The edge of the wings are blackish. Legs and feet are red and the bill is straw-coloured. Sexes alike. Young birds have more extensive feathering on their heads and their bare skin is yellowish.

Distribution: Scattered localities through South-east Asia, notably Vietnam, Malaysia, Sumatra, Java and Sulawesi.
Size: 100cm (39in).
Habitat: Coastal mudflats and mangroves.
Nest: Platform of sticks in a tree.
Eggs: 1–4, whitish.
Food: Fish and other vertebrates.

KINGFISHERS, CORMORANTS AND OTHER FISH-EATERS

The hunting strategies of this group of birds differ widely, but they are all well adapted to their environments. The way in which they have evolved in this respect is perhaps best illustrated by the collared kingfisher, which occurs in a huge number of different forms through its wide range.

Collared kingfisher

Mangrove kingfisher *Todiramphus chloris*

More than 50 distinctive races of the collared kingfisher are recognized across its extensive distribution. Many of the most distinctive evolved in relative isolation on remote Pacific islands, such as New Britain – their white areas are heavily suffused with an orange shade. On the southern Mariana islands, however, the white plumage is more extensive, covering virtually the entire head apart from bluish-green stripes behind the eyes. The diet of these birds is equally variable, ranging from crabs to cicadas, snails and even small snakes. When nesting, the collared kingfisher is highly territorial although pairs will drive away intruders at any time of the year.

Identification: Highly variable appearance depending on the subspecies, although the wings are invariably greenish blue with bright blue edges. Underparts are generally white and the collar is white as well. Many races have a greenish-blue crown with a black stripe running through the eyes. The beak is black, with a distinct paler base to the lower bill. Sexes are alike.

Distribution: Extends over a huge area from the Red Sea across southern Asia and the small Pacific islands on to northern and eastern Australia.
Size: 25cm (11in).
Habitat: Coastal areas. Sometimes inland.
Nest: Tree hole or an arboreal termite mound.
Eggs: 2–5, white.
Food: Invertebrates, crustaceans and small vertebrates.

Little pied cormorant

Microcarbo melanoleucos

Distribution: Extends from eastern Indonesia to the Solomon Islands and New Caledonia, and south to Australia and New Zealand.
Size: 65cm (26in).
Habitat: Coastal areas and inland waters.
Nest: Platform of sticks usually with trees nearby, which will be used for nesting purposes.
Eggs: 3–5, pale bluish.
Food: Fish and other aquatic creatures.

The appearance of these cormorants varies noticeably through the range. The New Zealand race (*M. m. brevirostris*), for example, displays a variable amount of white plumage on the underparts. These cormorants obtain their food by diving, seeking not just fish but also amphibians, crustaceans and other invertebrates, with the prey varying according to the cormorant's habitat. Although they are occasionally seen in loose groups, little pied cormorants tend to fish independently and may even take up residence in public parks where they feed heavily on goldfish in the ponds.

Identification: Distinctive appearance. Has a predominantly white head with black plumage to the crown area that extends down the back of the neck. Underparts may be entirely white or black, depending on the race. Has a long black tail and a small crest on the head. The bill is yellowish. Feet and legs are black. Sexes alike.

Brown booby

White-bellied booby *Sula leucogaster*

These boobies hunt a variety of fish relatively close to the shoreline, so usually they dive into the water from a low height, hitting the surface at an angle rather than entering vertically. This means that they penetrate the water less deeply. They are effective underwater swimmers, using their webbed feet and their wings to help them. The brown booby has an interesting relationship with its masked relative (*S. dactylatra*) when their distribution overlaps. They sometimes harry masked boobies for food in flight, stealing their catch. Rare mixed pairings between these two species have given rise to hybrid offspring.

Identification: Blackish head and upper chest, with browner suffusion to the feathers of the back, wings and tail. The underparts are white and the feet are yellow. Has a powerful bill which is bluish at the base, becoming dull yellow towards the tip. Hens are larger in size.

Distribution: Extends from the western Pacific to the east coast of Africa. Also present in the Atlantic, the Caribbean, and the western coast of Central America.
Size: 74cm (29in).
Habitat: Inshore waters.
Nest: Hollow on the ground.
Eggs: 2, bluish white.
Food: Fish.

Silver gull (*Chroicocephalus novaehollandiae*): 43cm (17in)
Extends from the coast of Ethiopia around the Asiatic coastline south to mainland Australia and Tasmania. Also occurs as far east as New Caledonia. Has a predominantly white and silvery-grey back, with black evident on the flight feathers. Orange-red ring around the eyes. Bill red, as are the legs. Sexes alike.

Black-tailed gull (*Larus crassirostris*): 48cm (19in)
Ranges from eastern coast of Asia and the shores around Japan southwards; wide range after breeding period reaches as far south as Australia. Distinctive U-shaped black area on the tail with a white tip, wings dark grey and black at the ends with a prominent white border along the rear edge. Remainder of the plumage is white. Bill yellowish with a dark tip, legs and feet yellowish. Young birds brownish, with no black on the tail, and greyish legs.

Pacific gull (*Larus pacificus*): 63cm (25in)
Restricted range, from Port Hedland in western Australia right along the southern coast and Tasman Sea. Also present on the south-east coast as far north as Sydney. White head and underparts, greyish-black wings with whitish tips. Bill is large and yellowish with red and black markings at its tip. Legs and feet yellowish. Young birds brownish-grey, with pale edging.

Little black cormorant (Little black shag, *Phalacrocorax sulcirostris*): 65cm (26in)
Ranges from New Guinea westwards to Indonesia and then southwards to Australia, including Tasmania, and on to New Zealand. Occurs both in coastal and inland areas. Has black plumage, a black bill and black feet. Traces of white feathering above the eye are only evident during the breeding season. Sexes are alike.

Striated heron

Green-backed heron, mangrove heron *Butorides striata*

The great variation in the appearance of the striated heron has led to more than 30 distinctive races being recognized by taxonomists. It is not just differences in coloration that sets them apart, but also their size because the Australian races are larger than those from elsewhere. These herons are equally at home in saltwater areas, such as mangroves, as well as fresh-water lakes, although they prefer areas where there is dense cover as this enables them to keep their presence hidden. Their shy nature is also reflected in their feeding habits. The striated heron often prefers to seek food at night, if the tide is favourable.

Identification: Very variable, even between members of the same race. Blackish plumage on the crown. Underparts are often pinkish greyish with a white stripe down the centre of the body, but can range from light brown to grey. Usually a bare area of yellow skin is most conspicuous in front of the eyes. Wings dark. Sexes are generally alike.

Distribution: Pan-global: ranges from the Indian subcontinent through South-east Asia to northern and eastern parts of Australia.
Size: 48cm (19in).
Habitat: Shallow water.
Nest: Built of twigs in a tree or bush.
Eggs: 2–5, pale blue.
Food: Fish and other aquatic life, reptiles and mice.

WADING BIRDS

These birds are well equipped to forage in wetland areas, with their long legs enabling them to wade through the shallows easily, while also giving them a good field of vision to detect possible prey. A sharp bill and rapid reflexes make them formidable hunters of small aquatic creatures. They may also be encountered in fields close to stretches of water.

White-necked heron

Pacific heron *Ardea pacifica*

The main distribution of these herons is centred on Australia. Although less common here, they also congregate in areas such as Irian Jaya in New Guinea. Following prolonged periods of rainfall, flooding means that these herons have greater feeding opportunities so populations can shift quite widely in search of flooded areas. They may be seen in coastal areas but prefer freshwater localities. White-necked herons breed in colonies of 20 or so pairs, building their nests in trees at least 15m (49ft) off the ground. Occasionally, much larger groups of as many as 150 pairs have been observed. They often nest in trees with other birds, such as spoonbills. Juvenile birds can be distinguished by greyish, rather than white, plumage on their head and neck.

Identification: The head and neck are white, and have slight black streaking in the centre of the lower throat and upper breast when out of breeding condition. Wings are blackish with a grey overlay. The underparts are blackish with white streaking. The bill, legs and feet are dark. Sexes alike.

Distribution: Found in southern New Guinea. Also present throughout Australia, apart from the central area.
Size: 106cm (41in).
Habitat: Shallow waters.
Nest: Platform of sticks.
Eggs: 3–4, pale blue.
Food: Small fish, vertebrates.

Eastern cattle egret

Bubulcus coromandus

Distribution: Exceedingly wide pan-global distribution. Asiatic race extends from southern and eastern parts of Asia into parts of Australia and New Zealand.
Size: 56cm (22in).
Habitat: Shallow waters and even relatively dry areas.
Nest: Sometimes in reedbeds, often on a platform above the ground.
Eggs: 2–5, pale blue.
Food: Invertebrates, amphibians and other small vertebrates.

The sharp bills of these egrets allow them to catch their quarry easily, although in urban areas they can often be seen scavenging around markets and in rubbish dumps. Now split from the Western species (*B. ibis*) the Eastern cattle egret is the largest and tallest of the two. Banding studies have revealed that cattle egrets will fly long distances, with those birds occurring in north-eastern Asia moving south in the winter. Ringed birds have turned up as far afield as the Philippines. This tendency to roam widely has allowed these egrets to colonize many of the more remote islands in the Pacific. Indeed, distinct seasonal movements have even been recorded in Australia.

Below: The egret's buff plumage is replaced largely by white during the breeding period for display purposes.

Identification: Pale buff coloration on the head and throat, extending down to the breast; also on the back and rump. The remainder of the plumage is white. There may be traces of white plumage around the yellow bill. The legs and feet are also yellow. Sexes alike.

Sarus crane

Antigone antigone

These large, long-lived birds pair for life, which can be for 30 years or more. They are easily spotted from some distance away in open, wet countryside, usually in pairs. In areas where food is plentiful, however, larger numbers of sarus cranes may occasionally gather together, with as many as 60 individuals recorded in one locality. These cranes are relatively fearless, often stalking among cattle in fields to pounce on small animals, such as frogs, that have been disturbed by the herd. In common with other species of cranes, their courtship involves a spectacular dancing ritual which is accompanied by loud calls.

Identification: Grey plumage, with a characteristic red head and long neck. Has an area of black plumage on the wings. The tertiaries drooping over the grey tail are pale, verging on white. Straight greenish, horn-coloured bill that tapers to a point. Legs are reddish and very long. Sexes alike.

Distribution: Ranges from the Indian subcontinent east and south across Cambodia and Laos, Vietnam as far as north-eastern Australia.
Size: 152cm (60in).
Habitat: Wetland areas, including paddy fields.
Nest: Platform of vegetation on the ground.
Eggs: 2, pinkish-white. May have brown markings.
Food: Invertebrates, fish, frogs, and some vegetable matter.

Plumed egret (*Egretta intermedia plumifera*): 72cm (28in)
Subspecies of intermediate egret. Extends from New Guinea to eastern Indonesia and south to Australia. White body, with delicate plumes over the back and on the chest. The bill and the area around the eyes are yellow. Top part of the legs are yellowish. The feet are greyish. Sexes alike.

Australasian bittern (brown bittern, *Botaurus poiciloptilus*): 76cm (30in)
Found in south-west and south-east Australia, including Tasmania, plus New Zealand, New Caledonia and the Loyalty Islands. Has white plumage on the throat and running down on to the neck. Brownish elsewhere but with black markings. The depth of coloration varies among individuals. Pale stripe above the eye. The bill and legs are pale yellow.

Black-necked stork (*Ephippiorhynchus asiaticus*): 137cm (54in)
Two populations: one is confined essentially to India; the other is in northern and eastern Australia. Glossy black plumage on the head and neck. The body is white apart from prominent black areas on the wings. Strong, powerful black bill. Legs and feet are red.

Straw-necked ibis (*Threskiornis spinicollis*): 76cm (30in)
Found in New Guinea and Australia apart from central and central-southern areas. Bare black head with white collar over much of the neck and buff area beneath. Rest of the upper breast area, back and wings are all greenish. Underparts white. Legs are red. Hens smaller.

Glossy ibis

Plegadis falcinellus

These ibises are often seen flying high in groups to and from their feeding grounds, and they usually roost on trees adjacent to, or surrounded by, water. This helps to protect them from predators such as foxes. Glossy ibises nest in colonies, and pairs are only territorial within the immediate vicinity of their chosen site. The chicks start to leave the nests once they are about 10 days old, and will form groups with the young of neighbouring pairs. In parts of Australia, the dry season may afford sightings of many thousands of birds in a single location, although actual numbers vary from year to year.

Distribution: Wide. Extends from the Red Sea via northern India to the eastern coast of Asia. Also present in Australia, the Philippines and Indonesia.
Size: 66cm (26in).
Habitat: Shallow areas of water.
Nest: Platform of sticks, built above water.
Eggs: 2–6, deep green to blue.
Food: Invertebrates, plus crustaceans and small vertebrates.

Identification: Dark brown overall but with some white streaking on the head. The wings and rump are green. Legs and bill are dark. When not in breeding condition, they are a duller colour. Sexes are alike.

RAILS, CRAKES AND JACANAS

Although shy by nature, some members of this group are seen in cultivated areas. Their large toes help to prevent them sinking into marshy ground. Sadly, the flightless nature of some rails from this region, such as the Tahiti rail (Gallirallus pacificus) has left them vulnerable to introduced predators, especially feral cats, and a number of the most distinctive Pacific island species, including this species, are now extinct.

Tasmanian nativehen

Tribonyx mortierii

Distribution: Confined to Tasmania and smaller offshore islands.
Size: 51cm (20in).
Habitat: Wetland areas with vegetative cover nearby.
Nest: Large, cup-shaped.
Eggs: 3–9, yellowish-buff with brownish markings.
Food: Mainly seeds and plants.

These large rails are flightless, and it is believed that the Australian mainland population died out as a result of hunting by dingoes less than 5,000 years ago. Their main defence is to run quickly away from danger. They are capable of reaching speeds equivalent to 48kph (30mph) over short distances. These birds sometimes graze in agricultural areas, even taking fruit from orchards. They live in groups, and when conflict breaks out with newcomers, the combatants jump into the air up to 1.5m (5ft), lashing out with their powerful feet until the weaker individual backs down.

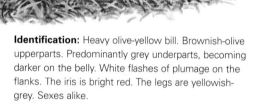

Identification: Heavy olive-yellow bill. Brownish-olive upperparts. Predominantly grey underparts, becoming darker on the belly. White flashes of plumage on the flanks. The iris is bright red. The legs are yellowish-grey. Sexes alike.

Watercock

Kora *Gallicrex cinerea*

In much of their range, these rails move south during the winter when they are mainly found on the island of Sumatra. Watercocks are most active at twilight, hiding away during the daytime, although in recently planted rice paddies they will often remain quite conspicuous until the plants grow larger and conceal their presence. They have characteristically jerky tail movements, that highlight their buff undertail coverts. Pairs call loudly for up to 30 minutes at a time during the breeding period but are quieter during the rest of the year.

Distribution: Across southern Asia from Pakistan and India east to China, Japan and the Philippines. Then south through South-east Asia to Sumatra and other islands.
Size: Cock birds up to 43cm (17in); hens 36cm (14in).
Habitat: Swampland, including rice paddies.
Nest: Cup-shaped mass of vegetation.
Eggs: 3–6, varying from whitish through yellowish to pink with darker spots.
Food: Mainly vegetation, including rice. Also invertebrates.

Identification: The cock in breeding condition has an unmistakable upright red horn extending back over the eyes, with mainly blackish plumage and scalloping over the wings. The iris, legs and feet are red. It resembles the adult hen for the remainder of the year, but is larger in size. The hen is predominantly brown, with a dark area on the head and scalloping on the wings. Dark barring to the plumage on the underparts.

Dusky moorhen (Black moorhen, *Gallinula tenebrosa*) Australian birds up to 40cm (16in); New Guinea birds as small as 25cm (10in). Extends from Sumatra, Borneo, Sulawesi and New Guinea to Australia. Breeding birds have a bright red beak and shield with a yellow tip. Greyish-black plumage. Joints of the orangish legs and feet are dark. Outside the breeding period, the bill is olive as are the legs and feet.

Red-legged crake (*Rallina fasciata*): 25cm (10in) Present in South-east Asia from north-eastern India south via Malaysia to Sumatra, Java, Borneo and neighbouring islands. Has reddish-chestnut plumage on the head, neck and breast. Browner on the back with black and white barring on the wings and underparts. Legs and feet red. Hens display cinnamon shade of coloration on the head and narrower black barring on underparts.

Slaty-breasted rail (*Gallirallus striatus*): 30cm (12in) Ranges eastwards from India to China and across South-east Asia to the Sunda islands and the Philippines. Chestnut-brown feathering runs from the head to the base of the neck. Underparts from the chin to the lower belly are a dark slate-grey. The rest of the plumage is dark brown with white stripes. Mainland birds tend to be much paler overall than the nominate race, which is found in eastern parts of the species' range.

White-breasted waterhen

White-breasted swamphen
Amaurornis phoenicurus

These wide-ranging crakes show a regional variation in size, with island races exhibiting the greatest diversity. It is not uncommon for island birds to have irregular white patches of feathering in areas that would normally be dark. This characteristic is described as partial albinism. These waterhens show little fear of human contact and can be seen in irrigation canals and similar stretches of water. They are not very strong flyers, but can swim and dive for food.

Distribution: From Pakistan and India to China and Japan. Present on Sri Lanka and through South-east Asia to the Sundas and other islands, including the Philippines.
Size: 30cm (12in).
Habitat: Swampland, sides of lakes and similar water.
Nest: Cup-shaped pad of vegetation.
Eggs: 3–9, cream to pinkish-white with darker markings.
Food: Mainly invertebrates and small fish.

Identification: White extends down over the chest and upper abdomen. Flanks are black. The upperparts are dark slate-grey, although browner over the rump. Has a red area on the top of the yellowish bill. Reddish plumage extends from near the vent to the undertail coverts. Sexes alike, but hens have a more olive tone to bill.

Pheasant-tailed jacana

Hydrophasianus chirurgus

The very long toes of these birds may not actually enable them to walk on water, but by distributing their weight effectively in this way, they can walk on mats of vegetation and the leaves of aquatic plants such as water lilies and lotuses, which is why they are also known as lily-trotters. They can swim if necessary, however, and dive on occasions, too. When breeding, cock birds incubate on their own, rearing the resulting chicks, while the hen moves on to seek another mate and lay again.

Distribution: Runs eastwards from India as far as China and south through South-east Asia to the Greater Sundas, via Sumatra, Java and Borneo. Present in the Philippines.
Size: 30cm (12in).
Habitat: Areas of still or slow-flowing water, such as marshes and ponds.
Nest: Pad of vegetation.
Eggs: 2–5, pale brown with darker markings.
Food: Invertebrates and vegetation.

Identification: White plumage on the head down to the upper breast with white also on the sides of the wing. A black area runs down the back of the head and a broad yellow band runs on top of this. Underparts are dark brown, but lighter in colour on the back. The long, blackish tail is missing outside the breeding season. The underparts are white apart from a greyish band on the breast, while the upperparts are much paler. Distinctive long toes. Sexes alike.

WATERFOWL

This group of birds has diversified to occupy a wide range of habitats and has adopted a correspondingly broad range of lifestyles, from grazing wetland areas to an almost entirely aquatic existence. Breeding habits vary, too, with some members of the group preferring to breed on the ground, while others choose the relative safety of tree hollows for their nest site.

Cape Barren goose

Cereopsis goose *Cereopsis novaehollandiae*

Distribution: Found in parts of southern Australia, including Tasmania. Breeds in four main areas: the Furneaux islands, Spencer Gulf islands, islands of the Recherche Archipelago and off Wilson's Promontory.
Size: 99cm (39in).
Habitat: Pasture and open country.
Nest: Made of vegetation, built on the ground.
Eggs: 3–6, white.
Food: Grasses and sedges.

These geese live almost entirely on land, only taking to water as a last resort when danger threatens, or when, during the moult, they are unable to fly for a period. They breed on small islands, where they are relatively safe from disturbance, nesting among the tufts of grass and other vegetation which they browse using their strong bills. Male birds have a much louder call than hens, whose vocalisations have been described as pig-like grunts. They weigh up to 5.3kg (12lb) but are still powerful in flight, their wing beats being both shallow and fast.

Identification: A distinctive grey colour with a paler whitish area on the head. Tail is black. Some irregular darker spotting on the wings, most pronounced in young birds. Reddish legs with black feet. Greatly enlarged greenish-yellow cere encompassing the nostrils. Bill is black. Hens are smaller in size.

Above: Cape Barren geese graze in flocks on grass: they are highly sociable birds by nature.

Cotton pygmy goose

White pygmy goose *Nettapus coromandelianus*

These geese spend most of their time on the water, frequently favouring deep areas. They are most commonly observed in pairs or small groups, although they occasionally congregate in much greater numbers outside the breeding season. These geese feed by dabbling under the water, only diving down occasionally, and often choosing vegetation growing above the water's surface. When flushed out, they fly quite low and generally not very far. The breeding season begins at the onset of the rainy season. Pairs nest individually and tend to remain close to the water. In some parts of their range, most notably in Australia, the numbers of cotton pygmy geese have declined as the result of wetland drainage.

Identification: A black stripe runs from the bill over the top of the head. A black collar runs around the upper breast and this is intersected with an area of white plumage. Underparts are mainly pale grey and the wings are blackish. Female is duller: mainly grey with black eye stripe. When not in breeding plumage, cock birds resemble hens, apart from a larger, white area on the wing.

Distribution: India eastwards across Asia. Also in Indonesia and eastern Australia.
Size: 37cm (14in).
Habitat: Deep water with plant growth.
Nest: Tree hollows lined with down.
Eggs: 6–16, ivory white.
Food: Aquatic plants and invertebrates.

Hardhead

White-eyed duck *Aythya australis*

Although these pochards are usually only encountered in Australia, they do irrupt on occasion and can then be seen much further afield in countries as far apart as Java and New Zealand. It is thought that such behaviour is usually triggered by severe droughts. It is believed that the remote population on Banks Island originated as a result of an irruption of this kind, rather than from a deliberate human introduction, and these immigrants have successfully established a separate breeding population. In Australia, there has been a decline in the number of hardheads over recent years as a by-product of drainage schemes.

Identification: A rich chocolate-brown colour with white lower breast and belly. Has white plumage around the vent. Bill is greyish, with a light band and a black tip. Iris is whitish. Females are very similar, but have dark eyes and may be slightly lighter and browner overall. There is no eclipse plumage. Juvenile birds resemble females but have russet-brown feathering on the abdomen.

Distribution: Australia, apart from central and central-southern parts. Isolated colony on Banks Island.
Size: 59cm (23in).
Habitat: Large, well-vegetated lakes and marshes.
Nest: Platform of vegetation.
Eggs: 9–13, greenish-grey.
Food: Mainly plant matter, some invertebrates.

Chestnut-breasted shelduck (Australian shelduck, *Tadorna tadornoides*): 72cm (28in)
Occurs mainly in western and south-eastern parts of Australia, including Tasmania, in shallow stretches of water. Drakes have glossy dark green head and neck with a narrow white collar separating this area from the chestnut breast. The remainder of the body, apart from the chestnut rump, is dark. The broad white area in the wing is most visible in flight. Ducks are recognizable by white edging around the base of the bill and eyes. They have greyish-brown bodies in eclipse plumage.

Pacific black duck (*Anas superciliosa*): 61cm (24in)
Found in Indonesia, New Guinea and islands to the east, as well as Australia, New Zealand and neighbouring islands. The basic coloration varies from brown to black, with lighter scalloping on the feathers. Has green speculum in the wing. Dark crown, and an eye stripe with buff lines is evident on the face as well. The bill is greyish and the legs and feet are a yellowish-grey. Hens tend to have browner plumage on the upper-parts of the body.

Magpie goose (*Anseranas semipalmata*): 85cm (34in)
Present in southern New Guinea and northern Australia and extending down the east coast. The body is white apart from glossy, blackish plumage on the head and rear of the body. There is a swollen area on the crown of the head. The bare facial skin is reddish. The legs are a golden yellow. Hens are smaller, and the swollen area is less pronounced.

Lesser whistling duck

Lesser tree duck *Dendrocygna javanica*

This is the smallest of the tree ducks, and like other members of the group, it prefers to roost in trees at night rather than on the water. The breeding habits of the lesser tree duck are unusual because although it does sometimes nest on the ground, it usually prefers to choose a site in a suitable tree. Pairs tend to either adopt a tree hollow for this purpose or to take over an abandoned platform nest made from sticks that would have been constructed originally by herons or a bird of prey. Only at the northern edge of their current distribution do these birds head south in the winter.

They used to occur in Japan, but, sadly, they were hunted to extinction in the early 20th century.

Distribution: From India and Pakistan eastwards across mainland Asia to China. Wide distribution across South-east Asia. Also south to Indonesian islands, including Java and Sumatra, and the island of Borneo.
Size: 40cm (16in).
Habitat: Shallow water edged with trees.
Nest: Either on the ground or in trees.
Eggs: 7–12, creamy white.
Food: Plant matter and aquatic snails.

Identification: Brownish, with a darker streak across the top of the head. Underparts are slightly pinkish. White area around the vent. Dark brown back and wings with lighter scalloping. Grey bill, legs and feet. Sexes alike.

FROGMOUTHS AND OWLS

These hunting birds are all cryptically coloured, with none of them displaying the bright plumage seen in the case of some woodland birds. Their hearing and keen vision help to alert them to the presence of possible prey. In spite of their popular image, however, not all owls are nocturnal hunters, with some being seen on the wing throughout the day rather than solely becoming active at dusk.

Large frogmouth

Batrachostomus auritus

These frogmouths seem to be rare on the Asiatic mainland, and so relatively little is known about their habits. What we do know is that they hunt off a perch, seeking invertebrates, such as grasshoppers or cicadas, which they swoop down on and seize in their bill. Large frogmouths have a very wide gape that allows them to feed easily. They are nocturnal creatures, hunting from dusk onwards. They are reminiscent of owls, in terms of cryptic coloration and calls.

Identification: These birds are much larger than other frogmouths. They have dark rufous-brown upperparts and white spotting forms a collar around the back of the neck. There are both white spots on the wings and buff barring on the flight feathers. The throat and breast are similar in shade to the upperparts, with white spotting on the breast and buff plumage on the belly. Forward-pointing bristles mask the bill. The eyes are relatively large. Hens are duller in colour and smaller overall.

Distribution: Ranges from peninsular Thailand and through Malaysia to Sumatra and Borneo.
Size: 41cm (16in), making this species twice as large as other frogmouths.
Habitat: Lowland forest.
Nest: Pad of down on a tree.
Eggs: 1, white.
Food: Invertebrates.

Collared owlet

Glaucidium brodiei

These owlets are unusual members of the owl family in that they hunt during the day, and may be seen in the vicinity of open clearings. Their vocalizations are unusual too, consisting of a series of quite musical call notes. In spite of their small size, these birds are aggressive hunters, and can take birds and even lizards as large as themselves. Their strong feet and fearsome-looking talons enable them to hold down their prey with ease as they kill it with their strong bill. It is not unusual for these owlets to be mobbed by groups of other birds. The disturbance that results from the driving mob can provide a means of identifying the owlets' presence in an area.

Above: The spots on the back of the collared owlet's head resemble eyes. This serves to deter possible predators.

Identification: Greyish-brown barred plumage. Has lemon-yellow eyes and white eyebrows and throat area. The underparts are also whitish. Greenish-yellow feet. Hens larger in size.

Distribution: Ranges from the Himalayan region east to China and southwards through much of the Malay Peninsula, then on to parts of Sumatra and Borneo.
Size: 15cm (6in).
Habitat: Hill and mountain forests with clearings, ranging up to an altitude of around 3,200m (10,500ft).
Nest: Tree hollow. The owl either uses a natural hole or takes over a chamber created by a woodpecker or barbet.
Eggs: 3–5, white.
Food: Large invertebrates and small vertebrates.

Barred eagle-owl

Malay eagle-owl *Bubo sumatranus*

Hard to spot during the daytime, barred eagle-owls frequently choose to roost in a concealed locality out of sight, well disguised by foliage, with their barred pattern of markings helping to provide them with additional camouflage. They are also not especially common, simply because pairs occupy large territories. These owls are thought to pair for life and will return annually to the same nest site, with pairs occurring in Sumatra and Java not infrequently choosing a large bird's nest fern (*Asplenium*), rather than a tree hollow.

Identification: Large, fairly horizontal tufts of feathers on the top of the head, directed to the sides, with white streaks above dark brown eyes. Barred blackish-brown and buff plumage, with a finer pattern of barring across the breast. Underparts whiter overall, but still with distinct barring. Bill and feet are a pale yellow. Hens may be larger.

Distribution: From southern Myanmar (Burma) and Thailand across the Malay Peninsula to Borneo, Sumatra, Java, Bali and adjacent islands.
Size: 46cm (18in).
Habitat: Tropical forests up to 1,600m (5,250ft).
Nest: Tree holes and ferns.
Eggs: 1, white.
Food: Invertebrates and smaller vertebrates.

Spotted wood owl (*Strix seloputo*): 47cm (18¹/₂in)
Found across South-east Asia over the Malay Peninsula to coastal areas of Java. Also present on Palawan in the Philippines and may occur on Sumatra. Rufous-buff facial disc. No ear tufts. Brownish barring on the underparts, may have areas that are whitish to more definite shades of buff. Eyes brown. Bill greyish. Hens larger.

Brown hawk-owl (*Ninox scutulata*): 32cm (13in)
Extends from the Indian subcontinent and South-east Asia to some Indonesian islands, Japan and the Philippines, then via the mainland to eastern Siberia. White underparts with brown streaking. Some subspecies may have underparts of lighter brown than the streaking. Brownish back and wings. Greyish-black bill. Hens are usually smaller.

Oriental bay owl (*Phodilus badius*): 33cm (13in)
Ranges across South-east Asia to Indonesia. Also present on Samar in the Philippines. An isolated population exists in south-west India and on Sri Lanka. Whitish facial disc, resembling a mask, with a speckled collar beneath. The wings are reddish-brown with speckling; underparts paler. A distinctive v-shaped frontal shield extends from between the eyes to the base of the yellow bill. Females are usually bigger.

Buffy fish owl (*Ketupa ketupu*): 48cm (19in)
Extends from southern Myanmar (Burma) into Thailand, through the Malay Peninsula to various Indonesian islands. Predominantly brown back and wings. The underparts are a pale yellowish-brown. Unfeathered, pale yellowish legs. Yellow eyes and black bill. Females larger.

Mountain scops owl

Spotted scops owl *Otus spilocephalus*

Inhabiting relatively inaccessible areas such as deep ravines, these owls become active at dusk when they begin to hunt their invertebrate prey. Males occupy relatively small territories and sing regularly, even outside the breeding period, with their calls sounding like a double whistle. Hens call far less often with their single note being heard in response to that of the cock bird, before merging into it. Although little has been recorded about their hunting habits, it is thought these scops owls obtain at least some of their prey on the wing, with moths as well as beetles featuring significantly in their diet.

Identification: Quite a small size compared to other owls. Some regional variation in colour. White feathering runs along the upper part of each wing. Underparts are brownish and have white areas crossed by black marks that are said to resemble arrowheads. Bristles are apparent on the face. Yellow eyes. The bill is cream. Sexes are alike.

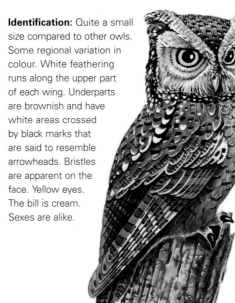

Distribution: Indian Himalayan region, parts of Nepal, Pakistan and Myanmar (Burma), to south-eastern China, Taiwan and south through the Malay Peninsula to Sumatra and Borneo.
Size: 18cm (7in).
Habitat: Humid upland areas of forest.
Nest: Tree holes, sometimes excavated by other birds.
Eggs: 2–5, white.
Food: Invertebrates.

CUCKOOS, WOODPECKERS AND BEE-EATERS

These birds all hunt invertebrates but they have evolved very different techniques for this purpose. While bee-eaters often target flying insects, woodpeckers prefer to hunt those that hide out of sight, using their bills to expose and then capture them. Cuckoos, on the other hand, have no specialized feeding strategy but eat whatever they are able to catch, locating their prey by keen observation.

Himalayan cuckoo

Cuculus saturatus

Distribution: Migratory races breed in northern parts of eastern Russia, Japan and the Himalayan region, before moving to South-east Asia in the winter.
Size: 26cm (10¹/₂in).
Habitat: Forest.
Nest: Those of other birds.
Eggs: 1 per nest, the colour of the egg corresponds to those of the foster species.
Food: Invertebrates.

Resident and migratory populations of these birds appear not to mix very much, with the migratory cuckoos often encountered at lower altitudes. It is actually said to be possible to distinguish between the non-migratory and migratory types of this cuckoo by their calls: the former will repeatedly utter a four- rather than three-note call. During the breeding season, the cuckoo utters its call more frequently so that it is easier to locate in the forest canopy. In northern parts of their range, these cuckoos frequent coniferous forests. In Asia, nests of the chestnut-crowned warbler (*Seicercus castaniceps*) are often parasitized by the Himalayan cuckoo.

Left: These cuckoos fly long distances and overwinter widely through Indonesia.

Identification: Has grey head and wings. Grey barring on white underparts, with a bare area of bright yellow skin around the eyes. Hens tend to be indistinguishable, but occasionally they are predominantly brownish with black barring in place of the grey areas. These are sometimes described as hepatic (liver-coloured) females and are a very rare sight.

Speckled piculet

Picumnus innominatus

These tiny woodpeckers are similar in habits to their larger relatives, using their bills to probe stems and branches for food. They are also sufficiently nimble in flight to feed on the wing, and can swoop down on spiders moving across bark. Speckled piculets are often observed foraging for food in the company of other birds, including various flycatchers and babblers, fire-tufted barbets and drongos. It is thought that the movements of these other birds help to stir up invertebrates, so making them easier for the piculets to catch. The nesting chamber excavated by speckled piculets is very small, measuring just 15cm (6in) in height and 6cm (2¹/₂in) in width and depth. They often prefer to nest in rotten timber as this is easier to bore into with their bills. When breeding, these small piculets are most likely to be located by their persistent tapping rather than actually seen.

Identification: Olive back, with a short tail. Has characteristic black and white spotted underparts. Black plumage runs through the eyes and is bordered by white streaks top and bottom. Cocks can be easily distinguished from hens by the orange patch on their forehead.

Distribution: From northern Pakistan and India east to southern China and down across the Malay Peninsula to Sumatra and Borneo. An isolated population exists in India's Western Ghats region.
Size: 10cm (4in).
Habitat: Trees, shrubs and stands of bamboo.
Nest: Hole excavated in bamboo or tree.
Eggs: 2–4, white.
Food: Insect larvae, spiders and other invertebrates.

Brush cuckoo (*Cacomantis variolosus*): 24cm (9½in)
Widely-distributed across Thailand and the Malay Peninsula, across the Sundas, south to Australia and east to the Philippines and the Solomon Islands. Head and upperparts are brownish-grey. Rufous underparts, with greyish tone to the throat and upper breast. Yellow eye ring. Sexes alike.

Chestnut-winged cuckoo (*Clamator coromandus*): 45cm (18in)
Distribution extends from east India to southern China and across South-east Asia to the Greater Sundas, Sulawesi and the Philippines. Has a black head and a spectacular tufted crest. The collar is whitish and there is chestnut on the wings. The breast is a buff colour and there are grey underparts. The back and wings are blackish. Sexes are alike.

Great slaty woodpecker (*Mulleripicus pulverulentus*): 50cm (20in)
Extensive distribution from northern central parts of India through Nepal east to south-west China. Also occurs in Vietnam, Thailand and Malaysia. Present in western Indonesia east to Borneo and Palawan. Slaty-grey underparts. Paler edging to the feathers, forming white spots on the neck. Red flashes below the eyes only apparent in cock birds. Buff plumage on the throat.

Bamboo woodpecker (*Gecinulus viridis*): 28cm (11in)
Extends from Myanmar (Burma) eastwards to parts of Thailand, northern Laos and Malaysia. Cocks are predominantly greenish with a large crimson area on the head. The rump too is red. Bill greyish. Hens lack the red area on the head.

Greater yellownape

Greater yellow-naped woodpecker *Chrysophlegma flavinucha*

During the breeding season, the distinctive crest of these woodpeckers is used as part of their display. The sound of drumming can be heard at this time as the cock bird taps quickly and repeatedly on the side of a tree to attract a mate. Both parents help to construct a breeding chamber, which is located 2–6m (6.5–20ft) off the ground. Both also actively incubate the eggs and feed the chicks. After fledging, the young will call loudly and repeatedly if they become separated from the family group. It is quite common to encounter these woodpeckers foraging in small parties. These birds find food largely by probing in rotting vegetation rather than excavating holes in the bark. They rarely descend to ground level.

Distribution: From the Himalayan region of north-west India through Nepal to Myanmar (Burma) across South-east Asia to China. Also isolated distribution through the Malay Peninsula to Sumatra.
Size: 34cm (13in).
Habitat: Forested foothills and mountain slopes.
Nest: Rotten tree.
Eggs: 3–4, white.
Food: Wide range of invertebrates and even frogs.

Identification: Predominantly green body, with a black tail and brown and black barring on the flight feathers. Distinctive yellow crest at the back of the head. Yellowish plumage on the throat with white spots beneath. Hens have more streaking on the throat.

Red-bearded bee-eater

Nyctyornis amictus

These bee-eaters are more likely to be seen in the middle and upper parts of the forest canopy, rather than in the darker undergrowth. Here they catch a wide variety of invertebrates in flight, preying not just on bees but also beetles, wasps and ants. They rest quietly on a chosen branch, waiting for their quarry to come within range, then fly fast and with great agility to capture it. Trees adjacent to clearings are often favoured, as these breaks in the forest provide an open area to capture prey. When breeding, the bee-eaters excavate tunnels, which can extend back 1.2m (4ft) into cliff faces and similar localities.

Identification: Pink plumage extends from in front of the eyes up over the crown. A red area beneath the bill leads down on to the chest. Yellow underside to the tail with black tips. The remainder of the body is green. The bill is dark and curves downwards at its tip. Hens have less pink plumage on the head.

Distribution: Through the Malay peninsula, apart from the southern tip, to Sumatra and Borneo.
Size: 30cm (12in).
Habitat: Lowland forested areas.
Nest: Hole in a vertical bank.
Eggs: 3–5, white.
Food: Invertebrates, including bees.

HONEYGUIDES, HORNBILLS AND BARBETS

The hornbills include some of the most magnificent birds found in the forests of Asia, not so much for their bright coloration but rather for their spectacular size and incredible bills. Barbets may be smaller, but they too have stocky bills, which in this case are used to bore into rotten wood, although they are not as talented in this respect as woodpeckers.

Malaysian honeyguide

Indicator archipelagicus

The Malaysian honeyguide is an Asian representative of a family whose members are more commonly distributed in Africa. Honeyguides have a zygodactyl perching grip, which means that their toes are arranged in a 2:2 perching configuration. They are hard to spot in the canopy, thanks both to their dull coloration and small size, and are normally solitary by nature, so very little has been documented about their habits. They do have a distinctive call, however, that consists of two notes: the first resembles the miaowing of a cat, and this is closely followed by a rattling noise. Honeyguides feed on bees as they emerge from their nests. This helps people pinpoint the nests of wild bees and find honey, which is how these birds acquired their name.

Identification: Dark olive-brown upperparts, with red irises and grey bill. Underparts greyish-white, becoming increasingly white on the lower underparts, with dark blackish streaking on the flanks. Hens lack the narrow yellow shoulder patch.

Below: The honeyguide feeds on bees, snatched from the air as they emerge from their nests.

Distribution: Ranges over the Malay Peninsula south to Sumatra and Borneo.
Size: 18cm (7in).
Habitat: Forested areas, typically in the lowlands up to an altitude of 1,000m (3,300ft).
Nest: Tree holes.
Eggs: Presently unrecorded.
Food: Bees and wasps.

Rhinoceros hornbill

Buceros rhinoceros

Distribution: In South-east Asia south through the Malay peninsula to Sumatra, Java and Borneo.
Size: 110 cm (43in).
Habitat: Lowland and hill forests.
Nest: Tree hollow.
Eggs: 2, white.
Food: Fruit and smaller vertebrates.

Right: The distinctive, long bill of this hornbill helps them to pluck fruit from otherwise inaccessible places.

The upturned casque on the top of the bill of these hornbills resembles the horn of a rhinoceros, which is, of course, why they got their name. They are most likely to be seen close by fruiting figs, which are one of their favourite foods. Deforestation of the areas inhabited by these large birds is a serious threat to their future, especially as they do not live at high densities. Individual pairs will roam over wide areas and depend on large trees for nesting purposes. As with related species, the male rhinoceros hornbill incarcerates his mate in the nest chamber, sealing the entrance with mud. He returns here regularly to feed her and their brood until the family are ready to break out of the chamber. This barrier is believed to guard against would-be predators, such as snakes.

Identification: Has a black head, breast, back and wings with a white abdomen. The tail is also white, but with a broad black band. Bill is yellowish, redder at the base with a distinctive horn-like casque above. Cock birds have a red iris, but this can range from whitish to blue in hens. Otherwise, sexes are alike.

Bushy-crested hornbill (*Anorrhinus galeritus*): 70cm (28in)
Ranges from the Malay Peninsula to Sumatra, Borneo and north Natuna. Predominantly black in colour with a loose crest at the back of the head. Has a greyish-brown tail with a black band at the base. Blue areas of skin present on the throat and around the eye. Cock birds have red irises and black bills while hens have black irises and whitish bills.

Black hornbill (*Anthracoceros malayanus*): 75cm (29¹/₂in)
Found across the Malay Peninsula south to islands, including Sumatra and Borneo. Body is entirely black apart from white edging to the tail feathers. The bill and casque are whitish and the iris is red. Hens have greyish bills and pinkish skin surrounding the eyes.

Wreathed hornbill (*Rhyticeros undulatus*): 100cm (39in)
Ranges from eastern India to south-west China, through South-east Asia and on across the Malay Peninsula to Sumatra, Java, Bali and Borneo. Has a cream-coloured head, with a reddish stripe extending from the nape. The back, wings and underparts are black. There is an unfeathered yellow gular pouch on the throat. Hens have black upperparts, a blue gular pouch and small casque.

Yellow-crowned barbet (*Psilopogon henricii*): 21cm (8¹/₂in)
Extends from the Malay Peninsula to Sumatra and Borneo. Mainly green, but darker on the wings. Has a prominent yellow forehead that extends back over the eyes. Blue plumage is present on the throat and at the back of the head. A black stripe passes through the eyes, and reddish spots are present on the nape and at the sides of the neck. Sexes are alike.

Great hornbill

Buceros bicornis (E)

There is some variation in size through the extensive range of these hornbills. Mainland populations tend to be slightly smaller than their counterparts occurring on the islands. Great hornbills are most likely to be seen flying over the forest, as their large size and rather noisy flight means they are more obvious. They may also be spotted feeding in the canopy, jumping from branch to branch as they do so. Their loud call sounds rather like the barking of a small dog.

Right: The cock bird finds food and brings it to the nest for its young.

Distribution: Range extends from India to South-east Asia, across the Malay Peninsula to Sumatra.
Size: 125cm (49in).
Habitat: Forested areas.
Nest: Tree hollow.
Eggs: 2, white.
Food: Fruit and small vertebrates.

Identification: A black band encircles the face and base of the lower bill, with a cream area behind that runs down on to the upper breast. Wings predominantly black, with a white band across. White also apparent across the tips of the flight feathers when the wing is closed. Lower underparts white, as is the tail apart from a broad black band relatively close to the rounded tip. Bill yellowish, with flat-topped casque above. Cocks have red irises while hens have cream-coloured irises. Sexes are otherwise alike.

Fire-tufted barbet

Psilopogon pyrolophus

The relatively long tail and short bill of these barbets sets them apart from other species occurring in Asia. They are noisy and active by nature, often hopping from one branch to another, and occurring in small groups where food is plentiful. If danger threatens, however, fire-tufted barbets are likely to freeze, which makes them hard to observe. When roosting, they often perch with their long tails held in a vertical position. This stance allows them to roost and breed in quite small nesting chambers, which they excavate using their powerful bills.

Identification: Predominantly green, although darker on the wings and lighter on the underparts. Has a black collar around the chest with an area of yellow plumage above. Areas of black, grey and green plumage are also present on the head, with brown extending down the back of the head. Has prominent forward-pointing bristles with reddish tips evident above the upper bill. The beak itself is greenish-yellow, with two black spots on each side. Sexes alike.

Distribution: Confined to the Malay Peninsula and Sumatra.
Size: 26cm (10¹/₂in).
Habitat: Forested areas up to 1,500m (4,900ft).
Nest: Tree holes.
Eggs: Presently unrecorded.
Food: Mainly fruit and invertebrates.

PITTAS AND TROGONS

These brightly coloured woodland birds are surprisingly hard to spot in their natural habitat, not just because they are often shy, but also because they merge into the background thanks to the various shades and markings on their bodies. Pittas spend much of their time on or near the forest floor, while trogons tend to occupy the lower reaches, too, with the shafts of light helping to obscure their presence.

Giant pitta

Hydrornis caeruleus

The large, powerful bill of the giant pitta is used to feed mainly on snails, which are broken on particular stones in the pitta's territory. Cock birds maintain and defend their own areas vigorously. Earthworms are also a favoured food and occasionally they catch small snakes. These birds turn over leaf litter on the forest floor where they feed, seeking edible items. They build their nest quite close to the forest floor, usually in the fork of a suitable tree. Pairs tend to stay together throughout the year, but they can be hard to observe, as they hop away through the undergrowth at the slightest hint of danger.

Identification: A distinctive blue back, wings and tail, with pale buff underparts. The head has a blackish stripe down the centre, another extending back from the eyes and a black collar around the back of the neck. The remainder of facial plumage is a greyish colour but with some black edging. The hens have a blue tail but the rest of the plumage on the back is chestnut brown rather than blue. Their head is brownish rather than grey.

Distribution: Extends from Myanmar (Burma) and Thailand through the Malay Peninsula to Sumatra and Borneo.
Size: 30cm (12in).
Habitat: Lowland and hill forests.
Nest: Dome-shaped, with entrance at the front.
Eggs: 2, whitish with brown speckling.
Food: Mainly invertebrates, and some small vertebrates.

Hooded pitta

Pitta sordida

There are approximately a dozen recognized subspecies of hooded pitta, resulting in a considerable variation in appearance through these birds' wide range. Hooded pittas tend to be solitary by nature, seeking out food on the ground, although they will sometimes perch at least 7m (23ft) off the ground. Both members of the pair are involved in nest-building, and use a variety of vegetation to create a dome shape. The nest is well concealed on the ground, with access to the interior via a side-opening. In some parts of their range, hooded pittas are migratory by nature, and can travel long distances, often flying at night. At the onset of the rainy season they will call after dark.

Identification: Generally has a black head, with green wings and a whitish blue flash on each wing. There is a variable crimson area around the vent, which travels up to the centre of the abdomen. An area of black plumage may appear on the front. White wing patches are sometimes evident. Sexes alike.

Distribution: Sporadic distribution from the foothills of the Himalayas through the Malay Peninsula to Indonesia, New Guinea, the Philippines and other islands in the region.
Size: 30cm (12in).
Habitat: Forested areas.
Nest: Dome-shaped mass of vegetation.
Eggs: 3–5, white with darker, often brownish spots and markings.
Food: Invertebrates.

Blue-winged pitta (*Pitta moluccensis*):
20cm (8in)
Migratory in northern parts of its range; winters in more southerly localities. Occurs in China, Myanmar (Burma), Vietnam, Laos, Cambodia, Thailand and then south through the Malay Peninsula to Sumatra, Borneo and neighbouring islands, occuring at lower altitudes. Has a black crown and black stripe running through the eye that are separated by a brown band. White throat. Green on the back and wings. Underparts buff, becoming crimson around the vent. Violet-blue wing coverts and rump, with a white area here also. Very short tail. Sexes are alike.

Javan banded pitta (*Hydrornis guajanus*):
24cm (9¹⁄₂in)
Found in Java. Yellow to orange stripe above the eyes, with black plumage below, running across the sides of the face. Some white on the throat. Upperparts are chestnut-brown and the tail is a rich shade of blue. The underparts are barred in hens but violet-blue in most cock birds. Banded pittas were formerly a single species however they are now split from Malayan banded pittas (*H. irena*) and Bornean banded pittas (*H. schwaneri*).

Red-naped trogon (*Harpactes kasumba*):
33cm (13in)
Ranges from the Malay Peninsula down to Sumatra and Borneo. Black head, with a white collar across the chest and red plumage beneath. Red collar around the nape of the neck. Bill and bare skin around the eyes are bluish. Underside of the long tail is whitish. Back is brown. Hens are paler, with a greyish head, and buff collar and underparts.

Garnet pitta

Erythropitta granatina

These stunningly beautiful birds are fairly well concealed in their forest habitat, thanks to their preference for thick undergrowth and the deep purplish coloration on their upperparts. They are more likely to reveal their presence to the observer by their distinctive song. This sounds like a whistle that becomes louder and then stops suddenly. It can carry over quite a distance. Having once located the presence of a garnet pitta, it is usually possible to get quite close to the bird without scaring them away, as they are not really particularly shy. They often disappear from tracks in the forest, preferring instead to hunt for food on the forest floor.

Distribution: From Thailand through the Malay Peninsula to northern parts of Sumatra and Borneo.
Size: 15cm (6in).
Habitat: Lowland forests.
Nest: Domed cup of vegetation.
Eggs: 2, glossy-white with reddish-brown spots.
Food: Mainly invertebrates.

Identification: Some regional variation in the markings, with more black on the head of the Bornean race. In common, they have a fiery red area of plumage on the head, the rest of which is black apart from a pale bluish streak on the side of the head. This separates the two colours. Purplish chest and back, with rich crimson underparts. Lighter blue area on the wings. Sexes alike.

Red-headed trogon

Harpactes erythrocephalus

These trogons tend to occupy the lower levels of the thick forest in which they live. They hunt a variety of invertebrates, using a suitable perch as a watchout point before swooping down on their quarry. Like other trogons, these have the 2:2 zygodactyl perching grip, where two toes are directed forwards and two provide support behind the perch. When breeding, these birds seek out tree hollows, which may be natural spaces or created by other birds such as woodpeckers.

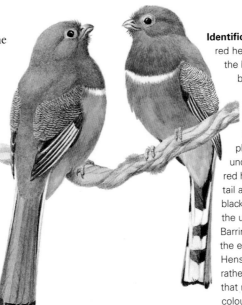

Identification: A bright red head contrasts with the bluish bill and blue, bare skin around the eyes. A white stripe across the breast separates the more pinkish plumage on the underparts from the red head. Wings and tail are brown, with black edging around the upper tail feathers. Barring is present on the edge of the wings. Hens have brownish rather than red heads, that merge into the colour on the back.

Distribution: Ranges widely from the Himalayas across Asia to southern China and south via the Malay Peninsula to Sumatra.
Size: 30cm (12in).
Habitat: Hill forest.
Nest: Tree holes.
Eggs: 2–3, buff.
Food: Invertebrates.

PHEASANTS AND OTHER FOREST-DWELLERS

This group of birds are all likely to be encountered on or certainly near ground level. Some, such as the lyrebird and great argus, have difficulty in flying any distance because of their ornate plumage, whereas the brown kiwi, like others of its kind, has lost the ability to fly altogether.

Superb lyrebird

Queen Victoria's lyrebird *Menura novaehollandiae*

The lyrebird resembles a pheasant and is sometimes known, misleadingly, as the native pheasant. Lyrebirds are shy and hard to spot, but the lyrebird is a talented songbird and the cock's powerful, far-carrying and lyrical song will often reveal his presence. The hens, though, have a quieter call. These birds are most likely to be glimpsed as they scurry across roads and open ground, although they can fly. They seek food on the ground, raking over leaf litter with their powerful feet. The cock bird also uses its feet to scrape up soil to form his display mounds.

Above: The lyrebird's tail feathers are more than 60cm (2ft) in length.

Identification: Dark, brownish upperparts with a coppery hue on the wings. Underparts are greyish. Adult cock birds have a distinctive train of lacy tail plumes with two long outer feathers, known as lyrates, that measure at least 60cm (24in). The tails are made up of seven pairs of feathers, with the central pair the longest. The tail itself is usually carried horizontally. Hens have shorter, more pointed tails without the filamentous plumes.

Distribution: Found in eastern Australia, from southern Queensland to Victoria. Also introduced successfully to Tasmania.
Size: Cock 100cm (38in); hen 86cm (34in).
Habitat: Wooded terrain.
Nest: Large dome-shaped nest constructed from vegetable matter.
Eggs: 1, ranges from grey to purple-brown with dark grey markings.
Food: Invertebrates, including crustaceans.

Golden pheasant

Chrysolophus pictus

Distribution: Occurs naturally in central China. Introduced to a few localities elsewhere, most notably in eastern England.
Size: Cock 115cm (45in); hen 70cm (27½in).
Habitat: Wooded areas with shrubs and bamboo.
Nest: A scrape on the ground.
Eggs: 5–12, buff.
Food: Vegetation and invertebrates.

Adult cock golden pheasants are naturally polygamous, living with two or three hens, but very little else has been documented about the habits of these birds in the wild. They occur in areas where there is dense vegetative cover, and because they live on the ground, observing them in these surroundings is difficult. They feed mainly on the leaves and shoots of a variety of plants, especially bamboo, as well as eating the flowers of rhododendrons.

Identification: Golden-yellow feathering on head, lower back and rump. The underparts are vibrant scarlet, merging into chestnut. The ruff or tippet on the neck is golden with black edging to the plumage and the upper back is green. Has long, mottled tail feathers. Hens in comparison are smaller and a duller colour, being essentially brown with mottling or barring on the feathers. Their tail feathers are pointed at the tips. Young birds resemble hens but have less pronounced markings.

Chestnut-breasted partridge (*Arborophila mandellii*): 28cm (11in)
Ranges from north-east India via Bhutan to south-eastern Tibet. Chestnut crown, paler on the sides of the face, with black speckling. A greyish streak extends back from the eyes. White band with narrow black stripe beneath lies above chestnut breast feathering. Rest of the body is greyish with chestnut speckling on the flanks. Wings browner with black scalloping. Sexes alike.

Crested partridge (Roul-roul, *Rollulus rouloul*): 26cm (10¹/₂in)
Extends from southern Myanmar (Burma) and Thailand through the Malay Peninsula to islands including Sumatra and Borneo. Highly distinctive reddish crest, edged with white. Red skin around the eyes. The rest of the plumage is dark. Hens lack the crest, and are greenish with a greyish head and brownish wings.

Crested fireback (*Lophura ignita*): Cock 66cm (26in): hen 56cm (22in)
Ranges from South-east Asia to the islands of Borneo and Sumatra. Dark bluish crest, with lighter blue wattles around the eyes. Rump is reddish. Dark blue underparts are streaked white or orange. White or buff tail feathers, depending on subspecies. Hens are predominantly brown, even blackish, with blue facial markings. White scalloping to the feathering on the underparts.

Southern brown kiwi

Common kiwi *Apteryx australis*

Distribution: Confined to New Zealand and present on both North and South Island as well as Stewart Island and some smaller islands.
Size: 56cm (22in).
Habitat: Forest.
Nest: In a burrow.
Eggs: 1–2, white or greenish.
Food: Invertebrates and a little fruit.

Identification: The reddish-brown plumage with darker streaking, has a distinctive hair-like texture. Long yellowish bill with bristles at the base. Strong, powerful legs. Sexes alike, although hens are larger with a longer bill.

The kiwi has become New Zealand's national emblem. These highly unusual flightless birds are essentially nocturnal in their habits. They have sensitive nostrils at the end of their bill and locate their food by smell, which is handy in the dark. They also use their bills like levers to pull out worms found in the forest soil. Hens lay what is proportionately the largest egg in the avian world relative to body size, and the yolk is relatively bigger too. This helps to nourish the chick through what is a very long incubation period, typically lasting 12 weeks. The male carries out incubation duties. Young brown kiwis resemble the adult but are smaller.

Great argus

Argusianus argus

The magnificient train created by the tail feathers of the male great argus can be up to 1.2m (4ft) long. Unfortunately, they are shy, solitary birds by nature and, therefore, hard to observe. While hens can fly without difficulty, the enlarged flight feathers of the cock, coupled with its long train affects its ability to fly any distance at all. It is not until a young male is three years old that the elongated feathers start to develop, with their transformation occurring gradually over successive moults over the next four years. They are generally used for display purposes.

Identification: Head and neck are blue, with a short blackish crest at the back of the head. Has white spots over brown plumage on the body. Large eye-like markings called ocelli in the wings. Upper breast is rusty-red. Grey coloration on the central tail feathers. Hens are much smaller, with a paler blue head and barred markings on the short tail.

Distribution: The Malay Peninsula, but absent from the south. Also found on Sumatra and Borneo.
Size: Cock 200cm (79in); hen 76cm (30in).
Habitat: Primary and logged areas of forest.
Nest: Hollow lined with grass.
Eggs: 2, creamy white.
Food: Plant matter and ants.

Left: The final stage of the cock's display involves bowing to the hen with his magnificent tail feathers held erect.

BROADBILLS AND OTHER SMALLER WOODLAND BIRDS

A number of Asian birds have ornamental rackets at the tips of their tail feathers, which are attached by so-called shafts, which like the racket are a continuation of the feather and quite flexible. They tend to be used for display purposes, although other ornamentations of the plumage, such as crests and bright coloration, can be seen in many broadbills.

Green broadbill

Calyptomena viridis

Distribution: From Myanmar (Burma) and western Thailand to the Malay Peninsula, Sumatra and Borneo.
Size: 17cm (7in).
Habitat: Lower levels of rainforest. Very rarely encountered in forests that have been logged.
Nest: Made of plant fibres.
Eggs: 1–3, whitish.
Food: Fruit.

These broadbills are so-called because of the size of their gape, or mouth-opening, rather than the size of their bill. They feed by foraging for fruit and their wide gape allows them to eat it whole. Their bill is very weak and lacks a cutting edge so they can only eat soft fruits such as members of the fig family. The green broadbill helps to maintain structure and diversity within the rainforest, since their feeding habits mean that they help to distribute the indigestible seeds of such plants via their droppings as they move around the forest. Their nest is an elaborate construction, resembling a bottle gourd in shape. It is suspended from a very thin branch as this helps to protect the birds from possible predators.

Identification: Has dark green plumage with three black bars across the top of the wings. A black circular area lies behind each eye. The very short tail emphasizes the outline of the plump body. The crest above the bill is larger in males. Hens are green all over but it is a lighter shade than the cocks.

Lesser cuckooshrike

Coracina fimbriata

Despite their name, these birds are related to neither cuckoos nor shrikes, but are actually a relative of the crow family, according to DNA studies. They are so-called because they resemble the cuckoos in shape and appearance, and yet are equipped with a strong, hooked bill like shrikes, which is used for seizing invertebrates. Lesser cuckooshrikes are birds of the forest canopy. They even nest in the canopy and are most unlikely to be seen on the ground. These cuckooshrike's young have very different colouring, with barring evident over what is primarily white plumage. These birds have relatively harsh calls which are most likely to be uttered when they are in a group, although individuals have been known to sing on occasion.

Identification: Mainly grey, although the sides of the face, wings and tail are blackish. There is white edging to the tips of the tail feathers. The eyes are dark brown. Hens are paler and have pale grey, rather than black, feathering on their face, plus some distinctive barring on underparts.

Distribution: Ranges across the Malay Peninsula to Java and Sumatra in the Greater Sunda islands. Also Borneo.
Size: 20cm (8in).
Habitat: Lowland and hill forest.
Nest: Cup-shaped, made of vegetation.
Eggs: 3 olive-green, with brown markings.
Food: Invertebrates.

Orange-bellied leafbird

Chloropsis hardwickii

The relatively long bills of these birds are used to search for invertebrates among the leaves, and to probe flowers in search of nectar. The eponymous coloration of the orange-bellied leafbird allows it to blend effectively into a background of vegetation. Young, recently fledged birds are entirely green. Their nests are well hidden in forks of trees. These leafbirds are solitary by nature, although they are more likely to be seen in pairs during the breeding season. They have quite loud, meliforous calls, with cocks singing more frequently during the breeding period. Leafbirds are also talented mimics and can master the song of other birds.

Identification: Mainly green upperparts with a black mask that extends from the cheeks down on to the chest. This is broken by a blue streak that runs down below the bill. Underparts are orange-yellow. There is some dark blue plumage in the wings. The tail is dark blue. Hens are essentially green with matching underparts but have lighter blue streaks on the sides of the long bill.

Distribution: Extends from the Himalayan region to southern China and south to areas of South-east Asia down to the Malay Peninsula.
Size: 20cm (8in).
Habitat: Hill forests.
Nest: Loose cup.
Eggs: 2–3, buff-cream with pale red markings.
Food: Mainly invertebrates. Also nectar and fruit.

Greater racket-tailed drongo

Dicrurus paradiseus

Distribution: Ranges from India eastwards through South-east Asia to China and down across the Malay Peninsula to the Greater Sundas. Is present on Sumatra, Java and Bali as well as Borneo.
Size: 36cm (14in).
Habitat: Lowland forest.
Nest: Cup-shaped, made from vegetation.
Eggs: 3–4, creamy-white with dark markings.
Food: Invertebrates.

Identification: Has bluish-black plumage, with a short crest above the bill. Sharply forked tail with narrow tail shafts that end in twisted enlargements known as rackets. During the moulting period, however, the rackets may be missing or simply not developed to their full extent. The sharp, pointed bill is black as are the legs and feet. Sexes alike.

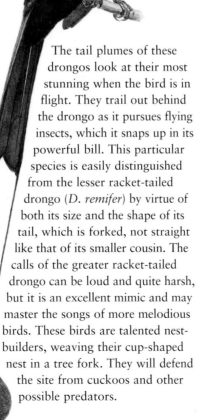

The tail plumes of these drongos look at their most stunning when the bird is in flight. They trail out behind the drongo as it pursues flying insects, which it snaps up in its powerful bill. This particular species is easily distinguished from the lesser racket-tailed drongo (*D. remifer*) by virtue of both its size and the shape of its tail, which is forked, not straight like that of its smaller cousin. The calls of the greater racket-tailed drongo can be loud and quite harsh, but it is an excellent mimic and may master the songs of more melodious birds. These birds are talented nest-builders, weaving their cup-shaped nest in a tree fork. They will defend the site from cuckoos and other possible predators.

Long-tailed broadbill (*Psarisomus dalhousiae*): 25cm (10in)
Sporadic distribution where suitable habitat is found from the eastern Himalayas across much of South-east Asia to Sumatra and Borneo. Black plumage on the top and rear of the head, with small blue and yellow areas. White collar around the neck. Greenish underparts and dark green over the back. Some blue on the wings. Blue tail. Hens may have faint yellow area on the nape.

Banded broadbill (purple-headed broadbill, *Eurylaimus javanicus*): 23cm (9in)
From Indo-China and Malaysia to Java, Sumatra and Borneo. Purple-maroon plumage on the head and underparts. Has an obvious black breast band that is absent in hens. Yellow markings on the back and wings, which are otherwise dark in colour. Bill pale blue and yellower at the tip.

Dusky broadbill (*Corydon sumatranus*): 25cm (10in)
Ranges from Indo-China down across the Malay Peninsula to Sumatra and Borneo. Pinkish-purple bill and bare skin around the eyes. The plumage is paler on the throat and blackish-brown elsewhere. Sexes alike.

Large woodshrike (*Tephrodornis virgatus*): 22cm (8¹/₂in)
Found in western India, and from the Himalayas across South-east Asia to southern China and south through the Malay Peninsula to Java, Sumatra and Borneo. Ten races recognized: larger birds with browner back in northern areas; smaller greyer populations in the south. Black stripe running through the eye. Rump whitish, as is the area under the throat. Underparts pale grey. Hens similar to cocks, but with browner tails.

PIGEONS AND DOVES

The diversity that exists within this group of birds can be seen at its greatest in the Australasian region, which is home to some of the most bizarre and distinctive members of this widely distributed family of birds. Vivid red, yellow and blue hues are apparent in the plumage of a number of species from the area, especially in the case of the fruit doves forming the genus Ptilinopus.

Nicobar pigeon

Caloenas nicobarica

These highly distinctive pigeons are found on many islands, particularly those least affected by human habitation. They are largely terrestrial, although if disturbed on the ground, they fly up noisily to branches close to the forest canopy. Here, their dark coloration makes them hard to spot. Nicobar pigeons have a particularly thick-walled gizzard, which allows them to grind up and digest large, heavily coated seeds without difficulty. Inevitable food shortages on small islands mean that these pigeons are often forced to forage further afield, crossing the sea to nearby larger islands, particularly during the breeding season when they are feeding their chicks.

Identification: Predominantly dark slaty-grey with green and coppery iridescent tones evident over the wings. Trail of long, relatively narrow feathers hanging down from the neck. White tail feathers and prominent swelling, known as a caruncle, on the top of the bill. Sexes alike.

Distribution: Found on islands in the Bay of Bengal eastwards as far as Palau and the Solomons. Larger numbers on breeding islands.
Size: 34cm (13in).
Habitat: Coastal forest areas.
Nest: Loose platform of twigs in a tree or bush.
Eggs: 1, white.
Food: Mainly seeds and fruit, some invertebrates.

Victoria crowned pigeon

White-tipped crown pigeon *Goura victoria*

Distribution: Northern New Guinea. Extends from Geelvink Bay to Collingwood Bay. Also found on a few smaller offshore islands here, such as Biak, Salawati and Seram.
Size: 74cm (29in).
Habitat: Lowland forest areas where the pigeons spend much of their time on the ground.
Nest: Platform of sticks, palm leaves and other vegetation.
Eggs: 1, white.
Food: Fruits, seeds and invertebrates.

This is one of three species of crowned pigeon occurring in New Guinea. These birds are likely to be encountered wandering in groups of up to ten individuals through forested areas, although in recent years they have become much scarcer near settlements as the result of being heavily hunted. If disturbed, crowned pigeons will fly up on to branches. Pairs also nest off the ground. The young bird is much smaller than its parents on fledging. It grows slowly, and will not be fully independent until more than three months old.

Identification: Has unique white tips to the blue lacy fan-like crest on the head. Remainder of the body primarily pale bluish grey, with a maroon breast and bluish underparts. Area of maroon also on the lower edges of the wing, with pale blue wing bar above. Lighter blue tip to the tail. Black feathering extends over the red irises. Sexes alike. Some individuals will display more black areas in their plumage than others.

Pied imperial pigeon (*Ducula bicolor*):
38cm (15in)
Found on islands across southern Asia down to
Australia. Frequently in coastal areas; scarce in
the Lesser Sundas. Creamy white with black flight
feathers and broad blackish area on the tail. Dark-
greyish bill and eyes. Some races have black
barring on the undertail coverts. Sexes alike.

Wedge-tailed green pigeon (*Treron sphenurus*):
33cm (13in)
Ranges from Himalayan region to southern China,
across the Malay Peninsula to Sumatra, Java and
Lombok. Greenish, with claret areas on the wings
adjoining the shoulders. Pale blue wash and slight
orangish hue on the breast, depending on race.
Dark green barring on yellow undertail coverts.
Long, wedge-shaped tail. Hens are greener.

Jambu fruit dove (*Ptilinopus jambu*):
24cm (9½in)
Ranges from southern peninsular Thailand to
Sumatra, western Java and Borneo. Red mask on
the face, with a paler breast and white plumage
on the lower underparts. Back of the head, wings
and tail are green. Undertail coverts are brown.
Hens are dark green overall, with a dull purple
area on the face and greyish tone to the breast.

Barred cuckoo-dove (*Macropygia unchall*):
37cm (14½in)
Extends from Himalayan region to China, parts of
South-east Asia and the Malay Peninsula. On to
Java, Sumatra, Bali, Flores and Lombok. Greyish-
pink on the head and neck, greenish suffusion on
the neck. Black, with chestnut markings on the
back, wings and long tail. Barring on the chest.
Hens have black and chestnut underparts.

Wompoo fruit dove

Ptilinopus magnificus

Distribution: Present
throughout New Guinea,
except the central
mountainous region. Also
extends down the eastern
side of Australia.
Size: Races vary widely, from
29 to 48cm (11½ to 19in).
Habitat: Mainly evergreen
rainforest.
Nest: Loose platform
constructed off the ground.
Eggs: 1, white.
Food: Fruit.

Identification: Pale greyish head,
with red eyes and a red bill with
a yellow tip. Back, wings and tail
are dark green, with a contrasting
yellow wing bar. Claret breast,
with the lower part of the body
and under-wing feathering bright
yellow. Greyish undertail coverts
are edged with yellow. Underside
of the flight feathers and tail are
greyish. Sexes alike.

Wompoo fruit
doves are so-
called because
of the sound of
their distinctive
calls. Living in
rainforest areas
means that there
will be sources
of fruit available to
these birds throughout the year, and they
have been documented as feeding on more
than 50 different types. Indigestible seeds
pass through their bodies and are deposited
elsewhere in the forest, and this helps to
maintain their food supply in the future.
Like other fruit pigeons, they have a very
wide gape, enabling them to swallow fruits
whole, as they are unable to bite into them
with their rather weak bills. Young chicks
grow very rapidly and will leave the nest at
just under two
weeks old.

*Left:
Although
both sexes
will share
incubation
duties, the
cock tends
to sit the
longest.*

Pheasant pigeon

Otidiphaps nobilis

Distribution: Much of New
Guinea and various small
islands.
Size: 46cm (18in).
Habitat: Hill forests.
Nest: Sticks on the ground in
a tree buttress.
Eggs: 1, white.
Food: Seeds and fruit.

These unusual pigeons
have no close relatives,
although they actually walk
a little like pheasants, with
their head held forwards and
their tail feathers moving
rhythmically. They are seen
on their own or in pairs. Being
both shy and alert by nature,
pheasant pigeons are very hard
to observe in the field, however,
unless the observer is well hidden.
When displaying during the breeding
period, males will swoop down from
a perch, flapping their short wings to
create an unusual sound that has
been likened to a gunshot.

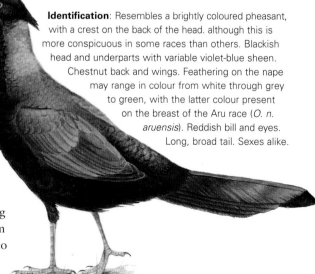

Identification: Resembles a brightly coloured pheasant,
with a crest on the back of the head. although this is
more conspicuous in some races than others. Blackish
head and underparts with variable violet-blue sheen.
Chestnut back and wings. Feathering on the nape
may range in colour from white through grey
to green, with the latter colour present
on the breast of the Aru race (*O. n.
aruensis*). Reddish bill and eyes.
Long, broad tail. Sexes alike.

CORVIDS

Blackish plumage predominates in members of the crow family, although there are some spectacularly coloured members of the family found in the Australasian region, such as the vivid green hunting cissas. Corvids are an adaptable group of birds, found in a wide range of habitats, and are not easily overlooked, thanks often to their loud calls.

Forest raven

Tasmanian raven *Corvus tasmanicus*

These ravens are often seen in flocks, sometimes scavenging on rubbish tips for food. Pairs do not breed communally, preferring to seek out separate sites in tall trees, lining the inside of their nest with animal hair or wool. The colour of the eyes provides a means of aging these corvids. They are bluish grey prior to fledging and brownish by the time of fledging. It is not until they are three years old that the characteristic white coloration becomes evident.

Identification: Stocky outline with relatively short wings and tail. Glossy black coloration, with a purplish-blue, or greenish-blue, suffusion. The plumage on the abdomen tends to be held quite loosely rather than lying sleekly. Iris is whitish. Heavy, blackish bill and feet. Hens are slightly smaller.

Distribution: Tasmania and offshore islands, as well as the south-eastern corner of the Australian mainland.
Size: 52cm (21in).
Habitat: Most common in wooded areas.
Nest: Bulky cup of twigs and sticks.
Eggs: 3–6, greenish with darker markings.
Food: Carrion, invertebrates and vegetable matter.

Common green magpie

Cissa chinensis

The plumage of the common green magpie can undergo an unusual but spectacular change, depending on its environmental conditions. When these birds live in relatively open country, the stronger sunlight actually bleaches their plumage. This results in the green areas becoming transformed into a light sky blue shade, while the chestnut patches change to a darker, duller shade of brown. The magpies usually occupy the lower reaches of the forest, searching in small parties through the shrubbery for invertebrates and will even eat carrion on occasions. Pairs breed on their own. The young birds have yellow bills and legs once they fledge.

Identification: Predominantly light green, with black bands running through the eyes. Broad chestnut areas cover the wings, with characteristic black and white barring where the wings meet. The undersides of the tail feathers are also black and white. Bill, legs and feet red. Sexes similar.

Distribution: Occurs over an extensive area from north-west India down to South-east Asia, as well as on the islands of Sumatra and Borneo.
Size: 39cm (15in).
Habitat: Edges of hill and lowland forests.
Nest: Cup-shaped platform of vegetation.
Eggs: 3–7, white through to pale green with darker markings.
Food: Invertebrates.

Slender-billed crow (*Corvus enca*):
47cm (18¹/₂in)
Malay Peninsula and numerous offshore islands,
including Sumatra, Java, Bali, Borneo, and the
Sula islands. Entirely black plumage. Relatively
slim bill shape. Culmen curves quite gently and
is bare of feathers at its base. Sexes alike.

Large-billed crow (*Corvus macrorhynchos*):
43–59cm (17–23in)
From Himalayan region and eastern Asia to
Siberia and China, through South-east Asia to
the Malay Peninsula. Present on many islands,
from Sumatra, Java and Borneo north to Japan
and the Philippines. Entirely black but with
arched and long bill. Broad wings. Hens are
slightly smaller.

Brown-headed crow (*Corvus fuscicapillus*):
45cm (18in)
Found in northern New Guinea and neighbouring
islands. Has a dark brown rather than blackish
head and a short, square tail. The bill is large and
distinctly curved. Sexes are alike, but young
birds can be distinguished by their yellowish
rather than black bills.

Grey crow (Bare-faced crow, *Corvus tristis*):
45cm (18in)
Widely distributed through New Guinea. Variable
coloration depends partly on age. Adults blackish,
with browner tone to underparts. Patches of bare
skin around pale blue eyes. Hens usually smaller.
Young birds are greyer overall, paler on the head
and underparts than the wings.

Crested jay

Platylophus galericulatus

Distribution: From Thailand
and the Malay Peninsula
south to Sumatra, Java and
Borneo.
Size: 33cm (13.5in).
Habitat: Lowland forest
areas.
Nest: Platform of twigs.
Eggs: Presently unrecorded.
Food: Invertebrates.

Identification: Highly distinctive
tail and reasonably broad crest.
Adults vary from a shade
bordering on black to reddish-
brown, depending on
the race. In all
cases, a broad
white area is evident
on the side of the neck. Bill and
legs are blackish. Sexes are alike.
Juvenile birds display barred
plumage on their underparts.

With their distinctive crest, these jays are
instantly recognizable, but relatively little
is known about their habits through their
wide range. They are quite bold by nature
and not instinctively given to flying away
from people, especially when searching
in the branches for food. They move their
crest feathers up and down readily, and
call quite loudly as well, uttering
notes that have been likened to
a rattle. The most distinctive of
these races (*P. g. coronatus*) is
found on Borneo and Sumatra.
It is a reddish-brown overall,
which is not dissimilar to
the basic colour of
young birds from
other races.

Hooded treepie

Crypsirina cucullata

These particular treepies are
thought to have become
much rarer over recent
years as a direct result of
the deforestation of their
natural habitat. These birds
hunt their prey in vegetation
rather than on the ground.
They may sometimes
be seen in small parties, but
pairs will breed on their own
rather than in colonies. The nest
itself is often partly covered with a
dome made of spiny branches, which
offers increased protection against nest-
raiders. Young birds can be identified for
a year or so after fledging by the orange
skin inside their mouths. This turns yellow
during their second year and finally black.
Their plumage is darker than an adult bird's.

Identification: Mainly pale grey with a
narrow white band below the black head.
Has black wings and central tail feathers
enlarged at their tips. Other tail feathers are
fawn grey. The irises are dark. Sexes alike.

Distribution: Exclusively
present in Myanmar (Burma),
but particularly observed in
central areas.
Size: 30cm (12in).
Habitat: Lowland forest.
Nest: Cup-shaped, made
from vegetation.
Eggs: 2–4, creamy to
greenish white with dark
markings.
Food: Invertebrates, and
some berries.

BIRDS-OF-PARADISE AND BOWERBIRDS

The magnificent appearance of mature cock birds of these species is totally unique. There are approximately 43 distinct species of birds of paradise and 18 recognized species of bowerbird. Their distribution is centred on New Guinea, extending to neighbouring islands, south as far as Australia. Hens in contrast are much duller, as are their offspring who take several years to reach adult coloration.

Golden bowerbird

Newton's bowerbird *Prionodura newtoniana*

Cock birds are quite flamboyantly coloured, with their longer crest feathers being erected for display purposes. They are so-called because the males construct ornate structures called bowers, which are used to attract would-be mates. These bowers are carefully built from twigs and other vegetation, and well maintained. The golden bowerbird may be the smallest of all bowerbirds, but it constructs the largest bower, up to 3m (10ft) in height. The eggs are laid in a separate site by the hen.

Identification: Cock bird has a yellow-olive head, with a short yellow crest. Wings are olive, with the underparts a rich, glistening golden shade, extending to the tail feathers. Hens have much duller coloration, with olive-brown upperparts. Underparts are greyish, with slight streaking on the throat and breast. Hens are also smaller in size.

Distribution: North-eastern Queensland, Australia
Size: 25cm (10in).
Habitat: mountain rainforest
Nest: Cup-shaped, made of vegetation.
Eggs: 2, creamy white.
Food: Fruit such as wild figs, plus insects.

Red bird-of-paradise

Paradisaea rubra

Hard to spot against a forest background, in spite of their striking appearance, these birds-of-paradise are most likely to reveal their presence by their shrill calls, which echo through the trees. Cock birds live in groups, separate from hens, and will gather at specific trees traditionally used for display purposes. Red birds of paradise tend to call down from branches in the canopy and their calls are uttered rapidly – about once every second. They forage up and down tree trunks.

Distribution: Western Papuan islands of Batanta, Waigeu and Saonek.
Size: 33cm (13in).
Habitat: Dense tropical forest.
Nest: Cup-shaped.
Eggs: 1, creamy with darker streaks.
Food: Predominantly fruit and also invertebrates.

Identification: Long, delicate red feathering on the flanks. Green plumage extends over the top of the head. Unusual curled, ribbon-like tail wires, which can be as long as 59cm (23in) when extended. Hens are less bright but have a yellow nuchal collar.

Great bowerbird (Queensland bowerbird, *Chlamydera nuchalis*): 37.5cm (15in)
Present in northern Australia from Broome in the west of the area to the coast of Queensland. The cock has grey on the underparts, mottled upperparts and a whitish edging to the brownish plumage over the wing and rump. A striking lilac crest is apparent on the nape of the neck. Hens may lack this crest feathering and are paler with less mottling.

Arfak astrapia (black astrapia, *Astrapia nigra*): 76cm (30in)
Restricted to the Arfak mountains of Vogelkop, north-western New Guinea. Cock has a broad purplish tail, bluish-green coloration on the throat and a blackish chest area with a copper-coloured surround. Head and wings dark, with back and underparts being green. Hens are greyish-brown, with barring on their tail and underparts.

King bird-of-paradise (*Cicinnurus regius*): 15cm (6in)
New Guinea and nearby islands. Cock bird has red upperparts and white underparts. Very short tail, with two wires terminating in green discs. Bill yellowish. Both sexes have blue legs. Hens are mainly brownish-greyish, with barred underparts.

Wilson's bird-of-paradise (*Diphyllodes respublica*): 17cm (7in)
Solely confined to the Western Papuan islands of Waigeo and Batanta. Cock birds have a blue cap on the head, yellow mantle, red back and wings. The underparts are green. The short tail is black and the tail wires spiral. Hens also have a blue cap and a black area over the rest of the head, but the wings and back are greyish brown, and the underparts are heavily barred.

Magnificent riflebird

Ptiloris magnificus

The distinctive display of the cock bird involves puffing out its chest feathering and stretching out its wings. Tall trees, often covered in vines and other creepers, are favoured as display sites. The sudden explosive calls of cock birds resemble the sound of a rifle firing, although distinctive regional dialects exist in the two separate New Guinea populations. The magnificent riflebirds found in the east – in Sepik, for example – make a more guttural noise than the westerly populations. These birds are sometimes seen foraging on trees in the company of babblers and pitohuis, seeking out invertebrates that have been disturbed by their companions.

Identification: Cocks dark with short tails and a long bill, and an iridescent bluish area on the crown and breast. Females also have a long elongated bill, but are basically brown in colour, with barring on their underparts.

Distribution: Parts of New Guinea and Queensland, Australia.
Size: 37cm (14¹⁄₂in).
Habitat: Forested, usually upland areas.
Nest: Deep cup-shaped nest, often built in a palm.
Eggs: 2, creamy with some darker markings.
Food: Fruit and invertebrates.

Black-billed sicklebill

Drepanornis albertisi

Distribution: North-west, central and east New Guinea.
Size: 35cm (14in).
Habitat: Mountain forests.
Nest: Broad cup-shape.
Eggs: 1, pinky cream with red and grey blotching.
Food: Fruit and invertebrates.

It is thought that the long, narrow curved bill of these birds probably helps them to feed. Although not rare, very little is known about the black-billed sicklebill's habits and this is partly because they usually occur in the upper branches of the tallest trees, making them hard to observe. In addition, their coloration enables them to blend into their surroundings very effectively. It is thought that they feed in a woodpecker-like fashion on tree bark, using their long bills to probe for invertebrates that might be lurking in holes in the trunk or under loose bark. Their distribution does not appear to be consistent throughout their range, even in areas of apparently identical habitat. On occasions, the powerful musical call of a cock bird may be heard.

Identification: The stunning beauty of the cock bird is most apparent during the display, when the tufted areas of feathering on the sides of the body are held erect. Hens lack these fan tufts, and are brownish with mottled plumage on the underparts and also have longer, more pointed tail feathers, which are darker in colour than those of cocks.

CASSOWARIES AND PARROTS

These distinct groups include not just one of the largest birds of the world, in the guise of the southern cassowary, but also a representative of the group of smallest parrots in the world, which are appropriately known as pygmy parrots. They represent two extremes within the avian order that can be encountered within the forest environment in the Australasian region.

Southern cassowary

Double-wattled cassowary *Casuarius casuarius*

Distribution: New Guinea, apart from northern-central region and the central highlands. Also on the Aru Islands. Two separate Australian populations found in north-eastern Queensland.
Size: 130–170cm (51–67in).
Habitat: Rainforest areas.
Nest: Depression on the ground.
Eggs: 3–5, pale to dark green.
Food: Mainly fruit, some animal matter.

These gigantic birds of the forest are quite able to kill a person if cornered, disembowelling them with a blow from the long inner claw present on their feet. The colour of the bare skin on the cassowary's head and neck changes with mood, becoming more brightly coloured when the bird is excited or angry. Hens mate with a number of different cock birds, leaving the male to hatch and rear the chicks on their own. The young cassowaries stay with the male for up to nine months.

Identification: Massive, predominantly black flightless bird with immensely powerful feet. Has a large blade-like casque on the head and a powerful bill. Head tends to be bluish overall with two striking reddish wattles hanging down the neck. Hens have a larger casque and are also much heavier, weighing up to 58kg (128lb), whereas males rarely exceed 34kg (75lb).

Red-breasted pygmy parrot

Mountain pygmy parrot *Micropsitta bruijnii*

As their name suggests, the pygmy parrots are the smallest of all parrots, with their distribution confined to islands off South-east Asia. This particular species is found at higher altitudes than are other pygmy parrots, and also uses trees rather than arboreal termite nests as breeding sites. They have jerky movements, rather reminiscent of nuthatches (*Sitta* species), and cling close to the bark as they search for the lichens growing on trees, which form the major part of their diet.

Identification: Has a buff-red crown, becoming bluish-purple at the back of the neck. The throat and cheeks are also buff-red and become yellowish around the bill. The remainder of the underparts are red while the back and wings are mainly dark green. Hens have a blue crown with buff orange cheeks, although these areas are a paler shade than in the cock.

Distribution: Buru, Seram and central New Guinea east to the Bismarck Archipelago and the Solomon Islands.
Size: 8cm (3in).
Habitat: Forest areas.
Nest: Tree holes.
Eggs: 3, white.
Food: Plant matter.

Edwards's fig parrot

Psittaculirostris edwardsii

These chunky parrots are very agile when feeding, and can consume food while hanging upside down from a branch with very little difficulty. As their name suggests, figs form an important part of their diet, and hundreds of these small parrots may congregate in an area where the fruit is freely available. More commonly, however, they live in pairs or small groups, and can be hard to spot in the canopy where they feed, despite the fact that they are not especially shy birds by nature, because their size makes them less conspicuous.

Distribution: Restricted to north-eastern area of New Guinea.
Size: 18cm (7in).
Habitat: Lowland forest.
Nest: Tree holes.
Eggs: 2–3, white.
Food: Fruit and some invertebrates.

Identification: Cock birds have a green crown with a narrow black stripe extending behind the eye. Yellow area beneath eye, along with some sky blue feathering, while the cheeks, breast and abdomen are scarlet, broken with variable violet markings across the throat. Hens are duller in colour, with green rather than red plumage below the collar. Young birds of both sexes resemble the hen, although their ear coverts are of a more greenish-yellow shade.

Brehm's tiger parrot (*Psittacella brehmii*): 24cm (9¹/₂in)
Three distinct populations: exist in the central highlands of New Guinea; north-east Huon Peninsula; and Vogelkop, where they live in areas of mountain forest. Cock bird has an olive-brown head, with a partial yellow collar on either side, and displays green underparts and red undertail coverts. Green feathering on the back is edged with black. Hens similar but display barring on the breast and lack any yellow plumage on the neck.

Pesquet's parrot
(*Psittrichas fulgidus*):
46cm (18in)
Two distinct populations are present on New Guinea. One is more localized, confined to the Vogelkop, while the other extends through the central area of the island towards the Huon Peninsula and the south-east.T These parrots are unmistakable, with bare skin on the head, predominantly black plumage with barring on the chest and brilliant scarlet red areas on the wings and underparts. Their profile in flight is more like that of a vulture than a parrot, soaring readily above the forest. Sexes are alike.

Papuan king parrot
(green-winged king parrot, *Alisterus chloropterus*):
38cm (15in)
Found in northern, central and south-eastern parts of New Guinea. Cocks have a red head and underparts, green wings with distinctive yellow-green barring and purple over the back, which may be darker in shade than that on the wings, depending on the race. These king parrots also have a long dark tail. Hens are duller than cocks and more uniform in colour, with a green head, breast and wings. The exception is the northern race (*A. c. moszkowskii*), where hens generally resemble the cocks, but with a green mantle.

Eclectus parrot

Eclectus roratus

This species represents the most extreme example of sexual dimorphism among all parrots. It was thought for many years following their discovery that the cock and hen were actually two separate species. There are around ten distinct races, and it is the appearance of the hen birds that differs most markedly. The feeding habits of these parrots are such that they are often seen in agricultural areas, readily feeding on crops ranging from bananas to maize. They are dependent on mature trees as nest sites however, choosing chambers that may be up to 6m (20ft) in depth.

Identification: Thick-set, with quite short, broad tails. Mostly green, with a yellowish upper bill and a red patch on the flanks. Hens have black bills. They are bright red, typically with purplish markings on the underparts, although these markings depend on the race. You can determine a juvenile's sex in the nest, from the colour of its plumage.

Distribution: Centred on New Guinea, but extends widely, to islands to both the west and east. A small population is also present on the Cape York peninsula, Australia.
Size: 35cm (14in).
Habitat: Lowland forests, often in coastal regions. Also in mangroves.
Nest: Tree hollow.
Eggs: 2, white.
Food: Fruit, buds and seeds.

LORIKEETS AND OTHER PSITTACINES

Cockatoos, with their distinctive crest feathers that can be raised when an individual is alarmed or excited, are confined to islands off South-east Asia, extending as far as Australia. Their plumage differs significantly from that of other parrots in another, less obvious way, however, in that it lacks the so-called blue layer. As a result, cockatoos tend to be either black or white.

Papuan lorikeet

Charmosyna papou

The beautiful, active and agile lorikeets are likely to be encountered in groups in the vicinity of flowering trees. They tend to bound from branch to branch, rather than flying. Their long tongues are specially adapted, as in the case of other lories and lorikeets, with special brush-like papillae that can be raised to sweep tiny pollen granules into the mouth. The melanistic form occurs in those populations, such as Stella's lorikeet (*C. p. stellae*), that are found in the eastern part of their range. Such birds tend to be found at higher altitudes. They interbreed freely with their red-coloured cousins, and both forms can be present in the same nest.

Identification: Four different races exist, all of which have long, narrow tail streamers. Predominantly red with a violet and black area on the back of the head. Has violet-blue under-parts. Green wings and tail, which is yellowish at the tip. Hens distinguished by yellow rump. Also occurs in a melanistic form, with black replacing the red plumage, except on the back and under the tail.

Left: The melanistic form of the papuan lorikeet is a naturally occuring mutation of the species.

Distribution: Confined to New Guinea, with populations in Vogelkop, central areas and down to the south-east. Also occurs in isolation on the Huon Peninsula.
Size: 42cm (16¹/₂in) including tail plumes.
Habitat: Woodland areas from 1,500–3,500m (5,000–11,500ft.)
Nest: Tree hollow.
Eggs: 2–3, white.
Food: Mainly nectar, pollen and fruit.

Palm cockatoo

Goliath cockatoo *Probosciger aterrimus*

Distribution: Found through much of New Guinea, aside from the central region. Also present on western Papuan and neighbouring islands, and the northern tip of the Cape York peninsula of Australia.
Size: 64cm (25in).
Habitat: Forest areas, especially edges of rainforest.
Nest: Hollow tree.
Eggs: 1, white.
Food: Nuts, seeds and fruit.

The very distinctive appearance of these cockatoos sets them apart from other species. They call frequently and loudly, with their calls having been likened to the braying of a donkey, when heard from some distance away. Their powerful bills allow them to crack the thick-shelled nuts of forest trees with little difficulty. Male birds often drum with a piece of stick, using this to bang rhythmically on the side of a tree trunk during the nesting period, as part of a territorial display. Unlike other cockatoos, they also line their chosen nesting cavity with a platform of sticks. It is thought this behaviour may help to prevent either the egg or chick being lost as a result of flooding during heavy rains.

Identification: Predominantly black, with a large, distinctive, erectile crest. Bare patch of reddish facial skin. Massive, powerful bill, which is smaller in hens. Sexes are otherwise alike. Juvenile birds have a paler patch of facial skin, and the skin around their eyes is whitish.

Yellowish-streaked lory

Chalcopsitta scintillata

These lories are adaptable in terms of the countryside where they can be observed, seeking out the flowering trees on which they depend for their food. They may subsequently invade orchards, in search of ripening fruit, and can sometimes be spotted feeding in the company of other lories. Yellowish-streaked lories are quite social by nature, and so they are often observed flying in small flocks, calling out noisily at the same time. Even when perched, they often reveal their presence by their calls, which sound like persistent squealing. Young birds may be harder to recognize, due to the lack of red plumage on the forehead.

Identification: Has a bright red area above the bill. The head is blackish, becoming browner on the breast with lighter streaking. Wings, back and underparts are mainly green, but have yellowish streaking on the abdomen. Thighs are red. Bill black, legs and feet are grey. Sexes alike.

Distribution: The southern part of New Guinea from Triton Bay and Geelvink Bay in the west to Port Moresby in the east. Also occurs on the Aru islands.
Size: 31cm (12¹/₂in).
Habitat: Forested areas, including coconut plantations.
Nest: Tree holes.
Eggs: 2–3, white.
Food: Nectar, pollen and fruit.

Orange-fronted hanging parrot (Papuan hanging parrot, *Loriculus aurantiifrons*): 10cm (4in)
Occurs through much of New Guinea, especially lowland areas, with the notable exception of the south-central region and small offshore islands. Predominantly green. Has a yellow crown and an orangish area on the throat. The rump is red with a yellow border. Hens lack the yellow crown. They have green heads with a bluish tinge to their cheeks and their bill is black. These parrots are so-called because of their habit of roosting upside down.

Fairy lorikeet (Little red lorikeet, *Charmosyna pulchella*): 19cm (7¹/₂in)
Found in central parts of New Guinea. Relatively small, with a mainly red head. The breast is red and streaked with a row of yellow feathers. Has a black area on the back of the head, with violet on the back and sides. The long tail is reddish on its upperparts. Hens display yellow plumage on the rump and the adjacent area of the back.

Red-cheeked parrot (Geoffroy's song parrot, *Geoffroyus geoffroyi*): 21cm (8¹/₂in)
Found on various islands from Lombok and the Moluccas eastward via New Guinea to Rossel, which is part of the Louisiade Archipelago. Also present on Australia's Cape York peninsula. Predominantly bright green, often with a red shoulder patch. Plum-coloured head with violet crown and nape. Broad and short-tailed. Blue visible under the wings. Hens have brown heads with black bills.

Whiskered lorikeet (Plum-faced lorikeet, *Oreopsittacus arfaki*): 15cm (6in)
Three separate populations in the mountainous areas of New Guinea. Predominantly green. Bright red area on the top of the head. White streaks below the eyes are on a mauve background and edged with black. Reddish underside to the tail. Hens have a green, rather than red, area on top of the head. Sexes otherwise alike.

Great-billed parrot

Tanygnathus megalorynchos

These parrots frequently move between smaller islands, although their fractured distribution means that five different races have been identified through their range, each varying slightly in terms of plumage. Great-billed parrots move in search of food, congregating in relatively large numbers at favoured feeding sites. They may even be encountered in mangroves. In flight their large bill and short tail means that they can be identified quite easily. Their strong bills enable them to crack nuts with ease.

Distribution: Present in the Moluccas, the western Papuan, Lesser Sunda and Tanimbar islands, as well as islands around Sulawesi. Thought to have been introduced to Balut in the Philippines.
Size: 41cm (16in).
Habitat: Forested coastal areas and foothills.
Nest: Tree hollow.
Eggs: 2–3, white.
Food: Nuts and fruit.

Identification: Massive reddish bill. Bright green head and greenish-yellow underparts. Has a bluish suffusion over the back and a black area on the shoulders. Golden edging is most apparent on the feathers on the upper part of the wing. Lower feathers are a dull green and the rump is light blue. The relatively short tail is green with a yellowish tip. Sexes are alike.

BIRDS OF PREY

Although dense stretches of woodland may not appear to represent the best hunting possibilities for birds of prey, it is remarkable how these predatory birds have adapted to this environment. This is also reflected by the way in which a number of species have become highly specialized in their hunting habits, such as the crested honey buzzard.

Blyth's hawk-eagle

Nisaetus alboniger

These strong aerial hunters seize their prey in the upper levels of the forest, taking not just birds but also lizards, bats and other mammals. They are watchful hunters, like other hawk-eagles, often swooping on their quarry from a favoured perch that affords good visibility of any movements in the canopy. On occasions, these eagles are mobbed by groups of smaller birds, such as drongos, seeking to drive the bigger birds away, and the resulting disturbance draws attention to the birds' presence. These hawk-eagles may also be seen circling and soaring over the forest. They are quite rare through their range, occurring at low population densities.

Identification: Darkish coloration on the head and back, with a long crest at the back of the head. Throat is white. Black barring on the breast and white barring to the dark feathers on the underparts. Has a greyer, broad band on the tail. Sexes alike.

Distribution: From southern Myanmar (Burma) through the Malay Peninsula to Sumatra and small nearby islands. Also present in north Borneo.
Size: 58cm (23in).
Habitat: Upland forest areas.
Nest: Bulky nest built at the top of a tree.
Eggs: 1, whitish with darker markings.
Food: Vertebrates.

Papuan eagle

New Guinea harpy eagle, Kapul eagle *Harpyopsis novaeguineae*

These forest eagles are formidable hunters, taking a wide range of prey, including tree kangaroos and wallabies and even domestic animals such as puppies. The distinctive ruff of feathers around the face helps them trace the source of sounds, and these birds also have keen eyesight. In addition to swooping down on their quarry, these eagles run and bound over the ground for short distances using their long legs. Breeding pairs return to the same site every year, choosing a tree with no lower branches and amassing a large platform of sticks near the crown at a height of 20m (66ft).

Identification: Brown upperparts with darker barring across the tail, which ends in a dark tip. The breast is brown and the underparts white. Long unfeathered legs with yellow feet. Has a crest that can be raised at the back of the head, and a pronounced ruff of feathers around the face. Hens are larger, but otherwise alike.

Right: Barred markings can be seen under the wings when the bird is in flight.

Distribution: Confined to the island of New Guinea.
Size: 90cm (35in).
Habitat: Rainforest up to 3,200m (10,500ft).
Nest: Platform of sticks.
Eggs: 1, white with darker markings.
Food: Vertebrates.

Crested serpent eagle

Spilornis cheela

There is a considerable variation in the size of these eagles through their wide range. The largest examples occur in northern India and Nepal and the smallest individuals are found further south on the Nicobar islands, off India's coast. Their name partly derives from the snakes that are a regular feature of their diet. The crested serpent eagle is likely to be observed soaring over the forest, although when hunting it usually rests on a perch, swooping down to grab snakes or lizards from either trees or the ground. Crested serpent eagles will sometimes prey on other vertebrates, including aquatic species such as eels, and have also been observed catching crabs.

Identification: Blackish brown upperparts, but has more variable underparts that range from reddish to dark brown and broken by white markings. The bill is blackish at the tip and yellow at its base. Broad greyish bar across the tail feathers. Sexes alike.

Distribution: India and Sri Lanka eastwards to China. Across South-east Asia and the Malay Peninsula south to Sumatra, Java and Borneo.
Size: 41–75cm (16–29¹/₂in).
Habitat: Wooded areas, but not dense forest.
Nest: Small cup-shaped with grass lining.
Eggs: 1, whitish with darker markings.
Food: Primarily reptiles.

Lesser fish eagle (*Haliaeetus humilis*): 60cm (24in)
Extends from Kashmir through the Himalayas into Myanmar (Burma) and Hainan, then south through the Malay Peninsula to Sumatra, Borneo, Sulawesi and neighbouring islands. Cock has a greyish head and neck, with brown back, wings and tail. White underparts. Greyish hooked bill and legs. Sexes are alike.

Long-tailed honey buzzard (*Henicopernis longicauda*): 60cm (24in)
Found on the west Papuan islands, Aru islands and New Guinea. Light and darker brown barring on the wings and tail. The head is brown with lighter chestnut ear patches. Whitish streaking around the neck and down on to the breast. The abdomen has a buff rather than whitish tone. Hens are larger.

Little eagle (*Hieraaetus morphnoides*): 55cm (22in)
Present all over New Guinea apart from the central mountainous region, and throughout Australia apart from Tasmania. These eagles occur in both a light and a dark form. The darker morphs are a deeper shade of brown, especially on the head and underparts. Lighter individuals have whitish areas on the greater wing coverts. Hens are larger.

Doria's goshawk (*Megatriorchis doriae*): 69cm (27in)
Present on New Guinea and neighbouring Batanta Island. Light brown with black barring on the upperparts. Grey tail with black banding. White underparts with dark streaking, which is most pronounced on the chest. Hens are larger.

Crested honey buzzard

Pernis ptilorhynchus

The far-north Asiatic population of the crested honey buzzard winters in the far south of the species' range on the Greater Sundas. It is possible to distinguish between these birds and the resident population, however, thanks to the former's lack of a pronounced crest. The feeding habits of these buzzards are highly distinctive, since they attack the nests of wild bees and wasps, eating not just the insects and their larvae but also the honeycomb. Although crested honey buzzards prefer to raid tree nests, they are quite able to use their strong feet to dig out nests on the ground. They also prey on other social insects such as ants and termites.

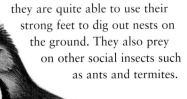

Distribution: Across India and South-east Asia, south across the Malay Peninsula to islands including Sumatra, Java and Borneo. Also a northern population, which ranges eastwards through southern Siberia.
Size: 57cm (22in).
Habitat: Wooded areas up to 1,800m (5,900ft).
Nest: Platform of twigs.
Eggs: 2, whitish with brownish markings.
Food: Wasps and bees.

Identification: Variable. Brown predominantly, which ranges from a light to dark shade depending on the individual. Broad greyish band across the tail feathers. Has white markings in the vicinity of the neck and on the underparts. Crest may be evident on the back of the neck. The bill is grey. Legs and feet are yellow. Sexes are alike.

CHATS AND OTHER INSECTIVOROUS BIRDS

All these birds, ranging from the tiny emu-wren to the pied currawong, hunt invertebrates, although they adopt very different feeding strategies. The savanna nightjar hunts on the wing and is a nocturnal hunter, whereas the fairy martin also hunts on the wing but during the hours of daylight. Others, such as the chats, prefer to look for their food on the ground.

Rufous-crowned emu-wren

Stipiturus ruficeps

Distribution: Extends from western Australia east to Queensland. Separate population in the south-east.
Size: 14.5cm (5¹/₂in).
Habitat: Dry, treeless country.
Nest: Oval structure made from vegetation.
Eggs: 2–3, white with brownish blotching.
Food: Invertebrates, and occasionally seeds.

The habitat requirements of these birds appear to be precise as they are found in areas of spinifex and porcupine grass, especially where there are isolated shrubs. Their small size makes it difficult to track their exact distribution, particularly as they skulk in the vegetation for long periods, although they sometimes reveal their presence by high-pitched calls. If disturbed, they fly a short distance before returning to the grass. Emu-wrens get their name from their tail feathers, which are long and stiff, resembling those of emus. They are unique in having just six tail plumes, fewer than any other bird in the world.

Identification: Upperparts are brownish with black streaking. The greyish-blue feathering on the eyebrows and cheeks is streaked with white. Also has greyish-blue feathering on the throat and the upper breast. Lower underparts are orangish-brown with a white area in the centre. Hens lack the greyish-blue areas on the throat and breast but do possess the white streaking on the eyebrows and cheeks.

Savanna nightjar

Allied nightjar *Caprimulgus affinis*

Nocturnal by nature as their name suggests, the persistent vocalizations of these nightjars helps to reveal their presence. They will call almost constantly for approximately half an hour, both at dusk and dawn, uttering a distinctive and repetitive cheeping sound. During the day, these nightjars rest in a relatively secure location on the ground, where their cryptic coloration helps to conceal their presence. They have also adapted well to urban living, however, and are not averse to resting out of sight on the roofs of buildings. The savanna nightjar is also drawn to hunt around electric lights, such as street lamps, as these attract night-flying invertebrates such as moths.

Identification: Short tail. Dark brown and black overall with barring on the tail and body. Has white outer tail feathers. Small bill is surrounded by bristle-like feathers. The white throat band is split into two. Hens lack the white outer tail feathers and have a more rufous-brown coloration.

Distribution: Extends eastwards from India to southern China south across South-east Asia to the Sunda islands, Sulawesi and the Philippines.
Size: 22cm (9in).
Habitat: Dry, open coastal areas.
Nest: Scrape on the ground.
Eggs: 2, buff with darker markings.
Food: Invertebrates.

Desert chat

Gibberbird *Ashbyia lovensis*

These chats are most likely to be observed on the ground, where their upright gait helps them to run fast if necessary. When flying short distances, they flutter low across the ground but they can fly strongly too, as befits a nomadic species that moves from one area to another in search of favourable conditions. The desert chat lines a scrape on the ground with vegetation to disguise its presence. It is not uncommon to see pairs together, although they are easily overlooked as they are well concealed on the ground. Occasionally, flocks of up to 20 individuals may be spotted, and often pairs choose to nest quite close together.

Identification: Brownish-black, mottled upperparts, with white tip to the black tail. Yellowish underparts, although the rump is a more orangish colour. Narrow, pointed, black bill. Dark eyes. Hens are similar but duller in appearance. Both sexes adopt an upright pose when standing.

Distribution: Southern-central parts of Australia near border areas between New South Wales, Queensland, Northern Territory and South Australia, although the precise range is not well known.
Size: 12.5cm (5in).
Habitat: Arid areas.
Nest: Scrape on the ground.
Eggs: 3, white with reddish-brown markings.
Food: Invertebrates.

Long-tailed shrike (Black-capped shrike, *Lanius schach*): 25cm (10in)
Extensive range from Iraq and India east to China, and south across the Malay Peninsula to the Greater Sundas and other islands, including the Philippines and New Guinea. Has either a black and grey or black head depending on the race. Mainly white underparts, with a rufous-brown mantle, back and flanks. Wings are black with a white area. Has a long tail and black on its upperparts. Sexes are alike.

Fairy martin (Cliff swallow, *Petrochelidon ariel*): 12.5cm (5in)
Widely distributed across Australia apart from the south-western corner and the northern part of the Cape York peninsula. Normally absent from Tasmania. Has a pale rust-red colour to the crown and whitish underparts. Wings and tail are blackish. The rump is white. Sexes alike.

Pied currawong (Pied bell-magpie, *Strepera graculina*): 49cm (19in)
Occurs down the entire eastern side of mainland Australia. Predominantly black, with a long, black, powerful bill and striking yellow eyes. There are white areas on the flight feathers, as well as at the base of the tail and in the vicinity of the vent. The tip of the tail is also white. Sexes are alike.

Pied butcherbird (Black-throated butcherbird, *Cracticus nigrogularis*): 37.5cm (15in)
Occurs all over Australia apart from the south-west corner and the south-east coastal region. Black head. Black areas on the wings and tail. The rest of the body is white. The sexes are alike. Young birds have brownish rather than black coloration.

Crimson chat

Ephthianura tricolor

These smallish birds are one of Australia's most nomadic species and travel across huge distances of inhospitable territory. They survive even when invertebrates are scarce. As these form the bulk of their diet, the crimson chat feeds instead on nectar gathered from desert plants. Remarkably, these plants can produce large amounts of nectar and this encourages the chat to fertilize their flowers by transferring pollen between the blooms as they feed on them. Probably correlating with flowering times, crimson chats are sometimes seen in quite large numbers where they have not occurred before, and then disappear as suddenly as they came.

Distribution: Across the interior of Australia from the west coast, although generally absent from other coastal areas.
Size: 12cm (5½in).
Habitat: Shrubland and open country.
Nest: Cup-shaped, located just off the ground.
Eggs: 3–4, white with darker spots.
Food: Invertebrates and nectar.

Identification: Crimson cap. Has blackish-brown sides to the face that extend over the mantle and back, although the wing feathers have paler edges. The throat is white; the underparts are crimson. Hens are easily distinguished by the light brown colour of their crown, and the red patches on their white underparts.

AUSTRALIAN PARAKEETS

Although grass parakeets are smaller than rosellas, both have comparable habits, having evolved to feed primarily on the ground, searching out grass seeds and other similar titbits. Members of both groups occur widely through Australia. Rosellas are easily distinguished from parakeets of similar size by means of the scalloping on their back and wings.

Bourke's parrot

Bourke's parakeet *Neopsephotus bourkii*

The relatively large eyes of these small parrots are an indication that they are most active at dusk and daybreak, resting when the sun is at its hottest, and have been known to fly after dark. They feed on the ground, moving on to new localities if a shortage of food or water threatens. Although these birds are usually encountered in small groups, much larger congregations, of up to a thousand birds, have been observed at larger waterholes in times of drought. Where conditions are favourable, they rear two rounds of chicks in succession: the first-round offspring disperse rather than stay near the nest site.

Identification: Has unusual coloration with brownish upperparts that often have a slightly rosy hue. The underparts are very pinkish, especially the abdomen. Has blue plumage on forehead, white around the eye and flecking on the face. Has violet-blue flight feathers and paler blue undertail coverts. Sexes are similar, although hens do not have the blue forehead-plumage.

Distribution: Interior of Australia, from Geraldton in Western Australia eastwards to South Australia. Separate population in south-west Queensland and the adjacent area of New South Wales.
Size: 20cm (8in).
Habitat: Scrubland and lightly wooded areas.
Nest: Tree hole.
Eggs: 3–6, white.
Food: Grass seeds and other vegetation.

Scarlet-chested parrot

Scarlet-chested parakeet, Splendid parrot *Neophema splendida*

Distribution: Southern-central parts of Australia and western and south Australia.
Size: 22cm (9in).
Habitat: Semi-desert areas.
Nest: Hollow tree.
Eggs: 3–6, white.
Food: Grass seeds and other vegetation.

These nomadic parrots move readily from the Great Victoria Desert region into neighbouring areas. These irruptions are triggered by a search for more favourable conditions. They can survive quite well without ready access to drinking water, however, as succulent plants help to meet much of their fluid requirement. They feed mainly on grass seeds and are most commonly sighted in areas of spinifex. Scarlet-chested parrots have developed clever feeding techniques whereby they hold down seed heads with one foot and prise the seeds out with their bill.

Identification: Scarlet plumage on the breast and yellow lower under-parts distinguishes the cock bird from all other grass parakeets. The facial area is blue, becoming paler around the eyes. Crown, neck, back and wings are green, apart from blue areas on the edge of the wing. Hens are similar but duller, with a green breast and paler blue face.

Adelaide rosella

Platycercus elegans adelaidae

Some ornithologists believe that this subspecies is a naturally occurring hybrid between the crimson rosella (*P. elegans*) and the yellow rosella (*P. e. flaveolus*). Even so, these parakeets breed true, and it is estimated that they have a population of more than 50,000. Those birds whose colouring closely resembles the yellow rosella may be termed *P. e. subadelaidae*.

Distribution: Southern Australia, being present in the Mount Lofty and southern Flinders ranges.
Size: 36cm (14in).
Habitat: Lightly wooded areas.
Nest: Tree holes.
Eggs: 4–5, white.
Food: Mainly seeds and fruit.

Identification: Variable coloration but appearing an orange-red colour overall. Often a little lighter at the top of the wings, with the scalloped patterning here both yellow and orange, depending on the individual. Wings are mauvish in the vicinity of the flight feathers and the tail. Sexes alike. Young birds are less colourful and do not acquire adult plumage until their second year.

Turquoise parrot (Turquoisine grass parakeet, *Neophema pulchella*): 20cm (8in)
Found in eastern Australia, from Queensland south via eastern New South Wales into Victoria. Blue area surrounding the black bill, extending back to the eyes. Yellowish underparts, but more orange on the breast. Crown, back, wings and tail are green, apart from the red bar and the prominent areas of blue on the wings. Hens lack the red plumage on the wings and have whitish lores, which help to distinguish them from hen scarlet-chested parakeets.

Blue-winged parrot (Blue-banded parakeet, *Neophema chrysostoma*): 20cm (8in)
Often migrates across the Bass strait to breed on Tasmania, returning to overwinter on mainland Australia and can be found as far north as Queensland. Yellow area around the bill, with a dark and light band of blue above, connecting the eyes. Olive-green upperparts and chest, with yellow abdomen. Prominent areas of dark blue on the wings. Hens are less brightly coloured.

Pale-headed rosella (Mealy rosella, *Platycercus adscitus*): 30cm (12in)
Found in north-eastern Australia, from the Cape York peninsula down to northern New South Wales. Yellowish plumage on the top of the head and white on the sides. Has blue cheek marking (depending on the race) and underparts. Red undertail coverts. Yellowish-white scalloping to the black feathers on the back, with blue on the wing. Sexes are alike.

Eastern rosella

Platycercus eximius

Distribution: From south-eastern Queensland, continuing southwards along the coast into the south-eastern part of South Australia. Also found on Tasmania.
Size: 33cm (13in).
Habitat: Grassland to wooded areas.
Nest: Tree hole.
Eggs: 4–9, white.
Food: Seeds and fruit.

Rosellas form part of the 'broadtail' group of parakeets, so-called because their tail feathers do not taper to a point unlike those of many other parakeets. The eastern rosella is a highly adaptable species. Small introduced populations are now established in New Zealand, where it has successfully adapted to living in pine forests. Eastern rosellas often feed on the ground and can be seen hunting for seeds on roadside verges, especially early in the morning. They then roost quietly through the warmer hours of the day. The hen incubates the eggs alone, although the cock bird may join her in the nest.

Identification: Bright red head with white cheek patches. Has yellowish-green underparts that become green towards the vent and red undertail coverts. The scalloped edging on the back varies from yellow to green, depending on the race. The rump is green. The tail feathers become bluish at their tips. The red is slightly duller in hens and the white cheek patches are not so clearly defined.

AUSTRALIAN PSITTACINES

Although the budgerigar is the best-known of all Australia's psittacines, this is a large group of birds which display a considerable diversity in appearance. In Australia, the terms 'parrot' and 'parakeet' tend to be used almost interchangeably. Elsewhere, however, the description of 'parakeet' is usually applied to psittacines with long tails.

Princess parrot

Princess of Wales parakeet, Queen Alexandra parrot *Polytelis alexandrae*

Distribution: Australian interior, from the Great Sandy Desert of Western Australia east to the Northern Territory via Alice Springs and as far as the extreme west of Queensland.
Size: 46cm (18in).
Habitat: Arid country.
Nest: Tree hollow.
Eggs: 4–6, white.
Food: Mainly seeds.

Very little is known about these enigmatic parrots, which turn up unexpectedly in a region and then disappear again for many years. It used to be thought they were truly nomadic, but recent studies suggest the centre of their distribution is in the vicinity of Lake Tobin, from where they irrupt at intervals to other parts of their range. These parrots are opportunistic when breeding, with pairs usually choosing to nest when food is plentiful. They seek their food on the ground.

Identification: Delicate pastel shades predominate in the plumage. Pale blue is evident on the crown and a pinkish hue on the throat. Has bright green plumage across the back and a bright blue rump. Hens lack the pale blue crown and their back is duller in tone.

Superb parrot

Barraband's parakeet *Polytelis swainsonii*

There is some seasonal movement of these parrots as they often move further north at the approach of winter. During the breeding season, small flocks of male superb parrots often forage for food alone. Pairs may nest in a loose colonial system of as many as six pairs, so hens are in the neighbourhood at this time. Superb parrots are quite opportunistic when seeking food, and they are not averse to feeding in agricultural areas, often descending into fields to pick up any seeds remaining after the harvest. These birds generally prefer feeding on the ground, although they will forage in the trees as well.

Distribution: Mainly confined to the Australian state of New South Wales, but also found to the south just across the border in northern Victoria.
Size: 42cm (16½in).
Habitat: Open woodland.
Nest: Suitable hole in a tree.
Eggs: 4–6, white.
Food: Seeds, fruit and vegetation.

Identification: Stunning yellow face, with a red band separating it from the breast. The remainder of the plumage is bright green apart from the tip of the tail and the flight feathers which are a bluish-black. The bill is red. Hens lack the bright yellow facial colouring and instead have a blue tinge to their green facial plumage and at the bend of the wing.

Cockatiel

Nymphicus hollandicus

Distribution: Occurs over most of Australia, although generally not in coastal areas, and absent from central-southern parts. Not present on Tasmania.
Size: 30cm (12in).
Habitat: Mainly arid areas.
Nest: Tree hollow.
Eggs: 4–7, white.
Food: Seeds and fruit.

These elegant relatives of the cockatoo live in flocks and are relatively nomadic by nature. Their whistling calls are much quieter than the cockatoos', and cock birds vocalize more than hens. Large flocks, hundreds of birds in size, may be seen in agricultural areas. Cockatiels often prefer to feed on the ground, with some flock members acting as sentinels, warning of the approach of possible danger. Once alerted, the whole flock will wheel away, so it can be quite difficult to approach these cockatiels closely.

Identification: Grey overall with white areas on the wings. Crest feathers are yellow with yellow sides to the face and orange ear coverts. Dark grey tail. Hens are duller. They have a greyish-yellow colour on the head. Their tails are barred on the underside with yellow and this is also seen on the underside of the wings in flight.

Regent parrot (Rock pebbler, *Polytelis anthopeplus*): 41cm (16in)
There are two widely separated populations on Australia: one is found in the south-west of Western Australia, while the other extends east across the South Australian border. Yellowish with a green mantle and reddish area on the wing. Bluish-black flight feathers and tail. Hens are greener, with a greyer tone to their underparts.

Australian ringneck (Port Lincoln parrot, *Barnardius zonarius*): 44cm (17in)
Ranges from western to central parts of Australia, mainly across the southern part of the continent. Has a blackish head, dark blue cheek patches and a yellow collar around the neck. The remainder of the body is mainly green, with a yellower abdomen, depending on the race. There may be a red frontal band. Hens are duller in colour.

Eastern bluebonnet (*Northiella haematogaster*): 30cm (12in)
There are three distinct populations present in the southern half of Australia and these range from the western side of the continent to Queensland. Has a prominent dark blue area on the face. The rest of the plumage has greyish tones, apart from the abdomen which is pale yellow with reddish markings. Undertail coverts may be red, depending on race. Blue area on the sides of the wings. Hens are less blue on the face.

Budgerigar

Melopsittacus undulatus

Distribution: Ranges over most of Australia, apart from coastal areas. Not present on Tasmania.
Size: 18cm (7in).
Habitat: Arid country.
Nest: Tree holes.
Eggs: 4–8, white.
Food: Mainly grass seeds.

Wild budgerigars are much smaller, more streamlined birds than their domesticated cousins, with the garish, domestic colour variants virtually unknown in wild flocks. When flocks are harried by a bird of prey, the budgerigars fly in tight formation, making it hard for the would-be predator to target an individual unless there is a straggler. Budgerigars are vulnerable to water shortages and so in times of drought, their numbers may plummet, but thanks to their free-breeding nature, their population recovers quickly when conditions are more favourable.

Identification: Facial area is mainly yellow with some spots evident. The underparts are light green. Black and yellow barring extends down over the back and there is scalloping over the wings. Tail feathers are bluish-green. Uniquely among psittacines, the budgerigar can be sexed by the colour of its cere, which is blue in cocks and brownish in hens.

AUSTRALIAN PARROTS AND PARAKEETS

Some of the most unusual parrots in the world are found in Australia and New Zealand, such as the ground parrot, which has evolved in the relative absence of predators. In part, the diversity in appearance and lifestyles reflects the harsh environments in which the birds occur, ranging from the searing heat of the Australian desert to the mountainous areas of New Zealand.

Golden-shouldered parrot

Psephotellus chrysopterygius (E)

These beautiful parrots have a very restricted range, and the entire wild population is made up of no more than around 500 birds. Habitat changes have contributed to their decline, as changes in the grazing patterns of sheep have restricted the availability of grass seeds which form the basis of their diet. Unusually, the golden-shouldered parrots nest in termite mounds, rather than adopting tree holes like most parrots. They prefer conical-shaped mounds, excavating an entrance which leads via a tunnel to a rounded chamber, around 25cm (10in) in diameter.

Identification: Yellow band on the forehead, with a black cap behind, extending down the back of the head. Greyish mantle and wings. Has an extensive golden yellow area at the shoulder. Sides of the face are bluish-green. The abdomen is orangish-red on a pale yellow background. Hens are mainly yellowish-green, with reddish markings on the abdomen.

Distribution: Four distinct populations are present on the Cape York peninsula in northern Queensland, north-east Australia.
Size: 27cm (11in).
Habitat: Lightly wooded grassland areas.
Nest: Terrestrial termite mounds, hence occasionally known as the ant bed parrot.
Eggs: 5–7, white.
Food: Grass seeds.

Night parrot

Pezoporus occidentalis (E)

Distribution: Arid central area of Australia. Absent from coastal regions.
Size: 25cm (10in).
Habitat: Arid scrubland near lakes.
Nest: Tunnel lined with sticks within a tussock of spinifex grass.
Eggs: 4–5, white.
Food: Spinifex grass seeds and other vegetation.

These parrots are very hard to observe, thanks to their cryptic coloration, nomadic nature and nocturnal habits. There were suggestions that they had become extinct, but during the 1990s, sightings to the south of Cloncurry confirmed their continued survival. Night parrots are most likely to be encountered among patches of marsh samphire in dried-up lake areas, and in spinifex grass, where they construct a tunnel lined with sticks as a nest site. As their name suggests, night parrots are active after dark when the desert cools down. These birds have few natural predators, but their numbers may have suffered because of introduced mammals such as cats and foxes.

Identification: Mainly green, with a yellower abdomen. Has striations and barring on the body and tail. Similar to the Eastern ground parrot (*P. wallicus*), but a duller green with no red frontal band above the bill. Also has shorter, browner tail feathers. Dark iris. Sexes alike.

Sulphur-crested cockatoo

Cacatua galerita

These raucous cockatoos can often be heard screeching from some distance away as they fly overhead, particularly in the early morning and then again towards dusk. They are highly adaptable and found in a wide range of terrain. They are not even averse to attacking agricultural crops, particularly as these are ripening. A close approach is difficult, especially in areas where they are persecuted. Several of the flock members watch for danger while their companions feed, emitting a harsh alarm call as warning which results in the entire party flying off. Pairs may often rest in trees during the heat of the day, and this is when they preen each other.

Identification: Large white body. Has prominent yellow crest feathers which can be erected if the bird is excited or alarmed. Tail is relatively short. Some yellowish suffusion under the wings. Powerful black bill. Greyish-black legs. Has a white eye ring, but this is pale blue in some races. Iris is black in cock birds and appears reddish-brown in a good light in hens.

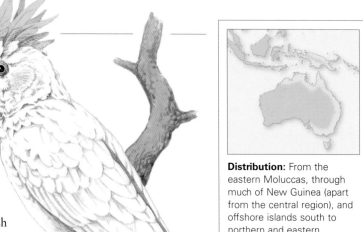

Distribution: From the eastern Moluccas, through much of New Guinea (apart from the central region), and offshore islands south to northern and eastern Australia, the south-eastern corner, and Tasmania. Introduced to New Zealand.
Size: 51cm (20in).
Habitat: Open country to woodland.
Nest: Tree hollow.
Eggs: 2, white.
Food: Seeds, nuts and fruit.

Kea (Mountain parrot, *Nestor notabilis*): 46cm (18in)
Occurs in mountainous areas of North Island, New Zealand – frequently above the treeline. Predominantly olive brown, with darker edges to the individual feathers and a reddish-brown rump. Dark band on the tail. Elongated black upper bill. Hens are smaller. Young birds have yellow not black ceres. Keas have been heavily persecuted in the past, as their habit of scavenging on sheep carcasses has unfairly bred the assumption that they are the killers.

Galah (Roseate cockatoo, *Eolophus roseicapilla*): 38cm (15in)
One of the most common and widely distributed cockatoos, occurring over virtually the whole of Australia. Less common on Tasmania, and are scarce in the Western Desert area. Has grey upperparts with rose-pink underparts and a compact, pinkish-white crest. Some variation in depth of coloration may be apparent, and on rare occasions, galah cockatoos with white rather then grey upperparts have been recorded in flocks. Hens have a reddish-brown iris.

Long-billed corella (*Cacatua tenuirostris*): 41cm (16in)
Found in south-eastern Australia, in the Murray-Darling area. Predominantly white in colour, with pronounced pinkish suffusion in the vicinity of the eyes and on the upper breast. Blue skin around the eyes. Has a distinctive long upper bill which is often used for digging up roots. A yellowish hue can be seen on the underside of the wings and tail in flight. Has a short, broad white crest. Sexes are alike.

Eastern ground parrot

Swamp parrot *Pezoporus wallicus*

As their name suggests, ground parrots are largely terrestrial in their habits, but they can fly in a zig-zag pattern after being flushed, and then dip back down into cover. Their presence is most likely to be revealed by their whistling calls. These are typically uttered just before sunrise and at sunset, although they may be heard during the day. Cocks croak rather like frogs near the nest, and this is well concealed with a tunnel-like entrance on the ground. Their distribution in heathland areas will suffer when the ground is swept by fire. Once the diversity of vegetation has been restored, it is likely to take four years until pairs start breeding successfully again.

Identification: Similar to, but more brightly coloured than the night parrot (*P. occidentalis*). Distinctive wingbar and a long, tapering tail which can measure up to 20cm (8in) overall. Red frontal band present in adult birds. Sexes alike.

Distribution: Narrow coastal strips in eastern and south-eastern Australia. Also present on Tasmania.
Size: 33cm (13½in).
Habitat: Heathland and sedge.
Nest: Cup of vegetation on the ground.
Eggs: 2–6, white.
Food: Seeds and some invertebrates.

PIGEONS AND DOVES

This group of birds are highly adaptable, as reflected by their reproductive habits. They breed quickly under favourable conditions, often nesting repeatedly in suitable surroundings. This in turn means that they can survive well in fairly inhospitable conditions, such as Australia's arid interior, taking advantage of the unpredictable rains that trigger a resurgence in the plant life.

Diamond dove

Geopelia cuneata

Distribution: Most of Australia, apart from southern and eastern coastal regions.
Size: 20cm (8in).
Habitat: Lightly wooded areas and grassland. Commonly encountered in the outback.
Nest: Loose platform of twigs and vegetation.
Eggs: 2, white.
Food: Mainly small seeds.

These doves live in small parties and usually tolerate quite a close approach, even when walking on the ground. They spend long periods here, seeking seeds and other edible items. When displaying, the cock bird bows in front of the hen and fans his long tail feathers, cooing loudly. The eye ring of the cock becomes more prominent during the breeding season. Pairs tend to be opportunistic breeders, and nest whenever conditions are favourable. In common with many members of this family, incubation duties are shared, with the cock bird sitting for much of the day. The chicks grow rapidly and leave the nest as young as 12 days old, even before they are able to fly well. Diamond doves have been known to spread occasionally outside the usual area of distribution.

Identification: Predominantly greyish brown, with white spots dotted irregularly over the wings. Has chestnut flight feathers. White underside to the tail. Prominent crimson eye ring, especially in cocks during the breeding season. Otherwise sexes alike. Young birds are brownish and lack the white spotting.

Left: The diamond dove's eye ring is a distinctive characteristic.

Crested pigeon

Ocyphaps lophotes

These large pigeons are usually seen in flocks, which may consist of more than 100 individuals, frequently foraging for food on the ground. They have benefited from the spread of agriculture in Australia, not simply because of the increase in crops but also the provision of waterholes for livestock on ranches in more remote areas. Crested pigeons are very adaptable, able to forage for native seeds or cereals and other crops. If disturbed, these pigeons fly up to a nearby tree, often jerking their tails vertically when they land on a branch. They often seek out the protection of a thorn bush or similar shrub when nesting, particularly in the more treeless parts of their range. The colourful areas on the wing form part of the cock bird's display.

Identification: Prominent narrow crest on the top of the head. The underparts are pinkish-grey. The back and wings are brownish and show black barring. Purplish areas are evident towards the rear of the wing. Sexes are similar.

Distribution: Australia, apart from north of the Northern Territory, Cape York peninsula, and the south-east region.
Size: 33cm (13in).
Habitat: Lightly wooded and open areas of country.
Nest: Platform of twigs in a bush.
Eggs: 2, white.
Food: Seeds, other plant matter and invertebrates.

Flock bronzewing (Harlequin pigeon, *Phaps histrionica*): 30cm (12in)
Found in northern parts of Australia away from the coastal zone. Highly nomadic by nature. Chestnut mantle, wings, back, tail and lower abdomen. The head is black with a white forehead and a C-shaped marking extending to the cheek from the eye. Also has a white patch on the upper chest and breast. The upper abdomen is greyish. Hen is dark brown. The grey on the throat is surrounded by a white area extending up above the bill. Has greyer underparts.

Squatter pigeon (*Geophaps scripta*): 28cm (11in)
Present in eastern Australia where it ranges north as far as the central area of the Cape York peninsula and south as far as north-eastern New South Wales. Predominantly brown on the upper chest, back and wings with white breast and flanks. Has black and white patterning on the sides of the face. The skin around the eye is red in northern populations. Sexes are alike.

Partridge pigeon (*Geophaps smithii*): 27cm (10¹/₂in)
Found in northern Western Australia, with a separate population in the tip of the Northern Territory. Also present on Melville Island. Mainly brown with a white area extending from the shoulder region and down the sides of the flanks. Some slight barring across the upper breast. Bare area of reddish or orange orbital skin with white area below, bordered by black. Sexes alike.

Red turtle dove

Red collared dove
Streptopelia tranquebarica

These doves are usually spotted in pairs but may also be seen feeding in the company of other related birds such as the laughing dove (*Spilopelia senegalensis*) in the east of their range. They tend to feed on the ground, and are especially numerous in agricultural areas where cereals are cultivated. Red turtle doves are not sedentary throughout their range, however, and leave the northerly parts of their range such as Taiwan during the winter months to head further south. Breeding in warmer climates can take place at any stage during the year, although the fragile nature of this dove's nest – a platform of twigs – means that it may sometimes collapse, resulting in the loss of both eggs and chicks.

Identification: Greyish head, becoming darker on the crown, with a prominent black collar across the back of the neck. Underparts are vinous-pink. Wings are brick red. Flight feathers are black and the tail is grey. Hens are brown and more buff-coloured than pink on the underparts. They also have a black collar.

Distribution: Extends across the Indian subcontinent east as far as China and offshore islands, including the Philippines, and south across South-east Asia. Has recently occurred on Java.
Size: 23cm (9in).
Habitat: Open countryside.
Nest: Platform of twigs.
Eggs: 2, whitish.
Food: Seeds.

Distribution: Three distinct populations in northern Australia. Chestnut-bellied form occurs in north-west; the white-bellied form in northern-central region and southern part of Cape York peninsula.
Size: 20cm (8in).
Habitat: Arid areas, where spinifex grass predominates.
Nest: Scrape concealed on the ground.
Eggs: 2, whitish.
Food: Seeds, some invertebrates.

Spinifex pigeon

Plumed rock pigeon *Geophaps plumifera*

Despite inhabiting the arid interior of the Australian continent, these pigeons rarely stray far from water. They favour areas where there are rocky outcrops, often breeding in this terrain and concealing their nest close to a rock. Spinifex pigeons spend much of their time on the ground, where they are encountered much of the time in groups. When they do take to the wing, they fly with their long crest lying back over the neck. If not directly threatened, these pigeons often prefer to run off and only fly away as a last resort. When displaying, cocks will bow and spread their tail feathers in front of a hen. This behaviour is also used as a threatening gesture to other males.

Identification: Rich chestnut, with black barring on the wings and neck area. Long narrow crest on top of the head. Greyish forehead and grey on sides of the face. White area under the throat. Bare reddish skin around the eyes is bordered by black. Whitish area on the belly, depending on the race. Hens may have shorter crests.

EMUS, MALLEEFOWL AND FINCHES

Birds have evolved a number of different breeding strategies, but surely one of the strangest is that of the malleefowl, whose eggs are hatched entirely by artificial means. This is in distinct contrast to the breeding cycle of the emu, which results in the cock bird remaining constantly with the eggs until they hatch weeks later, often going without food and water for much of this time.

Emu

Dromaius novaehollandiae

These flightless birds are well-adapted for running to escape danger and are capable of sprinting at speeds equivalent to 48kph (30mph) over short distances. They usually walk with little effort at a speed of about 7kph (4mph) and are able to cover more than 2.7m (9ft) in a single stride. When resting, emus lie down on their haunches in the open. They cool themselves by holding out their rudimentary wings, so that heat can be dissipated from the veins flowing close to the skin. After hatching their eggs, the cock rears the chicks on his own, although the group remains together for at least eight months.

Distribution: Most of Australia, apart from desert areas in the interior and some parts of the south-east. Not present on Tasmania.
Size: 190cm (75in).
Habitat: Plains and open woodland areas.
Nest: Scrape on the ground.
Eggs: 5–24, dark green, almost blackish.
Food: Omnivorous.

Identification: Very large. Brownish and shaggy-feathered with long legs and three toes on each foot. Black feathering on the face and down the back of the neck. The sides of the neck are bluish in colour. Has a black bill and reddish eyes. Hens are heavier, weighing up to 55kg (121lb) with deep blue coloration on the face and black feathering on the throat. Young birds have prominently brown-and-white striped backs.

Malleefowl

Leipoa ocellata

Distribution: Australia. Western coast up to Northern Territory and east to New South Wales.
Size: 60cm (24in).
Habitat: Mallee and other scrubland.
Nest: Mound.
Eggs: 16–33, pinkish.
Food: Omnivorous.

The condition of the soil is very important to malleefowl, which favour areas of sandy soil that they can excavate easily. Pairs construct a natural incubator for their eggs, in the shape of a massive mound up to 1m (3ft) high and 5m (16ft) in diameter. A hole is dug which is filled with vegetation and left over the winter before being covered with sand. The female then lays her eggs and buries them in the mound where the heat from the decomposing vegetation keeps them warm, at 33°C (91°F). The cock adjusts the temperature by moving the sand. Seven weeks later, the newly hatched chicks dig themselves out.

Identification: Head and neck greyish, with an inconspicuous black crest. Has barred wings, and a blackish line runs down the centre of the breast. Heavily barred upperparts, with brown, black, grey and white markings. Sexes similar but cocks have a booming call and hens crow.

Right: Chicks emerging from the incubation mound.

Zebra finch

Taeniopygia guttata

Living in flocks, these noisy finches are a common sight. Their calls are likened to the sound of toy trumpets. They often perch in the open, on fences, and can be spotted on the ground alongside roads, hopping along and searching for grass seeds. If necessary, they can fly with some agility, catching insects on the wing. Their nest is relatively large and untidy, with extra material often added through the incubation period. Pairs tend to breed repeatedly when conditions are favourable. The nest itself is sited in a variety of localities, ranging from inside the eaves of agricultural buildings to hollow trees.

Identification: Light grey head. Prominent chestnut-orange ear coverts, with a black stripe in front. Has fine zebra-like barring on the chest. The underparts are white and white-spotted chestnut areas extend down the flanks. The back is brownish. The tail is black and white. Hens are much duller, with a brownish-grey head and chest and creamy underparts. Bill is paler than that of the cock and they lack orange ear coverts.

Distribution: Lesser Sunda Islands of Indonesia and most of Australia apart from the far north and the east coast.
Size: 10cm (4in).
Habitat: Scrub, plains, open woodland.
Nest: Made of vegetation.
Eggs: 3–7, pale blue.
Food: Grass seeds and some invertebrates.

Painted finch (Painted firetail, *Emblema pictum*): 11cm (4¹/₂in)
Extends from western and central parts of Australia to western Queensland. Red face, back, rump and belly. The head, mantle, wings and tip of the tail are brown. Has a black area on the breast and flanks which is broken by white spots. Hens have virtually no red feathering on the underparts and feature a greatly reduced red area on the face.

Star finch (*Neochmia ruficauda*): 10cm (4in)
Widely distributed across northern parts of Australia but is more localized around the Cape York peninsula. Bright red plumage on the sides of the face extends to just behind the eye and down around the throat and is broken by fine white speckling. The breast and flanks are greyish with larger spots. The underparts are whitish. The back and wings are olive-green and the tail is reddish. Hens have a much more restricted area of red on the face, from the bill to the eyes, and are a duller shade overall.

Chestnut-breasted mannikin (Chestnut-breasted munia, *Lonchura castaneothorax*): 10cm (4in)
Present on New Guinea and northern and eastern Australia. Also found on some Pacific islands. Has a prominent chestnut area on the breast, with a black border beneath. Underparts are mainly white and there is black barring on the flanks. Undertail coverts are black. There are black areas with paler streaking on the sides of the face, with grey above, and these extend down to the nape. Brown mantle and wings. Golden-yellow rump and tail. Sexes are alike but the hen may be slightly duller in colour.

Scaly-breasted munia (Spotted munia, Spice finch, *Lonchura punctulata*): 10cm (4in)
Extends from the Indian subcontinent east to China, through South-east Asia and the Malay Peninsula to the Greater Sundas, Sulawesi and other islands. Introduced in some areas. Head and upperparts are rich brown, with black or dark brown crescent-shaped patterning on the white of the underparts. Spotted rump and yellowish tail. Sexes are alike.

Gouldian finch

Erythrura gouldiae

The gouldian ranks as one of the most stunningly-coloured finches in the world. Unfortunately, its numbers are in a severe decline. This appears to be at least in part due to a tiny parasite which spreads to nestlings via their parents and invades their airways. This leads to severe breathing difficulty and, frequently, premature death. The head coloration of this finch naturally varies – most often it is black or deep red, while, less commonly, it is an orangish yellow. These are not separate subspecies, but rather they are naturally occurring colour variants within a flock due to free interbreeding among these colourful birds.

Identification: The colour of the head is variable but the rest of the finch's body is consistent in colour. Has a bright blue collar around the head. Mantle and wings are green. Has a purple area on the breast. The underparts are yellow and the rump is blue. Pointed tail. Hens are duller with a shorter tail.

Distribution: Northern parts of Australia.
Size: 13.5cm (5in).
Habitat: Grassy plains with some trees.
Nest: Ball-like, often located in a hollow tree.
Eggs: 4–8, white.
Food: Mainly grass seeds and some invertebrates.

BIRDS OF PREY

Keen vision, fast flight and agility allow many birds of prey to hunt effectively, but those that feed primarily on carrion, in the form of dead animals, require a different strategy, as exemplified by vultures. While acute vision is also vital for them, they need to stay airborne with minimum effort, covering large distances while searching for the carcass of a large herbivore on the ground below.

Australian hobby

Little falcon *Falco longipennis*

These small, adaptable falcons may be seen flying during the day, and through into the night, particularly where there are artificial lights which attract insects, moths and similar invertebrates after dark. They catch their prey in flight, and are agile enough to take fast-flying quarry such as swallows. Farmers often welcome their presence because they feed on sparrows. Australian hobbys will build their nest in a tree, although other less conventional sites such as electricity poles may sometimes be used, especially in areas where alternatives are not readily available. After nesting, hens, especially, migrate north, leaving Australia for the winter. Populations elsewhere, in the Lesser Sundas for example, are sedentary.

Above: Australian hobbys have long, narrow wings, which helps their agility when hunting other birds.

Identification: Brown forehead, becoming blackish on the sides of the face with a white area from the throat up the sides of the neck. Streaked white on the breast, becoming rufous on the underparts. Wings are slate-grey with lighter edging. Barred tail has a white tip. Hens larger.

Distribution: Australia including Tasmania, ranging to New Guinea, New Britain and the Moluccas outside the breeding period. Also occurs on the Lesser Sundas.
Size: 35cm (14in).
Habitat: Open and wooded areas.
Nest: Platform made of sticks.
Eggs: 2–4, white with reddish-brown markings.
Food: Small birds, bats and invertebrates.

Grey-faced buzzard

Frog hawk *Butastur indicus*

These buzzards are frequently seen in areas close to water, where they hunt amphibians, which form a significant part of their diet. The grey-faced buzzard seeks a good vantage point and then uses its keen eyesight to pinpoint its prey before swooping down to seize it. These birds come together to form massive flocks, which may number thousands of birds when on migration. The migration routes may stretch along the Pacific coastline of Japan to the Philippines, with a separate route via Korea on the Asiatic mainland. When migrating in such numbers, grey-faced buzzards are vulnerable to being shot by hunters, and certainly in some areas, they are declining in numbers because of this threat.

Identification: White throat, broken by a black central area, with a white stripe above the eyes. Has a greyish-brown head and brown back and chest. The underparts are white with much brown barring. The tail is brown with black barring. Long wings. Yellow legs and feet. Sexes alike. Young are less colourful.

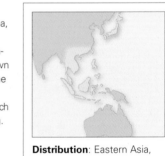

Distribution: Eastern Asia, Japan and the Philippines. Widely distributed through South-east Asia, down across the Malay Peninsula to the Greater Sundas, Sulawesi and neighbouring islands.
Size: 46cm (18in).
Habitat: Open country with nearby wooded areas.
Nest: Small platform of twigs in a tree.
Eggs: 2–4, white.
Food: Frogs, reptiles and rodents.

Himalayan vulture

Gyps himalayensis

These massive vultures glide almost effortlessly over long distances, relying primarily on their keen eyesight to locate the carcasses of large herbivores and other creatures on the ground. The size of this vulture means that it can drive off its smaller relatives at feeding sites, with the exception of the more assertive Cinereous vulture (*Aegypius monachus*). Large numbers are drawn to a suitable feeding site, where they rip the flesh off the carcass quickly and efficiently using their powerful hooked bills. Their largely bald heads mean they can feed without their plumage becoming matted with blood.

Identification: Variable, whitish-buff. Bare purplish-pink skin at the base of the neck. Greyish face. Wings and tail dark brown. Sexes alike. Young birds are darker in colour than adults.

Distribution: Himalayan region, from Pakistan to western and central parts of China.
Size: 115–150cm (45–59in).
Habitat: Mountainous regions, from 900–5,000m (3,000–16,500ft).
Nest: Sticks on cliff-face.
Eggs: 1, white with traces of red markings.
Food: Carrion.

Black falcon (*Falco subniger*): 56cm (22in)
Found in central and eastern Australia. Black with light edging on back and wing feathers and a white tip to the tail. Black bill and cere. Looks broad-winged in flight. Hens are larger.

Spotted harrier (*Circus assimilis*): 61cm (24in)
Present on Sulawesi, the Sula Islands, and mainland Australia. Has white spotting on the underparts and pale grey markings over the wings. Chestnut face, with greyish collar. The tail is barred. Hens are larger.

Black-breasted buzzard (Black-breasted kite, *Hamirostra melanosternon*): 61cm (24in)
Found in northern and western areas of Australia. Blackish crown, face, breast and back. Chestnut-orange plumage on the back of the head and neck and on the underparts. White areas on the wings. Dark tail. Powerful, greyish bill with dark tip. Hens are larger.

Indian vulture (E) (Long-billed vulture, *Gyps indicus*): 80–100cm (32–39in)
Ranges from south-eastern Pakistan and all India (apart from the extreme south) into Indo-China and the northern Malay Peninsula. Has a bare greyish head with white plumage at the base of the neck. The wings are brown, but become blackish on the flight feathers and tail. Underparts are buff-brown. The bill is more slender than in related species. Sexes are alike.

Western marsh harrier

Circus aeruginosus

Unlike many birds of prey, this harrier is a truly opportunistic hunter. It raids the nests of other birds, as well as catching the birds themselves, and also hunts mammals, such as rabbits, by swooping on them in the open. Its food varies, partly depending on its range, and may change throughout the year. During the winter, even the carcasses of dead whales washed ashore in coastal areas may feature in its diet. In Asia, these birds tend to migrate southwards at this time of year. Pairs regularly return to the same nest site in the following spring.

Identification: Plumage varies according to the race. Head is brownish with white streaks. Darker streaking on a buff chest. The abdomen is entirely brown. Wings are brown with rufous edging to the feathers. White and grey areas are also apparent. Tail is pale greyish. Hens are larger, with a yellowish-cream suffusion on the head, throat and shoulder. Young birds resemble hens but have darker shoulder markings.

Distribution: Extensive, being found in Africa and Europe as well as western Asia, where one population is centred across the entire Indian subcontinent and Sri Lanka. Further north, the species extends from Asia Minor eastwards to Mongolia.
Size: 48–56 cm (19–22in).
Habitat: Marshland and nearby open country.
Nest: Pile of reeds in a secluded reedbed.
Eggs: 2–7, pale bluish-white.
Food: Birds, plus other small vertebrates.

NECTAR-FEEDERS AND SEED-EATERS

Within the parrot family, some members of the group feed mainly on seeds, whereas others such as the lorikeets rely on their specially adapted tongues to feed on nectar. Small birds, notably sunbirds, also feed on nectar, but use their long, narrow bills to reach it. While this restricts their distribution largely to the tropics, other species such as pigeons and doves have more adaptable feeding habits.

Crimson rosella

Pennant's parakeet *Platycercus elegans*

Inhabiting a variety of localities, these colourful parakeets can become really quite tame. Although they prefer to feed on the ground, they will take food such as seed placed on bird tables readily and visit gardens on a regular basis. Their presence there is not always welcomed, however, as they may also strip off branches and eat blossoms, attacking fruit crops as well on occasion. The immature plumage is surprisingly variable, with birds from northern areas tending to have more red plumage than those in southern populations, which are mainly green on fledging. It takes the crimson rosella up to 15 months to attain its adult plumage.

Identification: Crimson head and underparts. Has black scalloped patterning over the wings. Prominent blue cheek patches. Has blue on the edge of the wings as well as on the tail. Sexes alike. Young birds are often predominantly green on fledging.

Distribution: Two distinct populations in coastal parts of eastern and south-eastern Australia. Introduced to New Zealand.
Size: 37cm (15in).
Habitat: Woodland, agricultural areas and gardens.
Nest: Tree hollow.
Eggs: 5–8, white.
Food: Seeds and other plant matter.

Coconut lorikeet

Trichoglossus haematodus

There is considerable diversity in the appearance of these lorikeets, approximately 6 different races have been identified over the islands where they occur and 7 subspecies are now classified separately. The variation is mainly in the colour of the neck and breast plumage, giving rise to local names such as the green-naped lorikeet (*T. h. haematodus*). Coconut lorikeets are conspicuous, noisy birds with bold natures. In some parts of eastern Australia, wild flocks regularly visit campsites, where they are a major tourist attraction, feeding on trays of sponge cake soaked in honey water held up for them by visitors. They are more active during the early morning and late afternoon and tend to roost quietly when the sun is at its hottest.

Above: The tip of the rainbow lorikeet's tongue is covered with tiny papillae, which effectively sweep up the pollen grain as it feeds on flowers.

Identification: Dark bluish head and green back and wings. Often has barring on the underparts. Breast is yellow to red, with a variable amount of scalloping. Collar varies from green through yellow to red, depending on the individual. Sexes are alike.

Distribution: Islands from Bali eastwards through the Moluccas and New Guinea to the Solomon Islands and New Caledonia. Occurs in Australia south from the Cape York Peninsula along the east, south-east and south coasts to the Eyre Peninsula. They also move between islands.
Size: 26cm (10in).
Habitat: Woodland, farmland and gardens.
Nest: Tree hollow.
Eggs: 2–3, white.
Food: Nectar, pollen, fruit and some seeds.

Spotted dove (Mountain dove, *Spilopelia chinensis*):
31cm (12¹/₂in)
Wide distribution from eastern Afghanistan across southern parts of Asia to China and offshore islands. South through the Malay Peninsula to the Sundas and the Philippines. Introduced to numerous areas, including parts of Australia and New Zealand. Has a distinctive black neck patch that is spotted with white markings. Greyish head. Has pinkish-buff underparts. The wings, back and tail are a brownish shade, often with darker markings apparent. Sexes alike.

Bar-shouldered dove (*Geopelia humeralis*):
29cm (11¹/₂in)
Northern and eastern parts of Australia and southern New Guinea. Has a copper-coloured patch on the neck and black barring over much of the brown upperparts. The forehead and sides of the face, as well as the breast, are greyish. The underparts are predominantly pink-buff. Sexes alike.

Black-capped white-eye (*Zosterops atricapilla*):
11cm (4¹/₂in)
Extends through the Malay Peninsula to Sumatra and Borneo. Has distinctive blackish feathering on the front and sides of the face and a white eye ring. The upperparts are olive green. The underparts are yellowish with grey flanks. The tail is also dark. Sexes alike.

Purple-throated sunbird (*Leptocoma sperata*):
14cm (5¹/₂in)
Extends from eastern Pakistan, mainly through coastal parts of South-east Asia, east to the Philippines then south to the Sunda islands and Sulawesi. Cocks may appear almost entirely black but have a purplish throat with crimson on the belly and upper abdomen. Hens have a characteristic greenish-yellow belly and undertail coverts, with dark olive upperparts and a black tail.

Oriental white-eye

Zosterops palpebrosus

The relatively narrow yet stocky and slightly curved bill of this bird is used not only to probe flowers for nectar, but also to grab invertebrates. The bill is not especially powerful, however, and this results in oriental white-eyes tending to stab at fruit rather than biting off chunks. White-eyes are seen in loose flocks, often foraging through vegetation in the company of other birds. These birds are very active and extremely agile and can be observed hopping from branch to branch. They call frequently to other members of the group, with their calls consisting of a series of twittering notes, combined when necessary with sharper alarm calls. When breeding, pairs of these birds build compact, well-constructed nests that are usually hidden and supported in the fork of a tree.

Distribution: From northern India eastwards to southern China. Present across South-east Asia and the Malay Peninsula to the Greater Sunda islands.
Size: 11cm (4¹/₂in).
Habitat: Vegetation in lowland areas.
Nest: Cup-shaped in vegetation.
Eggs: 2, pale blue.
Food: Invertebrates, nectar and fruit.

Identification: Yellowish-green upperparts with a characteristic narrow, white ring of plumage around the eyes. Underparts may be entirely yellow or the flanks may be greyish, depending on the subspecies. Sexes are alike.

Olive-backed sunbird

Yellow-breasted sunbird *Cinnyris jugularis*

Although sunbirds are quite common on mainland Asia, the olive-backed variety is the only species present on Australia. They use their long bills to obtain nectar from plants, and also hunt invertebrates, with spiders being a favoured food. In spite of its small size, the olive-backed sunbird is quite bold, even to the extent of siting its nests under the roofs of verandas and porches and in the vicinity of other outbuildings. It uses the gossamer threads of spiders' webs rather like cotton to bind the nest fibres together, frequently incorporating a trailing tail beneath as part of the design. The internal area of the nest is lined with softer materials such as down feathers. The young in the nest are reared almost exclusively on insects.

Identification: Brownish-green upperparts and bright yellow underparts. Adult cocks easily identified by a dark purplish metallic area on the throat, which is more extensive in breeding plumage. Narrow black bill. Short tail. Young birds resemble adult hens.

Distribution: From China across South-east Asia and the Malay Peninsula to parts of Indonesia and New Guinea. Extends south to north-eastern coastal region of Australia.
Size: 11cm (4¹/₂in).
Habitat: Areas where there are trees in the vicinity.
Nest: Pendulous, made of vegetation.
Eggs: 2–3, grey-green with mottling.
Food: Nectar, invertebrates.

HONEYEATERS, FAIRYWRENS AND OTHER AUSTRALASIAN SPECIES

There is a clear divide between birds found in Australia and New Guinea, and those occurring on the mainland of Asia and the Greater Sunda chain of islands. This division in distribution was first identified by the Victorian zoologist William Wallace, after whom the Wallace line is named, which marks the border between the Asiatic and Australasian zones. This border runs between the islands of Bali and Lombok.

Plain honeyeater

Nondescript honeyeater *Pycnopygius ixoides*

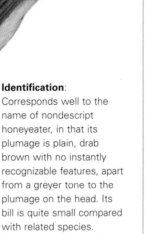

Its drab plumage means that the plain honeyeater is easily overlooked, especially when it occurs in the company of other related species. It is quiet by nature, which presents a further difficulty in assessing its numbers with any accuracy. Some ornithologists suggest that these honeyeaters are quite rare, although others think that they are in fact quite common but are not easily observed. When these honeyeaters feeds on flowers that produce large amounts of pollen, the pollen may stain their heads temporarily, giving them a yellowish hue. Honeyeaters as a group have a very important role in pollinating flowers as they feed, not just from pollen transferred on their heads, but also from pollen on their brush-like tongue.

Identification: Corresponds well to the name of nondescript honeyeater, in that its plumage is plain, drab brown with no instantly recognizable features, apart from a greyer tone to the plumage on the head. Its bill is quite small compared with related species. Brown irises. Sexes alike.

Distribution: All of New Guinea, apart from the southern Trans-fly region.
Size: 18cm (7in).
Habitat: Lowland areas, but has been known to extend up into the hills.
Nest: Cup-shaped.
Eggs: 2, pinkish with darker spotting.
Food: Fruit, nectar and invertebrates.

Little wattlebird

Brush wattlebird *Anthochaera chrysoptera*

In spite of its name, and unlike its close relative the red wattlebird (*A. carunculata*), this species has no fleshy swellings, or wattle, on its neck. The heavily streaked plumage on the little wattlebird's body helps to conceal its presence well when it is seeking food among its favourite shrub, the banksia. Little wattlebirds tend to be rather bold by nature, especially in areas such as gardens, and will allow a relatively close approach. They are also quite noisy and have a varied repertoire of calls. They raise their tails when they are excited, and will rattle their bills without actually giving voice. Their nest is concealed in a shrub and is usually lined with a soft material such as loose bark stripped from eucalyptus trees.

Identification: Heavily streaked plumage with lighter underparts. The silvery streaking is most apparent on the sides of the head and neck. Rufous patches on the wings are apparent in flight. White tip to the relatively long tail feathers. Black pointed bill. Sexes alike.

Distribution: South-western and south-eastern parts of mainland Australia. Also present on Tasmania.
Size: 30cm (12in).
Habitat: Woodlands, parks and gardens.
Nest: Cup-shaped, made of twigs.
Eggs: 1–2, salmon-pink with darker reddish spots.
Food: Invertebrates, fruit and nectar.

Left: Invertebrates feature prominently in the diet of young little wattlebirds.

Superb fairywren

Superb blue wren *Malurus cyaneus*

Despite their small size, superb fairywrens are notoriously aggressive and territorial when nesting, even to the point of both sexes attacking their reflections in a window or a car hubcap parked by a verge. After the breeding period, the family stays together, although hens leave the group in the spring. Young cocks remain and help to feed the first round of chicks in the following year, and this allows the adults to build a new nest and breed again very quickly. These fairywrens have adapted well to garden life, searching out invertebrates in the plants.

Identification: Cock bird in breeding plumage has a bright blue head, extending back along the sides of the neck to the mantle. Has a blackish intervening area. Breast is a characteristic bluish-black, with whitish underparts. Long, dark blue tail. Wings brownish. Hen is brown with a whitish throat, while the underparts are fawn-white in colour. Tail is brown with a bluish wash. Reddish-brown feathers around the eye and similar-coloured bill distinguish hens from out-of-colour cock birds, whose bills are black.

Distribution: Eastern and south-eastern Australia, including Tasmania.
Size: 14cm (5^1/2in).
Habitat: Dense, low vegetation.
Nest: Domed structure made of plant fibres.
Eggs: 3–4, pinkish-white.
Food: Mostly small invertebrates.

Noisy friarbird (*Philemon corniculatus*): 35cm (14in)
Found down the eastern side of Australia, although not in the extreme north or the far south. Brownish back, wings and tail with a ruff of creamy feathers around the neck and long silvery plumes on the upper part of the breast. Underparts greyish-white. Head bare and black with a swelling on the upper bill close to the base. White tips to the tail prominent in flight. Sexes alike.

Striated pardalote (*Pardalotus striatus*): 11.5cm (4^1/2in)
Present in various forms through much of Australia including Tasmania and other islands. Variable appearance, depending on race. Blackish crown with white markings. Greyish back with pale orange to red streak above the eyes. Grey and yellow evident on the underparts. Short blackish tail. White edging to the flight feathers. Hens are duller in overall coloration.

Australasian figbird (*Sphecotheres vieilloti*): 30cm (12in)
Present south-eastern New Guinea, and the north and eastern coastal areas as far as New South Wales in Australia. Has black plumage over much of the head, and bare area of red skin around the eyes. Green wing and rump, with black tail. Underparts vary from green to yellow, depending on the race. Whiter around the vent region. Hens have speckled underparts with brown or greenish back, wings and tail.

Pallid cuckoo (*Cacomantis pallidus*): 33cm (13^1/2in)
Found over much of Australia, including Tasmania. Undertakes seasonal movements and is occasionally seen in the Moluccas and New Guinea over the winter. Has a dark area around the eyes, a white area on the nape and white markings on the wings and flight feathers. The underparts are relatively pale. The long tail has whitish edging. Sexes are alike.

Flame robin

Petroica phoenicea

These birds are unusual among the many robins found in Australia and Tasmania, simply because they form flocks outside the breeding season, with hens usually predominating in these groups. When nesting, these birds occur in wooded areas, before moving into more open countryside for the rest of the year. Although the flame robins are more conspicuous in the open, the hens' dull-coloured plumage means that it can prove difficult to identify them correctly. The site chosen for the cup-shaped nest is variable, ranging from a fork in a tree to a cavity in the trunk, and may even be situated beneath a rocky overhang. The construction process usually takes at least two weeks. The nest is bound using the thread from a spider's web.

Distribution: South-eastern Australia including Tasmania
Size: 14cm (5^1/2in).
Habitat: Wooded and open country.
Nest: Bulky, cup-shaped.
Eggs: 3–4, greenish-white with dark markings.
Food: Invertebrates.

Identification: The head, wings and tail are dark grey apart from a prominent white area above the bill and white wing patches. Throat area is brownish too. Has buff and white markings across the wings and orange-red underparts. Hens have greyish-brown upperparts and white underparts.

STARLINGS, MYNAS, SPIDERHUNTERS AND LAUGHING THRUSHES

The starling family Sturnidae is well represented both in Asia and Australia, where the European starling (Sturnus vulgaris) has been introduced alongside native species. Mynas are a distinct grouping within the starling family, with this description being applied to large, short-tailed species with iridescent black plumage. Laughing thrushes, however, are found only in Asia, and have an attractive song in many cases.

Singing starling

Aplonis cantoroides

Distribution: New Guinea and neighbouring islands extending to the Bismarck Archipelago and the Solomon Islands.
Size: 19cm (7¹/₂in).
Habitat: Mainly open country.
Nest: Cavity in a tree hole or elsewhere.
Eggs: 2–3, pale blue with brown and violet spotting.
Food: Mainly fruit but also eats invertebrates.

During the breeding season, singing starlings are likely to be observed in pairs or even singly, but after the chicks have fledged, they join up to form large flocks comprised of both adult and juvenile birds. Perhaps surprisingly, in spite of their name, singing starlings are not talented songsters, although their calls are less harsh than those of many starlings. These starlings are seen predominantly in coastal lowland areas, and are a common sight in towns there. They have even been known to nest in buildings on occasions.

Identification: Predominantly black in colour with a marked green-metallic iridescence, depending on the light. Plumage on the back of the head and neck is elongated, forming hackles. The square, short tail is blackish. Iris is a bright contrasting orange-red. Bill and legs are black. Sexes alike. Young birds very different, having brown wings with some greenish suffusion, while the underparts are whitish with brown streaking. Iris brown.

Yellow-faced myna

Papuan mynah *Mino dumontii*

Studies have revealed how these mynas have different dialects in parts of their range. Those living in the vicinity of New Guinea's main town – Port Moresby – have call notes consisting primarily of two syllables, whereas in mynas living elsewhere through their range, three or more distinct notes running together can be identified. Yellow-faced mynas are believed to pair for life, even though they may congregate in large flocks comprised of hundreds of individuals at times. When nesting, a pair may be assisted by members of their previous brood. Once the chicks have hatched, insects and even small vertebrates assume greater importance in their diet to provide protein.

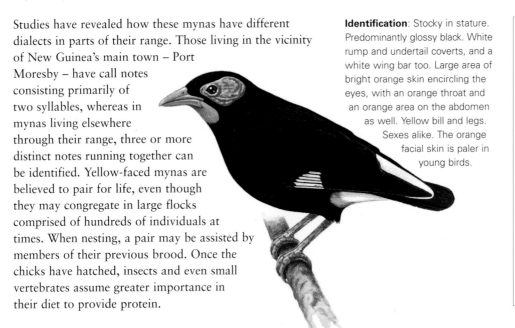

Identification: Stocky in stature. Predominantly glossy black. White rump and undertail coverts, and a white wing bar too. Large area of bright orange skin encircling the eyes, with an orange throat and an orange area on the abdomen as well. Yellow bill and legs. Sexes alike. The orange facial skin is paler in young birds.

Distribution: New Guinea, apart from the mountainous central zone, and adjoining islands.
Size: 26cm (10¹/₂in).
Habitat: In or near wooded areas.
Nest: Tree hole.
Eggs: 1–2, light blue with dark markings.
Food: Fruit and invertebrates.

Common myna

Indian mynah *Acridotheres tristis*

Distribution: Extends from south-eastern Iran and Afghanistan across central and southern Asia. Range is extending in some areas and the common myna has been introduced to many islands around the world from Madagascar to Hawaii, Australia and New Zealand
Size: 25cm (10in)
Habitat: Open country.
Nest: Usually built in a cavity
Eggs: 2–6, bluish
Food: Fruit, invertebrates

As their name suggests, these mynas are a common sight through much of their range, in agricultural areas as well as in towns and cities. They are very adaptable and this is reflected in their choice of nest sites. Common mynas have been recorded breeding in lamp posts, under the eaves of houses, in old machinery and even in air-conditioning units. An equally wide range of materials, from grass and leaves to pieces of plastic and paper, may be used in the construction. Common mynas are often seen in pairs, frequently foraging on the ground in parks and gardens for invertebrates. This is one of just a few avian species that has actively benefited from changes in the landscape arising from human development.

Identification: Black head with broad yellowish bare patch of skin around the eyes. Wings and body brownish with a white patch on the wings, white undertail coverts and a white tip to the tail. Yellow bill. Sexes alike.

Chestnut-cheeked starling (*Agropsar philippensis*): 18cm (7in)
Breeding grounds are centred in northern and central parts of Japan, with overwintering occurring further south, in Borneo, southern Sulu islands, parts of the Philippines and elsewhere, although the exact range has yet to be defined. Rarely seen on the Asiatic mainland in China. Cock bird has pale chestnut-coloured patches on the cheeks, greyish underparts, white wing bar and violet back. Hens by comparison are brownish-grey overall with paler underparts. A wing bar is also apparent.

Crested myna (Chinese jungle myna, *Acridotheres cristatellus*): 26cm (10½in)
Occurs in central and south-eastern China, extending to northern Indo-China. Also occurs on Hainan and Taiwan, and sometimes seen in western parts of Japan. Black, with a low crest extending back from the bill towards the eyes. Distinctive ivory bill. White patch on the wing and yellow iris. Sexes alike.

Chinese hwamei (Melodious laughing thrush, *Garrulax canorus*): 21.5cm (8½in)
Occurs in northern Indo-China and southern parts of China, including Hong Kong, as well as Hainan. Predominantly brown, with darker wings and tail. The tail is barred. Has dark streaking on the head and breast. The white plumage around the eye extends back to form a stripe running down each side of the neck. Has a "hwamei", which translates as "beautiful eyebrow". Sexes alike.

Spectacled spiderhunter

Greater yellow-eared spiderhunter *Arachnothera flavigaster*

Distribution: Extends from western Myanmar (Burma) through southern Thailand and the Malay Peninsula to Sumatra, Java and Borneo.
Size: 21cm (8in).
Habitat: Open forests and scrub.
Nest: Suspended structure.
Eggs: 2–3, pinkish with dark markings.
Food: Invertebrates, nectar.

Flowers that are red or orange in colour and shaped like trumpets tend to attract these nectar-feeding birds, which are members of the sunbird family in spite of the lack of iridescence in their plumage. They can be very aggressive, particularly during the breeding season, with an established cock bird chasing rivals away without any hesitation. At this time, the long, pointed bill of these birds is used rather like a needle to sew the nest in place, using gossamer threads of spiders' webs for this purpose. Spiderhunters are very bold birds by nature, and can often be seen in the open, particularly during the morning and later part of the afternoon, searching for food.

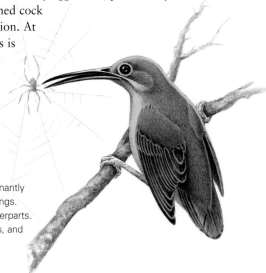

Identification: Relatively large spiderhunter. Predominantly olive green, darker in colour on the head, back and wings. There is a yellow suffusion to the plumage of the underparts. Yellow circles resembling spectacles encircle the eyes, and there are adjoining yellow ear patches. Narrow, long, down-curving black bill. Sexes alike.

BULBULS AND OTHER GARDEN BIRDS

There is a wide range of birds that may be encountered in garden surroundings, and they can be quite bold in this type of environment. A number are valuable allies of people, catching invertebrates that would otherwise become pests, particularly in tropical areas, although they also inflict damage on crops in some regions, especially when these are maturing.

Red-whiskered bulbul

Pycnonotus jocosus

These lively bulbuls are quite conspicuous through their range, occurring in small groups. They sing for quite long periods from the same perch, especially at the start of the breeding season, although the crest may not always be clearly visible at this stage. Sometimes they may be seen on branches but they will also perch on telephone cables in the open. Red-whiskered bulbuls are rarely seen on the ground, preferring to seek their food in trees. They are also sufficiently agile to be able to catch invertebrates in flight. When breeding, their nest is typically constructed up to 3m (10ft) off the ground in a bush or tree, being made of plant matter and lined with smaller plant fibres.

Identification: Head black, with a tall crest extending back towards the rear. Red patch behind the eyes, with white cheeks and throat broken by thin black lines. The wings and back are brownish. The underparts are buff in colour, apart from the vent area, which is red. Sexes alike.

Distribution: Extends from India eastwards to China and South-east Asia. Introduced in various localities including Australia.
Size: 20cm (8in).
Habitat: Open wooded areas and villages.
Nest: Cup-shaped, made of vegetation.
Eggs: 2–4, pinkish white with darker markings.
Food: Fruit and invertebrates.

Edible-nest swiftlet

Aerodramus fuciphagus

Distribution: Found on many offshore islands, including the Andamans, Nicobars and the Sundas. Also present on parts of the South-east Asian mainland at lower altitudes, including Myanmar (Burma), Thailand and the Malay Peninsula.
Size: 13cm (5in).
Habitat: Scrubland and towns.
Nest: Made entirely of saliva.
Eggs: 2, white.
Food: Invertebrates.

Although they fly in daylight, edible-nest swiftlets also rely on echolocation, rather like bats, which enables them to fly around caves in darkness. The rattling sounds that they utter reverberate off nearby objects, allowing them to fly without hitting any obstructions. The nests made by these swiftlets are constructed from saliva, and are traditionally harvested as the key ingredient of birds' nest soup. Over-collection of these nests and the resulting disruption of long-standing breeding colonies has led to a decline in the populations of edible-nest swiftlets at a number of localities through their range.

Identification: Upperparts blackish-brown, with brown underparts. Rump colour is variable, depending on the distribution. It is palest, bordering on white, in the case of birds originating from Singapore, and much darker in those found further north.

Right: These swiftlets breed communally in caves used over several generations.

Straw-headed bulbul (yellow-crowned bulbul, *Pycnonotus zeylanicus*): 28cm (11in) Extends through the Malay Peninsula down to the Greater Sunda islands. This is one of the larger bulbuls. It has a straw-yellow head and a white throat. Black lines run through the eyes and extend backwards from the side of the bill. Has a greyish chest with white streaking. This becomes grey on the belly and has a yellow vent. Olive-brown back, with whitish streaking near the neck. Sexes alike.

Collared finchbill (*Spizixos semitorques*): 23cm (9in) Found in central, eastern and southern parts of China and Taiwan. Has olive-green upperparts with the underparts a more golden-olive shade. The bill is short and thick and less pointed than in other bulbuls. Has a low, rounded crest on a black head. Has white streaking on the sides of the face, white lores and a white collar. The tail has a black tip. Sexes alike.

House crow (Indian crow, *Corvus splendens*): 43cm (17in) Occurs mainly in Asia from India eastwards to the western parts of South-east Asia, but also present in localities in the Middle East and Africa. Lighter greyish neck, back and underparts than other crows but with a jet black face, crown and throat. Sexes alike.

Coppersmith barbet

Crimson-breasted barbet *Psilopogon haemacephala*

The monotonous, repetitive calls of the coppersmith barbet resemble the sound of hammering on metal, which accounts for its unusual name. Their calls can be repeated as frequently as 100 times or more per minute, and this behaviour has led to them becoming known less flatteringly as "brainfever birds". They can also use their stout bills just like a hammer to tap away at rotten wood to create a suitable nesting cavity, which may be used for roosting purposes as well. In common with other barbets, the coppersmith displays the characteristic outward-curving longer feathers around the base of its bill, which are responsible for the common name of this group of birds ("barbet" actually means "bearded").

Distribution: Ranges from western Pakistan across Asia to south-western China, and through the Malay Peninsula to Sumatra and Java. Occurs on some Philippine islands.
Size: 15cm (6in).
Habitat: Wooded areas, often in cities and gardens.
Nest: Tree cavity.
Egg: 2–3, white.
Food: Fruit and invertebrates.

Identification: Red area above stocky, dark bill and across the breast, separated by pale yellow, which is also present above and below the eyes. Crown and lower part of the cheeks are black. Lower underparts light greyish with dark green streaks, while the upperparts are olive green. Legs reddish. Sexes alike.

Java sparrow

Rice bird *Lonchura oryzivora*

These members of the munia group are drawn to areas where cereals are ripening and flocks can inflict considerable damage on rice crops at this stage, especially when they descend in large numbers. Java sparrows are quite conspicuous finches, thanks to their large size and unusual coloration. Groups often settle in the evening on top of buildings before heading to their roosting sites. They frequently engage in a behaviour known as "clumping" when resting for any length of time, with the birds perching against each other. Pairs may nest under the eaves of buildings, although often they will use tree cavities for this purpose.

Identification: Black head with white cheek patches, grey chest and back with pinkish belly and white undertail coverts. Rump and tail above are black. Prominent reddish ring around the eyes. The large bill is pinkish. Both the eye ring and the bill may appear slightly enlarged in cock birds during the breeding season. Sexes are otherwise alike.

Distribution: Naturally found on Bali, Java and Kangean (part of the Greater Sunda islands) but introduced elsewhere both in the region – on Lombok, for example – and further afield in Venezuela and Puerto Rico, among other localities.
Size: 13cm (5in).
Habitat: Cultivated grasslands and gardens.
Nest: Domed nest with side entrance.
Eggs: 3–8, white.
Food: Cereal seeds such as rice, plus invertebrates.

HOW BIRDS LIVE

 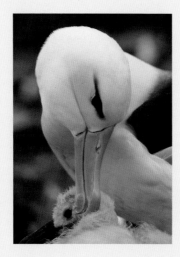 

Birds may differ dramatically in appearance, yet they all share a unique

characteristic – the presence of feathers on their bodies. Their lightweight

skeletal structure, often remarkably similar in different species, is an important

aid to flight, and it is apparent that even the few groups of flightless birds, such

as penguins (Spheniscidae), are descended from flying ancestors. The other

feature unique to birds is that they all reproduce by means of calcareous eggs.

Incubation may, in some cases, be the task of the male parent, while some

parasitic birds, such as the cuckoo (*Cuculus canorus*) or cowbird (*Molothrus

ater*), will transfer this duty to an unrelated species by laying in their nests. The

feeding habits of birds show even greater diversity, as reflected by differences

in bill structure and also digestive tracts. Birds' dietary preferences play a critical

part in their local environment. In tropical rainforests, for example, many fruit-

eating species help to disperse indigestible seeds through the forest, thus

ensuring the natural regeneration of the vegetation, and their food supply.

Left: A pair of gannets (Morus bassanus) *in breeding condition. The allegorical reference to greed in the term*
"gannet" originates from these birds' habit of swallowing their catch whole while feeding underwater.
Above from left: Black-headed oriole (Oriolus larvatus) *at nest, black-browed albatross* (Thalassarche melanophris) *with*
chick, male great frigatebird (Fregata minor) *displaying its inflated throat pouch.*

THE ORIGINS OF BIRDS

Vertebrates – first flying reptiles called pterosaurs, and later birds – took to the air about 190 million years ago. Adapting to an aerial existence marked a very significant step in vertebrate development, because of the need for a new method of locomotion, and a radically different body design.

The age of *Archaeopteryx*

Back in 1861, workers in a limestone quarry in Bavaria, southern Germany, unearthed a strange fossil that resembled a bird in appearance and was about the size of a modern crow, but also had teeth. The idea that the fossil was a bird was confirmed by the clear evidence of feathers impressed into the stone, as the presence of plumage is one of the characteristic distinguishing features of all birds. The 1860s were a time when the debate surrounding evolution was becoming fierce, and the discovery created huge interest, partly because it suggested that birds may have evolved from dinosaurs. It confirmed that birds had lived on Earth for at least 145 million years, existing even before the age of the dinosaurs came to a close in the Cretaceous period, about 65 million years ago. As the oldest-known bird, it was given the name *Archaeopteryx*, meaning "ancient wings".

Pterosaurs

A study of the anatomy of *Archaeopteryx*'s wings revealed that these early birds did not just glide but were capable of using their wings for active flight. Yet they were not the first vertebrate creatures to have taken to the skies. The pterosaurs had already successfully developed during the Jurassic period, approximately 190 million years ago, and even shared the skies with birds for a time. In fact, remains of one of the later pterosaurs, called *Rhamphorhynchus*, have been found in the same limestone deposits in southern Germany where *Archaeopteryx* was discovered. The pterosaur's wings more closely resembled those of a bat than a bird, consisting simply of a membrane supported by a bony framework, rather than feathers overlying the skin.

Some types of pterosaurs developed huge wingspans, in excess of 7m (23ft), which enabled them to glide almost effortlessly over the surface of the world's oceans, much like albatrosses do today. It appears that they fed primarily on fish and other marine life, scooping their food out of the water in flight. Changes in climate probably doomed the pterosaurs, however, since increasingly turbulent weather patterns meant that gliding became difficult, and they could no longer fly with ease.

Avian giants

In the period immediately after the extinction of the dinosaurs, some groups of birds increased rapidly in physical size, and in so doing, lost the ability to fly. Since their increased size meant that they could cover large distances on foot, and as they faced no predators because large hunting mammals had not yet evolved, these large birds were relatively safe. In New Zealand, home of the large flightless moas, such giants thrived until the start of human settlement about a millennium ago. The exact date of the final extinction of the moas is not recorded, but the group had probably died out entirely by the middle of the 19th century.

Above: An impression of how Archaeopteryx *may have looked. It is impossible to be sure of its coloration from its fossilized remains.*

Below: The largest species of moa would have dwarfed a man.

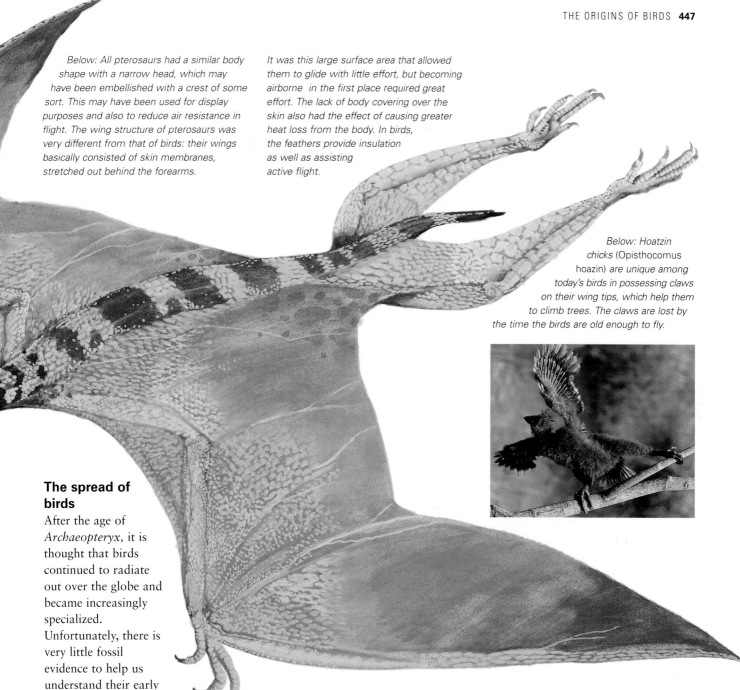

Below: All pterosaurs had a similar body shape with a narrow head, which may have been embellished with a crest of some sort. This may have been used for display purposes and also to reduce air resistance in flight. The wing structure of pterosaurs was very different from that of birds: their wings basically consisted of skin membranes, stretched out behind the forearms.

It was this large surface area that allowed them to glide with little effort, but becoming airborne in the first place required great effort. The lack of body covering over the skin also had the effect of causing greater heat loss from the body. In birds, the feathers provide insulation as well as assisting active flight.

Below: Hoatzin chicks (Opisthocomus hoazin) are unique among today's birds in possessing claws on their wing tips, which help them to climb trees. The claws are lost by the time the birds are old enough to fly.

The spread of birds

After the age of *Archaeopteryx*, it is thought that birds continued to radiate out over the globe and became increasingly specialized. Unfortunately, there is very little fossil evidence to help us understand their early history. This lack of fossils is partly due to the fact that the small carcasses of birds would have been eaten whole by scavengers, and partly because their lightweight, fragile skeletons would not have fossilized easily. In addition, most birds would not have been trapped and died under conditions that were favourable for fossilization.

By the end of the age of the dinosaurs, birds had become far more numerous. Many seabirds still possessed teeth in their jaws, reflecting their reptilian origins. These probably assisted them in catching fish and other aquatic creatures. It was at this stage that the ancestors of contemporary bird groups such as waterfowl and gulls started to emerge. Most of the forerunners of today's birds had evolved by the Oligocene epoch, some 38 million years ago.

Some groups of birds that existed in these times have since disappeared, notably the phororhacids, which ranged widely over South America and even into parts of the southern United States. These birds were fearsome predators, capable of growing to nearly 3m (10ft) in height. They were equipped with deadly beaks and talons, and probably hunted together in groups.

Recent finds

During the mid-1990s, the discovery of avian fossils in China that were apparently contemporary with those of *Archaeopteryx* aroused considerable interest. Like its German relative, *Confuciusornis* possessed claws on the tips of its wings, which probably helped these early birds to move around. Similar claws are seen today in hoatzin chicks. *Confuciusornis* resembled modern birds more closely than *Archaeopteryx* in one significant respect: it lacked teeth in its jaws. Further study of the recent fossil finds from this part of the world is required, however, as some may not be genuine.

THE SKELETON AND PARTS OF A BIRD

The bird's skeleton has evolved to be light yet robust, both characteristics that help with flight. To this end, certain bones, particularly in the skull, have become fused, while others are absent, along with the teeth. The result is that birds' bodies are lightweight compared to those of other vertebrates.

In order to be able to fly, a bird needs a lightweight body so that it can become airborne with minimal difficulty. It is not just teeth that are missing from the bird's skull, but the associated heavy jaw muscles as well. These have been replaced by a light, horn-covered bill that is adapted in shape to the bird's feeding habits. Some of the limb bones, such as the humerus in the shoulder, are hollow, which also cuts down on weight. At the rear of the body, the bones in the vertebral column have become fused, which gives greater stability as well as support for the tail feathers.

The avian skeleton

In birds, the greatest degree of specialization is evident in the legs. Their location of is critical to enable a bird to maintain its balance. The legs are found close to the midline, set slightly back near the bird's centre of gravity. The legs are powerful, helping to provide lift at take-off and absorb the impact of landing. Strong legs also allow most birds to hop over the ground with relative ease.

There are some differences in the skeleton between different groups of birds. The atlas and axis bones at the start of the vertebral column are fused in the case of hornbills, for example, but in no other family.

Feet and toes

Birds' feet vary in length, and are noticeably extended in waders, which helps them to distribute their weight more evenly. The four toes may be arranged either in a typical 3:1 perching grip, with three toes gripping the front of the perch and one behind, or in a 2:2 configuration, known as zygodactyl, which gives a surer grip. The zygodactyl grip is seen in relatively few groups of birds, notably parrots and toucans. Touracos have flexible toes so they can swap back and forth between these two options.

The zygodactyl arrangement of their toes helps some parrots to use their feet like hands for holding food. Birds generally have claws at the ends of their toes, which have developed into sharp talons in the case of birds of prey, helping them to catch their quarry even in flight. Many birds also use their claws for preening, and they can provide balance for birds that run or climb.

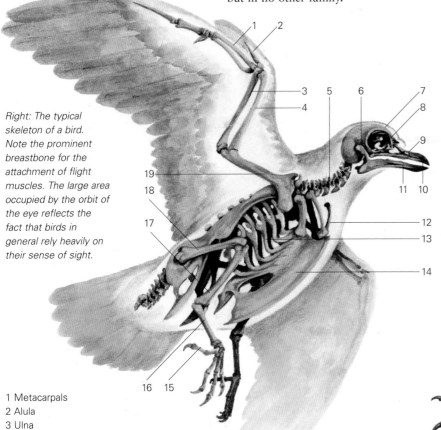

Right: The typical skeleton of a bird. Note the prominent breastbone for the attachment of flight muscles. The large area occupied by the orbit of the eye reflects the fact that birds in general rely heavily on their sense of sight.

1 Metacarpals
2 Alula
3 Ulna
4 Radius
5 Cervical vertebrae
6 Ear
7 Cranium
8 Eye socket
9 Nostril

10 Bill (upper mandible)
11 Bill (lower mandible)
12 Clavicle (wishbone)
13 Ribs
14 Sternum (breastbone)

15 Metatarsals
16 Tarsus
17 Tibia and Fibula
18 Femur
19 Humerus

Parrot

Above: Parrots use their feet for holding food, in a similar way to human hands.

Bird of prey

Above: In birds of prey, the claws have become talons for grasping prey.

Wader

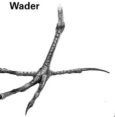

Above: Long toes make it easier for waders to walk over muddy ground or water plants.

Duck

Above: The webbed feet of ducks provide propulsion in water.

Above: The narrow bill of waders such as this curlew (Numenius arquata) enables these birds to probe for food in sandy or muddy areas.

Above: Birds of prey such as the golden eagle (Aquila chrysaetos) rely on a sharp bill with a hooked tip to tear their prey apart.

Above: Cranes have strong, pointed bills, which they use like daggers to seize prey such as frogs between the upper and lower parts.

Above: Flamingos have bills that enable them to feed with their heads trailing backwards in the water.

Above: The hyacinthine macaw (Anodorhynchus hyacinthinus) has one of the most powerful bills of any bird.

Above: Shoebills (Balaeniceps rex) have large bills that allow them to scoop up quite large vertebrate prey.

Bills

The bills of birds vary quite widely in shape and size, and reflect their feeding habits. The design of the bill has a marked impact on the force that it can generate. The bills of many larger parrots are especially strong, allowing them to crack hard nut shells. In addition, they can move their upper and lower bill independently, which produces a wider gape and, in turn, allows more pressure to be exerted.

Wings

A bird's wing is built around just three digits, which correspond to human fingers. In comparison, bats have five digits supporting their fleshy membranes. The three digits of birds provide a robust structure. The power of the wings is further enhanced by the fusion of the wrist bones and the carpals to create the single bone known as the carpometacarpus, which runs along the edge of the wing.

At the front of the chest, the clavicles are joined together to form what in chickens is called the wishbone. The large, keel-shaped breastbone, or sternum, runs along the underside of the body. It is bound by the ribs to the backbone, which provides stability, especially during flight. In addition, the major flight muscles are located in the lower body when the bird is airborne.

Darwin's finches

In the 1830s, a voyage to the remote Galapagos Islands, off the north-west coast of South America, helped the British naturalist Charles Darwin to formulate his theory of evolution. The finches present on the Galapagos Islands today are all believed to be descended from a single ancestor, but they have evolved in a number of different ways. The changes are most obvious in their bill shapes. For example, some species have stout, crushing beaks for cracking seeds, while others have long, slender beaks to probe for insects. These adaptations have arisen to take full advantage of the range of edible items available on the islands, where food is generally scarce. Some species have even developed the ability to use cactus spines and similar items as tools to extract seeds and invertebrates. In total, there are now 12 recognized species found on these islands, and nowhere else in the world.

Below: The finches of the Galapagos Islands helped to inspire Charles Darwin's theory of evolution. They are thought to be descended from a common ancestor, and have diverged significantly to avoid competing with each other for food. This is reflected by their bill shapes. The woodpecker finch (Camarhynchus pallidus) has even acquired the ability to use a tool, in this case a cactus spine, to winkle out grubs hiding in tree bark.

FEATHERS

The presence of feathers is one of the main distinguishing characteristics that set birds apart from other groups of creatures on the planet. The number of feathers on a bird's body varies considerably – a swan may have as many as 25,000 feathers, for instance, while a tiny hummingbird has just 1,000 in all.

Aside from the bill, legs and feet, the entire body of the bird is covered in feathers. The plumage does not grow randomly over the bird's body, but develops along lines of so-called feather tracts, or pterylae. These are separated by bald areas known as apteria. The apteria are not conspicuous under normal circumstances, because the contour feathers overlap to cover the entire surface of the body. Plumage may also sometimes extend down over the legs and feet as well, in the case of birds from cold climates, providing extra insulation here.

Feathers are made of a tough protein called keratin, which is also found in our hair and nails. Birds have three main types of feathers: the body, or contour, feathers; the strong, elongated flight feathers on the wings; and the warm, wispy down feathers next to the bird's skin.

A diet deficient in sulphur-containing amino acids, which are the basic building blocks of protein, will result in poor feathering, creating "nutritional barring" across the flight and tail feathers. Abnormal plumage coloration can also have nutritional causes in some cases. These changes are usually reversible if more favourable environmental conditions precede the next moult.

The functions of feathers

Plumage has a number of functions, not just relating to flight. It provides a barrier that retains warm air close to the bird's body and helps to maintain body temperature, which is higher in birds than mammals – typically between 41 and 43.5°C (106 and 110°F). The down feathering that lies close to the skin, and the overlying contour plumage, are vital for maintaining body warmth. Most birds have a small volume relative to their surface area, which can leave them vulnerable to hypothermia.

A special oil produced by the preen gland, located at the base of the tail, waterproofs the plumage. This oil, which is spread over the feathers as the bird preens itself, prevents water penetrating the feathers, which would cause the bird to become so

Below: Feathering is highly significant for display purposes in some species, particularly members of the Phasanidae family. The Indian peafowl (Pavo cristatus) has a very elaborate train of feathers, which it fans open to deter rivals and attract mates.

Above: A bird's flight feathers are longer and more rigid than the contour feathers that cover the body, or the fluffy down feathers that lie next to the skin. The longest, or primary, flight feathers, which generate the most thrust, are located along the outer rear edges of the wings. The tail feathers are often similar in shape to the flight feathers, with the longest being found in the centre. Splaying the tail feathers increases drag and so slows the bird down.

1 Primaries	9 Auricular region (ear)
2 Secondaries	10 Nape
3 Axillaries	11 Back
4 Rump	12 Greater under-wing coverts
5 Lateral tail feathers	13 Lesser under-wing coverts
6 Central tail feathers	
7 Breast	
8 Cere	

Above: The vulturine guineafowl (Acryllium vulturinum) is so-called because of its bare head and neck, which is a feature of vultures, although it is not a carnivorous species itself.

waterlogged that it could no longer fly. The contour feathers that cover the body are also important for camouflage in many birds. Barring, in particular, breaks up the outline of the bird's body, helping to conceal it in its natural habitat.

The plumage has become modified in some cases, reflecting the individual lifestyle of the species concerned. Woodpeckers, for example, have tail feathers that are short and rather sharp at their tips, providing additional support for gripping onto the sides of trees. Vultures, on the other hand, have bare heads because plumage here would soon become stained and matted with blood when these birds fed on a carcass.

Social significance of plumage

Plumage can also be important in social interactions between birds. Many species have differences in their feathering that separate males from females, and often juveniles can also be distinguished by their plumage. Cock birds are usually more brightly coloured, which helps them to attract their mates, but this does not apply in every case. The difference between the sexes in terms of their plumage can be quite marked. Cock birds of a number

of species have feathers forming crests as well as magnificent tail plumes, which are seen to greatest effect in peacocks (*Pavo cristatus*), whose display is one of the most remarkable sights in the whole of the avian world.

Recent studies have confirmed that birds that to our eyes appear relatively dull in colour, such as the hill myna (*Gracula religiosa*) with its blackish plumage, are seen literally in a different light by other birds. They can visually perceive the ultraviolet component of light, which is normally invisible to us, making these seemingly dull birds appear greener. Ultraviolet coloration may also be significant in helping birds to choose their mates.

Moulting

Birds' feathering is maintained by preening, but it becomes frayed and worn over time. It is therefore replaced by new plumage during the process of moulting, when the old feathers are shed. Moulting is most often an annual event. However, many young birds shed their nest feathers before they are a year old.

Moulting may also be triggered by the onset of the breeding season in some species, as is the case in many whydahs and weavers. These birds resemble sparrows for much of the year, but their appearance is transformed at the onset of the breeding period. Whydah cock birds develop lengthy tail plumes, and the birds also become more strikingly coloured. Hormonal alterations in the body are important in triggering this process, with external factors such as changing day length also playing a part.

Iridescence

Some birds are not brightly coloured, but their plumage literally sparkles in the light, thanks to its structure, which creates an iridescent effect. One of the particular features of iridescence is that the colour of the plumage alters, depending on the angle at which it is viewed, often appearing quite dark, almost black from a side view. This phenomenon is particularly common in some groups of birds, notably members of the starling family (Sturnidae), hummingbirds (Trochilidae) and sunbirds (Nectariniidae), which are described as having metallic feathers as a result.

In some cases, the iridescent feathering is localized, while in others, it is widespread over most of the body. Green and blue iridescence is common, with reddish sheens being seen less often. Iridescence is especially common in cock birds, helping them to attract mates. In some cases, therefore, it is seen only in the breeding plumage, notably on the upperparts of the body and the wings rather than the underparts.

Below: A blue-chinned sapphire hummingbird (Chlorestes notata) displays its iridescent plumage.

Right: The feather shaft holds the feather in place in the skin. The barbs run off the shaft at regular intervals, rather like the branches of a tree, and divide into smaller branches called barbules. These have tiny hooks attached to them that reinforce the structure of each flight feather, making it more rigid.

Barb   Barbule

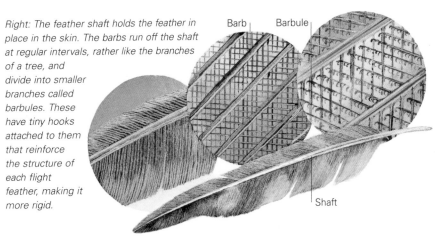

Shaft

FLIGHT

Some birds spend much of their lives in the air, whereas others will only fly as a last resort if threatened. A few species are too heavy to take off at all. The mechanics of flight are similar in all birds, but flight patterns vary significantly, which can help to identify the various groups in the air.

In most cases, the whole structure of the bird's body has evolved to facilitate flight. It is important for a bird's body weight to be relatively light, because this lessens the muscular effort required to keep it airborne. The powerful flight muscles, which provide the necessary lift, can account for up to a third of the bird's total body weight. They are attached to the breastbone, or sternum, in the midline of the body, and run along the sides of the body from the clavicle along the breastbone to the top of the legs.

Weight and flight

There is an upper weight limit of just over 18kg (40lb), above which birds would not be able to take off successfully. Some larger birds, notably pelicans and swans, need a run-up in order to gain sufficient momentum to lift off, particularly from water. Smaller birds can dart straight off a perch. Approaching the critical upper weight limit for flight, the male Kori bustard (*Ardeotis kori*) is the world's heaviest flying bird, although it prefers to run rather than fly because of the effort involved in becoming airborne.

Below: A typical take-off, as shown by a Harris's hawk (Parabuteo unicinctus).

Above: Birds such as the Andean condor (Vultur gryphus) can remain airborne with minimum expenditure of energy, by gliding rather than flying.

Wing shape and beat

The shape of the wing is important for a bird's flying ability. Birds that remain airborne for much of their lives, such as albatrosses, have relatively long wings that allow them to glide with relatively little effort. The wandering albatross (*Diomedea exulans*) has the largest wingspan of any bird, measuring about 3.4m (11ft) from one wing tip to the other. Large, heavy birds such as Andean condors (*Vultur gryphus*) may have difficulty in flying early in the day, before the land has warmed up. This is because at this stage, there is insufficient heat coming up from the ground to create the thermal air currents that help to keep them airborne. In common with other large birds of prey, Andean condors seek out these rising columns of air, which provide uplift, and then circle around in them.

The number of wing beats varies dramatically between different species. Hummingbirds, for example, beat their wings more frequently than any other bird as they hover in front of flowers to harvest their nectar. Their wings move so fast – sometimes at over 200 beats per minute – that they appear as a blur to our eyes. At the other extreme, heavy birds such as swans fly with slow, deliberate wing beats.

Lightening the load

It is not just the lightness of the bird's skeleton that helps it to fly. There have been evolutionary changes in the body organs too, most noticeably in the urinary system. Unlike mammals, birds do not have a bladder that fills with urine. Instead, their urine is greatly concentrated, in the form of uric acid, and passes out of the body with their faeces, appearing as a creamy-white, semi-solid component.

1. When resting, a bird typically has a relatively upright stance.

2. As it leans forwards for take-off, it raises its wings and starts to lift its legs.

3. Leaving its perch, the bird pushes off into the air, and opens its wings.

Above: Birds such as this broad-tailed hummingbird (Selasphorus platycercus) *have unparalleled aerial manoeuvrability, thanks to their rapid wing movements.*

Below: The black-browed albatross (Thalassarche melanophris) *and its relatives often skim just above the waves.*

The aerofoil principle

Once in flight, the shape of the wing is crucial in keeping the bird airborne. Viewed in cross-section from the side, a bird's wing resembles that of an aircraft, and is called an aerofoil, as aircraft use the same basic principle in order to fly.

The wing is curved across the top, so the movement of air is faster over this part of the wing compared with the lower surface. This produces reduced air pressure on top of the wing, which provides lift and makes it easier for the bird to stay in the air.

The long flight feathers at the rear edge of the wings help to provide the thrust and lift for flight. The tail feathers, too, can help the bird remain airborne. The kestrel (*Falco tinnunculus*), for example, having spotted prey on the ground, spreads its tail feathers to help it remain aloft while it hovers to target its prey.

A bird's wings move in a regular figure-of-eight movement while it is in flight. During the downstroke, the flight feathers join together to push powerfully against the air. The primary flight feathers bend backwards, which propels the bird forwards. As the wing moves upwards, the longer primary flight feathers move apart, which reduces air resistance. The secondary feathers further along the wing provide some slight propulsion. After that the cycle repeats itself.

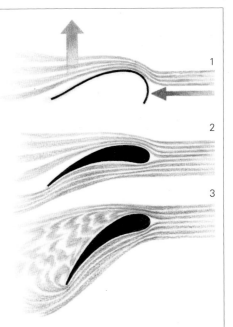

Above: The flow of air over a bird's wing varies according to the wing's position.
1. When the wing is stretched out horizontally, an area of low pressure is created above the wing, causing lift.
2. As the wing is tilted downwards, the flow of the air is disrupted, causing turbulence and loss of lift.
3. When the wing is angled downwards, lift slows, which results in stalling. The bird's speed slows as a consequence.

Flight patterns and formations

Different species of birds have various methods of flying, which can help the birdwatcher to identify them. For example, small birds such as tits (Paridae) and finches (Fringillidae) alternately flap their wings and fold them at their sides, adopting a streamlined shape, which helps to save energy. This produces a characteristic dipping flight. Large birds such as ducks and geese maintain a straighter course at an even height.

In some cases, it is not just the individual flying skills of a bird that can help it to stay airborne, but those of its fellows nearby. Birds flying in formation create a slipstream, which makes flying less effort for all the birds behind the leader. This is why birds often fly in formation, especially when covering large distances on migration.

4. Powerful upward and downward sweeps of the wings propel the bird forwards.

5. When coming in to land, a bird lowers its legs and slows its wing movements.

6. Braking is achieved by a vertical landing posture, with the tail feathers spread.

LOCOMOTION

For most birds, flight is the main means of locomotion. However, the ability to move on the ground or in water can be vital, particularly when it comes to obtaining food. Some birds have even lost the ability to fly, relying instead on their swimming or running skills to escape predators and find food.

Not all birds possess the ability to fly, but this does not mean they are handicapped in their natural environment. Penguins may appear to be rather clumsy shuffling around on land, but they are extremely well adapted to life in the water. Like other primarily aquatic birds, their webbed feet enable them to swim very effectively. Webbing is a common feature seen in aquatic birds. The skin folds linking the toes turn the foot into an effective paddle, allowing the bird to maximize its propulsive forward thrust by pushing against the water. On land, however, webbed feet do impose certain restrictions, because being linked together in this way means that the individual toes are not as flexible.

Aquatic locomotion

When penguins dive, their sleek, torpedo-shaped bodies allow them to swim fast underwater, reaching speeds equivalent to 40km/h (25mph). Their flippers, which evolved from wings,

Below: A group of king penguins (Aptenodytes patagonicus) leap in and out of the water as they swim along, in a form of movement known as porpoising.

help them to steer very effectively as they pursue fish, which form the basis of their diet. Like flying birds, penguins need effective wing muscles to control their movements, so their skeletal structure bears a close similarity to that of flying birds.

Flightless ducks and other aquatic birds, such as the flightless cormorant (*Phalacrocorax harrisi*), use a different method of locomotion: they rely entirely on their feet rather than their wings for propulsive power. Their skeletons differ from those of flying birds in that they lack the prominent keel on the sternum for the attachment of flight muscles.

Flightless land birds

A number of land birds have lost the ability to fly. Typically, they are birds that inhabit islands where, until the arrival of cats and rats brought by ships from Europe, they faced few if any predators. The arrival of predators has left them vulnerable, and many have since become extinct, including the dodo (*Raphus cucullatus*), a large, flightless pigeon from the island of Mauritius in the Indian Ocean. A high percentage of flightless birds evolved

Above: Penguins such as the chinstrap (Pygoscelis antarcticus) *are less agile on land than they are in the sea, where their body shape lessens water resistance.*

on the islands of New Zealand, but many have since vanished, including all species of moa (*Dinornis* and related forms). Moas represent the most diverse group of flightless birds ever recorded. The last examples probably died out about the time of European settlement of these islands in the 19th century.

The giant moa (*Dinornis maximus*) was the largest member of the group and, indeed, the tallest bird ever to have existed. It would have dwarfed today's ostriches, standing up to 3.5m (11½ft) high. There may have been as many as a dozen or more different types of moa, which filled the same sort of niche as grazing mammals, which were absent from New Zealand.

In the absence of predatory mammals, the moas faced no significant threats to their survival until the first human settlers reached New Zealand and started to hunt them. Their large size made them conspicuous, and, having evolved in an environment where they had been safe from persecution, they had lost their ability to fly. Moas were not even able to run fast, in contrast to modern flightless birds such as ostriches. These defenceless giants were soon driven to extinction.

Circulation

The circulatory system is vital in supporting the activities of both flighted and flightless birds, ensuring that their muscles are well supplied with oxygen. The heart acts as the pump, driving the blood around the body. The basic design of the heart is similar to that of a mammal, with the left side being highly developed because it does more work. Overall, the heart rate of birds is much more rapid than mammals of similar size, having been measured at 1,000 beats per minute in the case of canaries at rest. The heartbeat rises dramatically during flight, but soon returns to normal when the bird touches down.

The respiratory system

Birds have lungs, located close to the vertebral column, but these do not expand and contract in the same way as those of mammals. Instead, birds rely on a series of air sacs that act rather like bellows, to suck air through their respiratory system. In some cases, these link with the hollow limb bones, and thus help to meet the bird's high requirement for oxygen when flying. A bird's respiratory rate is a reflection of its body size, as well as its level of activity and lifestyle. Common starlings (*Sturnus vulgaris*), for example, typically breathe about 85 times every minute, whereas domestic chickens, which are more sedentary, have an equivalent respiratory rate of only about 20 breaths per minute.

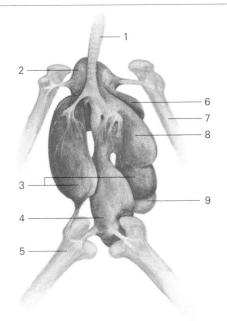

1 Trachea
2 Interclavicular air sac
3 Lungs
4 Abdominal air sac
5 Femur (leg bone)
6 Cervical air sac
7 Humerus (wing bone)
8 Anterior thoracic air sac
9 Posterior thoracic air sac

Above: The razor-sharp inner claw of the cassowary (Casuarius unappendiculatus) *is able to disembowel a person, making these birds very dangerous.*

Ratites

Not all flightless birds are helpless in the face of danger, however. The large, flightless birds known as ratites, including cassowaries, ostriches, emus and rheas, are particularly well able to defend themselves. Their strong legs are quite capable of inflicting lethal blows, especially in the case of the cassowaries (Casuariidae), found in parts of northern Australia, New Guinea and neighbouring islands. These birds have an elongated and deadly sharp claw on their innermost toe. If the cassowary is cornered and unable to run away, it lashes out with its legs and is quite capable of disembowelling a person with its sharp claws. The bird also has a hard, bony crest called a casque, which protects the top of its head.

The large ratites all share a similar shape, having bulky bodies, long legs and long, slender necks. Like all flightless birds, they do possess wings, which assist them in keeping their balance and may also be used for display purposes. Most birds have four toes on each foot, but ratites have no more than three toes, and less in some cases. Ostriches have just two toes on each foot. The fastest birds on land, they can run at speeds equivalent to 50km/h (31mph). The reduction in the number of toes may help these birds to run faster.

Emus (*Dromaius novaehollandiae*) have the most rudimentary wings of all ratites, which are not even used for display purposes. The rheas (Rheidae) of South America have the most prominent wings of the ratites. They cover the rump, but they do not enable these birds to fly, even when they are young.

Kiwis (Apterygidae) are also ratites, but they are much smaller birds with shorter legs. Unlike other ratites, they are not fast runners, but rely on camouflage and their nocturnal habits to conceal their presence from predators, rather than speed to escape.

Running in flighted birds

Some birds that are able to fly still prefer to use their running abilities to obtain food and escape danger. They include the roadrunners (*Geococcyx californianus*) of North America. With their short wings, these birds can fly clumsily, but prefer to use their strong legs to overtake and pounce on prey. In general, flying uses considerable energy compared to running or hopping. Many birds will elect to move swiftly over the ground to pounce on a food item or avoid an enemy if they judge that the situation does not warrant flight.

Above: The height and keen eyesight of ostriches (Struthio camelus) *means that they are hard to ambush in open country. Their pace allows them to escape from danger with little difficulty, while their long stride length when running enables them to cover large amounts of ground in a single step.*

AVIAN SENSES

The keen senses of birds are vital to their survival, in particular helping them to find food, escape from enemies and find mates in the breeding season. Sight is the primary sense for most birds, but some species rely heavily on other senses to thrive in particular habitats.

All birds' senses are adapted to their environment, and the shape of their bodies can help to reflect which senses are most significant to them.

Sight and lifestyle

Most birds rely on their sense of sight to avoid danger, hunt for food and locate familiar surroundings. The importance of this sense is reflected by the size of their eyes, with those of

starlings (*Sturnus vulgaris*), for example, making up 15 per cent of the total head weight. The enlargement of the eyeballs and associated structures, notably the eye sockets in the skull, has altered the shape of the brain. In addition, the optic lobes in the brain, which are concerned with vision, are also enlarged, whereas the olfactory counterparts, responsible for smell, are poorly developed.

The structure of the eye also reveals much about a bird's habits. Birds of prey have large eyes in proportion to their head, and have correspondingly keen eyesight. Species that regularly hunt for prey underwater, such as penguins, can see well in the water. They have a muscle in each eye that reduces the diameter of the lens and increases its thickness on entering water, so that their eyes can adjust easily to seeing underwater. In addition, certain diving birds such as little auks (*Alle alle*) use a lens that forms part of the nictitating membrane, or third eyelid, which is normally hidden from sight. Underwater, when this membrane covers the eye, its convex shape serves as a lens, helping the bird to see in these surroundings.

Eye position

The positioning of the eyes on the head gives important clues to a bird's lifestyle. Most birds' eyes are set on the sides of their heads. Owls, however, have flattened faces and forward-facing eyes that are critical to their hunting abilities. These features allow owls to target their prey.

There are disadvantages, though – owls' eyes do not give a rounded view of the world, so they must turn their heads to see about them. It is not just the positioning of owls' eyes that is unusual. They are also able to hunt effectively in almost complete darkness. This is made possible in two

Above: Kiwis (Apteryx australis) *rely much more heavily on their sense of smell than other birds, as is reflected by the fact that their eyes are smaller.*

ways. First, their pupils are large, which maximizes the amount of light passing through to the retina behind the lens, where the image is formed. Second, the cells here consist mainly of rods rather than cones. While cones give good colour vision, rods function to create images when background illumination is low.

The positioning of the eyes of game birds such as woodcocks (*Scolopax rusticola*) allows them to spot danger from almost any angle. It is even possible for them to see a predator sneaking up from behind. Their only blind spot is just behind the head.

Smell

Very few birds have a sense of smell, but kiwis (Apterygidae) and vultures (forming part of the order Falciformes) are notable exceptions. Birds' nostrils are normally located above the bill, opening directly into the skull, but kiwis' nostrils are positioned right at the end of the long bill. They probably help these birds to locate earthworms

---

Field of vision

The positioning of a bird's eyes on its head affects its field of vision. The eyes of owls are positioned to face forwards, producing an overlapping image of the area in front known as binocular vision. This allows the owl to pinpoint its prey exactly, so that it can strike. In contrast, the eyes of birds that are likely to be preyed upon, such as woodcocks, are positioned on the sides of the head. This eye position gives a greatly reduced area of binocular vision, but it does give these birds practically all-round vision, enabling them to spot danger from all sides.

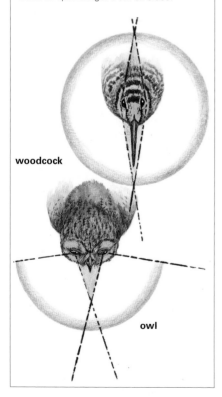

woodcock

owl

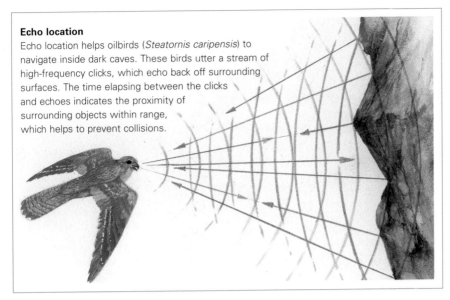

Echo location

Echo location helps oilbirds (*Steatornis caripensis*) to navigate inside dark caves. These birds utter a stream of high-frequency clicks, which echo back off surrounding surfaces. The time elapsing between the clicks and echoes indicates the proximity of surrounding objects within range, which helps to prevent collisions.

in the soil. Vultures have very keen eyesight, which helps them to spot dead animals on the ground from the air, but they also have a strong sense of smell, which helps when homing in on a distant carcass.

Taste

The senses of smell and taste are linked, and most birds also have correspondingly few taste buds in their mouths. The number of taste buds varies, with significant differences between groups of birds. Pigeons may have as few as 50 taste buds in their mouths, parrots as many as 400.

Birds' taste buds are located all around the mouth, rather than just on the tongue, as in mammals. The close

Below: Birds have good colour vision. It is this sense that encourages hummingbirds, such as this long-billed starthroat (Heliomaster longirostris), to home in on red flowers.

links between smell and taste can lead vultures, which feed only on fresh carcasses, to reject decomposing meat. They may start to eat it, but then spit it out once it is in their mouths, probably because of a combination of bad odour and taste.

Hearing

Birds generally do not have a highly developed sense of hearing. They lack any external ear flaps that would help to pinpoint sources of sound. The openings to their hearing system are located on the sides of the head, back from the eyes.

Hearing is of particular significance for nocturnal species, such as owls, which find their food in darkness. These birds are highly attuned to the calls made by rodents. The broad shape of their skull has the additional advantage of spacing the ear openings more widely, which helps them to localize the source of the sounds with greater accuracy.

Hearing is also important to birds during the breeding season. Birds show particular sensitivity to sounds falling within the vocal range of their chicks, which helps them to locate their offspring easily in the critical early days after fledging.

The oilbird (*Steatornis caripensis*), which inhabits parts of northern South America, uses echo location to find its way around in the dark, rather like bats do. Unlike the sounds bats make,

however, the clicking sounds of the oilbird's calls – up to 20 a second in darkness – are clearly audible to humans. The bird interprets the echoes of its call to avoid colliding with objects in its path, although it also uses its eyesight when flying. Cave swiftlets (*Collocalia linchi*) from Asia, which also inhabit a dark environment, use echo location in a similar way to fly.

Touch

The sense of touch is more developed in some birds than others. Those such as snipe (*Gallinago* species), which have long bills for seeking food, have sensitive nerve endings called corpuscles in their bills that pick up tiny vibrations caused by their prey. Vibrations that could suggest approaching danger can also register via other corpuscles located particularly in the legs, so that the bird has a sensory awareness even when it is resting on a branch.

Wind-borne sensing

Tubenoses such as albatrosses and petrels (Procellariiformes) have a valve in each nostril that fills with air as the bird flies. These are affected by both the bird's speed and the wind strength. The valves almost certainly act as a type of wind gauge, allowing these birds to detect changes in wind strength and patterns. This information helps to keep them airborne, as they skim over the waves with minimal effort.

Below: A combination of senses, especially touch, helps oystercatchers (Haematopus ostralegus) to detect their prey, which is normally hidden from view.

PLANT-EATERS

All over the world, many birds depend on plant matter as part of their diet, with seeds and nuts in particular providing nourishment. A close relationship between plants and birds exists in many cases. Birds fertilize flowers when feeding on nectar, and help to spread their seeds when eating fruit.

Many different types of birds are primarily plant-eaters, whether feeding on flowers, fruit, nuts and seeds, or other plant matter. Plant-eating species have to eat a large volume of food compared to meat-eating species, because of the low nutritional value of plants compared with that of prey such as invertebrates.

In the last century or so, many species have benefited from the spread of agriculture, which now provides them with large acreages of suitable crop plants to feed on. These birds' feeding habits bring them into conflict with farmers when they breed rapidly in response to a swift expansion in their food supply. For example, populations of little corellas (*Cacatua sanguinea*) have increased quickly in Australia thanks to the spread of arable agriculture there, and the

Below: Birds such as the cactus wren (Campylorhynchus brunneicapillus) have a close association with particular plants. This wren not only feeds on the plants after which it is named, but also takes advantage of their protective thorns when nesting.

associated provision of reservoirs for irrigation purposes. These birds have bred up to form huge flocks comprising many thousands of individuals, which inflict massive damage on crops as they ripen. They are now labelled as pests in some areas.

Adapting to changing seasons

Birds from temperate areas exist on a varied diet that is related to the seasons. Bullfinches (*Pyrrhula pyrrhula*), for example, eat the buds in apple orchards in spring – when they can become a pest – while later in the year, they consume seeds and fruit. Their bills, like those of most other members of the finch family, are stout and relatively conical, which helps them to crack seeds effectively.

Some birds store plant food when it is plentiful, to sustain them through the winter. Nutcrackers (*Nucifraga*) collect hazel nuts, which they feed on in winter until the following year. Acorn woodpeckers (*Melanerpes formicivorus*) drill holes in trees that they fill with acorns, creating an easily accessible larder for the winter, when snow may cover the ground.

Flowers

A number of birds rely on flowers rather than the whole plant as a source of food. Pollen is a valuable source of protein, while nectar provides sugars. Not surprisingly, flower-feeders tend to be confined to mainly tropical areas, where flowers are in bloom throughout the year. Hummingbirds (Trochilidae), for instance, use their narrow bills to probe into flowers to obtain nectar. Some hummingbirds have developed especially curved or elongated bills, which allow them to feed on particular flowers. These birds help to pollinate the plants on which they feed by transferring pollen from flower to flower on their bills or even on plumage.

The digestive system

Birds lack teeth, so their food must be swallowed whole. Birds have a storage organ known as the crop, which is located at the base of the neck. From here, food passes down into the proventriculus, where the digestive process starts, before entering the gizzard, which is equivalent to the mammalian stomach. Nutrients are then absorbed through the wall of the small intestine.

The digestive system of plant-eaters differs in various respects from that of predatory species. Vegetable matter is less nourishing than meat, so plant-eaters generally need longer digestive tracts to process the large quantities of food they must consume in order to obtain enough nourishment. In addition, digesting plant matter poses certain difficulties. The gizzards of seed-eating species such as many finches (Fringillidae) have especially thick muscular walls, which serve to grind up the seeds.

1 Oesophagus	6 Large intestine
2 Crop	7 Liver
3 Proventriculus	8 Spleen
4 Pancreas	9 Small intestine
5 Gizzard	

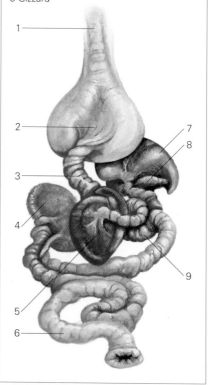

Above: Feeding on plants comes at a price, as many contain potentially harmful chemicals. Various parrots, such as these macaws (Ara species), make daily visits to cliffs to eat clay, which is believed to have a detoxifying effect on their digestive systems.

Sunbirds (Nectariniidae) found in Africa and Asia fill a similar evolutionary niche to hummingbirds, which they resemble in their small size and bright, often iridescent, plumage. Unlike hummingbirds, however, they are not sufficiently agile to feed in flight, but have to perch within reach of the flower. Various members of the parrot family also feed on flowers, notably lories and lorikeets. Their tongues are equipped with tiny, bristle-like projections called papillae, which enable them to collect pollen easily.

Fruit

Exclusively frugivorous (fruit-eating) birds such as fruit doves (*Ptilinopus*) are found only in the tropics, where fruit is available throughout the year. These species usually dwell in tropical rainforests, where they have a valuable role to play in protecting the biodiversity of the forest. The seeds of the fruits they eat pass right through their digestive tracts unharmed, to be deposited far from the parent plant, which helps the plants to spread.

Plant matter

Relatively few birds rely almost exclusively on herbage for their diet. The primitive hoatzin (*Opisthocomus hoazin*), from the rainforest of South America, is one example of a bird that does. Equally unusual are the turacos (Musophagidae) of Africa, which also feed mainly on leaves, which they pluck along with fruits. Some parrots such as the eclectus (*Eclectus roratus*) are also believed to feed largely on plant matter rather than seeds or fruit.

The breakdown of vegetation presents considerable difficulty, since birds do not possess the necessary enzymes to digest the cellulose in plants. Birds such as grouse (Tetraoninae), which feed regularly on plant matter, have evolved long, blind-ending tubes known as caeca. These contain beneficial microbes that can break down cellulose.

Nuts and seeds

These dry foods are a valuable resource to many different types of birds, ranging from parrots to finches. However, cracking the tough outer shell or husk can be a problem. Finches such as grosbeaks have evolved a particularly strong bill for this purpose. Hawfinches (*Coccothraustes coccothraustes*) are able to crack cherry stones (pits) to extract the kernel.

Above: Red-billed queleas, or weavers (Quelea quelea), are the most numerous birds in the world. Massive flocks of these birds will wipe out crops of ripening millets in parts of Africa, to the extent that they are sometimes called "feathered locusts".

The most bizarre example of bill adaption for eating seeds is seen in the crossbills (*Loxia*) of northern coniferous forests. These birds have literally twisted upper and lower mandibles, which help them to crack open the seeds inside the larch cones, which they eat. Some cockatoos such as the salmon-crested (*Cacatua moluccensis*) have bills that are even strong enough to open coconuts.

Below: Pink-footed geese (Anser brachyrhynchus) can be a problem in agricultural areas, since they will sometimes descend in large numbers to graze on young cereal crops.

PREDATORS AND SCAVENGERS

Just as with other vertebrates, there is a food chain within the avian kingdom. Some species hunt only other birds, while others seek a more varied range of prey, including, commonly, invertebrates. Even birds that feed mainly on seeds catch protein-rich insects to feed their chicks in the nest.

Some birds are active predators, seeking and killing their own food, while others prefer to scavenge on carcasses. Many predatory birds are opportunistic, hunting when food is plentiful but scavenging when food becomes scarce. Both hunters and scavengers have evolved to live in a wide range of environments, and display correspondingly diverse hunting skills to obtain their food.

Birds of prey have sharp bills that enable them to tear the flesh of their prey into strips small enough to swallow. Eating whole animals can potentially cause digestive problems for these birds because of the bones, skin, feathers and other relatively indigestible body parts. Owls overcome this problem by regurgitating pellets composed of the indigestible remains of their prey. Kingfishers produce similar pellets of fish bones and scales. These are of value to zoologists studying the feeding habits of such birds.

Below: Peregrine falcons (Falco peregrinus) are adept aerial hunters, with pigeons – including homing pigeons – featuring prominently in their diet. These birds of prey display not just speed, but also superb manoeuvrability in flight, when pursuing their quarry.

Birds of prey

Some avian predators feed mainly on other birds, such as the sparrowhawk (*Accipiter nisus*) – which is so-called because of its preference for hunting house sparrows (*Passer domesticus*). Another bird-eater, the peregrine falcon (*Falco peregrinus*), is among the most agile of all hunting birds. Strength is a feature of some species that prey on mammals, such as the golden eagle (*Aquila chrysaetos*), which has the potential to lift a young lambs in its powerful talons, but often feeds on carrion. Other birds target different groups of vertebrates as a

Above: Vision is the main sense that allows most birds of prey, such as golden eagles (Aquila chrysaetos), to target their victims. These eagles have keen sight.

food source, including fish and reptiles, while a great many avian species hunt insects and other invertebrates.

Hunting techniques

Many predatory birds hunt during the day, but not all, with most owls preferring to seek their prey at night. Mice and other creatures that are caught by owls are killed and eaten immediately. In contrast, shrikes (*Laniidae*) have a grisly reputation because they kill more prey than they can eat immediately. They store the surplus as a so-called larder. They impale invertebrates such as grasshoppers, and even sometimes small vertebrates, onto sharp vegetation, and return to feed on them later. Caching, as this behaviour is known, is especially common during the breeding period, and presumably developed as a way of ensuring that the shrikes have sufficient food to rear their young.

Some birds have evolved particular ways of overcoming prey in certain localities. In parts of Egypt, for example, eagles have learnt to prey on

Above: Like other cormorants, the great cormorant (Phalacrocorax carbo) brings fish that it catches underwater up to the surface before swallowing them.

Cormorants (Phalacrocoracidae) dive down after fish, and can remain submerged for some time. Kingfishers (*Alcedo atthis*) have sharp eyesight. Having detected the presence of a fish from the air, they dive into the water, seizing their quarry in their pointed bill and then re-emerging immediately. They then kill the fish by battering it against their perch. The speed at which the kingfisher dives provides the momentum to break through the surface, and it closes its wings once submerged to reduce resistance.

Birds hunting over areas of sea or fresh water always try to swallow their aquatic prey head first. That way, gills and scales do not get stuck in their throat. On land, predatory birds that hunt victims such as rodents employ a similar technique so they do not choke on fur and tails.

Scavengers

Vultures are the best-known of all scavengers. They can home in on carcasses from a great distance away, and so have become regarded as harbingers of death. Bearded vultures (*Gypaetus barbatus*) have developed a technique that allows them to feed on bones that their relatives cannot break open. They smash the bones into pieces by dropping them from a great height. It is a skill that they learn to perfect by choosing the right terrain on which to drop the bones.

The small Egyptian vulture (*Neophron percnopterus*) survives by

Above: Precise judgement allows a kingfisher (Alcedo atthis) to strike with deadly accuracy from a perch. These birds frequent stretches of clear water for this reason.

using its small size, which is no match at the site of a kill, to advantage: it can become airborne soon after dawn – before the thermal air currents needed by its larger relatives have been created – and seek out overnight casualities. In some parts of Africa, these vultures smash tough ostrich eggs by repeatedly throwing stones at them.

Other scavengers exist besides vultures. Road kills of birds and other animals offer rich pickings for a host of such species, ranging from corvids such as crows and magpies to road-runners (*Geococcyx californianus*).

Below: Griffon vultures (Gyps fulvus) and similar scavengers usually have bald heads, because any plumage here would quickly become matted with blood.

tortoises by seizing the unfortunate reptiles in their talons, and then dropping them onto rocky ground from the air to split open their shells.

Not all birds of prey are aerial predators. Species such as secretary-birds (*Sagittarius serpentarius*), which range widely across Africa in grassland areas, prefer to seek their victims on the ground. Secretarybirds have developed long, strong legs and yet have surprisingly small feet. Snakes feature prominently in the diet of these birds, which raise their wings when confronting one of the reptiles. This has the effect of breaking up the bird's outline, making it harder for the snake to strike. Meanwhile the bird uses its feet to stun the reptile by jumping up and down on it, before killing it with a stab of its sharp bill.

Aquatic predators

The osprey (*Pandion haliaetus*) is an unusual bird of prey that literally scoops up large fish swimming close to the water's surface while in flight. Other birds actually enter the water in search of their prey. They may not have sharp talons, but many have powerful bills that enable them to grab slippery fish without difficulty.

Pelicans are equipped with a large, capacious pouch beneath the lower part of their bill, which they use like a net to trawl the water for fish.

DISPLAY AND PAIRING

Birds' breeding habits vary greatly. Some birds pair up only fleetingly, while others do so for the whole breeding season, and some species pair for life. For many young cock birds, the priority is to gain a territory as the first step in attracting a partner. Birds use both plumage and their songs to attract a mate.

A number of factors trigger the onset of the breeding period. In temperate areas, as the days start to lengthen in spring, the increase in daylight is detected by the pineal gland in the bird's brain, which starts a complex series of hormonal changes in the body. Most birds form a bond with a single partner during the breeding season, which is often preceded by an elaborate display by the cock bird.

Bird song

Many cock birds announce their presence by their song, which both attracts would-be mates and establishes a claim to a territory. Once pairing has occurred, the male may cease singing, but in some cases he starts to perform a duet with the hen, with each bird singing in turn.

Singing obviously serves to keep members of the pair in touch with each other. In species such as Central and

Above: A male ruff (Calidris pugnax) at a lek, where males compete with each other in displays to attract female partners. Ruffs do not form lasting pair bonds, so the hens nest on their own after mating has occurred.

Below: Male masked weavers (Ploceus) build nests as part of their displays to attract the females. The techniques involved in nest-building are extremely complex and can be mastered only with practice. Hens are likely to choose older males as partners because they have superior nest-building skills.

Below: A cock Wilson's bird-of-paradise (Diphyllodes respublica) displaying. Bright plumage is often a feature of members of this family, but cock birds gain their breeding finery only slowly by progressive moults over several years. They move up through the display hierarchy until they can obtain a mate.

South American wood quails (*Odontophorus*), the pair co-ordinate their songs so precisely that although the cock bird may sing the first few notes, and then the hen, it sounds as if the song is being sung by just one bird. Other birds may sing in unison. In African gonoleks (*Laniarius*), it may even be possible to tell the length of time that the pair have been together by the degree of harmony in their particular songs.

Studies have revealed that young male birds start warbling quite quietly, and then sing more loudly as they mature. Finally, when their song pattern becomes fixed, it remains constant throughout the bird's life.

It is obviously possible to identify different species by differences in their song patterns. However, there are sometimes marked variations between the songs of individuals of the same species that live in different places. Local dialects have been identified in various parts of a species' distribution, as in the case of grey parrots (*Psittacus erithacus*) from different parts of Africa. In addition, as far as some songbirds are concerned, recent studies

Above: Mute swans (Cygnus olor) *are one of the species that pair for life. They become highly territorial when breeding, but outside the nesting period they often form flocks on large stretches of water. In spite of their common name, they can vocalize to a limited extent, by hissing and even grunting.*

have shown that over the course of several generations, the pattern of song can alter markedly.

Birds produce their sounds – even those species capable of mimicking human speech – without the benefit of a larynx and vocal cords like humans. The song is created in a voice organ called the syrinx, which is located in the bird's throat, at the bottom of the windpipe, or trachea.

The structure of the syrinx is very variable, being at its most highly developed in the case of songbirds, which possess as many as nine pairs of separate muscles to control the vocal output. As in the human larynx, it is the movement of air through the syrinx that enables the membranes here to vibrate, creating sound. An organ called the interclavicular air sac also plays an important role in sound production, and birds cannot sing without it. The distance over which bird calls can travel is remarkable – up to 5km (3 miles) in the case of some species, such as bellbirds (*Procnias*) and the bittern (*Botaurus stellaris*), which has a particularly deep, penetrating song.

Breeding behaviour

Many birds rely on their breeding finery to attract their mates. Some groups assemble in communal display areas known as leks, where hens witness the males' displays and select a mate. A number of different species, ranging from cocks-of-the-rock (*Rupicola*) to birds-of-paradise (Paradisaeidae), establish leks.

In other species, such as the satin bowerbird (*Ptilonorhynchus violaceus*), the male constructs elaborate bowers of grass, twigs and similar vegetation that he decorates with items of a particular colour, such as blue, varying from flowers to pieces of glass. Male bowerbirds are often polygamous, meaning that they mate with more than one female. Weaver birds, such as the red bishop (*Euplectes orix*), demonstrate the same behaviour. The males moult to display brightly coloured plumage at the onset of the breeding season, and construct nests that are inspected by the females. Hens are often drawn to the older cocks, whose nest-building abilities are likely to be more sophisticated.

Pair bonding

Many birds form no lasting male-female relationship, although the pair bond may be strong during the nesting period. It is usually only in potentially long-lived species, such as the larger parrots and macaws, or relatively long-lived waterfowl such as swans, that a life-long pair bond is formed.

Pair bonding in long-lived species has certain advantages. The young of such birds are slow to mature, and are often unlikely to nest for five years or more. By remaining for a time in a family group, the adults can improve the long-term survival prospects of their young.

Below: The dance of red-crowned cranes (Grus japonensis) *is one of the most spectacular sights in the avian world, reinforcing the life-long pair bond in this species. Dancing starts with the trumpeting calls of the birds as they stand side-by-side. Both sexes then start to leap into the air and display, raising their wings and tail feathers. Sometimes the birds even pick up sticks and toss them into the air.*

NESTING AND EGG-LAYING

All birds reproduce by laying eggs, which are covered with a hard, calcareous shell. The number of eggs laid at a time – known as the clutch size – varies significantly between species, as does egg coloration. Nesting habits also vary, with some birds constructing very elaborate nests.

The coloration and markings of a bird's eggs are directly linked to the nesting site. Birds that usually breed in hollow trees produce white eggs, because these are normally hidden from predators and so do not need to be camouflaged. The pale coloration may also help the adult birds to locate the eggs as they return to the nest, thus lessening the chances of damaging them. Birds that build open, cup-shaped nests tend to lay coloured and often mottled eggs that are camouflaged and so less obvious to potential nest thieves.

Nesting holes

Many birds use tree holes for nesting. Woodpeckers (Picidae) are particularly well equipped to create nesting chambers, using their powerful bills to enlarge holes in dead trees. The diameter of the entry hole thus created

Below: Ostriches lay the largest eggs in the world, which can weigh up to 1.5kg (3¹/₃lb). In comparison, a chicken's egg, shown in front of the ostrich egg, looks tiny. The egg nearest to the viewer is a hummingbird egg. These tiny birds lay the smallest eggs in the avian world, weighing only about 0.35g (0.01oz).

Above: A northern flicker (Colaptes auratus) – a member of the woodpecker family – returns to its nest hole. Tree holes offer relatively safe nesting retreats, although predators such as snakes may sometimes be able to reach them.

is just wide enough to allow the birds to enter easily, which helps to prevent the nest being robbed. Hornbills (Bucerotidae) go one stage further – the cock bird walls the hen up inside the nest. He plasters the hole over with mud, leaving just a small gap through which he can feed the female. The barrier helps to protect the nest from attacks by snakes and lizards. The female remains entombed inside until her young are well grown. At this stage she breaks out and then helps her mate to rear the chicks, having walled them back up again.

Nest-building

Some birds return to the same nest site each year, but many birds simply abandon their old nest and build another. This may seem a waste of effort, but it actually helps to protect the birds from parasites such as blood-sucking mites, which can otherwise multiply in the confines of the nest. Most birds construct their nests from vegetation, depending on which

The reproductive systems

The cock bird has two testes located within his body. Spermatozoa pass down the vas deferens, into the cloaca and then out of the body. Insemination occurs when the vent areas of the male and female bird are in direct contact during mating. Cock birds do not have a penis for penetration, although certain groups, such as waterfowl, may have a primitive organ that is used to assist in the transference of semen in a similar way.

Normally only the left ovary and oviduct of the hen bird are functional. Eggs pass down through the reproductive tract from the ovary. Spermatozoa swim up the hen's reproductive tract, and fertilize the ova at an early stage in the process. Generally, only one mating is required to fertilize a clutch of eggs. Spermatozoa may sometimes remain viable in the hen's body for up to three weeks following mating.

1 Kidneys	8 Isthmus
2 Testes	9 Egg with shell
3 Vas deferens	contained
4 Cloaca	in the hen's
5 Ova	reproductive tract
6 Infundibulum	10 Cloaca
7 Magnum	

Male   **Female**

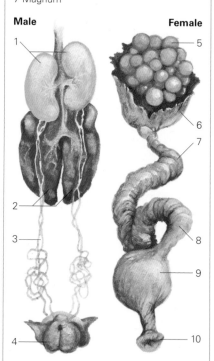

materials are locally available. In coastal areas, some seabirds use pieces of seaweed to build theirs. Artificial materials such as plastic wrappers or polystyrene may be used by some birds.

Nest styles

Different types of birds build nests of various shapes and sizes, which are characteristic of their species. Groups such as finches build nests in the form of an open cup, often concealed in vegetation. Most pigeons and doves construct a loose platform of twigs. Swallows are among the birds that use mud to construct their nests. They scoop muddy water up from the surface of a pond or puddle, mould it into shape on a suitable wall, and then allow it to dry and harden like cement.

The simplest nests are composed of little more than a pad of material, resting in the fork of a tree or on a building. The effort entailed in nest construction may reflect how often the birds are likely to nest. The platforms of pigeons and doves can disintegrate quite easily, resulting in the loss of eggs or chicks. However, if disaster does befall the nest, the pair will often breed again within a few weeks. At the other end of the scale, albatrosses expend considerable effort on nesting, because if failure occurs, the pair may not breed again for two years or so.

Cup-shaped nests are more elaborate than platform nests, being usually made by weaving grasses and twigs together. The inside is often lined with soft feathers. The raised sides of the cup nest lessen the likelihood of losing eggs and chicks, and also offer greater security to the adults during incubation. The hollow in the nest's centre is created by the birds compressing the material here before egg-laying begins.

Suspended nests enclosed by a domed roof offer even greater security. They are less accessible to predators because of their design and also their position, often hanging from slender branches. Some waxbills (*Estrilda*) build a particularly elaborate nest, comprising two chambers. There is an obvious upper opening, which is

*Above: The piping plover (*Charadrius melodus*) from North America breeds in the open and so must also rely on camouflage to hide its presence when sitting on the nest.*

always empty, suggesting to would-be predators that the nest is unoccupied. The birds occupy the chamber beneath, which has a separate opening.

Nest protection

Some birds rely on the safety of numbers to deter would-be predators, building vast communal nests that are occupied by successive generations and added to regularly. Monk parakeets (*Myiopsitta monachus*) from South America breed in this way. Their nests may weigh up to 200kg or more.

Other birds have evolved more sophisticated methods not only of protecting their nests, but also of minimizing the time that they spend

incubating their eggs. Various parrots, such as the red-headed lovebird (*Agapornis pullarius*) from Africa, lay their eggs in termite mounds. The insects tolerate this intrusion, while the heat of the mound keeps the eggs warm. Malleefowl (*Leipoa ocellata*) from Australia create a natural incubator for their eggs by burying them in a mound where the natural warmth emitted by decaying vegetation means that the chicks eventually hatch on their own and dig themselves out.

Other birds, such as the cowbirds (*Molothrus*) of North America, simply lay and abandon their eggs in the nests of other species. The foster parents-to-be do not seem able to detect the difference between their own eggs and that of the intruder, so they do not reject the cowbird egg. They incubate it along with their own brood, and feed the foster chick when it hatches out.

Birds that nest on the ground, such as the stone-curlew (*Burhinus oedicnemus*), are especially vulnerable to predators and rely heavily on their fairly drab plumage as camouflage. Skylarks (*Alauda arvensis*) have another means of protecting their nest site – they hold one wing down and pretend to be injured to draw a predator away.

*Below: Most eggs have a generally rounded shape, but seabirds such as murres (*Uria aalge*) breeding on rocky outcrops lay eggs that are more pointed. This shape helps to prevent the eggs from rolling over the cliff.*

HATCHING AND REARING CHICKS

Birds are vulnerable to predators when breeding, especially when they have young in the nest. The chicks must be fed frequently, necessitating regular trips to and from the nest, which makes it conspicuous. The calls of the young birds represent a further danger, so the breeding period is often short.

Most birds incubate their eggs to keep them sufficiently warm for the chicks to develop inside. Larger eggs are less prone to chilling during incubation than small eggs, because of their bigger volume. In the early stages of the incubation period, when the nest may be left uncovered while the adult birds are foraging for food, eggs can withstand a lower temperature. Temperature differences also account for the fact that, at similar altitudes, incubation periods tend to be slightly longer in temperate areas than in tropical regions.

The eggshell may appear to be a solid barrier but in fact contains many pores, which are vital to the chick's well-being. These tiny holes allow water vapour and carbon dioxide to escape from the egg, and oxygen to enter it to reach the embryo.

Incubation

The incubation period often does not start until more than one egg has been laid, and sometimes not until the entire clutch has been completed. The interval between the laying of one egg and the next varies – finches lay every

Below: A fertile chicken's egg, showing the development of the embryo through to hatching. 1. The fertilized egg cell divides to form a ball of cells that gradually develops into an embryo. 2. The embryo develops, nourished by the yolk sac. 3. The air space at the rounded end of the egg enlarges as water evaporates. 4. The chick is almost fully developed and ready to hatch. 5. The chick cuts its way out, and its feathers dry off.

day, whereas gannets may lay only one egg every six days. If incubation does not start until egg-laying has finished, the chicks will all be of a similar size when they hatch, which increases their overall chances of survival.

The cock and hen may share incubation duties, as in the case of most pigeons and doves, or just one member of the pair may incubate. This is usually the hen, but there are exceptions. For example, in ostriches

Above: Breeding in one of the coldest places on Earth means that emperor penguins (Aptenodytes forsteri) *can lay only a single egg, which they incubate on top of their feet, where special blood vessels help to warm it. After hatching, the chick is carried here too.*

(*Struthio camelus*) and most other large flightless birds, it is the male who incubates the eggs and cares for the resulting chicks. Anis (*Crotophaga*) breed communally, and all members of the group share the task of incubation.

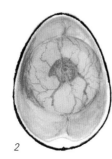
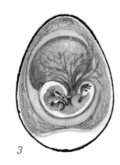

1   2   3   4   5

Nest parasites
Nest parasitism is common in many species of cuckoo, such as the common cuckoo (*Cuculus canorus*). The males do not establish breeding territories, but mate with females at random. The females lay a single egg in the nests of host species such as reed warblers (*Acrocephalus scirpaceus*). The rapid development of the cuckoo's egg is vital so that the chick hatches first, and can then throw the other eggs or chicks out of the nest. In this way, it monopolizes the food supply brought by its foster parents. Any other chicks that do survive this initial stage die later, as they lose out in competition for food with their gigantic nest mate.

Below: Foster parents such as this reed warbler continue to feed the young cuckoo even when the imposter dwarfs them in size.

Hatching

Incubation periods vary among bird species, ranging from as few as 11 days in the case of cowbirds (*Molothrus*), to over 80 days in some albatrosses (Diomedeidae). Before hatching, the chick uses the egg tooth on the tip of its upper bill to cut through the inner membrane into the air space at the blunt end of the shell, which forms as water evaporates from the egg. The chick starts to breathe atmospheric air for the first time. About 48 hours later, it breaks through the shell to emerge from the egg.

Chicks hatch out at various stages of development, and are accordingly able to leave the nest sooner or later.

Species that remain in the nest for some time after hatching, including parrots (Psittaciformes) and finches (Fringillidae), hatch in a blind and helpless state and are entirely dependent on their parents at first. Birds in this group are known as nidicolous. If not closely brooded, they are likely to become fatally chilled. In contrast, species that leave the nest soon after hatching, known as nidifugous, emerge from the egg and are able to move around on their own at this stage. They can also see and feed themselves almost immediately. The offspring of many game birds such as pheasants as well as waterfowl and waders are nidifugous, which gives them a better chance of survival, as they can run to escape from predators. Young waterfowl cannot take safely to the water at first, however, because they lack the oil from the preen gland above the base of the tail to water-proof their feathers.

Rearing and fledging

Many adult birds offer food to their offspring, even some nidifugous species. This can be a particularly demanding period, especially for small birds that have relatively large broods. Great tits (*Parus major*), for example, must supply their offspring with huge quantities of insects. They typically feed their chicks up to 60 times an hour, as well as keeping the nest clean.

Young birds usually leave the nest from about 12 to 30 days after hatching. However, some species develop much more slowly. Albatross chicks are particularly slow developers, spending up to eight and a half months in the nest.

When they first leave the nest, many young birds are unable to fly, simply because their flight feathers are not fully functional. If these feathers are not fully unfurled from the protective sheaths in which they emerged, they cannot function effectively. The strength of the wing muscles also needs to be built up, so it is not uncommon for young birds to rest on the sides of the nest, flapping their wings occasionally, before finally taking to the air for the first time. Chicks that

Above: Eurasian blue tits (Cyanistes caeruleus) are typical of many birds that leave the nest before they are able to fly effectively. The young remain hidden in vegetation and are fed by their parents in these critical early days after leaving the nest.

are unable to fly immediately on fledging remain reliant on the adults, especially the cock, for food until they become fully independent.

For some young seabirds, fledging is a particularly hazardous process. From their cliff-ledge nests, they may simply flop down on to the water, where they are at risk from drowning until they master swimming skills. If they get swept out to sea, they may be caught by predators such as killer whales.

Below: The broad and often colourful gape of chicks allows parent birds such as this Eurasian blackcap (Sylvia atricapilla) to feed their offspring quickly and efficiently. Weak chicks that are unable to raise their heads and gape at the approach of a parent will quickly die from starvation.

SURVIVAL

The numbers of a particular species of bird can vary significantly over time, affected by factors such as the availability of food, climate, disease and hunting. When the reproductive rate of a species falls below its annual mortality rate, it is in decline, but this does not mean it will inevitably become extinct.

For many birds, life is short and hazardous. Quite apart from the risk of predation, birds can face a whole range of other dangers, ranging from starvation and disease to the those caused by human intervention. The reproductive rate is higher, and age of maturity lower, in birds with particularly perilous lifestyles, such as blue tits (*Cyanistes caeruleus*). Such species often breed twice or more each year in quick succession.

Rising and falling numbers

Some birds have a reproductive cycle that is geared to allow them to increase their numbers rapidly under favourable conditions. In Australia, for example, budgerigars (*Melopsittacus undulatus*) multiply rapidly when the rains come. Rainfall not only ensures the rapid growth of the grasses that form the basis of their diet, but also fills the waterholes in the arid interior where these parakeets can be found. During periods of drought, however, when food and water become much harder

Below: Galahs (Eolophus roseicapilla) *have not just benefited from increased availability of food and water in their natural habitat thanks to agriculture, but they have also adapted to other changes in the environment too, such as roosting together on this aerial.*

Above: Many birds watch over their offspring when they hatch, but are ill-equipped to defend them from predators, as in the case of this male wood duck (Aix sponsa).

for these nomadic birds to find, the population plummets. But it can grow again rapidly when conditions become more favourable.

Regular fall-offs in populations can occur on a cyclical basis, as shown by the case of snowy owls (*Bubo scandiacus*) in North America. As the numbers of lemmings, which form a major part of their diet, rise, so too does the snowy owl population. This is the result of more chicks per nest being reared successfully, rather than dying of starvation. When numbers of lemmings then fall rapidly, thanks to a shortage of their food, owls are forced to spread out over a much wider area

than normal in search of food, and their breeding success plummets accordingly. Later they gradually increase again over successive years, as the lemming population recovers.

Group living

Birds that live in flocks find mates more easily than other birds, and group life also offers several other advantages, including the safety of numbers. An aerial predator such as a hawk will find it harder to recognize and target individuals in a flying mass of birds, although stragglers are still likely to be picked off.

Coloration can also increase the safety of birds in flocks. In Florida, USA, there used to be feral budgerigar flocks made up of multicoloured individuals. The different colours reflected the diversity of colour varieties that were developed through domestication. Today, however, green is by far the predominant colour in such flocks, as it is in genuine wild flocks, simply because predators found it much easier to pick off individuals of other colours. Greater numbers of the

Cryptic coloration

Camouflage, also known as cryptic coloration, enables a bird to hide in its natural surroundings. It offers distinct survival benefits in concealing the bird from would-be predators. Cryptic coloration has the effect of breaking up the bird's outline, allowing it to blend in with the background in its habitat. Posture and, in particular, keeping still can also help, as movement often attracts the attention of would-be predators.

Below: Blending into the background can be useful for predators too, as in the case of this scops owl (Otus senegalensis), *which often hunts insects in flight, as they fly within reach.*

always the case. The expansion of agriculture in countries such as Australia has resulted in the greater availability of water in what was formerly arid countryside. This, in turn, has enabled birds such as galahs (*Eolophus roseicapilla*), a type of cockatoo, to spread over a much wider area and reproduce so rapidly that they have reached plague proportions. Shooting has helped to control numbers of these birds, but, overall, galah populations have expanded in recent years because of changes brought by humans.

Other birds have benefited more directly from human intervention, as is the case with the common starling (*Sturnus vulgaris*). These birds have spread across North America, following their introduction from Europe in the late 1800s.

Similarly, the common pheasant (*Phasianus colchicus*) is now native across most of Europe, thanks to human interest in these game birds, which are bred in large numbers for sport shooting. Many more survive than would otherwise be the case, thanks to the attention of gamekeepers who not only provide food, but also help to curb possible predators in areas where the birds are released.

Slow breeders

Birds that reproduce slowly, such as albatrosses (Diomedeidae) and sandhill cranes (*Antigone canadensis*), are likely to be highly vulnerable to any changes

Above: Snowy owls (Bubo scandiacus) *are often seen near coasts outside the breeding season. They are opportunistic hunters, even catching fish on occasion.*

in their surroundings, whether caused by human interference, climate change, disease, or other factors. Great concern has recently been focused on albatross numbers, which are declining worldwide. Many of these birds have been caught and drowned in fishing nets in recent years. Albatrosses are normally very long-lived and breed very slowly. Any sudden decline in their population is therefore likely to have devastating consequences that cannot easily be reversed.

Below: Sandhill crane (Antigone canadensis) *with chick. Long-lived, slow-breeding birds such as cranes are the least adaptable when faced with rapid environmental changes of any kind.*

green budgies survived to breed and pass on their genes to their descendants, and so green became the dominant colour in the feral flocks.

Group living also means that when the flock is feeding and at its most vulnerable, there are extra eyes to watch out for predators and other threats. Within parrot flocks, birds take it in turns to act as sentinels, and screech loudly at any hint of danger.

Effects of humans

It is generally assumed that human interference in the landscape is likely to have harmful effects on avian populations. However, this is not

MIGRATION

Some birds live in a particular place all year round, but many are only temporary visitors. Typically, species fly north into temperate latitudes in spring, and return south at the end of summer. They have a wide distribution, but are seen only in specific parts of their range at certain times of the year.

Many species of birds regularly take long seasonal journeys. The birds that regularly undertake such seasonal movements on specific routes are known as migrants, and the journeys themselves are known as migrations. Migrations are different from so-called irruptions, when flocks of certain types of birds suddenly move to an area where conditions are more favourable. Birds migrate to seek shelter from the elements, to find safe areas to rear their young and, in particular, to seek places where food is plentiful. Birds such as waxwings (Bombycillidae) irrupt to a new location to find food when supplies become scarce in their habitat, but such journeys are less frequent and are irregular. The instinct to migrate dates back millions of years,

Right: This diagram illustrates the main migratory routes in the Americas, where birds fly either down the Central American isthmus, or across the Caribbean via the local islands. In following these traditional routes over or close to land, the birds avoid long and potentially hazardous sea crossings.

Below: The routes taken by birds migrating back and forth to Africa from parts of Europe and western Asia are shown here. Again, crossings are not always made by the most direct route, if this would entail a long and possibly dangerous sea journey.

to a period when the seasons were often much more extreme, which meant that it was difficult to obtain food in a locality throughout the year. This forced birds to move in search of food. Even today, the majority of migratory species live within the world's temperate zones, particularly in the Northern Hemisphere, where seasonal changes remain pronounced.

Migratory routes

The routes that the birds follow on their journeys are often well defined. Land birds try to avoid flying over large stretches of water, preferring instead to follow coastal routes and crossing the sea at the shortest point. For instance, many birds migrating from Europe to Africa prefer to fly over the Straits of Gibraltar. Frequently

Banding birds

Much of what we know about migration and the lifespan of birds comes from banding studies carried out by ornithologists. Bands placed on the birds' legs allow experts to track their movements when the ringed birds are recovered again. The rings are made of lightweight aluminium, and have details of the banding organization and when banding was carried out. Unfortunately, only a very small proportion of ringed birds are ever recovered, so the data gathered is incomplete, but now other methods of tracking, such as radar, are also used to follow the routes taken by flocks of birds, which supplements the information from banding studies.

Below: A mute swan (Cygnus olor) *wearing a band. Coloured bands can help to identify individual birds from some distance away.*

birds fly at much greater altitudes when migrating. Cranes (Gruidae) have been recorded flying at 5,000m (16,400ft) when crossing the mountainous areas in France, and geese (*Anser*) have been observed crossing the Himalayas at altitudes of more than 9,000m (29,500ft). Even if the migratory routes are known, it is often difficult to spot migrating birds because they fly so high.

Speed and distance

Migrating birds also fly at greater speeds than usual, which helps to make their journey time as short as possible. The difference can be significant – migrating barn swallows (*Hirundo rustica*) travel at speeds of between 3 and 14km/h (1.8–8.7mph) faster than usual, and the greater altitude at which they fly means that the air is thinner, and resistance less.

Some birds travel huge distances on migration. Arctic terns (*Sterna paradisaea*), for example, cover distances of more than 15,000km (9,300 miles) in total, as they shuttle between the Arctic and Antarctic. They fly an average distance of 160km (100 miles) every day. Size does not preclude birds from migrating long distances, either. The tiny ruby-throated hummingbird (*Archilochus colubris*) flies over the Gulf of Mexico from the eastern USA every year, a distance of more than 800km (500 miles).

Preparing for migration

The migratory habits of birds have long been the subject of scientific curiosity. As late as the 1800s, it was thought that swallows hibernated in the bottom of ponds because they were seen skimming over the pond surface in groups before disappearing until the following spring. Now we know that they were probably feeding on insects to build up energy supplies for their long journey ahead.

Even today, the precise mechanisms involved in migratory behaviour are not fully understood. We do know that birds feed up before setting out on migration, and that various hormonal changes enable them to store more fat

Above: Many birds, including this bluethroat (Luscinia svecica), *set out on migration after moulting. Damaged plumage can make the task of flying harder.*

in their bodies to sustain them on their journey. Feeding opportunities are likely to be more limited than usual when birds are migrating, while their energy requirements are, of course, higher. In addition, birds usually moult just before migrating, so that their plumage is in the best condition to withstand the inevitable buffeting that lies ahead.

Navigation

Birds use both learned and visual cues to orientate themselves when migrating. Young birds of many species, such as swans, learn the route by flying in the company of their elders. However, some young birds set out on their own and reach their destinations successfully without the benefit of experienced companions, navigating by instinct alone. Birds such as swifts (Apodidae) fly mainly during daytime, whereas others, including ducks (Anatidae), migrate at night. Many birds fly direct to their destination, but some may detour and break their journey to obtain food and water before setting out again.

Experiments have shown that birds orientate themselves using the position of the sun and stars, as well as by following familiar landmarks. They also use the Earth's magnetic field to find their position, and thus do not get lost in cloudy or foggy weather, when the sky is obscured. However, the way in which these various factors come together has yet to be fully understood.

BEHAVIOUR

The study of bird behaviour, known as avian ethology, is a very broad field. Some patterns of behaviour are common to all birds, whereas other actions are very specific, just to a single species or even to an individual population. Interpreting behaviour is easier in some cases than in others.

All bird behaviour essentially relates to various aspects of survival, such as avoiding predators, obtaining food, finding a mate and breeding successfully. Some behaviour patterns are instinctive, while others develop in certain populations of birds in response to particular conditions. Thus the way in which birds behave is partly influenced by their environment as well as being largely instinctual.

Age also plays a part in determining behaviour, since young birds often behave in a very different way to the

Above: The posture a bird adopts while sunbathing can appear to indicate distress, as is the case with this common blackbird (Turdus merula), *which is resting with its bill open and wings outstretched.*

adults. Some forms of bird behaviour are relatively easy to interpret, while others are a great deal more difficult to explain.

Garden birds
One of the first studies documenting birds' ability to adapt their behaviour in response to changes in their environment involved blue tits (*Cyanistes caeruleus*) in Britain. The study showed that certain individuals learned to use their bills to tap through the shiny metallic foil covers on milk bottles to reach the milk. Other blue tits followed their example, and in certain areas householders with milk deliveries had to protect their bottle tops from the birds.

The way in which birds have learned to use various types of garden feeders also demonstrates their ability to modify their existing behaviour in response to new conditions when it benefits them. A number of new feeders on the market designed to prevent larger creatures, such as

squirrels, from stealing the birds' food exploits the latter's ability to adapt in this way. The birds have to squeeze through a small gap to reach the food, just as they might enter the nest. Once one bird has been bold enough to enter in this fashion, others observe and soon follow suit.

Preening
Although preening serves a variety of functions, the most important aspect is keeping the feathers in good condition. It helps to dislodge parasites and removes loose feathers, particularly during moulting. It also ensures that the plumage is kept waterproof by spreading oil from the preen gland at the base of the tail.

Preening can be a social activity too. It may be carried out by pairs of males and females during the breeding

Aggression
Birds can be surprisingly aggressive towards each other, even to the point of sometimes inflicting fatal injuries. Usually, however, only a few feathers are shed before the weaker individual backs away, without sustaining serious injury. Conflicts of this type can break out over feeding sites or territorial disputes. The risk of aggressive outbreaks is greatest at the start of the breeding season, when the territorial instincts of cock birds are most aroused. Size is no indicator of the potential level of aggression, since some of the smallest birds, such as hummingbirds (Trochilidae) can be ferociously aggressive.

Below: A dispute breaks out between a pair of spotted nutcrackers (Nucifraga caryocatactes). *Birds often fight with their wings outstretched, as they seek to batter their opponent into submission.*

season, or among a family group. This behaviour is seen in a variety of birds, ranging from parrots to finches. Some parrots perform mutual preening throughout the year, which reinforces the pair bond. In some species of psittaculid parakeets, however, such as the Alexandrine (*Psittacula eupatria*), the dominant hen allows her mate to preen her only when she is in breeding condition, as a prelude to mating.

Bathing

Preening is not the only way in which birds keep their plumage in good condition. Birds often bathe to remove dirt and debris from their plumage. Small birds wet their feathers by lying on a damp leaf during a shower of rain, in an activity known as leaf-bathing. Other birds immerse themselves in a pool of water, splashing around and ruffling their feathers.

Some birds, especially those found in drier areas of the world, prefer to dust-bathe, lying down in a dusty hollow known as a scrape and using fine earth thrown up by their wings to absorb excess oil from their plumage. Then, by shaking themselves thoroughly, followed by a period of preening, the excess oil is removed.

Sunbathing

Sunbathing may be important in allowing birds to synthesize Vitamin D3 from the ultraviolet rays in sunlight, which is vital for a healthy skeleton. This process can be achieved only by light falling on the bird's skin, which explains why birds ruffle their plumage at this time. Some birds habitually stretch out while sunbathing, while others, such as many pigeons, prefer to rest with one wing

raised, leaning over at a strange angle on the perch. Vasa parrots (*Coracopsis*), found on the island of Madagascar, frequently behave in this fashion, although sunbathing is generally not common in this group of birds.

Maintaining health

Some people believe that when birds are ill, they eat particular plants that have medicinal properties, but this theory is very difficult to prove. One form of behaviour that does confer health benefits has been documented, however: it involves the use of ants. Instead of eating these insects, some birds occasionally rub them in among their feathers. This causes the ants to release formic acid, which acts as a potent insecticide, killing off lurking parasites such as mites and lice. Jays (*Garrulus glandarius*) and also starlings (Sturnidae) and common blackbirds (*Turdus merula*) are among the birds that have been observed using insects in this way. Members of the crow family have also been seen perching on smoking chimney pots or above bonfires, ruffling their feathers and allowing the smoke to penetrate their plumage. The smoke is thought to kill off parasites in a process that confers the same benefits as anting.

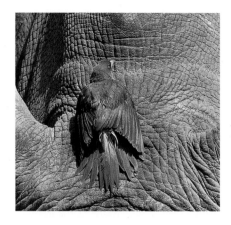

Above: Birds such as the African yellow-billed oxpecker (Buphagus africanus) form unusual associations with large mammals. These members of the starling clan frequently hitch a ride on the backs of animals such as buffaloes and rhinoceroses, where not only are they relatively safe from predators, but they also feed on the animal's resident colony of ticks.

Below: The European green woodpecker (Picus viridis) is hunting here for invertebrates on the ground.

Right: The natural waterproofing present on the plumage ensures that birds do not become saturated when swimming or caught in a shower of rain. This would destroy the warm layer of air surrounding the body created by the down feathering, and leave them vulnerable to hypothermia. Nevertheless birds do need to dry their plumage, which is what this American anhinga (Anhinga anhinga) is doing, with its wings outstretched.

BIRDWATCHING

Thanks to their widespread distribution, birds can be seen in virtually any locality, even in the centre of cities. You don't need any special equipment to watch birds, but a pair of binoculars will help you to gain a better insight into avian behaviour, by allowing you to study birds at close range.

Birdwatching can be carried out almost anywhere around the world. Many people enjoy simply watching the birds that visit their garden. A greater variety of species can be seen if the birdwatcher ventures further afield, to local parks, woods or wetlands for example. Birdwatching expeditions and sponsored birdwatching competitions offer opportunities to see an even greater variety of birds in different localities. Seasonal changes in bird populations mean that even if you visit the same area through the year, you will see new species at different times.

Above: At many major reserves where birds congregate, special permanent birdwatching hides have been set up to give visitors a good view without disturbing the birds themselves.

Getting a good view

Binoculars can be purchased from camera stores and similar outlets, but it is important to test them before deciding which model to buy, particularly as they vary quite significantly in price. When purchasing binoculars, you will need to consider not only the power of magnification, but also how closely the binoculars can be focused, particularly if you going to use them at home, where the bird table is likely to be relatively close.

Binoculars vary according to their power of magnification and the diameter of the objective lens in millimetres. The lens' diameter and magnification are given in the specifications: binoculars described as 8x45 multiply the image by 8 in comparison with how it would appear to the naked eye and have an objective lens of 45mm (1.8in), which determines how much light is gathered.

Two important considerations stem from the power of magnification. First, the depth of field is important, since it affects the area of the image that is in

---

Drawing birds for reference

1. Sketching birds is relatively straightforward if you follow this procedure. Start by drawing an egg shape for the body, with a smaller egg above, which will become the head, and another to form the rump. A centre line through the head circle will form the basis for the bill. Now add circles and lines to indicate the position of the wings and tail. Add lines for the legs and then sketch in the feet and claws.

2. Use an indelible fine-line felt-tip pen to ink in the shape of the bird that you have drawn previously in pencil, avoiding the unwanted construction lines.

3. Coloured pencils will allow you to add more detail after you have rubbed out any unwanted pencil markings.

4. If you take a number of prepared head shapes with you into the field, you can fill in the detail quickly and easily, enabling you to identify birds later.

focus. The greater the magnification, the shallower the depth of field. A deep depth of field can be helpful, since it ensures that a larger proportion of the birds on view are in focus, which avoids the need to refocus constantly. If the depth of field is shallow, only the birds in the centre will be in focus. Second, the degree of magnification also affects the field of vision – the area that you can see through the binoculars. A wide field of vision will help you to locate birds more easily.

Buying binoculars

A number of other factors may be considered when buying binoculars.
• Weight is important. Consider buying a lightweight pair if you intend using binoculars for long periods. They should also feel balanced in the hands.
• For people with large hands, small binoculars may be hard to adjust and not very comfortable to hold. Pay attention to the focusing mechanism – it should be easy to operate.
• Try the eyecups of the binoculars to see how comfortable they feel. If you wear spectacles, it is important that the cups give you a full field of vision. Binoculars with adjustable eyecups are more suited for spectacle-wearers.
• Is the design of good quality? It could be worthwhile paying extra for waterproofing. The better-quality

Below: A view of a hide. External camouflage, easy access and good viewing positions are essential features in the design of such units. Even so, it may take birds some time to accept the presence of a hide.

Above: A garden bird table will attract many species to feed, and if it is carefully sited, you should be able to see the birds easily, even from inside your home.

Right: Hanging cages are a compact type of food dispenser. They should be filled with special peanuts that are safe for birds. They may attract a wide variety of birds, including various tits, finches and even more unusual species, such as this great spotted woodpecker (Dendrocopos major).

models have their chambers filled with nitrogen gas to prevent any condensation developing.
• The design should be robust, with a solid protective casing.

Fieldscopes

Apart from binoculars, dedicated bird-watchers often use birding telescopes, called fieldscopes. These are ideal for use in hides as they can be mounted in various ways, using either a bench clamp fitting or a tripod. Fieldscopes are equipped with lenses similar to those in binoculars, but are more suited to long-term use, when you are watching a nest for example, as you do not have to keep holding the scope while waiting for a bird to return. Instead, attach the scope to a branch or bench and train it on the nest, then simply be patient until you see the bird return.

Making notes

When observing birds either in the garden or further afield, it is always useful to have a notebook handy to write down details and make sketches.

When sketching, proceed from a few quick pencil lines to a more finished portrait as time allows. Water-soluble pencils are helpful for colouring sketches, as the colours can be spread using water and a small paintbrush. If you spot a bird you cannot identify, jot down the details quickly in your notebook. Note the bird's colours and markings. Notice the length of its neck and legs, and the shape of its bill. Assess the bird's size in relation to familiar species, and try to decide which family you think it belongs to. Your notes can then be compared with a field guide or other sources of information to identify the bird.

FIELDCRAFT

If you are seriously interested in birdwatching, you will need to develop fieldcraft skills. There is a significant difference between watching birds casually in a garden and tracking down particular species in remote areas, where preparation is important. Don't neglect your own safety in the wild.

Left: Hand-held binoculars or a viewing scope attached to a tripod can help you to study both common and rare species. Taking notes is useful, especially if you intend to write up details of your observations.

Photography

In the past, birdwatchers relied on 35mm SLR cameras and telephoto lenses to record their sightings. Today, however, birders are increasingly using digital cameras. These work very well when combined via a connector to a viewing scope that magnifies the image, like a telephoto lens. Digital cameras have the further advantage that they do not require film, but store images in their memory. Unwanted pictures can simply be deleted, while the best images can be transferred to a computer and printed out. Although you will not run out of film, digital cameras do use a surprising amount of power, so remember to take spare

Research and careful preparation are vital to the success of any field trip. You should also select clothing and equipment suited to the particular place where you intend to study birds.

Clothing and equipment

Suitable clothing is vital to keep you warm and dry when birdwatching. Waterproof footwear will be needed when visiting wetlands, or after rain. Dull-coloured clothing will allow you to blend in with the landscape so you can approach the birds more closely. A camping mat can be useful if you intend spending time on the ground.

In addition to packing your binoculars, camera equipment and perhaps a viewing scope, you may also want to take a notebook or sketchpad. A field guide will help to identify birds, while a waterproof rucksack will protect all your belongings.

Preparation

It always helps to do your homework before setting out. Investigating the habits of the birds you hope to see will help you to decide on the best place to go, and the time of day when they are most likely to be seen. It may be useful to draw up a checklist highlighting key features of the species concerned in advance. You can then refer to these in the field. Studying a local map prior to your visit will help you to orientate yourself in new surroundings. Good preparation is especially important in areas where you are likely to be unfamiliar with the birds concerned.

Below: Plumage details, such as the handsome markings of this spotted nutcracker (Nucifraga caryocatactes), may be captured using a conventional camera with a telephoto lens, or using a digital camera or camcorder linked to a viewing scope.

batteries with you on field trips. Digital camcorders can also be linked with viewing scopes, and are more flexible than cameras. Not only does a camcorder enable you to record the bird's song – which can be significant, especially if there is any doubt about identification – but you can also obtain a sequence of still images, especially if you can see the bird from different angles. Flight patterns can be recorded in this way, which again can help with identification. Even in relatively dark surroundings, some camcorders will function well.

Using hides and cover

On recognized reserves, there are likely to be hides in the best localities for birdwatching. Hides allow you to observe birds at relatively close quarters, and also offer excellent opportunities to photograph or film birds in their natural habitat. Even so, patience is likely to be needed for successful birding, as there will be no guarantees that you will see the species you hope to spot.

In areas where no hide is available, take cover behind shrubs, tree trunks or raised banks, or even in a parked car. Birds are highly attuned to the

Below: There are now many organized trips taking keen birders to far-flung parts of the world, offering unique opportunities to see new birds in exotic localities.

Above: In some areas, there may not be any natural cover or hides available. To get close to birds, you will need to dress inconspicuously so that you blend into the background, and try to keep as still as you possibly can. Bird-watching requires plenty of patience.

slightest hint of danger, such as humans approaching. In areas where no cover is available, stand, kneel or lie in a comfortable position and try to move as little as possible. When approaching birds, make sure your position is downwind, so the sounds of your approach don't frighten them away.

Seeking rarities

Birdwatching magazines can be useful in identifying sites where rarities have been spotted. For up-to-the-minute news, you will need to seek out either a regularly updated website or an information phone line giving details of the latest sightings. Birders with access to email can also receive

bulletins listing where particular rarities have cropped up. These are most likely to be recorded after bad weather such as fierce storms which can blow migrant birds off-course.

Bear in mind that many people will be drawn to a place where an unusual species has been sighted, and it is important not to create a disturbance or to trespass on private land. Similarly, it is a criminal offence in some areas to disturb breeding birds. Always act in a responsible manner when birdwatching.

Getting the best results

• Plan well beforehand, including checking tide times if relevant. Tidal areas can be particularly hazardous where there is quicksand.
• Remember that bird populations may vary according to the time of year.
• Never neglect your own safety. Let someone else know where you are going, and when you intend to return.
• Check the weather forecast first, and take a mobile phone in case you get into difficulties.
• Take a local map and also a compass to guide you if you get lost. Allow enough time to locate and then observe the birds.

WHERE BIRDS LIVE

Birds have adapted to thrive in virtually every type of habitat around the globe, ranging from arid deserts to equally inhospitable polar regions. Some migrate long distances between breeding and wintering grounds each year, while others are more sedentary, and rely upon a specific type of habitat in which to live and breed. The adaptable nature of many birds is revealed by the way in which various species are now commonly seen in urban areas, where the presence of human habitations has produced a markedly different environment to their natural habitats. Observing birds can prove a very relaxing, casual pastime easily carried out at home or in a local park, although for the serious ornithologist, willing to travel longer distances or visit remote regions, careful planning is vital in order to increase the likelihood of spotting a particular species. Personal safety is an important consideration for these birdwatchers, as natural hazards such as rising tides can catch the keen observer unawares.

Left: Burrowing owls (Athene cunicularia) *rely on existing animal burrows for their nesting sites. The extermination of a number of burrowing rodents as "pests" is now posing a severe threat to these tiny owls.*
Above from left: Cape sugarbird (Promerops cafer), *mountain pygmy owl* (Glaucidium gnoma),
white-fronted bee-eater (Merops bullockoides).

ZONES AND HABITATS

Birds have been exceedingly successful in colonizing the planet. Their warm-blooded nature and ability to fly have helped them to reach and then adapt to life in some of the world's most inaccessible places. They are found naturally on all continents, even successfully inhabiting Antarctica.

Zoologists divide the world into broad geographical zones, within which there are many different habitats. This approach reflects the movements of the Earth's landmasses through geological time, and so helps to show relationships between species occurring in various parts of the world today.

The Americas

In the distant past, North America was separated from its southern neighbour, and they had different origins. North America was originally attached to what is now Europe and later drifted westwards, while South America was once joined to a huge southern landmass that geologists call Gondwana, which included what is now the Indian subcontinent, Australia, Africa and Antarctica. South America split off at an earlier stage in

geological history than did North America – more than 100 million years ago – at a time when dinosaurs were in the ascendancy and the skies were occupied by flying reptiles called pterosaurs, rather than birds.

When birds began to evolve on this southern continent, they did so in isolation from the rest of the world. For this reason, the bird life that occurs today in this southern zone is known as neotropical, to distinguish it from that found in North America, which is known as nearctic. Later the avian populations of the Nearctic and Neotropical zones mingled somewhat by way of the Central American land bridge that was created when these two vast landmasses joined. However, unique forms still exist that are found only in South America, reflecting their isolated development in prehistory.

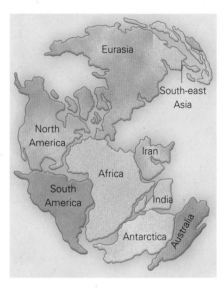

Above: This map shows how the different continents are believed to have formed and divided, giving rise to the familiar continents that we know today (see map below). These continental movements have had a direct impact on the distribution of avian populations.

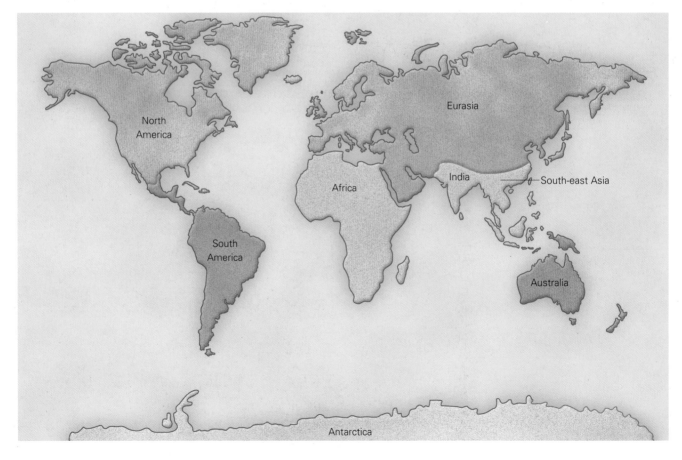

Above: The Indian subspecies of the rose-ringed parakeet (Psittacula krameri manillensis) has succeeded in adapting to a free-living existence in suburban areas around European cities, including London and Amsterdam. Here the birds survive the winter mainly on bird-table offerings of seed put out for native birds.

The Palaearctic

Europe has been separated from North America by the Atlantic Ocean for more than 50 million years, but the bird species of these now separate areas still show some evidence of their common past. In prehistory, Europe formed, and still forms, part of a much broader area known as the Palaearctic realm, which extends right across the northern continent from Iceland eastwards to Japan. Fossilized remains suggest that this region was the cradle of avian evolution, where the first members of the group probably originated more than 80 million years ago. Most zoologists believe that the oldest bird known to humankind, *Archaeopteryx*, was not in fact the first of the avian line, but that its ancestors have not yet been discovered.

The distribution of avian species in the Northern Hemisphere has been affected in the more recent geological past by the spread and subsequent retreat of the ice sheets from the far north. Today, Europe and Asia experience a climate similar to that of the corresponding area of North America, ranging from arctic to subtropical according to latitude. The two regions even have some birds in common, especially in the far north, where certain species have a circum-polar distribution – they are found right around the polar region.

Africa, southern Asia and Australasia

As part of the great southern continent of Gondwana, Africa used to be attached to South America, but subsequently remained in contact with what is now the Indian subcontinent during the critical early phase in avian evolution, approximately 60 million years ago. This distant history is reflected even today by the large number of avian species found south of what has become the Sahara Desert. This zone is now described as the Ethiopian realm, although it covers virtually all of Africa.

The Indian subcontinent became a separate landmass when Gondwana broke up. It ultimately drifted north, colliding and eventually joining with what is now the Asian landmass, and creating the Himalayan mountains in the process. As in Africa, the broadly tropical climate and the landscape have altered little since then, which has meant that a number of the species that evolved here are found nowhere else in the world.

East and south of India lie the islands that comprise the Australasian realm, which includes Australia, New Guinea and New Zealand. These islands once formed part of the vast landmass of Gondwana, but later broke away and have been isolated from the rest of the world for millions of years. A diversity of bird species found nowhere else in the world can be seen here as a result.

Present distribution

Birds' current distribution throughout the world is affected by a number of different factors, as well as the history of their evolution. The ability to fly has allowed birds to become very widely distributed, as has their warm-blooded nature, which has meant that they are far less vulnerable to climatic factors than cold-blooded creatures. Lifestyle, and particularly the range of foods that are available, also play a part. When birdwatching, there are certain groups of birds that you will be most likely to encounter in specific types of habitat as a result of all these factors. The major avian habitats of the world are as listed on the pages that follow.

Below: Common, or European, starlings (Sturnus vulgaris) are now well established outside their natural range. This picture was taken in the USA, where the species was introduced in the 1800s. It has since spread widely across North America, and can also be seen in other localities, including Australia.

THE SEA

The world's oceans provide a very rich source of food for all birds able to exploit it. Fish and invertebrates such as squid and krill form the basis of the diet of seabirds, some of which range extensively across the world's oceans and are frequently sighted long distances from land.

The huge expanse of the oceans, and the difficulty of observing seabirds, means that relatively little is known about many species. This lack of knowledge was confirmed by the case of the Bermuda petrel (*Pterodroma cahow*). This species was believed to have become extinct during the 1600s, but, remarkably, a surviving population was rediscovered in 1951 after more than three hundred years. Seabirds survive out at sea with the help of special salt-excreting glands in

Above: Birds have come to recognize trawlers as sources of fish, swooping down to feed on whatever is thrown overboard, and haunting shipping lanes. Fulmars (Fulmarus glacialis) and gannets (Morus bassanus) can be seen here in the wake of a trawler off the Shetland Islands of Scotland.

Below: Not all seabirds feed on fish. This Elliot's storm petrel (Oceanites gracilis) is feeding on planktonic debris, while paddling with its feet on the surface of sea.

the nasal area (just above their bills) that allow them to drink seawater without getting dehydrated.

Breeding habits

Many seabirds are social by nature, forming huge breeding colonies on rocky outcrops by the sea. Indeed, one of the main factors restricting seabird populations can be the lack of nesting sites. By congregating in large groups, these birds can maximize their reproductive success while reducing the harmful effects of predators. Nest-raiders such as black-backed gulls (*Larus marinus*) may be unable to inflict major damage on a breeding colony if the birds are so densely packed that the raiders cannot land.

Feeding

The feeding habits of seabirds have a significant impact on their lifestyle. Albatrosses (*Diomedeidae*), for example, spend most of their lives flying above the oceans. Their large wingspan allows them to glide almost effortlessly for long periods, swooping down to take food from the surface or even catching flying fish above the waves, rather than entering the water. Other species, such as gannets (Sulidae), dive beneath the surface to feed.

Right: The sea can be a hostile environment, with rough weather sometimes making feeding conditions difficult. High winds can batter birds and blow them off course, while oil spillages have presented a new threat in recent times. Ultimately, all seabirds are forced onto land to reproduce. Many species seek out remote oceanic islands to do so. There they can breed without being harassed by people or encountering introduced predators such as domestic cats.

Birdwatching tips

• Seabirds such as albatrosses are attracted to passing ships because of the food that is thrown overboard. This means they are relatively easy to locate in certain areas – for example near shipping lanes.

• Ornithologists can often take trips on local boats to view seabird colonies. These and other sea crossings may present a good opportunity to watch birds feeding out at sea.

• If you are prone to seasickness, don't forget to take medication beforehand if you think you may feel ill on a trip.

• Binoculars can easily be lost overboard from a small boat in choppy seas. Always sling them (and any camera equipment) around your neck, rather than simply holding them in your hands.

Typical sightings in seas and oceans, depending to some extent on location:
• Auks
• Gannets
• Albatrosses
• Petrels

Below: For most ornithologists, organized charter boat trips present the only way to reach seabird colonies.

1 Great black-backed gull
2 Sea eagle
3 Black-headed gull
4 Cormorant
5 Puffin
6 Razorbill
7 Little auk
8 Peregrine falcon

SEASHORE AND ESTUARY

Tidal rhythms have a significant impact on the habits of birds found on seashores and estuaries. These birds usually group together to feed on mudflats and sandbars that are uncovered at low tide. As the incoming tide encroaches, the birds are forced to retreat to the shoreline.

Gulls typify the image of the seashore more than any other group of birds, being a familiar sight on coasts the world over. These adaptable birds also venture well inland, especially to locations where food is available, such

Above: Sanderlings (Calidris alba) demonstrate the features of a typical wader. The daily lives of such birds are directly influenced by the movements of the tide.

Below: Black-headed gulls (Chroicocephalus ridibundus) are a species that differ significantly in appearance in winter. At this time their black head plumage is restricted to a crescent-shaped area on each side of the head.

as public parks with ponds and even the less salubrious surroundings of refuse dumps.

Lifestyle and feeding

Wading birds that frequent seashores typically have relatively long legs compared with perching birds, which enable them to walk through shallow water. Their narrow bills allow them to probe for invertebrates concealed in the mud. Some waders have evolved more specialized feeding habits, which are reflected in the shape of their bills. The oystercatcher (*Haematopus ostralegus*), for example, has a chisel-like tip to its bill that allows it to split open mollusc shells.

Shorebirds feed on a range of creatures, and can therefore be sighted further inland, even if only seeking sanctuary from storms. Some shorebirds are migratory, spending summer as far north as the Arctic Circle before heading south for winter again.

Breeding habits

Many birds that live close to the shoreline have to breed in the open. The eggs and chicks of such species,

which include curlews (*Numenius arquata*) have markings that conceal them well among the sand or pebbles. Even the coloring of the adult birds often helps to conceal their presence, with typical shades of grey, brown and white plumage merging into the background of the shoreline.

Within the tropics, a number of shorebirds have adapted to living in coastal mangrove forests, the roots of which are submerged by the incoming tide. They include some of the most spectacular members of the group, such as the scarlet ibis (*Eudocimus ruber*). These birds use the mangroves for roosting and breeding because they can nest off the ground there.

Right: The day-to-day distribution of seashore and estuarine birds is likely to be influenced by the weather. If conditions are stormy, birds often retreat to estuaries and coastal lagoons; in icy winter weather, a variety of unexpected species may be seen at estuaries, since these stretches of water do not freeze over, unlike surrounding areas of freshwater such as lakes.

1 Peregrine falcon
2 Snipe
3 Barnacle goose
4 Mediterranean gull
5 Sooty albatross
6 Gannet
7 Arctic skua
8 Storm petrel
9 Whimbrel
10 Oystercatcher
11 Dunlin
12 Long-tailed duck
13 Black-headed gull
14 Common sandpiper

FRESHWATER LAKES, PONDS AND RIVERS

The speed of the water flow in freshwater habitats has a direct impact on the vegetation that grows there, which in turn influences the types of birds that may be seen. Some birds are drawn to lakes, ponds and rivers mainly for food, whereas others seek sanctuary from would-be predators there.

A wide variety of birds can be encountered by lakes, ponds and rivers, but not all are easy to observe. In areas of slow-flowing or still, shallow water where reed beds are well established, rails of various types (Rallidae) are often present, but these birds are shy by nature. Their mottled plumage provides camouflage, while their slim, tall body shape coupled with long, narrow toes allows them to move quietly through the vegetation.

Finding food

Many birds of prey hunt in freshwater habitats, swooping low over the water to seize fish by day and even at night. Fishing owls (*Scotopelia*) have sharp spines on the undersides of their feet that allow them to tighten their grip on fish hooked by their sharp talons. Other hunters rely on different strategies to catch food. Herons (Ardeidae) wait in the shallows and seize fish that swim in range of their sharp, powerful bills. Some fish-eating birds, notably some kingfishers (Alcedinidae), dive to seize their prey, which they may feed to their young in river bank nests.

Nesting

Some birds are drawn to lakes and rivers not so much by food but by nesting opportunities. Swallows (*Hirundo rustica*) collect damp mud from the

Above: A sharp bill, narrow head and powerful neck mean that birds such as the red-necked grebe (Podiceps grisegena) *are well equipped to seize aquatic prey.*

water's edge to make their nests, and may also catch midges flying above the water. Most birds that actually nest by ponds and rivers seek seclusion when breeding. They hide their nest away, or make it hard to reach by choosing a spot surrounded by water, while taking care to avoid sites that may flood. Mute swans (*Cygnus olor*) construct large nests, which restricts their choice of sites. Both sexes, but especially the cob (male), defend the nest ferociously. These largish birds are capable of inflicting painful, damaging blows with

their wings on would-be wild predators, dogs or even people who venture too close.

Birdwatching tips

• Patience is essential when watching freshwater birds, as many species are shy and easily frightened away.
• Certain localities, such as large lakes and gravel pits, are particularly good for spotting waterfowl in winter. Check local details in field guides or websites.
• Quietly paddling a canoe up a river can be a good way to spot birds, but plan carefully and be alert to possible dangers, such as strong currents, weirs or waterfalls on the route.
• Take great care near rivers when there is a risk of flooding, such as after heavy rain.

Typical sightings by lakes, ponds and rivers, depending on location:
• Ducks, geese and swans
• Rails
• Herons
• Birds of prey

Below: The keen eyesight and long legs of birds such as the great blue heron (Ardea herodias) *help them to hunt effectively in freshwater habitats.*

Below: An African jacana (Actophilornis africanus) *on a hippopotamus. This bird's long toes support its weight when walking over lily pads, so it does not sink down.*

Right: Reedbeds associated with freshwater habitats provide cover for many species of birds. The dense vegetation in such areas means that birdwatching can be difficult. The narrow body shape and agility of many freshwater birds allow them to move easily through dense vegetation, avoiding detection. Fortunately, birds swimming into open water will be much easier to spot.

1 Spoonbill
2 Grey heron
3 Mallard
4 Tufted duck
5 Glossy ibis
6 Ringed plover
7 Coot
8 Common kingfisher
9 Muscovy duck

TEMPERATE WOODLAND

The temperate woodlands of the Northern Hemisphere have altered significantly over time owing to climate change, receding in cold periods and expanding in warmer eras. Coniferous forests extend north to the treeless area known as the tundra, where it is too cold for even hardy trees to grow.

Bird life in coniferous forests is less varied than in deciduous, broad-leaved woodlands, largely because there are fewer feeding opportunities. Nonetheless some species manage to thrive in this cooler habitat.

Coniferous woodlands

Clark's nutcracker (*Nucifraga columbiana*) of North American forests is one such success. Their curving bills allow these specialized members of the crow family to extract the seeds from pine cones effectively.

The food supply in this habitat is not guaranteed, however. There are barren years when the trees do not produce as many cones as usual, forcing the birds to abandon their regular haunts and fly elsewhere. These unpredictable movements, known as irruptions, occur when birds suddenly appear in large numbers outside their normal range, searching for alternative sources of food. They later disappear

Below: Some predatory birds have adapted to life in temperate forests, especially owls such as this long-eared owl (Asio otis). These hunters depend largely on rodents for food.

Above: Ground birds such as the western capercaillie (Tetrao urogallus) breed on the ground, concealing their presence as far as possible. Their chicks are able to move immediately after they hatch out.

just as suddenly as they arrived, and may not return again for years. In northerly areas the landscape is covered in snow for much of the winter. Some species, including various corvids and woodpeckers, prepare for the cold weather by burying stores of nuts or hiding them in trees.

Owls are frequently found in coniferous forests, preying on the rodents that can be quite plentiful there. However, owls may also be forced to hunt elsewhere if the numbers of their prey plummet, as occasionally happens when there is a shortage of pine cones.

Deciduous woodlands

A greater variety of feeding opportunities exists for birds in deciduous forests. Such woodland is more open, which means that there is a significant understorey of vegetation and insects are more plentiful. Migratory birds take advantage of the feeding opportunities in these forests in summer. Ground birds of various types, including wild turkeys (*Meleagris gallopavo*), are also found here. During the breeding season they congregate in forest clearings to display and mate. These birds eat a

Above: A pileated woodpecker (Dryocopus pileatus) male returns to the nest site. Trees provide relatively safe nesting havens, especially for birds such as woodpeckers that can create their own nesting holes.

variety of foods, ranging from seeds to berries and invertebrates, depending on the time of year.

Birdwatching tips

• Spring is a good time to spot birds in deciduous woodlands, before the trees are covered in leaves.
• Woodlands and particularly coniferous forests can be disorientating, so take a map and compass if you're going any distance in case you lose your bearings.
• In summer, woodland glades attract invertebrates, which in turn attract insectivorous birds in search of prey.
• Stand quietly in woodlands and listen – the song of woodland birds helps to reveal their presence.

Typical sightings in temperate woodlands, depending to some extent on location:
• Woodpeckers
• Finches
• Owls
• Warblers

Right: In many ways, temperate woodland is an ideal avian habitat during the warm months of the year, providing a wide range of food, excellent cover and a variety of nesting sites. During the winter months, however, life here can become much harsher. Once the leaves have fallen, the birds will be much more conspicuous, and food is likely to be scarcer. Survival will become even harder if snow blankets the ground.

1 Magpie
2 Black woodpecker
3 Sparrowhawk
4 Common pheasant
5 Wren
6 Blackcap
7 Woodcock
8 European greenfinch

TROPICAL RAINFOREST

Over long periods, tropical rainforests have provided relatively stable environments compared with temperate forests, and are home to some spectacular species. Unfortunately, many tracts of forest are not easily accessible. Choose locations carefully to maximize your chance of seeing a wide range of birds.

Many of the birds inhabiting rainforest areas are brightly coloured, but their vibrant plumage is very effectively concealed in this dark, shadowy environment. Only flashes of colour may be seen as the plumage is lit by shafts of sunlight penetrating through the dense canopy of the forest.

Rainforest diversity

The stable environment of the rainforest has undoubtedly contributed to the diversity of bird life found there. Fruit is especially plentiful, and specialist fruit-eating birds, known as frugivores, are therefore numerous. Their presence is essential to the long-term well-being of the rainforest, as they help to distribute the seeds of fruits on which they feed. The seeds are excreted in their droppings, often some distance away from where the fruit was originally eaten. This method of seed dispersal helps to ensure the continued regeneration of the forest.

Birds of prey can also be observed in tropical rainforests, having adapted well to forest life, and there are even a

Below: A yellow-naped Amazon (Amazona auropalliata) feeding. The unchanging climatic conditions in rainforests mean that food is readily available here through the year.

number of species that specialize in hunting other birds. These predators are relatively few in number, however, compared with the overall numbers of birds found in this habitat.

Many rainforest species have localized distributions. Toucans, for example, are confined just to the Americas, whereas the range of the spectacular birds of paradise is centred on the island of New Guinea in south-east Asia. Vast tracts of the world's rainforests are still so remote and inaccessible that, even today, particularly in South America, new species of birds are still regularly being discovered by explorers each year.

Threatened habitat

It is well known that the world's rainforests are being felled alarmingly quickly. The fast rate of destruction means that it is possible that some species may become extinct before they have even been identified. Museum collections around the world contain various hummingbirds (Trochilidae) and tanagers (Thraupidae), for example, that are known only from single specimens. The birds' distributions are unrecorded and nothing more has been documented about them.

Above: Toucans are among the most distinctive of all birds found in tropical rainforests. Their large but lightweight bills assist them in reaching fruits that would otherwise be inaccessible.

Birdwatching tips

• Rainforests are potentially dangerous places, so go with an experienced guide or group, and don't be tempted to wander off into the forest on your own.
• You are often more likely to hear rather than see birds in this leafy environment.
• Pausing quietly for a time should allow you to spot bird life more easily.
• Photography is often difficult in the forest because of the low light.
• The high humidity, almost daily rainfall and biting insects in rainforests can create additional problems.

Typical sightings in tropical rainforests, depending to some extent on location:
• Parrots
• Barbets
• Cotingas
• Trogons

Right: The dense upper canopy of the rainforest provides both a screen and a vantage point for birds, depending on their lifestyle. Hunters may perch among the tallest trees or fly over the canopy, seeking signs of possible prey beneath, while nearer to the ground, nectar-eating birds seek flowers to feed from. Fruit is also abundant in these lush forests, so frugivorous species are commonly encountered here too.

1 Red-fan parrot
2 Motmot
3 Quetzal
4 Scarlet macaw
5 Purple honeycreeper
6 Harpy eagle
7 King vulture
8 Saffron toucanet
9 Mountain tanager

TUNDRA AND POLAR REGIONS

Birds have successfully colonized many harsh environments, including the treeless tundra and freezing Antarctic. A surprisingly wide range of birds may be sighted on the tundra, especially in summer, when many migratory birds arrive to breed.

The treeless lands of the far north are inhospitable in winter, so many birds visit only for the summer. Icy Antarctica is even harsher, yet birds such as penguins are year-round residents on coastlines.

Antarctic survivors

As the huge landmass of Antarctica drifted gradually southwards millions of years ago, so the seabirds there adapted their lifestyle to survive the harshest conditions on Earth. The freezing cold and biting winds combine to create a numbing wind-chill factor that few creatures could survive, but penguins have adapted to thrive in this habitat. The lack of nesting material and the threat of fatal chilling if the eggs or young are exposed to the elements for even a few seconds have affected their breeding habits. Emperor penguins (*Aptenodytes forsteri*) lay only a single egg, which is kept wedged between the top of their flippered feet

Above: A rock ptarmigan (Lagopus muta) *hidden in the snow. This bird's white winter plumage provides excellent camouflage, and it becomes immobile at the hint of danger to complete its disguise.*

and their abdomen. Emperors have an increased number of blood vessels here, to convey heat to the developing embryo through the eggshell.

Penguins have reversed the general evolutionary path of birds to survive in this harsh environment. In the course of millions of years, most birds evolved increasingly lightweight bodies to facilitate flight, but the body weight of penguins increased because of a build-up of the subcutaneous fat that helps to insulate them against the bitter cold. The evolution of their wings into

flippers and their streamlined shape combine to make them highly effective marine predators.

The northern tundra

In the far north, the treeless tundra landscape is transformed during the brief summer months when the snow melts. The topsoil also thaws and the ground becomes boggy as the melt water cannot drain away through the permanently frozen layer beneath. Instead, water forms shallow pools at the surface, where mosquitoes and other insects breed in large numbers. These invertebrates and other food attract a variety of birds as temporary visitors. The migrants nest and quickly rear their young before the weather turns cold and they head south again.

Right: Many birds found in areas where snow often blankets the ground and there is little natural cover have mainly white plumage. This is true of both predators such as snowy owls (Bubo scandiacus) *and also prey. Other adaptations that assist survival in cold habitats include extra feathering over the body extending to the feet, and greater reserves of body fat.*

Birdwatching tips

• Wear pale or dull-coloured clothing to conceal your presence in these cold, treeless areas where there is little natural cover. Of course, all clothing must be warm as well.

• Take mosquito repellent when visiting the tundra during the summer.

• Allow for the bright light when photographing in snowy landscapes. Glare reflecting off the snow may distort your camera's light readings, so you may need to compensate.

• An increasing number of ornithological trips to the Antarctic allow you to visit this part of the world accompanied by experienced guides.

Typical sightings in tundra or polar landscapes, depending on your location in the Northern or Southern Hemisphere:

• Waterfowl
• Snowy owls
• Waders
• Penguins

Below: Antarctic seabirds such as the cape petrel (Daption capense) *benefit from the rich food supply in the southern oceans. These birds fly north to escape the worst winter weather, and only return to the shores of Antarctica during the brief summer to nest.*

1 Snow goose
2 Gyrfalcon
3 Cape petrel
4 Great shearwater
5 Snowy owl
6 Adélie penguin
7 Storm petrel
8 Emperor penguin
9 Ptarmigan

GRASSLAND, STEPPE AND MOORLAND

Grasslands and moorlands offer relatively little cover to birds, and some are harsh places where both water and food may be scarce. A number of birds found in these areas are ground-dwellers, and they are often well camouflaged, which makes them hard to spot unless flushed from their hiding places.

Moors and grasslands are among the best habitats in which to spot predatory birds as they fly overhead seeking live quarry or carcasses to scavenge. Prey species are also present in numbers, but they are more difficult to spot because of their camouflage.

Spotting predatory birds
Large predators and scavengers such as condors (Cathartidae) fly high over grasslands, utilizing the warm air

Above: A male greater prairie chicken (Tympanuchus cupido) shows off the barred plumage that is a feature of many birds found in moors and grasslands.

currents known as thermals, which allow them to remain airborne with minimal effort. Smaller hunters such as hawks swoop down much lower over the open countryside as they search for the small mammals or birds that form the basis of their diet.

Flightless grassland birds
Perhaps surprisingly, one of the ways in which birds of open country avoid being attacked by predators is by being large and conspicuous. With the exception of the cassowaries (*Casuaris*) of New Guinea and Australia, which inhabit dense forest, all the world's other giant flightless birds – the rheas (Rheidae) of South America, the African ostrich (*Struthio camellus*) and the Australian emu (*Dromaius novaehollandiae*), inhabit grassland areas. Here their large size acts as a deterrent to potential predators, including mammals. If a hunter attacks, their ability to run fast allows

Left: Not all kingfishers live in forested areas. The laughing kookaburra (Dacelo novaeguinae) occurs in open country in Australia.

them to escape from danger. If neither of these strategies works and the birds are trapped, they can lash out and inflict a potentially fatal kick with their powerful feet.

Moorland camouflage
On moorlands and steppes the weather can become cold and snowy in winter. Some of the birds found in this terrain undergo a seasonal moult at the onset of winter, from which they emerge transformed by lighter-coloured plumage to help conceal their presence.

Birdwatching tips
• Seek a good vantage point to increase your chances of spotting and following birds of prey.
• You will need a pair of powerful binoculars in grassland environments, as you will be combing relatively large and distant expanses of sky and land in search of birds.
• Use whatever natural cover is available to conceal your presence, such as tall vegetation and outcropping rocks.
• Horse riding can be a good way to cover long distances in grasslands and yet have a reasonable chance of spotting bird life, because birds are often less fearful of people on horseback.

Typical sightings in grassland habitats, depending to some extent on location:
• Eagles
• Vultures
• Grouse
• Hawks

Right: Avoiding predators is difficult in open countryside – especially hunters flying overhead. For prey species, the best strategy is to blend into the background and avoid being seen. While a relatively large number of mainly terrestrial birds are found in grasslands, therefore, these birds are often almost impossible to spot unless they take fright and fly up as you walk across the landscape. On the other hand, grasslands offer one of the best environments for observing birds of prey, since these birds are forced to spend relatively long periods on the wing searching for food.

1 Golden eagle
2 Brent goose
3 Red kite
4 Willow
ptarmigan
5 Raven
6 Merlin
7 Wheatear
8 Skylark
9 Grey partridge

URBAN LIFE

Some birds display a remarkable ability to adapt to modern life, occurring right in the centre of cities. They use buildings for nesting and, in the case of birds of prey, as vantage points for hunting, just as they would use trees or rocky crags in the wild. City parks, in particular, have become major refuges for birds.

Cities tend to be slightly warmer than the surrounding countryside, and this warm microclimate offers a number of advantages for birds. Drinking water is less likely to freeze in cold weather, and in spring, insects are more abundant at an earlier time, as plants bud and grow more quickly because of the warmth.

Residents and visitors
Some birds live permanently in cities, taking advantage of parks, whereas

Above: Out of all birds, the feral pigeon (Columba livia) has adapted best to urban life, to the extent that it is now a common sight in cities around the world.

Below: Some birds of prey, such as this black kite (Milvus migrans), photographed flying over Bombay in India, have adapted to hunt in cities. Urban environments also offer many opportunities for scavenging – for example, from streetside refuse bins or city dumps.

Above: Buildings can represent safe localities for nest-building. White storks (Ciconia ciconia) such as these have nested on town roofs for centuries in some parts of their range.

others are more casual visitors, flying in to roost at night from outlying areas, or pausing there on migration. Deserted buildings offer a snug and relatively safe retreat for birds that roost in flocks, whereas birds of prey seek the inaccessible ledges of high-rise buildings. The abundance of feral pigeons (*Columba livia*) in built-up areas attracts peregrine falcons (*Falco peregrinus*), proving that they are just as adaptable as their prey. The falcons may keep pigeon populations in check, but if not, their numbers can be also curbed by feeding them with corn, which acts as a contraceptive.

A life above the bustle of city streets generally offers predatory species a fairly safe existence, compared with more rural areas where they risk being shot illegally. There are still dangers lurking on the city streets, however. High-rise office blocks with large expanses of glass can lure birds to a fatal collision.

Migrating birds still pass through cities on occasion, notably huge flocks of common starlings (*Sturnus vulgaris*). These congregate not just in city parks, but also roost on buildings and tree-lined streets when breaking their journey, creating a noisy chatter and plenty of mess.

Birdwatching tips
• City parks offer the best chances of spotting the largest number of species in urban environments, particularly if there is a sizeable pond or lake.
• Early morning is a good time to spot birds at close quarters in cities, before many people are on the streets.
• Don't forget about the dangers of traffic in your enthusiasm to spot particular birds.
• Join the local ornithological society to gain insight into the more unusual species found in local towns and cities.

Typical sightings in urban environments, depending to some extent on location:
• Falcons
• Owls
• Pigeons and doves
• Gulls

Right: The spread of cities inevitably influences the local avian populations, by altering the neighbouring habitat. When new development encroaches on surrounding land, for example, it becomes increasingly hard for birds that have fairly specialist feeding requirements, such as white storks, to obtain enough food for themselves and their young. Only opportunists such as pigeons are likely to thrive in crowded city centres, but a wider variety of birds use the oases of city parks.

1 White stork
2 Collared dove
3 Jackdaw
4 Kestrel
5 Swallows
6 House martin
7 Feral pigeon
8 Black redstart
9 House sparrow

GARDENS

An amazingly wide variety of birds have been recorded as regular garden visitors. It is possible to observe as many as 40 species regularly visiting bird tables in north-western Europe and North America. Feeding stations undoubtedly help to draw birds to gardens, but birds also visit as part of their natural behaviour.

Tidy, immaculately manicured gardens generally support less bird life than well-established gardens with plenty of mature shrubs that can be used for roosting and nesting. If there are stands of trees nearby, or even just lining the road outside, the range of birds visiting the garden will increase, and larger species will become more common. Artificial nesting sites, such as nest boxes of various types and sizes, can also help to increase the variety and numbers of birds that visit gardens regularly.

Birds face a major danger in gardens in the guise of the domestic cat. Huge numbers of individuals fall victim to these pets annually. The majority of the casualties are young fledglings, which lack the awareness and caution of adult birds. In areas where the cat population is especially high, there

Above: Bird tables and feeders help to attract birds into gardens by providing them with additional food sources. These are especially valuable during cold winter weather.

may be local declines in bird numbers. However, studies suggest that bird populations do not seem to be adversely affected by cats overall.

Helpers and pests

Birds are often regarded as gardeners' friends because they help to control the number of invertebrate pests in gardens. For example, tits (*Parus*) eat aphids on rose bushes, and thrushes (*Turdus*) hunt snails. At certain times of year, however, some birds can themselves become pests. Pigeons (*Columba*), in particular, often dig up newly planted seeds and eat them before they can germinate, unless the seeds are protected in some way. Later in the year, some species eat ripening berries.

Residents and migrants

Some birds are resident in garden settings throughout the year. Others are temporary visitors, migrating to warmer climates for the winter period. Hummingbirds (Trochilidae), for example, are resident in northern parts of North America for only part of the year, and head south for the winter. Meanwhile, winter migrants from further north may descend on gardens

in place of the species that have left, as in the case of the fieldfare (*Turdus pilaris*) in Europe. There is increasing evidence that actual shifts in the behaviour and distribution of birds are occurring because of the availability of the kind of habitat and the provision of food there. The common blackbird (*Turdus merula*) has become a common sight in gardens, while in North America, the American robin (*Turdus migratorius*) has moved from its traditional woodland haunts into this type of environment too.

Above: A wide choice of bird food is currently available, along with various types of feeder to dispense it. These American goldfinches (Spinus tristis) have been photographed eating sunflower seeds.

Right: In many respects, gardens offer an ideal habitat for birds. Food is readily available in these surroundings, as well as trees and shrubs, which provide good opportunities for roosting and nesting. Unfortunately, gardens can often be dangerous places for birds to visit, thanks to the popularity of cats as pets. Nor are cats the only danger in this type of habitat. Predatory birds, notably magpies (Pica pica), will raid the nests of smaller birds, taking both eggs and chicks.

Birdwatching tips

• You can encourage invertebrate-eating birds to visit your garden by creating a wild area or by establishing a compost heap where invertebrates can multiply.

• Positioning a bird table near a window will allow you to watch birds from inside the house, but take care to site it well away from cover where cats could lurk and ambush the birds.

• Keep a pair of binoculars handy indoors so you can get a better view of the bird table and any unexpected visitors to it, plus a notepad to record descriptions of any unusual birds you see.

• Try to avoid using insecticides on your garden, as these reduce the food that will be available for birds.

• Ordinary slug pellets will poison slug-eaters such as thrushes feeding in your garden. Use pellets that are described as safe for birds instead.

Typical sightings in gardens, depending to some extent on location:
• Tits
• Thrushes
• Starlings
• Hummingbirds

1 Ruby-throated hummingbird
2 Great tit
3 Virginian cardinal
4 Magpie
5 Cactus wren
6 Rose-ringed parakeet
7 Collared dove
8 Common blackbird
9 Common starling
10 Nuthatch

GLOSSARY

avifauna: The birds of a specified region or period of time.

breeding plumage: The often brightly coloured plumage that the cock birds of some species adopt before the breeding season. Also referred to as summer or alternate plumage.

carpal: The area of plumage at the top of the leading edge of the wings, corresponding to the wrist.

carrion-eaters: Birds such as vultures that feed on the carcasses of dead creatures they themselves have not killed.

cere: The fleshy area encompassing the nostrils located above the bill. Often especially prominent in parrots.

cline: A gradual change in a characteristic of a species – size, for example – or the frequency of this characteristic, over a geographical area.

cob: A male swan.

columbiformes: The group of birds that comprises doves and pigeons.

contour feathers: The smaller feathers covering the head and body.

corvid: A member of the Corvidae family, such as crows, ravens and jays.

coverts: The specific contour feathers covering the wings, and also present at the base of the tail.

cryptic: Refers to coloration or formation that conceals or camouflages.

culmen: The central ridge of the bill.

down: Plumage of a loose texture that primarily serves to conserve body heat.

eclipse plumage: A transitional plumage seen, for example, in the drakes of some species of duck, occurring after they have moulted their breeding plumage, and which tends to resemble that of a female. Also seen in finches, weavers and other birds.

frugivore: A species that eats mainly fruit.

irides: The coloured area around the pupil,

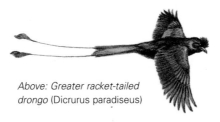

Above: Greater racket-tailed drongo (Dicrurus paradiseus)

corresponding to the iris.

irruption: An unpredictable movement of large numbers of birds, typically in search of food outside their normal range.

lek: An area where the male birds of some species, such as the capercaillie (*Tetrao urogallus*), perform courtship displays to attract females.

lores: The area between the bill and the eyes on each side of the face.

mantle: The plumage of similar colour on the back and folded wings of some birds.

melanistic: A dominance of black pigment in the plumage, such as in a particular colour phase of some species.

migrant: A bird that undertakes regular seasonal movements, breeding in one location and overwintering in another.

moustachial: An area of plumage, usually a stripe, running from the bill under the eye, resembling a moustache in appearance, as seen in the Inca tern (*Larosterna inca*).

nidicolous: Refers to newly-hatched young that remain in the nest for some time.

nidifugous: Refers to newly hatched young that leave the nest almost immediately.

nuchal: The plumage at the nape of the neck.

orbital: The skin around the eye.

pectoral: Of or located on the breast.

precocial: Refers to newly-hatched young that are covered with down and fully active, able to run around at this stage.

race: A geographically isolated population below the level of species, which differs

slightly, typically in size or colour, from other races of the same species.

racket/racquet: Enlargements at the tips of otherwise bare shafts of tail feathers, as seen in the greater racket-tailed drongo (*Dicrurus paradiseus*).

raptor: A bird of prey that actively hunts its food.

ratite: Any of the large, flightless birds, such as the ostrich (*Struthio camelus*), that have a flat breast-bone without the keel-like ridge of flying birds.

scapular: Of or on the shoulder.

spatule: Spoon-shaped or spatula-shaped feathers, on the wing or the tail.

speculum: A distinctive patch of colour evident in the flight feathers of certain birds, particularly ducks and parrots.

syrinx: The voice organ of birds, located at the base of the trachea (windpipe).

tarsal: Refers to the area at or below the ankle in birds, as in tarsal spur.

torpidity: A state of dormancy, usually undertaken to conserve energy and combat possible starvation in the face of adverse environmental conditions.

tousling: Territorial behaviour by pairs during the breeding period, in which the pair attacks the chicks of other birds, or even their own chicks, if they venture too close.

vagrant: A species or population seen far from its normal range.

wattle: A wrinkled, fleshy, often brightly coloured piece of skin that hangs from the throat or chin of certain birds, such as the long-wattled umbrellabird (*Cephalopterus penduliger*), or may be present elsewhere on the head, as seen in the hill mynah (*Gracula religiosa*).

zygodactyl: The 2:2 perching grip, with two toes holding the perch at the front and two at the back.

USEFUL WEBSITES

African Bird Club
www.africanbirdclub.org

American Birding Association
www.aba.org

Birdlife Australia
www.birdlife.org.au

Bird Canada
www.birdcanada.com

Birdlife International
www.birdlife.org

British Trust for Ornithology
www.bto.org

European Ornithologists' Union
www.eounion.org

Oriental Bird Club
www.orientalbirdclub.org

Ornithological Society of the Middle East
www.osme.org

Royal Society for the Protection of Birds
www.rspb.org.uk

Wildfowl and Wetlands Trust
www.wwt.org.uk

Below: Parrots have a zygodactyl perching grip.

INDEX